SPINNING AND WEAVING

Radical Feminism for the 21st Century

Elizabeth Miller, Contributing Editor

Tidal Time Publishing, LLC

TidalTimePublishing, LLC

Spinning and Weaving: Radical Feminism for the 21ˢᵗ Century

Contributing Editor: Elizabeth Miller
Cover art copyright © 2021 by Kayla Worley

Tidal Time Publishing, LLC
Mason, MI, U.S.A
www.tidaltimepublishing.com

ISBN: 978-0-9971467-4-5 (Paperback Edition)
ISBN: 978-0-9971467-5-2 (e-Book Edition)
ISBN: 978-0-9971467-6-9 (Kindle Edition)

Library of Congress Control Number: 2021930183

ABOUT THE COVER

Our beautiful cover, designed by Kayla Worley, depicts a web woven by feminist thinkers, in front of a portal to envision the ideal future.

Radical feminism is comprised of ideals and logical truths that encompass the female experience, and the way women have been caught up in the webs of expectations that are spun in patriarchal society and in our interpersonal relationships. Women can become encapsulated in these webs if we are not careful, and if we do not fight back. Conversely, if we utilize the tenacious nature of a web to our own advantage, as we advocate for women as whole and equal people, we allow for a new web to spin—to be woven. These webs we create, catching ideas from strong radical feminist women, help us to become a collective community of women who share the same vision, viewing our network of strong principles as a portal into a world free from patriarchy.

"This book is about the journey of women becoming, that is, radical feminism. The voyage is described and roughly charted here. I say 'roughly' by way of understatement and pun. We do not know exactly what is on the Other Side until we arrive there—and the journey *is rough*. The charting done here is based on some knowledge from the past, upon present experience, and upon hopes for the future. These three sources are inseparable, intertwined. Radical feminist consciousness spirals in all directions, discovering the past, creating/ dis-closing the present/future. The radical be-ing of women is very much an Otherworld Journey. It is both discovery and creation of a world other than patriarchy."

—Mary Daly (1928–2010), describing radical feminism in her book *Gyn/Ecology: The Metaethics of Radical Feminism*

DEDICATION

To my mother, the first feminist who shaped me, to all the feminists of earlier generations who paved the way for the rights we have now, to my sister feminists of my generation who fight fiercely alongside me to protect and expand our rights, and to our daughter and granddaughter feminists of future generations. May they complete the work of liberating all women and girls from patriarchy.

ACKNOWLEDGEMENTS

This book exists because I wanted to give voice to my radical feminist sisters, whom I am privileged to fight alongside. It could not exist without the hard work and brilliance of my sisters who wrote the pieces in this book. You have my admiration, my devotion, and my love.

Thank you to Kayla Worley, who created our inspiring cover art.

Thanks to Ruth Barrett, of Tidal Time Publishing, LLC, who brought the *Female Erasure* book into being, and who inspired and helped me to publish this book and led me through the process. Thank you for your tireless guidance.

Thanks to Mary Daly for giving us the inspirational imagery of the spinster and the weaver, the women who create by spinning and connecting the fabric of the world.

Finally, thank you to my sisters in the Chicago Feminist Salon, with whom I organize and strategize and agonize and analyze. You nurture me and feed my soul and give me hope.

And here's to the future spinsters and weavers who will take women's liberation forward into the 21st Century and beyond.

A NOTE ON THE TEXT

The authors who contributed to this book come from across the world; many come from countries that use British spelling when writing in English. Where an author used British spelling in her writing, I have retained it. However, for the sake of uniformity, I conformed punctuation to American usage throughout the book. For pieces that were originally published elsewhere, I have also retained the citation form used in the original piece.

TABLE OF CONTENTS

INTRODUCTION

Radical Feminism for the 21st Century and Beyond

by Elizabeth Miller, Contributing Editor

Why publish a collection of writings on contemporary radical feminist theory? Because women are under attack. Women are always under attack. The status of women since patriarchy began is attack by misogynist forces, mostly male, but also by female handmaidens of the patriarchy who center men and help them oppress women. Women as a class and all over the world have been oppressed by men as a class since men invented the patriarchal system: by slavery, forced marriage, forced breeding, compulsory heterosexuality, witch burning, female infanticide, foot binding, female genital mutilation, rape, murder, and the threat of those things to keep us in line. Men as the ruling class have treated us as their property and their resources, and have terrorized us into not objecting to any of it. Then there are the things they have taken from us, or prevented us from having: the right to own property, the right to vote, access to education, access to training for professions and well-paid work under good conditions, the legal right to work for money in work we choose, the right to serve in government and to participate in governing ourselves, in making the laws that govern us. Even basic literacy. Even our own bodily autonomy. All of these things men have kept from us. These days, radical feminists are perhaps most immediately worried about our oppression by the transgender movement. Transgender activists are engaged in a society-wide campaign to define women out of existence, to take away the few legal rights we have managed to wrest for ourselves by denying that women exist at all, except as an idea in men's heads that men can appropriate for themselves. While the trans juggernaut is truly terrifying, it is only the newest flavor of male oppression of women.

Because men never tire of finding new ways to control, own, and torture women, radical feminism is necessary. Radical feminist political theory as a blueprint for helping women achieve our liberation from patriarchy is necessary. It has always been necessary, but only in the last two or three hundred years (when women finally wrested the right to literacy and education from men's denying hands) have women had the means, tools, and opportunity to develop and to put in writing a formal political theory naming men's oppression of us. We are naming our right to be liberated from that oppression, and beginning to write a plan for a path forward. We are naming the methods by which we will liberate ourselves, the worldwide class of the female sex, from that oppression.

Radical feminism is the political theory recognizing that males for the past several thousand years have forcibly structured society in a power hierarchy imposed by violence and the threat of violence. This hierarchy of dominance keeps males in power over females on the basis of our membership in the biological sex class of females.

Radical feminism is root feminism—"radical" is from the Latin rādix ("root")—meaning that radical feminism recognizes that the root of women's oppression is our sex and men's construction of the patriarchal system to control and exploit us based on our sex. Radical feminism names the patriarchal system as the root of women's oppression. Radical feminism identifies women's liberation as what is needed to free ourselves from that patriarchal system.

Radical feminism has its roots in the political theory originated by Mary Wollstonecraft in the 18th century and developed in the 19th century by the female slavery abolitionists and suffragists. These abolitionists and suffragists fought for women's rights to vote, own property, refuse marriage, and access education and paid work outside the home. In the first half of the 20th Century, world wars and the Great Depression pushed women's fight for our rights to the back burner. The perceived need to repopulate Europe after the world wars pressured women to devote their lives to marriage and childrearing. In the United States, Europe, and much of the Western world, there was a Second Wave of radical feminism in the 1960s through the 1980s. This Second Wave was followed by another backlash of political conservatism and the reemergence of men's sexual rights movements that again pushed women's fight for our rights to the back burner.

So-called liberal feminism, or equality feminism, which focuses on getting equal rights to economic and political resources for women, while leaving the patriarchal structure intact, has been on the ascendancy since the 1980s. This "equality feminism" is not really feminism at all. Equality feminism is a mere sop to women, offering us perceived equality in name only while seemingly conceding that it is fine for women to be only a token numerical minority in positions of political and economic power. This feminism says that it's fine for the "sexual revolution" to consist solely of women being "freer" to have heterosexual sex on men's demand and to abort unwanted fetuses that result. Instead of patriarchy dressed in liberal feminist clothing, radical feminism seeks a sexual revolution where women have unquestioned control over our own bodies in all circumstances, and where it is not assumed that we will marry men, have their children, take on most of the responsibility of raising those children, and keep house for the man who fathers them. But society tells women that liberal feminism is the most we can hope for. And liberal feminism in turn redirects our attention to appreciating our "right" to have sex with all men who want to access us for sex, whether in dating, marriage, or "sex work." We are told to find this focus liberating. We are redirected into forgetting about dismantling the rotten societal structures that limit our choices to those which men find it convenient for us to have.

All of this shows us that radical feminist activism and radical feminist theory are as needed as ever to enable our work for liberation. New radical feminist theory must continue to develop in response to changes in societal conditions and changes in the guises (e.g. transgenderism, the rebranding of sex trafficking as "empowering sex work," etc.) in which men oppress women. The camouflage in which men put our oppression changes (and sometimes men wear those disguises themselves, when they put on lipstick and call themselves "she"). But their underlying goals of controlling us and appropriating our bodies, reproductive capacity, labor, and experiences as resources for themselves stay the same from generation to generation. Because men find new ways to disguise the means of their oppressing us in different eras, radical feminists need to stay nimble. We need to write radical feminist theory that recognizes, names, and calls out that oppression, and that exhorts women to liberate themselves from patriarchy. We can give ourselves the vision and the words we need as tools to liberate ourselves.

Hence, this book.

As a radical feminist who is actively engaged with other radical feminists in real life but also online, I noticed some things: There has not been a broad-ranging anthology of radical feminist essays published in many years, and not because there is no radical feminist political theory being developed. To the contrary, every day I see women writing radical feminist brilliance online, in blogs, in articles on websites, in social media posts and social media comments on other people's posts. Too much of this brilliance has been evanescent. Social media posts and comments in particular scroll away into obscurity within a day or a few days, simply because of the ever-renewing nature of social media. Even blog posts and website articles soon become buried when new material is written. I wanted the voices of the women I was reading and admiring to be raised up, to be amplified to more listeners, to be held so that it could last over time.

I decided to reach out to these women whose posts and articles inspired me, and ask them to share some of their radical feminist theory in a book, this book. I reached out to over 100 radical feminist women whom I know online or in real life, and some whom I don't know, but whose work I've admired.

I reached out to radical feminist Black women and women of color, women in Europe, the Middle East, India, Pakistan, South Korea, Central and South America, Australia, New Zealand, the U.S., and Canada—those who write in English, and whose work I'm aware of. Not everyone answered me, and some of those who answered and intended to contribute to the book became too busy to do so—and these contributions were also being written during the 2020 COVID-19 pandemic! I know that there is vast radical feminist work being done all over the world, and I wish I had better ways to learn of the work of women in Africa, Asia, Central and South America. English-speaking social media has not been a very likely place to connect with these sisters, and I would be lost in non-English speaking social media. So this collection reflects a smaller swathe of the radical feminist thought currently being developed in the world. This is another project for radical feminists—we have to find ways to share our work with each other across language barriers. For example, South Korean feminists recently hosted Sheila Jeffreys at a conference on her work, and are translating some of her books into Korean. The Women's Human Rights Campaign (founded in the U.K.) hosts a live Feminist Question Time webinar every week, platforming feminists from around the world. But there is so much more to be done to bring us together. How about a billionaire radical feminist to build us a United Nations-like radical feminist building where we can meet and have headphones with simultaneous translation in our ears as we speak to each other? J.K. Rowling, can you help us out? All of this to say that I wish the book reflected more voices of Black women, women of color, and women from more countries. I do feel good about the efforts I made as one woman bringing this book together.

Conservatives say that no progress for women is necessary. Liberal feminists believe that progress for women is linear; that women have the vote, the right to own property, and the right to enter professions—and that therefore we have triumphed over patriarchy. Alternatively, liberal feminists believe that there no longer is a need to fight for women's liberation—that prostitution, pornography, and being choked by men IS women's liberation. Liberal feminists will say that these things are "empowering" because men tell us they empower us, and liberal feminists believe them. Radical feminists are realists: we understand that the fight for women's liberation from patriarchy is cyclical, not linear. Every time we make progress women become complacent and men stop paying attention, and we have to win the fights all over again. The threats to our autonomy and liberation come from both the Right and the Left. Trump appointed three conversative religious zealots to the Supreme Court and now the right to abortion is in more danger than it has been in decades. We won the right to same-sex marriage and the trans movement rode in on the LGB movement's coattails. Transgender activists and allies spent the past 10 years telling women that men can be women, and that men who say they are women should get to be housed in women's prisons and play on women's sports teams and undress in women's locker rooms and get elected to the New York legislature in a position set aside for women. The sexual liberation movement in the 1960s turned out mostly to "liberate" women to be ever more available as a resource for men. Prostitution is called liberation. Allowing gay men to use our bodies as surrogates to gestate babies for them is called liberation. Having pornography made of us is called liberation, including the pressure to perform the sexual acts common in violent pornography. Being pressured to shave our vulvas and cover ourselves in makeup and wear "slutty" clothes and have plastic surgery to appeal to men's fetishes is called liberation. Everything that men want to take from us is rebranded as "liberatory" for women and sold back to us as something we are supposed to want.

And yet, despite—or perhaps because of—the intensification of the hellscape that men build for women every day, the 21st Century, and particularly the past 10 years, has seen a renaissance of radical feminism around the world. Women are forming new radical feminist and gender critical and lesbian feminist organizations, like Feminists in Struggle in the U.S., and the Women's Human Rights Commission, Get the L Out, and the LGB Alliance around the world. Women are founding websites and podcasts and radio shows, and radical feminist journals and zines, and organizing radical feminist conferences and publishing books like this one. Women are meeting in radical feminist consciousness-raising groups and feminist salons across America. Polish women by the hundreds of thousands are protesting on the street for a month at a time to demand their reproductive rights. After mass street protests by millions of Argentinian women, a bill legalizing abortion was enacted by the Argentina's Congress in December 2020, making Argentina the largest country in Latin America to legalize abortion. Mexican women seized Mexico City's National Human Rights Commission building to protest femicide in Mexico. Women in South Korea have launched the Reject the Corset movement, in which they stop purchasing cosmetics, plastic surgery, and uncomfortable "feminine" clothing, cut their hair short, and in some cases, boycott romance, marriage, sex, and childbearing with men. Women around the world crusade for the abolition of Female Genital Mutilation. Thousands of women in Iran have defied Iran's compulsory hijab laws, removing their hijab in public and in many cases posting videos of themselves doing so, even though hundreds of women have been arrested and imprisoned for breaking the modesty law. Young women in Sudan led a public protest movement against the 30-year-long dictatorship of Omar Hassan Ahmad al-Bashir. In India, female college students created the "Pinjra Tod" (break the cage) campaign at college campuses nationwide, to protest curfews for women students living in college hostels or dorms. Hundreds of thousands of women in Pakistan organized Aurat Marches (women's marches), demanding a society without exploitative patriarchal structures, the right of women to make decisions about their own bodies, and ending harassment, forced religious conversions and the sexist portrayal of women in the media, among other things. Bangladeshi police launched an all-female unit to tackle a rise in online abuse and harassment targeting women. Grassroots women's organizations across Nigeria, Uganda, Democratic Republic of the Congo, Lesotho, and Sudan are organizing around feminist issues including reproductive health, food security, and education. Women in Belarus are the driving force of a movement aimed at toppling President Alexander G. Lukashenko, a leader known as "Europe's last dictator." There are countless more examples of our sisters' fierce commitment to making the world better for women and girls.

This book was inspired by Mary Daly's metaphors of radical feminists spinning and weaving creation, and by interactions with my worldwide community of radical feminist sisters both in real life and in online communities, as we co-spin and co-weave our work of women's liberation.

> *A woman whose occupation is to spin participates in the whirling movement of creation. She who has chosen her Self, who defines her Self, by choice, neither in relation to children nor to men, who is Self-identified, is a Spinster, a whirling dervish, spinning in a new time/space ....*

Daly also gifted us the imagery of women weaving a feminist world:

> *Sparking means building the fires of gynergetic communication and confidence. As a result, each Sparking Hag not only begins to live in a lighted and warm room of her own; she prepares a place for a loom of her own. In this space she can begin to weave the tapestries of her own creation. With her increasing fire and force, she can begin to Spin. As she and her sisters Spin together, we create The Network of our time/ space.*
>
> *The force of Spinsters' Spinning is the power of spirit spiraling, whirling. As we break into The Third Passage we whirl into our own world. Gyn/Ecology is weaving the way*

past the dead past and the dry places, weaving our world tapestry out of genesis and demise.

—Mary Daly, Gyn/Ecology: The Metaethics of Radical Feminism.

As Mary Daly visioned, may fierce radical feminists the world over continue to arise, to fight, to take to the streets, to take back our freedom and our power, to say "No!" to the patriarchal forces that assail us. May we continue to spin and weave ourselves into a liberatory future! Solidarity, my sisters!

Elizabeth Miller
January 2021

PART I:

FOUNDATIONAL RADICAL FEMINIST THEORY FOR THE 21ST CENTURY

CHAPTER 1

On Twenty-First Century Patriarchy, and the Place of Women's Hearts in Women's Movement

by Renée Gerlich

I believe that each and every one of us has within our hearts a hidden feeling and that this feeling is moving us to find a channel of energy, light and hope.

Dona Enriqueta Contreras[1]

If what we need to dream, to move our spirits most deeply and directly toward and through promise, is discounted as a luxury, then we give up the core—the fountain—of our power, our womanness; we give up the future of our worlds.

Audre Lorde, *Poetry is Not a Luxury*[2]

Women's heartbreak is the most potent force for freedom in this world. Women carry the pain of living under patriarchy, a system in which one in three women are raped during their lifetime, and over 130 women are murdered each day around the world, by men they know. A network of institutions including the military, prostitution, surrogacy and marriage sustain patriarchy and ensure women are overworked, un(der)paid and otherwise punished for being female. These institutions shape the gender norms of male dominance and female subordination according to which we are all conditioned, and this universal conditioning means that women's heartbreak is not only a matter of individual trauma or "mental illness." It is a pervasive reality and a constant cultural undercurrent.

This heartbreak is the fuel of the women's movement. It represents a longing to know real love, real joy and real expression in this one wild and precious life,[3] and it is a bullshit radar that cannot be placated with compromise or negotiation. What we call women's liberation movement is the cumulative, ongoing work of individual women who transmute our heartbreak into something creative, something freedom making.[4]

Embarking on a path toward freedom involves some rewards and challenges that are similar for all of us, regardless of our specific circumstances. For example, choosing loyalty to ourselves over social norms lifts some of the weight of shame that was never ours to bear. As that happens however, we are punished for the changes we make. Our individual responses to these rewards and challenges, what we create from them, is our own contribution to the collective movement of women's liberation. That movement is made up of women's collective efforts to use our pain to free ourselves.

Because this path involves so many common experiences, it is worth thinking about it *as* a path, about the social, emotional and spiritual demands it makes upon us—and also about how our responses are shaping the movement we name after ourselves as women. Then we can step back and ask ourselves questions, like: do we recognise the feminism of today as a movement toward freedom? I'm not talking about the pseudo-feminism of pop culture, but women's liberation. In being part of this movement, do we feel, deep in our bones, and in every cell, excited and released? Is the work we do day to day in the name of feminism winning us more autonomy, or draining us? Does that matter? If there is a *war on women*, if sexual politics are a *battleground* in which only one side is armed, does it *matter* how feminism "feels," and whether it is stressful or freeing? What do you think? Does the feminism you know and do really reflect your own chosen response to heartbreak?

Second Wave

During the second wave of women's liberation in the 1970s and 80s, women gathered in consciousness-raising groups to do the work of liberation. They shared their life experiences and discovered something that changed the course of history. Women discovered that their heartbreak was not personal, because while it was indeed alienating, its causes were too formulaic, predictable, and tied up with culture, power, sex and gender to be purely "personal." Women also realised they had more power than they had been led to believe, to heal their heartbreak and change the circumstances of their lives.

Through consciousness raising, women learned to name social patterns: of feminine conditioning, of male violence, of patriarchal power and control tactics in private and public. Women divorced abusive husbands, broke up with boyfriends, promoted lesbian visibility and some went separatist[5] to dedicate their lives to women. They gave up feminine grooming rituals and the "corset," and put the freed energy into themselves and each other, into art, music, theatre and political action just as radical as the changes they were making to their own lives. They started rape shelters, feminist presses and periodicals, women's lands, Reclaim the Night marches, and strategised and organised to change law and institutional policy.

For all the political and institutional victories of the second wave, this was a time when a deep desire for freedom and autonomy, not just for "equality" and reform, shaped the women's movement. The great works of that moment—the essays, books, novels, artworks, songs, speeches, badges, patches, posters, presses, poems, and periodicals; books like *Sister Outsider* and *Gyn/Ecology*; poems like *The Dream of a Common Language* and *Monster*—were created by passionate visionaries. To these women, individual freedom and collective liberation were not separate, polarised intellectual ideas—one liberal, fantasy based and irresponsible; the other radical, materially based and moral. In this women's liberation movement, individual freedom indeed meant responsibility. It meant taking back responsibility for one's own life, something that is stolen from women. Collective liberation was not only about a shared moral obligation to shift the material conditions of oppression on behalf of those worst affected, or for future generations. It was about sharing in the challenges, thrills, and new forms of expression that come with reclaiming ownership of one's own mind and life. The second wave mantra, "the personal is political," implies that liberation, too, is both.

When women start treating anger and heartbreak as important signals in our personal lives—as they did in the consciousness-raising groups of the 70s and 80s—we become more loyal to ourselves, and begin to move away from our feminine conditioning and out of our socially accepted roles. As Harriet Lerner wrote in her 1989 book *The Dance of Anger*, when we make changes like this, they are likely to be met with resistance in others as well as in ourselves. This resistance may extend to demands reaching "almost to absurd proportions, in a powerful effort to protect... from the strong anxiety that standing on one's own can provoke in parties who are close to each other."[6] In the political sphere, that resistance is called "backlash." In our personal lives, Lerner refers to it in the language of "countermoves" or "Change back!" reactions. What are some common countermoves, she asks? They often involve the attempt to evoke guilt: "We may be accused of coldness, disloyalty, selfishness, or disregard for others."[7]

We can learn a lot about the current political and cultural climate by understanding that gaslighting and backlash work much the same in private as they do in public. Large scale backlash followed the women's liberation movement of the 1970s and 80s just as inevitably as it followed the radical personal changes that women made. Naomi Wolf and Susan Faludi documented its media and beauty industry iterations in their books *Backlash* and *The Beauty Myth*. The books *The Sexual Liberals and the Attack on Feminism* and Somer Brodribb's *Nothing Ma(t)ters* analyse the coup that took place in universities and other public institutions following the second wave, largely through the vehicle of postmodern ideology and the substitution of women's studies with queer theory and gender studies.[8]

Though postmodernism is said to have arisen in response to the rise of "metanarratives" and totalitarian ideologies in the early twentieth century, feminists have another perspective on its timing. As Brodrib comments,

> *Strange timing. The explosion of consciousness and responsibility, the death of meaning, is being proclaimed by postmodernism. All this is occurring as feminist critiques of the economy of patriarchal ideological and material control of women emerge from women's liberation movements.*[9]

Feminism is distinct from ideology and "metanarrative," because feminist theory does not begin with rigid, constructed ideas. It is constantly being shaped as feminists pose questions about the position of women and the facts of our lives in relation to existing structures and systems, and discover patterns. As Catharine MacKinnon writes in her magnificent essay *Points Against Postmodernism*, "Feminism's development as theory is impelled by the realities of women's situation."[10] The analysis is not rigid, predetermined, and detached, but ever developing on the simple premise of women's humanity. It is ironic that postmodernism usurped women's studies by replacing it with an academic paradigm that claims to be fundamentally democratic, but now supports the monolith of neoliberalism.

Literary theorist Terry Eagleton calls postmodernism a "cult of ambiguity and indeterminacy" that has bred "political illiteracy and historical oblivion."[11] In its cultivation of collective amnesia, postmodernism employs the gaslighting tricks of patriarchs. Judith Herman could have been talking about postmodernism in her book *Trauma and Recovery*, when she described gaslighting as follows,

7

In order to escape accountability for his crimes, the perpetrator does everything in his power to promote forgetting. Secrecy and silence are the perpetrator's first line of defense. If secrecy fails, the perpetrator attacks the credibility of his victim. If he cannot silence her absolutely, he tries to make sure that no one listens. To this end, he marshals an impressive array of arguments, from the most blatant denial to the most sophisticated and elegant rationalization... The more powerful the perpetrator, the greater his prerogative to name and define reality, and the more completely his arguments prevail.[12]

By the 1980s, the literature and proponents of second wave feminism were being marginalised, and their ideas were slowly captured, appropriated, commercialised and domesticated. Gaslighting does not just involve denial, after all, but distortion. Postmodernism in turn did not simply disappear feminism, but appropriated and distorted its insights, employing the tactic that George Orwell called "doublespeak" and Mary Daly called "reversal." In mind boggling displays of this doublespeak, ideas and practices that arose as part of the backlash to second wave feminism are now quite literally being sold to women as "feminism" itself. This is the primary context for women's struggle for freedom today.

Feminism points out that all hierarchies require a supporting ideology, and that the ideology of patriarchy is dualistic. It divides the world into two categories: "superior" and "inferior." Concepts like man, white, mind, and civilisation all become associated by virtue of their superior position, and defined in opposition to "inferior" concepts like woman, black, body, nature, and so forth.[13] The system works as long as we ourselves continue to identify with all that is deemed superior at the expense of all that is not. Feminism challenges this system by pushing us to shift our loyalties to all that is repressed, rediscovering the life and wholeness in what we have been told has no value.

One of the most "sophisticated and elegant" strategies that postmodernism employs to "promote forgetting" is the practice of "queering." As the feminist academic Susan Cox explains, this strategy takes the feminist revelation of dualistic hierarchies and turns it into an argument for deconstructing material reality:

> ...[Q]ueer theory views oppression as springing not from one class of people subordinating another, and exploiting them for labour and resources for their material benefit; but ... from the very act of labelling these groups in a binary fashion, which is seen as restrictive, and oppressive... People cannot express their authentic selves in this binary opposition.[14]

This sort of practice allows the feminist call to destigmatise female sexuality to become a justification for relabeling prostitution "sex work," and celebrating it as a form of individual female empowerment. It takes the feminist analysis of the patriarchal family as constructed and oppressive, and twists it into a defense of the surrogacy industry.

Today, the postmodern, beauty industry and media backlash against women's liberation have converged with transgenderism. Transgenderism takes the feminist critique of gender as a method of maintaining power relations between the sexes, and distorts it into an argument that biological sex in general, and females in particular, do not exist except as linguistic constructs and modes of social performance. This argument somehow gives men the right to claim this apparently non-existent, otherwise unreal femaleness, as their own identity or game to play. Ideologically, transgenderism is a prime example of a postmodern, patriarchal ideology that flourished as gender studies pillaged from women's studies departments before moving into mainstream media, pop culture and law.

Contrary to popular belief, transgenderism does not represent good intentions to "include" the marginalised, gone wrong. Nor is it strictly an academic invention. It represents what Lerner calls a "countermove," a set of old and fundamental patriarchal positions and gaslighting tactics elaborately and absurdly intensified. Patriarchal power structures have always relied on myths of male motherhood to justify themselves—God, the creator of the universe, is generally assumed to be male; Adam bore Eve miraculously from his rib; Zeus delivered Athena from his head; Jesus was more the son of God, his father, than of Mary, who is idealised not for mothering the boy, but for surrendering to his father's will with the line, "do unto me according to thy word."

The mantra "transwomen are women" encapsulates all the traditional myths and behaviours of patriarchy—the violation and myths of male motherhood that justify it; the game playing, gaslighting and magician's tricks; the propaganda, dualistic privileging of mind over body, and the simultaneous sexualisation and stigmatisation of female and lesbian sexuality. It updates this package to suit the political economy and technology for our era—one that is secular and postmodern, while it reveres consumerism and Big Pharma. Transgender ideology borrows too much from religion to be considered original—it is patriarchal ideology in a concentrated, neoliberalised form.

Transgenderism is such an absurd and elaborate countermove against the idea of women's autonomy that making sense of it necessitates a far-reaching assessment of politics and culture. Since transgenderism only makes sense as a contemporary manifestation of old and fundamental patriarchal myths and practices, feminism is the only way to answer the questions it prompts. So, as transgender ideology becomes more visible and public, and its lies more transparently nonsensical, many women reach "peak trans," as the cognitive dissonance of accepting "transwomen are women" becomes too much—and they are rediscovering, or newly discovering, feminism. This process can also awaken us to the aggressiveness and absurdity at the core of patriarchal power structures, the same structures that dictated our own girlhood conditioning, the same structures that tell us how to dress, eat, sleep, work, vote and parent daily. Coming to terms with transgenderism and its widespread acceptance coaxes many women into a thorough reassessment of our lives, roles and priorities.

Many of us are responding to this situation by creating and volunteering for campaigns against new, fast-moving sex self-identification laws that enable men to access female-only spaces. These campaigns involve strategic public advocacy, branding, slogans, flyers and merchandise, volunteers, and a lot of disagreement about how "feminism" is best "represented" (nicely, or angrily? With apology and disclaimers, or without? Through direct action or negotiation? With compromise, or without? With men, or without?). These campaigns call for governments to protect the interests of all women (or "female people," as we are now sometimes called, to avoid being confused with... *male* women).

As the work of women's liberation becomes more and more formalised, more and more civilised, it pays to remember that feminism is not just about campaigns. To wake up to all the lying and posturing is to embark on that path toward freedom, and to become open to the rewards and punishments that nonconformity, and pointing out the Emperor has no clothes, inevitably bring. This path is not just about the moral obligation to present truth to power. It is a path of the heart that wants more than to sleepwalk through life. And as we persist on the path, it is the heart that seeks sustenance.

Attachment

One of the important lessons of radicalism is about the nature of politics itself. Radical thinkers teach that people's political views, as well as their defensive reactions, countermoves and backlash, are not primarily based on values, underlying ideas, misguided intentions, or diverse understandings of the world. Politics is about *loyalty* and identification with power, about big money and vested interests. Politics is how people express their loyalties and their relationship to power above all—ideas and values are secondary justifications. That's why people in politics so often contradict themselves—why conservatives, for instance, preach self-responsibility as paramount but then consider men best placed to make laws about women's bodies. It's loyalty to the man of the house that matters, not moral, rhetorical or intellectual consistency.

Knowing that loyalties and power relations are based on investment rather than reason, has always driven radicals to prioritise resistance over tactics based on civil disagreement, debate, and "free speech." It is the understanding that loyalty trumps reason that led Frederick Douglass to say that, "power concedes nothing without a demand. It never did and it never will." It is why Martin Luther King Junior echoed this with the words, "freedom is never voluntarily given by the oppressor; it must be demanded by the oppressed." It is why Malcolm X declared that "Any time you beg another man to set you free, you will never be free. Freedom is something you have to do for yourselves." And why the inimitable Assata Shakur said: "Nobody in the world, nobody in history, has ever gotten their freedom by appealing to the moral sense of the people who were oppressing them."

Radicals know that people also cannot be expected to change their political views or identifications with power *through* reasoning or dialogue. It is not that ideas and conversation never influence people deeply, just that we cannot place our hopes in negotiation as a primary strategy for social change. The filmmaker Nina Paley puts it this way: "It all comes down to this. Can people change? Yes. Can you change them? No."

It is the same with individuals and our addictions and attachments. Attachment is to the individual what investment is to politics, and the two have the same source—the power structures and gender norms that define our society. The system of male dominance that we live within creates loyalty to men's interests in politics, and attachment to gender norms in individuals, by conditioning people to conform to these norms. As a society, we teach boys to repress the aspects of their humanity that patriarchy has deemed womanly or "feminine," and to become men who rely on power over women to fill the hole—power gained by using women for sexual gratification, and emotional and domestic labour. Girls and women are, in turn, taught to repress aspects of our own humanity, like the impulse to be seen and heard as we are, to have strong bodies, adventurous lives, a public voice. We are supposed to live these experiences vicariously, through relationships with the men and boys we care for, as they use us. As Janice Raymond writes in *A Passion for Friends*, "Women are assimilated by the hetero-relational ideology that men are a woman's greatest adventure. Women learn not to expect a lively future with women."[15] The role that women are designated has been given many names, like the "helpmate," or "handmaiden."

Harriet Lerner describes the dynamic between the sexes in terms of "overfunctioning" and "underfunctioning." Where one sex is expected to overfunction, as men are in, say, public life, women are expected to underfunction. Where women are expected to overfunction, as we are in the realm of emotionality, it is to enable men to *underfunction*, forego responsibility, and stay disconnected from their humanity in order to remain "masculine." That is what emotional labour is, in the "helpmate" role—it has little to do with authentic emotional expression and empathy, and everything to do with getting stuck compensating for somebody else's habit of using avoidance and repression to stay in control.

The reason why it is so difficult to break out of these conditioned roles, and the reason why these roles can lead people to believe absurdities like "biological sex does not exist," is not because it is all so well-reasoned and convincing. This dualistic system of gender, of ensuring that all of us—boys, girls, men and women—are identified with men's interests, this system of conditioning people from childhood to conform to norms of masculinity and femininity, does not operate through the power of persuasion, but through the power of *pain*. We are taught early on that we will be abandoned if we do not conform. It is taught from a time in our lives when the pain of repression really *is* preferable to the pain of abandonment, and when we are too young to be conscious of what is going on.

The impact and the prevalence of lifelong repression for the sake of acceptance is the subject of Gabor Maté's book *When the*

Body Says No.[16] Maté is an expert on addiction, and for him, addictions develop as a way of coping with the emotional numbing and chronic stress that arise from repression of needs, boundaries, and emotional pain that stem from power-based social systems like capitalism, racism and gender. Maté explains how the needs, boundaries, and traits that women repress for the sake of acceptance do not simply disappear, and neither does the hurt, shame, or anger involved with having to hide ourselves behind a mask to be accepted. It all becomes unconscious, trapped in the body, even confusing the immune system. Maté shows how the inability to say "No," is correlated with some autoimmune illness and cancers seen in women.

What happens when repression and hurt fester in the unconscious is that stress not only results, but it also becomes a kind of fuel that we depend on. Emotional numbing cuts us off from our most authentic sources of energy and motivation, and stress becomes a form of compensation, a way we know we're switched "on." We develop addictions that help us switch the stress *off* again and relax (like social media scrolling, television, alcohol) as well as to *feel alive*—thrilled and euphoric. Many of the world's major industries are based on these addictions and coping mechanisms.

This pattern of repression, numbing, and compensating with stress and addiction becomes a system through which we cope, and find a semblance of balance. It becomes our comfort zone, even what we recognise as our self. To threaten any aspect of this system then, is to threaten the balance, to risk exposing what should be repressed, and to finally risk rejection and abandonment. It feels life threatening. Gender is basic to the way we learn to survive in the world. This is why nobody can just be talked out of gender. We were never convinced of it in the first place. As a condition of social acceptance, it was deep under our skin before we knew what was happening, and we were hooked.

Because our conditioning goes deep and affects many areas of our lives, when women first encounter feminism and start to recognise systemic misogyny, our equilibrium is thrown. And even though this time, the discomfort really is "for our own good," finding a new way to live is no small task.

Shame

One of the most immediately powerful things about radical feminism is the way it interacts with our conditioning, specifically the habit of guilt and shame. Shame requires us to take things personally, and radical feminism *de*personalises the experiences that create feelings of unworthiness in women, by identifying patriarchy as a common condition and destroying the illusion of isolation. As the second wave feminist militant Andrea Dworkin said,

> *Women were left to face battery alone. Why? Why were we alone? ... If it's done to you because you're a woman, it's not done to you because you're Andrea or Susan or Felicity. It's done to you because you're a woman. And somebody noticed that you are a woman and somebody decided to hurt you because they wanted to hurt a woman. Not you in particular—a woman, any woman. You also. And you're not free of it. The question is, how are you ever going to be free of it?*[17]

When women learn to see the misogyny that is in front of us, to call it what it is, we awaken to a morality that is based in reality and not ideology. Feminism flips the moralism of patriarchy on its head, simply by putting women's experiences in a collective context and teaching us that morally, we are not accountable to any patriarch, male deity, policeman, Mr. Right, or even our fathers—either as they appear in the world or as they have been absorbed into our conscience. Feminism teaches that women are morally accountable to women, and most of all to those who are worst affected by male violence and poverty. As we see that women share a common condition with which we need not struggle alone, a layer of shame lifts.

When I began to read feminism, to feel this lifting of shame, and to realise I needed to forge a new path for myself, I was involved with the political left, particularly with protests against militarism and corporate free trade. I had become an activist in the first place because of my social conscience, because I was looking for answers about why the world is so unjust, and because I wanted to resist. In an essay from *Our Blood,* called *Redefining Nonviolence,* Dworkin talks about the role that the left delegates to women of conscience— the role of the "helpmate":

> *Politically-committed women often ask the question, "How can we as women support the struggles of other people?" This question as a basis for political analysis and action replicates the very form of our oppression—it keeps us a gender class of helpmates. If we were male workers, or male blacks, or male anybodies—it would be enough for us to delineate the facts of our own oppression; that alone would give our struggle credibility in radical male eyes.*
>
> *But we are women, and the first fact of our oppression is that we are invisible to our oppressors. The second fact of our oppression is that we have been trained—for centuries and from infancy on—to see through their eyes, and so we are invisible to ourselves.*[18]

I wrote my first essays on prostitution and transgenderism in 2015, and the backlash or "countermoves" began the following year, including from my activist "comrades." It hit hard. I remember sensing that many people on the left who were transactivists or supportive of prostitution seemed to froth at the mouth at finding a woman they could label a "SWERF" or a "TERF," to get stuck into.

I had taken risks, and been arrested twice, among these people, in the name of a greater good. I realised I needed to make better distinctions between the political risks that make martyrs of women, or rely on conditioned self-sacrifice on our part—and the kind of political risks that we make on our own terms, in our own interests and based on our own understandings. Dworkin's work helped me to see the difference. As I was shaken out of the political left, as so many women are today, Dworkin also helped me to continue peeling back the layers of shame rather than succumb to it. In *Our Blood*, she asserts: "The internal mechanism of female masochism must be rooted out from the inside before women will ever know what it is to be free."[19]

Dworkin's insistence that women stop behaving in overly accommodating and ultimately self-defeating ("masochistic") ways, assisted me with two things. It encouraged me to continue shedding the inclination toward taking on a "helpmate" role in my own political life. Transgender ideology itself demonstrates how detrimental it really is when women accept the ideal of self-sacrifice as a basis for our political ideas and actions. In the name of casting our own concerns aside to "help others," women on the political left are now participating in the rollback of centuries of feminist political gains. The endorsement of transgenderism by women on the political left demonstrates exactly why Dworkin really wanted women to stop being "helpful," instead of looking out for our own best interests. As it turns out, this willingness to take the shirt off our backs for the sake of anyone who asks for it *isn't even "helpful"*—it is as intellectually blinding and politically reckless as it is personally draining.

Dworkin's teaching also guided me to resist any urge to take the backlash I faced personally, as though it was directed at me as an individual. While I have often found the backlash I've dealt with to be stressful and hurtful, Dworkin stopped me from indulging in the response women are conditioned to have when we are criticised, bullied or rejected. We are supposed to respond by ruminating on "what's wrong with me?" trying to locate some personal defect to fix so we can avoid causing upset again. This is the expected response of a "helpmate" who is supposed to cope with life by seeking the relative comfort that comes from pleasing others, and never offending by saying "No" or having ideas of our own.

So instead of asking what I did "wrong" to provoke another person to criticise my decisions, I allowed myself to assess their behaviour first. I formed a habit of asking myself "is this an okay way to treat a woman?" and responding in kind. The question brought me perspective. In situations when the answer to my question was "no," I would follow it up with another—I would ask myself what sort of responses to misogyny I wanted there to be more space for women to make. I wasn't interested in which responses made me look good, just which ones there needed to be more space for.

For instance, I wanted women to stop accommodating men's bullying behaviour. I wanted to see us name abusive behaviour for what it is, rather than excusing it or treating it as innocent. I wanted us to seek accountability so that it's not so easy for men to harass us. I wanted women to stop letting anger eat us up from inside while we ask what's "wrong" with us, and why we feel bad, and how we can fix ourselves, and be nice for people. So, I made it my aim to name sexist behaviour for what it was, set boundaries around it, seek accountability, and express justified anger clearly. That was my new path.

Anger

I began to see the expression of anger as being part of what it means to stand for women's humanity. Maté addresses the physiological importance of anger when he writes,

> *Why do we have anger? In the animal world, anger is not a "negative emotion." An animal experiences anger when some essential need is either threatened or frustrated.*
>
> *...A cornered animal turns to face his pursuer with a fierce display of rage. Anger may save his life, either by intimidating the hunter or by enabling the prey to resist successfully.*
>
> *...For anger to be deployed appropriately, the organism has to distinguish between threat and non-threat. The fundamental differentiation to be made is between self and non-self. If I don't know where my own boundaries begin and*

18

end, I cannot know when something potentially dangerous is intruding on them. The necessary distinctions between what is familiar or foreign, and what is benign or potentially harmful, require an accurate appraisal of self and non-self. Anger represents both a recognition of the foreign and dangerous and a response to it.[20]

I came to see anger not as a toxic emotion, but as my body's way of alerting me to my own boundaries, inviting me to restore them. Lerner's book *The Dance of Anger* had an especially profound influence on me, and this process of learning about myself, about misogyny, resistance, "countermoves" and backlash was central to my politicisation and radicalisation as a feminist.

The initial backlash I faced in New Zealand involved a bullying pact composed by the "community liaison" from our government funded sex trade lobby, the New Zealand Prostitutes Collective. My workplace was targeted, I was banned from community events, routinely censored (articles I had published on a prominent left wing website simply "disappeared"; my interview with the state broadcaster was mysteriously "lost in the system"), and I was harassed with threats, defamation and parody social media accounts. I found organisations designed to support people with online harassment, discrimination and media complaints to be unhelpful at best, and complicit.

I quit my job due to workplace bullying, moved out of the city, and lost my savings while I threw myself into more research, writing, and activism. Through this work, I met more people who shared my concerns, and began bringing them together in a group I started online on Christmas day in 2016. I am forever glad, too, that I went to WoLF Fest that year, to meet other feminists. Before that, I knew all of about four people in the country who were sympathetic, and none outside. Now, when New Zealand women wake up to the dangers of transgenderism and prostitution, they make an instantaneous connection to a large, real and online feminist community. The situation has changed a lot—as recently as 2016, those connections and support did not reach New Zealand.

Meeting women was energising, and so was discovering that friends of mine were sympathetic. Feminism gives women a connection that allows certain masks to come off, and that adds strength, richness, and new levels of honesty to friendships. So finding women and bringing them together was exciting, and it made me feel like I could see a future, however far off, in which we would at some point start shifting the culture together, and making room for ourselves to speak and relate openly without having to confront the punishment with too little support.

For me, the real threat that transgenderism represents does not lie in the passing of specific pieces of legislation, but in the way the ideology isolates, alienates and dehumanises women while shoring up old and fundamental patriarchal positions in the culture at large. For years, I felt this tactic of gaslighting, shaming and alienating women who dissent was the most crucial thing for feminists to resist—and that resisting it with grassroots solidarity was much more important than, for instance, starting campaigns designed to have popular appeal. It comes down to recognising transgenderism as a backlash, a "countermove." As Lerner writes, "Our job is to keep clear about our own position in the face of a countermove—not to prevent it from happening or to tell the other person that he or she should not be reacting that way."[21] She says,

> It is our job to state our thoughts and feelings clearly and to make responsible decisions that are congruent with our values and beliefs. It is not our job to make another person think and feel the way we do or the way we want them to. If we try, we can end up in a relationship in which a lot of personal pain and emotional intensity are being expended and nothing is changing.[22]

This was the way I was thinking, working and believing when, by mid-2018, the group I started had grown to include about fifty

20

people. I had enjoyed the group, but I left at that point, because I was still working pretty much independently and I wanted to have smaller and more focused conversations. After I left, the group formed a public lobby in which women pool their own money and resources to put toward campaigns against sex self-identification that are designed to influence media, politicians, and public opinion. From the outset, this lobby minimised, hid, or denied its relationship to me and my work, claiming the decisions were tactical and based on a "pragmatic" approach. Because I had already been marked as a "TERF" and tainted in the process, the group believed it would not be prudent to associate with me politically and/or publicly.

Heartbreak, on my part, followed. The lobby invited a liberal politician who had tried to make women she called "TERFs" unwelcome at Pride Parades, to speak at one of their first public events. They gained a venue and publicity for another event with the help of the leader of New Zealand's libertarian political party. But they still would not name or associate with me for any reason, for fear it would have a negative impact on their public image. While I believe that women and feminist groups should be able to speak with whomever they like in politics, this group made the decision to work with, offer platforms to, and accept disagreement with, high-powered people who are overt misogynists whilst sweeping me under the rug. To me, this could only be seen as a double standard and an expression of loyalties, not tactics.

I found this situation tough. I think that for many women who come this far in feminism, the idea of losing the solidarity you've found is a nightmare. A group of feminists seems like the last social support network you'll ever be able to find. For me this was a nightmare with a silver lining.

Aloneness

There is a feeling that many writers, healers and spiritual teachers identify as sitting right in the middle of that pseudo "balance" we create, where we repress authentic aspects of ourselves, as well as hurt and anger, and then live by the energy of stress, survival and trying to please. The feeling in the middle is the feeling of aloneness. These days it is popularly called "disconnection." Marx called it "alienation." In *Trauma and Recovery*, Judith Herman calls it "helplessness." In *Daring Greatly*, Brené Brown calls it "vulnerability." Many feminists refer to it with the language of silence and invisibility.

In *Diving Deep and Surfacing*, Carol Christ calls this feeling "the experience of nothingness." Her book explores the way that violation, self-negation, and social and cultural invisibilisation compound with this human experience, for women—and how this is expressed in women's fiction writing. She says that among female protagonists in women's fiction,

> *The experience of nothingness often precedes an awakening, similar to a conversion experience, in which the powers of being are revealed. A woman's awakening to great powers grounds her in a new sense of self and a new orientation in the world. Through awakening to new powers, women overcome self-negation and self-hatred and refuse to be victims.*[23]

I read Christ's book while I was trying to accept the reality of dedicating myself to creating a community, only to find myself left effectively abandoned by it. During this period, I began to spend more time with a very dear, wise friend of mine who was active in second wave feminism, and is also a healer and Aikido practitioner. I talked with her about how, since becoming a feminist and speaking about it, it was hard to find like-minded people, and how the threat and pressure from these millennial ideologies and their assimilative power seemed to make it near impossible for me to build lasting solidarity and trust, in anything resembling a group or community, and apparently even among people who don't buy the ideas. My friend told me what to do when you are faced with a threat, according to Aikido: you hold your centre, and you "go underneath," allowing the force and mass of the perpetrator to spend itself.

This advice reminded me of a prophetic talk given by Mary Daly in 1980, called *The Fire of Female Fury*. Daly encourages women away from "reactivity" and toward "creativity"—since creativity demands that we assess things more deeply. Daly says that "we are living on a planet in which patriarchy... is raping the earth to death," so she asks,

> *How do you fight necrophilia with love of life? I suggest it is most urgent that we do not waste our energies re-acting. They will always have something for us to re-act against. Probably one of the most astonishing things in the 80s is going to be the constant erection of pseudo-feminism, so that they'll have us, hopefully (from their point of view) at each other's throats... the capturing of women's studies, the confusion of women who identify as "feminist"...*
>
> *The priority, then, the way of warfare, is creativity. I suggest how we fight is by not reacting, by refusing, powerfully, to react—and instead choosing to create.*[24]

The conclusion I drew about what happened with this lobby group is that the conditioned inclination to act as a "helpmate" and identify with the powerful gets so deeply embedded in women, it so much becomes our "comfort zone," that we can even fall into this role when we take up causes in which we have a chance at self-definition, and men have no inside influence. This system of repression, validation and stress that we create in our lives has such a powerful hold that we may continue to abandon ourselves and each other in preference of the familiarity of an ethic of charity work, "selflessness," and a bitter negotiation with men as leaders, even when nobody is demanding that we do it. As Lerner explains, when the need for change becomes clear, the temptation to stay in old roles and fight familiar battles is powerful. She writes, "Fighting and blaming is sometimes a way both to protest and to protect the status quo when we are not quite ready to make a move in one direction or another."[25] This line makes me think about those feminist reformists who work with the powerful but whose concession making undermines their central premise, their loyalty to women and themselves.

I realised I had abandoned myself, too. I started to see something I had not seen clearly while my thinking had been so deeply and consistently collective. The forced dependency that patriarchy cultivates in women requires us to become overinvested in relationships with men partly to avoid our aloneness. This aloneness contains all the treasures of our uniqueness as people, our truest desires, creative spirit, and individual responses to the world, but we collude in repressing these aspects of ourselves to stay connected. It becomes hard to face being alone, because when we do, we find feelings of pain, disappointment and regret that come from self-neglect and lost potential.

Feminism does not free women of these habits, avoidance patterns and coping mechanisms immediately and automatically. So, as we begin to question and reduce our conditioned dependency on men, we are likely to initially transfer it onto women. Consciously or unconsciously, we may expect feminists to look after our best interests and shield us from the prospect of aloneness. It is not a crazy or illogical expectation, but it does make for a movement full of projected insecurity and high stakes conflict.

There is an aloneness that is distinct from alienation, an aloneness that is painful but necessary to face if we wish to improve our lives, relationships, and social movements. Elizabeth Cady Stanton wrote about it in her 1892 speech *The Solitude of Self*: "We come into the world alone, unlike all who have gone before us, we leave it alone, under circumstances peculiar to ourselves." Our power as individuals is hidden in this solitude: our power to know, to name, to decide, to envisage, to create, to become physically strong. A desire to know that power as fully as possible, and with it, to cultivate our own unique, creative response to the world, exists within us. Both Lerner and Maté write about this when they distinguish between *responsibility*, that weight of moral obligation many women carry, and *response-ability*, the reality that none of us can "fix" the world, nor is it our duty—but we are each gifted with the ability to respond. Having only one life, this ability is sacred. It is not to be flitted away on virtuous "helping" and homework. What sort of feminist movement would we have if we each reckoned with this?

Negotiation

Imagine a movement of women who have learned to find riches in solitude, who are committed to knowing their own creative power, and who come together on that basis to move the obstacles that stand in our way as a sex. That is the movement I want to be part of. Only, there is nowhere to sign up—this movement has no name, no website, no spokespeople, no membership subscription and no e-mail address. It will grow like fruit from a tree as women discover each other in the process of rediscovering ourselves.

I no longer believe that anything less than a dedication to tending the fire inside that cannot be put out is worthy of women, as individuals or as a sex. Nor do I believe that anything less than this can be called politically practical. I agree with Maté when he says, in a talk titled *The Power of Addiction and the Addiction of Power*:

> *the addiction to power is always about the emptiness that you try to fill from the outside... and so as we look at this difficult world with a loss of the environment and global warming and the depredations in the oceans, let's not look to the people in power to change things. Because the people in power, I'm afraid to say, are very often, some of the emptiest people in the world and they are not going to change things for us. We have to find that light within ourselves, we have to find the light within communities and within our own wisdom and our own creativity. We can't wait for the people in power to make things better for us, because they are never going to, not unless we make them.*[26]

People have called me naïve for not being "pragmatic" enough to accommodate the so-called "political realities" of compromise and concession making in my work. But like Douglass, Luther King, Shakur, and Malcolm X taught—institutions do not respond to negotiation, they respond to pressure. Their positions are not based on best practice theory or innocent misunderstandings, but on investment and attachment to power. So, in my view, it is the tactic of polite political negotiation that is based on assumptions that I would call naïve, because political negotiation assumes that politicians and institutions respond to reason and negotiation *at all*—that they are interested in things like common ground, goodwill, good ideas and coherent thinking. They are not.

When we build a movement based on negotiation, it hurts us in two main ways: firstly, because it ignores the way that institutions truly operate. Transgenderism and its denial of biological sex and female existence has turned the statement "women are female" into a political one. What this statement (which used to be a mere fact) now represents, is not an argument or a piece of information, but the reassertion of a boundary that is being violated in the interests of power. When feminists make the now-political assertion that "women are female," but make concessions in the process of negotiating with the powerful (for instance by referring to "transwomen," or "trans rights," in campaigns against sex self-identification laws, by calling men who wear feminine clothing "she" out of "respect," or by shunning women who don't comply with these compromises), these concessions undermine the very boundary that their political truth telling was intended to assert in the first place. We will not get very far, for very long, like that.[27]

Feminists who engage with political lobbying based on compromise, palatability, and negotiation also often deny that women *want* very much. The feminist negotiator insists that women do not want much, because they think it would be political suicide to tell the truth: that we want autonomy and adventure, that we want to live full lives, and that this means we want to recreate the culture we live in from scratch. The negotiator has a lot to say about what we "*just* want." We *just* want safehouses. We *just* want our *prison cells to be sex-segregated*, because we just want to be safe from rape in jail. We *just* want our changing rooms and bathrooms and sports teams to be for us and not for *strange men*. We *just* want a turn to speak, after we have *finished listening*. (As Brodribb wrote in 1992, "I have to make arguments which sound extravagant to my ears, that women exist. That women are sensible."[28])

In her book *Women, Sex and Addiction*, Charlotte Kasl terms the feminine or "helpmate" role codependency, and says that "codependency is women's basic training."[29] She explains the cost to us when she says,

> *Codependency is difficult to describe because it is often about what a person does not do, which is basically to live her life. She doesn't follow the path of her own interests or let her passions flow through her. She is afraid of strong feelings and power. If the addict overindulges in sensory pleasures, the codependent starves herself of them. Or if she does indulge, she immediately feels guilty and can't enjoy them because at her core she feels undeserving.*

How sad this is, when, as *Untamed* author Glennon Doyle says, "the blueprints of heaven are etched inside the deep desires of women."[30]

Think about it: if choosing the path of politeness, palatability, and compromise really worked as a political strategy, even though it mirrors our conditioning, it would have succeeded already. Because if it were possible to condense the sound of women's voices over five thousand years of patriarchy, into a single sound recording—on playing it, you would hear this very sound of negotiation. As Gerda Lerner writes in *The Creation of Feminist Consciousness*—

> *This ultimate consequence of men's power to define—the power to define what is a political issue and what is not—has had a profound effect on women's struggle for their own*

emancipation. Essentially, it has forced thinking women to waste much time and energy on defensive arguments; it has channeled their thinking into narrow fields; it has retarded their coming into consciousness as a collective entity and has literally aborted and distorted the intellectual talents of women for thousands of years.[31]

This leads to the second reason why a reformist approach, based on negotiation and debate, is not as sensible as its advocates like to think: it necessitates that we ignore the way that oppression really works. Oppression does not leverage the power of persuasion, but the power of *pain*. If we become loyal to power through pain, attachment, and addiction, and not through persuasion, then the challenge of politicising is not just the challenge of becoming persuasive either, nor only of coming to terms with material reality and moral obligation. It is the challenge of confronting pain—mostly, our own. It is the challenge of confronting our own addictions, habits and attachments, and our own inner resistance to living for our own selves.

When we ignore this work, or minimise its importance, we risk doing something truly tragic: building a movement that reproduces the dynamics of self-sacrifice, obligation, stress and burnout, in which we martyr ourselves all over again, instead of transforming pain into something that can help us to relearn what it means to feel alive, and allow us to experience, in our own lifetimes, what it is like to be part of a culture created by countless women doing the same. A movement loved by women is the only kind that will ever create lasting and meaningful change.

Love

Today feminists are generally offered two alternative conceptions of freedom. In one, freedom will come after you release your body from that restrictive clothing you're wearing by signing up to these pole dancing classes; in the other, because women are oppressed as a class, no woman can be free until all women are free. To me, both of these narratives contain a fantastical element. Surely, an individual woman who is in denial about collective oppression cannot liberate herself as an individual, and certainly not by swinging around a pole in a g-string; but just as surely, a group of people who do not believe that they can liberate themselves, cannot liberate an entire sex class. As the Buddha taught,

> *It is not possible... that someone stuck in the mud could pull out another who is stuck in the mud. But it is possible that someone not stuck in the mud could pull out another who is stuck in the mud.*[32]

And in the words of the Tsultrim Allione, whose work explores the relationship between women and Buddhism,

> *In order for women to find viable paths to liberation, we need the inspiration of other women who have succeeded in remaining true to their own energies.*[33]

The women's liberationists of the seventies acted neither on the assumption that freedom is purely personal, nor that it is something we cannot experience ourselves, but only work for out of a moral obligation to future generations. Of course, freedom is not compatible with denial about our circumstances, but neither is it some hypothetical social order that people may or may not be able to agree on or bring about in a vaguely imagined, distant future.

Freedom lives in a woman's body. Our bodies know freedom, and point the way. They tell us when aspects of our lives, habits, beliefs, relationships or circumstances are antithetical to a state of ease, a state of growth, a state of expansion, and a state of freedom. Liberation is the work of learning how to listen to these signals and act for ourselves, whatever resistance we may face. Repression is the work of ignoring these signals, trying to *stop* the body from insisting that we seek conditions more conducive to the natural state of freedom. As Doyle puts it, "it takes a lot of effort for a live human being to stay half dead."[34]

The feminists who started women's lands during the second wave also teach us something about this energy and the way that women's freedom exists already, locked inside our bodies, so long as we insist that negotiation with power is the only path to change. In Australia, Chris Sitka helped to establish women's lands and says that she is committed to the cause of women's liberation, "Not because I intellectually prefer it, but because I have emotionally experienced it." As difficult as it might be to conceive of building new women's lands now, Sitka's writing captures the way that freedom is real for her, and not just a political concept. She explains,

The land Herself embraced me and nurtured me. She gave me confidence and strength. Both my body and mind muscles grew. I walked and ran and swam and rode on horses and loved my own body deeply and unconditionally. Not least because no-one, including the women I lived amongst, ever judged me for how I dressed, or didn't dress at all; or how wild and unkempt my hair was as I tangled with vines and got dirty churning up clay.

She recalls,

We sang day and night. We sang our joy and our hope for women. We sang to the land and to each other. It was a primal kind of love. An expanding love that circled the Earth and boomeranged back to us.[35]

Margot Oliver writes how, on the same women's lands,

I learnt about the absence of fear. In a contemplative moment I calculated that with the three local Women's Lands and the surrounding Crown Lands, there were about five

square miles to roam where we would only be accosted by other women—or by no-one else at all. We might meet a snake or three—a shy red-belly black or a diamond python highly likely, on occasion a brilliant green and yellow tree snake, or even a deceptively harmless looking brown snake—but no male violence.

It was extraordinary to decompress from this fear that all women carry, and also to be with other women realising the same liberation of body and psyche; experiencing that, in this fundamental way, we were safe.[36]

Of course, the foremothers of the second wave were the freedom fighters and suffragists of the first. And in her book *Sisters in Spirit: Haudenosaunee (Iroquois) Influence on Early American Feminists*, Sally Roesh Wagner asks the question, "How did the radical suffragists come to their vision, a vision not of Band-Aid reform but of a reconstituted world completely transformed?" She concludes, "They believed women's liberation was possible because they knew liberated women, women who possessed rights beyond their wildest imagination: Haudenosaunee women."[37] Haudenosaunee women (commonly known as Iroquois) were not bought and sold in marriage, not ashamed of their bodies, not subordinate, not afraid of the men of their own clans or of the "dark." Barbara Mann, of Seneca heritage, writes that,

The notion of such formalized woman-power may startle Europeans and their descendants, but it is an old and mature idea among Native Americans, especially those east of the Mississippi River. All eastern Nations recognised the political, economic, spiritual and social roles of clan mothers.[38]

Feminist mothers and advocates for home birth and women's rights in childbirth, like MaryLou Singleton and Michelle Peixinho in the United States and author Janet Fraser in Australia, also know about reclaiming this female sovereignty. As Fraser says in her book

Born Still, "What women really lack is autonomy in our lives, and thus in our birthing as well."[39] In *Wisdom Rising,* Tsultrim Allione recalls giving birth to her daughter in a way that captures so much about the shift from negotiation and "niceness," to tuning into the body and acting for the self, despite the discomfort of others:

> *By evening, I had been in hard labor for eight hours when the doctor arrived from Seattle. My labor wasn't progressing, and he thought the baby's head was in the wrong position. Suddenly I thought: I have to get this baby out! It's up to me, no one else can do this. What do I need to do?*
>
> *I tuned in to my body, got off the bed and onto the floor on my hands and knees, and told the doctor to leave me. I began weaving and shaking back and forth, up and down. My husband tried to approach me to tell me to be calm and breathe quietly, but I told everyone to get out of the way. I wasn't nice and calm; I was fierce and clear... And before long, I held my newborn daughter in my arms.*[40]

Doesn't this also amount to an argument that yes, it is not only right, but imperative that women, as individuals, not only commit ourselves to the "cause" of feminism but honour our own bodies, lives, sexuality, desires and potential as we get ourselves *free*? Incidentally, many liberal women echo this message poignantly. In Doyle's words,

> *Selfless women make for an efficient society but not a beautiful, true, or just one... What we need are women who are full of themselves.*[41]

In her TED talk *12 truths I learned from life and writing,* Anne Lamott says,

Our help is usually not very helpful. Our help is often toxic. And help is the sunny side of control. Stop helping so much. Don't get your help and goodness all over everybody.[42]

In *Big Magic*, Elizabeth Gilbert pleads,

Whenever anybody tells me they want to write a book in order to help other people I always think "Oh, please don't."

Please don't try to help me.

I mean it's very kind of you to help people, but please don't make it your sole creative motive because we will feel the weight of your heavy intention, and it will put a strain upon our souls.

Your own reasons to make are reason enough. Merely by pursuing what you love, you may inadvertently end up helping us plenty. ("There is no love which does not become help," taught the theologian Paul Tillich.) Do whatever brings you to life, then. Follow your own fascinations, obsessions, and compulsions. Trust them. Create whatever causes a revolution in your heart.[43]

At its essence, women's movement is created not only out of women's intellectual efforts or political commitment but out of women's pain and our desire to be free of it. This pain represents our longing to feel alive, not used, not exploited, not bored, not stressed to the bone, not tired, not foggy, not half asleep. When we use pain as a signal that we need to free ourselves from oppressive roles, habits, and circumstances, we inevitably face resistance inside ourselves, in our private lives, and in the public sphere.

Still, transmuting pain to freedom is the only way. In a world made up of institutions that will budge under nothing but pressure, the only collective strategy that can actually be considered pragmatic for women is the creation of movements that are not only "helpful" and righteous, **but that we love deeply, in our bones**. The movement we love is the one that is for us, and that we will commit to.

33

Of course, such a movement can involve committee meetings and seats at negotiation tables—but without question, it cannot begin in those places. Women's liberation movement really does begin with us—with each impulse felt, each word spoken, each action taken, each thing made from the love of freedom that lives in a woman's heart—refusing, ever and always, to go silent.

Endnotes

1   Contreras, Dona Enriqueta "Matriarchal Values with the Sierra Juarez Zapotecs of Oaxaca" in Heide Goettner-Abendroth (ed). *Societies of Peace*. Inanna Publications and Education Inc., 2009, pp. 76-8.

2   Lorde, Audre. *Sister Outsider*. The Crossing Press, 1984, p. 39.

3   The wonderful words of Mary Oliver, from her poem, *The Summer Day*.

4   Here I wanted to use the phrase "women's liberation movement" the way bell hooks does in *Feminist Theory: From Margin to Center* (South End Press, 1984). Hooks uses the word "movement" in this phrase not as a concrete noun pointing to something fixed and countable ("a social movement," "the women's movement"). Instead she uses "movement" as an abstract noun, denoting "the act of moving."

5   See Hawthorne, Susan. *In Defense of Separatism*. Spinifex Press, 2019.

6   Lerner, Harriet. *The Dance of Anger*. Pandora, 1989, p. 79.

7   Lerner, Harriet. *The Dance of Anger*. Pandora, 1989, p. 34.

8   Leidholdt, Dorchen and Janice Raymond (eds). *The Sexual Liberals and the Attack on Feminism*. Teachers College Press, 1990.

9   Brodribb, Somer. *Nothing Mat(t)ers: A Feminist Critique of Postmodernism*. Spinifex Press, 1992.

10 McKinnon, Catharine. "Points Against Postmodernism." Chicago Kent Law Review 75:3, 2000, pp.687-712.

11 Eagleton, Terry. *The Illusions of Postmodernism*. Blackwell Publishers, 1996.

12 Herman, Judith. *Trauma and Recovery*. Basic Books, 1992, p.8.

13 There is an excellent analysis of dualism and its origins in Foster, Judy. *Invisible Women of Prehistory*. Spinifex Press, 2013.

14 Susan Cox interviewed by Derrick Jensen for Resistance Radio, January 29, 2017. Accessed via YouTube. For more critiques of postmodernism, see also Mantilla, Karla. "Let Them Eat Text: The real politics of postmodernism." *Sisterhoodispowerful*, https://

sisterhoodispowerful.wordpress.com/2014/02/21/let-them-eat-text-the-real-politics-of-postmodernism/; Djinn, Anna. "Neoliberalism, Queer Theory and Prostitution." *The Feministahood*, 8 Nov. 2014, https://thefeministahood.wordpress.com/2014/11/08/neoliberalism-queer-theory-and-prostitution/, and Ekman, Kasja Ekis. *Being and Being Bought: Prostitution, Surrogacy, and the Split Self.* Spinifex Press, 2013.

15 Raymond, Janice. *A Passion for Friends.* The Women's Press, 1986, p. 180.

16 Maté, Gabor. *When the Body Says No.* Penguin, 2019.

17 Andrea Dworkin discussing her book Heartbreak in 2002 at The Radcliffe Institute's Schlesinger Library.

18 Dworkin, Andrea. *Our Blood.* Perigree Books, 1976, p. 70.

19 Dworkin, Andrea. *Our Blood.* Perigree Books, 1976, p. 61.

20 Maté, Gabor. *When the Body Says No.* Penguin, 2019, p. 174.

21 Lerner, Harriet. *The Dance of Anger.* Pandora, 1989, p. 35.

22 Lerner, Harriet. *The Dance of Anger.* Pandora, 1989, p. 39.

23 Christ, Carol. *Diving Deep and Surfacing.* Beacon Press, 1980, p. 13.

24 Daly, Mary. *The Fire of Female Fury.* 1980 talk, accessed via YouTube.

25   Lerner, Harriet. *The Dance of Anger.* Pandora, 1989, p. 33.

26 Maté, Gabor. *The Power of Addiction and the Addiction of Power*, TED talk, 2012.

27 Here I want to acknowledge the struggle that Julia Long in particular has waged to draw attention to this same political problem in the United Kingdom, where women like herself and Sheila Jeffreys are marginalised by more popular lobby groups like A Woman's Place UK, for their refusal to engage in concession making and compromise for instance by adopting the language of "trans rights" to placate those in power; for their loyalty to women including the female ex-partners of men who "transition," and for their willingness to consider direct action over negotiation with people in positions of power. Today, this sort of political integrity is more alienating than it should be for women, given that we are supposedly living in a time of radical, feminist, and radical feminist awakening.

28 Brodribb, Somer, *Nothing Mat(t)ers: A Feminist Critique of Postmodernism.* Spinifex Press, 1992, p. xviii.

29 Kasl, Charlotte. *Women, Sex and Addiction.* Harper and Row, 1989, p. 34.

30 Doyle, Glennon. *Untamed.* Dial Press, 2020, p. 121.

31 Lerner, Gerda. *The Creation of Feminist Consciousness.* Oxford University Press, 1993, p. 10. Gerda Lerner has no known relation to Harriet Lerner, also quoted in this essay.

32 Thiradhammo, Ajahn (ed.). *Treasures of the Buddha's Teaching.* Aruno Publications, 2013, p. 160.

33 Allione, Tsultrim. *Women of Wisdom.* Arkana, 1984, p. 20.

34 Doyle, Glennon. *Untamed.* Dial Press, 2020, p. 83.

35 Sitka, Chris in Sand Hall (ed). *Shelters and Building.* Shall Publishing, 2019, pp. 164-74.

36 Oliver, Margot in Sand Hall (ed). *Shelters and Building.* Shall Publishing, 2019, p. 33.

37 Wagner, Sally Roesch. *Sisters in Spirit: Haudenosaunee (Iroquois) Influence on Early American Feminists.* Native Voices, 2001, pp. 34-41.

38 Mann, Barbara. "They Are the Soul of the Councils: The Iroquoian Model of Woman-Power" in Heide Goettner-Abendroth (ed). *Societies of Peace.* Inanna Publications and Education Inc., 2009, pp. 57-69.

39 Fraser, Janet. *Born Still.* Spinifex Press, 2020, pp. 13-14.

40 Allione, Tsultrim. *Wisdom Rising.* Enliven Books, 2018, p. 14.

41 Doyle, Glennon. *Untamed.* Dial Press, 2020, p. 75.

42 Lamott, Ann. TED Talk, *12 truths I learned from life and writing.* https://www.ted.com/talks/anne_lamott_12_truths_i_learned_ from_life_and_writing.

43 Gilbert, Elizabeth. *Big Magic.* Riverhead Books, 2015.

CHAPTER 2

Radical Feminist Activism in the 21ˢᵗ Century

by Janice G. Raymond

This article was originally published in Labrys 27 (January 2015). Reprinted with permission.

When I was asked to speak at the 2014 radical feminism conference in London, the organizers asked me to talk about the future of radical feminism. The only way I could address the future was to evoke the past and the present, highlighting some of the milestones of radical feminist activism in my own life and work, with the hope that the history of radical feminist ideas and activism can generate some wisdom about the future.

I became a radical feminist in the late 1960s. But I was probably a budding radical feminist before that, since I grew up in an extended family of six boys. Luckily, I was the oldest. The period spanning the late 1960s and the 1970s was a vibrant time for feminism, not without its differences, however, between the so-called brands of feminism.

During part of that period, I was in graduate school. For many U.S. students at this time, it was impossible to be engaged in academic work without being involved in the major political issues of the day—civil rights, the anti-war movement as the United States was attempting to crush Vietnam, the environmental movement and of course, feminism. I was fortunate to study with Mary Daly and to be part of a radical feminist group of graduate students from many different universities in the Boston area who became activists.

At the time, I was working on a Ph.D. with a concentration in medical ethics. Legal abortion was one of the controversial debates of the day in the United States. Prior to the U.S. Supreme Court decision in 1973, which legalized abortion until fetal viability, I had begun to speak publicly in various states and public forums about a woman's right to abortion. Many of these invitations came to me because at the time, I was technically a member of a progressive religious community of Catholic nuns. Of course, a Roman Catholic nun speaking out in favor of women's right to abortion generated publicity and hastened my formal exit from the community.

In the mid-1970s, I was hired at the University of Massachusetts in Amherst, one of the largest public universities in the United States, where for 28 years, I was a professor. At the time, Women's Studies was a new academic field on U.S. university campuses. Many faculty in the Women's Studies programs of this era were socialist feminists, and radical feminists were definitely in the minority. This was before the advent of post-modernist theory, when many of the socialist feminists became post-modernists and when this brand of theory came to dominate a large number of Women's Studies programs.

At the same time, the feminist women's health movement was evolving, initially to challenge many medical practices that impacted women. The feminist women's health movement also generated women's health centers in which women's health problems were addressed and treated—injuries from women being battered, vaginal infections, menstruation, menopause, contraception, abortion, sterilization abuse of African American women in the United States and internationally, and self-help learning.[1]

Much of my teaching, writing and activism at the time focused on the use of technologies that were destructive to women's bodies and minds—for example, behavior control and modification

40

technologies such as psychosurgery (formerly called lobotomies) and electroshock therapies. In the United States, these technologies were used much more frequently on women than on men. As I began to write about these so-called therapies, I encountered women who had been subjected to them. One was a lesbian feminist activist whose parents, when she was a young woman, had her involuntarily confined in a mental institution, and subjected to lobotomy because a psychiatrist claimed it would cure her lesbianism. Instead, the surgery inflicted severe memory loss, periodic catatonia and chronic headaches lasting into adulthood.

Reproductive Technologies

At a conference in Groningen in the Netherlands in 1984, I met a group of radical feminist activists and academics, and we founded an international women's rights group called FINRRAGE that would monitor government policies and programs on reproduction, reproductive technologies, genetic engineering and the rapid development of new techniques such as surrogacy and reproductive drugs that were being targeted for use on women worldwide. The women in our founding group came from Australia, Argentina, Bangladesh, Switzerland, the UK and the US. We spoke at many conferences on the new reproductive and genetic technologies, testified before state and national bodies, and edited a journal called *Reproductive and Genetic Engineering*.[2] Some of us also wrote books on these issues. Mine was entitled, *Women as Wombs: Reproductive Technologies and the Battle over Women's Freedom*.[3]

Although most discussions of technological reproduction are focused on western technologies such as in vitro fertilization and freezing embryos, the reproductive use of women is being played out on an international medical stage where women's bodies are being trafficked for reproduction and/or utilized in reproductive tourism. Surrogate brokers, for example, quite candidly admit that they seek new and more inexpensive markets for women who will breed children for other people since the going rate is cheaper and the so-called labor supply more unquestioning. India has become the center of this reproductive tourism with a proliferation of surrogacy centers that advertise women for hire, and babies for westerners, through the use of poor Indian women as surrogates.

Lesbian Feminism

Also during the 1980s, the so-called "sexuality wars" surfaced within the feminist movement in the United States and elsewhere, primarily raised by the issue of pornography. Lesbians were particularly involved in these sexuality debates. In the 1970s, lesbianism had not been separated from feminism because many lesbians identified especially as radical feminists. Lesbian feminism was a politics of commitment to women and women's rights, not a biological destiny, and not simply a lifestyle. During the 1980s, lesbianism became a sexual identity without a feminist politics. Nothing contributed as much to this divide—between those who viewed lesbianism as only a sexual identity and those who identified as lesbian feminists—as the emergence of a sexual libertarian culture that staked its claim to a liberated lesbian sexuality grounded in the male-demand modes of sexual behavior—pornography, prostitution, and lesbian S&M.[4]

The debates about lesbian sexuality dominated Britain's first lesbian summer school, held in July of 1989. At this gathering I gave a talk, which became a published article called "Putting the Politics Back Into Lesbianism." Basically, I argued that there was little difference between a conservative worldview that locates women in this world primarily as sexual objects of men's fantasies and desires, and a lesbian libertarian lifestyle that is increasingly preoccupied with fucking as the be-all and end-all of lesbian existence. It is difficult to see what is progressive or rebellious about a position that locates female desire and that imprisons female sexual dynamism, vitality and vigor in the male-demand practices of sexual objectification, subordination and violence, this time engaged in by women. It was predictable that the lesbian feminist view would be categorized as anti-sex, and as puritanical radical feminism; and that those of us who made certain forms of lesbian sexual behavior problematic would be accused of being dogmatic and having no fun![5]

Radical feminism historically has called for the de-sexualization of women in the media, the marketplace and the world in general. What the sexual libertarians and liberals achieved was the re-sexualization of women using feminist and lesbian liberation rhetoric to assert that sexuality is a radical impulse. But sexuality is no more radical than much else. There are certain expressions of it that may be radical and there are other expressions of it that are not. It is ironic that the sexual libertarians want to reinvigorate the male-demand forms of sexuality on which they base their claims to sexual liberation.

I don't want to leave you with the impression that lesbians did not resist this view of sexuality. Certainly many lesbians did resist, and are still in the forefront of, for example, the anti-pornography movement. Lesbians are fighting internationally against global systems of prostitution and sexual slavery. But whereas formerly, you could count on a political movement of lesbian feminism, that political effort now seems diminished. Lesbian feminism was a movement based on the power of a "we"—not on an individual woman's sexual fantasy or self-expression—a shared politics, which maintained that prostitution, pornography and sexual violence could not be rationalized in the name of free choice, and that sex trafficking is globalized prostitution.

Sex Trafficking and Prostitution

In the 1990s, I became co-executive director with Dorchen Leidholdt of the international Coalition against Trafficking in Women (CATW).[6] For many years, I have worked with women in many different parts of the world to combat the prostitution and sex trafficking of women and children. As a feminist abolitionist activist visiting over 50 countries, I have met hundreds of women who have been in systems of prostitution and whose lives have been ravaged by it. I have met women who thought they were migrating out of their countries for work and ended up in the sex industry. I have met runaway girls in my country, who ran away because a male relative had sexually abused them at home, only to find themselves smoothtalked and pimped into the sex industry. I have been in brothels where I have seen young children servicing male buyers. And I have talked with men who are habitual prostitution users who feel entitled to use women's and girls' bodies to meet their alleged sexual needs.

As an activist, I have learned that working against the sex industry is like working against nothing else. The industry has friends in high places and has become a major lobbyist on behalf of national and international legislation that would favor its expansion. One wonders where all the anti-globalization activists are when it comes to confronting the globalized sex industry. Instead, the debate over prostitution has focused mainly on women's choice and consent. From the critics of international capitalism, we hear very little about the role of the sex industry and its economic and sexual exploitation of women. There is a dominant academic perception that prostitution is just sex, not sexual exploitation; just sex, not a sex industry; and that we must preserve whatever calls itself "sex." We are urged to swear loyalty oaths to any practice that gets represented as sex. The very language of "sex work" and "sex worker" helps to launder the system of prostitution throughout the world.

In pro-prostitution discourse, prostitution is sex work, not sexual exploitation. Pimps are third party business agents who women choose to protect themselves and manage their economic interests, not first-class exploiters. In Victoria Australia, pimps who are legal brothel owners are designated as sex work service licensees. Prostitution users are customers or clients who provide women with incomes, not abusers. Brothels are safe spaces for women to ply their trade, not quarters where women are controlled and kept in check. Women in prostitution are sex workers, not victims of sexual exploitation. And victims of trafficking are migrant sex workers whose passage from one country to another is facilitated migration by helpful people movers. Even the words escort and escort agencies make the system of prostitution sound more chic and safe. This rhetorical strategy lends support to a global sex industry by supporting its goals to normalize prostitution as work and sanction its perpetrators as simply entrepreneurs and cordial capitalists.

The global system of prostitution is based on gender. Most of the studies that have interviewed prostitution users—those men who exploit women for the sex of prostitution—have documented that gendered views of women feature largely in why men buy women for sexual activities. From the British guy who admits "I want my prostitute ... to be a pretend girlfriend...to be genuinely attracted to me," to the outright misogynist who responds proudly, "At just the right moment I leaned forward and shot my load on her face! She was surprised and shocked, this got me more excited than the act"—men's views and actions as prostitution users are based on ideas about women that conform to their gendered views of who women are, and how women are expected to act.[7]

Transgender

There is gender and there is transgender. When I first published The Transsexual Empire in 1979,[8] the word gender was understood to be separate from the word sex. Sex was what defined a person biologically, and gender was understood to mean the sex- appropriate behavior that was socially constructed. In her new and brilliant book, Gender Hurts, Sheila Jeffreys looks at the history of the word gender and emphasizes the fact that radical feminists used the term to talk about gender roles, the "gender order," or the gender hierarchy, but in each of these usages, it was clear that it meant a social and political construction of male and female behavior. Now, as Jeffreys points out, gender has replaced the word sex, "as if gender itself is biological."[9] The conflation of sex and gender is achieved in

45

the construction of the category transgender. The term transgender, replacing transsexual, has expanded to include not only those who undergo surgery but also those who avoid the surgery, use only opposite-sex hormones, or simply self-identify as member of the opposite sex.

People sometimes ask me, "What's the big deal about transgender," and why is it such a significant issue, especially in the schema of pressing issues that feminists concern ourselves with. As I saw it then and see it now, transsexualism and transgender raise questions of what gender is and how to challenge it. Advocates of transgender argue that it is a radical challenge to gender—transgressing gender expectations and rigid boundaries of socially appropriate sex-role behavior—if a person undergoes surgery or hormone treatment to configure one's body to the opposite sex, or simply claims membership in the opposite sex by self-identification. If we have to change our bodies in order to challenge gender norms, we are not transcending gender, i.e., we are not free from gender. We are exchanging one gendered identity for the other. What good is a gender outlaw who is still abiding by the rules of gender?

The "transsexual empire" is the conglomerate of medical specialties that join together to make transsexual treatment and surgery possible. As with prostitution and sex trafficking, people ignore the medical industry that has colonized gender dissatisfaction. As a wide swath of conduct and personal struggles are labeled as psychological problems or as syndromes requiring medical solutions, all sorts of behaviors are treated with drugs, surgery, and other technical means. More and more personal, ethical, and social conflicts are defined as medical problems when they are actually human problems in living that conflict with social and political norms.

Carrying the medical model to the extremities of enforcing gender conformity, the Indian state of Madhya Pradesh is investigating claims that up to 300 girls were surgically turned into boys for parents who wanted sons. Women's rights campaigners have denounced the practice stating that transsexual surgery makes a "mockery of women in India."[10]

Since the Islamic revolution in 1979, Iran has become the second country after Thailand to perform more transsexual surgeries than any other, where many male homosexuals and some lesbians experience pressure to transition surgically as a means of normalizing their homosexuality. In a country where homosexual acts are criminalized and punishable by execution, persons who undergo sex reassignment surgery can exist without fear. The law serves to encourage, if not compel, homosexuals to undergo surgery to escape harassment and punishment. Authorities have proposed transsexual surgery as a way of "hetero-normalizing" persons with same-sex desires or who engage in same-sex relations. Although Iran has some of the most repressive laws against women and same-sex relations, it has a liberal and lucrative medical sex change industry in which much of the cost of the surgery is covered by the government.[11]

Especially troubling in the west is the institutionalization of hospital-based gender identity clinics that treat children who act out opposite-sex behavior. A primary effect of defining gender identity as a medical problem to be solved by hormonal treatments and surgery is to encourage parents to view their children as in need of transgender treatment. Children then undergo psychiatric evaluation and hormone treatment, often followed by surgery. These clinics are multiplying in countries such as the United States, Britain, and Australia.[12]

Any woman who has experienced the agony of not fitting into a society where gender is defined by rigid roles is hardly insensitive to the suffering that transsexuals and those who identify as transgender experience. Like persons who want to change gender, many women have felt dissatisfied with their bodies and found themselves in a psychically disjointed state because they could not accept their role. However, through a process of consciousness-raising, many feminists have learned that there is a whole male power structure that defines who and what we are allowed to be.

47

Today, there are more women who identify as trans men than when I published my book in 1979. Nevertheless, it is still mostly a one-way traffic of men moving down the transgender highway.[13] And it is certainly a one-way flow of men who identify as trans women moving down the online highway, demanding the recognition of their "womanhood" and attacking mainly radical feminists who refuse this acknowledgment, trying to silence our public speech and even threatening us with violence and death.

The debate about transgender has succeeded in dividing many feminists. However, if we can't agree on what is a woman, how can we agree on much else? How can we claim to defend women's rights if we cede our womanhood to men? Do hormones, surgery and or self-identification make a woman? The tragedy is that many women no longer acknowledge that being born female conveys a common history and a life of biological, social and political significance. When abortion rights organizations are being pressured to stop using the word women about those who become pregnant and seek abortions, and to include in their literature that men can become pregnant (i.e., persons who identify as trans men), where have all the feminists gone?

Men who claim they are women, and their advocates, have devoted enormous energy to ensure that a man, whether he has gone through transsexual surgery or whether he simply self-identifies as a woman, is allowed into women's bodies, events, meetings, music festivals and the like. It appears that the bedrooms of lesbians are now the topic du jour of the transgender press and blogosphere. Certain transgender forums have been organized specifically to discuss and strategize how lesbians could be pressured to date and have sex with those who identify as trans lesbians. As one transgender activist put it, "Trans women's bodies are female bodies, whether or not we have penises." Perhaps the epitome of this incongruity is that men who claim to be lesbians are now claiming that they have a lesbian penis or, as one transgender activist worded it, a "lady stick." Yet lesbians who reject that men can be lesbians are slurred as transphobic.[14]

This is the world of Alice in Wonderland—where Alice is the radical feminist and Humpty Dumpty is the transgender advocate—as exemplified in the following conversation between the two. First, Humpty Dumpty states with a full dose of male certitude: "When I use a word, it means what I choose it to mean. Neither more nor less!" To which Alice responds, "The question is whether you CAN make words mean so many different things." To which Humpty Dumpty admitted: "The question is who is to be master, that's all."

Radical feminism and the future

Indeed, the question of who is to be master is the question of political power. And this brings me to the question of the future of radical feminism. I have no special wisdom in predicting the future. However, I do know that a radical feminist future must take the question of power very seriously, and women must be prepared to act in a larger context of worldliness than just the radical feminist community. Throughout history, women in most parts of the globe have lacked influence in and control over the political world in which we live because of women's victimized and derivative status in patriarchy, or because in some radical feminist contexts women have chosen to dissociate from the political world. In conclusion, I want to focus on a radical feminist vision of worldliness for the future.

Working in the world means a confrontation with power and an ability to challenge patriarchal power, especially powerful institutions and industries that subject women to violence and exploitation. It is to realize that women's oppression—whether through technologies that manipulate and mutilate the female body, or through systems of trafficking and prostitution that sexually exploit the female body, or through medical treatment that allegedly constructs a female body from one that is male—has become industrialized, and that what we are challenging are powerful industries.

49

I have always believed that radical feminism is not and cannot be separated from the world in which we exist. Even radical and voluntary dissociation from the world, originally undertaken as a radical separatist stance, can produce a worm's-eye view of the world that removes us from a share of what should be a common world and a radical feminist influence on that world, a world that increasingly is becoming more and more globalized by the industries that manage and control large populations of women—for example, the medical industry and the sex industry, which have joined in promoting both sexual and reproductive access to women's bodies as they internationalize both prostitution and surrogacy to promote sexual and reproductive trafficking.

The radical feminist activism in which I participated during the 1970s and that has continued through most of my activist life involves a lot of talks and testimonies in non-feminist forums, citizens' groups, and governmental commissions and legislatures in various parts of the world. It involves new ways of translating feminist ideas into public policy and legislative forums, crafting an ability to translate feminist politics into public forums. It entails sometimes working with people that we may never have thought we would work with, such as the police or conservative legislators who are ready to pass legislation, for example, which gives protection and assistance to victims of trafficking. And it has involved working with women whom I would never have typed as radical feminists but who in their work for women are radical in the most fundamental sense of that word.

Groups who strive to make political change have to search for ways to act across differences in ideology and tactics. Sometimes, this effort results in organizations acting in loose association. Sometimes, it results in coalitions of those with whom we would never be able to link with on other issues such as anti-war or reproductive rights. African American activist, Fannie Lou Hamer, reminds us that a coalition is not a home. As U.S. civil rights leader, Bayard Rustin, stated, "The issue is which coalition to join and how to make it responsive to your program...the difference between expediency and morality in politics is the difference between selling out a principle and making smaller concessions to win larger ones."

The radical feminist activists of the future will find themselves challenging those who should be our natural allies, e.g., so-called human rights organizations, such as Amnesty International, who draft policies that aim to decriminalize pimping, brothels and prostitution users. Certainly, radical feminists face a difficult road in that we are often fighting both the right and the left, including the left's version of women's sexual and reproductive liberation and the right's version of women's sexual and reproductive morality. Even within feminism, radical feminism has taken on issues that other feminists either avoid or choose to be on the opposing side of, such as in the battles over reproductive technologies, pornography, prostitution and transgender.

What is important for the future of radical feminism is that those of us who are radical feminists engage with the world. We have got to take back this world for ourselves and for other women.

For over 35 years, I have been privileged to work in an international context with some very worldly radical feminists. Over the decades I have been a radical feminist, radical feminism has become more global. I think the radical feminism of the future will continue that global community. I could not have engaged in much of the work that I have done without a community of global feminists. The group of women who founded the Coalition Against Trafficking in Women, Asia Pacific were mainly political prisoners who were detained and some tortured during the Marcos dictatorship in the Philippines. They were victims of a brutal regime who used their victimization not only to confront a political dictatorship but also later to oppose the globalized sex industry. Rachel Moran in her book Paid For has used her personal experience of sexual exploitation to turn experience into reflection on public policy on prostitution, and worked to create national legislation that targets the men who buy women for the sex of prostitution.[15] The organizers of this conference have worked to do just that—create a conference—and against great odds secure a venue over the protests of transgender advocates who would limit radical

51

feminist speech—and in the process of doing so, I'm sure, they have learned a lot of lessons about radical feminist organizing and what it takes to create a public forum.

No one says that this is an easy task. But radical feminism has made great gains. When Kathleen Barry gave new life to feminist abolitionism of prostitution in the 1970s,[16] it was almost impossible to challenge the accepted political ideology that legalization of prostitution protects women and is the progressive system of prostitution legislation. The male buyer was invisible, and few wanted to talk about the male demand for the sex of prostitution. It wasn't until the 1990s that feminist abolitionists were taken seriously by legislators that legalization is not the answer, and that the alternative was to penalize the prostitution users—the men. Feminist abolitionists started with one country, and over a decade of activism, fought to change Sweden's legal system of prostitution to criminalizing the male buyers and decriminalizing the prostituted women. Today, most of the Nordic countries have legislation criminalizing the purchase of sexual activities. The Republic of South Korea and the Philippines have similar laws as does Northern Ireland and Canada. France and the Republic of Ireland are considering anti-demand legislation.

As radical feminists, we may find ourselves in positions where our political activism carries the hazards of being ostracized from our families or peer groups, or being fired from our jobs, but we seldom have to die for our beliefs and politics.

The most important task of activism is to act. Find your own location of activism, whether it's anti-militarism or environmental activism, and imbue that location with radical feminist direction. The task of radical feminist activism is to develop strategies that improve women's lives and thus the human condition. This kind of activism requires critical thinking, participation in the world, and it requires making judgments and acting on them. Find some way to revitalize radical feminist activism in the world.

· Endnotes

1   The Boston Women's Health Book Collective first published *Our Bodies, Ourselves* in booklet form. The original book edition was republished by the New England Free Press in 1971 and sold for 40 US cents.

2   See the Prologue in *Made to Order: the Myth of Reproductive and Genetic Progress*. Eds. Patricia Spallone and Deborah Lynn Steinberg (New York: Pergamon Press), 1987. Written by the founders of FINRRAGE, the prologue illustrates the group's history and goals and how reproductive technologies affect women in different parts of the world.

3   Janice G. Raymond. *Women as Wombs: Reproductive Technologies and the Battle Over Women's Freedom* (San Francisco: HarperSanFrancisco), 1993.

4   See Dorchen Leidholdt and Janice G. Raymond, Eds. *The Sexual Liberals and the Attack on Feminism* (New York: Pergamon Press), 1990.

5   Janice G. Raymond. "Putting the Politics Back into Lesbianism." In *Classics in Lesbian Studies*. Ed. Esther D. Rothblum (London: Haworth Press), 1997.

6   For more information, visit the website of the Coalition Against Trafficking in Women (CATW) at www.catwinternational.org.

7   For a fuller discussion of male attitudes towards women in prostitution, see Chapter II, "Prostitution on Demand: The Prostitution Users," in Janice G. Raymond. *Not a Choice, Not a Job: Exposing the Myths about Prostitution and the Global Sex Trade* (Potomac Books, an imprint of the University of Nebraska Press), 2013.

8   Janice G. Raymond. *The Transsexual Empire: The Making of the She-Male* (Boston: Beacon Press), 1979. For an updated discussion of the politics of transgender, see "Fictions and Facts about The Transsexual Empire" at https://janiceraymond.com/.

9   Sheila Jeffreys. *Gender Hurts: A Feminist Analysis of the Politics of Transgenderism* (London: Routledge), 2014. p. 5.

10 "Indians Pay Surgeons to Turn Girls into Boys." The Telegraph, June 27, 2011, http://www.telegraph.co.uk/news/worldnews/asia/india/8601488/Indians-pay-surgeons-to-turn-girls-into-boys.html. Accessed May 2, 2012.

11 Sasha von Olderhauser. "Iran's Sex-Change Operations Provided Nearly Free-of-Cost." Huffington Post, June 6, 2012. http://www.huffingtonpost.com/2012/06/04/iran-sex-change-operation_n_1568604.html. Accessed May 2, 2012.

12 Jeffreys, *Gender Hurts*, Chapter 6.

13 For example Az Hakeem, in his gender identity disorder clinic in London, writes, "The ratio of biological males to females referred to the service is approximately six to one." Az Hakeem. "Psychotherapy for Gender Identity Disorders." *Advances in Psychiatric Treatment*, 18, pp. 17-24.

14 Kitty Barber. "A Tranny Close to Home." November 27, 2012. http://kittybarber.wordpress.com/tag/ladystick/ Accessed January 25, 2013.

15 Rachel Moran. *Paid For: My Journey Through Prostitution* (Dublin: Gill & Macmillan Books), 2013.

16 Kathleen Barry. *Female Sexual Slavery* (Englewood Cliffs, N.J.: Prentice-Hall), 1979.

CHAPTER 3

Radical Feminism: The Survival of Women

by Tamarack Verrall

Ihave long called myself a radical feminist, an identity that has been under attack for many years. It identifies what I believe, that action is needed to shift from a global society held in place by violence, specifically from a global patriarchal society dominated by men, locked in place through violence toward women and girls.

I was one of those much-maligned feminists of the 1970s as we found our ways to each other, our meetings focused on action, to provide women's centres as safe spaces for women to find help and to speak with each other, documenting what changes were needed, and pressing the Canadian Government to provide money for shelters, for women to escape violence.

Much of our work was not well reported in the conventional news so we developed our own news media, before computers. Telephone lines, travelling to meet, learning how to lay out those early women's liberation newsletters, we found each other and taught each other, sharing our skills. We learned from women visiting from other countries and from women coming into our centres and shelters. Feminist was the word that cut through any doubt. We were focused on discrimination and violence toward women, bringing it into the light and holding it there. But a difference between feminism and radical feminism arose. Radical feminism is firmly committed to go far beyond a few (usually) white women gaining access to well-paying jobs. Radical feminism goes to the root cause of inequity, of the accepted violence, of every form of mistreatment of women, everywhere. Radical feminism is unapologetic, expecting radical change. Radical feminism continues to illuminate what women face, this continually increasing aggression. We speak out about every aspect of oppression, and about the radical change needed in how countries, societies, individuals treat women and girls, in how business is done, how laws are made, how culture is defined with little or no leadership by women. Radical feminism means leadership by women in all aspects of society. Radical feminism means radical change. Radical feminism is determined to expose this patriarchal system of control and to undo it, creating a system in which some will lose privilege and in which all will benefit.

Radical feminism demands an end to this patriarchal system of men holding the power to keep in place a global society in which women are not only side-lined, but punished with rape, torture, imprisonment, murder for speaking out or simply for being women. We are working for a world that recognizes the importance of women's voices and the necessity of change. A world that is not simply a few more women in power with hands tied. A world that does not intentionally hide the contributions women have made in the past, and does not turn away from the need to end every form of violence and control over women and girls globally.

I identify as a radical feminist because I am calling for radical change and unapologetically and critically point to the violence being done by men toward women and girls, including what is being done in the name of customs and in the name of religions that promote discrimination, control and violence, specifically toward women and girls.

Through the 1970s as we set up women's centres and rape crisis centres, raised International Women's Day to a new level, and created public venues to speak out, the word feminist and more so radical feminist was spat back at us in a way that caused many women to privately tell us that though they agreed with everything we were saying, they could not or would not define themselves as a feminist. That it was too risky for them. We were considered too dangerous to be hired, fair game to be maligned. By then I was a feminist, a radical feminist and a radical lesbian feminist, the latter combination that would bring almost certain loss of job if "out" and at the least, the suspicion of being biased and therefore un-hireable. Not trusted as we were for calling for a radical change in society globally, for an end to male supremacy and violence against women, and an end to poverty and indentured labour, our intent has been to fundamentally shift the world economy, dependent on the free labour of women, ending a system in which men, in particular very rich white men, were controlling and continue to control the world economy, and in which all men are still given the message that they are not only allowed to, but expected to control women in their homes, their lives, their jobs, even in the streets.

As we radical feminists became increasingly vocal, growing in numbers, daring to meet to share experiences and ideas, the violence against us increased and a twisted message was spread: the assumption that we wanted to do what men have done to us. There was an outrage that we pointed to the many ways that men continue to dominate women. Even speaking about it proved that we were "man-haters." Hate is a strong and ugly word. The strategy of calling us man-haters has been an effective ploy to cause women to dissociate from even the concept of radical feminism. We have been attacked from the political left and right, the left accusing us of not addressing capitalism despite our clear intention that we end poverty, focused on the majority, who are poor, and most often women of colour. We have been accused of being against men while we have made it clear that it is violent control by men that we are against. We have been strangely accused of being anti-pornography with the argument that stopping pornography is unrealistic and undemocratic. As a radical feminist I see pornography as integral to holding the patriarchal system in place as it provides psychologically damaging material, increasingly violent, a free training school to draw men and boys into addictive behaviour that violates women and girls, and continually feeds a culture that is dangerous to us all. We have been accused of being too radical to imagine a world in which no woman is forced into prostitution, as from circumstance of no other options, of being trafficked into it, or sold into it, this is the reality being described by women and girls desperate to get out of it.

From the start radical feminists have been accused of being anti-male for meeting with each other in women-only spaces. We are accused of hating men for opening women's centres and for simply wanting to meet as women. Recently the hateful term "TERFs" (trans exclusive radical feminists) has arisen as a cry against women-only space, and new forms of violence have been levied against lesbian feminists in particular claiming that meeting as radical feminists or meeting as radical lesbian feminists, even meeting as women, is discriminatory and exclusive.

What has been missing from this argument, which has become a widely accepted series of attacks on those of us who do want to meet without men, is the important detail that we need this, to heal from male violence we have experienced, and to provide healing space for those who have not felt safe to speak about, or even allow themselves to remember what has been done to them by men. It is in these women-only spaces that we can fully look at our past and find support without defensiveness, or fear of having confidentiality broken and be pushed into even more dangerous situations. It is in these women-only spaces that we are able to speak freely about the patriarchal system, understand what it is, share stories on how it has happened, on what women have been doing to change this, to simply feel safety, physical safety, to heal from the violence and to explore how to create a safe world for women and girls. All women and girls.

As a radical feminist I am appalled at the resistance to this simple need. Some time to speak only with each other as women. The many forms of violent responses to this only serve to keep the system that oppresses women in place. We need, at the very least, these moments to heal, to document our experiences, and to create a new plan. The resistance to women meeting is a tactic to prevent change. To attack radical feminism is to undermine the creating of a plan to undo male control over women, to undo a patriarchal system and replace it with a society that is peaceful and respectful of all people. The resistance to women meeting together feeds the current system of keeping women's ideas suppressed. These are discussions that pertain to ourselves as women, documenting what is holding us back. Radical feminists protect this basic right, for women to meet with women without fear, with a safety not available to us yet in the larger public, with the freedom to remember, to envision a different world, and simply, out of respect.

We are working for a world in which there is no more killing girls at birth for being girls, no more dowry systems, forced marriages, trafficking of girls into prostitution, FGM or breast ironing, with the right for girls to go to school, an end to menstrual huts, every girl with the menstrual pads she needs, an end to persecution of widows, and a restructuring of who does labour for free and under what circumstances. An end to beatings, to lack of access to paid work, to being told what to wear and what not to wear, the right to be in public safely, the end of any form of pain inflicted on our bodies and our psyches and the complete freedom to choose what we do with our lives, always.

For everyone, the eradication of poverty, free access to education for all, free medical care, freedom from all violence, the end to all wars, the eradication of trafficking people for labour and sex, the end of slavery and commitment to taking care of this Earth.

What needs to be recognized, understood and respected is that in the time that we have with each other meeting as women and girls we have been doing this work. For anyone to refuse the right for us to have this necessary time to heal ourselves and to provide a healing environment for others, for anyone to interpret this as hateful and discriminatory towards men, is to assume that men deserve the right to tell us what to do. If this small amount of privacy for all of these reasons outlined is still seen as discriminatory or radical, we still have a long way to go toward freedom for women.

I challenge why this is seen as discriminatory or something to disallow. Is it that those opposing are afraid of what we are working toward, because we are speaking of a need for vast and radical change? If this simple time together is what we need, I question the opposition. Do they not want us to remember? To heal? To grow strong in ourselves? To know where and how this violence is happening and to know what needs to change? This is what is made more difficult by the resistance to allow us the freedom to meet when we want to and need to, as women. The motives behind labelling this as discriminatory feels all too familiar as a tactic to keep us from fully knowing, fully healing and gathering the energy we need to continue to offer brief times of safety for women escaping violence and to create this enormous change.

Why I am still a radical feminist

There is so much violence against women even after more than a half century of the women's movement being the main focus of my life. Billions are injured, tortured, killed every day on this planet, and most women still not free to choose our lives, working for little or no money, doing most of the unpaid labour in the world and trying to fix it at the same time. The need for radical change calls for radical action. I am a radical feminist because I refuse to be satisfied with small gains for a few, leaving the majority of women with no change at all. I am a radical feminist in my commitment to anti-racism and to a global community in which no one is left out, a global community in which everyone of us has choice in how we live our lives, in which poverty is eradicated and our planet cared for.

We need this, as a humane society. We need the leadership of women, women who know what needs to be changed, having lived the experience of surviving in a world in which our perspectives have been and continue to be so violently suppressed, a world in which we have been working for what we all need.

A Love Poem to Global Sisters

Far away, deep in my heart
I call out your names in joy
 I carry your stories and how we have met
This is a new ecstasy.
Now that this ancient dream is coming true
This dream that we carried Before we were born –
We are finally,
Finally meeting each other In this lifetime.
Now I have met you
Where you are
Who you are
I have read what you have to say
I have read from you what we can do
Across barriers of time and distance In which we have
always known
That each other was there
And now stories and photos
Of your beautiful faces
And the faces of all those girls and women
That you are gathering in your loving arms
Your voices carry across the oceans
I call out your names
I hear you singing and dancing together
"Until every woman is heard, Until every woman is heard"*
And we sing back and drum and dance from here
The same ancient dance
We are here to do this
And in this life time
We are finally,
Finally Meeting each other.

-- written for my World Pulse Sisters 2015 from
Poems for Daring Women by Tamarack Verrall
[*sung by the Power Women Group, Kenya]

CHAPTER 4

Radical Feminism and the Actualization of Woman

By Bríd

The Dialectic

The life process is anything but linear. From one moment to the next, we spiral through time, exploring the way of the world and discovering ourselves in the process. As we spiral, we abandon ourselves to our convictions and pursue them to their end, only to discover the weaknesses, faults and contradictions of our logic. But at the instant that our failures seem to spell sure ruin—at the apex of one spiraling moment—a new spiral is born, springing forth with a new logic, a new way of being, a new attempt at life. With each spiral, we learn from our past. By incorporating our very contradictions, we neutralize past errors and forge new, stronger selves. This is actualization.

Thesis

The woman of the Twenty-First Century is free. No longer confined to the chains that held her mother imprisoned—to husband, house or child—her potential is unbounded. Should you ask her, she'd say her only oppression now is the pressure to prove woman is deserving of the freedom now afforded her, the pressure of limitless possibility. Her foremothers had smashed the fragile notion of woman, without which these chains had nothing to bind, and achieved in its stead a freedom they had left as yet undefined. The freedom that Twenty-First Century woman inherited waits in anticipation for our Twenty-First Century woman to define. This is the only task for our woman of today.

Remembering, but vaguely, the victimhood that came with the label "woman," our Twenty-First Century woman rejects any association with the term as her first act towards definition. *Person*. From now on, woman is nothing more than *person*. Equality, she reasons, lies in the Universal. Every treatise that speaks of the nature of Man, of the trials and tribulations of Man, she liberally revises to include herself in the philosopher's intentions. Universal Man becomes the prerogative of Twenty-First Century woman too. For she is free.

Unbounded, she charges into the world of Man as his equal, to find her place among men and there define her freedom. Here she is, poised at the onset of ~~womanhood~~ adulthood. But as she asserts herself into fraternity with men she senses something she had not expected: a kernel of change has occurred among them as well. Voices tinged with laughter have become set in baritones behind stern faces fixed for public presentation. The lank muscular frames of puberty have bulked, pumped with a new bravado. These are no longer the boys of her childhood, she thinks. These men, too, have taken the possibility of their burgeoning adulthood and claimed a new fraternity. But theirs appears to be a fraternity of a different sort than our Twenty-First Century woman dreamed for herself. Sitting among them in the wide-open spaces of the Universal, she senses that these men have carved out for themselves a secluded corner she cannot access. By their shared posture, their grammar, it appears these men enact a script she simply hadn't learned. Nervous now—unaware that adulthood comes with these new prerequisites and embarrassed by her mistake—she tries to mimic the nuances these men know so well, but in vain. Without knowledge of the secret handshake of this new fraternity, she is refused entry. Invisible, voiceless, useless, they hand her a stack of papers and volunteer her to staple them.

Nevertheless, she persists. Seeing and appreciating, now, the value of this fraternal script, she becomes awe-struck and enamored by the men who know it so well. If she sought to define her freedom by the Universal, she had better learn from these men—already so comfortable in their Universality—what it means to be free. Her tactics change. There was prior reading to be done, which she neglected. Realizing her failure and her need to catch up, she appeals to one of the men to be her tutor. What a good tutor he is: he tells her she is stupid and she learns.

What is the secret of Universal Man? What is the language that gains one access? He doesn't tell her outright—no, that is not the ways of a true guru—but after many months, a year, she finally becomes awakened to the secret behind her tutor's hints. He plays her music composed by his fraternity and tells her that it is good. He shows her films and she studies the jawlines of their heroes. He reads her books and tells her what it is to know. She thinks she understands at first. She plays a song she once knew and asks if it is good. He smiles at her simplicity and shakes his head. She offers a film of strong heroines but he points with a finger at the limitations of their stature. She tells him that she, too, will write a book, and he laughs and says this is not the way. All that she offers he refuses. All that she thinks for herself is wrong. All that she produces bars her from the Universal. She doesn't yet understand the secret, but she begins to predict its pattern.

One final lesson. The tutor has taken our Twenty-First Century woman to bed now and tells her she will give herself to him. She says *no*, and he advances. It is a lesson, one she's learned before: against Universal Man, woman's voice doesn't matter. How foolish she was to forget. He takes off her clothes, and she doesn't protest again. There is fear on her face, but she has learned it doesn't matter: our tutor won't see it. If she were to hold a mirror to her own face in this moment, she wouldn't see it either. No one can see it, for woman is invisible. She has learned this, and learned this so well, that she now can refuse to see it herself. She is a good student. He moves now to spread her legs. They clamp shut, but he continues, prying her legs apart. This must be another lesson, she thinks. In lessons prior, when her tutor corrects her behavior it is to impart new hints. She waits in trepidation, legs pried apart, to discover what he will teach her this time. In a gesture, Universal Man advances upon our Twenty-First Century woman, her legs pried apart. Man advances and our woman, legs pried apart, recedes from the body now under his control and into the recesses of her mind. He enters and she disappears, legs pried apart.

At last she understands. One final lesson, and, at last, she understands. The pattern—all that she offers he refuses; all that she thinks for herself is wrong; all that she produces bars her from the Universal—its secret is only this, that the Universal is all that she is not. For Universal Man to enter, *she* must disappear, her legs pried apart. At last she understands. She understands that her tutor did not *do* any prior reading. He did not *study* any secret handshake. The gates to the Universal were open to him, lying in wait for him, because the Universal was *made* for him. He is Universal because he is *Man* and Universal Man has always ever *been* Man. And she? She will forever lack this qualification. Lesson concluded, our Twenty-First Century woman crawls to a corner of the bed, crying tears that will go unseen, sobs that will go unheard and pain that will go unrecalled. For even she herself knows that in the world of Universal Man, Twenty-First Century woman cannot exist. She knows now she is not Man. She knows she will never be.

Spiraling, spiraling, she spirals down.

Antithesis

She stops. Our woman is frozen now in an interminable moment of indecision. Her task before was definition but she learned in the surest of ways that she does not define, she is *defined. Man* comes with definition. Man is definition. To be Man is to define. And she is not Man, so she does not define. She is *not-Man*, and as such she is *defined*. That is more certain a definition than she could ever procure. And so, she lies in wait for Man to define her. But Man, existing as he does in a world of Men, does not see her there, waiting. Why would he notice or care for that which cannot definite itself? Lying in wait for definition—because what else is not-Man to do?—she remains Nothing.

Nothing doesn't ask what her freedom is or could be. Freedom is a non-question for Nothing. Nothing forgets herself, erases herself. Nothing's task now (if it can be called such) is to shrink and shrink until not even a void could be found in her place. For Nothing is only a void so long as one believes something must fill its place, and this is only the delusion of her own mind. Her task is to accept within herself, for the sake of the world of Men, that she is *not*. She applies herself earnestly.

Nothing does not offer any opinions or suggestions anymore, for she has none. Nothing does not laugh freely, because to have a sense of humor is to *have*. Nothing cannot have. Nothing stops singing, because to sing is to be inspired, which simply should not be. Nothing lies in wait. She hasn't yet erased her own void yet—who can be surprised if in this task, too, she fails?—and so sometimes Man sees her there, taking up space with her emptiness. He gives her more papers to staple. As she shrinks, the world of Man begins to expand. Her mind now exists for him, and this is good. She asks how to do what it is she is told to do and only does as instructed. *How do you want me to staple these?* Learned uselessness brings her closer to erasure. Even then, she regrets that her void has been seen, but she does her best to shrink. She shrinks and Man fills her space.

She awaits her cues. At 3:45, she stares at the clock—*half an hour*. 4pm—*15 minutes*. 4:10—*5 minutes*. 4:15 she hears the car door slam. She holds her breath, preparing to be Nothing. The basement door opens and shuts. She waits. Footsteps on the stairs. She knows her role well. Another door—opened, closed. She is numb. He whistles. Mechanically a smile stretches across her face. "Hi

Dad!" she echoes and rises to answer his call. Nothing shrinks and his echo remains.

Four more hours before he goes to sleep.

Four hours later, in the moments when Man sleeps, Nothing releases the breath she has been holding in his company. She tries to keep it within her permanently, but she fails. Night by night she releases that stale breath. As faint and imperceptible as it is, she is sorry for it. Tonight, she steps into the shower and faces the onslaught of water, same as she does after each night of waiting. Tired, listless, she lets the same mechanic smile melt from her face. But tonight, with the water weighing against her, gravity doesn't stop at the smile. Despite herself, Nothing finds her whole body sinking along with it, beaten down beneath the water and washing into the drain. Her strength, her will, escape her and empty into the gurgling pipes. It is happening: after all her waiting, all her shrinking, all her performance of Nothingness, she is finally disappearing. The void, the wasted space, is finally washing down the drain. And Nothing, the pathetic, useless non-creature that she is, allows herself to disappear. Spiraling, spiraling…

But when she opens her eyes she is still there. Despite her certainty that this time she had truly faded to nothing, despite relinquishing everything so that the weight of the world could sink her through the grounds of the lowest pit and out of existence, she opens her eyes and realizes she is still there. She is in shock at the reality of her being. With nowhere to go, nothing else to do, she gets up.

Standing on shaky legs, she shuts the water off, surprised at the power of her limbs. She climbs out of the tub, weak, unsteady. She dries off and breathes, just like every other night. Just as if *this night* she *didn't* just collapse on the floor. Just as if tonight were like every other night in the world of Men. But *this night*, when she leaves the bathroom and before she goes to bed, she drifts down to the kitchen. In the dark, while Man sleeps, she grabs what she came for then glides back to bed. The sheets and blankets envelope her as they always do, a thin package of fading muscle and fragile bones.

But this night, she falls instantly into a heavy sleep. *This night*, she sleeps with a knife beneath her pillow.

When she wakes, she splashes water onto her face and stares at the person in the mirror. There she is. She looks at the color of the lips, the curve of the nose, at the person behind the eyes. Looking directly into this face, an old stranger she once knew, she asks herself why she brought a knife with her to bed last night. Frozen, she does not look away from the stranger. Holding the full honesty of the face there before her, she compels the stranger to answer: *because I am scared.*

I am scared. She thinks of the last time she said these words. Her dad is screaming at her mom, screaming at her because she tried to say *no.* He mocks her for *Putting her foot down!* and stomps his feet in front of her. He laughs at her, a wild, angry laugh. He sees Nothing there and softens his face. —*Why are you crying, Sweetheart?* —*You're scaring me.* —*Don't be scared of Daddy. Daddy loves you.*

And she understands. Staring at the face in the mirror, Nothing understands that the stranger's face is her own. She understands that the stranger—*she*—said these words once, *I am scared*, but was told they had no meaning. Although she would stop saying these words, she understands that she has been scared this entire time. Every time she said, *I love you*, she meant that she was scared. She wonders if it's been just as long that the face in the mirror was a stranger to her.

And she is still scared. Looking at her face now, she knows she is scared. She sees her face and believes it again. She knows. She does not know what this day is going to bring, or the next, but she does know *something*. Her face is telling her. *She knows.*

She splashes water on her face and watches the water spiral down the drain. She shuts of the faucet and, listening to the water spiraling, spiraling, she stands straight and walks away.

Synthesis

Our woman is not nothing. She is a corporeal reality. A body with a face that shows fear and a hand that holds a knife. But what can our woman be if nothing is not even an adequate option? She thought she was a person, but she learned that men have claimed the universal as their own. Knowing that she is not-man, she tried to erase her own void, but in vain. She survived. She sees her flesh now and knows that where her body is there can be no void. What can she be?

As she steps out into the world now, trying to understand what she is, our woman begins to see the bodies around her. Facing the reality of her face, her flesh, for the first time she beings to see others that resemble her. She looks to them for answers. In different shades and shapes, she recognizes the same outlines of her own body in these others. She looks behind their eyes and wonders if she sees the same person too. What is it she is looking for? What would make her know?

Then she sees it. There in front of her, she sees it and can't look away. A story told in bold headlines: "21-year-old woman murdered by boyfriend over Thanksgiving break." She sees her picture. She was a student in our woman's class. She didn't know her, but they were supposed to graduate together. Shannon was her name. Our woman looks at Shannon's eyes and can't look away. Holding Shannon's face there before her, our woman remembers only weeks ago staring at her own frozen image in a bathroom mirror. She remembers tunneling through dark pupils to discover the person that lies behind them, a terrified figure shaking in their depths. She remembers how long she pretended that creature wasn't there, but how, once she found her, she knew it was the only creature anyone *could* see. She looks at Shannon and knows that no one told her either, how to look behind her own eyes. How to see what they all could see. That behind her empty mask and mechanic smile, she was shaking with fear—day by day, night by night. *Why didn't anyone tell her? Didn't they know we were scared? Couldn't they see it in our eyes? Why didn't they tell us?*

And with Shannon before her, our woman realizes that she is speaking in terms of We. Like recognizing her own frightened image, it becomes obvious to her once she says it who *We* are. *We* are those bodies that shelter frightened figures. *We* are the ones that wear masks and smiles to pretend that those figures aren't there. *We* are the ones that erase ourselves so well that we can't even see what's hidden before us: fear.

We live in fear. The face of our woman grows stern. No false smile tries to find its way there now; the blank space that existed before has been filled. The knowledge of We and the dangers that threaten us fill her, showing itself on her face. There is anger there now, and that is all our woman sees, all she wants to see, all she wants anyone to see. Filled with the knowledge of We, the void our woman once was in the world of men disappears. But our woman does not disappear with it. No—she is full now. Filled with the knowledge of We, she exists. Ever so surely, she exists in spite of a world of men that wants her—*us*—to disappear. She exists so fully that her existence becomes identical with the very refusal to be erased. She becomes Opposition itself.

Our woman—knowing that she, and Shannon, and all of those with bodies like ours, faces like ours, eyes like ours, knowing that we are all the same We; knowing that Shannon's story *is ours*—our woman no longer shakes when she thinks of the knife she hid beneath her pillow. She no longer treats her survival as fugitive, something she steals in the dark while the world wants her to disappear. Resolutely, filled with the knowledge of We, our woman vows to fight for her existence, for our existence. With the power of her fists, in the light of day, she transforms the frail figure of nothing into the undeniable force of Opposition. She makes her body a weapon. With every strike, she thinks of the ones who make us scared, the ones who make us sleep with knives beneath our pillows, the ones who kill us. With every strike, the void that once was becomes a memory that only grows her force even more. She learns to fight, so that the next time she sees someone with fear behind her eyes, she can defend her.

Filled with the knowledge of We, our woman, Opposition, no longer can be contained. She finds herself, now, standing before seven teenage girls, their bodies shy, their faces uncertain. Looking at them, she sees herself, she sees Shannon. She sees them as the world of men wants to see us: voids that should disappear. Defying erasure, Opposition spills herself out before them: *Ok, ladies! We're doing push-ups today! Drop and give me ten!* They moan and refuse, their arms slouched by their sides. But our woman is already on the ground. *What if a man attacks you? Will you be able to defend yourself then?* Her smile is reassuring, but for the girls, the message of Opposition rings out clear. Their faces drop momentarily as they eye her, then so do they: seven teenage girls, on the ground, doing push-ups. With all their might, they struggle up and down, up and down. When the weight of the world becomes too much, they don't stop. With all their strength, they stay fighting, struggling alongside Opposition.

Fighting, because they know. They don't need explaining: intuitively, they know. Like staring into the face of a stranger in the mirror, only to admit you've known all along that face was your own—they know. They know what our woman knows, what We *all* know. They know that the reason we are united as a single *We* is because *men hurt women. Men hurt us.* Our male relatives, our partners, our colleagues, our friends, strangers in the street—they hurt us, any one of us. The teenage girls in front of our woman already know, because when they see their mothers, sisters, friends beaten, degraded and killed, these images and sounds of women in fear are identical to their own. Where the world of men sees voids, these girls see themselves. And so they already know: when one of us is made void, We *all* are.

They've known all along, but maybe they've never been told. Like no one told our woman, like no one told Shannon. Without saying it out loud, with *no one* saying it out loud, maybe they too pretended it wasn't there, opening the way for the stealthy advance of erasure to creep over their existence. Maybe they, too, thought it was imagination, the delusions of one who is in fact nothing. Maybe they, too, once named fear for what it was, but were filled instead with lies masquerading as truths: fear is love. Maybe they, too, took the knowledge that *men hurt women* and had already banished it inside them, banishing the knowledge of We along with it. Without We to fill them, maybe these seven teenage girls had already started to become living, breathing voids.

But their fighting bodies, here, now, say otherwise. Seven teenage girls on the ground, doing push-ups. Fighting with all their strength against the weight of the world, their bodies prove themselves as corporeal reality. Struggling against the specter of nothing hiding frail and timid behind dark pupils, they bring force into their frames. Banishing the void, they, too, become the Opposition of We. And our woman, spilling forth, spirals on. As she walks away, leaving them in their struggle, she overhears one of those teenage girls, one Opposition fighting with all her might, she hears her say, *I like her. She's strong.* She hears this, and a sob rises in our woman's chest, bursting through her in sorrow and in rage. From a depth she didn't know existed, the sob erupts within her. But when she hears it roar into the open air, our woman hears that it is no sob, but a battle cry—a cry of peace and struggle; of hope and despair; of celebration amidst a world of injustice. It flies from her like a canary escaping a mine. And with this roar, our woman knows now exactly who she is.

She spirals. She *is* not-man. Our woman does not *scare* teenage girls. She never *hurt* her mother. She did not *kill* Shannon. Unlike man, our woman fights with all her existence to *keep her sisters alive.* Our woman is not-man and nor would she ever want to *be* him. *She spirals.* Nor is she an empty universal. Our woman is full of life—she sees her body, she recognizes the face in the mirror, she can find the person behind the eyes—and that person is *not* nothing. She is *not* a void lying in wait for definition. Our woman is beyond any notion man has at his disposal to define her. *She spirals.* Our woman is member of no universal identified by man: she is united to a beautiful Sisterhood of *We.* A Sisterhood that knows what it is to celebrate Life, to mourn its loss, to fight with all the force of Opposition for its preservation. Our woman knows exactly who she is. She is Woman. *We* are *Women.* Knowing this, she is free.

In memory of Shannon

CHAPTER 5

"Feminism Allowed You to Speak":
Reinforcing Intergenerational Feminist
Solidarity Against Sophisticated Attacks

by Yagmur Uygarkizi

This article is part of a reflection developed for the first panel of Radical Girlsss called "Radical Courage: Can We Be Young, Feminist and Radical?" hosted by the 2019 FiLiA conference. I would like to thank my fellow Radical Girlsss (Alyssa Ahrabare, Natasha Noreen and Bec Wonders whom I spoke with) for their insights and contributions.

*L*ittle *Red Riding Hood* is the story of a little girl who on her way to her sick grandmother, encounters a wolf that asks her where she is headed to. In Charles Perrault's version, after the girl's naïve reply, the wolf arrives at the grandmother's house before Little Red Riding Hood. He deceives the grandmother into opening the door, eats her and dresses up as her. Once the little girl arrives, she does not recognise the wolf dressed up as her grandmother, she nonetheless remains quite puzzled by her granny's big teeth. There is only so much she can question the situation until the wolf eats her too. End of the story.

Wolves still dress up as grandmothers. They still deceive little girls. They tell them reality is irrelevant. They make them question themselves and their guts, the very same guts that rang all the alarm bells when Little Red Riding Hood saw the big arms, big legs, big ears, big eyes and big teeth. Notice how the wolf attacks the grandmother before attacking the granddaughter. He could have just eaten the girl in plain sight, but no, that would have been too obvious, too dangerous even for the wolf. The grandmother, the mother would have been alerted by their beloved daughter's absence. They would have sooner or later found the wolf. After all, wolves know that women do marvels when we come together.

In this context, where deceiving wolves have monopolised the discourse, maintaining intergenerational feminist transmission (radical feminism being a pleonasm, I dropped the adjective) seems more difficult than ever. It is no longer enough to expose misogyny for what it is to spark sex consciousness: various forms of oppressions have been turned into empowerment thanks to queer theory and its advocates. Simultaneously, material reality, women's lived experience is presented as the ultimate form of subjugation that must be eliminated. By taking a long premise to explain the context that enabled queer theory to rise, I would like to suggest that queer politics in public discourse is pernicious in that it fosters an essentialisation of misogynist practices, rendering any criticism against them impossible and by the same token hijacking any struggle against them. The problem has a name, but it can no longer be said. In this misogynist atmosphere, political consciousness and organisation of young women (but not only!) is a matter of urgency.

I. Postmodernity

To understand how we got to a situation where saying that "women don't have penises" has become tantamount to hate speech, we have to understand postmodernity. A rather fancy intellectual term, it is best understood as a reaction to the preceding positivist era of the 20th century in which scientific approaches to knowledge and ideologies dominated. Those "great narratives" –

all-encompassing visions and directions for society – faced crushing defeat with wars, totalitarian regimes and the failure of ideologies to deliver (e.g., capitalism hasn't been overthrown).[1] In response, new paradigms – micro-issues, diversity, relativism – have replaced the old, but all in deference to the continuing male reign.

Whereas long-term global political battles characterise the modern era (liberation of women from patriarchy), in postmodernity micro-issues come to predominate due to a lack of ambition and sight (as if make-up was sufficient to solve women's problems). By the same token, ethical relativism has replaced a universal morality; women's rights are now negotiable. Culture is a wonderful bypass for all sorts of abuse. Girls were exchanged in a form of morbid potlach during the Rotherham scandal where Asian men were allowed to rape teenagers by local authorities. Still in the name of culture known girl rapists receive cinema awards.[2] Multiculturalism, that is the most obvious manifestation of the widespread sex-differentiated rule of law (two sexes/two laws) is at heart a racist policy that purports that just because ones comes from a different country one does not deserve the same rights as the locals.[3] For example, too many accept that some women must be entirely covered in black veils just because it is the only way men allow them to leave the house; yet I doubt they would accept it for themselves.

The postmodern emphasis on diversity distracts from the much-needed recognition of our common experience as women: the "white feminism" discourse is nothing but a discrediting of misogyny. The only valid oppression would be racism that, what a coincidence, also concerns men. The minimisation of misogyny is a false reassurance for the ones that believe that money or skin colour can save us from our subordinate condition as women: let us not forget that even queens are forced to lie back and think of England. Intersectionality, as Fatiha Boudjahlat explains, is a crossroads where men always have a right of way.[4]

Most importantly, while in a modern era there is the possibility of finding the truth, making statements about reality and calling for change, postmodernity precludes this by preaching a vociferous relativism.[5] Subjectivity, not objectivity, is a key word; there are "alternative facts." This last expression was coined by the Trump administration: it should alert us over the fact that populists and the most evident representatives of postmodern culture – queer activists – are closer to each other than they themselves would like to believe. Their superficial division can be understood as a diversion tactic to better circle us women with nowhere to exit.

Queer theory

Despite what the wolves tell us, "queer" is not a synonym for lesbian or gay. The current queer craze – from TV shows like *Queer Eye* to the rewriting of history (no, Virginia Woolf was not queer)[6] – takes its origin from the academic work of queer theorists from the 1980 and 1990s, most notably Judith Butler.[7] While feminists had demonstrated that what were considered female traits were not linked to biology but to socialisation,[8] queer theorists went one step further and explained that sex itself is enforced by societal discourse. A core tenet of this theory is thus "gender is a doing": it is because we repeat certain behaviours, dresses, language, etc. that we enforce the idea that there are two sexes. In reality though, this is just an illusion maintained by the almighty and all-powerful of our societies (feminists?). In a nutshell, we would all be actresses performing our gender in the great drama of humanity.[9]

Performance is a key word here: it is informed by the notion of performative utterances, which is none other than a fancy way of saying speeches that are acts. If you say, "I promise," you are both saying the words and executing the action of promising. As such, performative utterances can never be true or false. If you don't keep your promise, I cannot say that what you said was not true, because you did say it. However, you did not stick to it, so it is "unhappy." Speech acts can only be "happy" or "unhappy."[10] This is where we can fully sense the deep divide between modern approaches and postmodern ones. According to performative utterances and by extension queer theory, if a man says he is a woman, his claim can only be happy or unhappy: he can only act upon it or not. It can never however be "false" because the notion of truth itself is irrelevant, if not entirely eradicated. By saying it, he is performing it. When we say no, this is not true, or something as terroristic as "women don't have penises," we are clearly *passé*. We are evolving in a positivist approach of truth and falsity that no longer has any place in *pomo* world. It's like shouting in a language no one else around you speaks because they already adopted another one you cannot learn. The means of expression are still monopolised by men and once again our voices bounce off deaf ears.

There is another tenet of queer theory that, although not directly relevant to this article, is worth mentioning because of its enormity and the danger it poses to women and girls. Since changing discourse is sufficient to change reality without ever acting materially, it follows that many practices that are perceived as problematic are only so because we say they are. Queer theory being more obsessed with sexuality than a horny Freudian, this approach is particularly germane for sexual practices. As Bec Wonders explains, for queer theory, any sexual normativity is bad – we can already sense one of the many self-defeating contradictions of this academic dogma, which I will return to later.[11] For example, prostitution is not the problem, stigmatisation is. Men abusing children are not paedophiles or *paedocriminals*[12] but are engaging in "cross-generational sex." This is what Gayle Rubin argues in her circle of "good" versus "bad" sexuality. She also equates the imaginary struggle of *paedocriminal* members of the infamous North American Man/Boy Love Association – a group built in 1978 to suggest that victims of abusive men are actually in love with them – to the one of homosexual activists, updating an old stereotype of gay men as *paedocriminals*.[13] She is not the only queer academic to come to the defence of *paedocriminals*. Well might we like to dismiss these words as the mere ravings of one or two academics who have chained themselves up in an ivory dungeon, they have become not only the dominant paradigm in universities but have swept through the media and politics too, with great political consequences for women and girls.

II. The consequences: identification with oppression

Judith Butler explains that the description of sex is already the attribution of it. Any definition of woman is ineluctably normative: saying that women *do* have XX chromosomes is to queer ears the same as saying that women *should* have XX chromosomes. As mentioned before, normativity being necessary exclusive is bad, so it is better not to define women and even better not to organise as women. The only possible political organisation is in the name of the deconstruction of womanhood.[14] This queer lesson in political activism is well integrated by a vocal number of young women (but not only!) who instead of organising around the female sex organise around female oppressions.

Three practices in particular seem to be recurring in mainstream media: prostitution, veiling and sex roles. Prostitution is presented as yet another sexual orientation on a par with homosexuality, itself equivalent to child abuse or sexual torture ("sadomasochism") according to Rubin. Therefore, a man does not rape a woman through prostitution, but the woman *is* a prostitute (even worse, a "sex worker") just like a man would be gay – her whole being is defined by the situation she is trapped in. She has it in her to be driven to this type of "sex." This approach is evident in pro-prostitution slogans like "strippers and women unite." The women abused by men are divested of their womanhood and reduced to whatever humiliations they have to bear in order to survive. The same old distinction between "normal women versus prostitutes," promoted by the johns or prostitution-rape afficionados themselves, is coated with titillating rainbow glitter.

There is a similar trend with veiling. Instead of being seen as a sex-based discriminatory practice that transfers the responsibility of sexual violence from men to women, it is turned into an identity. Women who practice veiling are "hijabis." This is a form of reverse objectification wherein in place of a woman turned into an object – a "cumdumpster" like in pornography – an object engulfs a woman to define her whole existence. You're no longer a woman, but "hijabi"; you're the cloth that hides you.

Finally, and most importantly, sex roles are no longer imposed but ingrained: gender becomes an identity. If you as a woman are foolish enough to abide by the stereotypes that constrain you, then that's your problem: you could have just identified your way out of it. This is the message the disparaging "cis women" expression hides.[15]

We are witnessing an essentialisation of our oppression: what men do to us is who we are apparently. If they rape us, we are the rape. If they veil us, we are the veil. If they stereotype us, we are the stereotype. One can sense a hint of victim-blaming here: just like a woman in prostitution/pornography might feel that she is only good at that, queer theory rehashes that yes, that is very true. Instead of taking material biological reality as the basis of an identity, socially constructed practices are taken as accurate indicators of someone's identity. What this means is that any criticism of those practices becomes a criticism of the person. Whorephobia. Islamophobia. Transphobia. The basis of the discrimination shifts from the female sex to the sex-based discrimination itself.

The paradoxes

When looking closer at this nerve-racking discourse, the con-tradictions become evident. We have seen the first one: saying that something is bad is itself bad. The whole queer current[16] seems to be operating on a self-defeating double negation.

Being gay is born that way, and by extension so is being a prosti-tute, "trans" people (prefix people?) are born in the wrong body; yet, one is not born a girl. Sex is created by discourse, one is assigned a sex — so sex is merely discursive — but sex simultaneously becomes very tangible when it provides so much work for women around the globe (the queer view of prostitution). Also, the existence of two sexes is too much to bear, it is a constraining binary, but it is replaced with another binary: the cis/trans one.[17]

Religion is the domain of belief, inherently abstract. "Gender" is fluid. Yet here we have this practice of covering up with veils only human members of the female sex, girls and women. In this immaterial world, there remains an insistence on defending the practice of something deeply tangible – the price being paid on the very real skin and hair of women.[18]

We have the materiality of the being, made most evident by the body, and the abstraction of the identity, elaborated socially, on the other. By loathing the body, the material, queer activists reveal their contempt for women. Indeed, in our cultures, women are body and men are mind. The rhetoric of "born in the wrong body" only enshrines that. The woman is body. The body is wrong. The woman is wrong. Again, we women with our terrifying inescapable visible, tangible, smellable biology are the terrible reminder of humans' inescapable corporality. We must therefore be eradicated.[19]

Also, talking about being born into a body makes it seem as if the body were a vessel entirely disconnected from the mind that one somehow slides into. It is reminiscent of the film *The Man with Two Brains* starring Steven Martin.[20] In it, Martin's character Dr Hfuhruhurr[21] falls in love with a female brain and goes on a quest to find her the "perfect body" to "fuck" (yet another coincidence, he finds one in the prostitution industry). This fiction captures reality well given that men seem to fall in love with only other men's brains: they celebrate each other's writings, films, findings, tap each other on the back with lavish award ceremonies, promote each other all the way to the top. What a wonderful world it would be if some doctors not too different from Dr Hfuhruhurr would create the "perfect" "fuckable" female-shaped bodies to host the marvellous male brain: male head and female body, male leader and female executioner; the structure of our patriarchal societies reproduced on the single.[22]

III. Why is this happening? Breaking intergenerational transmission

The contemporary queer movement as relayed by powerful media outlets like Condé Nast with *Them* or the BBC is a parody of feminism. It develops its own vocabulary, demands changes, it takes to the streets, but it's become grotesque. Just like the Fascist regime in Italy, it changes pronouns.[23] It enforces a newspeak. It is also reserved to a subversive happy few who are edgy enough to keep track, leaving the majority aside: anti-democratic at its core the queer is also profoundly anglophone since the linguistic reflection on gender it makes is not applicable to the many languages that are deprived of it. More generally the changes demanded denote not a struggle against the reality of oppression but a "struggle against reality" *tout court.*[24] It asks us to pretend not to see the obvious tensions and contradictions. It goes so far in its demands that it annihilates the credibility of other social movements.

Beyond its parodic function, there is the more insidious aim of digging an intergenerational gap between women. Feminism is for the old, queer is for the young. A close friend of queer politics, *Libby Lib Fem*, so-called neoliberal feminism, tells young women to put that harness on and get whipped. We young women must have no knowledge of what women have done for us before, nor should we ever meet them, and how could we, given that activism is reduced to a screen?

The personal is political. What happens in the public discursive sphere is in tandem with what is going on behind closed doors. Before sisterhood, there is motherhood — even when we don't want to. How many of us have thought "I don't want to end up like my mother"? Why would we? Our mothers are our first exposure to our female condition, clearly on the side of the oppressed in the *domus*. They represent the first potential female bond of our life. And yet, we do not identify with our mothers, as if doing so would protect us from the same fate. Our mothers are a temporal mirror that we break in a desperate attempt to remove our chains. Seven years of despair. More. Even if we are close though, we will be told to "cut the umbilical cord." There shall be no strong mother-daughter bond under patriarchy lest there be early sex consciousness. If there is no daughterhood and motherhood, there will not be any sisterhood.

Just like we personally do not recognise our mothers, the queer movement dismisses the women that came before. It trashes the work done by our foremothers. It is no coincidence if the theoretical precursors of queer theory are men. Queer theory has no mothers, only fathers. What we see today lies within a greater tradition of male creators, of birth fathers, first of all being "God." Jealous of the female power of creating life, men have come up with this figure, a male creator of all there is on earth. If we can be led to believe this story,[25] we sure can believe that men can get pregnant.

Where to next?

In a cramped lecture room in a university in London, a heated debate on pornography takes place. Debate is a strong word given that a handful of feminists condemn pornography in a room filled with young people saturated with it. Challenging the idea of consent in prostitution is always met with great anger and a woman in her twenties goes on about how much she enjoys having her hair pulled. An older woman curbs her enthusiasm and leaves the room: "Feminism allowed you to speak." We forget that. The hard-won battles seem so distant and when new ones appear, there is difficulty in identifying the problem: male violence.

Young women are flocking to activism as the protests against climate change and for the 25th of November show. The problem lies in the lack of analytical and expressive tools that render the operation clumsy if not entirely unproductive. "Fuck me not the planet" is a slogan that emerged in the Thunberg protests: written on a placard it is held by minor adolescent girls, sometimes with a phone number. Others say: "Destroy my pussy not my earth." The salvation of our planet lies upon an altar of raped girls, apparently.

Similarly, in protests against rape, some young women wear skimpy underwear with sexualised elements like the playboy bunny tail: complain against rape culture but stay "fuckable," darling.

The longing for change, the activism, the organisation at grass-root level are already there; the critical analysis is not. A first way to guide this vital energy is reading. Libraries can save lives. Many essentials in feminism are no longer edited. The ones that are available are forgotten. Titles need to be shared; book requests must be made in public libraries. Instead of sedimenting thought, we undertake a Sisyphean theoretical work at each generation. Young women are given answers, we need questions.

To ask questions we need a space. Reading, writing, learning is one thing, shaking up your preconceptions, disagreeing face to face and dancing wildly late at night is another. Radical Girlsss was specifically born for young women. The youth branch of the European Network of Migrant Women and Girls aims to foster a space of critical thinking, sisterhood and solidarity. Tired of fake activism behind our screens, the isolation that comes with it, the lies we are told about sexuality, lack of boldness, we fight back and we grow – from the root.

Sorry Cassandra...

Cassandra is the beautiful daughter of the king of Troy. In one version of her myth, the god Apollo falls in love with her. To seduce her, he gives her the power of predicting the future. She rejects him. He punishes her by revoking the gift he had made: she will still be able to predict the future, but no one will believe her. Her mouth left open; he spits in it. Her open mouth is his, she can shout but she will no longer be heard.[26]

People already thought she was a little crazy, but when she warns her fellow Trojans against the infamous horse, that was confirmed. She is laughed at. Discarded. Insulted. In a desperate attempt to fight the inevitable, she tries to burn the horse. She will be stopped. They will die.[27]

In the face of a mounting postmodern world order, the feminist movement is facing a dire attack. When we say: "Name the problem: male violence," queer activists reply: "Naming the problem is the problem." Don't shoot the messenger, or the message won't pass on to the next generations. For the principal danger of the current political discourse directed at young women is not just about making us active agents of male violence against ourselves but to build a wall between us and our feminist mothers. There are already signs of disgruntlement; after all, there can be only so much patience for nonsense. We must remain vigilant though: once the obsession with "gender" is exposed, it might even more difficult than before to make the case about sexual politics. When the sea retreats too far, a stronger wave comes in.

Endnotes

1 O'Byrne, Darren (2017) *Sociologia: Fondamenti e teorie.* (Sandro Bernardini trans) Milano-Torino: Pearson Italia.

2 While in the UK, religion is typically a free ride to abuse girls, that same function is fulfilled by "art" in France. For a wider study of the excuse men develop to justify their abuse of women (my favourite being a parody made by Liliana Ricci: "my mum tied my nappy too tight") see the work of Patrizia Romito later adapted by Lise Bouvet and Yael Mellul (2010) in *Intouchables? People, Justice et Impunité*, Paris: Balland, 2018.

3 Boudjahlat, Fatiha (2017) *Le Grand Détournement.* Paris: Les Editions du Cerf.

   Donati, Pierpaolo (2008) *Oltre il Multiculturalismo. La Ragione Relazionale per un Mondo Comune.* Roma -Bari : Laterza.

4 Boudjahlat, Fatiha (2018) "Fatiha Boudjahlat : 'Contre Le Racisme Des Bons Sentiments Qui Livrent Les Femmes Au Patriarcat Oriental.'" Le Parisien. (18 August 2018). http://www.leparisien.fr/societe/fatiha-boudjahlat-contre-le-racisme-des-bons-sentiments-qui-livrent-les-femmes-au-patriarcat-oriental-18-08-2018-7856688.php (Last accessed: 8 December 2019).

5 O'Byrne, Darren (2017) *Sociologia: Fondamenti e teorie.* (Sandro Bernardini trans) Milano-Torino: Pearson Italia.

6 Queer Portraits in History webpage entry on Virginia Woolf. https://www.queerportraits.com/bio/woolf (Last accessed 14 December 2020). Queer does not mean gay or lesbian or bisexual. Queer, first, obviously means weird, but second it is a political position, the one outlined in the article. Virginia Woolf was bisexual, not queer. Whether she would have considered herself "queer" today, is a matter of speculation, but to state she was queer at her time is historical revision.

7 In *Unpacking Queer Politics,* Sheila Jeffreys brilliantly criticises the hogwash of queer theorists, rendering it accessible to all.

   Jeffreys, Sheila (2003) *Unpacking Queer Politics: A Lesbian Feminist Perspective.* Cambridge: Blackwell Publishers Ltd.

8 A classical reference is *Little girls: Social conditioning and its effects on the stereotyped role of women during infancy* written by the Italian educatress Elena Giannini Belotti, first published in 1973.

Belotti, Elena G. (1973) *Dalla Parte delle Bambine*. Milano: Feltrinelli.

9 For those of you who are particularly nerdy or simply still not get the queer universe (which is probably their purpose), the Stanford Encyclopedia of Philosophy's page on the sex-gender distinction is accessible and exhaustive. It provides the necessary historical and academic background to understand the theoretical underpinnings of expressions like "pregnant person."

Mikkola, Mari (2019) "Feminist Perspectives on Sex and Gender," The Stanford Encyclopedia of Philosophy (Fall 2019 Edition), Edward N. Zalta (ed.). https://plato.stanford.edu/archives/fall2019/ entries/feminism-gender/ (Last accessed: 4 Dec 2019).

10 http://web.stanford.edu/class/ihum54/Austin_on_speech_acts.htm (Last accessed: 4 December 2019).

11 Wonders, Bec (2019) "Generation Feminist." Panel. FiLiA Conference.

12 I am here translating literally the French feminist neologism that sprang from the observations that men who abuse girls do not like children, contrary to what pedo*philia* suggests. I would like to add that I do not believe this neologism is good enough, though, it seems euphemistic not to mention the rape or abuse. It is a step forward and I encourage my English-speaking readers to continue thinking about ways to build our language.

13 Rubin, Gayle (1999) "Thinking Sex: Notes for a Radical Theory of the Politics of Sexuality," in: R. G. Parker & P. Aggleton (eds.), *Culture, Society and Sexuality: A Reader* (Psychology Press, 1999).

14 Mikkola, Mari (2019) "Feminist Perspectives on Sex and Gender," The Stanford Encyclopedia of Philosophy (Fall 2019 Edition), Edward N. Zalta (ed.). https://plato.stanford.edu/archives/fall2019/ entries/feminism-gender/ (Last accessed: 4 Dec 2019).

15 As a note, the expressions cis and transwomen are actually incorrect. Cissexed/cissexual or transsexed/transsexual would be more accurate. The prefix *cis-* means on the same side as and *trans-* means across. There is no such thing as across women (or maybe we are to understand that on the other side of women are men?). Also, the prefix *trans-* requires the definition of the word it is attached to. Transport means the means used to move objects or people around (across ports). A port is a harbour. Transnational: across nations.

Nation: a group of people sharing a sense of belonging in a given country. And so on and so forth. This is why the prefix *trans-* is more widely used than *cis-*. In the case of women though, no definition of woman is allowed, so it is not clear who is crossed (feminist?). The incorrect use of the two prefixes is made evident in the translation into romance languages like French or Italian – which are much closer to the Latin roots the prefixes originate from, where trans effectively becomes a suffix: "femmes trans" or "donne trans" (as opposed to "transsexuel" and "transsessuale").

16   There might be objections that the points I described about prostitution, veiling and gender identity are not strictly orthodox to queer academics. What matters to me here is not so much if queer theorists themselves have suggested all of those things exactly as I report them, but how queer theory is the basis of much faux-feminist discourse today.

17   Terragni, Marina (2018) *Gli Uomini ci Rubano Tutto*. Venezia: Sonzogno.

18   In the wonderful emojis provided by Apple, all characters come in two sexes. Only the pregnant woman and the veiled one have no male counterpart. The first one probably will not last long, but I highly doubt that the second will change. For some reason the contemporary "feminist" discourse targeting young women never challenges religiously motivated sex roles.

19   On an analysis of culture versus nature encapsulated by sex differences, read Susan Griffin's 1981 book *Pornography and Silence*. London: Women's Press.

20   *The Man with Two Brains* (3 June 1983). Film. Directed by Carl Reiner. USA: Warner Bros.

21   Queer theory draws inspiration from Monsieur Michel Foucault. It is a great irony that Foucault exposed the medical body for being shaped by political needs and that queer activists defend transsexualism following the exact same principle, that is by relying heavily, contrary to their claims, on the medical body to enforce their politics. It is after all the British Medical Association that came up with "pregnant person." The Endocrine Society is obviously over the moon. The pathologizing "phobia" is the preferred term for supposed discrimination, thus making medical and individual what is a collective political matter. (https://www.endocrine.org/topics/ transgender-medicine (Last accessed 17 December 2020).

22 I would like to thank Alex G. K. Pulsford for suggesting to me this way of seeing, for his help in revision and friendship.

23 Ajello, Nejo (2008) "La guerra dei pronomi nell' Italia in orbace." *La Repubblica* (Archivio). (27 January 2008). Available online: https://ricerca.repubblica.it/repubblica/archivio/repubblica/2008/01/27/la-guerra-dei-pronomi-nell-italia-in.html (Last accessed 4 December 2019).

24 This is taken from the inalienable rights scene from the film *The Life of Brian* (1980) by Terry Jones.

Stan: I want to be a woman. From now on I want you all to call me Loretta.

Reg: What!?

Stan: It's my right as a man.

Judith: Why do you want to be Loretta, Stan?

Stan: I want to have babies.

Reg: You want to have babies?!?!?!

(…)

Reg: What's the point of fighting for his right to have babies, when he can't have babies?

Francis: It is symbolic of our struggle against oppression.

Reg: It's symbolic of his struggle against reality.

25 I would have not come up with this point were it not for a conversation with my mother Uygar who highlighted the fundamental issue with veiling. "If we can believe that veiling is a choice," she said, "we can believe that anything is a choice. The veil is only a test of the extent of our gullibility."

26 Cremaschini, Marilena (2016) "Il Mito di Cassandra e l"Impossibilità di Comunicare." Dottssa marilena Cremaschini. (5 November 2016). http://www.marilenacremaschini.it/il-mito-di-cassandra-e-limpossibilita-di-comunicare/ (Last accessed: 4 December 2019).

27 https://mythologica.fr/grec/cassandre.htm (Last accessed: 4 December 2019).

CHAPTER 6

Therapeutic Ideology as a Way of Bringing Women Back Two Hundred Years

by Dana Vitálošová

Where we are

It is 2020 and therapeutic ideology is everywhere. It could be lurking under each stone, behind every tree. Thus, reading books can now be considered bibliotherapy, gardening horticultural therapy, dog walking canistherapy, manual work occupational therapy, going on holiday milieu therapy, painting pictures art therapy, taking pictures phototherapy, watching moving pictures cinematherapy, going on holiday to the sea Thalassotherapy and my favorite – taking rest after work or school – recreational therapy. However silly the therapeutic labels, all the activities mentioned above are at least, in and of themselves, harmless.

Sadly, some other contemporary therapies aren't. Consider, for example, the sort that purports to alleviate women's mental discomfort by surgically removing their healthy body parts.

Many women and girls now undergo mutilation therapy, widely known as sex-reassignment surgery, or, more recently as gender confirmation surgery (GCS). Of all procedures recorded by the American Society for Plastic Surgeons (ASPS), GCS was among the most rapidly increasing between 2016 to 2017.[1] GCS increased by 155% in this period, with a 289% increase for "transgender men,"[2] i.e., women who would like to stop being female.

New cures demand new "diseases." Thus, in the last decades, we have seen the invention of gender dysphoria and body dysmorphia as well as chest dysphoria, which stands for "significant discomfort with the presence of [one's own] breasts."[3]

The term "chest dysphoria" is a manifestation of another sign of therapeutic frameworks taking over our lives. Although it describes discomfort with the presence of female breasts, these are not mentioned. Such erasure is intentional, as women with "dysphoria," in other words those who would like to stop being female, often consider terms describing their secondary sex characteristics "triggering."[4]

The word "trigger" is again a psychological term, which has been used to describe sensations, images, or experiences that prompt recall of a traumatic memory. Body dysphoria, as transgender ideologues periodically remind us, can lead to suicide.[5] Thus, words describing women's body parts are made into triggers of guns, i.e., deadly weapons. So are different opinions. Consequently, trans-identified people often include trigger warnings before quoting ideas that are not 100 % aligned with their ideology.

The "triggerization" of discourse does not pertain only to the trans-identified world. Increasingly, it has been used by feminists to avoid dealing with unpleasant issues. To give an example from my life: in 2019, I was invited to lead a workshop at a Czech feminist conference. Before the event, I pondered devoting the session to the topic of fight against child pornography. However, the women organizers told me they found such a subject "too triggering."

I went along with this, as at the time I gave triggers greater importance than I do now. However, I was also angry. I thought: "who will stop child sexual exploitation when feminists are too fragile to even hear it mentioned?" Should we leave the fight to men who are most often the perpetrators? In fact, the reaction reminded me of the 19th century's trope of women fainting on couches when their nerves were stirred by shocking conversational topics. Mutilation therapy calls to mind another 19th century occurrence – the diagnosis of hysteria, treated by surgeons who removed healthy ovaries, uteri, and clitorises to relieve women of a nonexistent mental disorder. Incidentally, there are even more parallels between the 19th and the 21st centuries. I believe these present important clues to where we are, which is why I'm now going to explore them further.

Anyone can be a millionaire

At the beginning of the 1990s, the Internet boom began. This U.S. technology opened many new areas for business. Subsequently, seemingly anyone could become "someone" in the Wild West of the World Wide Web. Many men fell for the lie that anything that's touched by the Internet is a goldmine. Thus, they founded or invested in new businesses (startups), that were useless or terribly run. The result was the dot-com bubble, which burst in 1998.

This situation resembled the early 19th century. Instead of data-driven communication, in the 1820s, it was canal-building that inflamed male fantasies of grandeur. According to J.G. Barker-Benfield, canals "linked the settled round of home with the seas of freedom and recklessness."[6] Consequently, "three states brought themselves to the edge of bankruptcy; between 1816 and the Civil War more than $200 million was invested in canal construction."[7] Just as in the case of 21st century online businesses, many canals turned out to be useless when soon enough, railways replaced ships as the preferred way to transport cargo.

When the canal-building frenzy subsided, others appeared. The resources of the North American continent seemed bottomless – vast "free" land could be settled, gold mined, oil extracted, railways and factories built. These "crazes" were, just as in the case of the 1998s dot-com bubble, often followed by economic crises – e.g. one in 1819, another in 1837.[8]

93

Just as in the 21st century, although the poor were becoming poorer and the rich richer, the myth of "endless opportunities" persisted[9] and put men under a lot of pressure.

Men going crazy

In 1851, Dr. Edward Jarvis spoke before the Association of Medical Superintendents of American Institutions for the Insane: "no son is necessarily confined to the work...of his father... all fields are open... all are invited to join the strife.... They are struggling... at that which they cannot reach... their mental powers are strained to their utmost tension.... Their minds stagger ...they are perplexed with the variety of insurmountable obstacles; and they are exhausted with the ineffectual labor."[10]

According to Barker-Benfield, men "had to face the severe stresses of the competition between the equals of American democracy." They "could rise and sink again through all the grades that lead from opulence to poverty."[11]

No wonder many men went insane. The famous writer, Herman Melville, had to watch his father die mad because of repeated business failure.[12]

Similarly to the 19th century U.S., in this century of the globalized world, it has become increasingly obvious that not just anyone can ascend to the Internet heaven inhabited by the few richest men on the planet. Not just any Dick or Rajesh will replace Amazon founder, Jeff Bezos or any one other Internet giant that tries to step on his feet.

Wealth being out of reach, it is now also becoming clear that reaching online fame is not as easy as we believed just a few years ago. To catch people's attention – whether on YouTube, Facebook, Twitter, Instagram, Snapchat, TikTok, or any other online medium, you'd have to be truly outrageous or pay a lot of money to "boost" your visibility. Gone are the days when you could believe that a "viral post" was just a Tweet away. In terms of technology or content, the Internet has seen it (almost) all.

However, the true believers in succeeding in the World Wide Web are still out there. Every year, they meet at the not-so-Wild-anymore-West of the U.S.A. for TechCrunch Disrupt, a Silicon Valley event. Here, technological startups compete for a grand prize and the attention of potential investors. The fact that the event organizer is owned by a giant communications company called Verizon,[13] is an apt metaphor – instead of competing for becoming an owner, the techy men (and some token women) are now trying to get owned, their goal being bought by one of the giants.

To a man (as well as some women) who grew up in the world full of promise for the rise of talented individuals and is now stuck in a dead-end job and a video game addiction, this must be a disappointment.

In fact, in the U.S. alone, men's suicides have been increasing since 1999, the year after the burst of the dot-com bubble.[14]

Bachelors/"Men Going Their Own Way"

Another significant parallel between the 19th and 21st centuries is the rise in the number of males who avoid/ed women, in particular eschew/ed forming long-term relationships with them, let alone marrying them. In the 19th century, according to Barker-Benfield "the lone hunter of Cooper's Leatherstocking Tales, Natty Bumppo, realized the promise of total mobility because he was free of women."[15] Barker-Benfield adds that for many of the 19th century men "to marry was to 'fall,' to destroy the freedom of autonomy: marriage was a 'malady,' showing 'symptoms.' That is, it represented a threat to a man's body. It shackled and humiliated; according to the bachelors, sexual union was a painful and permanent form of subordination and women were perennial dangers."[16]

In the 21st century, male avoidance of long-term relationships with women has taken on various forms and in the second decade has gotten an increasingly aggressive flavor.

In 2008 Michael Kimmel wrote that long after college, many young men in the U.S. continued living with their male ex-classmates, frequently changing jobs, drinking, and playing video games, and engaged with women only through hook-ups.[17] At the same time that they were stuck in dead-end jobs, members of this "Guyland" were convinced that a great career was waiting around the corner, even though they were unwilling to put much effort into going around that corner.[18]

In the 2010s and beyond, Kimmel's *Guyland* that came out of his interviews with young men conducted between 2004 and 2008, turned into the land of increasingly aggressive online communities called Men Going Their Own Way (MGTOW) and Incels (involuntarily celibate men).

The reason? The career mentioned in *Guyland*, supposedly waiting around the corner, never materialized. Instead of blaming the man-made capitalist "laissez-faire" system spewing lies that anyone can become "someone," these unsuccessful men blame women and feminists in particular.

The communities that started online (MGTOW and Incels), motivated men to also commit gynocidal atrocities offline. In 2018, 25-year-old Alek Minassian intentionally drove a rental van into pedestrians on a busy pavement in Toronto.[19] The crowd of 10 killed and 14 wounded by his attack consisted predominantly of women. In a post on Facebook that Minassian made right before the attack, he praised Elliot Rodger, a 22-year-old man who, in 2014, murdered 6 women and men in California, motivated by his blaming women for his misery.[20]

Blame and punishment

Just as in the 21st century, in the 19th century men avoided criticizing the unfair man-made system as the cause of unhappiness it engendered. The rise in men's insanity was first blamed on many other culprits, e.g., not enough physical exercise, and subsequently, the experts turned on women.[21] Barker-Benfield writes that "as success became more remote and more threatened, male identity became more vulnerable, and the concern to discipline women increased."[22]

Barker-Benfield further quotes a 19th century doctor named Amariah Brigham who "claimed that women's nervous systems overloaded by mental excitement would have 'deplorable effects upon their offspring.'"[23] According to Barker-Benfield's analysis, unless women were directed back to a focus on the body, the United States would experience "dangerous consequences." Thus, in the words of Barker-Benfield "the responsibility for social insanity shifted to women."[24] The excitement and life of the mind was a consequence of women becoming more educated and active in the public domain – first in fighting for the common good and the rights of the oppressed, later in the forming of a women's movement.

Deformed transformed

As an example of deadly patriarchal reversals, in her 2006 book *Amazon Grace* Mary Daly quoted Robert F. Kennedy Jr. describing the Bush administration: "When they destroy the forest, they call it the Healthy Forest Law; when they destroy the air they call it the Clear Skies Bill."[25]

Similarly, 19th century doctors viewed the destruction of a woman's body as purifying. Gynecologist Augustus Kingsley Gardner wrote in 1872 about a visit of a chronically ill female patient:

> [T]he most marked evidence of the benefits to the whole character is seen in those early afflicted by that disease of lingering suffering (...). "What angelic serenity! What beatific gentleness and love! What mild radiance pervading the whole being of one of those afflicted! Those days and nights, those weeks and months of persistent agony have purified the whole nature, have seemingly eliminated every grain of gross alloy,

and left the fine gold, purified as by fire.. (...) this baptism of pain and privation has regenerated the individual's whole nature, and as the physical creature has been weakened and destroyed, the spiritual being, in humble, submissive resignation to the loss which it has sustained, has been nurtured and strengthened by resignation, and beautified, by the chastening made but a little lower than the angels.

Gardner also describes such female patients as "deformed transformed" and calls their scars "scaffoldings by which they have mounted into heaven."[26]

One form the destruction/purification/punishment of women takes in the 21st century is mutilation therapy. Comparing representations of this purification with Gardner's view of angelic disembodied women, we can take a look at photographic projects. Since at least 2015, multiple photographers have chosen to capture and expose images of women who wanted to purify themselves of their femaleness (commonly known as "trans men") and had their breasts removed, their flattened chests showing scars. In the description to one of the projects we can read about "the humility of a human [female] body."[27] We also learn about "personal experiences with overcoming huge hurdles"[28] that allude to Gardner's emphasis on persistent suffering benefitting the female character. "Rebirth" then points towards a transformation by deformation (see Gardner's "deformed transformed"). Emphasis on suffering pervades most narratives by women who undergo mutilation therapy: for instance, a statement by a photographed woman called Alex says, "[My] tattoo means strong because you have to be. Five and a half years of weekly injections, two surgeries, and I now finally feel comfortable in my body."[29]

Descriptions of mental and physical agony abound also in online forums devoted to females who would like to stop being female (known as "FTM (female-to-male)"; or "trans men"). Reminiscent of Dr. Gardner's allusion to "purification as by fire," female teenagers muse here about burning their breasts away: "Woah man..

y'know how girls burn their bras in moves [sic] when they're banding together against something/someone? We should.. burn our tids [sic] after they've been removed!"[30]

"Purification" of the world by the destruction of "evil females" with the help of fire was, incidentally, also used by Christian exorcists.[31] But, the type of purging used in 15th to 18th century Europe, i.e., the burning of whole women, using force, is now deemed barbaric. In the world of "progress," young women are the ones who desire to cut and burn away their femaleness, no external force applied, at least not visibly.

I believe Christian exorcists of the 17th century would be pleased to see such an effective, clean, and easy way to do their job. The 19th century doctors who wished women to focus on their bodies, not their minds, would probably be pleased with this development as well.

What to do about it

Feminists, the real ones, are not happy with such "progress." However, many of these well-meaning women, a huge percentage of whom claim that kids don't need sex reassignment surgery, also state: "those kids need therapy!" The most common narrative in online feminist forums is that young women who consider themselves "trans" are troubled, unhappy, damaged, are suffering from PTSD, are victims of sexual abuse and as such they need treatment.

There are many problems with these narratives. First, the well-meaning feminists usually do not realize that "the trans kids" undergoing hormonal or surgical treatment are already getting therapy. The females (and males) are being mutilated in the name of alleviating their mental distress, i.e., their bodily mutilation is a therapeutic intervention. Now, the therapy-promoting feminists would probably object to mutilation being real treatment. But who are they, as lay people, non-experts, to say what therapy is the most effective? Healing, in our technically obsessed society, is the realm

99

of supreme body and mind technicians, i.e., doctors, who are supposed to know the best.

If common sense or differing economic needs succeed, they may, at some point, collectively decide that mutilation therapy wasn't such a good idea. However, how do we make sure their next therapy would be any better? After all, not that long ago, psychiatrists considered lobotomy helpful.[32]

Another important point to make is that by pushing women and girls who wish to get rid of their femaleness into getting psychological help, we are supporting the notion that the problem lies in them, not in the way the society is structured. Thus, we are strengthening the patriarchal view of women as frail or damaged, susceptible to all kinds of diseases, that has been around since at least the myth of Eve and her Fall.

Convinced of her own faultiness (underlying trauma, etc.), a woman could then spend a lifetime discovering "what was wrong with her in the first place" that she fell for the lies of transgenderists.[33] She could focus on uncovering her childhood traumas, describing her non-functional family dynamics up to her great-great-great-grandmother's generation, discovering her hidden complexes and communication patterns, or learning about her archetypal subconscious whatevers. During all this therapeutic re-education, she could also try to heal her faultiness with dramatherapy, horticultural therapy, cinematherapy, dance therapy, recreational therapy, occupational therapy or canistherapy. Thus, the woman would be taken care of – she'd have no time for feminism – she'd be busy dissecting her psyche! At least she's not cutting off her body parts, you could say. But, should that be enough for us, as feminists?

Endnotes

1   Nolan, Ian T, et al. "Demographic and Temporal Trends in Transgender Identities and Gender Confirming Surgery." *Translational Andrology and Urology*, AME Publishing Company, June 2019, www.ncbi.nlm.nih.gov/pmc/articles/PMC6626314/.

2   Nolan, Ian T, et al. "Demographic and Temporal Trends in Transgender Identities and Gender Confirming Surgery." *Translational Andrology and Urology*, AME Publishing Company, June 2019, www.ncbi.nlm.nih.gov/pmc/articles/PMC6626314/.

3   Olson-Kennedy, Johanna. "Chest Dysphoria and Chest Reconstruction Surgery in Transmasculine Youth." *JAMA Pediatrics*, American Medical Association, 1 May 2018, https://jamanetwork.com/journals/jamapediatrics/fullarticle/2674039.

4   Montgomery, Steph. "Why I Call It Chestfeeding (And You Should, Too)." *Romper, Romper*, 18 Jan. 2017, www.romper.com/p/9-reasons-why-i-call-it-chestfeeding-you-should-too-31215.

5   Louie, Sam. "Trauma and Transgender Identity." *Psychology Today*, Sussex Publishers, 31 Dec. 2019, www.psychologytoday.com/us/blog/minority-report/201912/trauma-and-transgender-identity.

6   Barker-Benfield, G. J. *The Horrors of the Half-Known Life: Male Attitudes toward Women and Sexuality in Nineteenth-Century America*. Second ed., Routledge, 2000.

7   Barker-Benfield, G. J. *The Horrors of the Half-Known Life: Male Attitudes toward Women and Sexuality in Nineteenth-Century America*. Second ed., Routledge, 2000.

8   Tindall, George Brown., and David Emory. Shi. Dějiny Spojených statů amerických. Nakl. Lidové Noviny, 1996.

9   Barker-Benfield, G. J. *The Horrors of the Half-Known Life: Male Attitudes toward Women and Sexuality in Nineteenth-Century America*. Second ed., Routledge, 2000.

10   Barker-Benfield, G. J. *The Horrors of the Half-Known Life: Male Attitudes toward Women and Sexuality in Nineteenth-Century America*. Second ed., Routledge, 2000.

11   Barker-Benfield, G. J. *The Horrors of the Half-Known Life: Male Attitudes toward Women and Sexuality in Nineteenth-Century America*. Second ed., Routledge, 2000.

12 Barker-Benfield, G. J. *The Horrors of the Half-Known Life: Male Attitudes toward Women and Sexuality in Nineteenth-Century America.* Second ed., Routledge, 2000.

13 Patel, Nilay. "Verizon Just Bought Engadget and TechCrunch - Can They Stay Independent?" *The Verge*, 12 May 2015, www.theverge.com/2015/5/12/8590735/verizon-just-bought-engadget-and-techcrunch-can-they-stay-independent.

14 "Suicide Rising across the US." *Centers for Disease Control and Prevention*, 7 June 2018, www.cdc.gov/vitalsigns/suicide/index.html.

15 Barker-Benfield, G. J. *The Horrors of the Half-Known Life: Male Attitudes toward Women and Sexuality in Nineteenth-Century America.* Second ed., Routledge, 2000.

16 Barker-Benfield, G. J. *The Horrors of the Half-Known Life: Male Attitudes toward Women and Sexuality in Nineteenth-Century America.* Second ed., Routledge, 2000.

17 Kimmel, Michael. *Guyland.* HarperCollins E-Books, 2008.

18 Kimmel, Michael. *Guyland.* HarperCollins E-Books, 2008.

19 "Alek Minassian Toronto Van Attack Suspect Praised 'Incel' Killer." *BBC News.* BBC, April 25 2018. https://www.bbc.com/news/world-us-canada-43883052.

20 "Alek Minassian Toronto Van Attack Suspect Praised 'Incel' Killer." *BBC News.* BBC, April 25 2018. https://www.bbc.com/news/world-us-canada-43883052.

21 Barker-Benfield, G. J. *The Horrors of the Half-Known Life: Male Attitudes toward Women and Sexuality in Nineteenth-Century America.* Second ed., Routledge, 2000.

22 Barker-Benfield, G. J. *The Horrors of the Half-Known Life: Male Attitudes toward Women and Sexuality in Nineteenth-Century America.* Second ed., Routledge, 2000.

23 Barker-Benfield, G. J. *The Horrors of the Half-Known Life: Male Attitudes toward Women and Sexuality in Nineteenth-Century America.* Second ed., Routledge, 2000.

24 Barker-Benfield, G. J. *The Horrors of the Half-Known Life: Male Attitudes toward Women and Sexuality in Nineteenth-Century America.* Second ed., Routledge, 2000.

25   Robert F. Kennedy Jr. "Bush's Crimes Against Nature" *Truthout*.
     7 Oct. 2004, http://www.truthout.org/docs_04/100904G.shtml, in
     Mary Daly. *Amazon Grace*. 2006.

26   Gardner, K. A. *Our Children*. Hartford, USA: Belknap and Bliss.
     1872, in: Barker-Benfield, G. J. *The Horrors of the Half-Known Life:
     Male Attitudes toward Women and Sexuality in Nineteenth-Century
     America*. Second ed., Routledge, 2000.

27   Hickson, Alex. "Transgender Men Are Laid Bare in Beautiful
     Photoset Dubbed 'Work in Progress'." *Metro*, Metro.co.uk, 8 July
     2017, https://metro.co.uk/2017/07/08/transgender-men-are-laid-
     bare-in-beautiful-photoset-dubbed-work-in-progress-6765086/.

28   Hickson, Alex. "Transgender Men Are Laid Bare in Beautiful
     Photoset Dubbed 'Work in Progress'." Metro, Metro.co.uk, 8 July
     2017, https://metro.co.uk/2017/07/08/transgender-men-are-laid-
     bare-in-beautiful-photoset-dubbed-work-in-progress-6765086/.

29   TheAdvocateMag. "PHOTOS: The Bare Truths of Trans Men."
     ADVOCATE, Advocate.com, 29 May 2015, www.advocate.com/arts-
     entertainment/art/photography/2015/05/29/photos-bare-truths-
     trans-men?pg=full

30   cloudy_skies_ahead. "yo, i'm a dude why fuck do i have titties??"
     Reddit, 27 May 2020, https://www.reddit.com/r/ftm/comments/
     gqumm2/yo_im_a_dude_why_fuck_do_i_have_titties/

31   Daly, Mary. *Gyn/Ecology: the Metaethics of Radical Feminism*.
     Beacon Press, 2006.

32   Daly, Mary. *Gyn/Ecology: the Metaethics of Radical Feminism*.
     Beacon Press, 2006.

33   Boyce, Benjamin A, director. "Growing Out of Group Think
     | with Helena." *YouTube*, 4 Jan. 2020, www.youtube.com/
     watch?v=MXD1uDsbc8A.

CHAPTER 7

Ecocide, Biocide, Femicide… Omnicide.
The Final Stage of Patriarchy

by Agnes Wade

Women are described in animal terms as pets, cows, sows, foxes, chicks, serpents, bitches, beavers, old bats, old hens, mother hens, pussycats, cats, cheetahs, bird-brains, and hare-brains… "Mother Nature" is raped, mastered, conquered, mined; her secrets are "penetrated," her "womb" is to be put into the service of the "man of science." Virgin timber is felled, cut down; fertile soil is tilled, and land that lies "fallow" is "barren," useless. The exploitation of nature and animals is justified by feminizing them; the exploitation of women is justified by naturalizing them.

-Karen J. Warren, *Ecological Feminism*

Mother

There was a time when I bristled at the term, "Mother Earth." I saw it as yet another way women were dehumanized, used as a symbol for something men think should matter. Like the infamous PETA ads comparing farm animals to symbolically butchered women, it felt like another form of ownership, just a (supposedly) benevolent one. "She was important... she was someone's wife, someone's sister, someone's daughter." Not to mention, I have to admit a skepticism towards anything with the aroma of religion, I'm reluctant to accept things on faith. But.

One does not need to be particularly spiritually inclined to see that the Earth is alive, a living being made up of living systems of beings. As you walk across a meadow, the chorus of insects, each hard at work, rises in crescendo. Birds warn each other in pairs of your arrival. Your fingers transport a blackberry from the patch at the edge of the forest to your mouth, feed it to the micro-flora living in your gut. Salmon, born in small, fresh-water streams, grow strong enough to move into rivers, then into mixed fresh and saltwater estuaries, and finally to the Oceans, depositing nutrients and feeding predators all along the way. There, they grow before making their way back to the stream where they were born, where they breed and then die, their bodies -- now full of the Ocean -- feeding everything from micro-organisms to plant life to bears in the rivers and streams. The Amazon river, emptying into the Atlantic, dilutes its saltiness for 100 miles, and provides a bonanza of nutrients for phytoplankton -- base of the Oceanic food web and producers of roughly 80% of Earth's oxygen. Ocean currents carry warm tropical waters up the coast of South America, feeding to the rainforest the precipitation it needs to sustain the greatest variety of life on this Life Planet -- just one hectare of Amazonia may contain over 750 species of trees and 1500 species of plants. The Earth is manifestly, overwhelmingly, alive. So much so that, now, the pronoun "it" feels profoundly wrong to me. And "He" is impossible. Despite millennia of indoctrination with the idea of masculinity as the essence of maleness, the masculine as the positive, active, creative principle of humanity while the feminine lays passive and inert, incomplete, we know that creation is female. That's why her subjugation requires such violence.

We need Earth because we are of Earth. Life calls to Life. Being in nature, or even just looking at images of nature, has been shown to reduce anger, fear, and stress and increase feelings of calm and well-being. Researchers in hospitals have found that even putting a simple potted plant in a room can significantly impact stress and anxiety. Researchers at Exeter University have found that "precisely 120 minutes" a week spent in natural surroundings lowered blood pressure and stress hormone levels, reduced nervous system arousal, enhanced immune system function, increased self-esteem, reduced anxiety, and improved mood. None of this will come as much of a surprise. We bring plants and animals into our homes; we go camping and fishing to "unwind." Anyone who has spent some time in jail (or any man-made structure of concrete and steel, windowless and lit with fluorescent lights) knows the feeling of complete alienation and emptiness inside. Inmates being transported to court will pause for as long as their guards will allow, just to breathe real air; their eyes, thirsty for green and blue, will well up as, for a moment, they feel sane again.

But Americans now spend 93% of their time trapped indoors.[1] Businesses are trying to attract a "skilled work force" by providing a "quality outdoor experience." The society (some, but the who and the why of those "some" is a story for another time) men created to enshrine their supremacy, valorize the power to control over the desire to cooperate, and reverently baptized "civilization," is soul-destroying. It's pathological. Necrophiliac. Capitalism, man's latest scheme for efficient extraction, is nothing if not adaptable. So adaptable, and so capable at co-opting and swallowing up any idea or liberatory movement which poses a real threat, that it's managed to naturalize itself. We believe implicitly that what we have -- humans separate from and above nature, some men separate and above other men, all men separate and above women, the will to mastery and subjugation defining all -- is what's inevitable, that an economy based on hierarchies of exploitation is simply inescapable. Fighting it is a simpleton's exercise in futility. The inimitable Dr. Jane Clare Jones summed up what she called "the economy of entitlement" in relation to the dogmatic, quasi-religious, demand that women acquiesce -- immediately and without question -- to every dictate of the newly postmodern-ized politics of gender identity,[2] and it couldn't more perfectly delineate the belief system which is now eating Earth alive, flaying Her, setting Her ablaze like the witches who came before: "The readiness of people, both male and female, to identify with and elevate the pain of males not being given what they want, over and against the females who tell them "no," is the psychic substance that greases the wheels and gears of the whole patriarchal shit-show. And it is the psychic substance that serves to justify, exculpate, and explain away any violence used to press male claims." The extracting of more water, more minerals, more nutrient-rich soil overrides the need for living beings to keep being. The desire for more wood, more flesh, more energy, overrides the need of indigenous people to keep their way of life, to not to be re-located to civilization's slums. The majority of U.S. Federal prisoners incarcerated under "domestic terrorism" laws are environmental activists. Over the past 15 years, the number of murdered environmental defenders has more than doubled around the world, mostly in nations whose ruling classes are rushing to join ours in its orgy of consumption.[3] The correlation between global ecological destruction and the international onslaught against women's rights is too strong to be some terrible coincidence; the same monster is devouring all.

Hyper-exploitation, commodification, and extraction

Forests cover about 30% of Earth's land mass, just over 4 billion hectares, down from the pre-industrial area of 5.9 billion hectares.[4] According to a 2015 study in the journal *Nature*, half of Earth's trees have been felled since Man began to cut them to build his Civilization.[5] Half.[6] Keep in mind, too, that these figures don't consider tree farms -- a form of monoculture which no serious biologist could call a functioning ecosystem -- to be deforested. According to the University of Michigan, 90% of the old-growth forests which once covered the lower 48 states have been cut down since 1600, and most of what remains is on public lands. In the

Pacific Northwest of the United States, home of incredible redwood trees and cloud forests, 80% of this forestland is slated for logging. The Northwest Forest Plan, created to halt the destruction after tireless work from environmental activists, is under constant threat from logging corporations and their lobbyists, who misinform the public and buy their way in to the regulatory and legislative process.[7]

Globally, the average share of women in national legislatures is 24.1 percent. There are only 10 female heads of government, out of a possible 193. As of 2019, the U.S. rose from 77th to 75th, with women occupying 23.5% of total House seats. Globally, women do 66% of the world's work but, according to World Economic Forum, own less than 20% of the land. According to a recent study initiated by the United Nations Development Program, almost 90% of people are biased against women. Close to 50% of men said they had more right to a job than women, and almost a third thought they had a right to beat their partners.[8] According to studies published in Harvard Business Review, millennial men's attitudes towards women had substantially fallen in relation to their fathers' generation; the men had consistently exaggerated assessments of their male peers, despite unequivocal evidence that their female peers were performing better; in every biology class surveyed, a man was seen as the most accomplished student, even where women earned significantly higher grades; they generally overestimated the intelligence of male classmates over female ones; women, however, didn't display a bias, their assessments of their classmates tended to be accurate.[9] In a 2020 survey by the U.K. charity Hope Not Hate, half of Gen Z (16-24 year-old) males believe "feminism has gone too far" and negatively affects their lives, with only 21% disagreeing.[10] Meanwhile, gender roles are instilled in children ever more acutely in the form of toys and clothes and media. In a study of 2-5 year-olds, parents controlled the conversation of daughters more strictly, and fathers were more likely to talk over their children than mothers.[11] Girls are also given less freedom than boys,[12] do more chores,[13] and are given a smaller allowance.[14]

Prairies cover 20 to 40 percent of Earth's land mass, depending on how you define them. These biomes are one of the most complicated and diverse land ecosystems, surpassed only by rainforests, and are home to some of the last remaining megafauna. Grasslands keep most of the carbon they sequester from the air underground, while trees store it in their woody biomass and leaves. The increased rate and severity of wildfires, combined with slash-and-burn deforestation to make room for agriculture, around the world, means forest carbon is released into the atmosphere in sudden explosions. When fire burns grasslands, however, the carbon fixed underground tends to stay in the roots and soil, which makes them a more reliable carbon sink, with a sequestration rate of 0.3 to 1.7 tons per acre per year.[15]

Prairies once dominated the middle of North America, 40% of what is now the United States. The "sea of grass" supported 30-75 million bison (estimates vary), as well as elk, deer, and antelope and the wolves and grizzly bears who preyed on them. Hordes of smaller inhabitants, from birds to pocket gophers to coyotes, as well as the eponymous prairie dogs, made their homes here. Lewis and Clark described herds of bison "so numerous" that they "darkened the whole plains." As late as 1871, a young U.S. soldier named George Anderson described a herd in Kansas so "enormous" that it took him and his men six days to pass it. "I am safe in calling this a single herd," he wrote, "and it is impossible to approximate the millions that composed it." But "progress" had to push West, what choice was there? Destiny must Manifest.

In 1790, there were 3,900,000 European Americans, most of them living within 50 miles of the Atlantic Ocean. The U.S. census did not count indigenous people at the time, and most agreed with Alexis de Tocqueville's assertion that America was an, "empty continent… awaiting its inhabitants." But the 19th century painter George Caitlin, who traveled among Native Americans to paint hundreds of portraits and scenes of their life, estimated that their total population numbered 16 million. Estimates vary to this day, but there can be no doubt that what happened to the American

Indian population as a result of disease, famine, and genocidal war imported from Europe was an American Holocaust.

By 1830, there were 13 million European Americans, and by 1840, 4,500,000 had crossed the Appalachian Mountains into the Mississippi Valley.[16] They hunted the wildlife with abandon and mined the foothills for gold. They slaughtered the buffalo, churned the grasslands into mile-wide dust swathes, and polluted water sources. Treaties were made with the diverse and adaptable Native American tribes, and they were broken. In 1825, the Federal Government created a Permanent Indian Frontier, encompassing much of modern-day Kansas, Nebraska, and Oklahoma, which was to serve as a stable home for displaced Eastern tribes. Tribes already in the area, such as the Kansas, Wichita, Osages, and Pawnees, ceded lands to make room for tribes "removed" from the east, such as the Delawares and Kickapoos. But in 1854, the Kansas-Nebraska Act opened up vast areas for European American settlement. The Cheyenne, Sioux, and Arapaho, Comanches, and Kiowas, began to fight defensive, and ultimately tragic, wars.[17] The grasslands' new European inhabitants found the prairie soils useful for crop production, and the introduction of the mechanical reaper (and later, the combine harvester) and railroad did the rest. They reduced the tall-grass prairie to less than 1% of its original area in a century's time. They plowed deep into the topsoil, destroying the native grasses' ability to trap moisture during periods of drought and high winds. Their, and especially the famous "robber barons," greed caused the infamous "Dust Bowl," which blackened the skies and traveled east to choke cities as far as New York City and Washington, D.C. in the 1930s.

This culture's masters must expand, extract, compete for more. Above all, they need more bodies to plow their fields and guard their houses and run their machines and buy their products. Fight their wars. Women's wombs, long since taken out of the hands of midwives, are the most fundamental natural resource of all. At the time the United States Constitution was written, abortions before "quickening" were openly advertised and commonly performed. But in the mid to late 19th century, states began to pass laws outlawing abortion. Fear mongering about the high birth rates of immigrant women compared to "native" Anglo-Saxon women combined with the increasing power of male physicians to wrest that final shred of power out of female hands.[18] The respected early-twentieth century physician, Dr. Joseph DeLee, stated in a 1915 speech that, "The midwife is a relic of barbarism. In civilized countries the midwife is wrong, has always been wrong... Even after midwifery was practiced by some of the most brilliant men in the profession, such practice was held opprobrious and degraded." Dr. James Marion Sims, the "father of modern gynecology," gathered knowledge by operating on enslaved black women in the south, without consent or anesthesia.[19] And the moment reproductive freedom was regained by the second wave of women's organizing, the battle to keep it began. Crisis Pregnancy Centers began appearing almost immediately, handing out deceptive pamphlets and promising help to women and girls who agree to "choose life." Billboards with wide-eyed infants dot the interstate highway system. Their propaganda campaign has been so successful that many members of the public, politicians, and even some religiously-minded doctors now believe that aborted fetuses feel pain and "fight for their lives" and that "partial-birth abortion" is a common practice -- that an 8-month pregnant woman can just walk into a Planned Parenthood clinic and rid herself of a viable fetus on a whim. We are losing this war. State after state is introducing "heartbeat bills;" five have passed them. Increasingly draconian restrictions have passed, 300 in 2019 alone, which make safe abortion inaccessible for poor women. Women of color are targeted with rhetoric like, "the most unsafe place for an African American/Latina is in the womb." The Hyde Amendment disproportionately affects black women, and similar funding restrictions limit the ability of Native American women who receive care through the Indian Health Service to access abortion. The U.S. is the only developed country with an increasing rate of maternal mortality,[20] and Black women are dying at three to four times the rate of white women due to pregnancy-related issues.[21] Priority in childbirth is given to the infant, the husband, the doctor. Women's birth plans are ignored and trivialized, women are belittled and coerced into invasive and unnecessary treatments, and are generally treated as an inconvenience in the process of birthing a new human being.

According to the Food and Agriculture Organization of the United Nations, 90% of global fish stocks as a whole are now fully exploited, overexploited, or depleted.[22] However, recent research from Columbia University, which accounted for data omitted by the FAO (like artisanal fisheries, bycatch, and ubiquitous illegal fishing) found that global catches may have been 50% higher than the UN FAO's estimate, and that the true numbers indicate a fish population on "the verge of collapse."[23] This situation is worsened by fisheries subsidies, which are estimated to total $20 billion a year. 85% of these subsidies benefit large fleets; trawlers the size of football fields pull gill nets (including the nominally outlawed but still commonly used drift nets, the "curtains of death" ranging from 300 feet to seven miles in length). Bottom trawlers plow the Ocean floor, destroying up to 20 pounds of "by-catch" life for every pound of target catch.[24] They're emptying the Oceans. But exploitation on steroids is not the only war being waged on Earth's great waters, Her blue womb. Acidification, caused by the uptake of increasing carbon dioxide in the atmosphere, has already decreased ocean PH by a third since the dawn of the industrial revolution -- far faster than any known change in ocean chemistry in the last 55 million years -- and is projected to double by 2100.[25]

This, combined with warming waters, is why corals are experiencing the massive die-offs known as "bleaching events"; corals, oysters, sea snails, and other creatures with delicate carbonate shells or skeletons are weakened by even slight changes in the ocean's PH balance. The Great Barrier Reef, the only living structure visible from space, will likely be gone by 2050 on our current trajectory.[26] Pollution from large livestock farms, oil refineries, and coastal sewage, as well as non-point source pollution from runoff, spews millions of tons of heavy metals and chemical contaminants, killing

100,000 sea mammals and 1 million seabirds every year. Nitrogen pollution triggers the growth of massive algae blooms, like the one that led to Florida's catastrophic 2018 Red Tide event which littered Gulf Coast beaches with the bodies of manatees, dolphins, sea turtles, a whale shark, and thousands of fish. The ecosystem has not recovered. As algae blooms decompose, they consume oxygen, triggering the creation of "hypoxic zones,"[27] or "Dead Zones," where most marine life either dies or, if it's mobile, leaves. Habitats that would normally be teeming with life become biological deserts. The Mississippi River carries an estimated 1.5 million metric tons of nitrogen pollution into the Gulf of Mexico every year, creating a dead zone the size of New Jersey each summer. These oceanic dead zones have quadrupled in size since 1950, and their number has multiplied tenfold.[28] Ocean plastic pollution is increasing exponentially.[29] Swirling convergences of plastic debris make up 40% of Earth's ocean surfaces, and at current rates are expected to outweigh all fish (assuming there still are any) by 2050.[30] It is estimated that approximately 706 million gallons of waste oil enters the ocean every year, with over half coming from land drainage and waste disposal, 8% from offshore drilling, and the remainder from routine maintenance of ships.[31] Phytoplankton, the tiny plant-like organisms which make up the foundation of the oceanic food web and photosynthesize CO^2 into 50 to 85 percent of the oxygen in Earth's atmosphere, aren't doing well in warming waters. A study published in the journal Nature has shown that their populations have decreased by 40% since 1950.[32]

So, this is death, on such a breath-taking, gargantuan scale, that words are just insufficient. I use numbers to describe it, because narrative calls up a wave of grief which washes over me, submerges me until I feel like I can't breathe. Not even scientists can stay detached; Tim Brodribb, who has been measuring the ways global warming kills trees for the past 20 years, listens with a microphone to their last, labored breaths during one of the heat induced die-offs happening all over the world. He says, "We really need to be able to hear these poor trees scream. These are living things that are suffering. We need to listen to them."[33] Samuel McDonald, an activist at Resilience Project with a Master's in Environmental Management from Yale, writes in his essay *Collapse Despair:* "The idea that carbon capitalism is the best and only possible form of economic production is too thoroughly embedded in too many minds across the globe… there are moments when I walk down the street and look around at the people there and I feel surrounded by shades: mangled corpses, distracted slaves of indifferent Hades, forgotten dust drifting placidly."[34] I was in Florida the year before the record Red Tide. I drove down there with the man I married, to visit his family and friends and have a small wedding ceremony on the beach. I watched dolphins somersault and dance in the warm Atlantic waters painted magenta and orange by the setting sun. Everyone became animated as they recounted stories of life on the gulf: suddenly noticing a giant manta ray while swimming, bumping into a manatee with her calf while paddle boarding, finding themselves surrounded by a pod of dolphins after diving off of a dock. Many of those people have left now, after finding their favorite beach transformed into an abattoir. I've seen marine biologists break down in tears as they relate the massive scale of death they're witnessing; the astonishing life forms, many of them only beginning to be studied, gone forever. The origin of Life; used, polluted, discarded.

As in one birthplace, so in another. There are no precise figures for how many births have occurred as a result of commercial surrogacy, but the past two decades have seen a surge in the practice. According to the BBC, the global surrogacy industry is worth an estimated $6 billion a year.[35] According to a July 2020 article in the New York Times, a "movement" is forming "to fight for fertility equality." The "right" to leverage your greater resources to lease someone else's reproductive capabilities. It should come as no surprise that financially and socially vulnerable women are targeted as wombs for rent. A surrogate in Ukraine, for example, can have up to $20,000 dangled in front of her -- more than eight times the average yearly income in her country. With disparate laws governing the uterus trade in various countries -- Germany and France view it as violating the dignity of women, while in California it's seen as an expression of a woman's autonomy to receive payment for the use of her womb (no shock there) -- couples from countries which don't allow it travel to those with light (or no) regulations. Thailand, Cambodia, India, Nepal, Kenya and Nigeria have seen influxes of western "health tourists" in recent years; some have been forced to instate stricter regulations, or outlaw the practice entirely, after particularly egregious (and predictable) scandals erupt. A Japanese man ordered 16 babies from women in Thailand, for example.[36] A congressional hearing was called when an American woman, gestating twins for a Spanish couple, died.[37] A couple tried to force a Connecticut woman to abort after abnormalities were spotted on ultrasound.[38] 40 babies were rescued and 100 gang-members arrested (no word on the mothers' fate) in a puppy-mill style "baby factory" in China's Shandong province in 2015.[39] India was the biggest international destination for commercial surrogacy until foreigners were banned from the industry in 2015, when numerous abuses were uncovered[40]: Poor women, most of who couldn't read, many of them very young, were required to sign a contract, then housed in a bunker-style building where their every move was monitored and controlled, forced to give birth though C-section, and in the end, the "baby brokers" kept the lion's share of the fee.

Last year, 2019, the BBC reported 19 pregnant women and girls, aged 15 to 28, had been freed from a Nigerian "baby factory;" most of them had been abducted and raped "for the purpose of getting them pregnant and selling the babies." Police said that male babies would be sold for $1,400 and females for $830.[41] But we shouldn't have to list these abuses to prove that pregnancy is not a resource to be purchased, that babies are not a commodity, and that having blood offspring is not a "right," any more than we should have to bring up rape victims, pregnant teenaged girls, and women whose pregnancies will kill them in defense of abortion access. It's just the commodification of everything, combined with a sense of entitlement so deeply ingrained, it has distorted and bent the language of "rights" and "equality" to its will. Imagine thinking you have the right to access someone's reproductive system. To use your economic power to access her internal organs, and then erase her from the life of the child she created, because you're sad that you can't have a genetic copy of yourself. The enormous work a woman's body does to knit a human skeletal, nervous, and muscular system out of her own flesh and blood and bones is treated as nothing more than incubation. She "carries" someone else's baby. So long as there has been a "choice" there is "freedom," regardless of context.

Man's civilization extracts. It must extract. It has to grow, and to grow it has to feed. It must first clear the land base of everything living which can't be immediately converted into wealth. So, the soil degrades and erodes. Half of the planet's topsoil has been lost in the past 150 years.[42] The land is left not only less fertile, but more compacted, with higher salinity. Eroding topsoil clogs waterways, and degraded lands are less able to hold on to water, worsening flooding. In the U.S., soil on cropland is eroding 10 times faster than it can be replenished. According to Maria-Helena Semedo of the UN's Food and Agriculture Organization, if topsoil continues to be degraded at the current rate, the world could run out of it in about 60 years.[43] Agriculture accounts for over a quarter (26%) of global greenhouse gas emissions. Half of the world's habitable land is used for it. 70% of global freshwater withdrawals are used for it. 78% of global ocean and freshwater eutrophication (the pollution of water-ways with nutrient-rich pollutants) is caused by agriculture.[44] In fact, agriculture, deforestation, and other forms of land "use" generate a third of greenhouse gas emissions, including 40% of methane.[45]

Surrogacy, like other forms of trafficking in women and girls, is a symptom of the belief that women are a resource for extraction, nourished on backlash against our demands for liberation and fueled by the nitrous booster of technophilic capitalism. But there are far more ancient methods for acquiring a female body. Child marriage is not a "third world problem." Sherry Johnson[46] is among those fighting to end it in the U.S. The 20-year-old man who began raping her at age 8 was a member of her family's church. By ten, she was pregnant, and at 11 she was married to her rapist. Stories like hers happen far too commonly, but U.S. lawmakers have stubbornly resisted attempts to outlaw the practice of "child marriage." Not only do 48 states allow it, but 25 don't even have a minimum marriage age. According to data gathered from 41 states, 200,000 minors were married between 2000 and 2015, with the vast majority (87%) being girls, and in most of them (86%), they were married to an adult man. To put it bluntly, this is a legal loophole for pedophilia straight out of the Old Testament. Rape charges are dropped and, as is often the case, power over the child or teen's pregnancy goes from the parents to the rapist. The girls are 50% more likely to drop out of school, twice as likely to live in poverty, and three times as likely to be beaten by their "spouse" compared to a married adult. Globally, an estimated 12 million girls were child brides last year. Because their bodies are still developing, girls between the ages of 15 and 19 are twice as likely to die in childbirth as women 20 and over, and it's the leading cause of death for girls between the ages of 15 and 19.

Lies and Propaganda

The greenhouse effect, how carbon dioxide affects the atmosphere, was first described by renowned Swedish scientist and Nobel Prize Winner Svante Arhenius in 1896. In 1938, Guy Callendar showed that the Earth's temperature of Earth's atmosphere was already increasing.[47] By the 1950s, scientists knew that climate change presented serious risks. In a special address to Congress in 1965, President Lyndon Johnson warned that, "Air pollution is no longer confined to isolated places. This generation has altered the composition of the atmosphere on a global scale through radioactive materials *and a steady increase in carbon dioxide from the burning of fossil fuels.*" The role of greenhouse gases in heating the atmosphere was broadly acknowledged by scientists and world leaders long ago.

1988, the first of a now-familiar pattern of record-setting hot summers, was a milestone. Dr. James Hansen, climate scientist and director of NASA, testified before the U.S. Congress that scientific data had confirmed humans' role in climate change, and Congress introduced the National Energy Policy Act in an effort to reduce greenhouse emissions. The same year, the United Nations Intergovernmental Panel on Climate Change was formed. A year later, the IPCC issued its first report, warning that the average temperature increase needed to be kept below 1° C or we'd face "societal collapse." But the rate of emissions has only risen, and exponentially. More than half of the world's industrial carbon emissions have been released into the atmosphere since that year, and methane is increasing even faster. The 1°C mark has almost been reached, so the new goal is 1.5° or even 2°.

Already in July of 1977, a senior scientist at Exxon Corporation had delivered a detailed address to an audience of oilmen, explaining that the use of fossil fuels was warming the planet and could endanger humanity. "Present thinking," he said, "holds that man has a time window of five to ten years before the need for hard decisions regarding changes in energy strategies becomes critical."[48] Initially, the company saw this as an existential threat and launched its own rigorous research. But at the end of the 1980s, Exxon did an about-face, and abandoned its research into the effects of increased atmospheric CO_2 in favor of a denial campaign, blocking efforts to control greenhouse gas emissions.[49]

Now, in the face of overwhelming evidence, major fossil fuel companies tend to publicly acknowledge climate change, and even support efforts to address it (which ones they support deserves a long, hard look), but continue to covertly support groups which seek to undermine any real progress. Heartland Institute, Americans for Prosperity, and the Committee for a Constructive Tomorrow, among others, continue to shill for the bloated, insatiable monster that is fossil fuel. Examples of its malicious tactics are far too numerous to list here. They've threatened the climate scientist who published the pioneering "hockey stick graph," illustrating the recent spike in global temperatures,[50] with simulated anthrax.[51] Female scientists endure misogyny and sexualized threats.[52] Their strategies have been catalogued in detail by the Union of Concerned Scientists[53] in *The Climate Deception Dossiers, Internal Fossil Fuel Industry Memos Reveal Decades of Corporate Disinformation,* and by Naomi Oreskes and Erik M. Conway in *Merchants of Doubt.*[54]

> *The way to right wrongs is to turn the light of truth upon them.*
>
> -Ida B. Wells

If rape, wife battery, and femicide are the armed forces in the war on women, pornography must surely be its propaganda arm. Again, it is not my aim to cause distress, and I wish I could avoid it. But I know of no way to accurately describe the cruelty of sexually commodified females-as-entertainment without talking about what actually happens.

Because porn companies are privately held, and because illegal child porn represents a significant portion of the content produced and used, it's difficult to make an accurate estimate of its size. Some believe the industry's revenue is roughly $6 billion a year, others $10 billion, $15 billion, and even $97 billion.[55] Numerous other industries thrive on the profit generated by porn, too. The Hilton, Marriott, and Westin hotel chains. Cable and Satellite companies. AT&T- Comcast. News Corp. offers pornography channels. Yahoo! Has made lots of money selling ads and links to porn websites. In a strange coincidence, smartphone screens started getting bigger at exactly the same time mobile porn became available. The corporate power and reach of the porn industry are indisputable, and that's undoubtedly a major reason why the testimonies of the women and girls who've been harmed by it aren't heard by the majority of the public. Its proponents have no trouble publishing breathless articles about the liberatory nature of watching others endure punishing, degrading, and physically dangerous sex acts. But even they almost never mention the "performers" themselves. It's up to a minority of radical feminists and anti-porn campaigners to get their stories heard:

When I arrived on set, I expected to do a vaginal girl boy scene. But during the scene with a male porn star, he forced himself into me anally and would not stop. I yelled at him to stop and screamed 'no' over and over, but he would not stop. The pain became too much, and I was in shock and my body went limp.

-Corina Taylor.

My initiation into prostitution was a gang rape by five men, arranged by Mr. Traynor. It was the turning point in my life. He threatened to shoot me with the pistol if I didn't go through with it. I had never experienced anal sex before and it ripped me apart. They treated me like an inflatable plastic doll, picking me up and moving me here and there. They spread my legs this way and that, shoving their things at me and into me, they were playing musical chairs with parts of my body. I have never been so frightened and disgraced and humiliated in my life. I felt like garbage. I engaged in sex acts for pornography against my will to avoid being killed. The lives of my family were threatened.

-Linda Lovelace.

I got the shit kicked out of me... most of the girls start crying because they're hurting so bad... I couldn't breathe. I was being hit and choked. I was really upset, and they didn't stop. They kept filming. [I asked them to turn the camera off] and they kept going.

-Regan Starr.

I did gonzo porn at the start and that was the most degrading, embarrassing, horrible thing ever! I had to shoot an interactive DVD which takes hours and hours of shooting time with a 104 degree fever. I was crying and wanted to leave but my agent wouldn't let me, he said he couldn't let me flake on it. I also did a scene where I was put with male talent that was on my no list. I wanted to please them, so I did it. He put his foot on my head and stepped on it while he was doing me from behind. I freaked out and started bawling; they stopped filming and sent me home with reduced pay since they got some shot but not the whole scene.

-Jessi Summers.

My first scene was one of the worst experiences of my life. It was very scary. It was a very rough scene. My agent didn't let me know ahead of time... I did it and I was crying, and they didn't stop. It was really violent. He was hitting me.

-Sierra Sinn.

Some women hate it so much you can hear them vomiting in the bathroom between scenes.

-Shelley Lubben.

Guys punching you in the face. You have semen from many guys all over your face, in your eyes. You get ripped. Your insides can come out of you. It's never ending.

-Jersey Jaxin.[56]

Yeah, there are a lot of cover-ups going on. There is a lot of tragedy. There are a lot of horrible things.

-Anita Cannibal.

These are just a few of countless testimonies from former porn performers ("performers" is an uncomfortable word, but it's a little better than "actresses"), women whose names are known in the industry and who have taken part in its mainstream content. There seems to be no limit to the appetite for watching women, afraid and in pain, used for porn consumers. Anal sex, once niche, is completely mainstream, so double penetration and fisting were demanded. The female body – whose colon is smaller than a male's – simply could not take the abuse, and rectal prolapse became such a common injury that it spawned its own genre: "rosebudding" porn. Simple blowjobs weren't enough, the women's throats had to be aggressively penetrated, while tears stream down their faces, until they vomit. Interactive "fetish" sites were set up where viewers could contact the pornographers directly and tell them what they want to see done to a bound and gagged young woman with no ability to invoke a "safe word" (if we're going to pretend such a thing would be respected). Teenaged girls are aggressively targeted by porn companies, often while they're still minors, promising piles of cash and a rebellious, glamorous lifestyle to girls whose job prospects won't pay for a car, food, and an apartment; girls whose brothers at least have the chance of working unionized construction jobs, or girls facing crushing college debt and the need to feed themselves through school. They're assured that they'd never be asked to do anything they're not comfortable with, and they've already gone through the cultural grooming process which tells them that their bodies are the most interesting thing about them, that an expectation of mutual respect and sexual intimacy is "vanilla," boring, and emotionally needy, that being choked, hit, degraded and anally penetrated are just everyday sexual activities. "Teen" is one of the most popular search terms, scenes which start with a girl blowing out the candles on her 18th birthday are not uncommon. They're quickly funneled from "girl on girl" to "rough" to "kink." Those who survive it at all almost never last longer than six months, usually no more than three.

But that's the professional porn industry, and the "amateur" side is growing fastest, with little or no production cost and the promise of unlimited stimulation for the consumer. 6 million new videos a year are generated on Pornhub (owned by mega-parent company Mindgeek), the most popular site, with 42 billion annual views. Any claims of self-regulation here are a cynical joke, anonymous users can go through a simple registration process to upload clips of bruised girls and women with vacant, dead eyes, with titles like, "It's too big for her ass – Listen to her painful screams" and "Struggling slut fights rough anal abuse – fails miserably" and are paid for the number of views. Age verification is impossible, and not even the interviews purporting to demonstrate "consent" in mainstream videos are required.

Artist and trafficking survivor Suzzan Blac has been documenting the extreme misogyny enacted on Pornhub and other major platforms for years on her blog, "The violence of pornography."[57]

I'd like to really show what I believe the men want to see: violence against women. I firmly believe that we [pornographers] serve a purpose by doing that.[58]

-Bill Marigold, porn industry veteran.

There's nothing I love more than when a girl insists to me that she won't take a cock in her ass, because- oh yes she will!

-Max Hardcore, performer and pornographer, credited with popularizing the "Gonzo" genre.

My whole reason for being in this industry is to satisfy the desire of men in the world who basically don't care much for women and want to see the men in my industry getting even with the women they couldn't have when they were growing up. I strongly believe this... so we cum on a woman's face or somewhat brutalize her sexually: we're getting even for their lost dreams. I believe this. I've heard audiences cheer me when I do something foul on screen. When I've strangled a person or sodomized a person, or brutalized a person, the audience is cheering my action, and then when I've fulfilled my warped desire, the audience applauds.

-Bill Marigold, porn industry veteran and
Free Speech Coalition member.[59]

He [Sandler] dismissed the contention that his 'rape camp' web site would increase violence against women in Cambodia. 'I have nothing against women here.' He explained, 'it's not being marketed to this community' and since few Cambodians had internet access they weren't likely to see it. If his sexual bondage show caused violence against women in the United States -- the community of the target audience -- that was acceptable, even desirable. 'It might promote violence against women in the United States, but I say, 'Good.' I hate those bitches. They're out of line and that's one of the reasons I want to do this.

-Dan Sandler, pornographer.[60]

"*They're out of line, and that's one of the reasons I want to do this.*" And yet, the argument somehow still has to be made that porn is dangerous, that it causes harm. So, we point out the studies connecting it with the belief that women enjoy[61] rape[62] and[63] that we don't suffer much as a result of it.[64] That watching it leads to believing that rapists should receive less jail[65] time.[66] That it leads to a greater acceptance of violence[67] against women. That it's connected to increased self-reported likelihood[68] to[69] rape among adolescent boys[70] and adult men.[71] (If you're glancing down at the footnotes, you might've noticed a curious pattern -- the growth of the porn industry seems inversely correlated with motivation to study its effects). That it leads to creating more sexually violent fantasies to get aroused,[72] more sexual harassment[73] behaviors.[74] That[75] it is[76] associated[77] with having[78] engaged[79] in rape.[80]

The 1986 Report of the Attorney General of the United States' Commission on Pornography: Section 5.2.1 stated that, "...clinical and experimental research... [has] focused particularly on sexually violent material, [and] the conclusions have been virtually unanimous. In both clinical and experimental setting, exposure to sexually violent materials has indicated an increase in the likelihood of aggression. More specifically, the research, which is described in much detail in the appendix, shows a causal relationship between exposure to material of this type and aggressive behavior towards women."[81]

It doesn't matter how well we build our case, how many studies we find. How many Universities suspend future research after the detrimental and irreversible effects are shown over and over. Pornography and its brother sex industries continue to grow and expand because what they provide is something essential to this culture, something its males require to continue doing what they do. The bond created when they sneer over breaking the spirit of a girl, brutalizing her past the point of no return, is so much like the bond over felling a Redwood, or skinning a tiger, or burning a rainforest. It's the final mastery of destruction.

The average age of first exposure to pornography was 11 years old, with 10% of 12 to 13-year-olds expressing worry that they may be addicted, as of 2015.[82] After a recent surge of young boys convicted of criminal sexual behavior- the number of kids under 17 convicted of rape had almost doubled in four years,[83] the U.K. attempted to institute stringent age verification. Predictably, the "sexologists" and academic "sex work" fanboys came out of the woodwork (or wherever they spend their days), wailing about "government intrusion," and after a series of "technical problems," the plan was scrapped. Freedom.

It's a ticking time bomb. It's going to get worse; it's not going to get better.

-Demi Delia, porn performer.

What's coming

It's maddening, the lack of outrage. The dishonest, chicken-shit excuses for acts of such cruelty, your stomach tightens into a knot. We're all losing our minds a bit, here in this late stage of capitalism. We cling to our veneer of edgy detachment like a rotten life raft. The machines which we must worship as the manifestation of the inevitable march of "human progress" have us alienated to the point of psychosis; from each other, from meaning, from the Earth herself. As the ruling classes curate the detailed news which floods our myriad screens, the larger political patterns and processes which dictate our reality are obscured. 40 million Americans are on psychiatric drugs, many of them since childhood. Somehow, this pharmacological inundation has not prevented the now-common specter of school shootings and mass murder. Added to this is the drip...drip...drip of catastrophic ecological news in our social media feed. Someone, usually a "friend" we've never met, shares some article, about some scientific organization, which has projected the end of something by some year. Often, we don't read past the headline. We know it's bad, reading about just how bad will only make us feel bad, and then we won't be productive. To be productive, one must "think positive." We dutifully recycle and try to eat less meat (or, if we're contrarian, we share memes making fun of those who recycle and try to eat less meat). This is how a public which has largely accepted that "climate change is real" still believes that we should really "do something" for "future generations" with easy lifestyle changes. We've allowed ourselves to believe we can do our part by tweaking our consumption patterns and voting for the right member of the ruling class. We've been shielded, and shielded ourselves, from knowing and understanding just what's underway, and what lies ahead. So, this is going to be difficult, on a deep level. It's difficult to write, my mind keeps desperately searching for distractions as I do it, something -- anything -- else to focus my attention on. Please keep reading; this is hard for me, too.

Global average temperatures have already surpassed the 1° C increase limit put forward by the first IPCC report. As of 2019, the average temperature across global land and ocean surfaces was 1.1° C above the 20th-century average of 13.9° C, and the rate of increase has more than doubled since 1981. Until then, global temperatures had increased from pre-industrial levels at a rate of 0.07° C per decade; since then, it's been 0.18° C. From 1900 to 1980, a new high temperature record was set on average every 13 years, it's now every three. The five warmest years in the 1880-2019 record have all occurred since 2015.[84]

In 2015, it had become clear that limiting warming to 1° C was not going to happen, so when the world's countries met at the Paris climate summit, they revised it to 1.5° C, then 2°. The Geneva-based World Meteorological Organization has recently said that forecasts suggest there's a 20% chance the 1.5° C mark could be hit by 2024 for at least one year.[85]

So far, we've watched hurricanes intensify and floods increase as the oceans -- which absorb 90% of the increasing temperature -- warm. Mega-storms have gone from occurring once every 100 years, to once every 16 years.[86] The Gulf of Mexico and East Coast of the United States have found themselves scrambling to prepare as tropical storms spin into monstrous Category 4 Hurricanes in record time.[87] Warm water expands; warming oceans are the cause of half the sea level rise we've seen so far, and with 50% of the U.S. coastal population living in Florida, the state is on the brink. Already, salt water is pushing through bedrock into the water supply and overtaking the critical everglades ecosystem. It's predicted that much of Miami will be lost within three decades.[88]

Heat is the deadliest form of extreme weather in the U.S., causing more deaths than hurricanes and floods combined, more than twice as many deaths as tornadoes, and four times as many as from extreme cold.[89] Heat waves are occurring three times more often than they did in the 1960s,[90] with an increasing rate of increase.[91] From 1998-2017, more than 166,000 people died due to heatwaves, including more than 70,000 who died during the 2003 heatwave in Europe.[92] The summer of that year was the hottest European summer since at least 1540. Between 15,000 and 19,000 people died in France alone.[93]

In 2012, the central and western US was hit by a record drought, the driest in Texas history, which affected 81% of the country and cost $30 billion. A recent NASA study found that a drought which has been affecting (I almost said "ravaging") the Levant region of the Mediterranean has been the worst in 900 years.[94] More drought means more fire, and the past couple of years have seen a conflagration of wildfire headlines. Last year, 2019, we learned of megafires (100,000 acres – 40,000 hectares – 400 square kilometers or more). Brazil, the Democratic Republic of the Congo, the Russian Federation and the United States had all experienced these infernos by the close of 2019, with Indonesia burning as well. The burning of the world's largest tropical rainforests was intentionally caused by human ranchers and miners, but an unusually hot and dry fire season made their work easy. By the second week of January 2020, over 10 million hectares had burned in Australia, and an estimated billion animals perished. The western US has seen a 400% increase in wildfires,[95] with fires larger than 1,000 acres five times more frequent and burning ten times as large since the 1970s.[96]

A third of Earth's total land mass is under threat from desertification,[97] driven by climate change, expansion of croplands, unsustainable land management practices and increased pressure on land from population and income growth. According to a 2019 IPCC Special Report, desertification hot-spots extended by almost 10% between the 1980s and 2000s, effecting 500 million people in 2015. Unsustainable land use, coupled with droughts, has also contributed to increased dust storms, "associated with global cardiopulmonary mortality of about 402,000 people in 2005." Sandstorms and sand dune movements are disrupting transportation and solar and wind energy harvesting infrastructures.[98]

Maybe you've seen that famous National Geographic video of the starving polar bear.[99] I had to look it up again to footnote it, so now I know what kind of dreams are in store for me tonight. It's hard to describe the sorrow, the angry, desperate grief that seeing that creature fills me with. The *wrong*ness of it. But we're meant to be too cynical for such things. It's deeply uncool to be so moved. This year's Siberian heat wave triggered an outbreak of fires across the tundra, and temperatures in one arctic town hit 100° F. Each September, we wait to see if summer sea ice finally breaks down. When satellites first began monitoring it in 1979, the average area covered by sea ice was 40% larger and twice as thick.[100]

So. What's coming. The IPCC's assessment has projected that doubling atmospheric carbon over pre-industrial levels will cause average global temperatures to reach 2°C – 5.4°C by the end of the century. But the reflective effect of clouds, and dimming effect of aerosol pollutants, has proved challenging for climate modeling in the past. More recently, at least eight next-generation models released in 2019, projected the average at 5°C or as much as 8°.[101] Current carbon emission trends show exponential increase, and IPCC reports frequently skew conservative, in fact, despite spurious claims to the contrary. Observed green-house emissions, for example, have proved close to its worst-case projections, sea-level rise and arctic sea ice melt are also accelerating at a faster rate.[102] In addition, the IPCC scientists are always under political pressure from their respective governments, notably the United States, but not solely. But most crucially, the IPCC doesn't account for difficult to quantify feedback loops, or "tipping points," initiated as temperatures rise. Ice reflects solar radiation, while water absorbs it, so as ice melts the open water is warmed and more ice melts (the albedo effect). Hotter temperatures make forests more susceptible to diebacks and wildfires, turning a carbon sink into a massive carbon emitter, further heating the atmosphere. Permafrost, soil that stays below freezing for at least two years, covers 24% of Earth's exposed landmass, and it's melting all over the world, creating a particularly dangerous feedback loop whose effects are difficult to predict: permafrost contains almost twice as much carbon as is in the atmosphere today,[103] as well as an enormous amount of methane, a greenhouse gas which traps 86 times more heat than CO^2.[104]

Most frighteningly to scientists, the thousands of currents, gyres, and eddies that carry water around the planet as part of the Atlantic Meridional Overturning Circulation (AMOC), of which the Gulf Stream is a key part, have already slowed 15% since the middle of last century, with immediate effects on temperatures and weather patterns, and an exacerbating effect on other feedback loops.[105] Together, these and other tipping points threaten a cascade, with each one triggering the others, creating an irreversible shift. Melting Greenland ice has already driven a key component of ocean circulation to a thousand-year low. Further decline of the AMOC would lead to a shift in heat distribution around the planet, trigger a forest collapse in the Amazon, send Africa's Sahel region into near-permanent drought, disrupt Asian monsoons, and rapidly warm the Southern Ocean, causing a surge in global sea levels as the West Antarctic Ice Sheet collapses. This would bring about a new world scientists are calling "hothouse Earth."[106]

Three years ago, Stephen Hawking told BBC news that the domino effect may already be triggered, and that the end result will be something like what happened on Earth's sister planet, Venus, whose own oceans boiled away under a runaway greenhouse effect, turning it into the hellscape of boiling sulfur and acid rain it is today. Most scientists don't agree with quite that prediction, but James Hansen (remember him?) is one. Venus was his original focus of study at NASA, before he turned his attention to Earth's atmosphere, and he has written that, "If we burn all reserves of oil, gas, and coal, there's a substantial chance that we will initiate the runaway greenhouse. If we also burn the tar sands and tar shale, I believe the Venus syndrome is a dead certainty."[107] But even if all possibility of life isn't forever wiped out, even if what happens is "only" a repeat of the Great Dying that was the Permian-Triassic extinction event 252 million years ago, when 95 percent of marine and 70 percent of terrestrial species were destroyed, huge amounts of methane and carbon heated the atmosphere, the ocean lost 80% of its oxygen and warmed by 5° C, even if that happens and the possibility of life rebounding remains, that is unacceptable.

The Earth is currently warming faster than it did at the end of the Permian.[108]

In 2017, the American Institute of Biological Sciences published a letter,[109] the second declaration of its kind, warning that the biosphere was fast approaching the limits of what it could tolerate. They pleaded that we stabilize the human population – which has only swelled by 2 billion since the first letter was published in 1992, an increase of 35%. They stressed that, "Soon it will be too late to shift course away from our falling trajectory, and time is running out." In 2018, the World Bank concluded that 143 million people will be displaced by water shortages, crop failure, and rising sea levels in Sub-Saharan Africa, South Asia, and Latin America alone by 2050.[110] In the U.S., people will be pushed out of their homes by fire, arid croplands, and rising seas, "Including all climate impacts it isn't too far-fetched to imagine something twice as large as the Dustbowl," according to Jesse Keenan, climate adaptation expert at Harvard. By the end of the century, sea level rise alone is projected to displace 13 million.[111]

Writing for The New Humanitarian in 2018,[112] Oxfam director Winnie Byanyima spoke of the women in her native Uganda who walked 6 hours a day to bring their families water, and of the lengthening dry seasons threatening to make that walk longer still. She called out Arab Group countries which blocked attempts by the international community to address the increased pressure on girls and women from forced migration during the Warsaw climate summit, "It seems the mention of human rights, let alone women's rights, is too much for some countries to stomach." As the drought crisis deepens in Angola, girls are being taken out of school and trafficked into the sex trade to feed their families. 45 million people in southern Africa face hunger after repeated droughts, and girls as young as twelve are sold, "cheaper than a loaf of bread."[113] According to World Vision, the crisis has also increased incidents of child marriage and rape, with girls at heightened risk while walking long distances for water or to forage in the forest.

They keep telling us it's "us." "We" are slaughtering the wild, "we" are poisoning and emptying the oceans, "we" are razing Earth's forests and setting her atmosphere on fire. But in reality -- and I believe this -- the majority of people would make the necessary sacrifices if they really knew how, and what threatens them, and what hell world their children will see. What hell world our daughters will see. It's not "us." It's "them." And we know their names. Names like Darren Woods, CEO of Exxon. Feras Antoon, owner of Mindgeek. Ben van Buerden of Shell.[114] The mining and timber and agribusiness lobbyists making a joke of regulatory agencies.[115]

This is not the time for despair, but neither is it a time for some vague, fluffy hope that "human ingenuity" will save us all. The technology that we're told will deliver us exists in the service of those who would sacrifice us; its motivations are their motivations. The young girls who can't wait to turn 18, so that they can set up an Onlyfans site, will not be saved by technology; neither will the millions of shorebirds, scrounging for something to feed their babies from among the piles of plastic waste, now that the carp are gone. Yes, there is grief. Grief that inundates you and penetrates your bones, that threatens to paralyze like a nerve agent. We mustn't let it paralyze. We must spin it and weave it into a weapon. Into rage at the nihilism, the cruelty, that brought us here. Nothing about this was inevitable.

We know that the most important thing an oppressive system which divides people -- and living things generally -- into hierarchical classes of value requires is some way to naturalize itself. Africans were a "lower order," less rational, more prone to emotional outbursts; but also physically stronger and less able to feel pain, making them suited for enslavement. Women's "nature" has changed, depending on what was required by kings and Church Fathers and Presidents, but we, too, have been irrational, emotionally and physically frail; but also nurturing and self-sacrificing, perfectly suited for the role of help-mate and baby-raiser. Nature, "red in tooth and claw," is fundamentally cruel, both justifying Man's cruelty in subjugating Her, and explaining the need for such subjugation. I am not going to spend pages rebutting the spurious claims which have been made about the "women from Venus, men from Mars," "sexed brain," theories used to rationalize sex role stereotypes, or outlining the history of bad "science" propping up racism, or exploring the ways that cooperation and mutuality are far more representative of Nature than competition. Cordelia Fine has done an excellent job of knocking down neurosexism in her book "Delusions of Gender," as have Lise Eliot, Gina Rippon, and scores of other neuroscientists. For some behavior or other aspect of human experience to truly be innate, it has to be universal; but history, anthropology, and archaeology all show us that the sex roles which are familiar to us are far from immutable. It is worth noting, though, that of all of the different ways of arranging human societies, I know of none that had no sexual division of labor whatsoever, what varies is how rigid they are, and the hierarchical value assigned them. But also: the societies that have existed, and the few that survived long enough to be studied, which have been described as matriarchal -- matrilineal and matrilocal -- have egalitarianism in common, women didn't violently subjugate men. And none turned themselves into militaristic civilizations bent on conquest, destroying their natural environment and hunting its creatures to extinction. And that is curious.

In her oft-cited (though, I would argue, not nearly "oft" enough, these days) study[116] of rape-free vs. rape-prone societies, the ethnographer and professor of anthropology Peggy Reeves Sanday, who spent years of her life living with and studying the Matriarchal Minanhkabau people of West Sumatra, studied fraternity culture in American universities, and conducted cross-cultural research of 150 different tribal societies, found remarkable and important differences. She defined a rape-prone society as "one in which the incidence of rape is reported by observers to be high, or rape is excused as a ceremonial expression of masculinity, or rape is an act by which men are allowed to punish or threaten women." She defined a rape-free society as one in which rape is either infrequent or does not occur, but she clarified that, "I used the term 'rape-free' not to suggest that rape was entirely absent in a given society but as a label to indicate that sexual aggression is socially disapproved of and punished severely." By this measure, she found that of 95 band and tribal societies she had studied, 47% were rape-free and 18% were rape prone. She found that rape in tribal societies, "is part of a cultural conflagration that includes interpersonal violence, male dominance, and sexual separation." She found that, "Rape-prone behavior is associated with environmental insecurity and females are turned into objects to be controlled as men struggle to retain or to gain control of their environment... *Where men are in harmony with their environment, rape is usually absent* [emphasis mine]." I believe this is crucial. Something which has a beginning, has causative factors, was learned, can be un-learned. If it's a disease with a cause, it can be cured. Men rape and subjugate women when men set themselves up in struggle against Nature.

> *The common erotic project of destroying women makes it possible for men to unite into a brotherhood; this project is the only firm and trustworthy groundwork for cooperation among males and all male bonding is based on it.*
>
> -Andrea Dworkin, Our Blood

Speaking ill of the sex industry is forbidden in western liberal feminism; to do so earns one the ridiculous acronym "SWERF" -- even if you're speaking from direct personal experience. Wanting to end men's abuse of women in prostitution is "sex worker exclusionary." The likes of Susie Bright, and other reactionaries who believe that letting men rape the poor and disposable will protect them, have turned any criticism of the sex industry into sacrilege, and in the process gotten feminists to do the pimps' work for them. Veronica Vera has said that women in the industry are "practitioners of a sacred craft." I wonder what Veronica would think of the young woman who shared her story of entering the industry at 22:

My first agent told me I would make a better escort, so I started seeing clients as well. A few weeks later I flew to NY for a 'hardcore scene.' My agent didn't elaborate on hardcore, just emphasized it was money. I was beaten, given a black eye, and sodomized with a baseball bat. I wasn't allowed to end the scene unless I wanted a pay cut. I finished alright -- but was forever scarred. I ended up in the ER a few weeks later with lacerations in my anus... I was raped at gunpoint by people I met in the industry. I went from being a heavy drinker to shooting up coke, heroin, and meth... Despite all this, I didn't even leave the industry willingly. Not, at least, for a while... I was in and out of psych wards, rehabs, detoxes, and halfway houses.[117]

Professor and graduate program director at York University Shannon Bell would call her a "worker, healer, sexual surrogate, teacher, therapist, educator, sexual minority, and political activist." Imagine being so out of touch. Try to fathom the breathtaking privilege of someone who would call a sexually tortured girl a "worker" and a "healer." While the DVD series "Gag Factor" offers up "New whores degraded every Wednesday," and the promotional copy for "Anally Ripped Whores" advertises that, "We at pure filth know exactly what you want, and we're giving it to you. Chicks being ass-fucked till their sphincters are pink, puffy and totally blown out. Adult diapers just might be in store for these whores when their work is done," Slutwalk organizer Jaclyn Friedman shouted to a crowd in Boston, "If you've ever been called a slut, stand up and say it together – I am a slut... I am a slut, I am a slut. I am a slut!," undoubtedly making male porn consumers see the abused women they jerk off to with newfound respect; "If you like the roughest, it could be the Jessica scene... At one point, she stops the scene crying... if you like vomit, go for babydoll..." ("Panas," Adult DVD talk).

I believe this is an essential component of the "divide and conquer" strategy of hierarchical civilizations: Start by dividing the women into a descending hierarchy of value, destroy their solidarity and instill fear. Though most men know women whom they love, and even respect, they can be encouraged to turn against them; their freedom to do what they wish to women becomes the only freedom they have, it eases their discomfort with their own class status. Upper-class women can be deceived into thinking that they can escape the bonds of womanhood by leveraging their social capital, using it to put weight behind the argument that *they* are equal, that *they* aren't weak and stupid and untrustworthy like *them,* like *those* women. It's worth noting here that there was one case of men mobilizing in defense of women during the witch hunts: In 1609, the men of the Basque region were away fishing the annual cod harvest (there's that cod again), when they heard rumors that the French Inquisitor had gathered their wives, mothers, daughters, and sisters, that they had been stripped, stabbed, and some had already been executed. The fishermen returned, clubs in hands, and liberated a convoy of witches being taken to be burned, expelled the inquisitor, and successfully stopped the trials.[118]

I guess it's customary to end a piece of writing of this nature by outlining some sort of solution, preferably one which requires no discomfort, risk, or sacrifice. It's deeply unsatisfying to have injustices and threats delineated, with no resolution. I get that. It doesn't help that there's been at least a 40-year campaign to cripple leftist class analysis, to herd us all into silos of micro-identity, to the point that we can only see ourselves influencing society from the confines of our individualized bubbles (the nature of that campaign, from the deification of the first postmodernists to the capture of academia -- and through it every type of popular protest movement -- would double the length of this little treatise; I trust that others are doing that work). We're not solving this by changing our shopping habits, or by choosing the crypto-fascist over the fascist-fascist in the voting booth. We need to be questioning why we're expected to worship "civilization" as an intrinsic Good. It was a mistake. I'm not arguing that we can or should live in mud huts instead, that we need to abandon literacy or science, but we do need to take a long, hard, look at societies which have not practiced a way of life which terrorized its female population and destroyed the natural world. Or at the societies that women have already created to protect each other from endemic male violence. When Europeans first met the Iroquois, the idea of a sophisticated, successful culture in which women were not oppressed was so foreign, they assumed the women they saw participating in tribal government were concubines. In fact, the matrilineal Iroquois federation had women in positions of responsibility for defining the political, social, spiritual, and economic norms of the tribe. Women owned the land and tended the crops, and determined the consequences for crimes.[119] The Mosuo people of China consider themselves a matriarchy, with women in charge of business and men taking care of the animals. The women choose their sexual partners in a "walking marriage": men live in their mothers' house, and at night women walk to their partners. Paternity of babies is often unknown, but this carries no stigma.[120] In 1990, a group of 15 women formed a village in the Samburu grasslands of Kenya after being raped by British soldiers. Many had been shunned by their families or beaten by their husbands after surviving the assaults, and they had had enough. The village, Umoja, is surrounded by a fence made of thorns, and allows no male visitors. Women come to escape FGM, abusive husbands, and rape -- all of which are cultural norms among the local Samburu people.

This is why I get so frustrated when people make references to "human nature" in discussions about environmental destruction, or fall back on sex role stereotypes to explain male violence against women and children. We know that humans can live differently, and we need to, we must, learn from and emulate those people who have. We can bring back the grasslands and the buffalo, we can let the forests grow back, we can start to heal the terrible wounds of colonialism. We don't have a choice anymore. You know what I'm afraid of? The fear that haunts me, keeps me awake at night, and cemented my conviction that having children would be a terrible idea? The knowledge of where we're currently all headed. I imagine a young girl of twelve, 50, 40, maybe thirty years from now: She's walking hand-in-hand with her mother on a bridge over the water which has submerged what was once St. Petersburg, Florida. No insects buzz, no birds chirp. The only sound is the clicking of their regulation high-heeled shoes and the mechanical clangs of industry in the distance. The girl looks down at the still water through her oxygen mask, electric blue now that the plankton no longer color it green. What was crashing waves is now a stagnant pool, but she tries to remember the great breakers, struggles to imagine what it must have been to see a dolphin leap through the surf. Or even a whale. She tries to control her breathing as her mind attempts to conjure a creature so enormous, to imagine its haunting music. Her mother is fortunate to be allowed to walk alone -- when the Amazon Party beat the Nestle Party in the last election, the remaining vestiges of age of consent laws were finally done away with, and unaccompanied women had to register to travel. So, she taught her child the techniques of marketing her little body to members of the Law and Order squads whose drones hover over their heads. They are walking to meet them now; the uniformed, heavily armed patrolmen who keep the peace and oversee the laborers. If she's very good, the girl might become a Wife.

We can't stop the twin horsemen of the apocalypse, the war on the natural world and the war on women, they're here. But we can fight them. We can end the era of multi-national corporations stealing massive swathes of land from subsistence farmers and living ecosystems to strip it bare and plant it with monoculture crops for export and profit for shareholders. We can destroy the multi-billion dollar slave trade which goes by the name "global sex trafficking." We can stop the trawlers which scour the oceans for what life hasn't already been slaughtered, processed, and converted into dollar bills. We can dismantle the Female Genital Mutilation, the wife purchasing and "honor" killing, the sexualization of girlhood. We can end the destruction of everything living, replaced with endless miles of suburban wasteland and soybean fields and industry. A growing number of women are farming here in the

U.S, and they have a different approach; they're focused on feeding people and educating them about where their food comes from, they're community-focused, prioritizing keeping the land healthy long term.[121]

I did a quick calculation, based on data available online: If the U.S. prairies were allowed to return to their pre-colonization acreage of 142 million, they alone could sequester (based on median sequestration rates) the amount of carbon emitted by the United States in 2017 every ten years. Prairies are being destroyed at an even faster rate than rainforests, and greenhouse gas emissions are increasing exponentially, but imagine if this process was reversed. The alternative is a nightmare world in our lifetimes, it will take real sacrifice, real radical change to avoid it. To allow the natural world to even begin to restore balance, we have to decrease our demands on it, and fast. There's simply no avoiding the conclusion that our numbers have to drop; stopping suburban encroachment on the remaining wild lands, restricting the amount of meat consumed by wealthy countries, reducing air travel to a minimum, adopting regenerative agricultural practices, and similar measures which have been proposed will buy time, but there's just no way Earth can sustain another billion people every 25 years.

Unfortunately, in some circles, even suggesting putting a stop to population growth immediately calls up thoughts of eugenics, forced sterilization, and compulsory abortion. Authoritarianism and control of female reproduction are so built into this culture, it's unimaginable that we could build a society in which women are truly liberated, fully in control of childbirth (or lack thereof). Just teaching girls to read reduces birth rates substantially. Even the concessions which women in the west have been able to wrest from this system, incomplete and spottily enforced, have been sufficient to create sub-replacement fertility rates. The ruling classes of Poland (my native country) and the Russian Federation are responding to falling populations -- caused in no small part by Communist era ideals of sex equality -- by instituting draconian restrictions on reproductive freedom, Russia has basically decriminalized wife battery in the midst of an explosion in sex trafficking. Yes, many of the countries which are experiencing the biggest population booms are in the global south. But the problem is not the ethnic makeup of homo sapiens on this planet, it's the numbers. There are too many people in Canada, the U.S., and in Germany, too. We need the Hyde Amendment lifted, we need the Equal Rights Amendment ratified, and we need to give political asylum to women escaping gendered oppression.

Despite the patronizing insinuations of Western cultural relativism, women around the world are fighting back against their oppression, and they're well aware that it's sex-based. Ever since the U.S.-backed Ayatolla Khomeini rose to power in Iran and proceeded to dismantle women's rights, women have been organizing and resisting.[122] In South Korea, women are responding to a series of sex abuse scandals, and a system unmotivated to act. They're demanding female-only spaces, advocating separatism, and calling out the beauty industry for its part in subordinating women and girls.[123] This spring in Mexico, thousands of young radical feminists took to the streets in revolt, a response to the country's worsening femicide crisis.[124] In Uganda, a rising tide of eco-feminism is fighting back against the mining interests, sugar cane industry, and palm oil plantations destroying the incredibly diverse Bugonda forest on which they rely for food and medicine.[125] In the Amazon Basin, indigenous women, some from tribes which traditionally have not recognized female leadership, have formed a powerful coalition to stand up to the unchecked destruction of their rainforest home spearheaded by president Jair Bolsonaro and his corporate backers. Celia Xakriaba, one of the heads of the movement, is unequivocal about the connection between environmental destruction and violence against women and girls: "I like to say about the matrix of destruction that it's the *patrix* because it's based on patriarchy, not matriarchy." Women around the world are taking action. Meanwhile, in the U.S.A., we're calling trafficked girl children "juvenile sex workers." We're debating whether women are real.

The dominant ideology has women academics fired from their jobs and banned from public speaking for pointing out the obvious truth that women's oppression is based on sex and reproduction, and that buying and renting women for sexual exploitation is a cause and a consequence of that oppression. This culture has us believing that we can sit comfortably in our living rooms, signing online petitions and waiting for geoengineering to solve the climate crisis with nonexistent technology, while oil companies race to take advantage of melting Arctic ice and drill for still more petroleum. This ideology's weakness is the same thing which allowed it to spread so quickly -- it's reliant on us staying divorced from embodied reality, it's trans-humanist at its core. It can't forge real, lasting bonds between people; that requires time and patience and attention, a willingness to be uncomfortable sometimes. Yes, feminism has been turned into a parody of itself -- a toxic mimic -- but there are still young girls who see the patterns and who read voraciously (remember that? Remember finding a book and barely putting it down until it's finished?), there are still women alive who linked arms with their sisters decades ago and demanded liberation, who made a wall across every line of race and class and politics and every manner of social division and said *"No." "No, you won't do that to us. No, if you do it to her, you're doing it to me. No, we will not allow it."* We can learn the lessons of the past -- we can remember not to turn on each other, we can be careful not to allow some of us to be lionized, co-opted, and assimilated while others are left behind. We can find the courage to take risks again, even to make sacrifices. We know how this whole thing works now.

He says that woman speaks with nature. That she hears voices from under the earth. That wind blows in her ears and trees whisper to her. That the dead sing through her mouth and the cries of infants are clear to her. But for him this dialogue is over. He says he is not part of this world, that he was set on this world as a stranger. He sets himself apart from woman and nature... We are the bird's eggs. Bird's eggs, flowers, butterflies, rabbits, cows, sheep; we are caterpillars; we are leaves of ivy and sprigs of wallflower. We are women. We rise from the wave. We are gazelle and doe, elephant and whale, lilies and roses and peach, we are air, we are flame, we are oyster and pearl, we are girls. We are woman and nature. And he says he cannot hear us speak. But we hear.

--Susan Griffin, *Woman and Nature: The Roaring Inside Her*

Endnotes

1   Klepeis, Neil, William C. Nelson, & William H. Engelman. "The National Human Activity Pattern Survey (NHAPS): a resource for assessing exposure to environmental pollutants." *Journal of Exposure Science & Environmental Epidemiology*, 26 July 2001, nature.com.

2   Jones, Dr. Jane Clare. "TRAs, Rape-Logic, and the Economy of Entitlement." 23 July 2020, https://janeclarejones.com/2020/07/22/tras-rape-logic-and-the-economy-of-entitlement/.

3   Butt, Nathalie, Frances Lambrick, & Anna Renwick. "The supply chain of violence." *Nature Sustainability*, 2, 742-747, 5 Aug. 2019, https://www.nature.com/articles/s41893-019-0349-4.

4   "Forest area (% of land area)." https://data.worldbank.org/indicator/AG.LND.FRST.ZS

5   Pennisi, Elizabeth. "Earth home to 3 trillion trees, half as many as when human civilization arose." *Science Magazine*, 2 Sep. 2015, https://www.sciencemag.org/news/2015/09/earth-home-3-trillion-trees-half-many-when-human-civilization-arose.

6   "Forests - Our World in Data." https://ourworldindata.org/forests.

7   "Pacific Northwest Archives." forestlegacies.org, https://forestlegacies.org/programs/pacific-northwest/.

8   "Almost 90% of Men/Women Globally Are Biased Against Women." 5 March 2020, https://www.undp.org/content/undp/en/home/news-centre/news/2020/Gender_Social_Norms_Index_2020.html.

9   Kramer, Andrea S. and Alton B. Harris. "Are U.S. Millenial Men Just as Sexist as Their Dads?" *Harvard Business Review*, 15 June 2016, https://hbr.org/2016/06/are-u-s-millennial-men-just-as-sexist-as-their-dads.

10   Lott-Lavigna, Ruby. "Feminism Has 'Gone Too Far,' Say 50 Percent of Gen Z Men." *Vice World News*, 3 Aug. 2020, https://www.vice.com/en/article/y3zxmy/gen-z-men-attitudes-towards-feminism.

11   Law, Philippa. "Classroom Talk." BBC Homepage, Sept. 2014, http://www.bbc.co.uk/voices/yourvoice/classroom_talk.shtml.

12   "Girls have less freedom than boys while living with their parents," The Basque Youth Observatory, https://www.gazteaukera.euskadi.

eus/contenidos/informacion/estatistikak_2015/en_6778/adjuntos/
Berria_permisos_genero_en.pdf.

13 Gunnery, Mark. "Why Do Boys Get A Pass When It Comes to
    Household Chores? The Same Reasons Men Do." WAMU 88.5
    - American University Radio, 29 May 2019, https://wamu.org/
    story/19/05/29/why-do-boys-get-a-pass-when-it-comes-to-
    household-chores-the-same-reasons-men-do/.

14 Miller, Claire Cain. "A 'Generationally Perpetuated' Pattern:
    Daughters Do More Chores." *The New York Times*, 8 Aug. 2018,
    https://www.nytimes.com/2018/08/08/upshot/chores-girls-research-
    social-science.html.

15 Kerlin, Kat. "Grasslands More Reliable Carbon Sink Than Trees."
    climatechange.ucdavis.edu, 9 July 2018, https://climatechange.
    ucdavis.edu/news/grasslands-more-reliable-carbon-sink-than-trees/.

16 Zinn, Howard, *A People's History of the United States*. Harper Collins,
    1980.

17 *Encyclopedia of the Great Plains*. http://plainshumanities.unl.edu/
    encyclopedia/.

18 *History of Abortion - National Abortion Federation*. https://prochoice.
    org/education-and-advocacy/about-abortion/history-of-abortion;
    History of Abortion, https://feminist.com/resources/ourbodies/
    abortion.html.

19 Hohman, Maura. "How this Black doctor is exposing the racist
    history of gynecology." Health and Wellness, *Today*, 29 June 2020,
    https://www.today.com/health/racism-gynecology-dr-james-
    marion-sims-t185269.

20 Delbanco, Suzanne, Maclaine Lehan, Thi Montalvo, and Jeffrey
    Levin-Scherz. The Rising U.S. Maternal Mortality Rate Demands
    Action from Employers." *Harvard Business Review*, 28 June 2019,
    https://hbr.org/2019/06/the-rising-u-s-maternal-mortality-rate-
    demands-action-from-employers.

21 Novoa, Cristina and Jamila Taylor. "Exploring African
    Americans' High Maternal and Infant Death Rates." 1 Feb. 2018,
    https://www.americanprogress.org/issues/early-childhood/
    reports/2018/02/01/445576/exploring-african-americans-high-
    maternal-infant-death-rates/.

22 *Fisheries*. http://www.fao.org/fishery/en.

23 Luo, Azua (Zizhan). "Ocean Fish Stocks on 'Verge of Collapse', says IRIN Report." Feb. 2017, https://www.newsecuritybeat.org/2017/02/ocean-fish-stocks-on-verge-collapse-irin-report/.

24 Kituyi, Mukhisa and Peter Thomson. "90% of fish stocks are used up - fisheries subsidies must stop emptying the ocean." *World Economic Forum*, 13 July 2018, https://www.weforum.org/agenda/2018/07/fish-stocks-are-used-up-fisheries-subsidies-must-stop.

25 "Ocean Acidification." https://oceanacidification.noaa.gov.

26 Bragdon, Amber. "The Great Barrier Reef is at a critical tipping point and could disappear by 2050." 18 Oct. 2019, https://www.businessinsider.in/science/news/the-great-barrier-reef-is-at-a-critical-tipping-point-and-could-disappear-by-2050/articleshow/71655216.cms

27 "What is a Dead Zone?" https://oceanservice.noaa.gov/facts/deadzone.html.

28 Carrington, Damian. "Oceans suffocating as huge dead zones quadruple since 1950, scientists warn." 4 Jan. 2018, https://www.theguardian.com/environment/2018/jan/04/oceans-suffocating-dead-zones-oxygen-starved.

29 "Plastic Pollution." https://ourworldindata.org/plastic-pollution.

30 "Ocean Plastics Pollution, a Global Tragedy for Our Oceans and Sea Life." https://www.biologicaldiversity.org/campaigns/ocean_plastics/

31 "Oil Spills: Impact on the Ocean." http://www.waterencyclopedia.com/Oc-Po/Oil-Spills-Impact-on-the-Ocean.html.

32 Boyce, Daniel G., Marlon R. Lewis and Boris Worm. "Global phytoplankton decline over the past century." 29 July 2010, https://www.nature.com/articles/nature09268.

33 Berwyn, Bob. "'We Need to Hear These Poor Trees Scream': Unchecked Global Warming Means Big Trouble for Forests." *Inside Climate News*, 25 Apr. 2020, https://insideclimatenews.org/news/24042020/forest-trees-climate-change-deforestation.

34 McDonald, Samuel Miller. "Collapse Despair." *Activist Lab*, 18 Dec. 2017, http://www.activistlab.org/2017/12/collapse-despair/.

35 Fenton-Glynn, Claire. "Surrogacy: Why the world needs rules for 'selling' babies." 25 Apr. 2019, https://www.bbc.com/news/health-47826356.

36 Gecker, Jocelyn. "Thai surrogate offers clues into Japanese man with 16 babies." *Associated Press*, 3 Sept. 2014, https://www. thenationalnews.com/world/asia/thai-surrogate-offers-clues-into-japanese-man-with-16-babies-1.239982.

37 "American Surrogate Mom Dies." 12 Oct. 2015, www.cbc-network. org/2015/10/american-surrogate-mom-dies.

38 Cohen, Elizabeth, "Surrogate offered $10,000 to abort baby." 6 Mar. 2013, https://www.cnn.com/2013/03/04/health/surrogacy-kelley-legal-battle/index.html.

39 Mackay, Don. "Shocking pictures show Chinese baby factory where mothers are paid £10,000 for their newborns." 13 Jan. 2015, https:// www.mirror.co.uk/news/world-news/shocking-pictures-show-chinese-baby-4971128.

40 Saravanan, Sheela. *A Transnational Feminist View of Surrogacy Biomarkets in India.* Springer, Heidelberg University, Germany, 26 Mar. 2018.

41 "Nigeria Police Raid Lagos 'Baby Factory'." *BBC World News*, 30 Sept. 2019, https://www.bbc.com/news/world-africa-49877287.

42 "Soil Erosion and Degradation, Threats, WWF." https://www. worldwildlife.org/threats/soil-erosion-and-degradation.

43 Cosier, Susan. "The World Needs Topsoil to Grow 95% of Its Food – but It's Rapidly Disappearing." *The Guardian*, Guardian News and Media, 30 May 2019, www.theguardian.com/us-news/2019/may/30/topsoil-farming-agriculture-food-toxic-america.

44 Ritchie, Hannah & Max Roser. "Environmental impacts of food production." Jan. 2020, https://ourworldindata.org/environmental-impacts-of-food.

45 Hersher, Rebecca & Allison Aubrey, "To slow Global Warming, U.N. Warns Agriculture Must Change." 8 Aug. 2019, https://www.wnyc. org/story/to-slow-global-warming-un-warns-agriculture-must-change/.

46 Lagrone, Paul. "Tampa woman forced to marry her rapist at 11 years old, fights to end child marriage in America." 12 Feb. 2018, https:// www.abcactionnews.com/news/state/tampa-girl-forced-to-marry-her-rapist-at-11-years-old-fights-to-end-child-marriage-in-america.

47 Seidenkrantz, Marit-Solveig. "80 Years Since the First Calculations Showed That the Earth Was Warming Due to Rising Greenhouse

Gas Emissions." 5 June 2018, https://phys.org/news/2018-06-years-earth-due-greenhouse-gas.html.

48 Kusnetz, Nicholas. "Exxon's Own Research Confirmed Fossil Fuels' Role in Global Warming Decades Ago." 16 Sept. 2015, https://insideclimatenews.org/news/15092015/Exxons-own-research-confirmed-fossil-fuels-role-in-global-warming.

49 "The Chilling Effect of Oil & Gas Money on Democracy." Spring 2016, https://www.cleanwateraction.org/, file:///C:/Users/ATHENA~1/AppData/Local/Temp/Money_in_Politics_05%20 03%2016a_web%20-%20FINAL.pdf

50 Mann, Michael E., Raymond S. Bradley. and Malcolm K. Hughes. "Global-scale temperature patterns and climate forcing over the past six centuries." 23 Apr. 1998, www.meteo.psu.edu/holocene/public_html/shared/articles/mbh98.pdf.

51 "How the Fossil Fuel Industry Harassed Climate Scientist Michael Mann." 12 Oct. 2017, https://www.ucsusa.org/resources/how-fossil-fuel-industry-harassed-climate-scientist-michael-mann.

52 "As Climate Scientists Speak Out, Sexist Attacks Are on the Rise." 22 Aug. 2018, https://www.scientificamerican.com/article/as-climate-scientists-speak-out-sexist-attacks-are-on-the-rise.

53 "The Climate Deception Dossiers." *Exxon's Climate Denial History, Union of Concerned Scientists*, 29 June 2015, https://ucsusa.org/resources/climate-deception-dossiers.

54 Oreskes, Naomi and Erik M. Conway. *Merchants of Doubt.* Bloomsbury Press, 2010.

55 Benes, Ross. "Porn Could Have a Bigger Economic Influence on the U.S. than Netflix." *Quartz*, 20 June 2018, https://qz.com/1309527/porn-could-have-a-bigger-economic-influence-on-the-us-than-netflix.

56 "Porn Stars Speak Out." *Collective Shout*, https://www.collectiveshout.org/porn_stars_speak_out.

57 "The Violence of Pornography." https://www.theviolenceofpornography.blogspot.com.

58 Soller, Robert J. and I.S. Levine. *Coming Attractions: The Making of an X-rated video.* Yale University Press, 1996.

59 Soller, Robert J. and I.S. Levine. *Coming Attractions: The Making of an X-rated video*. Yale University Press, 1996.

60 *What Pornographers Really Think of Women,* Deutsche Presse-Agentur, 14 Oct. 1999.

61 Weisz, M.G. and C.M. Earls. "The effects of exposure to filmed sexual violence on attitudes toward rape." *Journal of Interpersonal Violence*, 10, 1 Mar. 1995, pp. 71-84.

62 Ohbuchi, K., T. Ikeda, & G. Takeuchi. "Effects of violent pornography upon viewers rape myth beliefs: A study of Japanese males." *Psychology, Crime & Law*, volume 1, 1 Mar. 1995, pp. 71-81.

63 Zillman D. and J. Bryan. "The effects of repeated exposure to violent pornography, nonviolent dehumanizing pornography, and erotica" in *Pornography: Recent research, interpretations, and policy considerations*. Eribaum, 1989, pp. 159-184.

64 Check, J. and N. Malamuth. "An empirical assessment of some feminist hypotheses about rape." *International Journal of Women's Studies*, 8(4), 1985, pp. 414-423.

65 Linz, D.G., E. Donnerstein, and S. Penrod. "Effects of long term exposure to violent and sexually degrading depictions of women." *J. Pers. Soc. Psychol., PubMed.gov.,* Nov. 1988, https://pubmed.ncbi.nlm.nih.gov/3210143/

66 Hald, G., N. Malamuth, Carlin Yues, & C. Yuen. "Pornography and attitudes supporting violence against women: revisiting the relationship in nonexperimental studies." *Aggressive Behavior*, 36, Jan. 2010, pp. 14-20.

67 Zillman, Dolf, & Jennings Bryant. *Pornography and sexual aggression: Effects of massive exposure to pornography.* Elsevier, 1984, pp. 115-138.

68 Rostad, Whitney L., Daniel Gittins-Stone, and Lindsay Orchowski. "The Association Between Exposure to Violent Pornography and Teen Dating Violence in Grade 10 High School Students." *Archives of Sexual Behavior*, 15 Jul. 2019.

69 Boeringer, S.B. "Pornography and sexual aggression: Associations of violent and nonviolent depictions with rape and rape proclivity." *Deviant Behavior*, 15, 1994, pp. 289-304.

70 Bonino, Sliva, Silvia Ciairano, Emanuela Rabaglietti & Elena Cattelino. "Use of Pornography and Self-Reported Engagement

in Sexual Violence Among Adolescents." *European Journal of Developmental Psychology*, vol. 3, Issue 3, 17 Feb. 2007, pp. 265-283.

71 Koss, Mary, Tamara Addison, and Neil M. Malamuth. "Pornography and Sexual Aggression: Are There Reliable Effects and Can We Understand Them?" *Annual Review of Sex Research*, Vol. 11, 2000, pp. 26-91.

72 Malamuth, Neil. "Rape fantasies as a function of exposure to violent sexual stimuli." *Archives of Sexual Behavior*, 10, 1981, pp. 33-47.

73 Vega, V. and N. Malamuth. "Predicting sexual aggression: The role of pornography in the context of general and specific risk factors." *Aggressive Behavior*, 33, 2007, pp. 104-117.

74 Barak, A., W.A. Fisher, S. Belfry and D.R. Lashambe. "Sex, guys, and cyberspace: Effects of internet pornography and individual differences in men's attitudes toward women." *Journal of Psychology and Human Sexuality*, 11, 1999, pp. 63-92.

75 Baron, L. and M. Strauss. "Sexual stratification, pornography, and rape in the United States." in Malamuth, N. and E. Donnerstein (Eds), *Pornography and Sexual Aggression*, Academic Press, 1984.

76 Carr, J. and K. Van Deusen. "Risk factors for male sexual aggression on college campuses." *Journal of Family Violence*, 19, 2004, pp. 279-289.

77 Crossman, L. "Date rape and sexual aggression by college males: Incidence and the involvement of impulsivity, anger, hostility, psychopathology, peer influence and pornography use." *Dissertation Abstracts International: Section B: The Sciences and Engineering*, 55, 1995, p. 4640.

78 Bergen, Raquel K. and Kathleen A. Bogle, "Exploring the Connection Between Pornography and Sexual Violence." *Violence and Victims*, Vol. 15, Feb. 2000.

79 Simmons, C.A., P. Lehmann, and S. Collier-Tenison, "Linking male use of the sex industry to controlling behaviors in violent relationships." *Violence against women*, 14, 2008, pp. 406-417.

80 Marshall, W.L. "The use of sexually explicit stimuli by rapists, child molesters and non-offenders." *Journal of Sex Research*, 25, 2, 1988, pp. 267-288.

81 *Attorney General's Commission on Pornography: final report* Washington, D.C.: U.S. Dept. of Justice (1986).

82 Howse, Patrick. "'Pornography addiction worry' for tenth of 12 to 13-year-olds." *BBC News*, 31 Mar. 2015, https://www.bbc.com/news/education-32115162?ocid=socialflow_facebook.

83 Drury, Ian. "Extreme internet porn is fuelling a surge in sex attacks by children: Number of under-17s convicted of rape almost doubles in four years." *The Daily Mail*, 12 Feb. 2017, https://www.dailymail.co.uk/news/article-4217768/Extreme-porn-fuelling-surge-sex-attacks-children.html.

84 Lindsey, Rebecca and Luann Dahlmann, "Climate change: Global temperatures." 16 Jan. 2020, www.climate.gov.

85 Achoui-Lesage, Nadine and Frank Jordans. "UN: World could hit 1.5 degree warming threshold by 2024." 9 July 2020, https://news.yahoo.com/un-world-could-hit-1-093754762.html.

86 "Climate Impacts." July, 2020, *Union of Concerned Scientists*, https://www.ucsusa.org/climate/impacts.

87 "Climate change and Florida: What you need to know." *The Climate Reality Project*, 16 Oct. 2018, https://www.climaterealityproject.org/blog/how-climate-change-affecting-florida.

88 Luscombe, Richard. "Will Florida be lost forever to the climate crisis?" *The Guardian*, 21 Apr. 2020, https://www.theguardian.com/environment/2020/apr/21/florida-climate-crisis-sea-level-habitat-loss.

89 "Weather Fatalities 2019." *National Weather Service*, hhtps://www.weather.gov/hazstat.

90 "U.S. Heat Wave Frequency and Length are Increasing." *U.S. Environmental Protection Agency*, https://www.globalchange.gov/browse/indicators/us-heat-waves.

91 Diffenbaugh, Noah S. "Verification of extreme event attribution: Using out-of-sample observations to assess changes in probabilities of unprecedented events." *Science Advances*, Vol 6, No. 12, 18 Mar. 2020.

92 *Heatwaves,* World Health Organization. https://www.who.int/globalchange/publications/heat-and-health/en.

93 Bamat, Joseph. "France takes steps to avoid repeat of deadly 2003 heat wave." 7 Jan. 2015, https://www.france24.com/en/20150701-france-paris-heat-wave-alert-deadly-2003-summer-guidelines.

94 "The facts about climate change and drought." *The Climate Reality Project*, 15 June 2016, https://www.climaterealityproject.org/blog/facts-about-climate-change-and-drought.

95 Lieberman, Bruce. "Wildfires and climate change: What's the connection?" *Yale Climate Connections*, Jul 2, 2019, https://yaleclimateconnections.org/2019/07/wildfires-and-climate-change-whats-the-connection/.

96 Gray, Ellen. "Satellite Data Record Shows Climate Change's Impact on Fires." *NASA*, 10 Sept. 2019, https://climate.nasa.gov/news/2912.

97 Kukreti, Ishan. "Desertification expands in areas on front line of climate change." *Down to Earth*, 13 Sept. 2019, https://www.downtoearth.org.in/news/climate-change/desertification-expands-in-areas-on-front-line-of-climate-change-66494.

98 "Special Report: Special report on climate change and land." *Intergovernmental Panel on Climate Change*, 8 Aug. 2019, https://www.ipcc.ch/srcc.

99 Gibbens, Sarah. "Heart-Wrenching video shows starving polar bear on ice-less land." *National Geographic,* 7 Dec. 2017, https://www.nationalgeographic.com/news/2017/12/polar-bear-starving-arctic-sea-ice-melt-climate-change-spd/.

100 Dunne, Daisy. "Interactive: When will the Arctic see its first ice-free summer?" *Carbon Brief*, https://interactive.carbonbrief.org/when-will-the-arctic-see-its-first-ice-free-summer.

101 Voosen, Paul. "New climate models predict warming surge." *Science*, 16 Apr. 2019, https://www.sciencemag.org/news/2019/04/new-climate-models-predict-warming-surge.

102 "How the IPCC is more likely to underestimate the climate response." *Skeptical Science*, July, 2015, https://skepticalscience.com/ipcc-scientific-consensus.htm.

103 Macdougall, Andrew H., Christopher A. Avis, and Andrew J. Weaver, "Significant contribution to climate warming from the permafrost carbon feedback." *Nature Geoscience* 5, 9 Sept. 2012, pp. 719-721, https://www.nature.com/articles/ngeo1573.

104 Cho, Renee. "Why thawing permafrost matters." *Earth Institute*, Columbia University, 11 Jan. 2018, https://blogs.ei.columbia.edu/2018/01/11/thawing-permafrost-matters/.

105 Berwyn, Bob. "Scientists say ocean circulation is slowing. Here's why you should care." *Inside Climate News*, 7 May 2018, https://insideclimatenews.org/news/07052018/atlantic-ocean-circulation-slowing-climate-change-heat-temperature-rainfall-fish-why-you-should-care.

106 Pearce, Fred. "As climate change worsens, a cascade of tipping points looms." *Yale Climate Change 360*, 5 Dec. 2019, https://e360.yale.edu/features/as-climate-changes-worsens-a-cascade-of-tipping-points-looms.

107 *How likely is a runaway greenhouse effect on Earth?* Jan 13, 2012. MIT Technology Review. https://www.technologyreview.com/2012/01/13/256801/how-likely-is-a-runaway-greenhouse-effect-on-earth/.

108 McDonald, Samuel Miller. "Collapse Despair." *Activist Lab*, 18 Dec. 2017, http://www.activistlab.org/2017/12/collapse-despair/.

109 "15,364 Scientist Signatories, World Scientists' Warning to Humanity: A Second Notice." American Institute of Biological Sciences, *Bioscience*, Volume 67, 12 Dec. 2017, pp.1026-1028.

110 "Groundswell: Preparing for Internal Climate Migration." *The World Bank*, 19 Mar. 2018, https://www.worldbank.org/en/news/infographic/2018/03/19/groundswell---preparing-for-internal-climate-migration.

111 Milmann, Oliver. "We're moving to higher ground: America's era of climate mass migration is here." *The Guardian*, 24 Sep. 2018, https://www.theguardian.com/environment/2018/sep/24/americas-era-of-climate-mass-migration-is-here.

112 Byanyima, Winnie. "What to do about climate change? Ask women – they have the most to lose." *The New Humanitarian*, 18 Dec. 2018, https://www.thenewhumanitarian.org/opinion/2018/12/18/what-do-about-climate-change-ask-women-they-have-most-lose.

113 Batha, Emma. "Cheap as bread, girls sell sex to survive drought crisis in Angola." *Thompson Reuters Foundation*, 31 Jan. 2020, https://www.timeslive.co.za/news/africa/2020-01-31-cheap-as-bread-girls-sell-sex-to-survive-drought-crisis-in-angola/.

114 Aranoff, Kate. "It's time to try fossil-fuel industry executives for crimes against humanity." *Jacobin Magazine*, 5 Feb. 2019, https://jacobinmag.com/2019/02/fossil-fuels-climate-change-crimes-against-humanity.

115 Scherbakova, Anastasia. "Mining for favors: The impact of lobbying on regulatory enforcement." *Academy of Management*, 30 Nov. 2017, journals.aom.org, https://doi.org/10.5465/AMBPP.2017.11351abstract.

116 Sanday, Peggy Reeves. "Rape-Prone Versus Rape-Free Campus Cultures." *Violence Against Women*, Vol. 2 No. 2, June 1996, pp. 191-208.

117 "They Raped Me at Gunpoint": True Stories From a Former Escort and Porn Performer." *Fight the New Drug*, 19 Sept. 2019, https://www.fightthenewdrug.org.

118 Federici, S. *Caliban and the Witch*, pp. 189.

119 Iroquois Women, Oct. 1, 2001. Portland State University, web.pdx.edu.

120 Marsdane, Harriet. "International Women's Day: What are Matriarchies, and Where are They Now?" *The Naga Republic*, 8 Mar. 2018, http://www.thenagarepublic.com/global-national-local/international-womens-day-what-are-matriarchies-and-where-are-they-now/.

121 Bates, Anna Thomas, "Female Farmers Often Take a Smaller, Educational Approach, Report Says." *Milwaukee Journal Sentinel*, 9 Aug. 2013, https://www.archive.jsonline.com.

122 Hakakian, Roya, "The Flame of Feminism is Alive." *Foreign Policy*, 7 Mar. 2019, https://foreignpolicy.com/2019/03/07/the-flame-of-feminism-is-alive-in-iran-international-womens-day/.

123 Izaakson, Jen and Tae Kyung Kim, "The South Korean Women's Movement: 'We Are Not Flowers, We Are a Fire,'" *Feminist Current*, 15 June 2020, https://www.feministcurrent.com/2020/06/15/the-south-korean-womens-movement-we-are-not-flowers-we-are-a-fire/

124 Phillips, Tom. "'This is Our Feminist Spring': Millions of Mexican Women Prepare to Strike Over Femicides." *The Guardian*, 7 Mar. 2020, https://www.theguardian.com/world/2020/mar/07/mexico-femicides-protest-women-strike.

125 Lewton, Thomas. "Uganda's Eco-Feminists are Taking on Mining and Plantation Industries." *Conservation News*, 2019, https://news.mongabay.com/2019/10/ugandas-eco-feminists-are-taking-on-mining-and-plantation-industries/.

CHAPTER 8

Female Separatism: The Feminist Solution

by Sekhmet She-Owl

Introduction

Feminists have been debating female separatism as a political act for decades. While most radical feminists have been fully supportive of and interested in female-only spaces, non-separatist and anti-separatist women have always vastly outnumbered the separatists in the feminist movement. Separatism has been called "too extreme" by feminist women who themselves are regarded as extremists in this anti-feminist world, and female separatists are often shunned, criticized, and maligned by these other feminists, to say nothing of the anti-feminist population. Not much has changed in the separatism conversation over the last fifty years, and if radical feminism exists fifty years from now, feminists will probably be having the same argument about separatism then. It's an important discussion for us to have. The question at the heart of this argument is really the question at the heart of feminism itself: are we serious about pursuing our own liberation and well-being as women or are we willing to settle for less?

What female separatism is and is not

Female separatism is the feminist choice to create and maintain personal relationships primarily, if not exclusively, with other
women. A female separatist's friendships, familial relationships,
and romantic relationships (if she has any) are with women. She
actively seeks out connections with other women and avoids social
entanglements with men. She excises her pre-existing relationships
with men, whatever their nature, easily and permanently, only
making exceptions for sons and other biological relatives if they are
worthy enough to remain in her orbit. She is ready to cut loose any
male exception to her separatism the moment he proves to be more
toxic and parasitic than not. The female separatist woman always
puts the women in her life first, ahead of any men she might choose
to tentatively keep around. She doesn't think twice about eliminating a man she's connected to if she discovers he's committed any
kind of ethical violation against a woman or a girl.

Female separatism is not and has never been about withdrawing completely from mainstream, male society to go live on a rural
women's commune. While most female separatists would probably
take advantage of such an opportunity if it presented itself, most
have never had the financial means to even consider such a lifestyle
change, whether we're talking about the separatists of the late 20th
century or today. Certainly, a female separatist would never willingly
live with males in the same household, but she is also not going to
jeopardize her own survival by abandoning the financial, medical,
and social resources she depends on in male society. Poverty class,
working class, and middle class women obviously can't afford the
secluded women's commune life, yet these are the women who have
always comprised the majority of female separatists. Anti-separatist
women who claim that female separatism is unrealistic because
women can't afford to live in female-only, self-contained communities that hardly exist are dishonestly characterizing separatism as
something it's not. Most of us will spend our lives working with
men and living in the male-inclusive cities and towns of the world,

156

whether we like it or not. We are still separatist where it counts: in our personal lives.

Some women might imagine or choose to express separatism through seeking services exclusively from other women: deliberately choosing female doctors, dentists, therapists, lawyers, store clerks, etc. They may also experiment with consuming media created by women exclusively or purchasing goods only from woman-owned businesses. While these choices are wise and offer their own benefits for both the female consumer and the female provider, they are not necessary to separatism and pale in comparison to the central decision to conduct significant, personal relationships only with other women. A woman who only uses female doctors and only reads books written by women but who lives with her husband is not a female separatist. Likewise, an actual female separatist probably won't think twice about having a man ring up her groceries or watching a TV show created by men; her social life and household, meanwhile, will reflect her conscious choice to only get emotionally involved with women.

Female separatism deals the ultimate blow to male power

It has been said that female separatism is radical feminism's natural and logical conclusion. Most radical feminists have chosen not to follow their politics all the way to that end and do what they can to avoid, ignore, or deny it. Anti-separatist feminists engage in what has been called "thought termination," meaning the act of refusing to follow one's own thoughts to their logical conclusions, in order to justify their decision to stay connected to males. They also encourage this thought termination in other women, wanting to undermine female separatism as a legitimate political and personal choice for their own selfish reasons.

When making political and feminist analysis or when attempting to determine in your own life if a particular decision is feminist or anti-feminist, it is useful to ask the ancient Roman legal question:

"Cui bono?" or "Who benefits?" Of course, women do stand to gain certain rewards and privileges from engaging in male loyalism, misogyny, and anti-feminist actions, but whatever the matter at hand, an anti-feminist and anti-female decision will ultimately benefit males the most. When we ask "Who benefits the most?" from women and girls choosing to lead male-inclusive and male-centric lives, the answer is clear: males do.

The most recent studies have found that heterosexual marriage makes men happier and women more unhappy overall. The overwhelming majority of domestic labor and childcare continue to fall on the wife's shoulders in heterosexual marriage throughout the developed world, and this is true even while most married heterosexual women in developed countries work full-time throughout adulthood. Heterosexual and bisexual women openly admit to experiencing sex in their heterosexual relationships that ranges from inorgasmic and boring to violent, humiliating, and painful. Outside of heterosexual relationships, women and girls often find themselves on the losing side of unequal relationships with male family members and friends who take advantage of their labor, emotional and otherwise, and do not reciprocate or bother suppressing their sexism.

The power struggle between males and females has always been sexual, both in the carnal and reproductive sense. Even the word *patriarchy* rests on the sexual, social, and familial arrangements that exist in a predominantly heterosexual, mixed society where men and women live in constant contact with each other: *rule of the father* assumes that women and girls are in a position to be ruled, both socially and physically. It assumes the *presence* of a man.

Female separatism is the unavoidable, ultimate conclusion of radical feminist politics for the simple reason that separatism alone prevents the male objective driving men's oppression and domination of the female sex: using women and girls as sexual, domestic, social, and economic resources. If this is the point of patriarchy, how can anything other than female separatism be the solution to it? In a system where males already have all the power and control, women and girls will never be able to change their own status or achieve liberation from oppression through cooperating with males and granting them everything they demand.

Males want sexual access to female bodies above all else, and furthermore, they rely on women and girls to perform the domestic labor, social labor, and professional labor that keep men comfortable physically, emotionally, and psychologically. For thousands of years, men universally made sure that women and girls could not survive independently of them by locking us out of education, paid work, and the political arena and refusing to give us basic rights to own money and property. They knew and feared that if women had the option to survive and thrive apart from men, most of us would choose to do exactly that.

The only reason women now have the legal rights and protections that allow us to reject heterosexual marriage and motherhood is because we fought hard for those rights and protections over the course of at least a hundred years in developed countries, and we are still fighting all over the world, not only to gain what we lack but to protect what we have. Men have never yielded any political concessions to women willingly, easily, or readily. They have resisted us every step of the way, and they will never cease their attempts to take back the progress we've made.

If female separatism was of no consequence to the male sex, they wouldn't have spent all of recorded history making it virtually impossible. They wouldn't now be going out of their way to destroy any and all female-only spaces, both physical and digital, in the name of transgenderism. They would not have lorded physical and sexual violence over us since the beginning of time as punishment for our resistance and disobedience.

Why men will never tolerate female separatism

To understand why female separatism is necessary and good for women, we must recognize the results of women leading male-centric lives for what they are. The overwhelming majority of women in the world live male-centric lives, and this has always been the case. These women are male-identified, as radical feminists of the 1970s used to say, meaning that they identify with males rather than with females and see the world and themselves from the male, anti-feminist perspective. Male-identification in women is inevitable when they conduct relationships with men uncritically and certainly when they live male-centric lives, and a woman cannot be a feminist as long as she is male-identified. While there are degrees of male identification and loyalty to men in the female population, ultimately all women who live male-centric lives are voluntarily supporting and protecting males in some way. Their support and protection of males keep patriarchy alive, which is why they're rewarded for it in the form of social status, economic opportunities and privilege, and less overall aggression and overt contempt from men.

Men and women have always had a parasitic relationship: men being the parasites and women being the hosts. Men feed off of female energy, labor, and attention, using these resources to bolster their egos, free up their time for leisure and career pursuits, and lead far more materialistically and domestically comfortable lives than they would on their own. Women make it possible for men to be the professionals and the artists they've always been without making any personal sacrifices, and they provide men with all the creature comforts human beings crave in their living environments. Meanwhile, beyond feeding off female domestic and emotional labor, men use women's bodies for sex and reproduction, the two prizes they seek most of all, without caring what the female experience of heterosexual intercourse and reproduction is. Heterosexual relationships have never been about the reciprocal, loving meeting of needs between two equals; they have always been about men taking what they want from women, while women settle for whatever measly compensation they can get in return. Remember that for most of human history, women had no choice but to enter heterosexual marriage, and they often didn't even get to choose the men they married. Men never asked what women and girls wanted for their own lives because men never cared. It is only because of feminist struggle against male laws, traditions, and violence that any woman or girl has a choice today.

The opposite of female separatism is granting males access to females physically, sexually, emotionally, mentally, and spiritually. Males depend on this access for their survival and pleasure; they will never willingly, peacefully surrender access to us. Even temporary female-only spaces enrage males because they fear that women and girls will like the freedom and safety and joy of those spaces so much, they'll decide to become separatists. Women taking our attention away from men and dedicating it to ourselves offends men, as it suggests we care about ourselves and each other as women—even temporarily—more than we do about them. The act of separating also begins to unravel the male lie that women depend on men for survival and comfort, when the truth is it's the other way around. Every potential result of women gathering in female-only space increases the likelihood of those women becoming full-time separatists, and that is the outcome males fear most.

All feminist consciousness-raising takes place in female-only spaces. The 20th century feminist movement came into being only because of women gathering together away from male surveillance and talking honestly with each other about their experiences of misogyny. There is no feminism without female-only space, and males know this. They also know that a woman with feminist consciousness is far more likely to choose female separatism than her male-identified counterparts. Male objections to female-only space boil down to preventing women from becoming feminists and abandoning males altogether as a result.

As my feminist predecessors have pointed out long before me, female separatism and female-only spaces also enrage males for representing female power and self-sovereignty: only the powerful have the ability to control who has access to them and to draw their own boundaries. Males are boundary violators by nature, which is why they commit rape—the ultimate boundary violation—with clear conscience. As far as males are concerned, women and girls are not supposed to have boundaries, and for most of history, males successfully made it impossible for us to deny them access to us by tying our physical survival to heterosexuality. Now that we have the choice in developed nations to survive outside of heterosexual marriage and prostitution and the choice to live female separatist lives, the female-only space has become intolerable to men and boys more than ever before.

The personal benefits of female separatism

The benefits of female separatism for individual women and girls are equally as important and compelling as the political rewards. Leading a female separatist lifestyle supports the holistic well-being of any woman or girl who does it, positively affecting her physically, mentally, emotionally, and spiritually. Female separatism, like radical feminism, has never just been about delivering a blow to male power or escaping male oppression; it's also about loving and prioritizing women, including yourself.

The physical benefit of female separatism is the most obvious: a dramatic increase in physical safety that no other protective or defensive measure can match. You cannot be raped, beaten, or killed by a male who isn't in the room with you. Given that the overwhelming majority of rapes, femicides, and sexual assaults of women and underage girls are committed by males that the women and girls know personally, using female separatism as a method of risk reduction is the most rational and logical choice we could make. Anti-separatist women who insist that this conclusion is "victim-blaming," being transparently motivated by their own loyalty to men, try to argue that it should not be women's responsibility to avoid men but men's responsibility to refrain from violence and sexual predation. This is a futile argument and a moot point, as men will never stop doing what they want to do and have always done to us. Women and girls can't control men; we can only control ourselves. Denying males physical access to us significantly reduces our chances of being sexually or violently attacked by them, and to date, anti-separatist women have failed to provide a plausible theory of maintaining personal relationships with men that is equivalently low-risk to women and girls.

The emotional and mental benefits of female separatism bleed into each other, encompassing both harm reduction and more positive female/female relationships. Living a female separatist life means investing all of your time, energy, emotion, psychic space, and resources in other women: your female friends, female family members, female lovers (if you choose to romantically engage with women), and whatever broader female community you decide to actively participate in. Dedicating yourself to relationships with other women and girls enriches both your own life and theirs, promoting the mental health of all women involved and significantly increasing the odds of you enjoying true reciprocity in your closest relationships. Without a husband, boyfriend, sons, or other males to serve, a woman is free to nurture her relationships with other women to a degree that married heterosexual women don't and can't reach. The quality time, connection, and affection possible between women who live independently of men make those relationships beautifully, satisfyingly deep, intimate, and rewarding. Many of us can remember having friendships with other girls in early and middle childhood that were exceptionally intense, sweet, and loving, and we experienced those friendships precisely because we were young enough to actively avoid and reject male company and spent little to no time thinking about males. Instead, we focused on each other and the feelings of tenderness we shared with other girls, which were the highlight of our emotional lives at the time. That kind of female friendship does not have to end with girlhood. In a female separatist's life, friendship with other women always keeps its potential for profundity.

While oppression can and does take place between women along the axes of race, class, sexuality, ability, and even sex itself, the kind of misogyny males in particular exhibit toward all women and girls will always be absent between women. The power imbalance between a man and a woman based on sex cannot and does not exist between two women. The kind of violence, degradation, and exploitation that women experience at the hands of males will not enter your personal life if all of your personal relationships are with other women, and simply knowing that can give you tremendous peace of mind. We know for a fact that stress negatively affects human health, both physical and mental, and men are often the biggest source of stress in a woman's life. Remove that source, replace it with the love and friendship of other women, and notice how much easier it is to live a calm, happy life.

A word on lesbian separatism

Lesbian separatism—the deliberate practice of lesbians forming personal relationships only with other lesbians—serves the same purposes as female separatism and goes a step further: insulating lesbians from the oppressive behaviors of heterosexual and bisexual women, while redirecting lesbian resources back into our own community. Needless to say, lesbian separatism is a difficult lifestyle to pursue, given how few women are lesbians and the lack of lesbian-only spaces and in-person community. Even lesbians who do not consider themselves separatist but long for lesbian friendship have a hard time finding other lesbians locally these days, especially if they live outside metropolitan cities. The scarcity and inaccessibility of lesbian community in material reality is one reason for the "lesbian loneliness" that so many lesbians, especially young ones, describe online. It is not a loneliness for a romantic partner but for a network of rich friendships with other lesbians and for lesbian culture.

Heterosexual and bisexual women have always been lesbian-hating to some degree, and their fixation on men, particularly their husbands and boyfriends, chafes at many lesbians regardless of politics. Lesbian separatism is both a strategy and statement of self-love, self-respect, and self-preservation for lesbians, a way to further purge their personal lives of lesbian oppression and experience affirmation from other lesbians instead. Every adult lesbian knows what it's like to encounter lesbian oppression in interactions with heterosexual and bisexual women, and often, those women are friends or family members who claim to care about or even love the lesbians in their lives. Yet without a willingness to ruthlessly examine and acknowledge their own words, thoughts, and actions when it comes to lesbians, these heterosexual and bisexual women will always end up acting out their deeply ingrained anti-lesbian prejudice against their lesbian friends, sisters, daughters, cousins, etc. Heterosexual and bisexual women refusing to take responsibility for their hurtful words, actions, and attitudes—which is usually the case—only makes the experience of prejudice worse for the lesbian. The injustice of bigotry makes true intimacy, trust, and reciprocal love impossible between androphilic women and lesbians, and lesbian separatism is a natural, rational answer to the impasse.

Lesbians investing their time, energy, love, and resources into other lesbians ultimately enriches lesbian lives and contributes to the development of lesbian community. Concentrating on positive relationships with other lesbians as a lesbian supports lesbian self-esteem, success, and mental health in ways that navigating relationships with non-lesbians never quite does. The unique and profound experience of being truly seen, understood, and celebrated can only ever happen to a lesbian through friendship with other lesbians, and while rewarding relationships with heterosexual and bisexual women and even gay men can and do occur in lesbian lives, these other relationships forged in spite of social inequality can't substitute for the bond between identical equals.

Conclusion

If feminism's true goal is the global liberation of all female human beings from male oppression and if the individual feminist's goal is the highest possible level of liberation in her personal life, we must recognize female separatism's place in our cache of political strategies designed to help us achieve those goals. While female separatism is not the only way to move toward collective and personal liberation, while it can be considered the final step rather than the only step, female separatism can and will ultimately do what no other feminist act can do for us as women. You are not required to become a separatist in order to genuinely possess feminist consciousness or to participate in other feminist acts, but your feminist impact on the female condition will remain stunted as long as you continue to support men physically, sexually, emotionally, psychologically, financially, and otherwise. While no one woman can destroy patriarchy through her separatism, every female separatist brings the sum total of our ranks closer to the elusive tipping point of female liberation. Every separatist counts. Beyond this, the female separatist lives a life of unparalleled potential for joy, growth, peace, authenticity, security, well-being, and love with other women. Female separatism gives us as women the opportunity to live with dignity, self-respect, mental clarity, and hope for ourselves as individuals, despite the unchecked misogyny that always surrounds us.

Acknowledgements

I must thank and credit the female and lesbian feminist separatists who came before me and who contributed valuable work on the subject of separatism and to the feminist movement broadly. Many of them are no longer alive, but their legacy and influence survive them. Without their work, I would not have raised my own consciousness and become a female-identified, lesbian-identified female separatist and feminist woman. I list some of their published work below for your study.

Dykes Loving Dykes by Bev Jo, Linda Strega, and Ruston

Lesbian Nation: The Feminist Solution by Jill Johnston

For Lesbians Only: A Separatist Anthology edited by Sarah Lucia Hoagland and Julia Penelope (See "A Black Separatist" by Anna Lee from this anthology on feminist-reprise.org)

The Politics of Reality: Essays on Feminist Theory by Marilyn Frye (See especially "Some Reflections on Separatism and Power," available on feminist-reprise.org)

"Separation in Black: A Personal Journey" by Jacqueline Anderson, from *Lesbian Ethics*, Vol. 3 No. 2 (available on feminist-reprise.org)

CHAPTER 9

To My Radical Feminist Sisters

by Dr. Jessica Taylor

To my radical feminist sisters around the world,
I am writing this open letter to all of you to uplift you and to remind you of your strength. Our strength.

Dale Spender wrote in 1986 that with every wave of feminism, comes a backlash of misogyny. The first wave feminists who were killed, tortured, abused, humiliated, force fed and beaten, changed the world for women, forever. As their power grew, the backlash grew.

As women found each other, loved each other, and stood together, men in the patriarchy created disgusting, ugly public caricatures of them as witches, barren, old, haggard, and hated. The point of this strategy was two-fold: to break their spirits and to hold them up as an example to the other women – of what would happen to them if they dared to join the suffragettes. Women pushed on. They fought for us. They gained our voting rights and property rights. They did this at huge personal cost, and at the time, they were hated viscerally and openly.

In the second wave of radical feminism in the 1960s onwards, women joined arms once again. The second wavers, many of whom are still here with us (love and respect to you all, we owe you incredible amounts), progressed and achieved more than we realise. Our second wave sisters gave us rape support centres, domestic violence refuges, women's shelters, single sex spaces, equality law, changes in divorce and custody law, feminist consciousness raising, feminist groups, and contraception. Women in the second wave threw light on the way women were being discriminated against in every aspect of their personal and public lives. They continued the work of the first wave, by publicly and intelligently criticising and challenging the male establishment. They did this despite constant portrayals as man-hating, controlling, abusive, ugly, childless lesbians.

As you can probably see, there is a pattern forming here.

Our current feminism is not much different. The old stereotypes of us are still raging on from 100 years ago. Men still mock us for being feminists and concerned with women's rights. The memes look exactly like the old suffragette postcards. Shit has not changed one fuckin bit.

We have again made massive strides, although we are more divided these days. As radical feminists, our purpose is to remain dedicated to the liberation of all women and girls from oppression around the world. This means rejecting white, upper class feminism which confines feminism to big words and protected bookshelves of academics and philosophers. It means debating with and often disagreeing with, liberal feminism. It means calling out misogyny within feminism, and misogyny that parades as feminism. Over time, uneducated onlookers have become annoyed and confused. Women are expected to club together and be homogenous. The fact that our feminism differs so much is the source of much amusement to men who don't understand a jot of feminism. Of course, women are all so simple, that we must all agree.

This also means that we need to stand our ground as the next wave of misogyny hits us and attempts to push us back. Feminism is taking a real battering at the moment. Women who comply with the abuse and ridicule of feminists are rewarded with temporary protection from misogyny. People who publicly attack women are congratulated and awarded.

170

With every wave of feminism, there is a wave of woman-hate. We are more powerful than we have ever been, more connected than we have ever been, more educated than we have ever been, and better resourced than ever.

The backlash and the upsurge of misogyny is heavy because we are making such collective progress. Women have platforms. We are talking about rape, domestic abuse, child sexual exploitation, trafficking, femicide, FGM, harassment, pay gaps, and gender-role stereotypes. Society is listening. Society is watching.

Every time we speak out, write a blog, make a video, or sit on a panel, we influence another woman or girl to realise the strength she really has. The power she really has. Don't ever underestimate the power of your influence as a strong female role model. Whatever position you take up as a radical feminist role model, you will change so many lives.

The misogyny will continue to hit us because we continue to push forward. We have bigger platforms than we have ever had. This means thousands of men have access to us, and can abuse us with ease. It is clear from the violence and abuse we are subjected to online, that the crimes committed against all of us every single day are being ignored. Many of us are told that the abuse we are subjected to is simply a consequence of being "in the public eye" or "having radical feminist views."

It's frankly amazing how people have conceptualised radical feminism over the years. We've been branded as the crazies. Likened to genocidal dictators, murderers and serial paedophiles. The character assassination continues. We scare them because we stand firm and because we are not ashamed of our commitment to women and girls' rights.

It paints a bleak picture. Or does it?

Are you not surrounded by radical feminists? Are you not able to read this essay? Are you not able to meet with your sisters online?

Do you see the activism around you? The lobbying and arguing and campaigning and world-changing?

Every woman has the power to make a change, whether that is small or huge. We must continue to talk to girls about radical feminism, and the incredible progress we have made since our first wave sisters stuck their necks out. Don't allow radical feminism to become a dirty phrase again. Don't succumb to pressure.

Do not throw women under the bus because it protects you for a little longer. Do not stay silent whilst your sisters around the world are oppressed and murdered. Do not laugh along as men abuse and oppress women, thinking, "That will never be me."

Use your strength. Use your resources. Platform women and girls. Protect them, support them, influence them, and inspire them. Be the woman you needed to look up to as a girl.

Radical feminists are hated for two reasons:

1. We unapologetically centre women and girls in our feminism, and we have no interest in bending to the pressure of patriarchal values or norms.

2. We are women.

That's pretty much it. People will come up with many different bullshit reasons why we are such disgusting women, but every one of them smacks of the same shit thrown at our first wave and second wave sisters. Stop feeding into it. See it for what it is. It's recycled misogyny from 100 years ago because they can't think of anything else to say or do to us.

This is about collectively and individually reframing us as the old, haggard, witches, bitches, mad, hysterical, evil, childless lesbians who hate men and want them all to die. They have nothing else left. They personally attack us because they have nothing else.

This is what happens when women attempt to do something for each other – men are so entitled and so accustomed to being centred, that they cannot handle being sidelined for a bit whilst we focus on the oppression of women and girls. See it as nothing more than a tantrum. Whataboutery in all its pathetic beige, beardy, boring, repetitive "glory."

Women can hate us too. I see them. I see them often. The "egalitarians" who hate feminism. The "feminists" who tell us to go kill ourselves or die in a fire or call for our resignations. The women who internalise misogyny, use it against themselves whilst attacking other women for the oppression they are subjected to. The women who rush to the aid of the NAMALT crew. It really is incredible that those women would use all of the rights, powers, voices, and platforms that they have because radical feminists gave it to them over the last 100 years – to bully and abuse radical feminists. Irony doesn't even touch the sides of that one.

The deeper irony being, that we will all keep fighting for their rights, even if they hate us. Even if those women say they don't need feminism. Even if they say they hate feminism. Even if they say they don't want those rights. Even if we disagree with them. We have been protecting women and girls (even the ones we don't like) for decades.

I know how hard it is right now. I see so many of you struggling, giving up, getting tired and being abused. I see you trying to thicken your skin to face another day talking about the most basic shit, because you know you will have another day of abuse and threats. I see society get more and more misogynistic every day. I watch as some of the world's biggest abusers and misogynists run our countries, royalty and governments.

My sisters, you are the force that the world needs right now. Every time you take a stand, you do something brilliant. You are a raging fire.

Women's anger is pathologised because it is so powerful. We do not use our power to commit millions of murders and rapes each year. We do not use our power for worldwide warfare and genocide. We do not use it to dick-measure with our nuclear weapons. We do not use it to exploit developing countries. We use it to change the world. We use it to challenge the system. We use it to support other women. We use it to relentlessly defend our human rights. We use it to write essays and blogs that start debates and conversations. We set up conferences and groups. We create charities and grassroots projects.

We are the powerhouse that the world ignores but always expects to be there to look after the kids and clean up after the men.

I want to remind you that the shit being thrown at us is disgusting, violent, and abusive because it has a purpose: to silence and intimidate the most powerful female voices we have.

What people seem to forget is that within our radical feminism, we are made up of some of the strongest women in the world. We are refugees and asylum seekers, we are single mothers, we are trafficking survivors, we are women fighting cancer, we are women who have been beaten, raped, abused, strangled, tortured, imprisoned, and discriminated against. We are ex-sex workers and women who have escaped prostitution. We are lesbians. We are activists, we are lawyers, we are academics, we are police officers, we are social workers, we are politicians, we are writers and performers, we are business owners and consumers. We are politically and economically active. We are voters. We have all lived through shit that people cannot even begin to imagine. We are living, breathing, and dying in this feminism.

They cannot extinguish the fire we have set alight. The only reason they seek to weaken us, is because they recognise our power.

Now, you need to recognise your power, too.

Get back up, focus on your feminism and your love of women and girls, and get back to work. There is so much to do. Do not allow the accusations of hatred and abuse to blur your vision. We know we don't hate minority groups. We know we do not engage in transphobia. We know we don't abuse and hate those who are different to us. We know we do not align with or support right wing, racist, homophobic groups who proclaim to be feminists and radical thinkers. These accusations are set ups. Deliberate conflations to encourage the hatred of feminists.

Radical feminism is the liberation of women and girls from the global oppression that is the patriarchy. Gender role stereotypes have oppressed and harmed us for so long. We have been minimised, ignored, gaslit, abused, attacked, and silenced for so long. Yet, we are still here running the rape centres, the shelters, the helplines, the support groups, the women's services, the households, the families, the communities, and the female-led companies.

But we will keep going.

Millions of women and girls rely upon the work we do, whether we do it silently, covertly, or publicly and loudly.

In sisterhood,

Dr Jessica Taylor
Psychologist
VictimFocus
Email: Jessica@victimfocus.org.uk
Website: www.victimfocus.org.uk
Tweet: @DrJessTaylor
Fbook: www.facebook.com/JessicaForenPsych

CHAPTER 10

Self & Sisterhood in a Narcissistic World

by Thistle Pettersen

We have seen that the Female Self is The Enemy targeted by the State of War. This Self becomes ultimately threatening when she bonds in networks with other Self-accepting Female Selves. Since we have been conditioned to think quantitatively, feminists often begin the Journey with the misconception that we require large numbers in order to have a realistic hope of victory. This mistake is rooted in a serious underestimation of the force/fire of female bonding. It occurs when Amazons fall into the trap of imagining that sisterhood is like male comradeship. Because of the inherent weakness of its cogs, the male machine does require large numbers of self-sacrificing comrades. Because of the inherent strength of a woman who is Friend to her Self, the force of female bonding does not require multitudes.

~ Mary Daly, Gyn/Ecology

Face it. All you really possess consistently throughout your life-time is your body to take care of and your inner life, your mind, your spirit, and the sum total being, of what we call the "self."

For this reason, we are naturally self-centered because fundamentally, the self holds all the information we know that has come to us and been perceived through our senses from the universe that exists outside of our bodies. It is through the self that we know the world outside our bodies that we interact with in a constant energy exchange. This experience is stored within the mind and psyche that reside, obviously, in the body, in the folds of the brain. Marks of our experience are also stored in other parts of the body, such as in the muscles and on the skin in the form of scars, or even tattoos. All of it, stored and based in the body, is the sum total of who we are, and who others come to know as a person, or a self separate from others, and distinct.

The self should not be confused with selfishness or narcissism, however.

To the contrary, it was Mary Daly who wrote about the possibility of woman becoming herSelf after coming into consciousness about how patriarchy dissolves woman's selfhood. Male rule requires that women be subordinate to men and essentially relegates woman to a servant class position that includes child-raising and sexual relations upon demand.

In the atmosphere or "universe" of patriarchy, it is no wonder a woman's Self is compromised at best and annihilated at worst.

In addition, what does it mean to cultivate selfhood in this age of runaway narcissism fostered by the internet? Look at any YouTube video of a young girl "transitioning gender" and you'll see what I mean by "runaway narcissism." Transactivism, in its obsession with body hatred and harm as a method of reaching selfhood, only confuses and alienates, rather than facilitating the building of relationships we need to be a strong, diverse, and accepting society. The kind of comradeship "trans" and "non-binary" youth establish is fake and provides no real comfort. Our girls are literally killing themselves through dark narcissistic pathways that lead to tragedy and fake female friendships. This is the exact opposite of Mary Daly's vision of individual woman's Selfhood leading towards a small, but tightly knit and effective sister circle.

How do we become ourSelves, like Mary Daly was talking about, and not become self-centered and competitive with other women for the spotlight or to have admirers, to be the smartest, the most beautiful, the bravest, or the best in our arenas?

I am not saying that we should not hold up women who step forward and up for women in big ways in our many feminist, detransitioning, and lesbian arenas. Indeed, they/we are under so much fire on the frontlines of the War on Women, that it is essential that we show solidarity.

But I am saying that too often, I see the same women being revered and not a lot of room for other women to step up to the spotlight. It sometimes makes me wonder if our women's movement is still bound by our patriarchal socialization that has taught us to be skeptical and to compete, rather than to trust and collaborate. Recently, we witnessed a refreshing change to this pattern just before the virus outbreak put us all in lockdown. Standing for Women and the Make More Noise collective organized a gathering for International Women's Day 2020 in Hyde Park in London, at the historic free speech zone known as Speakers' Corner.

People of any political or religious persuasion are encouraged to gather at Speakers' Corner to get up on their soapboxes and speak their minds to whoever will listen.

The Suffragists in the UK were doing this in that very spot over a hundred years ago in their fight for the vote in Britain.

At this particular grassroots speaking event, any woman could get up on her soapbox and express herself, which leveled the playing field for all women present to be heard. Among the many speakers present that day were Julia Long, Venice Allan, and Sheila Jeffreys. How empowering that must have been for women to stand up, join in with, and address them as peers! To follow the speaking event, organizers had also booked a pub in London which allowed participants to continue the gathering, and many women stayed on into the wee hours connecting, networking, and building friendships and female community with one another.

How exhilarating!

In contrast, women, under patriarchy, are socialized to hate

179

each other. I grew up in the 1980's, in the time of the movie Heathers and all of the sardonic attitudes that went along with it. Some of the girls I met at the public high school I attended were truly cruel to other girls and highly competitive in their hierarchical social circles. I am sure it is no different now and perhaps even worse, for girls in public high schools today.

Not only can we counter these socialized patriarchal behaviors in our women's culture in groups, but we can cultivate our own individual Selfhood, that will help us to function in groups and also to just love and accept ourselves as we are after years of being told we are never enough both by society at large, but also in our daily lives at school, work, and in our families and eventually, in our own heads.

I liken Mary Daly's Selfhood to that of a Mama Bear caring for her cubs. In the case of ourselves, we have a more child-like self and a more mature self that coexist in our psyches. Therefore, to cultivate the Self, it behooves women to remember how fiercely mother bears will defend their cubs against danger.

If we imagine that the child-like part of us is worthy (in the bear's mind this would not even be a question), creative, funny, and alive within us, we can also imagine that when the bullies come around to try to tear us down, the Mama Bear inside instinctively will come to the defense of her offspring.

For many of us feminist witches out there, our "off-spring" are extensions of ourSelves and come out in the form of creative works such as songs, music, poems, art, and writing. But our creativity is not limited to the arts and philosophical pursuits; it is also well-harnessed in collaborative group projects that create villages of artists' and women's "children" that can then smash the patriarchy and set all women free.

Sometimes in my Journey, there has been no one who would stand up for me against misogynistic attacks. For those of you new to me and my story, it is a long one.

I was pushed out of my teaching job after being shunned and ostracized by co-workers who publicly declared my feminist views to be "hateful and bigoted" after I held a sign at the Women's March 2017 that said "Don't Believe the Hype! Transactivism is Misogyny!" I lost my budding music career that included working on an album of music with my band, Thistle & Thorns, and playing regularly in the community at several venues. I lost my public Selfhood and the community in my hometown has lost a major contributor to leftist organizing in the environmental movement, a folk singer, and so much more – its Soul, it sometimes feels like.

Don't get me wrong, many women and some male allies have shown deep solidarity and support for me as a person with a Selfhood throughout my whole ordeal dealing with trans activist extremists who have convinced the Wilmar Neighborhood Center, just as one example, to ban me from performing on their stage.

But in day-to-day, individual situations, ultimately, it has been Mama Bear inside of me that has done most of my Self-advocacy work in my community. I have been the main organizer behind campaigns to hold up my case to the community, with all of its sordid details, so that Madison at least has the opportunity to reflect collectively on what has happened. At least TRAs (trans-rights activists) and Madison at large have been provided a look in the mirror to see how what has been done to me has been done to all women in the myriad of ways women can be publicly shamed, for what seems like all of eternity.

I plant a seed in the women's movement with this public advocacy work I continue to do for mySelf, in that Dalyian sense.

If you are persecuted by men's rights activists or TRAs, you don't just lay down and die! You get up and fight like a Mama Bear for her cubs.

You also come to understand that you are a target of such brutal attacks precisely because you and your cubs are valuable as well as powerful.

My songs are my cubs and my activist projects, such as Grassroutes Caravans (bicycle adventuring mobile villages), MAMA (Madison Action for Mining Alternatives) and WLRN (Women's Liberation Radio News), are the villages I co-create with

181

other like-minded Selves who wish to shift social reality from a basis of narcissism to one of Selfhood and care for one another.

I write this essay as a shameless advocate for mySelf in all of my brilliance, my talents, and my depths of being. I am here. I exist. I am strong and I am worthy and capable of building community and forming bonds with my sisters here and beyond! You can love, accept, and advocate for yourSelf too. Let's do it together. Sister, take my hand.

Woman am I
Spirit am I
I am the infinite within myself
I have no beginning
I have no end
all things I am
I will always always love thee
I will never never leave thee
Take my hand
we'll dance together
Take my hand
we'll dance forever
I will always always love thee
I will never forget thee

Poem (paraphrased) from Sonia Johnson's
SisterWitch Conspiracy.

PART II:

INTERSECTIONAL FEMINISM

CHAPTER 11

Women Aren't Men: A Radical Feminist Analysis of Indigenous Gender Politics

by Cherry Smiley

Trigger warning: A woman sharing thoughts.

> ...*[T]he issue of transsexualism is an ethical issue that has profound political and moral ramifications; transsexualism itself is a deeply moral question rather than a medical-technical answer.*[1]

> -- Janice Raymond

Transgender ideology harms women and girls. In Canada, the uncritical acceptance of the claims and demands of transactivists, academics, and others who promote transgender ideology has resulted in the rapid adoption of legislation and policy that disproportionately impacts Indigenous women and girls. There are three ways in which transgender ideology, legislation, and policy harms Indigenous women and girls in Canada: our stories are rewritten, we are silenced, and we are disproportionately impacted by policy experiments related to women-only spaces.

185

Let's rewrite Herstory: All the genders, pre-colonization

> *The imposition of colonial patriarchy has marginalized Indigenous women and Two-Spirit people[2] [emphasis added] through Indian Act governance systems, and by the Indian Act itself...until 1985, when amendments were made to the Indian Act, an Indigenous woman or female-presenting Two-Spirit person [emphasis added] who married a non-Indigenous man lost her legal status as an Indian, and was unable to pass on status to her children.[3]*

-- Chelsea Vowel

Manstitutions[4] have embraced, without adequate information, question, or reflection, the idea that "transwomen are women." Statements made by some Indigenous researchers, leaders, and advocates are wholly accepted as truth when it comes to the idea of gender identity,[5] genders,[6] and queerness among Indigenous peoples in the past and present. These kinds of statements, however, are only accepted when they align with the beliefs and analysis of "settlers." To claim that female-presenting Two-Spirit people lost Indian status when they married non-status men raises questions concerning validity of the claim and presentation of evidence, but more importantly, attempts to rewrite our past and present as one where Indigenous *peoples* experience sex[7] discrimination in the Indian Act. This is simply not true. The only Indigenous people discriminated against on the basis of sex in the Indian Act are women. Even if these women identify as Two-Spirit, they are still women. Given the intensity of the backlash from Indigenous and non-Indigenous manstitutions, the sexist attacks against generations of Indigenous women that continue today, and the terrible ways that women were, and are, treated for daring to fight for themselves and for other women to matter, descriptions of our herstories and current struggles deserve well-researched, thoughtful, and accurate treatment.

186

We often hear that pre-colonial Indigenous cultures in North America had many different genders and Two-Spirit individuals were valued and respected and were often medicine people and held leadership positions:

> All across Turtle Island, there are documented accounts of multiple gender roles beyond just man and woman, often acknowledging more than two genders. In all accounts, Two Spirit people were respected by their communities, valued for their gifts, and accepted for who they were...[t]hey were considered to have the power of both male and female spirits, and were therefore seen as having a close relationship with the Creator. Two Spirit people were often healers, visionaries, and medicine people within our nations. They were regarded as fundamental components of our communities, cultures, and societies.[8]

> -- Canadian Centre for Gender and Sexual Diversity

Maybe this was true and maybe it wasn't; maybe this was true in some nations and not true in other nations. However, my grandma's stories, historical research, common sense, and my tendency to float upstream (as grandma would say) brings up questions, lots of questions. I think asking questions is always a good thing.

Some questions

Generally, multiple genders are found in cultures where gender roles are rigid. In at least some, maybe many, pre-colonial Indigenous nations, it would make sense to have less rigid gender roles as opposed to more. When the rules are very strict about what "women do" and what "men do," for example, one sex is dependent on the other for certain needs. For example, if only men hunt, women are dependent on men to hunt; if only women prepare food to be eaten, men are dependent on women to have food that is safe to eat. This is more a reflection of modern culture than anything else. If only men knew how to hunt and hunted, what would happen if a number of men were injured or ill or died? If only women knew how to safely prepare foods, what would happen in the middle of a tough winter when everyone - women, men, and children - needed to pitch in extra? It would make sense that most or all members of a group, female and male, would need to know how to survive and be able to put that knowledge into practice meaning that ideas about what "women do" and what "men do" would be less strict and more fluid.

Where do babies come from?

Women know how babies are made and where babies come from. As female human beings whom can become pregnant and give birth, Indigenous women in pre-colonial times had to have as much control over their own reproduction as they could if they were to survive, whether this meant by abstaining from sex, using a method of birth control, aborting a fetus, or other means. If women were continually pregnant, this would have significant impacts on a group in terms of who is able to do what labour, the potential of complications or loss of life, the amount of assistance needed from others in the group before, during, and after giving birth, and population size relative to the lands and non-human relatives in the vicinity. Another consideration would be time of year, as most women would likely not want to give birth in the middle of winter or be pregnant during a very hot and humid summer if this could be avoided.

What this means is that Indigenous women had to know how babies were made, where babies came from, and in a heterosexual sexual encounter, which person could become pregnant. This means acknowledging the realities of immutable biological sex as female people or male people, no matter what gender a woman or man feels that they are on the inside.

Some self-reflection

I used to believe very strongly that most Indigenous nations in Canada were matriarchal and that women were respected and held leadership positions. Maybe this was true and maybe it wasn't; maybe this was true in some nations and not true in other nations. At the time, this claim supported the work I was doing for Indigenous women and girls. However, after some serious self-reflection, I've come to understand that I was mistaken to rely on this claim to advocate for our liberation. These kinds of claims, whether they are about women as respected leaders or about Two-Spirit people as medicine people and whether they work in our interest or not, silence discussion. "It used to be this way so it should be this way again…" is an impossible claim to prove, politically lazy, and in regard to ideas about gender in the past, abandons women from historically patriarchal cultures, invisibilizes women who refused the limits of gender and broke the rules, and has long been used to justify male violence against women and girls in many cultures, including ours today. It's important to note here that grandma's stories neither vilified nor valorized homosexuality – rather, it seemed that homosexuality was widely accepted and as such, wasn't considered "different" enough to be a topic of consistent mention.

Shut Up, TERF[9]

Indigenous women, who had fought for decades and longer for a national inquiry into murdered and disappeared Indigenous women and girls in Canada ("the inquiry") were sidelined in our own inquiry to make room for 2SLGBTQQIA[10] communities, without any notice or discussion. The inquiry acknowledged that the Commissionaires made the decision to include men who identify as Two-Spirit or Indigenous women or non-binary or genderqueer or Indigiqueer or any other number of identities, due to pressure from unnamed advocacy groups. As a result, disproportionate amounts

189

of time, resources, and energy went into discussing everyone else but Indigenous women in our own inquiry. If the issue of male violence against Indigenous 2SLGBTQQIA communities is as pressing as claimed and suffers from lack of research that examines the scope of the issue, a more effective strategy might have been to demand targeted research funding and a separate inquiry on that issue so that it could be thoroughly examined. This is not what happened.

The inquiry that Indigenous women called for was a place to prioritize women, not a place for "gender affirmation" or even a depoliticized place to remember the dead. If the inquiry thought that women mattered, men with gender feelings would not have been included and the really tough conversations would have been welcomed. It is not possible to have these tough conversations with all their messiness and debate and sometimes hurt feelings *and* simultaneously maintain a space as apolitical and "sacred." Actually, I should say that it is possible but I doubt feminist women would last long or be heard in such a place before being silenced or removed for the supposed crime of disrespecting families, not prioritizing men's feelings, or for clearly and boldly stating our reality.

In this way, the "wrong kind" of Indigenous women were silenced in terms of lack of access to the inquiry as an investigative and public platform and continue to be silenced for daring to say that we know who women are and that we will prioritize women in our liberation struggles. Dworkin theorized this lack of access to mainstream media and other manstitutions as some of the practical ways that feminist women are silenced.[11]

It's obvious to women when those in media or academia or other manstitutions are so disconnected from reality – their own and particularly ours – that the silence they advocate for us extends to cover and distort our own female bodies. For example, a public health organization in British Columbia uses "folx with a cervix" and "people" to mean women. A health organization should know that women are the only "folx" that have a cervix, and therefore women are the only "folx" who need pap tests for our health and well-being.

Options for Sexual Health @optbc · Mar 28, 2019

Real talk: Cervical screening guidelines have changed. This means that for folx with a cervix, most people don't need annual Pap tests*. Even though cervical screening is not recommended... instagram.com /p/Bvj7FuShS7e/...

We are pressured to use "inclusive" terms like "pregnant people" or "people with uteruses," even though women are already here, you don't need to include anyone else in these categories.

The silencing of lesbian women, in particular, goes even further and forcibly invades women's bodies. Using their experiences of being disproportionately passed over for promotions at work, women theorized the idea of the "glass ceiling," a description of the invisible barrier that men create to stop women from advancing to management positions. Women in corporate workplaces can only rise so far before they hit the "glass ceiling." Using their experiences of being passed over as potential sexual partners by lesbian women, men who identify as lesbian women theorized the concept of the "cotton ceiling," a term coined by Drew Deveaux, a man who identifies as a transgender woman. The "cotton ceiling" refers to women's underwear and describes a barrier that stops men who identify as lesbian women from being able to sexually penetrate lesbian women with their "female" penises – sometimes referred to as a "lady dick" – or with other male body parts. In the ways women are relegated to lower-paid jobs with less chance of promotion than their male counterparts, men who identify as lesbian women are relegated to the "friend zone" and only considered "woman" enough to socialize and politically organize with but are discriminated against by lesbian women who refuse sexual relationships with men.

When sharing a draft of this text with a friend who had not heard of the "cotton ceiling" before, she immediately thought it was a term invented by men who attempt to "correctively rape" lesbian women. When lesbian women's "Nos" are silenced or ignored and when manstitutions accept the gaslighting pro-rape theory of busting through the "cotton ceiling" as progressive simply because the men who promote this theory and behaviour identify as women, lesbian women particularly and women generally hear this as a threat, loud and clear.

Being silenced before we can even speak is an experience too common to women and girls:

>...[O]ne of the things I've learned in the last fifteen years is how much women are silenced through sexual abuse. The simple experience of being abused, whether as a child or as an adult, has an incredible impact on everything about the way you see the world around you, so that either you don't feel you can speak because you're frightened of what the retaliation will be, or you don't trust your experience of reality enough to speak - that happens to a lot of incest victims. Or you are actually physically kept from being able to speak - battered women do not have freedom of speech.[12]

I remember when I first read this paragraph, I cried because it spoke so loudly to me. It's taken me a long time to speak and this is true for so many women and girls. This is particularly true for Indigenous women and girls and sisters of colour as we survive (and sometimes do not survive) disproportionate amounts of male violence, often over the course of our lives and often starting in girlhood. Male violence teaches us that we don't matter. We learn to shut up and take it. We learn to stay quiet and hopefully it'll be over soon and we will get to stay alive. We learn that we don't matter and to keep our discomfort or worries or fears to ourselves. In the context of patriarchy, allowing a man who identifies as a woman into the safety of a women's transition house for battered women and their children affirms that women don't matter and puts women in crisis and who are in vulnerable circumstances in an impossible situation. If she is uncomfortable sharing women's space with a man, she will either say something and risk being told she is a hateful bigot that just needs to be educated and possibly asked to leave the shelter or she will say nothing out of fear or conditioning that has taught her she doesn't matter and this silence will be viewed by shelter workers, policy makers, and others as confirmation that women welcome men who identify as women into their spaces. We are forced to deny our own experiences of reality, male violence, and legitimate concerns we may have sharing an intimate space with a man that feels like a woman. To tell a woman that has just been attacked by a man that the man in front of her is a woman is absolutely appalling and shameful.

The pressure is increasing, lest we be figuratively burned at the stake like our rule-breaking foremothers, to stop talking, shut up, and why don't you understand that man has always been a woman you transphobic bigot, go die in a fire TERF. The silencing of concerns and critical discussion about transgender ideology and accompanying legislation and policies is dangerous for women and girls and particularly for Indigenous women, women of colour, and poor women who are disproportionately impacted in women's shelters and transition houses, detox centres, and prisons.

Harm

Research has consistently shown that Indigenous women and girls in Canada face disproportionate levels of male violence. Violence and the threat of violence not only impacts our health and wellbeing but also stops us from fully participating in social, economic, and political spheres. Patriarchy and male violence hurts all women but the male violence Indigenous women and girls face is *particular* to our historical and current circumstances as Indigenous women. There are specific reasons and solutions as to why women and girls, and in this case Indigenous women and girls, are harmed and attacked by men. Men attack Indigenous women because we *are* Indigenous women, not because we *feel* like Indigenous women (whatever that feeling may be). We are oppressed and attacked by men because of our sex, not our gender. The concept of gender itself is an attack on women.[13]

Vancouver Rape Relief and Women's Shelter (VRRWS) was recently defunded by the City of Vancouver for refusing to open their doors to men who identify as women. I used to work at VRRWS and when I attended conferences or events in the Ottawa/Montreal area I knew what to expect when I told others that I had worked at VRRWS. The immediate reaction was a look of shock and disgust and then a statement about how VRRWS is transphobic. Sometimes this statement would come from other current or former front-line anti-violence workers. It is misogynist behaviour to ignore all the work VRRWS has done for women as the first rape crisis centre in Canada and to ignore all the women who have come and gone as collective members, paid workers, volunteers, residents, and women seeking support and jump straight into immediate condemnation of this organization as hateful. Shame on you. I learned a lot at VRRWS and I think I was only able to flail about with all kinds of issues I wasn't ready to work through and learn because the space was women-only. It is heartbreaking to know that many women and girls in Canada today won't know what it feels like to be around only women, all day, by choice.

Women-only space is absolutely necessary for women who have been assaulted by men. Women's emotional and mental wellbeing are just as important as our physical safety and men, regardless of their gender feelings in their heads, can and do disrupt our safety and wellbeing without the use of physical violence. Perhaps some women do not mind having a male nurse perform a rape kit on them at the hospital or sharing intimate and traumatic details about rape to a man at a rape crisis centre or hearing the heavy footsteps of a male resident in a transition house for battered women in the middle of the night. I can confidently say that few, if any, women would refuse a female nurse and specifically request a male nurse to perform a vaginal exam after a rape or refuse a woman and specifically request to speak with a man about the details of a rape or refuse a female roommate and specifically request an unknown man as a roommate in a shelter with a lack of space and privacy as she and her children are escaping an abusive male partner. This is important and we could go back and forth about what women "like" or "prefer" or "tolerate" but this isn't really the point.

The point is:

Women need to know that women-only space *is an option* and that it is *entirely acceptable and understandable* that a woman who has been assaulted by a man would want to be around only other women and to get assistance from other women and work with other women who can understand what it is to be born female in patriarchy.

Whether it's after being attacked by a man or in order to organize politically for our own interests or to build and grow friendships or for whatever reason we decide, women need to know that women-only space *is an option* and that it is *entirely acceptable* to demand this and create this for ourselves.

Women are socialized to caretake others and particularly to ensure that men's feelings are not hurt. It has been my experience that when we women give each other permission to ask for, demand, support, and participate in women-only spaces and when we *actually prioritize ourselves* – our safety, wellbeing, and liberation – we feel more able to demand, create, and hold women-only space as an option for ourselves and for other women. Men who feel themselves to be women do not understand what it is to be a woman in patriarchy. Their experience is as men who feel themselves to be women in their heads but who are not women in patriarchy and all the male privilege, entitlement, and misogynist ideas that come along with that gender identity.

Given the high rates of male violence against Indigenous women and girls and the disproportionate number of Indigenous women that most rape crisis centres and transition houses work with, defunding VRRWS or any rape crisis centre or transition house, sends the message that Indigenous women matter less than men's feelings.

Morgane Oger seemed very invested in the City of Vancouver defunding VRRWS, referring to VRRWS as a "supremacist organization":

Morgane Oger @MorganeOgerBC · 15h

Tonight, a supremacist organization with a purity test on womanhood learned that cultivating exclusion and discrimination really does have a price.

I profoundly encourage Vancouver Rape Relief to reconsider its untenable policy to arbitrarily exclude some women.

♡ 87   ⟲ 5   ♡ 21   ⬆

The message we women receive is loud and clear: women and girls, and particularly Indigenous women and girls, who are attacked disproportionately by men, matter less than Morgane Oger's feelings and uniformed opinions. The City of Vancouver has sent the message that women-only space is *not* an option and that it *is entirely unacceptable and incomprehensible* that a woman who has been assaulted by a man would want to be around only other women and to get assistance from and work with other women who can understand what it is to be female in patriarchy.

The last time I was sexually assaulted, I think two years ago in Montreal, I went all the way across the city to get assistance from a woman-only rape crisis centre in part because Concordia's Sexual Assault Resource Centre provides services to "all genders." I did not want to speak with a male counselor or volunteer and I did not want to sit next to a man in the waiting area, regardless of the gender feelings of these hypothetical men. I can guarantee you that I am not the only woman who feels this way and I am not the only woman who wants to be around other woman after I have been attacked in a way that only women are attacked by men. My feelings and my wellbeing and the feelings and wellbeing of women everywhere matter.

It's important to note that the City of Vancouver is not the only manstitution to defund VRRWS for daring to work in the interest of women. The British Columbia Teacher's Federation had already chosen to defund VRRWS because VRRWS knows that women are female human beings. Women who centre women and who stand up for women-only space are bullied, targeted, and even assaulted.

VancouverRapeRelief
@VanRapeRelief

A follow up to the dead rat that was nailed to our door recently... this morning we found this writing scrawled across the windows of our storefront space that we use for support and training groups #Misogyny

Tweet your reply

The issue of male violence against women and children in the home has received more attention lately as the COVID-19 pandemic has highlighted that women and children are not always safe at home amongst suggestions and orders to quarantine, self-distance, isolate, and stay at home as much as possible in attempts to slow the spread of the deadly virus.

In a now-removed post on *Medium* dated April 12, 2020, author Laura Izaguirre began her article with the following statement:

The Vancouver Rape Relief Shelter (VRR), an infamous crisis counseling place run by TERF's who discriminate against trans women and sex workers, has been permanently stripped of over $30,000 in public funding from the city of Vancouver! This is excellent news.

The article states that "VRR's goal is to take vulnerable women and brainwash them with anti-trans propaganda...VRR's leadership is as committed to despising women as David Duke and Richard Spencer are to anti-Semitism." The article elaborates on different strategies to wipe out the VRR "den of TERF vipers" in order to make Vancouver safe for women. These strategies included attempting to cut VRRWS' public and private funding, infiltrating VRRWS and taking over the collective in a "bloodless coup," launching lawsuits, direct action targeted at VRRWS and VRRWS "leaders" who are identified by name with photographs and a suggestion to share this information so that other activists can "appropriately engage with them," deplatforming VRRWS from public engagements, bombarding VRRWS through social media, in-person, mail, email, or phone methods (all are listed) with opinions, modifying VRRWS' Wikipedia page to state that they are a hate group, and joining transactivist groups that worked very hard to defund VRRWS from City of Vancouver funding.

This is important. This is not a distraction from the current worldwide crisis we are in. Male violence against women and children in the home was a worldwide crisis before the pandemic, during the pandemic, and will be so after the pandemic. Izaguirre's article was shocking in its clarity, even among feminists who have been engaged in these debates for years, for decades. Oger and Izaguirre are not the first and won't be the last individuals to attempt to defund a women's transition house and rape crisis centre for working with women and the implications of these misogynist actions go beyond one women's shelter.

Indigenous women are overrepresented in women's shelters, transition houses for battered women and children, and rape crisis centres as well as in the prison system in Canada due to the impacts of patriarchy, racism, and capitalism. Research has shown consistently that many women and girls in prison in Canada have survived male violence and are disproportionately poor.

Women's shelters and women's prisons are two places where men who identify as women believe that they should be able to access. This is already happening and men who identify as women have assaulted and caused discomfort to women, who are disproportionately Indigenous, in shelters and in prisons. Women, such as Heather Mason and others, have been courageously speaking out about what happens when men are put in women's prisons. VRRWS is holding strong for women, as always, refusing to be bullied by Oger or the City of Vancouver or by anyone into deprioritizing women's interests and needs in the women's anti-violence movement.

As the self-identification of gender is promoted and the pressure for women to be inclusive of men's feelings in our healing from and political resistance to male violence against women and girls increases, Indigenous women and girls are the ones who are and will disproportionately pay a substantial price as policy makers come to realize that forcing women's transitions houses, that are supposed to be safe shelters for women and children fleeing male violence, to accept men who self-identify as women and housing men who self-identify as women, who are in prison for raping women or other violent crimes, in women's prison is distressing and dangerous for women and girls, and disproportionately for Indigenous women and girls. Again, the message is sent is that Indigenous women and girls don't matter and are not worth fighting for.

In conclusion

I don't believe in the idea of a gender identity. Biology is a material reality, human beings cannot change sex, and men oppress women on the basis of our sex. Gender is made-up rules, limitations, and expectations that harm women and benefit men. To say we are each born with a gender identity is an idea that can and should be debated and its impacts on our material realities as women thoroughly examined with a feminist framework. This is a very important point. The idea of gender should not be examined in isolation. When it is, those critical of transgender ideology are often right-wing, conservative, and/or religious men from organizations that advocate for sexist, racist, and classist policies that hurt women. The debate around gender is important for feminists because it forms a foundation for our movement. How can we even begin to form a feminist analysis and work for and with women if we are pressured to believe men are women if they say they are and we are told to not only include but *prioritize* the political goals of men who identify as transgender women in our work? How can we further our politics, strategy, and fight for women and girls when men are constantly demanding access to our spaces, some of which are spaces where we are most vulnerable?

Indigenous women who don't say and do what men want us to say and do are being silenced again, after lifetimes of silence, generations of silence. The message this sends is that *Indigenous women are only welcome to speak if you say what we want you to say – Indigenous women don't get to say no – Indigenous women don't matter.*

I recall events at York University in Toronto, Carleton University in Ottawa, and Concordia University in Montreal where I was giving presentations about my research on prostitution and male violence against Indigenous women and girls or listening to presentations given by others. I recall being asked about the lack of inclusion of transgender women in my research and I recall my character, not my research, being challenged as I was asked how I would treat a transgender person as if I would be violent or discriminatory. I recall individuals moving to other seats so they didn't have to sit beside me and hearing the whispers and watching the faces of women and men contort with disgust because of what I was saying, because of *me*; they were disgusted *by me*. I won't forget those faces as we women continue to fight for our own liberation. Disagree with us, challenge us, but what we have to say matters because women matter. Izaguirre's (later removed) article states:

> [VRRWS] threaten the safety and dignity of others and therefore deserve none themselves until they choose to be human once more... We can't all be like the heroic woman who came close to delivering a blow for justice on TERF Julie Bindle. Do what you can manage...

The idea that physically harming women in public spaces for questioning or challenging transgender ideology, legislation, and policy is warranted, justified, and even celebrated, speaks to our realities as women who are not always free to speak in the private spheres of our home and increasingly unable to speak in the public sphere. These threats have been realized against some women and this is misogyny at its finest: you deserve it TERF! Myself and other women spend way too much time, energy, and resources strategizing how to stay safe when giving public talks. For example, whenever I speak in public, I make sure to run through in my mind how I would get out of the room if need be. This happens everywhere, even at my own university.

The City of Vancouver, The British Columbia Teacher's Federation, universities and other manstitutions who have cancelled feminist talks, and others who have worked to silence or stop or harm women who speak out against transgender ideologies, legislation, and policies that directly impact women should pay attention to articles like Izaguirre's. Her ideas are not extreme or fringe, they are mainstream in transactivism, although perhaps presented in a more inviting way. As Izaguirre stated, "we should always remember that deplatforming works. Canceling them from communication platforms makes it harder for them to spread their propaganda." The continued use of many of Izaguirre's suggested strategies against VRRWS, other feminist groups, and against individual women by supposedly progressive organizations and governments should be cause for incredible concern – by the general public and also by these organizations and governments themselves. It seems impossible to defend such misogynist actions when they are laid out so publicly and so starkly, but I am not confident that "progressive" organizations have the desire to self-reflect or think critically or have the courage to stand with women who assert their boundaries and prioritize themselves.

For any reason, we women are allowed to say no; we women are allowed to say "today we are taking care of our needs"; "today we are prioritizing our feelings"; "today we are fighting for our own liberation because sure as hell no one else is going to do it for us." Women have worked so hard, with so little and sometimes nothing, to build transition houses and rape crisis centres from nothing with incredible opposition. Others are free to do the same for their own interests. It is not our job as women to politically organize for the interests of men. It is ok to say no and the more of us that do, the easier it is.

Endnotes

1   Raymond, Janice G. *The Transsexual Empire: The Making of the She-male*. Teachers College Press, 1994.

2   The term "Two-Spirit" was coined at the 3rd Intertribal Native American, First Nations, Gay and Lesbian American Conference in 1990. Initially the term spoke back to the erasure of Indigenous women and men in the wider LGBT movement and referred to being both homosexual and Indigenous. Today, the term is used more broadly to reflect many different gender identities that are claimed among Indigenous women and men and commonly refers to the idea of both a "female spirit" and "male spirit" inhabiting one human being.

3   Vowel, Chelsea. *Indigenous Writes: A Guide to First Nations, Métis, & Inuit Issues in Canada*. HighWater Press, 2016.

4   "Manstitution" refers collectively to Indigenous and non-Indigenous male-centred institutions such as governments, universities, non-governmental organizations (NGOs), the justice system, social services, activist groups, mainstream media, and the men who created and work in these institutions for the benefit of men.

5   According to gender ideology, "Gender identity" refers to "…your psychological sense of self. Who you, in your head, know yourself to be, based on how much you align (or don't align) with what you understand to be the options for gender." (www.genderbread.org). For example, gender ideology claims that you may have a male body but you identify, in your head, as a woman.

6   "Gender" refers to made-up rules, expectations, preferences, and behaviours that are assigned based on sex (for example, girls like pink, boys like blue). Feminist theory maintains that gender is a hierarchy, as opposed to a binary, and oppresses women while benefitting men. Feminists want to abolish gender.

7   Sex refers to our biological realities as human females and human males. There are sex differences such as chromosomes, gonads, sex hormones, and genitals that exist between females and males. For example, human females are able to become pregnant and give birth and human males are not able to become pregnant or give birth. There are some people who are born with an intersex condition but this is rare. It is not possible for human beings to change sex.

8   Canadian Centre for Gender and Sexual Diversity website, https:// ccgsd-ccdgs.org/1-who-are-two-spirit-people/.

9   A slur used to silence women who question gender and gender identity. The acronym stands for "trans-exclusionary radical feminist." TERF appears in statements such as "kill TERFs." See www.terfisaslur.com for more information.

10 Refers to Two-Spirit, lesbian, gay, bisexual, transgender, queer, questioning, intersex, allies.

11 See Dworkin, Andrea. "Dworkin on Dworkin," in Diane Bell & Renate Klein (Eds.), *Radically Speaking: Feminism Reclaimed.* Spinifex Press, 1996.

12 Dworkin, Andrea. "Dworkin on Dworkin," in Diane Bell & Renate Klein (Eds.), *Radically Speaking: Feminism Reclaimed.* Spinifex Press, 1996, pp. 203-217.

13 Millett, Kate. *Sexual Politics.* Columbia University Press, 2016; Jeffreys, Sheila. *Gender Hurts: A Feminist Analysis of the Politics of Transgenderism.* Routledge, Taylor & Francis Group, 2014.

CHAPTER 12

Intersectionality Hijacked

by Raquel Rosario Sánchez

Does intersectionality theory include women and girls? The mere question could be deemed ignorant or offensive. After all, when U.S. law professor Kimberlé Crenshaw coined the term in her 1989 academic paper "Demarginalizing the Intersection of Race and Sex: A Black Feminist Critique of Antidiscrimination Doctrine, Feminist Theory and Antiracist Politics,"[1] she was developing an explicit criticism of the realities which affect women, specifically Black women. It represented a Black feminist denunciation which sought to shed light on the intersecting forms of oppression impacting the lives of Black women, both though their race and, poignantly, their sex.

Crenshaw acknowledged the precedents set by fellow Black feminists such as Anna Julia Cooper, who in the 19th century similarly conceptualised this matter prior to Crenshaw's legal essay, yet it was Crenshaw's academic reasoning which catapulted intersectionality theory into the stratosphere of public thought. Published by the University of Chicago's *Legal Forum*, Crenshaw criticised what she described as "the single-axis analysis which assumed that race and sex are mutually exclusive categories in the lives of Black women," while utilising three legal cases which addressed both racial discrimination and sex discrimination in the United States:

DeGraffenreid v. General Motors, Moore v. Hughes Helicopter, Inc., and *Payne v. Travenol Laboratories, Inc.*

She argued that, up until that point, in US law, discrimination against white females represented the standard sex discrimination claim presented before the courts. And that, similarly, Black men represented the standard envisioned for racial discrimination. This left Black women in the invidious position of being unable to bring forward claims which had so far been deemed "not pure enough" to qualify as both:

> *The court's refusal in DeGraffenreid to acknowledge that Black women encounter combined race and sex discrimination implies that the boundaries of sex and race discrimination doctrine are defined respectively by white women's and Black men's experiences.*
>
> *Under this view, Black women are protected only to the extent that their experiences coincide with those of either of the two groups. Where their experiences are distinct, Black women can expect little protection as long as approaches, such as that in DeGraffenreid, which completely obscure problems of intersectionality prevail.[2]*

A powerful analytical tool was born. Unfortunately, it appears that, at the same time that it has slowly but surely gained ground in larger society, intersectionality theory has been hijacked to include everyone's privileges and oppressions, except those which affect women who advocate for their sex.

Intersectionality…without females

Today, it is through Crenshaw's analysis that we have arrived at what is sometimes called intersectional feminism. In July 2020 UN Women, the United Nations entity tasked with promoting the empowerment of women and "gender" (sex) equality, published an article advocating that the suitable way for enact feminist thought and practice was through an intersectional lens. UN Women defined it thusly:

> *Intersectional feminism centres the voices of those experiencing overlapping, concurrent forms of oppression in order to understand the depths of the inequalities and the relationships among them in any given context. Using an intersectional lens also means recognizing the historical contexts surrounding an issue.*
>
> *Long histories of violence and systematic discrimination have created deep inequities that disadvantage some from the outset. These inequalities intersect with each other, for example, poverty, caste systems, racism and sexism, denying people their rights and equal opportunities. The impacts extend across generations.[3]*

Note how in defining their preferred vision for feminism, the self-defined "global champion for gender equality," fails to mention women and girls... let alone the word female.

"Intersectional feminism" represents an inclusive label used interchangeably to also signify "liberal feminist," "third-wave feminism," "mainstream feminism," "postmodern feminism" and, because the vast majority of the population are not women's rights theorists: feminism.

In this article, I will write about the experiences of three women who, through their personal upbringing and professional work, ought to represent living and breathing examples of what intersectional feminism claims to champion, yet have been ostracised by proponents of the doctrine, as a result of their determination to defend their sex. These women are Indian filmmaker Vaishnavi Sundar, Nlaka'pamux and Diné scholar Cherry Smiley, and British criminal defence barrister Allison Bailey.

--Vaishnavi Sundar

Our first example is Vaishnavi Sundar, a self-taught filmmaker from Chennai, in South-Eastern India. She founded a production company called Lime Soda Films, which she utilises as a feminist vehicle creating women-centred films with her all-female, international crew. Sundar also created Women Making Films, an online global forum which promotes female filmmakers and their work through writing, workshops, screenings, film festivals and mentorship programmes.

Sundar conceived, produced and directed India's first full-length documentary on workplace sexual harassment, which was fundraised by the public. *But What Was She Wearing?* shed light on the sexual harassment women face in their places of work; ranging from corporate offices to construction sites. Sundar sought answers to questions such as "what constitutes a workplace?" "what happens if the harasser is your employer?" and to interrogate, "what rights do women have on paper (as policies) versus the reality of how these policies are implemented?"

Vaishnavi Sundar is a feminist go-getter from the Global South whose voice ought to be amplified and celebrated by intersectional feminists. Right?

Apparently not. In our current times of social media activism and cancel culture, it is not enough to be a woman so steadfast in her dedication to women's rights that she teaches herself how to produce feminist movies. Yes, of course. A woman could do that if she so chooses… but it will account for nothing unless she acquiesces to a set of tenets establishing the nothingness of females.

Writing an article on *Medium* about her experiences with intersectional feminism, Sundar disclosed how she was due to screen *But What Was She Wearing* in New York, on February 2020, having previously been invited by The Polis Project. This organisation prides itself on conducting research and journalism which contributes to "amplifying voices that are unique, critical and underrepresented" and to "speak truth to power." Posters for Sundar's film had already been designed for the event and she had been introduced to the moderator who would chair her screening.

But, not to be! A week before the event was due to take place, the organiser contacted Sundar to inform her that she had been cancelled due to what they deemed "her transphobic views." Intersectional feminists in India had learned of her scheduled screening in New York and complained to The Polis Project about social media exchanges Sundar had engaged in regarding the conflict between sex-based rights and "gender identity" issues, years before she produced her documentary.

But what had she said? Writing for *Spiked*, a political magazine based in London, Sundar reiterated her unconscionable ideas:

> *Biological sex is not a social construct. Women's sex-based oppression is real. Housing people with male genitalia in spaces with victims of male sexual violence can be harrowing to women inmates. Mental illnesses like autogynephilia and other dysphorias can cause dangerous, irrevocable damage. And gender theorists are erasing women, much like patriarchy does.*[4]

Where is the logic of shutting down professional opportunities for women like Sundar? How could this theoretical tool, which ought to include every intersection of oppression, have been weaponised to ostracise a woman whose sole crime has been to defend the rights of her own sex? Is intersectionality theory not wide enough to include her?

After the New York screening fiasco, writing opportunities dried up for this freelance writer. Magazines and film outlets which would previously accept every one of her submissions suddenly made excuses to exclude her voice from their pages. The current theocratic oath which negates sex-based rights ought to be spoken loud, proud, and often... or else.

--Cherry Smiley

As a feminist campaigner, researcher and artist from the Nlaka'pamux (Thompson) and Diné (Navajo) Nations, Cherry Smiley is a fighter through and through. She has worked as an anti-violence worker in rape crisis centres and transition houses for battered women and their children, as the assistant coordinator for a drop-in anti-violence group for Indigenous girls, and as a project manager for a national native women's organization. She is a recognised international speaker on the impact of sexualized colonial male violence against Indigenous women and girls, particularly in prostitution, and is currently a PhD candidate at Concordia University, in Canada, researching the topic.

Smiley is a co-founder of Indigenous Women Against the Sex Industry and founded *Women Studies Online*, a platform "informed and inspired by the radical feminist politics that initially guided the creation of Women's Studies programs in universities across Canada and elsewhere" and relies on the consciousness-raising feminist tradition. Smiley's intention in founding this effort is to put women back in the Women's Studies academic field.

A born fighter, Cherry Smiley did not anticipate having to battle those who should have supported her work and experiences. Due to her opinions in defence of sex-based rights, which she shared both in her activist social justice circle and her writing for platforms such as *Feminist Current*,[5] she has been subjected to the opprobrium of the intersectional feminist brigade who accuse her of committing violence through her words and thoughts. A violence so aggressively intolerant that people can barely finish her articles. She has been ostracised and deplatformed within academic circles, particularly those which claim to centre social justice as their pursuit.

Cherry Smiley knows violence very well. Her work has always centred the eradication of male violence against Indigenous women and girls. Yet instead of joining her fight against the male violence which harms her people, social justice inquisitors have converted

210

Smiley into the aggressor... enabling male perpetrators to disappear from their accusatory lens, both unchallenged and unaccountable.

Writing for Canadian platform *Feminist Current* against the ostracization of women who challenge doctrines of "gender identity" and defend sex-based rights, Smiley states:

> *Too often, activists and academics who claim to be working for justice choose to side with individuals who use bully tactics to shut women that they don't agree with up. There is nothing new or progressive or inclusive or diverse about telling feminist women to shut up. A strategy grounded in recognizing another's humanity would include engaging, debating, and disagreeing passionately and respectfully at public events or holding an event to highlight one's own particular political analysis and engaging in public discussion and advocacy around the issue at hand.*
>
> *Silencing women considered dangerous for having thoughts and sharing them is not how we treat each other when we recognize each other as equals. I encourage all dangerous women and allies to speak out against the no-platforming and assault on women who express radical feminist opinions or critical ideas about prostitution and gender.[6]*

In what can only be considered a devastating irony, Smiley describes her PhD research project using words which illustrate a reality she herself has been subjected to as a scholar:

> *Constructed as "squaws," Indigenous women and girls are seen as savage, subhuman and disposable. They are depicted as women and girls who always want sex and are sexually available to men at all times. Despite their over-representation in street prostitution, Indigenous women occupy marginal positions in sexual exploitation discourse. This research posits the sexual exploitation of Indigenous women and girls as a*

211

site to understanding expressions of colonial male violence and their impacts on Indigenous women and girls.[7]

In her own life and work, due to the demonisation of activists' sectors which have weaponised intersectionality theory, Smiley has been constructed as yet another savage, subhuman, and disposable Indigenous woman. In the attempts to assassinate the character of an up-and-coming scholar who has dedicated her life to ending male violence, and whose sole wrongdoing was veering from the patriarchal and colonial scripts assigned to her, the misogynist trope of the aggressive woman of colour becomes reified by those who claim to promote anticolonial and antiracist politics. Who benefits from putting an outspoken Indigenous feminist "back in her place" and reinforcing colonial stereotypes?

--Allison Bailey

The daughter of Jamaican immigrant parents born in east Oxford and raised in the working-class neighbourhood of Crowley, Allison Bailey knew she wanted to fight for justice from a young age. Her background presents us with a resolute Black woman whose work in community advocacy and defence of the rights of same-sex attracted people spans decades, attesting to her commitment to equality. At 17 years old, Allison Bailey came out as a lesbian in a community in which support for her same-sex attraction was not a guarantee. This was also a time when the United Kingdom operated under Section 28 of the Local Government Act 1988, which marginalised homosexuality by forbidding local authorities from "promoting" gay and lesbian relationships.

In her late teens, she moved to New York and then San Francisco, working and living in The Castro, a neighborhood considered ground zero for United States left wing political activism and LBGT rights, while the community was surviving the AIDS epidemic.

In 1992, on the night that the police officers who murdered a defenceless Rodney King were acquitted, Bailey peacefully protested the racial injustice taking place. She was arrested and imprisoned at the Santa Rita Women's Jail.

Today, Bailey is a very well-regarded criminal defence barrister and lifelong campaigner for racial equality, lesbian, gay, and bisexual rights. In 2018, her keen intellect detected that there was a serious conflict of rights brewing in the United Kingdom when the conservative government announced that they wanted to reform the Gender Recognition Act 2004, in order to include the nebulous concept of "self-identification" into the law. Individuals should be able to "self-identify" into the sex of their choosing through an expedited administrative process, the government maintained. The proposed reform was officially dropped in September 2020, but the years preceding the move witnessed social justice fighters embroiled a relentlessly acrimonious battle.

Radical and socialist feminist campaigners raised concerns that the proposed reform could create repercussions for the sex-based rights which are already enshrined in UK law through the Equality Act 2010; including the right to single-sex spaces such as women's refuges, prisons, and changing facilities. The broader concept of "sex self-identification" therefore conflicted with the rights both of same-sex attracted people and of females.

The virulence and intimidation levelled at women, especially women of colour, by the intersectional feminist contingency advocating for these policy reforms demanded, according to Bailey, a social reckoning. With the aim of tackling this problem, she helped set up the LGB Alliance in 2019.[8] She tweeted in support for the organisation she co-founded and witnessed all hell break loose in her professional life.

Ruefully, Bailey herself would not be safe from the Postmodern Inquisition. Not even her legal chambers in London would protect her. In fact, Garden Court stands accused of colluding with LGBT lobby group Stonewall, in an attempt to punish her for her entirely lawful beliefs. She had previously raised concerns with her chambers about Stonewall's "Diversity Champions" scheme, to which Garden Court subscribes because, in her opinion, it allowed an activist organisation to police employees thoughts and opinions. And that is exactly what she says happened to her at her place of work.

Garden Court's stated philosophy is that their legal practice is visionary and bold, affirming:

> *Our motto, "Do right, fear no one," embodies our longstanding ethos: we are dedicated to fighting your corner, no matter how formidable the opponent might seem. Equally, our approach is progressive. We help many clients use the law to advance social justice and equality.*[9]

Allison Bailey would soon learn otherwise. As she started to publicly voice her concerns about a brewing conflict in law, Stonewall complained to Garden Court, which publicly announced that they had started a process to "investigate" her.

She wrote in the text for her *Crowdjustice* effort:

> *I realised that the new trans activism operated a crude but effective system of punishment and reward: agree with every demand of the trans lobby and be safe; object and face vilification, abuse, boycott, character assassination and cancellation. The label of transphobic has been applied to me and to others like me who recognise that sex is immutable.*
>
> *A person may identify as they identify, and they should be protected and respected for their identity. However, a person's identity is not a license to cause distress or intimidation to others, and can never legitimately be used to put others to harm. There are necessary exceptions to the acceptance of males in female spaces, and those exceptions are necessary to protect women.*[10]

Bailey's experience suggests that Garden Court's progressive vision and fearlessness does not extend to protecting their own Black, lesbian human rights defender from persecution. On the contrary, her chambers dragged her through an internal complaints process, while allegedly secretively coordinating with the outside lobby group regarding her. The complaint against her was upheld and thus, the viciousness which has rained upon her ever since, much of it constituting racialised abuse, became legitimised.

Predictably, feeling emboldened by the fact that yet another institution backed down in response to their howls for symbolic female sacrifice, far from receding, the bullies demanded more. Intersectional feminist warriors complained to the crowdfunding platform that the text in which she describes her background and announced her legal fight to challenge both her chambers and Stonewall, was in itself discriminatory. That is, it was alleged that the words of this Black barrister with a life-long dedication to justice were so unconscionably harmful that they ought to be censored. And equally predictably, within hours of the complaint, Crowdjustice removed Allison Bailey's page from public view, but not before she was able to raise an astonishing £60K in less than 24 hours. Such was the support for her case.

In these dynamics, we all get to witness the spectre of an intersection of oppressive systems rearing its head to put this measured lawyer back into the cynical toy box where all the "angry black woman," "rampant black woman" and "ignorant black woman" stereotypes fester. Sticking the knife in, the same crowdfunding platform which took a cut from all donations people gave towards Bailey's legal battle went one step further by attempting to remove her voice from the public domain, as if this woman's words humanising herself were best sight unseen. Whose social justice is this?

Moving forward, group-think free

The aforementioned UN Women's article on intersectional feminism made a point of not linking this theoretical approach to the actual word "women." It does feature the voices of campaigners whose work focuses on women and girls, but the international agency itself recoils from making the connection to females. Instead, it speaks of an unexplained "we," an imprecise "those," and the importance of striving towards a better future "for all."

A feminist theory which does not centre women and girls. A liberatory movement without a clear subject. What is feminism, if we do not strive for women's liberation? A care-giving political enterprise, preoccupied with the class struggles of everyone but ourselves? Have we learned nothing from our histories of struggle? Far from outdated, the old adage which states that unless we make a point of explicitly naming and centring women's lives and experiences in our efforts, they become invisibilised (at best), remains the norm in public life.

Today, Vaishnavi Sundar continues both to produce documentaries and to write articles problematising the material conditions of women and girls in India. Far from shying away from the conflict between sex-based rights and "gender identity" theory, she is in the process of producing a documentary about it. Undaunted, Sundar poignantly writes:

> By being outcast, I was essentially being told that the feminism I live by – the feminism of Mary Wollstonecraft, Emmeline Pankhurst and Andrea Dworkin – was exclusionary because it rejected males in female safe spaces. My intersectionality wasn't expansive enough to accommodate men. My feminism did not embrace the "choice" of carrying water for patriarchy.[11]

Cherry Smiley ploughs through, as well. The academic rejection and the targeting she has experienced at the hands of those who would otherwise celebrate her, had it not been for her defence of sex-based rights, has been enacted with the purpose of breaking her spirit. But she refuses to acquiesce to her own erasure:

No woman owes anyone a justification as to why she dares to say, in public no less, that she and other women matter. No woman should ever be asked, expected, or feel pressured to reveal to anyone the hurt men have caused to her to justify her analysis of issues that impact her. We don't owe anyone an apology or an explanation or a justification for saying that we are not menstruators. We are women, and we matter. We will continue to describe our bodies and realities as we know them to be.[12]

Same with Allison Bailey. Doing right and fearing no one, the lady lawyer defends herself from the edict forced upon her by so-called justice warriors. She pushes through, committing the ultimate sin by becoming the witch who, having being caught, refuses to repent:

I reject the suggestion by trans activists and their supporters, including so called anti-fascist journalists, that women like me must give way in our activism to more worthy causes and just shut up about our concerns about the new trans activism, as advocated for by Stonewall. This argument seems itself racist, misogynist, naive and self-indulgent.

Just as there may finally be a reckoning about racial injustice, I hope there may also one day soon be a similar reckoning about male violence, oppression and woman-hatred; including a reckoning about this moment in history when men tried to run off with women's rights.[13]

Although they all are lifelong campaigners for the human rights of females, Vaishnavi Sundar, Cherry Smiley, and Allison Bailey are vastly different women. Each one has faced hardships and privileges which could not be replicated in each other, due to the particularities of their upbringing and position in the world. But apart from their sex and their dedication to women's rights, something which they share is the ostracism and virulence they have been subjected to by proponents of intersectional feminism.

It was never Kimberlé Crenshaw's intention to exclude women who defend their sex from the all-encompassing prism her theoretical analysis provides. On the contrary, she admits that there have been "distortions" to its purpose and reminds those who utilise her analytical tool that it was never meant to be "identity politics on steroids."[14]

The legal scholar's warning has gone, so far, unheeded by her own self-professed disciples. Perhaps because "intersectional feminists" do not want to respect her intentions, and instead prefer to project their own reinterpretations of the theory, as opposed to what Crenshaw truly meant. She acknowledges this crux, stating during an interview with left-wing political magazine *Vox*:

> *Usually with ideas that people take seriously, they actually try to master them, or at least try to read the sources that they are citing for the proposition. Often, that doesn't happen with intersectionality, and there are any number of theories as to why that's the case, but what many people have heard or know about intersectionality comes more from what people say than what they've actually encountered themselves.*[15]

By deeming the women presented in this article as unacceptable, the age-old stereotypes of the ignorant Indian woman, the savage Indigenous woman, and the angry Black woman become reified in society's consciousness. None of them are anything of the sort, yet the weaponising of intersectionality theory has opened the door to activists who are usually far more privileged than they are to put them back in the oppressive place which patriarchy, imperialism, racism, and colonialism designed for women with their background.

By removing sex from the intersectionality prism, activists who have taken up its mantle without researching its source render it toothless. A theory which cannot address the material conditions of half of the population, including the segment within that who is born Black, represents a diluted and ineffective way of enacting structural transformation. This is contrary to what Kimberlé Crenshaw meant to do, so the slap that so-called social justice warriors are inflicting with their defanging of intersectionality theory is not only to the faces of Sundar, Smiley and Bailey, but to its author as well.

Far from repeating platitudes about diversity and inclusion, we ought to critically examine the oppressive behaviour being excused through the hijacking of an analytical tool which was meant to be liberational. What happens to the women who agree that our experiences involve overlapping, concurrent forms of oppression (and privilege) which we must untangle in other to better understand the depths of inequalities, but who also fight to defend our sex? What happens to the women who also agree that we need a liberatory approach which illuminates the connections between all fights for justice, but who equally want to centre females?

Sadly, as of 2020, it appears those women are still best left off the margins.

Endnotes

1   Crenshaw, Kimberlé. "Demarginalizing the Intersection of
    Race and Sex: A Black Feminist Critique of Antidiscrimination
    Doctrine, Feminist Theory and Antiracist Politics. 1989,
    https://chicagounbound.uchicago.edu/cgi/viewcontent.
    cgi?article=1052&context=uclf.

2   Crenshaw, Kimberlé. "Demarginalizing the Intersection of
    Race and Sex: A Black Feminist Critique of Antidiscrimination
    Doctrine, Feminist Theory and Antiracist Politics. 1989,
    https://chicagounbound.uchicago.edu/cgi/viewcontent.
    cgi?article=1052&context=uclf, p. 143.

3   "Intersectional feminism: what it means and why it matters right
    now." *UN Women*, 1 July 2020, https://www.unwomen.org/en/news/
    stories/2020/6/explainer-intersectional-feminism-what-it-means-
    and-why-it-matters.

4   Vaishnavi Sundar. "I was cancelled for my tweets on transgenderism,"
    Spiked, 4 March 2020, https://www.spiked-online.com/2020/03/04/i-
    was-cancelled-for-my-tweets-on-transgenderism/.

5   *Feminist Current*, https://www.feministcurrent.com/tag/cherry-
    smiley/.

6   Smiley, Cherry. "An open letter to the left regarding silence." *Feminist
    Current*, 5 May 2018, https://www.feministcurrent.com/2018/05/05/
    open-letter-left-regarding-silence/.

7   Cherry Smiley. Trudeau Scholar, PhD Communication, Concordia
    University website, https://www.concordia.ca/sgs/student-profiles/
    cherry-smiley.html.

8   LGB Alliance website, https://lgballiance.org.uk/.

9   Garden Court Chambers website, https://www.
    gardencourtchambers.co.uk/about.

10 Allison Bailey: "I am suing Stonewall to stop them policing free
    speech," *Woman's Place UK*, 27 June 2020, https://womansplaceuk.
    org/2020/06/27/i-am-suing-stonewall-stop-policing-free-speech/.

11 Vaishnavi Sundar. "I was cancelled for my tweets on transgenderism,"
    Spiked, 4 March 2020, https://www.spiked-online.com/2020/03/04/i-
    was-cancelled-for-my-tweets-on-transgenderism/.

12 Cherry Smiley, "Transwomen are women or else," *Medium*, 16 June 2020, https://medium.com/@clsmiley/transwomen-are-women-or-else-a996e4ac02c5.

13 Allison Bailey: "I am suing Stonewall to stop them policing free speech," *Woman's Place UK*, 27 June 2020, https://womansplaceuk.org/2020/06/27/i-am-suing-stonewall-stop-policing-free-speech/.

14 Katy Steinmetz, "She Coined the Term 'Intersectionality' Over 30 Years Ago. Here's What It Means to Her Today," *Time*, 20 Feb. 2020, https://time.com/5786710/kimberle-crenshaw-intersectionality/.

15 Jane Coaston, "The intersectionality wars," *Vox*, 28 May 2019, https://www.vox.com/the-highlight/2019/5/20/18542843/intersectionality-conservatism-law-race-gender-discrimination.

CHAPTER 13

Oil and Water: Young Migrant Women and the Promises of Liberal Feminism

Interviewed by Bec Wonders

1. **Profiles**
2. **Laying the Groundwork: Feminist Principles**
   a. Defining "Feminism"
   b. Liberal vs. Radical Feminism
   c. Examples of Liberal Feminism
   d. Envisioning a Feminist World
3. **Young, Migrant, Female: Intersections**
   a. Influenced by the Migrant Journey
   b. Difficulties Facing Young Feminists Today
   c. Messages for Young Migrant Feminists
4. **Intergenerational Approaches: Thinking Through the Past, Towards the Future**
   a. Improving Intergenerational Cooperation
   b. Practical Steps to Incorporate Young Female Migrants
   c. Hopes and Plans for the Future of the Feminist Movement

Profiles
Interviewed by Bec Wonders

Bec Wonders

Bec is a 27-year-old feminist scholar. She was born in Sweden to Dutch and Canadian parents and grew up in Germany. Bec co-founded the Vancouver Women's Library in 2017 while pursuing a Masters in Publishing. She also founded the Frauenkultur Archive: an online repository of second-wave feminist book titles. Bec is currently completing her Ph.D. at the Glasgow School of Art in the history of feminist publishing during the Women's Liberation Movement.

In conversation with

Yağmur Uygarkizi

Yağmur is a 24-year-old feminist who was born in Turkey, grew up in Italy and France, and studied in the UK. She is interested in male violence or discriminatory practices against women that are not commonly perceived as such, specifically prostitution-pornography and veiling. She has translated, written, and spoken on those issues and she's always more than happy to sneak into random people's casual conversations about those practices if she senses nonsense. She is the co-creatress of Radical Girlsss, the young women's movement of the European Network of Migrant Women.

Natasha Noreen

Natasha is a 26-year-old feminist and activist advocating for migrant and women's rights in Italy and Pakistan. She is a member of the European Network of Migrant Women and Radical Girlsss. Natasha volunteers in several local associations that promote the inclusion of economic migrants and asylum seeker migrants within

Italian society. She is also the founder of Feminism Pakistan: a Facebook community that promotes feminist discussion in Pakistan.

Adriana Thiago

Adriana is a 27-year-old Portuguese-Brazilian feminist and graduated in International Relations. Born in Luxembourg to Portuguese and Brazilian parents, she currently lives in Belgium. She studied in Madrid and has lived in Rio de Janeiro to reconnect to her culture of origin. Adriana has worked both as an activist in civil society associations and governmental organizations within the migration sector in Europe and Latin America. She now works for the European Network of Migrant Women and is a co-convenor of its Young Women's Movement, RadicalGirlsss, where she strives for a global radical feminist perspective and the end of sexual exploitation.

Alyssa Ahrabare

Alyssa is a 25-year-old French feminist from Moroccan and Algerian origins. She has a Masters in International Law with a specialization in human rights and fundamental liberties and she is an international consultant on women and human rights. Alyssa is a spokeswoman for the French organization Osez le Féminisme! (trans. "Dare to be Feminist!") Alyssa is the Project Officer for the European Network of Migrant Women and a co-convenor of its young women's movement Radical Girlsss. She is also a member of the Women in Politics group of the European Women's Lobby, as well as the founder of a theatre company which uses art and pedagogy to promote equality between women and men.

Laying the groundwork: feminist principles

What does it mean to you to be a feminist? How do you define "feminism"?

225

Adriana: I think for me to be a feminist means to strive for the collective liberation of all women. It means to start from the personal, and then to try and find the balance between theory and practice. It's like pieces on a chessboard: it doesn't make sense to think of only one piece winning the game. We all must collaborate in order to be strategic in the struggle. Being a feminist means aligning oneself with sisters in the fight towards the collective liberation of women.

Alyssa: I also think that being a feminist involves sisterhood: this kind of deep and invaluable love that specifically exist between women who understand that we are in this together. It means realizing that the war against women exists and it is global. It's also about understanding that one of the best weapons of patriarchy is to divide us and prevent us from considering ourselves as a group, a class. Culturally, girls and women are often put in competition. We have countless representations of rivalry between women. It's really common to hear that we are mean to one another and that it's so much nicer to hang out with men. That's an intentional lie. Women can love and support each other because we are part of a class that shares a history, a memory, a combat, and a common goal. If we unite, if we manage to share a common consciousness of what it is to be a woman, we are a political and cultural force to be reckoned with. For me, that's the very essence of the feminist fight.

Natasha: I honestly had very similar thoughts. It's a long journey, feminism, and I can't limit it to one definition, because for me it began on an individual level, and then it grew to include the way I think about my family, to even further beyond that. But essentially it comes from within, it's the awareness of your womanhood. As a feminist you try to feel, analyze, and contextualize your own oppression, asking questions like "Where does it come from?" The more you question this, the deeper you go and the closer you come to what Adriana mentioned: the realization that you want to liberate all women, not just on a singular, individual level. So, for me, being a feminist is just being a woman, honestly, it's like when Maya Angelou said that it would be stupid not to be on my own side. So, being a feminist is being a woman but also understanding the core of womanhood: knowing that it's not a feeling, but a lived reality that we have to keep on living in from the time we are born to the time we die.

Yagmur: I think, in essence, that feminism is the ideology and movement that strives for the liberation of women and girls from the system of male dominance, which is patriarchy. I think that in practice what this means is realizing how much men hate women, you know. This idea comes from Germaine Greer who says that "women have very little idea of how much men hate them," which is also terrible because she says "them" and not "us," making the statement vague instead of specific. I always make this mistake as well, but I think this shows how unpopular it is to be on your own side. How can we realize our own subjugation when people constantly tell me that's not true? Well, I have a lot of empirical evidence to corroborate my claim, so it's about having the courage to realize the hatred that men have for us.

What are the differences between Liberal and Radical feminism?

Adriana: If I'm being really honest, perhaps it is kind of harsh but for me, it's the truth: I don't think you can put "liberal" and "feminism" in the same sentence. So-called "Liberal feminism" has made us believe that it's a legitimate feminist position and that we have the choice to stand on either side. But if we really want to strive for a global feminist movement and perspective, I think we really got to challenge the idea that a Capitalist mode of functioning can be called feminism. It just puts a price tag on our movement. The central difference, I would say, is that Liberal feminism is more than an ideology or modus operandi, it is a catch-all *inclusivity* movement that prevents women from naming ourselves as a class of people.

Alyssa: I agree, and I think it's also important to state that historically, Liberal feminism stems from political Liberalism and its economic manifestation: Capitalism. The notion of individual freedom is key to understanding this.

Adriana: Exactly. Radical feminism is really the basis, the root, the extremely uncomfortable and painful reality, but it's a fundamental analysis of the origin of our oppression. It goes beyond the reality of male violence and asks the question of *why* male violence exists in the first place. Getting to the root of the problem of patriarchy and understanding its various ramifications is what differentiates Radical feminism from the Capitalist movement that is Liberal feminism.

Natasha: As young women in the patriarchal system, we are never made to love the idea of feminism or of self-love. So, our first expression of self-love manifests as Liberal feminism, it doesn't come from within, it comes from this superficial, fake surrounding: it's an illusion. Young girls are being seduced with cute t-shirts, glitter, queer theory, and rainbows. Liberal feminism is the extreme manifestation of patriarchy, I one hundred percent agree with Adriana. Liberal feminism is an oxymoron. Within the patriarchal system, where choices are made for us already, Liberal feminism is the toxic choice for women and girls all around the world.

Alyssa: Totally. For Liberal feminists, the Capitalist society can be reformed and bettered. The system itself can remain untouched and as a result, the Liberal feminist approach serves perfectly to protect the structures of inequality.

Natasha: I also think that the issue of veiling is a perfect metaphor for Liberal feminism: just as you can't be Liberal and a feminist, you also cannot cover your face and your identity and engage in a deeply entrenched misogynistic culture while proclaiming that it is a feminist choice. These masks, whether they be veils or makeup, are fake costumes that cover up misogyny.

Adriana: I sometimes feel bad for the women who really believe that they are being feminist, because, ultimately, it's not really their fault. At the individual level, I can't help but feel sad for so many young women who are brought into this. I don't know if that makes sense.

Natasha: I totally feel the same because today, within Asian communities, there are women who have an extreme love for their tradition and their culture, which underneath are toxic women-hating practices. It's extremely painful to see how they romanticize these traditions. The conversation is increasingly taking men out of the equation and it's becoming about women versus women. This has been a very difficult shift to witness.

Bec: This is the great patriarchal lie that women have come to believe: Liberal feminism is the most rewarding and effective form of feminism. By reframing what is really anti-feminism as feminism, we end up in that situation that Natasha describes where women are pitted against women. It's very effective, and it's working.

Yagmur: It is taxidermy. It is men hunting down feminism, scraping out the inside, keeping the skin, and filling it up with basic patriarchal principles. They label it "feminism" and hang it on a wall as a trophy. This is exactly what's going on. Feminism has been reduced to "being," when it really should be about "doing." We're losing the idea of "deeds not words." Feminism is not an identity. I even struggle to find "feminism" being used as a standalone word, I struggle finding "woman" on its own. It's always "something"-woman, "something"-feminist. The more you put adjectives in front, the more it becomes about the adjective and less about the word that it's supposed to qualify.

It's such a huge request to ask women to realize that men hate us. Whether we like it or not, we are in bed with the enemy. That's quite unique because usually with other subjugated groups, such as racially discriminated communities, there exist geographically segregated spaces. The oppressor and the oppressed typically don't mix in physical spaces. But to open your eyes and realize that your father hates you because he watches pornography, your boyfriend hates you because he fetishizes other women, is just such a massive realization to make.

Alyssa: This also relates to how our oppression started with the idea of private property. The necessity for men to control their descendants in order to keep property in the blood line was at the basis of heteronormativity, monogamy and imprisonment of women in the domestic sphere. Women become a vehicle by which private property and the male lineage is maintained.

Yagmur: It reminds me of the story "The Princess and the Pea": the pea is on the bottom, layered beneath mattresses, the princess lays on top, and if she feels the pea, she is the genuine princess. Feminism is like that: can you *feel it* under all the layers of glamour and propaganda? Are you willing to realize what's going on? One of the ingenious ways in which the patriarchal ideology is achieved is to frame the discourse as a disagreement between women. In actuality, there is a conflict between men and women, but this historical power dynamic is made invisible when women are pitted against each other.

Bec: The one thing that I've been thinking about a lot is how really impossible women's liberation is. I don't mean to say that to sound cynical, or to say it's not worth fighting for. But to really understand the extent to which women are embedded in patriarchy is to understand that, you know, we are surrounded by men. This distinction you mentioned between other kinds of groups, that are in geographically different locations, are more likely to develop a sense of togetherness because they're physically in a different place to their oppressor. Women are everywhere. We're everywhere in every single facet of society in every class in every race and so, how to generate that sense of class consciousness between women, I think, is, you know, maybe to say impossible is a little bit hyperbolic but I think it's, it's extremely difficult.

Adriana: Can I just say, this made me think of a quote by Andrea Dworkin, who said that "The tragedy is that women so committed to survival cannot recognize that they are committing suicide." We're so committed to change and political activism, but there is always a chance that behind the next corner there is a man who will cut our throats with a knife just because he can. It can happen at any moment. So, like, the fact that we're putting ourselves out there and showing up, it can ultimately lead towards our demise as well.

Bec: This, to me, is feminism: taking risks, you know, confronting the violence in the world, and confronting it even though you know there will be repercussions as bad as rape or death. To me is what the political feminist movement is about. And I think that is a huge distinction: the actual feminist struggle involves dangerous territory, it is uncomfortable, it can lead to backlash, but we do it anyway.

What are some examples of Liberal Feminism in your own lives?

Yagmur: In my experience, the superficial notion of "consent" is having disastrous consequences. I have friends who are complying to things they don't want, simply because they say, "I consent." I have friends who are being tied up and being hit by their boyfriends, thinking that this is what sex entails. I had a friend who was confronted by a man who said he had never slapped a woman, and her immediate reaction was to assume that he had no sexual experience. Some of my male friends are really confused that women are defending violent sexual practices and prostitution so wholeheartedly. Everything is flipped. It's the classic tale of The Beauty and The Beast: an arranged marriage takes place, where they tell the woman that if she grins and bears it, and if she is kind enough, she will start to see him as a handsome man. I feel that it describes perfectly what's going on in the context of sexual violence: if we just grin and bear it, it's easier than actually challenging it.

Bec: What do you make of the fact that BDSM and rope tying is becoming really fashionable? In my context, it's mostly women who are requesting this and wanting to do this and arguing that it's empowering. How do you make sense of that?

Yagmur: I've recently come across this term which has been recently circulating in French feminist circles: "traumatic genital excitement." It essentially involves looking back to the thing that provided you pleasure, even though it might have been a traumatic experience. It's about being addicted to your own trauma, through sexual violence, because it might stimulate you. It's as if pain were pleasure. But the pleasure actually comes from *ending* the pain. Pain is still pain. So again, we have this state of reversal where things are things they're not: men are women, pain is pleasure, violence is kindness.

Natasha: It's also important to mention that from a global perspective, I have noticed that women are only getting the Liberal feminist messaging and are finding it very confusing. It is heartbreaking to see that these young women are being bombarded with these distorted notions of pleasing the man next to them. It hurts the core of my existence.

Alyssa: I think that the concept of "individual liberty" is one of those harmful messages which lies at the core of the Liberal feminist message. Take prostitution, for instance: from the Liberal feminist perspective, prostitution can be a free, empowering choice. But this is so clearly intellectual fiction! From a global perspective, women have less economic opportunities, we are poorer, we have been taught to understand our bodies as value-generating vessels, we are often abused and raped at a very young age, resulting in psycho traumas that make us more vulnerable to traffickers, the list goes on... If prostitution were a free choice, why are women and girls disproportionately represented, especially those of us with migrant backgrounds? How can it be a free choice when the median age of entering prostitution is 13? Liberal feminism cannot meaningfully contend with structural inequalities as long as individual freedom is heralded as the primary marker of liberation. I would go so far as to saying that Liberal feminism is entirely complicit in the system that oppresses us.

Natasha: I found out quickly that the only way to be accepted in Liberal feminist circles is to say "yes, sorry, yes ma'am, yes sir" like a puppet. Obviously, in a patriarchal society and male-dominated culture, women are never going to be heard. But now, even in women-only spaces and women's groups, there is a complete lack of dialogue. There is an entire set of questions and arguments that you cannot touch. This new normal turns those women who ask questions into the enemy, the monster. This is what I experienced. I never understood why I was being called names and vilified. These women are being made to see me as their enemy just because I am asking questions. I know that for me it has been crucial to ask questions. If I hadn't been able to ask questions or discuss my doubts, I wouldn't be sitting here today thinking, questioning, and trying to save other women's lives.

Even in the context of Indian subcontinent, it is very much the same. Older women are being eaten up by these Western Capitalist theories of equating male feelings about identity to women being killed and raped. This message is being conveyed so effectively, that even women who have actual grassroots knowledge of feminism and the clerical society, still cannot understand the consequences of having any dialogue in feminist spaces.

Adriana: I definitely agree with Yagmur. I'm noticing really worrying things about sex. It has affected me personally. Before I really understood the basic notions of feminism, I didn't consider myself a feminist because I didn't agree with the Liberal currents. So I thought, okay, I'm not a feminist because I don't believe in this message. I didn't realize that there were other streams of feminist thought.

I've also noticed a lot of worrying trends while being an activist in the migration sector for the last six years. There is a wave of depoliticization happening regarding migrant women, who are being made to believe that they can opt out of their oppression. It really makes me angry to see so many women in refugee centers, all the while Liberal feminists are talking about identity and self-empowerment. But what are they doing about the last girl? The last woman? There are still migrants being tortured in detention centers, little girls being raped in Libya, sex dolls coming from China with the bodies of five-year-old girls. We are making society stupid. I really think that we're turning young people into thoughtless, unquestioning people who don't have any capacity for critical thinking and just gobble down anything that is set in front of them.

Yagmur: When you were talking about refugee camps, it made me think about a good way to have a feminist barometer, by asking:

how does this message help stop female genital mutilation? How does this help stop rape? In other words: how does wearing a choker and nipple tassels on Instagram concretely tackle global femicide?

Adriana: Exactly. The inequalities that we have been trying to fight for decades, like race and class inequalities, are actually being exacerbated by Liberal feminism. They forget that their "feminism" has become an elite discourse for people who can read Judith Butler and other postmodern theorists. Meanwhile, as they label us "white feminists," the majority of women who cannot speak up for themselves are being left on the sidelines. They are turning women away who are not in the position to read or understand postmodern theory, and we're letting the elite lecture us about colonizing the discourse.

Yagmur: But it's also not good for themselves. It reminds me of Andrea Dworkin saying that "Feminism is a political practice of fighting male supremacy on behalf of women as a class, including all the women you don't like." Liberal feminists are trapped in their immediate bubbles of agreement and forgetting to think about women as a global class. This is why I'm also quite troubled by the objectivization of "white feminism," the idea that white women and rich women are horrible, I really don't believe that. I live in a quite wealthy neighborhood, and I can guarantee you that there is a systemic level of teaching women to be submissive in these circles. These women might think that they are free, because they have money, but it's not even their own money - it's their fathers, it's their husbands. Thinking that our affiliation to male categories of society will save us is simply not true.

Adriana: Yeah, and the fact that all the revolutionary movements are losing their energy. Because everything that is "anti-systemic" today is considered fashionable. But actually, people don't realize that they're fighting for the status quo to be maintained. And there's nothing revolutionary in adhering to norms that only serve to exacerbate our oppression. So, I think, there is a huge impact on all social movements. They are becoming catch-all terms for whatever the newest fashionable rhetoric is, rather than focusing on building coalitions across differences. Take, for example, the mass graveyards of black migrants in the Mediterranean Sea. Where is the outrage?

What would an ideal feminist world look like to you?

Natasha: My immediate thought was a world with no men. But beyond that, I envision a society in which female bodies are not controlled. But it is difficult to realize, because one of the main functions of patriarchal power convinces us that actually, we want to be controlled. I often imagine what it would be like without being socialized through generations of patriarchal history, without all the norms and values of male culture. Even thinking about "female domination" seems pretty patriarchal in its formulation.

Bec: I mean, that is a good point because really, it's an impossible question. How do you envision a feminist world from the point of view of being so embedded in patriarchy? It's like trying to imagine how birds view the world in ultraviolet color.

Yagmur: I think a feminist world would mean living out our full potentials, to do anything we would like to without that thing that is keeping us back (that thing obviously being male violence). The important question here being: What's next, after feminism? What would I be doing if I weren't doing feminism? Finding your passion is incredibly important as a way of defining yourself outside of the fight against male violence. Who are you without men?

Bec: Exactly, when feminism becomes too much of an identity, I suppose you fall into a situation of defining yourself against the world, and so you're always in opposition. I think it's so important to imagine the world that you are *for*, the world in which you can become someone who is defined by yourself, rather than by outside forces.

Adriana: For me it's a very difficult question, because there's literally no point of reference for a feminist world. It's not like we knew a time in which women were free. But I think a feminist world would be a world in which we don't see girls under 18 with their ears pierced. I know this might seem a little bit specific, but I'm from a

Latin culture in which newborn girls are immediately categorized in opposition to boys by getting their ears pierced. It is the first mark of the expectations of femininity and submissiveness. You can't even talk, you can't even say what your favorite color is, but you are already socialized as the "other."

Alyssa: I agree with Adriana, to me, an ideal feminist world is one where choices are not conditioned by one's sex. So, it is a world in which discrimination does not start as soon as the ultrasound shows the baby's sex. Boys and girls would play together, girls wouldn't feel less intelligent, sexual violence would be faced head-on, everyone would be taught that mutual desire should be at the basis of any human interaction and girls wouldn't have "eating disorders" because there would be no unachievable ideas of beauty.

Adriana: I have also been thinking a lot about "eating disorders." In an ideal feminist world, no woman would be sick. There wouldn't even be this measure of "eating too much" or "eating too little," because this is not something that we would impose on one another. We wouldn't have medicalized and sick girls.

Bec: I think that's such a good point, women would not be sick. The distinction between the self and the body would no longer be there, because the body would be liberated, and by the body being liberated, women become liberated. And so, in a feminist world there would be more of an identification with the body. Eating disorders, prostitution, rape, violence, compulsory femininity - all of this involves disassociation from your body. You have to remove yourself from your femaleness. Bridging that gap between the self and the body would completely change the way women position themselves and see themselves in the world.

Alyssa: Precisely, I think that a feminist world would mean that women are no longer trapped by high heels and tight clothes that prevent us from running, or long nails that prevent us from grabbing. It is also a world where men would be able to wear tight clothes and make up, where boys would be able to play with dolls and wear pink. Basically, we would be able to meaningfully control our own bodies.

Adriana: Exactly, everything is imposed on our bodies because it's the material site of violence in control and coercion is manifested. I just want to feel whole. In my ideal world women would be whole. We are not half of an orange - we're the entire fruit.

Young, migrant, female: Intersections

How has your migrant background influenced the way you think about feminism?

Yagmur: So, I'm Turkish and I've grown up mainly in France. One of the best ways I can describe the migration experience is like being in the back of a car. The car is going really fast, so you're moving, migrating, and you're seeing everything that's going on around you and it's beautiful. But you're stuck in the car. And that's the feeling that I have. I also think that this idea of cultural relativism is doing so much damage, because we must recognize that there are incremental improvements between countries and the way they treat women. I have to be honest and say that I would never want to live in Iraq or Iran as a woman. At the same time as a migrant woman you can't access "the better life" as easily as your fathers or brothers. There are two different articulations of patriarchy migrant women have to live with: the traditional family unit and the Liberal state of patriarchy.

A turning point for me was realizing that racism would stop the moment I step back into Turkey, but I am a woman wherever I go. This was the biggest realization for me in understanding the female condition.

Alyssa: It's interesting because even though I experienced sexism since childhood, I only noticed later on that the racism I encounter is inherently tied to me being a woman. I was born in France to Moroccan and Algerian parents, and I often experience sexual harassment on the basis that I am deemed "exotic." But this racism does not only react to my migrant background, it specifically aims at the fact that I am a *woman* with a migrant background. People assume that I am Muslim and so I constantly get asked why I don't wear a veil, and every time I appear on television or the press I am hounded with racist and sexist comments. This gave me a strong understanding of *intersectionality*, you know, in the way that different characteristics result in a specific kind of discrimination which cannot be separated. I also think it is important to integrate the concept of *universalism*, which is the notion that there are fundamental rights common to every human being, regardless of religious or cultural context. I understand universalism and intersectionality as complementary: the universal declaration of human rights must consider the intersections of oppression, while intersectionality must also avoid cultural relativism. This balance is incredibly important. My migrant background has taught me that it is impossible to be a feminist without taking a stance against Colonialism and Capitalism.

Adriana: I also think that my migration background has affected me, because I don't like saying that I'm Brazilian, for example. When I say that I'm Brazilian I'm automatically sexualized, and I believe that's one of the reasons why I've for so many years I've rejected my body. Just the simple fact of saying that I am Brazilian is very difficult for me, because I think it opens a door in men's mind that I'm sexually available and sexually more fun. This has placed me in competition with other women and brought so many problems that I never asked for.

I was born in Luxembourg to Portuguese and Brazilian parents, but I never really felt at home there. Even when I go back to Brazil, I'm considered the "gringa," you know, my skin tone is light even though my family is darker. My migration background has also influenced the way I talk about class and racism, and how I position myself in relation to women that are in far worse situations than I am. I don't know what it's like to be discriminated against for the color of my skin, but I've been sexually assaulted and have witnessed firsthand what happens to women in Brazil and Portugal. There is a certain level of sadness involved in not "belonging" to a specific country, but my background has also provided me with a unique lens through which global forms of misogyny and the common experience of women has become apparent.

Natasha: I'm trying not to cry because I can relate to exactly what you're saying. I was once asked about what it means to be a migrant woman, and before that I never thought of myself as belonging to this category. Now, after having lived in Italy for 11 years and moving to various other places within Europe, I have lost the concept of "migrant feminist." I no longer see women as being oppressed because of their nationalities, instead I have realized that it's because of our female bodies. Female bodies are being controlled universally, either in the name of Islam in Pakistan or in other Muslim countries, or by the name of Liberal feminism in Western Capitalist countries. This is what the migration experience has gifted me: the ability to connect on an emotional level with women everywhere.

Also, the cornerstone of this consciousness is realizing that women's suffering is often positioned simply as "humanistic" suffering. I have noticed that the women's sector in Europe and Pakistan has very little feminist analysis. The female struggle has become a fight to see women as equal to men – positioning men as the aspiration of what it means to be human. In other words: the more male-like presence you have, the more admiration and respect you will receive. Instead, the Radical feminist analysis allows us to understand our subjugation based on sex, which is a unique kind of domination that cannot be made sense of on the same plain as other forms of violence.

Adriana: From my perspective, what can often happen is that women are positioned against other women from the beginning of the migration journey. There is of course a need to be able to articulate the specifics of Latina, or black, or working-class women – but what is actually happening, in my experience, is that women are being increasingly subdivided into "othering" categories that prevent the overlap of our common experience.

Bec: Everything that you're saying echoes this phrase by Juliet Mitchell from her 1971 book *Woman's Estate*, where she talks about "the commonality underlying the diversity." It seems that difference and diversity is being accounted for, but the commonality isn't, and so we end up in this situation of division and unbreachable categories.

Yagmur: When we prioritize these different categories in trying to understand what it means to be a woman, it becomes overly individualized. How many women can you find that all share the same sub-categories of experience? The scope becomes reduced and it becomes impossible to name the common experience of women. Misogyny has one variable, and that is sex. Of course, as a woman you will have multiple identities and factors at play that determine the way you will be seen and treated in society, I'm not denying that. But when you are oppressed as a woman, across all nationalities, ethnicities, and cultures – it is the female sex which matters. And again, I cannot insist enough that whatever patriarchy gives, patriarchy takes. So, if you're advantaged because you have access to money, all that money will go towards your looks. It has become a race to the bottom. Women say they are privileged just because they can eat and are not subjected to daily violence. What should be basic human rights are now privileges that women must apologize for.

In your own context, what is the most difficult challenge about being a young feminist today?

Natasha: I'm still situated in a traditional family setup. So, my first difficulty is within my own room. I have been conditioned by traditions that I had no part in shaping. Within my family there are so many women that I would like to help, but I can't. There is a constant struggle of wanting to fight for the liberation of all women, yet within my own family I can do very little. The second most difficult thing is the constant brainwashing through mainstream media of being positive, upbeat and happy. I question myself continuously about whether I am on the right path, because the acceptable face

240

of feminism is covered in glitter, positivity and empowerment. My reality is very different – it is dark, painful and uncomfortable. This reality is not being named, and so it becomes impossible to address the problem.

Alyssa: In France, for me, the main challenge for young women is that there seems to be a general acceptance that the feminist fight ended some time ago. Most people do not acknowledge the overwhelming amount of untold, unpunished violence and injustice that still remains, for example pornography. Pornography is one of the main problems for young women because it promotes the idea that sexuality is inseparable from violence. It legitimates male violence against women and girls because it relies on an essentialist vision of the sexes: women actually enjoy being humiliated to experience sexual pleasure. Spanking, whipping, filmed rape... Pornography is teaching young girls (and boys) that women belong in a submissive role. Violence, humiliation and dehumanisation of women and girls are key to getting as many views as possible.

Adriana: The biggest challenge for me is this sense of doom that things are getting gradually worse. I also feel a lot of pressure and responsibility to act out of urgency, but there is also a general sense for young women that we cannot bring anything new to the table because we're too busy trying to find a job or getting university degrees. I'm actually scared for the future, especially considering all this talk about transhumanism, artificial intelligence and the increasing pornification of society. I'm really worried about the younger generations; my heart actually is bleeding for them. The main difficulty I experience is this constant feeling of not doing enough.

Yagmur: One of the main difficulties in my view is the fact that, as young women, we will often actively campaign against ourselves. And so, when we try to engage in feminist dialogue, we have to be prepared not only for men, but for many women being against us. You feel like you are in another era. We are forced into being clandestine. Meanwhile we know that there is a very powerful, unashamed pimp lobby which is rebranding women's subordination

241

as empowerment, a fact that is often met with disbelief by other women.

What message needs to be conveyed to other young migrant women, that they are not currently hearing? Is there a message you wish you would have heard as a young migrant girl, coming from older feminists?

Adriana: I would tell young migrant women to not let their oppression be morally and culturally normalized and sexualized. It's a hard question for me. As a young girl I would have loved to be introduced to more Second Wave feminist texts, but I would have also needed someone to explain how this theory relates to my own reality.

Alyssa: I want to relay to girls that they can challenge sexist representations of women. I would advise them not to reproduce the violence they see, and to not let themselves be dehumanized by anyone. That they learn to listen to themselves, their desires and their limits. That they open themselves to feminism and then support other girls to do the same. On the other hand, something which I would have wished to hear from older feminists is more teaching about the harms and dangers of online violence, whether that be on social media or pornography websites. This violence is not less worrisome just because it seems to be virtual, on the contrary, it has lethal consequences and it is too often wrongly brushed aside.

Yagmur: I would want other young migrant women to understand that their culture will not protect them. Something I wish I would have been told is that the body never lies. If your body says no, it means you are saying no. And you are allowed to verbalize that. But in general, I have been very blessed in the feminist relationships I have cultivated, and I always hear the words of Fiona Broadfoot: "Radical Feminism saved my life," which is my experience also. I have benefited a lot from older feminists being upfront and not being afraid to speak truth to power. This makes me really worried because I feel that younger women are not willing to discuss or debate things, as everything must increasingly be delivered with velvet boxing gloves. We are losing the ability to name the female experience.

Adriana: This reminds me of experiencing younger women writing each other off if one of them is confident and outspoken about a certain topic. It's like being clear and firm is a taboo, instead women must be vague and apologetic to be taken seriously. I think that we need to learn how to communicate better with younger generations.

Bec: It's one of the greatest tools of patriarchy: making women afraid of each other's true speech and resent each other for that, resent each other for what we could be, but what we're not.

Natasha: Personally, I would like to see my fellow girls, feminist or not, to have enough self-confidence from a very young age so they do not require male validation. I would have loved to know that, and to be encouraged to be vocal about things I disagree with. Being vocal about your anger, being unafraid to talk about trauma. I never had that feminist perspective because it was always portrayed as ugly and dark. I would like for young girls around the world to encounter clearer and more engaging feminist messages.

Intergenerational Approaches: Thinking Through the Past, Towards the Future

What is something that could improve intergenerational cooperation?

Alyssa: Recently I participated in a feminist video contest on the theme of the Women's Liberation Movement. We looked at feminist archives with interviews, pictures from protests, songs, and political posters. This was incredibly inspiring, and it can enable young feminists to realize that we are a part of something bigger than just our present condition. It has the potential of creating sisterhood between generations. I think that we should also create more spaces where we can meet, debate and learn from one another. I am always so moved by the emotion of older feminists when we meet in conferences, when they come to me to say that I am part of the new generation, as if they were passing me a torch. This realization is so important: we are not alone, we do not need to reinvent the wheel because we have inherited the thoughts, the words, the analysis, the defeats and the victories of our older sisters.

Natasha: The first thing that comes to mind is being able to dialogue better in between generations. When we talk about intergenerational problems, I feel like it comes from poor communication with each other. We are all at different stages of womanhood and a lot of what differentiates generations tends to get lost in translation. Empathic communication is needed to bring both ends to a constructive solution.

Adriana: I agree with Natasha that a lot of empathy is needed in both directions. A lot of people say that conflict within the feminist movement is a generational issue – but it's not – it's an ideological issue. I don't agree with some younger feminists when they define themselves in opposition to older feminists. Where would we be without the persecuted women who dared to resist? The blame is being put on older women, which misrepresents the structural forces of male culture. But at the same time, on a practical level, I wish that older women wouldn't expect so much of younger women. I used to flip burgers to be able to survive and militate in feminist organizations. I realize that there is virtually no money to pay young women to do feminist activism, but please don't expect me to be energetic because one day I will have a breakdown. It is no coincidence that most feminists are tired as hell, and many have mental health issues.

Bec: Yeah, there seems to be this dual necessity for empathy. On the one hand, older women, expecting a lot from the younger generation, but on the other hand young women today define themselves in opposition to older women and believe that they are going to correct the failures of history, which creates this artificial divide between generations. That really serves patriarchal methods. Women have rebelled and resisted since the beginning, and the idea that there were no women, or that only certain women are selectively recovered to fit a contemporary narrative, is very harmful.

Adriana: But this is something that is done on purpose. Gendered marketing instils this message into young women who are scared to grow up, scared to accept the effects of time on their bodies. They look at older women and think "I don't want to be like this. I don't want to be old." This also relates to trans activism, in the way that we are prevented from naming our mothers. They want to cut any ties that we have with previous generations so there's no continuum. I think we should be giving intergenerational dialogue a lot more thought because our livelihood depends on it.

Bec: As you say it's intentional in the way that each new generation of women must relearn lessons from the movement. There's no continuation of learning, and so every time the movement must re-energize and start from scratch, rather than building from previous efforts. This is very intentional.

Yagmur: It's interesting what you say about the fear of getting old. I often use the analogy of Little Red Riding Hood to explain what is going on: the wolf, who is disguised as a woman, eats the grandmother first. He doesn't just eat the little girl straight away. He makes sure that the old woman, the wise woman, is attacked first, to make sure that there will be no retaliation against him. It's really dangerous for men if we get close to that knowledge and wisdom which older women have cultivated.

What is a practical step that other women can take to better incorporate the experience of young migrant women in their feminist organizing?

Adriana: We have to remember that, even though we are all women, we have different cultural codes. I think it's easy for us as radical feminists to talk about sex and pornography, but many girls feel deeply ashamed and are unwilling to address these topics. So we must become creative with our language. Many radical feminists are online, but there are even more women around the world who

245

do not have an internet connection or a phone. These basic things sometimes need reminding of. We have to put into practice what we're learning in the books.

Alyssa: It is also important not to be "maternalistic" and for white woman to resist the attitude of knowing what's best. A migrant woman arriving from the "economic south" to a "developed country" will not necessarily be able to break free from her chains. To me, it is also key not to allow cultural relativism in the name of so-called tolerance. It is crucial to facilitate spaces for women of colour to be able to freely talk about the specific violence we face. When organisations want to include migrant women in their work, everyone involved should address their own behaviour in relation to the issue of racism. I am reminded of a phrase by Pat Parker, when she says that "the first thing you must do is forget I am Black. The second is never forget I am black." What she means is that, while treating every sister the same way, we must never forget the specific, intertwined violence that women face when oppressions intersect.

Natasha: In my experience we must scratch the surface, so that we can move closer to understand the layers in between. Especially within the migrant context, what we need to do is to encourage women to scratch the surface of their lives to come closer to who they are, outside of the norms and traditions that have defined them. Asking two or three general questions about their personal lives will help uncover their individual potential.

Yagmur: Women are not pieces of furniture as Anna Zobnina says, we are not for the taking, to be rearranged. I remember a quote by Malcolm X saying, "don't condemn if you see a person has a dirty glass of water, just show them the clean glass of water that you have." I think this is a useful attitude towards feminism that goes beyond the categorical subdivisions. You know, it's not in my interest that you join the movement, it's in your interest.

What are your hopes and plans for the future of the feminist movement?

246

Yagmur: I always visualize a feminist tribunal, where we will finally have recognition of the male violence that was done to us, recognition of our status as victims, retribution for the damage inflicted on us and reparations. That keeps me going.

Adriana: What you just said blew my mind, we need to be asking for reparations. There is a genocide of women, a femicide, and there always will be until we collectively refuse it. It's time to ask for reparations. On a practical level I think women in the feminist movement need to be communicating better with each other. We're scared to communicate and say how we feel. We're not honest with each other, when we really owe it to ourselves and each other to be honest. Our socialization gets in the way of our communication, and I think one of the biggest challenges is moving from the "saying" to the "doing."

Alyssa: I hope for more unity and collaboration between women, activists, artists, scientists, organisations, politicians, and funders. We all have something to contribute to the movement and a role to play in it. My focus is on changing the narrative through arts and communications, putting forward new stories, new views in order to transform attitudes. We need analysts and scientists collecting more data for activists. We need feminist women represented in the political system to implement legislative progress. We need women in high places and women remaining on the grassroots level to be able to speak up and protest. My hope is for every woman, every girl, to be able to think for herself and support her sisters. I want to see an international feminist movement that has a global perspective, united by sisterhood and a shared analysis.

Adriana: I also think the simplification, in terms of accessibility, of feminist content needs to be taken seriously. The continuum of our analysis is slowly dying, and we need to unclog the sink so that women can once more drink the riches of feminism.

Natasha: I hope that we are able to grant our future girls and women a better sense of self, that we can see ourselves as a complete whole. I am planning to encourage more open debate about Radical feminism in Pakistan over the next few years, until we can form an actual group. I would like to see, not just women, but feminist women represented in politics.

Yagmur: What about you?

Bec: I would wish for women to become friends with women in the past, even if they are long dead. I wish for more consciousness of the continuation of the struggle, placing ourselves on a temporal continuum from the first time that a woman raised her fist.

Adriana: All the hopes that we have, like collective remembering, communication, reaching our potential, everything that we want for the future we're beginning the process in this conversation. I feel really blessed to be able to have this conversation with other women. I'm a bit emotional because this is a beautiful moment. I wish all girls would have the privilege of having conversations like this.

Bec: I concur and I think it's not often that we have these intentional conversations about these topics. For me, this is more than just an interview, it's also about understanding my own thoughts better in relation to yours. I miss you and I wish we could do this together in person and we need to congregate soon.

Natasha: I want to give you all a huge hug!

Bec: Natasha gives the best hugs.

Natasha: It's true.

All: Bye sisters! Thank you so much! Love you!

CHAPTER 14

#SayHerName Speaks Out—Are You Listening?
Intersectionality in the Era of Erasure

by Danielle Whitaker

Originally published February 29, 2020 for Women's Liberation Radio News, WLRN;[1] updated June 21, 2020

When Kimberlé Crenshaw coined the concept of "intersectionality" over 30 years ago,[2] her focus centered on the unique lived experiences of black women—specifically in the way multiple characteristics such as sex and race intersect to create a compounded form of oppression distinct from that of white women or of black men, due to those classes' reality of race privilege and sex privilege, respectively:

> *With Black women as the starting point, it becomes more apparent how dominant conceptions of discrimination condition us to think about subordination as disadvantage occurring along a single categorical axis. I want to suggest further that this single-axis framework erases Black women in the conceptualization, identification and remediation of race and sex discrimination by limiting inquiry to the experiences of otherwise-privileged members of the group.*

The first time I heard the term *intersectional* four or five years ago, it was being thrown about by misogynists to accuse radical feminists of not being "intersectional enough"—in other words, of not centering white, "woman-identifying" members of the sex-privileged male class in the fight for female liberation. Today, though the term is frequently appropriated by those within identity politics to insist that feminism must expand its focus to "intersect" with male interests and demands, its original context remains painfully relevant.

I remember when #BlackLivesMatter first took hold in 2013, well before its much-needed resurgence today. I remember Trayvon Martin and the devastating image of his young, smiling face. I remember the other men whose deaths catalyzed the movement, and I remember the explosive support this initiative (quite rightfully) received. However, despite the fact that my journey into radical feminism began several years ago, it is only very recently that I became familiar with #SayHerName.

That's not because it's new. #SayHerName gained momentum— though significantly less than BLM—a full five years ago. However, despite a few heartbreaking articles about Sandra Bland's fate in 2015, I don't recall hearing about the movement or about the other black women highlighted within it since then—and that is precisely why this initiative is so important:

"What's most problematic about the contemporary conversation," Crenshaw herself stated[3] just three-and-a-half years ago, "is the complete irrelevance of women of color."

Spearheaded in 2015 by Crenshaw's organization the African American Policy Forum,[4] #SayHerName arose as a social movement in the U.S. to increase awareness and support for black female victims of police brutality—to address how existing both as a member of an oppressed race class and of the oppressed sex class contributes to these victims' experiences. While BLM did not explicitly seek to exclude black women from its focus, the ugly truth is, we live in a world where male is both default and dominant—everywhere, in every context, in every race, across every culture, for

250

virtually all of recorded history. When we have conversations about "people," spaces for "everyone," vague ideas of "equality" and so on, it is men—black or white, depending on circumstance—who always take center stage. It is only by carving out a space and focus specifically for women, for addressing the problems faced uniquely by the female sex under patriarchal oppression, that activists have ever been able to make headway in any angle of feminism.

Black feminist bell hooks expressed this succinctly when she described racism as "a divisive force separating black men and white men," and sexism as "a force that unites the two groups."[5]

hooks exposed what few others in the fight against racism have been willing to acknowledge: much like BLM today, despite the overwhelming support and vital contributions of black women, the civil rights movement was largely controlled by men invested in "reclaiming" their manhood by establishing and enforcing patriarchy within the black community:

> *Just as the 19th century conflict over black male suffrage versus woman suffrage had placed black women in a difficult position, contemporary black women felt they were asked to choose between a black movement that primarily served the interests of black male patriarchs and a women's movement which primarily served the interests of racist white women.*

#SayHerName doesn't seek to replace BLM or downplay its significance, but rather to eliminate this *irrelevance* that Crenshaw calls out—to address the fact that in the fight against racism, as in everything else, the primary focus is and always has been men. Black women activists were at the forefront of the BLM movement at its inception, standing up for men, but we still have not seen equivalent numbers of black men leading the fight for black women. The amount of media attention that the men of BLM received does not compare, by any standards, to the attention—or rather, lack thereof—received by their female counterparts such as Bland, Rekia

Boyd, Shelly Frey, Shereese Francis, Tyisha Miller, and countless others.

Even now, it is primarily within feminist and woman-centered media that I have witnessed any significant coverage of Breonna Taylor, the 26-year-old black woman killed by police in her own home in March 2020.[6] What's more shocking is that Taylor's murder occurred in March, yet I didn't first hear her name until after the tragedy of George Floyd catalyzed the social transformation we are witnessing today.

I think it's safe to assume that no black woman's death would have sparked the current movement taking hold across the globe.

Even if they manage to escape death, black women suffer at staggering rates. Right now, there are 64,000 black women and girls reported missing in the U.S. alone.[7] Despite the fact that they are only 7% of the country's population, they make up more than 10% of missing persons cases, many of which remain unsolved, and again, these are only the ones who have been reported—the actual number could be much higher.

On the other hand, names like Natalee Holloway and Elizabeth Smart—both of which I've cited from memory—have gained household familiarity. Media on all sides of the political spectrum are seemingly unashamed of their biased concern when it comes to crimes against young, attractive white women; cases like the two aforementioned garner international fame and coverage, whereas most of the black women's names listed above I had never heard until researching for this piece. This discrimination is so rampant and consistent they've even coined a name for it: missing white woman syndrome.[8]

It is no coincidence that within leftist politics and social ideology, anti-racism is far more supported than anti-misogyny; nowadays, even amongst so-called progressives, simply *acknowledging* the reality of women's sex-based oppression is controversial at best, "violent bigotry" at worst.

The reality is, fighting racism will always be more accepted than fighting misogyny—because racism also affects men.

It is fully possible—necessary, in fact—to understand that men too can be victims of male violence and that race-based violence against either sex is inexcusable, while also acknowledging that women of color *uniquely* experience police brutality and all other forms of male violence—whether from men of their own race or another—with an added layer of oppression. Rape and sexual assault, for instance, are infinitely more common against women in the "justice" system, and it is only women who face the risk of pregnancy.

We cannot ignore, either, the toxic patriarchal culture and anti-woman violence amongst male members of U.S. law enforcement. Research estimates that "domestic violence," which almost always means male violence against females, is *two to four times higher*[9] in this group than in the general population.

Let that sink in. The men who have sworn to protect us and our communities are two to four times more likely to abuse the women in their lives. More shocking (or not, depending on how long you've been a feminist), the research shows almost 30% of the accused officers still had their jobs a year later.

This is an epidemic—an epidemic being treated as an inconvenience.

It often feels as though we are swimming upstream in this era of erasure and obfuscation. From "I don't see color" and "all lives matter" to the assumption that feminism is no longer needed in the West despite an entire cult of males now staking claim to womanhood through the performance of gender stereotypes, it can easily feel as though we've scarcely made any progress at all.

Unfortunately, true progress is not always linear.

While the recent generations of Internet and social media have granted us the platforms necessary to spark important conversations, to more quickly and widely raise awareness of and address injustices, it also clearly exposes the uneven attention given to privileged classes over those who are oppressed. This is why we must continue to shed light on what is kept in the dark, to expose and speak the truth, to learn, to inform ourselves and those around us. It is no one else's job to educate us.

So start reading. Start listening. Start with Crenshaw's original essay. Explore the works of Audre Lorde and bell hooks and Chimamanda Ngozi Adichie. Read and watch interviews—not social media propaganda—with Stormé DeLarverie, the black butch lesbian who led the Stonewall Riots and who is being erased from her own history by the lesbophobic trans movement.

There is no shortage of black women's voices; it is our duty to listen.

If we can understand institutional race-based oppression yet deny institutional sex-based oppression—our activism, soapbox lamentations, and efforts for woke points are grounded only in what's popular and acceptable to speak up against in the given moment.

After all, it is only through exposure of injustice that we can begin to work toward justice.

Endnotes

1 https://wlrnmedia.wordpress.com/2020/02/29/sayhername-speaks-out/.

2 https://chicagounbound.uchicago.edu/cgi/viewcontent.cgi?referer=&httpsredir=1&article=1052&context=uclf.

3 https://www.law.columbia.edu/news/archive/kimberle-crenshaw-intersectionality-more-two-decades-later.

4 https://www.aapf.org/sayhername.

5 bell hooks, *Ain't I a Woman* (1999).

6 https://www.cnn.com/2020/05/13/us/louisville-police-emt-killed-trnd/index.html.

7 https://medium.com/the-blight/there-are-64-000-missing-black-women-in-the-usa-222001806a6e.

8 https://scholarship.law.wm.edu/cgi/viewcontent.cgi?article=1508&context=wmjowl.

9 https://www.theatlantic.com/national/archive/2014/09/police-officers-who-hit-their-wives-or-girlfriends/380329/.

CHAPTER 15

Racy Sex, Sexy Racism: Porn from the Dark Side*

by Gail Dines

In April 2007, radio show legend Don Imus finally overstepped the
mark with his vile description of the Rutgers University women's
basketball team as "nappy headed ho's." Following a concerted
campaign by the African-American community, CBS fired him
amidst a public outcry and a mass exodus of corporate sponsors
from his show. But what barely merited a comment, let alone outcry
from the media, was a press release issued three weeks later from
the porn company Kick Ass Pictures, announcing its intention to
donate one dollar from every sale of its new movie, titled *Nappy
Headed Ho's*, to the Don Imus retirement fund. And this movie is
just one among countless that have "hos" in the title, a shorthand
way the porn industry commonly refers to black women.

Over the years, thanks in a large part to the civil rights movement, blatant examples of racism that were once commonplace
in mainstream media have become less acceptable. The old
"StepinFetchit"-type movies that depicted black men as imbeciles

or *The Birth of a Nation*-type movies that showed black men as violent rapists of white women would not be tolerated today. This does not mean that racist depictions are a thing of the past, just that the media industry has to operate with some restraint since we have, as a society, made some surface attempt at reigning in the most vulgar and crass demonstrations of racism. Not so for the porn industry, which gets away with a level of racism that is breathtaking in its contempt and loathing for people of color.

Consider the August 2007 release of *Long Dong Black Kong* which caused quite a stir in the porn industry with charges of racism for using the word Kong to describe the black male performer. Invoking the "only a joke" defense, Peter Reynolds, VP of Adam and Eve, the movie's distributer, recommends that "we should all not take ourselves so seriously," as the "name is totally innocent."[1] Given the overtly racist titles of recent porn movies that feature black men – *Hot Black Thug, Black Poles in White Holes, Huge Black Cock on White Pussy,* and *Monster Black Penises* – the *Long Dong Black Kong* title does, at first glance, seem fairly tame by comparison. However, by referring to black men as monsters, this movie came too close for comfort for many porn producers. It exposed that which the porn industry would prefer to keep below the surface – that black men are routinely depicted as monstrous in their uncontrolled desire for white women.

The *Long Dong Black Kong* movie belongs to a genre called "interracial" by the industry. According to an article in *Adult Video News*, this is one of the fastest growing and most bootlegged sub-genres in gonzo pornography today.[2] While the term interracial suggests a grab bag of color with performers of different races having sex with each other, in reality, interracial porn features mainly black men with white (often blonde) women, with titles such as *Black on Blondes, White Pussy -Black Cocks,* and *White Sluts on Black Snakes.* If porn users want to see other racial or ethnic mix, they have to go to categories marked "Black" (which refers to porn with black women performers), "Asian," "Latin," or "Ethnic," all of which are burgeoning genres in porn.

The racial politics of the porn industry today mirror those of pop culture in that the majority of people involved in the production end of the business is white. This white control has led Jake Stead, a well-known black performer, to accuse the industry of "rampant racism,"[3] in its failure to provide black producers with the start-up capital, networks, or access to distribution channels that many white producers enjoy. Jesse Spencer, aka Mr. Marcus, performer and owner of the production company MSEX, similarly faults the industry for its over-representation of white producers and performers, and calls for a greater black presence. In an interview for XBIZ, he offers a solution to racism in porn: "I think it has to be up to the black performers to create product for our people and our market, because no one is going to do it for us."[4] Who exactly is included in the "us" category is unclear because it's hard to imagine how black women, or any women of color, would benefit from Mr. Marcus' proposal.

Black women do not fare well in the porn industry because the "plum" jobs for porn performers – the contract employment with the two major porn-feature studios, Vivid and Wicked – are reserved mainly for white women. These studios with their chic image, sophisticated marketing practices, and guarantee of regular work, afford their contract women an income and level of visibility that makes them the envy of the industry (Jenna Jameson, of course, is held up as the quintessential example of just how far a contract porn star can go). With surgically enhanced bodies, perfectly coiffed hair, and glamorous makeup, these women act as PR agents for the porn industry, showing up regularly on Howard Stern, E! Entertainment, or in the pages of *Maxim*. As the porn industry increasingly wiggles its way into pop culture, it is no surprise that they use mainly white women as the "acceptable" face of porn; their all-American-girl looks seamlessly mesh with the blonde-blue eyed images that grace the screens, celebrity magazines, and billboards across North America.

In porn, women of color are generally relegated to gonzo, a genre that has little glamour, security, or chic status. Here women

259

have few fan club websites, do not make it to pop culture, and have to endure the body-punishing sex. But while the sex acts are typical gonzo, the way the written text frames the sex is unique as it racializes the bodies and sexual behavior of the performer. In all-white porn, they never refer to the man's penis as "a white cock" or the woman's vagina as "white pussy," but introduce a person of color, and suddenly all players, white included, have a racialized sexuality, where the race of the performer(s) is described in ways that make women a little more "sluttier" and the men more hyper-masculinized.

It is this harnessing of gender to race that makes women of color a particularly useful group to exploit in gonzo porn, since gonzo porn works only to the degree that the women in it are debased and dehumanized. As a woman of color, the porn performer embodies two subordinate categories, such as Asian fuckbucket, Black ho, and Latina slut. All past and present racist stereotypes are dredged up and thrown in her face while being orally, anally and vaginally penetrated by any number of men. When men (irrespective of race) ejaculate on her face and body, they often make reference to her skin color, and her debased status as a woman is seamlessly melded with, and reinforced by, her supposed debased status as a person of color. In the process, her race and gender become inseparable and her body carries the status of dual subordination.

Racializing the slut: Women of color in porn

It is no surprise that Asian women are the most popular women of color in porn, given the long standing stereotypes of them as sexually servile Geishas, Lotus blossoms, and China dolls. Depicted as perfect sex objects, with well-honed sex skills, Asian women come to porn with a baggage of stereotypes that make them the idealized women of the porn world. In most sites and movies specializing in Asian women (Asian being used in porn as a shorthand for a whole range of ethnicities), we see a mind-numbing replaying of the image of Asian women as sexually exotic, enticing, and submissive, in both the text and pictures. Using words such as naive, obedient, petite, cute, and innocent, the websites are full of images of Asian women, who, we are told, will do anything to please a man, since this is what they are bred for. It seems however, from these sites that Asian women are only interested in pleasing white men because Asian men are almost completely absent as sex partners.

The introductory text on *Hustler*'s website, *Asian Fever*, sums up the way Asian women are caricatured in porn:

> *Asian Fever features scorching scenes of the sexual excesses these submissive Far East nymphos are famous for. No one knows how to please a man like an Asian slut can, and these exotic beauties prove it …*[5]

Notice here how Asian women are defined as being super slutty, thanks to their assumed sexual excesses, submissiveness, skill and beauty. Their supposed submissiveness is eroticized as they are presented as completely powerless to resist any sexual demands men may have. Their powerless is further enhanced by the ways these women are "childified" as they are presented as naive, innocent, and lacking any adult agency. The more childish the woman seems, the greater the ability of the male user to exploit, and manipulate.

The bodies of these women are similarly described as immature, and of course, given that this is porn, it is always their vaginas that are constructed as the most child-like. Words like tiny, little, and tight are used as a way to develop an image of a vagina that seems more like a child's than a woman's. Many of these sites promise the viewer the pleasure of seeing a "tight Asian cunt filled with a huge cock," thereby sexualizing female discomfort. In keeping with the gonzo script, these women are depicted as loving rough sex and are happy to take the abuse handed out to them.

For "authenticity" the web sites often write the English text in chopstick font, play Asian sounding music in the background, and have the women speaking in broken English. While all of these sites are deeply racist in the way they caricature Asian cultures, one of the worst offenders is a site called *Me Fuck You Long Time*, which offers the viewer movies of "Asian Sluts Getting Fucked by American Cocks." Referring to the women as "Fuckbuckets," this site has multiple images of women being gagged by so called "American cocks." On the right hand side of the site, is an American Flag, a tank, and the statue of Liberty, and on the left is an Asian woman holding a Chinese flag (although the banner on the site advertises "Japanese Fuckbuckets" not Chinese). Just below her is a streaming video of an Asian woman having ejaculate squirted on her face. The not-so-subtle message here is that no matter what really happened in the past, today the American's are the real winners as they get to fuck Asian women any way they want. To the winner, goes utter and complete access to the losing side's women, and what better way to represent this than to have a continuous video of the losing side's woman being degraded in the best way porn knows how: a face covered in ejaculate.

Sometimes the industries of trafficking and sex tourism, which supply western men with cut-rate women and girls, are referenced for an extra thrill. The text promoting the film *Asian Street Hookers* advertisers "real Asian freaks from southeast Asia," and to make really sure that the user knows that they are talking about trafficking in women, they boast that "The Oriental Express flies to Thailand and the Philippines - and once again imports the sexiest dolls around." Indeed if the pleasure in porn is watching a woman rendered powerless, then trafficked women are about as powerless as you can get. They are in a foreign country with no support systems, their passport is usually confiscated by the pimp, they have no money, often can't speak the language, and are at the mercy of the sex traffickers who would just as soon kill them as let them leave. In this subordinated state, the women have to submit to any sexual use and abuse brought to bear on her body. In porn world sex, this state of utter oppressions is about as hot as you can get.

Whereas Asian women are seen as biologically disposed to being subservient, black women are presented as the very opposite. The idea that black women are lacking the traditional feminine qualities of subservience is not something that porn invented; it has been around for some years, and has at times found its way into governmental reports, most notably the Moynihan Report which blamed black poverty on black women's emasculation of black men. As ridiculous as this is, black women in particular, and the black community in general, have paid a heavy price for the pathologizing of black women as unrestrained bitches steamrolling over black men. Now in porn, these women get their comeuppance.

Similar to the rest of society, black women are unequally treated in the industry, often earning less than their white female counterparts for the same acts and scenes, and very few black women actually become well-known, and are thus denied the added wealth that comes with having a name in the industry. In his book on the black porn industry, Lawrence Ross quotes the well-known black porn actor Lexington Steele as saying:

> In a boy/girl scene, one girl one guy, no anal sex, the market dictates a minimum of $800 to $900 per scene for the girl .... Now a white girl will start at $800 and go up from there, but a black girl will have to start at $500, and then hit a ceiling, of about $800. So the black girl hits a ceiling at the white girl's minimum.[6]

In an industry where all female flesh is disposable, black women seem to come and go even more often than white women, a sign no doubt of their low status and perceived interchangeability.

With names like *Juicy Black Butt*, *Horny Black Pussy*, *Bad Black Babes* and *Black Pussy Stuffed*, the race of the woman is clearly transmitted to the potential user. Wading through numerous sites featuring black women, what appears as a common theme is the framing of these women as aggressive and mouthy. They are constantly referred to as having an attitude, and the job of porn-sex is to train them – domesticate them if you will – into a subordinate state. They are presented as having a particularly excessive and uncontrollable type of sexuality that takes a real man, be he black or white, to handle her. The pleasure offered to the users could well revolve around watching a man become hyper masculinized in his ability to give the black woman just what she really deserves, supposedly a fucking so harsh, she is forced into a subordinate femininity.

A whole sub-genre of black porn is depicted as taking place in the ghetto, a location that is described as sexually lawless, debauched and brimming with hos, pimps, and gang bangers. The black women who populate the porn world become not just sluts and hos, but ghetto sluts and hos, which make them even more dehumanized than their white counterparts. On some of these sites the women are depicted as unkempt, poorly dressed, and lacking in style. The story here is that they need a pimp to turn her into a presentable prostitute, and not to worry, there is no shortage of pimps, usually black, eager to take on the job.

On *Pimp My Black Teen*, the headline on the site reads "We find ordinary black teens from the ghetto and pimp them out extreme-makeover style." This site, like many other pimp sites, has pictures of so-called "before and after makeovers" in which a teenage black woman is shown in sweatpants and jeans for the "before"—and sexy, revealing underwear for the "after." One caption reads "we caught up with Reneeka looking like a tattered hood rat. Once we styled her fine brown ass, her wet pussy took a long black cock just fine." Above the text are pictures of "Reneeka" giving oral sex to a black male, her face smeared with ejaculate. But while "ghetto" black women may try to clean themselves up to look more sexy and hot, there is no escaping their roots, exemplified in the case of Saxxx:

> *Saxxx tried to clean herself up, but there was no fooling us, she was still a low down dirty ghetto ho! So I rammed her head into the couch as I worked her snatch like a jack hammer, then proceeded to fire a messy load all over her face.*[7]

Indeed, it is their so called ghetto-style that seems to make them more appealing, as one fan, comparing white and black women performers, told Ross that white women "are all fake and shit, fake tits and fake ass on the camera, you know what I am saying? But the black chicks are the real deal. Like you could actually get with them."[8]

One image of black women that is common in both mainstream pop culture, especially hip hop and porn, is the reduction of them to a "big black booty." Some sites put booty in their title – like *Big Booty Cuties*, *Black Booty Cam* – while others make clear that the black women's buttocks are the focus of attention – *Sweet Chocolate Butt*, *Black Ass Fucks*, *Phat Ass Ebony*, and *Black Ass Fucking*. And virtually every black porn site talks about the "booty" in their promo text, promising lots of "big black round asses." African American writers such as Patricia Hill Collins[9] have explored how this fetishization of black women's buttocks is rooted in the belief that black women are especially promiscuous and that their "booty" is the only part worthy of notice, thus reducing black women to sexual objects devoid of humanity, individuality and dignity. Instead of a whole person, the black woman becomes an appendage to a big black booty, one that she is willing to shake at any man, no matter what his race.

It is impossible to know with any certainty who buys these movies with black women, but articles in *Adult Video News* and on the *XBIZ* website suggest that when both male and female porn performers are black, then it is mainly geared towards a black audience. Lawrence Ross, in his interviews with the fans of this genre, found the majority to be black, and their reason for buying these movies was that for them, "black porn is the manifestation of a fetish. Black skin is looked at as being a sort of hypersexuality, an explosive combination that is more exciting and hotter than general-market or white sex."[10] If Ross is correct, then the dominant white produced stereotypes of blacks as having what Cornel West mockingly refers to as "dirty, disgusting, and funky sex,"[11] would seem to have gained some traction with black men.

Also, black men have been socialized over the years by white controlled pop culture, as well as by the increasingly pornographic images in mainstream hip hop. Highly sexualized images of black women are a staple of these videos, and while, as some black critics argue, these images reinstate black women as sexually desirable in a society where the beauty standard is racist,[12] they do so in ways that objectify her body and teach boys and young men that they are not equal partners but rather fuck objects who deserve to be treated just like the women in porn videos. Hip hop helped develop the black porn genre, and Mireille Miller-Young argues that,

> *white pornographers were acutely interested in how black men consumed images of black women—how they fetishized them in popular culture—so that they could expand their market beyond the standard white male consumers who generally purchased adult tapes featuring black sexuality.*[13]

Hip hop was the main source of information for porn producers eager to open up the black male market; it would seem, given the growth in the number of black porn movies released, that it successfully provided a blueprint for porn imagery.[14]

There are now a growing number of sites that depict sex between white men and black women, and if the porn boards are any reflections of readership, the majority of these viewers appear to be white. It seems that when either the male or female porn performers is white, then the audience is mainly white men. This makes sense given how racial conflict is constructed, articulated and exploited as a way to enhance the sexual debasement of women. On the site *White Dicks in Black Chick* – where the banner reads "White Guys Violate Ebony Babes," – the sex is regular gonzo, but the text constructs a scenario of acute economic deprivation and subsequent sexual exploitation:

> *What a fuckin' hot day it was when we found Carmen. She was walking out of the grocery store with her shirt up*

and her big fat tits hanging out. We had to say something to her. A fine black woman like this. But when we tried to approach her, she wasn't having it. This woman may be the most racist black woman we've ever met. She couldn't stand the white man. Calling them perverts, ingrates, honkeys even threatening to get her gang members to kick the shit out of them. But we had an angle. See Carmen has two kids, and they need milk but Carmen is a little low on cash right now so we made her a proposition. One thousand bucks to fuck a white man. Our final offer. She accepted alright and when we got back to the house, she also got a mouthful of white cum to wash down that milk.[15]

On the site is a large picture of "Carmen" on all fours with a penis entering her anus. The message being here that her gender, race, and class locations have visually and viscerally brought her to knees.

For all the abuse encoded in the text – a desperate woman forced to sell herself to feed her children – this site is nothing compared to the actual sexual violence that black women in *Ghetto Gaggers* suffer at the hands of white men. Promoting itself as a site that delivers "Ghetto Fabulous Face Fucked Beyatches," the home page has many pictures of black women with lots of semen dripping off their faces. Surrounding this image are smaller ones of the women being anally, orally, and vaginally penetrated. Unlike much of gonzo, there is no attempt to even pretend that these women like the sex, as they are shown close to tears, grimacing and in many cases, thoroughly disgusted by the semen that is all over their eyes, mouth and nose. Although the entire site is very disturbing, one of the worst images is of "Vixen," who looks utterly exhausted. The text accompanying the images reads:

Vixen is a sassy ghetto fabulous beyatch with more attitude than Harlem has crack. She needed a learnin' by some white cocks to remove the sass from her chicken head

bobbin' back and forth ghetto ass. We did just that. Two cocks
in her holes, we ran train on her ass, slapped the taste out of
her mouth and dumped two loads all over that sexy beyatch.
Ghetto Gaggers, we destroy ghetto hoes, and it be showin' like
a mutha fukka!

It's apparent that these pornographers see sex as a punishment
for Vixen's failure to act like a subservient female. The violence of
this site is not lost on fans, who, on the porn discussion board Adult
DVD Talk, share their favorite scenes. Hotboy 1999 tells his virtual friends that "i (sic) love the hardcore face fucking, the women
drooling, the gagging, and the puke scenes" and asks for suggestions for more gagging and puke scenes. Panas answers "If you like
the roughest it could be the Jessica scene, where she is extremely
uncomfortable and at a point, she stops the scene crying. If you like
vomit go for Baby Doll, a scene where she starts vomiting from the
very start."[16] Indeed, on the free teaser, anyone can watch "Baby
Doll" vomit over and over again as she is gagged. The role of such
violence is to feminize her into being a real woman, and who better
to deliver this message in a racist society than white men.

Asian women and black women are not the only women to
be racially exploited by the porn industry; there is also a market
for other ethnic groups, especially Latina women, and lately for
Arab women. Irrespective of the ethnic group, the framing of the
narrative is exactly the same – their race makes them that bit sluttier than "regular," white porn women. For men the story is more
complicated; not all men of color are treated as that much more
hyper masculinized.

Racializing the stud: Men of color and porn

While there are literally thousands of images of Asian women
on these porn sites, there are very few Asian men as sex partners.
This mirrors pop culture, where apart from a few sagely old men,

dispensing wisdom in broken English, or a Kung-Fu-type fighter, Asian men are virtually absent in media, especially as intimate partners of Asian women, or any women for that matter. The lack of Asian male characters as lovers, husbands, boyfriends, or even porn performers is, according to Darrell Hamamoto, an Asian-American professor and porn producer at the University of California, Davis, due to the widely held stereotype of Asian men as asexual and geeky. But if we move over to gay porn, we see plenty of Asian men that are portrayed as anything but asexual. Some of these sites have Asian-on-Asian male sex, but when an Asian male is paired with a white man, he is described in much the same way as Asian women - cute, petite, innocent. The word that often appears with Asian men in porn is "twinks," a term used in gay slang to mean young looking attractive, slightly built, gay male. The stereotypes that make Asian men attractive as feminized gay men are the very ones that make them unappealing in straight porn since to be a feminized man would undo the strict gender demarcation present in all straight porn.

It seems that the hyper-feminization of Asian women in pop culture and porn leaks down to Asian men, where the group as a whole become feminized as the sexual object of white masculinity. This "de-masculinization" of Asian men in western culture was the topic of discussion on Adult DVD talk when a user asked why there are no Asian male porn stars? Mixed in with the predictable racist assumptions – "Asian men tend to have smaller genital size" – there was a range of posts that illustrated ways in which white men view Asian men as lacking masculinity. One user wrote "even if a white woman might like an asian (sic) male, she might not want to sleep with him because of the way people view the masculinity (or lack thereof)" to which another responded:

> But: porn isn't so much about "real life." Like any kind of show business, it emphasizes "image" and exaggerates. Since it is about sex, there is a tendency to exaggerate masculinity vs. feminity (sic). And like it or not, there is a tendency to

perceive individuals of certain races and/or "types" as more masculine (or feminine as the case may be) than others.

 I would say that in the eyes of many, black guys top the list in terms of masculinity (as defined in terms of size, muscularity, physical power, dick size, aggressiveness, and self-confidence), while the common *perception* of Asian guys among would put them lower on that list. White guys would fall, on average, somewhere in between ....[17]

What is remarkable about this post is the way the writer (Eduardo911) so neatly sums up how race is gendered to the degree that one group represents masculinity (black), one femininity (Asian), and one group (whites) floats somewhere in the middle of the continuum. When this racial landscape gets disrupted, porn users become somewhat uneasy, like in the case of the porn site *Asian Man*, which advertises itself as being about the "sexual adventures of an Asian man and beautiful girls from all over the world." The readers reviews on the *Sir Rodney* site are very mixed, with many reviewers unsure as to how Asian the site owner and performer, Rick, really is. Some insist he is Asian, while others, such as Anonymous, argue that "Asian-man is a ripped off (sic). This asshole who own (sic) the site is not even Asian or Chinese."

For those who believe that "Rick" is indeed Asian, there is a lot of support for having an Asian man as the lead male performer, or, as Anonymous puts it, "the site's unique feature is that it features an asian (sic) in the male role." But for all the hype about this site featuring an Asian man, the male porn performer goes to great lengths to conceal his racial identity. In every still image on the site he hides his face, sometimes to the point of chopping off the top of a picture, or even blacking out his head. In the movies, his face is buried in the body of the woman he is penetrating, or the camera is held at an angle that conceals his face. Although it is the norm in heterosexual porn to minimize the images of the male performer, perhaps for fear that the sight will make the viewer uncomfortable while watching (and possibly enjoying) another male become aroused, this site takes it to an extreme. It would seem that "Rick," or whoever the owner is, feels unsure about how well an Asian man would be received by consumers, so he makes him everyman by blocking out distinguishing racial characteristics.

One other site that further promotes Asian men as heterosexual porn performers is *Phuck Fu Masters*, owned by Asian-American porn producer, Jack Lee. The story told on the site is that two amateurs from Hong Kong come to America for instruction from a porn master in how to become the first-ever Asian male porn stars, and the viewers get to see them honing their skills on mainly white women. The text on the site both pokes fun at, and reinforces, traditional stereotypes of Chinese people with constant references to Chinese food delivery, kung fu, and Chi, as well as emphasizing just how new to porn sex these men are. Rarely in porn is reference made to the inexperience of the male performers since their masculinity is tied into their sexual prowess, but here on a site with Asian men, the theme is that the male performers need to be taught by a master. And who, in porn world sex, is the master best suited to teach Asian men how to have sex? A black man of course, in the form of Santino Lee, veteran porn performer and producer. So on this site, run by an Asian man, there is still a re-playing of the hyper masculine black male and the feminized Asian dichotomy by making the former the "master" of the latter.

Jack Lee has been quoted as saying that he started this website because "there's a demand from many Asian men to see guys like themselves portrayed as sex symbols," and that for him and his Asian viewers it "is an Asian Pride thing." These are almost the exact same sentiments expressed by professor and pornographer Darrell Hamamoto, although Hamamoto uses somewhat more scholarly language to justify his entry into the porn world. Creator of *Skin on Skin*, a porn movie using only Asian American performers, Hamamoto sees his porn movie as "a proudly erect statement on Asian American male sexuality."[18] How he gets to this somewhat twisted position is through a very reasonable assessment of how Asian-American sexuality has been "warped by White supremacist

271

thought/behavior, the history of anti-Asian exterminationism, colonialism, removal and relocation, deportation, and anti-miscegenation laws." There is no doubt that such overtly racist practices would have a major impact on every facet of life, including sexuality, and Hamamoto's outrage is well justified, given the racism that Asian-Americans continue to experience in this country.

But Hamamoto is really only outraged on behalf of Asian American men and demonstrates utter contempt for Asian-American women in his willful failure to adopt any critical analysis of how porn negatively affects the lives of Asian-American women. No stranger to sophisticated thinking on how images construct reality, media scholar Hamamoto suddenly sounds like an average porn consumer when he comments, in an interview, that finding Asian American women to appear in porn was easy because "There are tons of Yella womenz who want to appear on camera doing the Wild Thang." Well, certainly, if you surf the Asian porn sites, you will find "tons" of Asian women. But to conclude from this, as Hamamoto does, that Asian-American porn is about Asian-American women's desire to do the "wild thang," rather than a racist marketing ploy developed by primarily white men to make a profit off of long held racist stereotypes, is simply absurd.

What seems to be blinding Hamamoto to the exploitation of Asian-American women in porn, is his overwhelming desire to re-masculinize the Asian-American male. And this is where his project really turns bizarre, for while he critiques the dominant racist image of the emasculated Asian-American male, he ultimately uses the dominant sexist image of masculinity – one based on control and dominance of women – as his measure of what a remasculinized Asian man should look like. Within this framework, it makes sense why Hamamoto sees Asian-on-Asian porn as a way to change the image of Asian American men, since Asian men get to play out the ultimate act of masculinity – fucking (over) their own women. This might be, as both Jack Lee and Darrell Hamamato say, a proud statement for Asian American masculinity, but for Asian American women, it is business as usual with their sexuality still being used

272

in the service of proving the masculinity of the man who is fucking them.

For all the attempts to remasculinize Asian men, it seems that it will take more than a few porn sites to shift the stereotypes of Asian men that have long been part of the collective consciousness of white Americans. As long as Asian men are seen by whites as feminized, it is unlikely that they will ever be of much interest to white male porn users as this muddies the gender demarcation between women and men. If as argued elsewhere, men go to porn to shore up their masculinity, then they want to see men – real powerful men – fucking women who at the moment of penetration are utterly feminized by their subordinated role. The more masculine the man, the more likely he can subordinate, and the more the user/spectator gets to live his masculinity out vicariously as he watches the scene unfold before him.

If Asian men have occupied the feminized end of the masculinity continuum, then black men have been at the hyper-masculinized end of the continuum. Saddled with ugly stereotypes as violent thugs and rapists, black men are often held up as examples of masculinity run amok, the kind that is uncontained and out of control. In fact, this is the very masculinity that is idealized and glorified in porn, since every male in the porn world is hyper-aroused and ready to do what he has to in order to pleasure himself. It would appear that the long-held image of black men as spoilers of white womanhood were in fact tailor-made for porn, so it should be no surprise that the industry has cashed in on these stereotypes in the form of the very successful genre of interracial porn (IP). As one porn retailer puts it:

> My customers seem to enjoy black men "taking advantage" of white women, seducing their white daughters and wives. The more "wrong" a title is, the more appealing it is. The Blackzilla line is one of my best selling series. Oh No! There's a Negro in my Mom is also one that sells as soon as it hits the shelves. My customers don't want to see a loving interracial

couple; they want to see massive black dicks, satisfying or defiling pretty white girls.[19]

While the movie *"Long Dong Black Kong"* may have caused somewhat of a stir for its racism, it was in fact a perfect title for a porn movie featuring black men and white women as the original *King Kong* movie was probably the most dramatic rendering of black masculinity that this country had ever seen when it came out in 1933. Who can forget the image of an out of control black monster rampaging through the streets of New York, with a defenseless white woman clutched to his chest? No surprise that when the movie was released in Germany in 1934, it was renamed *King Kong and the White Woman*. Depicting blacks as monstrous is not something that *King Kong* invented, since this stereotype had been circulating long before the movie, but it was the first time a mass audience got to witness, visually and firsthand, just what a terrifying threat such a monster was. Although Kong did not have an identifiable penis, we were primed to imagine just what damage he could do to petite Fay Wray (and later Naomi Watts), as she lay helpless in his arms. Today we don't need to imagine, as we get to see, in movie after movie, just what violence an unconstrained black penis can do to white women who, unlike chaste Fay Wray, are such "dirty whores" that they actually seek out sex with these "black monsters" who have insatiable appetites and inhuman size penises.

Porn movies that pair black men with white women are very popular with porn consumers, the majority of whom are white, and *AVN* articles suggest that IP is being produced, marketed, and distributed mainly to a white audience. This seems strange given that a relatively short time ago, the thought of a black man just looking at a white woman was enough to work white men up into a lynch mob frenzy. And now they are buying millions of dollars' worth of movies that show, in graphic detail, a black man doing just about everything that can be done to a white woman's body. But it is actually less strange when we realize that in the world of porn, the more a woman – white or of color – is debased, the better the porn experience for the user. And what better way to debase a white woman, in the eyes of white men, than to have her penetrated over and over again by that which has been designated sexually perverse, savage and debauched? One interracial porn producer says that his most popular movies are those where "the purity of the sacred white women is compromised … even if the white girl is as dirty and diseased-riddled as humanly possible."[20] This explains why interracial porn geared towards white men is almost totally dominated by black male porn performers rather than any other ethnic group.

It is not an easy task in gonzo porn to make anyone group look more debauched than the next since everyone in porn is depicted as nothing more than a walking genitalia looking for penetration and orgasm. But even in this world, black men are more reduced to their penis than any other group of men, because the focus of the "plot" and action is, predictably, "the big black cock" that can't get enough "white pussy." Described as "huge," "enormous," "monstrous," "gigantic" and "unbelievable" with mind-numbing monotony, the black penis is filmed from every angle to give the porn user a clear image of its size and color. The female body, the one most usually scrutinized in porn, is only interesting in terms of how much of the penis she can tolerate in IP. The main focal point of these movies is the numerous ways in which the huge black penis can do damage to small white orifices, as constant mention is made of her inability to deal with such a large penis. Or as one fan put it, the best IP movies are those where "he is giving her more than she can handle." The site *White Meat on Black Street*, for example refers to the women as "victims," and promises users "interracial pussy splitting action" because "these horse-hung black dudes are packing so much meat it is a wonder that these tight white pussies don't recoil at the mere sight!"

The movies typically begin with the women expressing shock at the size of the penis, and in some cases, she tells the camera man that she is not sure she can do the scene. Whether fake or real, as the sex begins you watch the women grimace, shout out in pain, and move away from the penis, only to be dragged back towards it as it penetrates an orifice. In some of the movies there is more than one man, so she might have penises thrust into her vagina, anus and mouth at the same time. The usual gonzo sex goes on and on, and the viewer gets to see her gag to the point where tears are streaming down her face. While the penis is thrust into her vagina and the anus, and she is squirming, she says, often through gritted teeth, that she loves "big black cock."

The male porn performers are, like most men in gonzo, depicted as lacking empathy and completely uninterested in the pain or discomfort they are causing the women. While this kind of behavior reduces all men in gonzo to robotic fuckers of women's orifices, for black men this is described as part of their very biological makeup and hence carries the weight of authenticity. And porn users like authenticity – they want to know that what they are masturbating to actually happened to that woman. If they suspect they are being fooled, they get upset like in the case of some fans who are convinced that the penis attached to one of the men in *White Meat on Black Streets* is fake. As the users discuss the truth or falsity of the penis, one reader writes "the dick is clearly fake. Watch how he has to hold it on. It doesn't cum realistically either. Stupid niggers trying to fake big dicks."[21] Why the outrage? One possible answer could be that if the penis is fake, then maybe her pain is also fake, and this spoils the thrill of watching the action play out. Also, many of these white men seem somewhat entranced by the black penis, as they seem to be spending a lot of time studying it while masturbating.

In IP movies, the white penis is often held up as inadequate and lacking in potency when compared to black ones. An excellent example of this can be found in one of the most popular series of IP movies called *Blacks on Blondes* which feature white, blonde women with multiple black males. Like in most IP, the white performer is "applauded" for being able to take a black penis in her white mouth, vagina and anus. In one particular movie with "Liv Wylder" we see an example of a theme running through IP, namely the emasculation of the white man by the big black penis. The text on the site reads:

276

Bring out the cuckold mask again! Time for another white couple to live out their naughtiest fantasy, and thanks to Blacks On Blondes for making it happen! Liv and Hubby have been married for a few years, and she wears her ring proudly. But lately the spark has left the bedroom, if you know what I mean. A few e-mails later, and we've got Hubby in a cage while Boz and Mandingo work Liv over. And when I say they work her over, we mean it. She takes so much black dick it amazed even us. The best part of this whole deal was the end: after Liv has about a gallon of cum all over her face and clothes, and grabs a plastic bowl - for Hubby to beat off in. He does, and his wad was weak, and Liv lets him know that.[22]

The story that the text and images are telling in this movie has deep historical resonance as it is pitting the black male sexuality against white male sexuality, and the loser is without a doubt the latter. The white man's poor performance in the bedroom ("the spark has left the bedroom"), as well as his ineffectual semen ("his wad was weak"), stand in sharp contrast to the size of the black men's penises, the skill of their sexual performance ("they work her over, we mean it") and the amount of semen they produce ("a gallon of cum"). To add to the humiliation, the last line lets us know that Liv is only too happy to ridicule the husband in front of the black men. What we have here is a playing out of a stereotype that demarcates the white man as civilized, and therefore somewhat restrained in his bodily functions, versus the uncivilized, animal-like black man who, unencumbered by social norms and dictates of bodily control, really knows how to please a woman. And when push comes to shove, the white woman really prefers the unrestrained sexuality of black men. No wonder one popular series of IP films is called *Once You Go Black . . . You Never Go Back.*[23]

This mocking of white masculinity would see like an odd thing to do in a porn genre that is mainly targeted to white men. Men generally do not like to be ridiculed for having an ineffectual penis, so what possible pleasure could white men get from such movies?

One potential answer could be in the viewer's identification with the black male, as he gets to imagine what life would be like if he were, according to the image, an out-of-control savage black man, rather than a penis-challenged white man. This would not be the first time in history that white men have identified with black men as a way to enjoy the pleasures of the (assumed) unconstrained body. The Blackface Minstrel shows that swept through America in the 1830s and 1840s were very popular with white male audiences, and even though the minstrels were white men in blackface, some scholars suggest that once given the mask of blackness, white men could "sing, dance, speak, move, and act in ways that were considered inappropriate for white men."[24]

When white men watched the minstrels, they saw not white men in blackface, but what they thought was authentic black behavior being played out in front of them. The reason for this, argues Mel Watkins, is that whites assumed that the minstrel shows depicted something real and essential about blacks, because the shows:

> *Were advertised as the real thing. In fact, one group was called "The Real Nigs" ... they were advertised as "Come to the theatre and get a real look into what plantation life was like"... It was advertised as a peephole view of what black people were really like.*[25]

I would suggest here that IP is not so much a peephole as a peep-show into what whites think is real black sexual behavior. White men get a bird's eye view of "authentic" black sex at work. The *Blacks on Blondes* text above perfectly captures, albeit in an extreme form, the image of a white man, sexually caged by his race, peeping at uncaged, uninhibited black men performing sex in a way that really pleases slutty white women. The white man watching this, or indeed any IP movie, gets to shed his whiteness and identify, for the duration of masturbation and ejaculation, with that one group of men who seem to be tailor made for porn. As the white man unzips, he steps out of the socially constructed cage of whiteness and into a thoroughly debauched world of huge, semen filled black penises out to rip, tear, pummel, and hammer white women into the utter subordination of becoming a fuckee.

While this debasing of white women might well intensify the sexual thrill for the white user, it has real world implications for the black community. All forms of oppression, be they gender, race or class based, require a system of beliefs that justify why one group has power over another. This justification process often comes in the form of negative images of the targeted group as somehow less human than the group in power, and it is this less-than-human status that makes them especially deserving of exploitation, abuse, and degradation. In porn, all people are seen as less-than-human because everyone is reduced to an orifice, but for whites, this is not presented as a condition of their whiteness, since in our society, whiteness is colorless and hence invisible by virtue of its power status. For people of color, however, it is their very color that constantly makes them visible as a racialized group as they carry the marker of "difference" on their skin. This is why it is impossible in porn for a person of color to have just a vagina or a penis, as their orifices are always going to be racially visible as "Asian Pussy" or Black Cock."

The pornographic images that meld the racial with the sexual may make the sex racier, but they also serve to breathe new life into old stereotypes that circulate in mainstream society. While these stereotypes are often a product of the past, they are cemented in the present every time a user masturbates to them. This is a powerful way to deliver racist ideology, as it not only makes visible the supposed sexual debauchery of the targeted group, but it also sexualizes the racism in ways that render the actual racism invisible in the mind of most consumers and non-consumers alike. This is why Don Imus got fired, and the pornographers get rich.

Pornographers are not necessarily out and out racists; they are just amoral businessmen who will mobilize any stereotype they can if it means higher profits. In a glutted market with an increasingly desensitized consumer base, they need to push the gonzo envelope towards the more extreme. But in reality what is there left to do today to a woman's body, short of killing her? Or as one porn director succinctly put it, "how many dicks can you shove in a woman at any one time"? The porn industry seems to have dug a hole for itself as it went so hard core and cruel so quickly, that it is now having trouble keeping their desensitized and bored consumers interested. How indeed, is it going to keep meeting their needs for "more extreme stuff?"

Endnotes

1   Sullivan, David. 2007. "Jeff Mullen: Long Dong Black Kong 'Not Racist.'" *Adult Video News,* http://business.avn.com/articles/1699. html. August 8. Accessed August 9, 2008.

2   http://www.avnonline.com/index.php?Primary_Navigation=Editori al&Action=Print_Article&Content_ID=105809 (accessed December 20, 2005).

3   "Black Video: Forward or Back?" *Adult Video News,* http://business. avn.com/articles/13323.html . Accessed April 18, 2009.

4   Andrew, Steven. 2007. Mr. Marcus, Adult Video News, http://www. xbiz.com/articles/80453/Mr.+marcus. April 4. Accessed April 10, 2009.

5   Asian Fever, http://asianfever.com/mansion1/index2. php?s=3&p=1&w=368290&t=0&c=0. Accessed March 23, 2009.

6   Ross, Lawrence. *Money Shot: Wild Days and Lonely Nights Inside the Black Porn Industry.* New York: Thunder's Mouth Press, 2007, P. 14.

7   Raw Black Amateurs, http://www.rawblackamateurs.com/ft=ae2171-68af3d38/index.html?cf=0&pp=1. Accessed March 12, 2008.

8   Ross, ibid., 100.

9   Hill Collins, Patricia. 2007. *Black Sexual Politics.* New York: Routledge. 2007.

10 Ross, Ibid., 99.

11 West, Cornell. 1992. *Race Matters.* (Boston: Beacon Press. 1993. P. 83.

12 Miller-Young. Mireille. 2008. Hip-Hop Honeys and Da Hustlaz: Black Sexualities in the New Hip-Hop Pornography. *Meridians: feminism, race, transnationalism,* 8 (1) 261–292.

13 Miller, Ibid., 270.

14 While the explicit nature of the hip hop videos has helped to mainstream pornographic images through channels such as MTV and BET, what is even more powerful is the close financial relationship between hip hop and porn. Increasingly, hip hop artists are involved in making porn videos to go along with their music, and hip hop artists are using pornographic imagery and porn stars in their videos. According to writer P. Weasels:

hip hop porn can be divided into two broad categories: porn-centric and music-centric …. In the porn-centric movies, there doesn't tend to be much in the way of new music or original beats; the porn takes center-stage. In the music video-style porn, the artist has taken some time to make new tunes for the film, and generally it will be marketed that way.

(P. Weasels. *Porn 101: Hip Hop Porn Primer* http://www.gamelink. com/news.jhtml?news_id=news_nt_primer_hip_hop_porn. Accessed May 2, 2009.

AVN's Frank Majors (*Strange BedfellowsRock 'n' Rap Storm Porn, But Where Can It Go From Here? http://www.avn.com/video/ articles/15844.htm,* accessed January 7, 2009) traces the beginning of this relationship back to the 1990s, with artists such as DJ Yella, a founding member of NWA, both directing and acting in porn. But, as Majors argues, the relationship between porn and hip hop took off in 2001 when superstar rapper Snoop Dog joined with Hustler to make Snoop Dogg's *Doggystyle.* This became the best-selling porn movie of the year and was followed by Snoop Dogg's *Hustlaz: Diary of a Pimp,* which also became a top seller.

Following the Snoop videos, other hip hop artists jumped on the bandwagon and aligned themselves with the porn industry. Majors points out that "soon the market was flooded with the artists such as Mystikal's *Liquid City* (Hustler), Too Short's *Get In Where You Fit In* (Adam and Eve), Lil' Jon & The East Sidaz's *Lil' Jon's American Sex Series* (Video Team), and Ice-T's *Pimpin' 101* (Pleasure Productions)." Ice T is especially interesting as he is a one-time pimp turned actor and rapper. According to the director, Tony Diablo, Ice T's hands-on knowledge of pimping helped to make Pimpin' 101 more intense as "he broke down every sort of girl and he's sharing his own experiences" (Ice-T's Pimpin' 101, http://www. adultvideonews.com/otset/ots0103_02.html, accessed January 7, 2009). This is ironic given that Ice T plays a caring and empathetic police officer who deals with sex crimes against women on *Law and Order SVU.* As an unrepentant pimp and a producer of porn, Ice T gets to construct an image of himself on television that is greatly at odds with his lived experience.

15 White Dicks in Black in Black Chicks. http://www. whitedicksinblackchics.com/t1/?nats=NjM4Mjo3MjoyOA,0,0,0,0. Accessed March 24, 2009.

16 Adult DVD Talk. http://forum.adultdvdtalk.com/forum/ topic.dlt/topic_id=117363/forum_id=1/cat_id=1/ reply=1258433#post1258433. Accessed January 5, 2009.

17 Adult DVD Talk. http://forum.adultdvdtalk.com/forum/topic.dlt/ whichpage=1/topic_id=74110/forum_id=1/cat_id=1/74110.htm. Accessed January 5, 2009.

18 Wang, Oliver. 2003. Asian American Porn. http://modelminority. com/modules.php?name=News&file=article&sid=397. Accessed January 5, 2009.

19 Black Humor: The Marketing of Racial Stereotypes in Interracial Porn. AVN Online. http://www.mydigitalpublication.com/ publication/?i=12069 . Accessed March 3, 2009.

20 Ibid.

21 Anonymous Reviewer Submission for "White Meat on Black Street," http://www.sirrodney.com/singlereview/White+Meat+On+Black+St reet#readerreviews. Accessed December 13, 2005.

22 Blacks on Blondes, http://blacksonblondes.iwantanewgirlfriend.com. Accessed December 16, 2005.

23 For a description of the content of these movies, *see* "Once You Go Black . . . You Never Go Back" Movie Series http://www. searchextreme.com/series/Once_You_Go_Black..._You_Never_Go_ Back/97899206841 . Accessed December 28, 2005.

24 Butters, Gerald. (2002). *Black Manhood on the Silent Screen*. Kansas: University Press of Kansas. P. 10.

25 Mel Watkins Interview Excerpt, http://www.pbs.org/wgbh/amex/ foster/sfeature/sf_minstrelsy_5.html. Accessed December. 24, 2005.

PART III:

PORNOGRAPHY AND PROSTITUTION AS OPPRESSION OF WOMEN

CHAPTER 16

Harm and Its Denial: Sex Buyers, Pimps, and the Politics of Prostitution, with Particular Attention to German Legal Prostitution

by Melissa Farley, Ph.D. Prostitution Research & Education, San Francisco and Inge Kleine, Ph.D. Kommunikationszentrum für Frauen (KOFRA), München

"Legal prostitution is like making sure that the trains run on time." Inge Kleine, 2015

Some pimps, some sex buyers, and some governments have decided that certain women, in order to survive, can be sexually exploited or raped by many men each day. These women are usually poor and ethnically marginalised. In Germany, those who favor the abolition of prostitution call this "poverty prostitution." As a Canadian prostitution tourist commented about women in Thai prostitution, *"These girls gotta eat, don't they? I'm putting bread on their plate. I'm making a contribution. They'd starve to death unless they whored."* This self-congratulatory Darwinism avoids the question: do women have the right to live *without* the sexual harassment or sexual exploitation or serial rape of prostitution, or is that right reserved only for women with race or class or geographic privilege?[1]

"You get what you pay for without the 'no,'" a sex buyer explained. Non-prostituting women have the right to say "no," at least in theory, with legal protection from sexual harassment and sexual exploitation and rape. But prostitution is the business of sexual exploitation. A sex trade entrepreneur proudly displayed his architectural drawings for a legal brothel complex just outside Mexico City. Unrolling the delicate drawings, he pointed to the bars, the brothels, the video and sex toy shops, the restaurants, the buildings where the women lived, the childcare center, the strip clubs on each block. At the corner of one of the drawings was a larger, two-story building. "That's the medical clinic," he smiled. "That's where they get stitched up and can get right back to work."[2]

The existence of prostitution marks society's betrayal of women, its betrayal of all who are marginalized and vulnerable because of their sex, their ethnicity, their poverty, the location where they happen to live, and their history of abuse and neglect.

But how do men think about these realities? How do they justify to themselves their decision to buy a human being to use for their conception of what sex is? Men who buy sex have much to teach us about prostitution and sex trafficking. This article offers a summary of research on sex buyers, a discussion of German sex buyers' attitudes toward the sex trade during the COVID-19 pandemic, testimony from women in prostitution and from sex buyers, a discussion of legal German prostitution today and during the Nazi era, and barriers to progressive change that would reduce sex trafficking and move toward abolishing the abuse that is prostitution.

Is prostitution harmful?

To understand the role of sex buyers, it's necessary to understand what prostitution is and its impact is on the women, men, and transwomen[3] in prostitution. Sexual violence and physical assault are the norm for women in all prostitution, legal or not. A brothel owner in the Netherlands complained about an ordinance requiring that brothels have pillows in the rooms, "You don't want a pillow in the [brothel's] room. It's a murder weapon."[4] Aware of sex buyers' violence, the legal Dutch pimp knew that sex buyers are regularly murderous toward women. Women in prostitution experience violence that includes incest, rape, and battering. Survivors of prostitution explain, "It's like domestic violence taken to the extreme."[5] A Canadian prostituted woman said, "what is rape for others, is normal for us."[6]

Regardless of its legal status, prostitution harms the women and girls in it, according to extensive evidence. In addition to psychological trauma,[7] prostitution harms women physically. Heide (2016) and Bissinger (2019) have documented extensive harms caused by German prostitution to women's reproductive systems and immune systems.[8] Concluding that all prostitution, both legal and illegal, is contemptuous of women and humanity, built on exploitation and cruelty, Bissinger and others have documented the refusal to use condoms by a majority of sex buyers, whether in Germany as advertised by legal brothels, in Canada, India, or USA, exposing the women to venereal and in some cases deadly, disease.[9] Women in prostitution face overwhelmingly high rates of rape and homicide and are murdered at a rate that is among the highest ever documented among women.[10] The death rate of women in prostitution was forty times higher than that of the general population, according to a Canadian commission.[11] Another study reported a 36% incidence of attempted murder of women in prostitution.[12] Describing prostituted women as the most raped women on the planet, Susan Hunter at the Council for Prostitution Alternatives in Oregon reported that prostituted women were raped an average of once a week.[13] Eighty-five percent of prostituting women in Minnesota had been raped in prostitution.[14] In addition, prostituting women are regularly physically assaulted and verbally abused, whether they prostitute on the street, or in strip clubs, or in brothels.[15]

In Germany, 92% of prostituting women experienced sexual harassment, 87% suffered physical violence, and 59% suffered sexual violence.[16] Since prostitution was normalized as "sex work" in 2002, there have been 86 murders and 59 attempted murders of women in German prostitution.[17]

Poverty and homelessness are both antecedent to and a consequence of prostitution. Among 854 women, men, and transwomen in prostitution from Canada, Colombia, Germany, Mexico, South Africa, Thailand, Turkey, United States, & Zambia, 75% had been homeless at some point in their lives. Eighty-nine percent of these people in prostitution in 9 countries wanted to escape prostitution, but did not see other options for survival. The emotional consequences of prostitution are the same in widely varying cultures whether prostitution is legal or illegal, in a brothel, a strip club, a massage parlor, or the street. In 9 countries on 5 continents, two-thirds of women, men and transwomen in prostitution met diagnostic criteria for posttraumatic stress disorder. This level of extreme emotional distress is the same as that seen in the most traumatized people studied by psychologists: battered women, raped women, combat veterans, and survivors of state-sponsored torture.[18] Symptoms of emotional distress in all prostitution are off the charts: depression, suicidality, posttraumatic stress disorder, dissociation, substance abuse, and eating disorders. Across widely varying cultures, the traumatic consequences of prostitution were similar whether prostitution was legal, tolerated, illegal, whether indoors or outdoors.

Pimps and sex buyers commodify and dehumanize women in prostitution, removing her personhood. A sex buyer described prostitution as "renting an organ for 10 minutes."[19] Women in prostitution are not considered fully human. They are seen as body parts or temporary girlfriends whose feelings are irrelevant. A woman who prostituted for 19 years in Canada explained prostitution in much the same way that sex buyers did, "They own you for that half hour or that twenty minutes or that hour. They are buying you. They have no attachments, you're not a person, you're a thing to be used."[20] The sex buyer demands that she enact his fantasies about women and sexuality. She conveys that she is subordinate and sexually available. Her name changes, her appearance changes, her body movements change, her voice changes. As Norwegian women in prostitution explained, she is transformed in prostitution into a thing to be used for the sex buyer to empty himself into.[21] Andrea Dworkin wrote of the prostituted woman, "... she has no name. She is a mouth, a vagina, and an anus ...who is she? She is no one. Not metaphorically no one. Literally, no one."[22] Evelina Giobbe wrote about the aftermath of prostitution,

> *I feel like I imagine people who were in concentration camps feel when they get out.... It's a real deep pain, an assault to my mind, my body, my dignity as a human being. I feel like what was taken away from me in prostitution is irretrievable.*[23]

Dissociation permits psychological survival, whether the traumatic events are slavery, incest, military combat, torture, rape, or prostitution. Psychological dissociation is necessary so that she can survive the prostitution, so that she can create another person, another part of herself who does the prostituting: the not-me.[24] The real me is a daughter, a mom, a student. Dissociation is an elaborate escape and avoidance strategy in which overwhelming human cruelty results in fragmentation of the mind into different parts of the self. A primary function of dissociation is to handle the overwhelming fear and pain, to deal with the systematized cruelty encountered during prostitution by splitting. Dissociation in prostitution often repeats a protective psychological response for surviving childhood sexual assault. Survivors explain, "It was easy for me to turn a trick because I could just take myself out – like with my dad. It was like I took myself out of the situation and just focused on something else and it was like I wasn't even there."[25] Another woman explained, "You make yourself empty inside."[26]

Some sex buyers cause emotional distress in the woman they purchase because of their desire to playact the kind of relationship that they are unable or unwilling to have with non-prostituting women, euphemistically naming prostitution a "girlfriend experience." Constructing an imaginary pleasant emotional connection with the woman they buy for sex, they can keep thinking of themselves as nice guys. This scenario demands extensive and exhausting lies from her.[27] As survivor/activist Rachel Moran wrote to the "nice" sex buyer,

> *The truth, that you're so desperate to flee from, is that you are just like a gentle rapist... The damage you're causing is incalculable, but you tell yourself you're doing no harm here, and you use the smiles of the women you buy as some kind of currency; they allow you to buy your own bullshit. Every moment with you was a lie, and I hated every second of it.*[28]

Prostitution is many things at the same time. It is a tool of men's dominance, a tool of race/ethnic dominance, a tool of class dominance. It is violence against women. In states that legalize or decriminalize the sex trade, prostitution is a state-guaranteed infrastructure for the sexual use of women by men who pay a fee. Prostitution is the idea of sex without reciprocity, of one-sided sexual gratification in which one person dehumanizes the other person; she doesn't even have to be psychologically present since she can dissociate and disappear and seem to be someone that she is not. Feminists have struggled fiercely against this type of coerced sex. But for many men, this sex of prostitution remains normalized and most nations' laws do not even call it rape. It is deeply disturbing to see one's state or region endorse, even champion, the dehumanized, dissociated sex of prostitution. In their prostitution laws, their concessions to the sex trade's demands, and in their pandering to men who buy sex as their rightful entitlement, Germany, the Netherlands, New Zealand, Nevada, and other pimp states across the globe have sent a clear message to one half of their populations: a message of contempt.

Is prostitution a free choice?

Two common myths about prostitution are that it is a voluntary choice and that legalizing it makes prostitution safe. Neither myth is accurate, but the fantasy of a free choice allows societies to disregard and to dismiss the woman in prostitution as somehow different from other women, and through this dismissal, to justify her prostitution. Prostitution is then no longer understood as a male institution but instead as an institution that is a benefit to marginalized and women who are considered different from so-called nice women. Via pseudo-feminist sex trade marketers, the woman in prostitution has been transformed from the 19th century stereotype of a morally defective woman to the 20th century stereotype of a daring and rebellious entrepreneur. Both notions serve the same goal; they rationalize prostitution as *women's* creation, not men's. This shift in focus enables the sex buyer to maintain both social invisibility and a lack of accountability for harm.[29]

In Germany, these myths are believed even by some who are critical of prostitution. Nonetheless, the facts are clear: on average, 84% of people in prostitution were under the control of a pimp or trafficker.[30] Pimps and traffickers exercise extreme control: one person deceives or coerces another person into prostitution, keeps her in prostitution, and receives the majority of its profits. Pimps are traffickers.[31] Sigma Huda, the UN Special Rapporteur on Violence against Women and Children noted that most of the time, prostitution meets the legal definition of trafficking.[32] An organized crime expert estimated that more than 90% of women in German legal prostitution were controlled by pimps.[33] SOLWODI, a German NGO helping women escape prostitution, estimated that 80% of prostituted women were "under strong pressure and have no alternatives."[34] A 2014 European Parliament Briefing reported that 60%–90% of those in a number of national prostitution markets have been trafficked."[35] Chief superintendent Helmut Sporer, Kriminalpolizei, Augsburg explained,

It is very important to keep in mind that prostitution and human trafficking are closely connected. There is no such thing as clean and good prostitution that exists separately from the horrible realities of human trafficking and pimping.[36]

Choice implies the presence of alternatives. Prostitution, whether legal or illegal, is not a genuine choice because the conditions that permit real choice are not present: physical safety, economic non-discrimination, equal power with sex buyers, and real alternatives to prostitution. Almost everyone in prostitution is there because of a lack of alternatives, not because they freely chose it. In prostitution, one person wants sex, the other person does not. The money itself persuades, entices, or coerces the prostituted person to perform sex acts. Payment does not erase his sexual violence, verbal sadism, domestic abuse, and rape. Women are coerced into prostitution in many ways. A woman who flees a community where there are few jobs available to her and who travels to a city where she thinks she can make money quickly to send home may find herself imperiled by prostitution. A homeless woman, in exchange for food or shelter, may give in to prostitution. A woman who is expected to tolerate sexual assault in order to keep her non-sex-trade job may find she gets paid less in that job than in prostitution.

Rationalizing his exploitation of a trafficked woman, a sex buyer said, "If I don't see a chain on her leg, I assume she's made the choice to be there." According to this argument, if there's no physical evidence of force, then her prostitution is named voluntary or consenting. Most women are coerced into prostitution by *inequality*: sex inequality, race/ethnic inequality, economic inequality, and increasingly by geographic vulnerability to catastrophic climate change, wars, and other causes of refugee status.

Yet the knowledge that women in prostitution have been exploited, coerced, pimped, or trafficked does not deter sex buyers. Half of a research sample of London sex buyers said that they had used a woman in prostitution who they knew was under the control of a pimp. As one man explained, "It's like he's her owner."[37] Another

294

man said, "The girl is instructed to do what she needs to do. You can just relax, it's her job."[38]

What is known about sex buyers?

Sex buyers see but refuse to acknowledge the coercion and the terror, the disgust and despair, in the women they buy for sex. If she does not run screaming from the room yelling "help, police!" she is assumed to have consented to the prostitution, therefore she's not trafficked. "All of them are exploited," declared an Italian sex buyer with an attitude of chilling indifference. "However, they also have good incomes."[39]

A number of researchers have found that sex buyers are more likely than other men to commit sexual violence. Heilman interviewed men in Chile, Croatia, India, Mexico, and Rwanda and found that in all five countries, men who bought sex were more likely to rape.[40] The more often a Scottish sex buyer used women in prostitution, the more likely he was to also report having committed sexually coercive acts against non-prostituting women.[41] Other research found that men who buy sex share similar attitudes and behaviors to sexually aggressive men. To summarize, when sex buyers were compared with men who did not buy sex, the sex buyers exhibited the following attitudes and behaviors:

1. Sex buyers have a preference for impersonal or non-relational sex.
2. Sex buyers have significantly more sex partners (both in and out of prostitution) than men who don't buy sex.
3. Sex buyers fear rejection by women more than men who choose not to buy sex. Some of the sex buyers said they were shy, insecure, or feared being sexually judged.
4. Sex buyers had committed sexually aggressive acts in the past, telling researchers in anonymous interviews that

they had committed more rapes than men who did not buy sex.

5. Sex buyers said that they were more likely than non-sex-buyers to rape if they could get away with it.

6. Sex buyers have a hostile masculine self-identification. Their identity as men was based on domination of women, mistrust of women, and negative stereotypes about women.

7. Sex buyers report a greater number of arrests for crimes other than prostitution than men who don't buy sex.

8. Sex buyers lack empathy. "I don't want to know about her," a sex buyer said, "I don't want her to cry or this and that because that spoils the idea for me."[42] Another example of this failure of empathy is from a man who explained that prostitution is "like going to have your car done, you tell them what you want done, they don't ask, you tell them you want so and so done."[43]

Online chat forums reveal sex buyers' awareness of the brutal conditions of prostituted women's lives, but that awareness is accompanied by a lack of empathy for women in the sex trade. The COVID-19 pandemic in 2020 generated much discussion on German sex buyer online forums, revealing sex buyers' dehumanizing exploitation of extremely vulnerable women. German sex buyer forums were reviewed in April 2020 by sociologist Manuela Schon.[44]

German legal sex buyer #1: "Today I was strolling around and of course went after our hobby...To everyone who will now be outraged: Yes, I am aware of the current situation and I will not complain if there will be no intensive care bed or ventilator for me, just as I will not complain if I someday will catch the HIV virus." *Willing to risk his life in order to exploit a woman in prostitution – in this man's calculations of risk, he does not consider her risk.* Some men who buy sex are sexually aroused by the danger of intimate contact during the coronavirus pandemic.

German legal sex buyer #2: "I'm afraid the brothels won't reopen before next year... there will be more sexual assaults on women, since a lot of guys can't get rid of their pressure. A lot will change. Maybe there will be a lot of fresh meat." *Some men's rationalization for prostitution is: if I don't get to rape a woman who is available to me because she needs my money to survive, then I'll rape the "nice" women out there. So give me what I want or I'll have a rape-tantrum.* Of course prostitution does not prevent rape. But even women in prostitution have internalized this lie. A woman in Seattle escort prostitution pointed out that during the pandemic, "As things get stressed out, we can be a lot of peoples' outlets."[45]

German legal sex buyer #3: "I still fuck the whores without a condom. She can lick the caviar from my ass." *This man hates women.*

German legal sex buyer #4: "How do you fuck catholic [no condom] in corona times? One could take her doggy, hoping that the virus doesn't enter through the glans. Allegedly it is a respiratory virus, which is only absorbed through mouth, eyes and nose." *He wants what he wants and to hell with her health, his family's health, his community's health, his own health. He lies to himself about the risks.*

German legal sex buyer #5: "Anita is worth a lot in times of crisis (which means now). She only does outdoor meetings. Not without condom sorry needs to be said. But she offers a quite good oral service without condom with cumming into mouth or on the tits. What can I say? Beggars can't be choosers." *For this man, women's value is based on how fuckable he perceives them to be. He feels sorry for himself because he can't get her to do *exactly* what he wants her to do.*

German legal sex buyer #6: "At the moment they are all scared. Usually here in the Bremen area you need to pay 200€ when ordering someone to your place. I only paid 130€. The whores need money, so they make it for less money to have customers at all." *Did he think to himself: I saved some money by bargaining with a woman who was scared and hungry. What fun!*

German legal sex buyer #7: "I found a good solution [to the closure of German legal brothels], I now fuck my secretary. I always wished for that, but now it has happened due to the Corona Crisis. I am very satisfied with her." *All women are whores according to this man.*

A majority of sex buyers are aware of sex trafficking but choose not to assist the women and not to report it to the police. A Scottish trafficking hotline received only three calls from sex buyers in one year. According to a spokeswoman from the Glasgow Women's Support Project, "Men are very aware of the terrible circumstances some of these women are in but choose to do nothing."[46] A London study of 110 sex buyers found that half had knowingly bought a woman who was under the control of a pimp.[47] A sex buyer stated that prostitution had no negative effect on prostitutes because they had no feelings, yet he also said he had never tried to rescue a prostitute because *"you can get killed doing that."*[48] A sex buyer who was interviewed by a prostitution survivor explained,

SEX BUYER: I think the thing I am most ashamed of is that I've been to Asian massage parlors. And call me naive, but what I discovered after a couple of trips to these places is that many of these women are victims of sex trafficking. They're imported into the country under the ruse of getting a good job . . . And even after they work off their debt, often they just return to the sex industry, because they lack skills, they lack a verifiable work history, they don't speak very good English, and the sex work is what they know and it becomes, in a way, easy money. Thing is, they are not glassy-eyed robot slaves sobbing under their oppressor like you see in movies about this kind of thing.

INTERVIEWER: But it's not consensual. It's coercion. It's sex slavery.

SEX BUYER: And I felt very remorseful when I learned this. And then I did it again.[49]

Other sex buyers have articulated their awareness of exploitation and violence in prostitution. Here are some examples,

"The pimp controls her and forces her to do things she's not ready or wanting to do."

"She is definitely afraid of him. She'll get slapped around if she don't do what she's told."

"He controls her by hitting her. And by playing mind games with her."

"It's sad and obviously exploitive. One person is compromising themselves in a manner that they'd rather not for the benefit of another."

"The pimp is the owner and the prostitute is the slave to make money for the pimp."[50]

One study explored the impact of living in a region where legal prostitution exists by comparing men who live in or near legal prostitution zones with men who do not live in these regions. When college-aged young men in Nevada were compared with similar young men in regions of the U.S. where prostitution is not legal, it became clear that the state's support of prostitution in Nevada had a significant effect on men's attitudes and behavior toward women. Nevada university students endorsed a greater number of myths about prostitution that justified sexual violence, and they were significantly more likely than non-Nevada students to use women in prostitution, to go to strip clubs and massage parlors, and to use pornography. Influenced by the state's support for prostitution, the Nevada men normalized prostitution for their children as well as for themselves. They considered it acceptable for their future sons to use prostitutes and for their future daughters to become prostitutes. They failed to see prostitution as sexual exploitation, while at the same time justifying acts of sexual violence against women in prostitution—for example, they assumed that it would not be possible to rape an escort. These dehumanizing attitudes placed prostituted women in harm's way.[51]

Camouflage and denial regarding German prostitution

Given the evidence about the harms of prostitution, some writers' perspectives seem biased. Despite evidence that sex buyers are not like other men in terms of their misogyny, lack of empathy, and attitudes toward women, some researchers nonetheless declare that sex buyers are normal, everyday men.[52] These views then inform *ethical punter campaigns* that actually entrench and promote the sex trade. Such campaigns falsely present prostitution as a banal, victimless act.

Perceptions of sex buyers in Germany range from a neoliberal normalization of prostitution to detailed analysis of the extreme inequality and brutality of prostitution.[53] Some German academics put forward a romantic view of sex buyers that has evolved from sex trade advocacy groups' harm reduction programs. These groups assume that reduction of STD/HIV and reduction of prostitution's social stigma are all that are needed to eliminate or decrease prostitution's harms. German research on sex buyers promotes the myth that men who commit violence against women are mentally disturbed, easily recognisable psychopaths.[54] Victim-blaming is acti-vated when myths about sex buyers do not align with the evidence.[55] From the perspective of sex trade advocates and some sociologists, only a very few people in prostitution are truly victimized: children, victims of trafficking, which is defined in confusing and restrictive terms. Women who migrate to Germany because of extreme pov-erty or who are refugees from conflict zones, for example, are not considered genuine victims.

Sex buyers' motivations have been valorized by some research-ers. Velten, Kleiber and Grenz describe sex buyers as "disappointed romanticists" who suffer because of their wives' sexual deficits. Sex buyers are seen as liberal adventurers on the cutting edge or as brave hedonists. Ambivalent men buy sex and later regret their choice, but the reasons for their regret are unanalyzed.[56] At times, less idealizing and more critical of the inequality between the sex buyer and the woman sold in prostitution, Gerheim has noted sex buyers' motives: seeking sex with no fear of rejection, loneliness, contempt for women, emotional crisis, and enjoyment of danger.[57]

In the German media, the sex buyer may be ridiculed, but he is still seen as controllable, not dangerous, or even a victim. A recent media report failed to recognize stalking, which was instead roman-ticized. In the newspaper account, a sex buyer fell in love with a prostituting woman, fantasized a relationship with her, aggressively texted her and tried to meet her in person in order to go into her bathroom and shower with her. Writing about the sex buyer as a "nice idiot," or as a sucker conned by a prostitute, the journalist failed to analyze the sex buyer's behavior as *stalking*, a form of violence which is a threat regularly encountered by prostituting women.[58] After the murder of a Romanian woman in prostitution by her regular sex buyer in front of a Stuttgart brothel, men in a chat room minimised her death as a "relationship drama that ended in murder."[59] The killer was a 53-year old family man who was angry because he had spent a lot of money paying for sex and therefore he felt entitled to a genuine relationship with her. She disliked him intensely, preferring to walk 80 km to return to the brothel instead

301

of staying the night at a hotel with him. The community of sex buyers and the newspaper *Bild* described the killing as a "relationship drama"[60] rather than as the murder of a prostituted woman by an entitled, enraged sex buyer.

What sex acts are sold in legal brothels? The acts of prostitution cannot be adequately described in abstract terms; it is necessary to use concrete, even crude language. In German legal brothels, a condomless sex buyer can pay to deposit his semen in the mouth of a prostituted woman and demand that she swallow it; he can pay her to kiss him with a mouth full of semen; he can play with his feces on her body. He can pay to engage in what legal pimps call "blood sports," including cutting her. He can pay her to lick his testicles and anus. He can pay to perpetrate gang rape on her with his friends, all of whom will ejaculate on her face, eyes and nose. He can buy the right to have a woman defecate on him or he can defecate on the woman he buys. He can pay to have a woman urinate on him or to urinate on her. He can pay to have a woman drink his urine or he can drink hers. For a higher price, every sex act can be performed without a condom.[61]

Why is the harm of prostitution invisible even though it is in plain sight? A survivor of prostitution said, "It's like incest, no one wants to talk about it." Many people simply cannot stand to look at the despair, the vastness of the physical and psychological harm to those prostituted. It is too painful, too cruel, too ruthless. Denial of the harm of prostitution accompanies sex buying but it is also integral to neoliberal discussions about prostitution. Many words that refer to prostitution cover up its cruelty: the expressions, "migrant sex work" and "sex tourism" imply that prostitution is just another job that women travel to perform. Just as the words "field worker" or "house worker" or "assistant planter" deny the harm of slavery, so also the notion of "sex work" denies the violence in prostitution.[62]

The reality of the sex trade is further concealed by some individuals who describe themselves as sex worker advocates but who are in fact pimps. Some advocates identify themselves publicly as sex workers or sex worker advocates, although they are actually managers of women in the sex trade, some are pimps, and some have been arrested for pandering, brothel managing, or trafficking. Tanja Sommer is a sex worker advocate with Berufsverband erotische und sexuelle Dienstleistungen (BesD) (Business Association of Erotic and Sexual services). Sommer is a leader of BesD[63] and also manages a brothel in which other women prostitute.[64] Her colleague Holger Rettig who helped found BesD[65] and works closely with the group, is a leader of UEGD (Unternehmerverband Erotikgewerbe Deutschland, Business Association of Erotic Businesses in Germany), an organization consisting entirely of brothel-owning pimps. There is a blatant conflict of interest when individuals who are management/owners/pimps are in the same organization as those who are under their control. This misrepresentation is even more sinister and unethical when the brothel owners, managers, and pimps hide their affiliations, claiming to represent the interests of "sex workers." Hiding beneath the banner of labor unions, the pimps appeal to the Left's sympathies. Yet groups such as the New Zealand Prostitutes Collective, the International Union of Sex Workers (UK), Red Thread (the Netherlands), Durbar Mahila Samanwaya Committee (India), Stella (Canada), and Sex Worker Organizing Project (USA), while aggressively promoting prostitution as legitimate work, do not resemble what most consider to be labor unions. These pimp-led groups do not demand safety, shorter hours, higher pay, or that a smaller percentage of earnings be deducted by management or pimps. They do not demand exit services, which are what 90% of women in prostitution say they want. Instead, these groups promote a free market in human beings to be used for sex.[66]

Many are confused by the proposal that disabled men are entitled to sex. According to the pimps' logic, if disabled men cannot find a willing sex partner, they are entitled to buy one. Rather than challenging prejudice against people with disabilities, pimps suggest providing a disabled person with a woman in prostitution -- someone who is herself vulnerable and socially outcast. The plan rests on the assumption that all men have a right to sex. This prostitution scheme is marketed as "sexual assistance" and is promoted by Kassandra in Germany and advocacy groups such as "Soph!e" [sic] , member of the "Volkshilfe Wien" ("The People's Help," a social support and advocacy organization addressing a wide range of social concerns), or LIBIDA in Austria, who have obtained public funding for training women to provide prostitution to the disabled community.[67] The groups seek health insurance funding to pay for prostitution for disabled sex buyers,[68] and have offered training for certificates in "sexual assistance." It is unclear whether mentally or physically disabled men are themselves asking for prostitution, or whether their legal guardians actually operate as assistant pimps. These schemes are based on the unfounded assumption that disabled men are unable to form intimate sexual relationships. In practice, these programs are pimp scams in which prostituted women pay to earn meaningless certificates as "sexual assistants" instead of being offered what they seek -- exit support and legitimate job training.

When a state tolerates or promotes legal prostitution, as Germany does, then laws against sexual assault are in jeopardy and are sometimes even eliminated. Pro Familia, an agency similar to Planned Parenthood in USA, published a legal opinion in 2005 on "sexual assistance" that illustrates the ways that legal prostitution can contaminate civil society. Pro Familia advocated the provision of women in prostitution to men with "severe mental limitations." In Kassandra's ideology and in the Pro Familia legal opinion, *the abused are encouraged to become abusers.* Care homes are seen as legally obligated to provide in-home prostitution. The Pro Familia legal experts also addressed disabled men's capacity for informed consent and concluded that assessing men's ability to consent to prostitution would constitute "a moral examination" which would unjustly restrict the men's rights.[69]

Sex trade apologists assume that sex buyers are mostly nice fellows who will assist a trafficked woman if she asks for help. This benign viewpoint is the basis for "ethical sex buyer" campaigns that promote harm reduction. Despite the availability of condomless sex acts for sale in legal brothels, a Frankfurt program employed young women community educators in condom costumes who distributed postcards expressing support for prostitution while politely suggesting condom use, courtesy, and personal hygiene.[70] In reality, these programs were brothel marketing campaigns that reinforced men's entitlement to prostitution. While developers of the program expressed their concern that the *community educators* not be traumatized by rude or aggressive sex buyers, at the same time they ignored the fact that *prostituting women* were subjected to the men's abuse and violence. Another campaign postured as reducing the harms of exploitation and slavery[71] while warning sex buyers,

> *Forced prostitution is also fraud committed against men who are pulled into the grey area of organized crime.* Here you are being betrayed as a customer, *because the services to you are not rendered voluntarily. As a client you create the market for prostitution by your demand. You can influence it by your behaviour and react to its ills. (authors' emphasis).*[72]

Police investigated 49 cases of potential coercion resulting from this campaign, but the results were unclear because the law itself is vague.[73] Women avoid testifying against their pimps and traffickers because they are terrified. Even when information provided by a sex buyer results in a police investigation, the legal challenge can be overwhelming because of the difficulty of separating legal pimping from trafficking under legal prostitution.

The lack of clarity regarding pimping, coercive control, and violence in German prostitution laws affect the safety of all women, as evident in rape conviction rates which reached a historic low of 7.5% in 2016, with 85% of all rapes not reported. For example, a young woman's experience of trafficking, pimping, sexual assault and kidnapping was redefined as a "work accident" by a Hamburg court.[74] The reluctance to define "coercion" or "force" has hampered rape prosecutions as well as trafficking cases. This misogynist thinking was evident during ratification of the Istanbul Convention, which is an international agreement on prevention of violence against women. German rape laws did not meet the minimum requirements of the Istanbul Convention which states that "Consent must be given voluntarily as the result of the person's free will assessed in the context of the surrounding circumstances."[75] Consent is an oxymoron when the context is the placement of a woman in a legal pimp's brothel. *A state that accepts and taxes prostitution as a business model has difficulty in the legal rejection of rape.*

Another case exemplifies Germany's legal difficulties in protecting women from violence. In 2016, a young Eastern European woman was severely injured when she tried to escape from her pimps by jumping from a third-floor brothel window. The Hamburg Social Law Court declared that these events could be described as a "work accident."[76] The young woman had no German work permit, which made her vulnerable to her pimp's manipulative control. The pimp controlled her under conditions which have been defined as slavery elsewhere: he controlled all her activities including locking her in an apartment for several days, he raped her, held her legal documents, required her to be available for purchase at all times, required her to pay rent for rooms rented for prostitution, and he took 50% of her earnings. Appearing to side with the pimp, the court avoided use of the word rape, which would have required a legal investigation. Avoiding a straightforward response to her kidnapping and rape, the Social Court focused instead on the woman's labor status as independent contractor vs employee. The court's decision to mandate pimp/employer medical insurance payment for the woman's injuries was lauded by pro-prostitution advocates.[77] The elimination of legal accountability in this case of severe human rights abuse only makes sense if the camouflaging of prostitution as state-taxed work is understood as the context for this egregious disappearance of legal justice.

What can we learn from Nazi-era legal prostitution?

Germany has legalized the sex trade in the past as well as the present. There is extensive documentation of the National

Socialists' regulationist approach to prostitution both in theory and in practice.[78] The Nazis' regulations have many similarities to Germany's 2002 law that regulates prostitution. During the Third Reich 1933-1945, women in prostitution and other women socially defined as sexually deviant or promiscuous, were labelled "anti-social" and were regarded as "lost to the folk community," that is, they were seen as "unpure" people who should be segregated away from "good" Germans. Vice police were given extensive powers so that a wide range of women could be arrested. These included women in prostitution who were outside of the state-regulated brothels or outside of special streets zoned for prostitution such as the Herberstraße in Hamburg which exists today as a red-light zone. The NS vice police could also arrest women in bars or restaurants, including women without a male companion or women who were accused of sex outside marriage.

Women were jailed, deported to concentration camps or work-houses, committed to mental institutions where many starved to death, and many were forcibly sterilized under a law permitting sterilization of "those of less value." Women to be prostituted were selected from lineups of prisoners of war, from groups of Jewish women who had been deported from other parts of Europe, and from women prisoners already in the Ravensbrück concentration camp. Some German women political prisoners were also selected for concentration camp brothels.[79] Women were bribed into prostitution with promises such as release from imprisonment after six months' brothel service, but they were returned to their former camps physically degraded, sick, and sometimes forced to submit to medical experimentation.[80] The National Socialists viewed the women in the camp brothels as disposable humans who would not survive, thus there were no barriers to any abuse or torture of the women by either the men prisoners or by the SS. Nazi racial purity laws comfortably tolerated the deaths of these disposable women. The Rassenschande laws prohibited sex between Germans and Jews and between Germans and many Eastern Europeans. Thus, these women's deaths by any means meant that no racially contaminated children would be born.

The enslaved women in these brothels were from local communities. Any woman in an occupied country who was determined by a German official to be "a prostitute" -- young, single, unmarried women -- could be kidnapped for the Wehrmacht brothels. Women forced into prostitution at the concentration camps or at the army brothels were often given the "choice" of prostitution or labor camp. The fact that many women chose brothel prostitution has been used by the German state to deny them post-war compensation, as their decision is counted as "voluntary." Women offered the "choice" to prostitute in the Nazi brothels were in fact making a non-choice. If anything, they chose to stay alive instead of dying of starvation or being worked to death.[81] The charge that their prostitution was "voluntary" is the same judgment being made of desperate women in prostitution today. And today as well, if a woman is not shackled or if she does not have a gun aimed at her head, if she is prostituting in order to avoid starvation or death, then her prostitution is viewed as her choice, thus she is blamed for her own victimization. Moral judgment against women in prostitution existed during the Third Reich, continued among Holocaust memoirists, and still exists among today's historians.[82] "Research into Nazi-era prostitution challenges our use of the word *prostitution*, which suggests to some that a commercial exchange or choice occurred. In fact, Nazi-era prostitution is better described as *rape,* which emphasizes coercion or choicelessness.[83]

Publicly, the Nazis stated that they did not use Jewish women for prostitution because of racial purity laws.[84] In reality, Jewish women were prostituted by Nazis in concentration camps, although their rape/prostitution was both "submerged in the tide of murder" during the Holocaust,[85] and also hidden because the women were stigmatized and shamed as women for their prostitution which was a means of avoiding death by starvation in the camps. Some women were selected at Auschwitz for use in brothels.[86] The rituals of sexualized humiliation of both Jewish and non-Jewish women in

Nazi brothels are mirrored in the sex acts for sale in legal brothels in Germany today. Women in prostitution the world over describe poisonous verbal abuse as among their worst experiences in prostitution. Women prisoners were overpowered by the Nazis' sadistic verbal abuse at the KZ "saunas," where they were humiliated and dehumanized, and where they were selected for brothels or work camps or death camps.[87] Women in these Nazi selection zones described the lineup experience much like the women in legal brothels describe being lined up and selected for sexual use today. They felt like livestock who were being scrutinized, pinched, and rated by selection judges in the camps. The men were described as "wolves" or a "herd of SS," by one woman.[88] Women returned to Ravensbruck concentration camps as "wrecks," after enslavement in other camps' brothels, not only humiliated but also physically broken.[89]

Once women are controlled and subordinate in legal prostitution, then any dehumanization, abuse, or experimentation on them is considered reasonable. In 2001 in California, Donna Hughes and Melissa Farley interviewed Margaret Gruter, wife of an SS officer and gynecologist, Dr. Joaquim Gruter, who supervised women in NS brothels during the war. Margaret Gruter stated that her husband experimented on prostituted women in the Nazis' Italian brothels. As a result of that human experimentation, SS Officer Dr. Gruter developed an intrauterine device for birth control which he patented after resettling in the United States. In the 1950s, Nevada pimp Joe Conforte also experimented on women in legal brothel prostitution. According to Conforte's ex-wife, who spoke to a source interviewed by Melissa Farley, Conforte enabled a pharmaceutical company to experiment with various dosages of birth control pills for preventing pregnancy. No charges were ever filed against Conforte for this unethical and illegal experimentation on women in the brothel, although he was later convicted of income tax evasion and charged with bankruptcy fraud, money laundering, witness tampering, racketeering, and conspiracy. Conforte remains in hiding in Brazil where he continues to traffic women in the sex trade.

In 2020, the vast majority of women in legal brothels face the same choicelessness, acquiescing to prostitution in order to eat, obtain housing, or support their families. Just as historical sexist prejudice was aimed at Jewish and other women who survived the Nazi brothels, women in legal prostitution today are judgmentally assumed to be "voluntary prostitutes." The social stigma against women who were prostituted instead of starved in the concentration camps has stifled the testimony of survivors and witnesses.[90] An attitude of victim-blaming continues, resulting in feelings of shame by women who were prostituted and survived. Recently a member of a German NGO chastised a woman for having prostituted at an age that was deemed "old enough to know better," even after the woman had recounted the harrowing circumstances that channeled her into legal prostitution.

Like other occupying armies such as that of the United States in Vietnam, the Nazis feared STD epidemics. They also assumed that men's sexual needs compelled the sale of women for sex. The Nazis, including Himmler and other officials of the Third Reich, viewed carefully-regulated prostitution as way to prevent rape and homosexuality. Before 1942, the SS had already organized their own brothels in concentration and work camps; after 1942 women prisoners were offered to enslaved men prisoners as work incentives.

The Nazi regime established separate categories of brothels based on their own hierarchical rankings of the men who were to be serviced in the brothels. The German Army brothels, Wehrmachtsbordelle, were separated into brothels for officers, brothels for regular soldiers, brothels for concentration camp prisoners, brothels for foreign forced laborers, brothels for the Waffen-SS (Wehrmacht combat troops), brothels for the regular SS troops who enforced racial purity laws, brothels for foreign combat allies, brothels for foreign volunteers in the German army, brothels for Waffen-SS troops from non-German countries, brothels for troops from Eastern Europe who were considered racially superior "eastfolkish" people, brothels for employees of Todt (a military engineering company that was a crucial part of Nazi construction projects), brothels for the National Socialist Corps of Motor Vehicles, brothels for the commercial navy, and brothels for the state-owned railway, the Reichsbahn. With the exception of Denmark, historians assume that Wehrmachtsbordelle were established in all Nazi-occupied regions. Nazi brothels existed in Poland, Norway, Belgium, Greece, France, Italy, and the former Soviet Union (most frequently in Ukraine, Estonia, Latvia, and Lithuania).[91]

Almost all (90%) of the women in German legal brothels today are from outside Germany: Romania, Albania, Poland, Czechoslovakia, and Nigeria.[92] In other words, the women who are most frequently trafficked into German brothels are from some of the countries that were occupied by the Nazis during World War II.[93] Scooter Preston, a pimp who called himself a "pleasure guide," renamed trafficking of women to German brothels, *aggressive girl importing*:

> *Importing fresh girls from Czech Republic, Poland, and Slovakia every month, the Munich and Berlin red light districts are internationally famous in large part because of their reputation for aggressive girl importing from neighboring countries. It is common insider knowledge that there are more Polish working girls in Berlin than in Warsaw!*[94]

The concentration camps' brothels, *Sonderbauten*,[95] were established by Himmler in the final years of the Third Reich with the goal of motivating enslaved prisoners to increase their productivity. Special brothels were established to reward both the elite SS troops and the enslaved prisoners who were presumed to be inspired to work harder so that they could earn the right to use a woman in prostitution.[96] Peepholes provided voyeuristic sexual gratification to brothel guards. The observation of their prostitution humiliated the men who were sometimes coerced into using these enslaved, prostituted women. One man was forced by Nazi guards acting as pimps to visit the brothel as a reward. He was commanded to drop his pants, humiliating him into betraying his values by forcing him to use a woman for sex. This prisoner was coerced to become "a perpetrator, a rapist."[97] Most male prisoners in the camps however, dehumanized the women and treated them with contempt,[98] much the way sex buyers treat women today in state-sanctioned brothels.

Some sex buyers in the camps included young men who had no sexual experience and who were ambivalent about prostitution, as in the case of a young man who earned a visit to a camp brothel, and regretted it the moment he entered the brothel.[99] This same ambivalence of sex buyers is evident today. A sex buyer interviewed in London noted that he had only ever used one woman in prostitution. When asked why only one, he responded that while he was with the woman he had bought for sex, he looked in her eyes, and there he saw the same expression that he knew was in his own eyes when a German priest raped him as a child. That was the first and last time he bought sex. Understanding at a deep emotional level that prostitution was a form of sexual abuse, he made the choice not to buy sex again.

Nazi slogans were lies crafted to facilitate vast cruelties and human rights abuses, and to conceal genocide. The best known is "Arbeit macht frei." While this slogan is commonly understood as pacification for humans soon to be murdered, it also suggests that the slave labor to which some prisoners were subjected would lead to better outcomes, even freedom. Kidnapping, dehumanization, and enslavement were renamed "work." And today pimps argue that prostitution is "sex work" in order, they say, to dignify the worker. On the other hand, survivors say prostitution is named sex work in order to camouflage what is in reality paid rape. The transformation of prostitution into "sex work" normalizes it, mainstreams it, and makes invisible the overwhelming human cruelties and human rights abuses intrinsic to it and endemic in it. These are only two examples of the many euphemisms that camouflage human rights abuses in the legal sex trade. As recently as 2015, tour guides at Dachau concentration camp denied the existence of brothel prostitution under the Third Reich.[100] Today, prostituted women are regularly killed while in German legal prostitution. These facts are also looked away from, stubbornly avoided, or denied.

Will legal prostitution solve the violence and human rights abuses of prostitution?

It is a cruel lie to suggest that legal prostitution protects women. Legal prostitution in Germany has resulted in dramatic increases in the exploitive, harmful, and often sexually violent behavior of tens of thousands of men. Legalized prostitution conceals and at the same time promotes inequalities based on sex, ethnicity, poverty, and geography. If she says a sex act was unwanted, coerced, or performed because she was desperate for food or shelter, then that sex act should be defined as rape. A woman at a brothel in Nevada explained that legal prostitution was "like you sign a contract to be raped."[101] When the state is supported by taxation of brothels, the state itself assumes the role of pimp. When the state emboldens sex buyers and pimps by zoning, regulating, or legalizing prostitution, life becomes even more dangerous for women both in and out of prostitution.

Today, some still imagine that legalizing or regulating prostitution will help to reduce the human rights abuses that are built into it. Yet the violence and long term harm of prostitution are unrelated to prostitution's legal status. The greater the woman's poverty, the greater the violence against her in prostitution. The greater the number of men who buy her for sex, the more likely she is to suffer violence and severe physical health problems.[102] Evidence shows that legal prostitution is associated with increased rape and increased sex trafficking.[103]

Bureaucracies, management, regulation, health registration forms, educational campaigns to turn sex buyers into nice men who respect women's rights, unions, policies, legalization -- none of this has changed or will change what is fundamentally harmful in

313

prostitution. Legal prostitution's proponents have failed to explain how they will "monitor" prostitution in such a way that women's safety is ensured. A Dutch brothel with three emergency buttons in each tiny room nonetheless failed to "monitor" and prevent violence against the women inside. Its regulationist approach to prostitution has been acknowledged as a failed experiment by the Dutch.[104] Legal prostitution instead conceals many crimes that are integral to prostitution, such as coercion and trafficking, according to a Dutch prosecutor.[105] Police investigating trafficking networks noted organized criminals' efficiency in conducting and interfacing with legal prostitution. Chief Superintendent Helmut Sporer from Augsburg described a Hungarian trafficker's method of supplying women to legal brothels in Austria and Germany: the pimp carefully sorted women by size, hair colour, and body size. The women were commodities to be evaluated, tested, and used, with pimps permitting returns if their fellow pimps were not satisfied.[106]

The legalization of prostitution in Germany and elsewhere has resulted in an expanded market for sex purchase along with an escalation of pimping, trafficking and violence against women. Legalization solidifies structural violence against women in prostitution, especially pimping. As brothels and other prostitution venues become cities' new aesthetic and legal landscapes -- the state-endorsed prostitution infrastructure entitles men to 24/7 sexual access to women.

Following the legalization of prostitution, extremely dangerous sex practices increased as the economic bottom dropped out of the sex market. The poorest women in legal brothels were coerced into practices that Kraus described as "hell on earth,"[107] with violent, degrading abuse of women advertised for sale in legal brothels.

In theory, the 2002 Prostitution Act made it possible for women to select their buyers, choose what acts they performed, and choose the hours when they were sold for sex. In actuality brothel keepers rented rooms at extortionate prices, adding additional fees such as "entrance fees," and fees for toilet paper and bed linens, as well as chilling requirements such as money-back guarantees for dissatisfied sex buyers. In many cases the women were kept in debt-bondage while being euphemized as "independent contractors."

Legalization of the sex trade means that pimping can be camouflaged as "operational aspects of the sex trade." Under this camouflage, pimps are no longer pimps; instead, their involvement in the sex trade becomes that of agents, bookers, or managers which then makes it extremely challenging to prosecute traffickers. In theory, "forced prostitution," "exploitative pimping," and trafficking are still illegal in Germany. A legal definition of "exploitative" was not declared in law and has been interpreted in various ways. In most cases in Germany, attorneys must prove force or coercion in order to convict pimps. These terms are defined so narrowly in both German and U.S. law, that pimps and traffickers are able to evade accountability.

Prostitution does not exist in a social or legal vacuum. German rape laws are built on the same definitions of force and coercion that are used in the prostitution law, with similar results. Because Germany's laws and legal practice did not comply with the Council of Europe Convention on Preventing and Combating Violence Against Women and Domestic Violence (Istanbul Convention), the German penal code on sexual offenses was revised in 2016.

Despite the advantages of the prostitution law for pimps, and despite the mainstreaming of prostitution as work, legal pimps have nonetheless been convicted of trafficking and tax evasion, and recently (we are delighted to report) the largest brothel in Germany closed due to bankruptcy as a result of the economic stress generated by COVID-19 restrictions.[108] The coronavirus pandemic exposed the failure of legal and decriminalized prostitution to protect women from the violence of pimps, traffickers, and sex buyers. In response to COVID-19, Germany in 2020 closed down legal brothels and ejected desperately poor women because the women could not afford to pay the brothel pimps for the rooms they lived in.[109] The economic crisis of women in German legal prostitution is the same as the economic crisis that women suffer in illegal prostitution. In March 2020, the Berlin Senate and the Federal Ministry for Families,

Senior Citizens, Women and Youth asked an association of legal pimps (BesD) whether women who flee domestic violence during the pandemic, could be sheltered in the closed brothels during the pandemic. Because women were quarantined with their abusers and sought to escape, there was a national shortage of shelter for battered women in Germany.[110] Since their brothels were closed, the pimps welcomed the paid opportunity to house battered women in their brothels. The irony and the insanity of the government's proposal was not lost on historian Inge Kleine who pointed out that *prostitution itself* is a cruel variant of domestic violence. Although the Senate's proposal for pimp-sponsored housing for battered women was quietly rescinded, an alternative solution was not considered: municipalities could have taken over the brothels, kicked out the pimps and transformed the buildings into long-term housing for trafficked women.

After closing the legal brothels in response to the pandemic, the city of Stuttgart prohibited prostitution entirely. This meant that if a woman with no means of survival had been kicked out of a legal brothel, and if she then resorted to prostitution in order to feed herself or her family, she could be arrested. The cruelty of this policy was protested by survivor Huschke Mau, who noted that 80% of the women in the German brothels had been coerced into it by abusive pimps, boyfriends or husbands, or by extreme poverty. Thus, to arrest the women would be to compound the harm and to blame the victims, not the perpetrators. Mau saw that the arrest policy endangered women's health and their survival. She and other German feminists noted that the pandemic provided an opportunity for German cities to implement the Nordic law on prostitution. Under the Nordic law, sex buyers, brothelkeepers, and pimps are charged with crimes, *but the victim of the crime* is not arrested. Mau observed that the pandemic presented an opportunity for Germans to show solidarity with the most vulnerable -- those who are paid for in prostitution -- who should be provided support and exit services rather than arrest.[111]

Conclusion

A sex buyer declared, "Prostitution is where men have the freedom to do anything they want in a consequence-free environment." Most of the time, in most places in the world, men can buy sex with no negative consequences. It is time to change that. It is time to focus on the invisible perpetrator in the sex trade: the sex buyer. Prostitution eroticizes and institutionalizes the inequality between women and men. It is an institution so deeply exploitive and violent that it can only be abolished, not repaired, reformed, or regulated. The Nordic law on prostitution is a human rights-based approach that has been shown to be effective in reducing sex buying and trafficking.[112] In these abolitionist laws, now enforced in 8 countries, the sex buyer, pimp, and trafficker are *penalized.*[113] The prostituted person is *decriminalized*, and the government is obliged to provide *exit services* and *rehabilitation* to whoever wants to leave prostitution. Survivors of prostitution and service providers point out that it is crucial for exit and support services to be provided prior to -- not after -- arrests of sex buyers.

The big lies from the pimps, sex buyers, and their political allies at Amnesty International, the German Green Party, the Open Society Institute of George Soros, and the UN's World Health Organization can confuse even policymakers.[114] But the growing evidence regarding the severe harms of prostitution regardless of its legal status, poses a challenge for them. The testimony of survivors of prostitution crushes the myths about prostitution as a reasonable job choice. And the testimony of sex buyers, mirroring the testimony of prostitution survivors, destroys the notion that prostitution is simply a "service" provided by "sex workers." In their own words, sex buyers' attitudes of entitlement, their pleasure in dominating and hurting women, their misogyny, racism, and class prejudice could not be more clear.

The notion that legalizing prostitution makes it safer, is deeply flawed. After Germany's 2002 Prostitution Act was passed, the first informational pamphlets provided to women in Hamburg prostitution cited HIV as an occupational hazard which resulted in an increase in their mandatory health insurance fees by €500 per month.[115] Kassandra, a pro-sex trade advocacy group in Nuremberg, cautioned pimps and brothel keepers about the "legal particularities regarding prostitutes aged 18-21,"[116] but at the same time failed to warn young women about the harms they were likely to encounter at the hands of legal pimps. In a country with legal prostitution, the naming of injuries resulting from escape from a pimp's violence as "work accident," illustrates women's lack of safety even when legal redress or protection is sought. We hope that this discussion clarifies the fact that when prostitution is legalized, the legal bar for protecting women from male violence is drastically lowered. In German history and also today, it seems that *as long as the legal and administrative functioning of an institution is carefully regulated and smoothly operated*, then the massive human rights abuse at its center can be ignored.

Endnotes

1 Geographic privilege is when a person happens to be born in a place that is *not* severely impacted by climate change, or war, and the person is not on the poor side of a massive divide between the rich and the poor.

2 Interview with a pimp, Melissa Farley, Mexico City, 1998.

3 We note that in Germany the expression trans* is used to suggest inclusivity.

4 Suzanne Daley (2001, August 12). New Rights for Dutch Prostitutes, but No Gain. *New York Times*. Retrieved August 25, 2001 from http://www.nytimes.com/2001/08/12/international/12DUTC.html.

5 Diana Leone (2001, September 10). *One in 100 children in Sex Trade, Study Says*, Honolulu Star-Bulletin, http://starbulletin. com/2001/09/10/news/story1.html.

6 Melissa Farley, Jacqueline Lynne, and Ann Cotton (2005) Prostitution in Vancouver: Violence and the Colonization of First Nations Women. *Transcultural Psychiatry* 42: 242-271. Available at https://prostitutionresearch.com/prostitution-in-vancouver-violence-and-the-colonization-of-first-nations-women/.

7 See Melissa Farley. (2003) (Editor.) *Prostitution, Trafficking, and Traumatic Stress*. New York: Routledge.

8 Wolfgang Heide, M.D., Stellungnahme zur öffentlichen Anhörung zur Regulierung des Prostitutionsgewerbes im *Ausschuss für Familie, Senioren, Frauen und Gesundheit im Deutschen Bundestag* am 06. Juni 2016. See his deposition at https://www.bundestag.de/blob/42 5132/8d5f5d287762d764f17a9c1996b36b0e/18-13-76e_wolfgang-heide-data.pdf. See also Liane Bissinger, M.D. *The Physical Damage in Prostitution: Report by a Gynaecologist from Street Work.* https://prostitutionresearch.com/the-physical-damage-in-prostitution-report-by-a-gynaecologist-from-street-work/?highlight=bissinger.

9 Because sex buyers the world overpay more money for not using condoms, extremely risky sex acts "can always be purchased." Bebe Loff, Cheryl Overs, and Paulo Longo, 2003, Can health programmes lead to mistreatment of sex workers? *Lancet* 36: 1983.

89% of Canadian customers of prostitutes refused condoms in one study. (Leonard Cler-Cunningham & Christine Christensen, 2001,

Violence against women in Vancouver's street level sex trade and the police response. Vancouver: PACE Society).

An economic analysis of condom use in a brothel area of eastern India found that when desperately poor women insisted on condoms, they were paid 66%-79% less by sex buyers (Vijayendra Rao, Indrani Gupta, Michael Lokshin, Smarajit Jana, 2003, Sex Workers and the Cost of Safe Sex: The Compensating Differential for Condom Use in Calcutta. *Journal of Development Economics* 71 (2): 585-603).

In another study, 47% of women in U.S. prostitution stated that men expected sex without a condom; 73% reported that men offered to pay more for sex without a condom; and 45% of women said that men became abusive if they insisted that the buyers use condoms (Janice Raymond, Donna Hughes, & Carole Gomez, 2001, *Sex Trafficking of Women in the United States: International and Domestic Trends.* Washington, D.C. Department of Justice. Available at http://citeseerx.ist.psu.edu/viewdoc/download?doi=10.1.1.218.2120&rep=rep1&type=pdf).

10 See John J. Potterat, Devon D. Brewer, Stephen Q. Muth, Richard B. Rothenberg, Donald E. Woodhouse, John B. Muth, Heather K. Stites, and Stuart Brody, Mortality in a Long-Term Open Cohort of Prostituted Women. *American Journal of Epidemiology* 159; 778 (2004).

11 Report of the Special Committee on Pornography and Prostitution (1985) *Pornography and Prostitution in Canada.*

12 Leonard Cler-Cunningham & Christine Christenson (2001) Studying Violence to Stop It: Canadian Research on Violence Against Women in Vancouver's Street Level Sex Trade, *Research for Sex Work* 4, 25-26.

13 Hunter described them as most raped women on the planet. Susan K. Hunter (1993) Prostitution is Cruelty and Abuse to Women and Children, *Michigan Journal of Gender & Law* 1, 1-14.

14 Ruth Parriott (1994) Health Experiences of Twin Cities Women Used in Prostitution, Unpublished paper commissioned by Women Hurt in Systems of Prostitution Engaged in Revolt (WHISPER), Minneapolis.

15 Melissa Farley, Ann Cotton, Jacqueline Lynne, Sybille Zumbeck, Frida Spiwak, Maria E. Reyes, Dinorah Alvarez, Ufuk Sezgin (2003) Prostitution and Trafficking in Nine Countries: Update on

Violence and Posttraumatic Stress Disorder. *Journal of Trauma Practice* 2 (3/4): 33-74. Available at https://prostitutionresearch.com/ prostitution-trafficking-in-nine-countries-an-update-on-violence-and-post-traumatic-stress-disorder/

16 Erika Schulze, Sandra Isabel Novo Canto, Peter Mason, & Maria Skalin (2014) *Sexual Exploitation and Prostitution and its Impact on Gender Equality*. Policy Department C: Citizens' Rights and Constitutional Affairs. European Parliament (2014) Available at http://www.europarl.europa.eu/RegData/etudes/etudes/ join/2014/493040/IPOL-FEMM_ET(2014)493040_EN.pdf.

17 *Sex Industry Kills* (2020, August 22) Nonprofit documentation project by Manuela Schon, Germany, https://sexindustry-kills.de/ doku.php.

18 Melissa Farley, Ann Cotton, Jacqueline Lynne, Sybille Zumbeck, Frida Spiwak, Maria E. Reyes, Dinorah Alvarez, Ufuk Sezgin (2003) Prostitution and Trafficking in Nine Countries: Update on Violence and Posttraumatic Stress Disorder. *Journal of Trauma Practice* 2 (3/4): 33-74.

19 Melissa Farley (2007) "Renting an Organ for 10 Minutes:" What Tricks Tell Us About Prostitution, Pornography, and Trafficking. In David Guinn and Julie DeCaro (eds.) *Pornography: Driving the Demand for International Sex Trafficking* Pp 144-152. Los Angeles: Captive Daughters Media.

20 Pornography and Prostitution in Canada: Report of the Special Committee on Pornography and Prostitution (1985) 2. Minister of Supply and Services, Canada. p. 376–77.

21 Cecilie Hoigard & Liv Finstad (1986). *Backstreets: Prostitution, Money and Love*. University Park: Pennsylvania State University Press.

22 Andrea Dworkin (1997) Prostitution and Male Supremacy. In *Life and Death*. New York: Free Press. Andrea Dworkin was a survivor of prostitution.

23 Evelina Giobbe, founder of US-based WHISPER (Women Hurt in Systems of Prostitution Engaged in Revolt), 1985.

24 Sandra Norak (2020) Loss of Self in Dissociation in Prostitution; Recovery of Self in Connection to Horses: A Survivor's Journey, *Dignity: A Journal on Sexual Exploitation and Violence*, 4(4). https:// digitalcommons.uri.edu/dignity/vol4/iss4/6/

25 Melissa Farley (2013) Prostitution: An Extreme Form of Girls' Sexualization. In Eileen Zurbriggen and Tori-Ann Roberts (eds.) *The Sexualization of Girls*. Oxford University Press.

26 Ryan Bishop, & Lillian S. Robinson (1998). *Night Market: Sexual Cultures and the Thai Economic Miracle*. New York: Routledge, p. 47.

27 Sebastian Shedahi & Miriam Partington (2020, April 7). Coronavirus: offline sex workers forced to start again online. *BBC News*. https://www.bbc.com/news/technology-52183773.

28 Rachel Moran (May 19, 2014) An Open Letter to the "Good" Punter. *Survivor's View Blog*. https://prostitutionresearch.com/an-open-letter-to-the-good-punter/.

29 Kathleen Barry (1996) *The Prostitution of Sexuality*. New York: NYU Press; Kajsa Ekis Ekman (2013) *Being and Being Bought: Prostitution, Surrogacy and the Split Self*. North Melbourne: Spinifex Press; Janice Raymond (2013) *Not a choice, not a job: Exposing the myths about prostitution and the global sex trade*. Sterling VA: Potomac Books.

30 See footnote #14 in Melissa Farley, Kenneth Franzblau, and M. Alexis Kennedy (2014) Online Prostitution and Trafficking. *Albany Law Review* 77 (3): 1039-1094. Available at http://www.albanylawreview.org/issues/pages/article-information.aspx?volume=77&issue=3&page=1039.

31 Catharine A. MacKinnon (2011) Trafficking, Prostitution and Inequality. *Harvard Civil Rights-Civil Liberties Law Review* 46: 701-739. Available at https://prostitutionresearch.com/trafficking-prostitution-and-inequality/.

32 Sigma Huda (2006, Feb 20) *United Nations Economic and Social Council, Committee on Human Rights. Integration of the Human Rights of Women and a Gender Perspective: Report of the Special Rapporteur on the Human Rights Aspects of the Victims of Trafficking in Persons, Especially Women and Children*. 42 UN Document E/CN.4/2006/62.

33 Manfred Paulus, *Out of Control: On Liberties and Criminal Developments in the Redlight Districts of the Federal Republic of Germany* (2014, May 6) Prostitution Resources, http://ressourcesprostitution.wordpress.com/2014/05/06/m-paulus-out-of-control-on-liberties-and-criminal-developments-in-the-redlight-districts-of-the-federal-republic-of-germany/.

34 P Mendes Bota (2014). Prostitution, Trafficking and Modern Slavery in Europe. *Committee on Equality and Non-Discrimination Rapporteur*. https://ec.europa.eu/anti-trafficking/publications/prostitution-trafficking-and-modern-slavery-europe_en.

35 European Parliament (2014) *Briefing Paper: Sexual exploitation and prostitution and its impact on gender equality*. Available at http://www.europarl.europa.eu/RegData/etudes/etudes/join/2014/493040/IPOL-FEMM_ET(2014)493040_EN.pdf.

36 Helmut Sporer, Kriminalpolizei Augsburg. Quoted in Simon Haggstrom (2016) *Shadow's Law: The True Story of a Swedish Detective Inspector Fighting Prostitution*. Stockholm: Bullet Point Publishing, p 91.

37 Melissa Farley, Julie Bindel, and Jacqueline M. Golding (2009) *Men who buy sex: who they buy and what they know*. Eaves: London and Prostitution Research & Education: San Francisco. Available at https://prostitutionresearch.com/men-who-buy-sex-london-2009/.

38 Melissa Farley, Julie Bindel, and Jacqueline M. Golding (2009) *Men who buy sex: who they buy and what they know*. Eaves: London and Prostitution Research & Education: San Francisco. Available at https://prostitutionresearch.com/men-who-buy-sex-london-2009/.

39 Andrea Di Nicola, Andrea Cuaduro, Marco Lombardi, Paolo Ruspini (editors) (2009) *Prostitution and Human Trafficking: Focus on Clients*. New York: Springer. In reality, the vast majority of women in prostitution do not have "good incomes."

40 Brian Heilman, Luciana Herbert, & Nastasia Paul-Gera (2014). *The making of sexual violence: How does a boy grow up to commit rape? Evidence from five IMAGES countries*. Washington, DC: International Center for Research on Women (ICRW) and Washington, DC: Promundo. Available at https://prostitutionresearch.com/law-and-policy-sex-buyers-the-making-of-sexual-violence/?highlight=Heilman

41 Melissa Farley, Jan Macleod, Lynn Anderson, & Jacqueline M. Golding (2011) Attitudes and Social Characteristics of Men Who Buy Sex in Scotland. *Psychological Trauma: Theory, Research, Practice, and Policy* 3/4: 369-383. Available at https://prostitutionresearch.com/attitudes-and-social-characteristics-of-men-who-buy-sex-in-scotland/

42 Melissa Farley, Jacqueline M. Golding, Matthews, E.S., Neil Malamuth, Jarrett, L. (2015) Comparing Sex Buyers with Men

Who Do Not Buy Sex: New Data on Prostitution and Trafficking. *Journal of Interpersonal Violence* (August 2015) 1-25. Available at https://prostitutionresearch.com/men-who-buy-sex-have-much-in-common-with-sexually-coercive-men-new-study-shows-4/

43 Neil P. McKeganey & Marina Barnard (1996). *Sex work on the streets: Prostitutes and their clients.* Buckingham, UK: Open University Press.

44 Manuela Schon is co-founder of Abolition 2014: For a world without prostitution. http://abolition2014.blogspot.com/.

45 Kate D'Adamo (2020, March 13) COVID-19 Could be Uniquely Serious for Sex Workers. Slixa.com. https://www.slixa.com/blog/experience/coronavirus-impacts-sex-work/

46 Stephen Naysmith (2014) Exposing the invisible men who rate sex workers online," *Herald Scotland* 6 March 2014. Available at http://www.heraldscotland.com/news/13149175.Exposing_the__invisible_men__who_rate_sex_workers_online/.

47 Melissa Farley, Julie Bindel, and Jacqueline M. Golding (2009) *Men who buy sex: who they buy and what they know.* Eaves: London and Prostitution Research & Education: San Francisco. Available at https://prostitutionresearch.com/men-who-buy-sex-london-2009/

48 Melissa Farley (2007) "Renting an Organ for 10 Minutes:" What Tricks Tell Us About Prostitution, Pornography, and Trafficking. In David Guinn and Julie DeCaro (eds.) *Pornography: Driving the Demand for International Sex Trafficking* pp. 144-152. Los Angeles: Captive Daughters Media. Available at https://prostitutionresearch.com/renting-an-organ-for-10-minutes-what-tricks-tell-us-about-prostitution/

49 Antonia Crane (2012) Paying to Play: Interview with a John. *The Rumpus* June 6 2012. Available at http://therumpus.net/2012/06/paying-to-play-interview-with-a-john/.

50 Quotes from Melissa Farley (2007) "Renting an Organ for 10 Minutes:" What Tricks Tell Us About Prostitution, Pornography, and Trafficking. In David Guinn and Julie DeCaro (eds.) *Pornography: Driving the Demand for International Sex Trafficking* pp. 144-152. Los Angeles: Captive Daughters Media.

See also Melissa Farley, Julie Bindel, & Jacqueline M. Golding (2009) *Men who buy sex: who they buy and what they know.* Eaves: London and Prostitution Research & Education: San Francisco.

Available at https://prostitutionresearch.com/men-who-buy-sex-london-2009/and Melissa Farley, Jan Macleod, Lynn Anderson, and Jacqueline M. Golding (2011) Attitudes and Social Characteristics of Men Who Buy Sex in Scotland. *Psychological Trauma: Theory, Research, Practice, and Policy* 3/4: 369-383. Available at https://prostitutionresearch.com/attitudes-and-social-characteristics-of-men-who-buy-sex-in-scotland/

51 Melissa Farley, Mary Stewart, and Kyle Smith (2007) Attitudes toward Prostitution and Sexually Coercive Behaviors of Young Men at the University of Nevada at Reno in *Prostitution and Trafficking in Nevada: Making the Connections* 173-180.

52 Rachel Moran and Melissa Farley (2019, Feb 5) Consent, Coercion, and Culpability: Is Prostitution Stigmatized Work or an Exploitive and Violent Practice Rooted in Sex, Race, and Class Inequality? *Archives of Sexual Behavior.* Available at https://prostitutionresearch.com/wp-content/uploads/2019/03/Moran-Farley-Consent-Coercion-Culpability-2019.pdf.

53 Doris Velten: Aspekte der sexuellen Sozialisation. Eine Analyse qualitativer Daten zu biographischen Entwicklungsmustern von Prostitutionskunden. Berlin 1994 (Freie Universität Berlin, Dissertation, 1994); Dieter Kleiber und Doris Velten: Prostitutionskunden. Eine Untersuchung über soziale und psychologische Charakteristika von Besuchern weiblicher Prostituierter in Zeiten von Aids (Schriftenreihe des Bundesministeriums für Gesundheit. Bd. 30). Baden-Baden 1994, Sabine Grenz, (Un)heimliche Lust. Über den Konsum sexueller Dienstleistungen. Wiesbaden 2007; Udo Gerheim, Die Produktion des Freiers. Macht im Feld der Prostitution. Eine soziologische Studie. Bielefeld 2012 (Dissertation on sex buyers); Christiane Howe, Round table discussion at Missy Magazine, "Roundtable erotisches Kapital" – Missy Magazine, 25.02.2014 (letzter Zugriff 28.12.2016, 19.35) Women's magazine presenting as feminist, liberal. https://missy-magazine.de/blog/2014/02/25/roundtable-erotisches-kapital/ and Christiane Howe (2005): Non-Discriminatory Approaches to Address Clients in Prostitution. In: Sector Project against Trafficking in Women – GTZ, Gesellschaft für technische Zusammenarbeit (Hrsg.): Challenging Trafficking in Persons. Theoretical Debate and Practical Approaches.

Most recent: Susann Huschke, Peter Shirlow, Dirk Schubotz, D., Ellis Ward, Ursula Probst, C. Ni Dhonaill (2014, October) Research into Prostitution in Northern Ireland. Commissioned from

Queen's University Belfast by the Department of Justice; https://
www.academia.edu/17343071/Research_into_Prostitution_in_
Northern_Ireland and Susann Huschke und Dirk Schubotz (2016)
Commercial Sex, Clients and Christian Morals: Paying for Sex in
Ireland. Sexualities 19 (7), 869-887. http://pure.qub.ac.uk/portal/
files/56938886/Huschke_Schubotz_Paying_for_Sex_in_Ireland_
accepted_word_document.pdf.

54 Rape myths and rape myths acceptance: Gerd Bohner.
Vergewaltigungsmythen. Wien 1999, https://www.researchgate.net/
publication/236331106_Vergewaltigungsmythen_Rape_myths.

55 "I used to think all sex buyers were pigs," explained sociologist
Udo Gerheim who revised his view that prostitution was nothing
but pure patriarchal violence. (taz, Sep. 2, 2006: Interview mit Udo
Gerheim durchgeführt von Eiken Bruhn (letzter Zugriff 28.12.2016
http://www.taz.de/!477630/, 18.35) Summary of research on
punters in a national daily (quality paper). "Nor is the cliché true
that punters act like pashas. The punters I have interviewed were
all embarrassed rather. They want to be desired and say things like
'when the door closes she is the boss in the ring' […] The punters
we interviewed love their wives more than anything." Christiane
Howe in a discussion published in: Missy Magazine, 15 Feb 2014)
"Roundtable erotisches Kapital" – Missy Magazine, 25.02.2014
(letzter Zugriff 28.12.2016, 19.35) Women's magazine presenting as
feminist, liberal http://missy-magazine.de/2014/02/25/roundtable-
erotisches-kapital/.

56 Doris Velten, 1994, quoted in: Sabine Grenz, (Un)heimliche Lust.
Über den Konsum sexueller Dienstleistungen. Wiesbaden 2007, S.21.
In fact, many men view sex buyers as "losers" who cannot convince
women to have sex with them unless paid for.

57 Udo Gerheim (2012) Die Produktion des Freiers. Macht im Feld der
Prostitution. Eine soziologische Studie. Bielefeld (2012) S. 228 ff.

58 Ursula März, "Der nette Idiot" – Die Zeit, 17.11. 2016 (letzter Zugriff
28.12.2016, 19.55) https://www.zeit.de/2016/46/rotlichtviertel-
berlin-prostitution-akademiker-prozess.

59 Todesdrama am Paradise. Mann tötet Hure und sich selbst mit
Messer. Bild, Regional, Jul 17, 2016. https://www.bild.de/regional/
stuttgart/mord/zwei-tote-bei-messerstecherei-in-stuttgart-46860736.
bild.html SWR (regional public tv channel) "Bluttat in Leinfelden-
Echterdingen. Tatmotiv offenbar im persönlichen Bereich" Jul
17, 2016; Abendzeitung /dpa "Bluttat vor Bordell Paradise. Junge

Frau erstochen: Täter war ihr Kunde." Jul 18., 2016, https://www.
abendzeitung-muenchen.de/panorama/bluttat-vor-bordell-bei-
stuttgart-freier-53-ersticht-25-jaehrige-prostituierte-art-351861;
FAZ - "Angreifer war wohl Kunde von Prostituierter" Jul 18, 2016,
https://www.faz.net/aktuell/gesellschaft/kriminalitaet/identitaet-
der-beiden-toten-vor-bordell-geklaert-14345257.html; Stuttgarter
Zeitung "Mord in Leinfelden-Echterdingen. Prostituierte auf der
Straße erstochen." Article based on dpa by wolf-Dieter Obst, Jul 17.
2016, https://www.stuttgarter-zeitung.de/inhalt.mord-in-leinfelden-
echterdingen-prostituierte-auf-der-strasse-erstochen.b82f8e8a-660b-
4185-b282-536fac8e1e2d.html.

Writing on the AO Huren chat room (www.ao-huren.to/forum.
php), a punter wrote about the murder: *regarding the deed as such
... well ... I'm more surprised things like that don't happen more often
[...] when a punter knives a whore, she probably earned it. Whores
that don't just grab the money, but fool around with an 'unstable'
man's feelings, just fool around with the proverbial fire.*" Forum AO-
Huren, 18.07.2016, AO Huren.to zitiert nach "Chiquita/ Sofaficker"
at Sexindustry Kills Website https://sexindustry-kills.de/doku.ph
p?id=prostituiertenmoerder:chiquita." See also Manuela Schon,
"Prostituiertenmorde in Deutschland: keine singulären Ereignisse
– Wo bleibt der Skandal?" in Abolition 2014, Nov 17, 2016 http://
abolition2014.blogspot.de/2016/11/prostituiertenmorde-in-
deutschland.html#more (English version below the article).

60 See immediately preceding footnote for sources.

61 See http://archive.is/l0GR4; http://www.bw7.com/forum/
    showthread.php?t=319 ; bw7 is a forum for punters and women
    in prostitution, abbreviations and practices are listed in this thread
    cf. "Nasti" 24.01.2008, 17:52), cf also Archive at https://archive.is/
    x7yHH, and https://www.redlight.net/de/info/paysex-shortcuts.
    html, and https://www.hc-movie.com/blog/sex-abkuerzungen/

62 Melissa Farley (2015) Slavery and Prostitution: a 21st Century
    Abolitionist Perspective. In Bonnie Martin and James F. Brooks
    (eds.) *Linking the Histories of Slavery in North America and Its
    Borderlands.* Santa Fe: School for Advanced Research Press.
    Available at http://prostitutionresearch.com/wp-content/
    uploads/2016/07/Slavery-Prostitution-Farley-2015.pdf.

63 http://berufsverband-sexarbeit.de/en/contact/.

64 Der Spiegel, "Uncovered" March 28, 2015. shttp://www.spiegel.de/
    spiegel/print/d-132909484.html.

65 http://www.spiegel.de/spiegel/print/d-132909484.html.

66 Cecilie Hoigard (2015) *The Presence of Pain in the Debate on Prostitution.* Women's Front of Norway. Available at http:// kvinnefronten.no/wp-content/uploads/2015/05/Two-Articles-on-Prostitution.pdf.

67 See LIBIDA Sexualbegleitung: https://www.behindertenarbeit.at/ wp-content/uploads/alphanova-LIBIDA-Lehrgang-2017-2018.pdf, http://www.sophie.or.at and http://www.sophie.or.at/2020/10/21/ lehrgang-sexualbegleitung-sexualassistenz/. See also Kassandra e.V. Beratungsstelle für Prostituierte, "Sexualbegleitung" https:// www.kassandra-nbg.de/sexarbeit-von-a-z/#sexualbegleitung with detailed information at http://www.angehoerigenberatung-nbg.de/ sites/default/files/files/pdf/Qualifizierte%20Sexualbegleitung%20. pdf The market for "sexual assistance" or prostitution provided to disabled men, expanded in 2020. The publicly funded group Kassandra now advertises prostitution under the guise of "sexual assistance" at https://www.kassandra-nbg.de and https://www. kassandra-nbg.de/kontakte-sexualbegleitung/.

68 See N.N. Die Zeit Online: "Sexualassistenz: Grüne fordern Sex auf Rezept für Pflegebedürftige." Sex mit Prostituierten solle für Schwerkranke von den Kommunen bezuschusst werden, fordert die pflegepolitische Sprecherin der Grünen. Vorbild seien die Niederlande. Zeit Online, 8. Januar 2017 http://www.zeit.de/politik/ deutschland/2017-01/sexualassistenz-gruene-sex-schwerkranke.

69 Expertise. Sexuelle Assistenz für Frauen und Männer mit Behinderungen. Herausgegeben von ProFamilia, Gesellschaft für Familienplanung, Sexualpädagogik und Sexualberatung e.V., Mitarbeiterinnen dieser Ausgabe Anneke Bazuin (Sexuelle Assistenz in Europa), Renate Eisen-Raetsch (Redaktion), Sigrid Weiser (Projektleitung), Dr. Julia Zinsmeister (Juristische Gutachterin), p.40ff. https://www.profamilia.de/fileadmin/publikationen/ Fachpublikationen/expertise_sexuelle_assistenz.pdf.

70 *Freiersein. Eine Dokumentation über ein institutions- und zielgruppenübergreifendes Projekt zur Aufklärung von Männern/ Freiern,* (Being a John. A documentation of a project spanning several institutions and target groups for the enlightenment of men/punters.) ed. by Christiane Howe und Anna Erdelmann. (2006). Accessed online December 2016 at a website which has been removed, but its content is in possession of the second author. Under the 2016 prostitution amendment, sex without condoms was

criminalized. Enforcement of the prohibition is likely to be expensive if not impossible, and condomless sex acts will probably continue to be provided for a fee by vulnerable women.

71   FiM (Frauenrecht ist Menschenrecht) launched a 10-week campaign called "Stoppt Zwangsprostitution" during the 2006 FIFA World Cup.

72   FiM, (Hg.) "Stoppt Zwangsprostitution" Kampagne http://www. stoppt-zwangsprostitution.de . (Herausgegeben von Frauenrecht ist Menschenrecht, Frankfurt a.M. 2007 http://www.stoppt-zwangsprostitution.de/art/doku_kampagne.pdf).

73   The German laws on pimping and trafficking require both exploitation and physical force, and are difficult crimes to prove. See a legal discussion at Rahel Gugel (2011) Das Spannungsverhältnis zwischen dem Prostitutionsgesetz und Artikel 3 II Grundgesetz, Berlin p.82 and p.92 ff. Also see Manfred Paulus, *Out of Control: On Liberties and Criminal Developments in the Redlight Districts of the Federal Republic of Germany*, Prostitution Resources (May 6, 2014), http://ressourcesprostitution.wordpress.com/2014/05/06/m-paulus-out-of-control-on-liberties-and-criminal-developments-in-the-redlight-districts-of-the-federal-republic-of-germany/.

74   Sozialgericht (Social Court) Hamburg (2016) Urteil vom 23.06.2016, S 36 U. 118/14. http://grundundmenschenrechtsblog.de/wp-content/uploads/2016/08/Urteil-SG-HH-vom-01072016-Prostitution-und-Arbeitsunfall-SGB-VII-anonymisierte-Fassung.pdf.

75   Council of Europe (2011) *Istanbul Convention on Preventing and Combating Violence Against Women and Domestic Violence Article 36 No. 2*, https://rm.coe.int/168008482e.

76   http://grundundmenschenrechtsblog.de/wp-content/uploads/2016/08/Urteil-SG-HH-vom-01072016-Prostitution-und-Arbeitsunfall-SGB-VII-anonymisierte-Fassung.pdf.

77   The groups who funded and supported the legal battle were Institut für Menschenrechte and the kok, an antitrafficking consortium. Ironically, the pro-sex trade Institut für Menschenrechte will evaluate the 2016/2017 Prostitutes' Protection Law, a set of regulations that were an attempt by Germany to address the human rights failures of its 2002 prostitution law. https://taz.de/Rechte-von Sexarbeiterinnen/!5314684/; https://www.kok-gegen-menschenhandel.de/fileadmin/user_upload/medien/Pressemitteilungen/PM_2016_Koofra.pdf.

78 Third Reich prostitution policy varied according to the nation or
    territory being occupied, the ability to traffic/kidnap/coerce local
    women into prostitution, military strategies, occupation politics
    at different stages of the war, and experiences and knowledge of
    regional commanders.(Regina Muhlhauser, 2009, Between "racial
    awareness" and fantasies of potency: Nazi sexual politics in the
    occupied territories of the Soviet Union 1943-1945, in Dagmar
    Herzog (2009) *Brutality and Desire: War and Sexuality in Europe's
    Twentieth Century.* Hampshire, England: Palgrave-MacMillan; pp
    197-220, p 213. Eroberungen: Sexuelle Gewalttaten und intime
    Beziehungen deutscher Soldaten in der Sowjetunion 1941-1945;
    Catharine MacKinnon (2005) "Genocide's Sexuality" in *Political
    Exclusion and Domination* (Melissa S. Williams & Stephen Macedo,
    eds.) New York: NY University Press. p 313-356.

79 Christa Schikorra (2002) Prostitution of Female Concentration
    Camp Prisoners as Slave Labor. On the Situation of "Asocial"
    Prisoners in the Ravensbruck Women's Concentration Camp. In
    Wolfgang Benz and Barbara Distel, eds. *Dachau and the Nazi Terror
    1933-1945* Vol 2 Dachau.

80 Elizabeth D. Heineman (2002) Sexuality and Nazism: The Doubly
    Unspeakable? *Journal of the History of Sexuality* 11(1/2) Special
    Issue: Sexuality and German Fascism (Jan. - Apr., 2002), pp. 22-66.

81 The Nazis selected for prostitution Polish women, political prisoners,
    women of Aryan-appearing ethnicities, and women branded
    antisocial such as lesbians or women previously arrested for
    prostitution for sexual use. But there is also extensive documentation
    of sexually enslaved Jewish women in and outside of Nazi brothels.
    See Catharine MacKinnon (2005) "Genocide's Sexuality" in *Political
    Exclusion and Domination* (Melissa S. Williams & Stephen Macedo,
    eds.) New York: NY University Press. p 313-356.

82 Elizabeth D. Heineman (2002) Sexuality and Nazism: The Doubly
    Unspeakable? *Journal of the History of Sexuality* 11(1/2) Special
    Issue: Sexuality and German Fascism (Jan. - Apr., 2002), pp. 22-66.

83 Elizabeth D. Heineman (2002) Sexuality and Nazism: The Doubly
    Unspeakable? *Journal of the History of Sexuality* 11(1/2) Special
    Issue: Sexuality and German Fascism (Jan. - Apr., 2002), p 66.

84 Brothels controlled by the Nazis existed throughout occupied
    Europe despite Hitler's official policy condemning prostitution. See
    Christa Paul: *Zwangsprostitution. Staatlich errichtete Bordelle im
    Nationalsozialismus (Compulsory constitution. State-built brothels in*

national socialism.) Edition Hentrich, Berlin 1994, cited by Catharine MacKinnon (2005) "Genocide's Sexuality" in *Political Exclusion and Domination* (Melissa S. Williams & Stephen Macedo, eds.) New York: NY University Press. p 313-356.

85 Catharine MacKinnon (2005) "Genocide's Sexuality" in *Political Exclusion and Domination* (Melissa S. Williams & Stephen Macedo, eds.) New York: NYU Press. p 321.

86 Christa Paul (1994) cited by Catharine MacKinnon, 2005 in "Genocide's Sexuality."

87 Naáma Shik (2009) Sexual Abuse of Jewish Women at Auschwitz-Birkenau. In Dagmar Herzog (2009) Brutality and Desire: War and Sexuality in Europe's Twentieth Century. Hampshire, England: Palgrave-MacMillan; pp 221-246.

88 Naáma Shik (2009) Sexual Abuse of Jewish Women at Auschwitz-Birkenau. In Dagmar Herzog (2009) *Brutality and Desire: War and Sexuality in Europe's Twentieth Century*. Hampshire, England: Palgrave-MacMillan; pp 221-246. Quoting Ada Halperin testimony, Yad Vashem Archives, 31 January 1994, p 31 (Hebrew). Also H. Tischauer testimony, Yad Vashem Archives O.36/42, 23 September 1946, p 11 (English).

89 Christa Schikorra (2002) Prostitution of Female Concentration Camp Prisoners as Slave Labor. On the Situation of "Asocial" Prisoners in the Ravensbruck Women's Concentration Camp. Wolfgang Benz and Barbara Distel, eds. *Dachau and the Nazi Terror 1933-1945* Vol 2 Dachau.

90 Naáma Shik (2009) Sexual Abuse of Jewish Women at Auschwitz-Birkenau. In Dagmar Herzog (2009) *Brutality and Desire: War and Sexuality in Europe's Twentieth Century*. Hampshire, England: Palgrave-MacMillan; pp 221-246. See also Mareike Fallet & Simone Kaiser (2009) *The Main Thing Was to Survive at All.* der Spiegel http://www.spiegel.de/international/germany/concentration-camp-bordellos-the-main-thing-was-to-survive-at-all-a-632558.html.

91 Respondek, A.S. (2019) "Gerne will ich wieder ins Bordell gehen...": Maria K.`s freiwillige Meldung für ein Wehrmachtsbordell. Hamburg: Marta-Press, p. 203.

92 Forschungsprojekt PRIMSA vorgestellt: "Prostitution, Menschenhandel und sexuelle Ausbeutung – eine Realität in dieser Gesellschaft" (2016) http://www.blick-aktuell.de/Berichte/Forschungsprojekt-PRIMSA-vorgestellt-230212.html.

PRIMSA was/is a project with participation of abolitionist NGO SOLWODI. Roshan Heiler now works with the German Bundeskriminalamt (Federal Criminal Police Agency) in a project about human trafficking.

"Über 90 Prozent der Betroffenen haben einen Migrationshintergrund. Die größte Gruppe stellen dabei Frauen aus Rumänien dar, gefolgt von Albanerinnen und Nigerianerinnen." More than 90% have migrated to Germany. Most are Romanian women, second most frequently Albanian women, third most frequent Nigerian women.

93 "According to various studies, including one by the European Network for HIV/STI Prevention and Health Promotion among Migrant Sex Workers (TAMPEP), 65% to 80% of the girls and women come from abroad. Most are from Romania and Bulgaria." (2013) http://www.spiegel.de/international/germany/human-trafficking-persists-despite-legality-of-prostitution-in-germany-a-902533.html.

94 This advertisement was located on a website that advertised German legal prostitution which has been removed. The content is in possession of the first author.

Green Party politician Volker Beck promoted the legalization of prostitution, stating that if prostitution is not legalized, "....then it will just happen in places that are difficult to monitor." In Cordelia Meyer, Conny Neumann, Fidelius Schmid, Petra Truckendanner, & Steffen Winter (2013) Unprotected: How Legalizing Prostitution Has Failed. *der Spiegel*. http://www.spiegel.de/international/germany/human-trafficking-persists-despite-legality-of-prostitution-in-germany-a-902533.html.

An Amsterdam legal brothel was monitored with 3 emergency buttons, but this failed to prevent violence. Organized criminals have taken over Dutch legal prostitution, just as they have taken over control of German legal prostitution. In Melissa Farley (2006) Prostitution, Trafficking, and Cultural Amnesia: What We Must *Not* Know in Order to Keep the Business of Sexual Exploitation Running Smoothly. *Yale Journal of Law and Feminism* 18:109-144. FN 183. Like the National Socialists, traffickers and their criminal colleagues commodify women and don't see them as fully human; Manfred Paulus (2014, May 6) *Out of Control: On Liberties and Criminal Developments in the Redlight Districts of the Federal Republic of Germany*. Prostitution Resources, http://ressourcesprostitution.

wordpress.com/2014/05/06/m-paulus-out-of-control-on-liberties-and-criminal-developments-in-the-redlight-districts-of-the-federal-republic-of-germany/.

95 One translation is "special constructions." Euphemisms for the sex trade are also common today in such concepts as "migration for sex work," and "sugar daddy dating." Recently, Germany and Switzerland have added "Verrichtungsboxen" – "performance boxes" or "getting something done" boxes. These are bus-stop-like facilities where woman are selected to perform sex acts in cars or in "eco-toilets" in Berlin, which were constructed for women prostituting in the street since the closure of legal brothels during the COVID-19 pandemic.

96 Christa Schikorra (2002) Prostitution of Female Concentration Camp Prisoners as Slave Labor. On the Situation of "Asocial" Prisoners in the Ravensbruck Women's Concentration Camp. Wolfgang Benz and Barbara Distel, eds. *Dachau and the Nazi Terror 1933-1945* Vol 2 Dachau.

97 Robert Sommer (2009) "Forced Sex Labour in Nazi Concentration Camps." In Dagmar Herzog (2009) *Brutality and Desire: War and Sexuality in Europe's Twentieth Century.* Hampshire, England: Palgrave-MacMillan; pp 168-196. p 186 quoting Jean Michel, "Dora, the Concentration Camp where Modern Space Technology was Born and 30,000 Prisoners Died." London, 1979. p 156.

98 Christa Schikorra (2002) Prostitution of Female Concentration Camp Prisoners as Slave Labor. On the Situation of "Asocial" Prisoners in the Ravensbruck Women's Concentration Camp. p 254. Wolfgang Benz and Barbara Distel, eds. *Dachau and the Nazi Terror 1933-1945* Vol 2 Dachau.

99 Robert Sommer (2009) Camp Brothels: Forced Sex Labour in Nazi Concentration Camps. In Dagmar Herzog (2009) *Brutality and Desire: War and Sexuality in Europe's Twentieth Century.* (pp. 168-196). London: Palgrave Macmillan.

100 A Dachau tour guide told Inge Kleine in 2016 that until recently tour guides were prohibited from mentioning the concentration camp's brothel. The following reasons were offered for this policy of denial: a) the brothel had never been used or it had been boycotted (which was also said about gas chambers in Dachau), and b) they did not want to feed the voyeuristic interests of visitors, and c) children or teenagers who came to see what a concentration camp was like - would presumably be frightened if they knew about the brothel.

101 Melissa Farley (2007) *Prostitution and Trafficking in Nevada: Making the Connections.* San Francisco: Prostitution Research & Education.

102 Ine Vanwesenbeeck (1994). *Prostitutes' Well-Being and Risk.* Amsterdam: VU University Press; Ruth Parriott (1994). Health Experiences of Twin Cities Women Used in Prostitution. Unpublished survey initiated by WHISPER, Minneapolis.

103 For example see Seo-Young Cho, Axel Dreher, & Eric Neumayer (2013) Does legalized prostitution increase human trafficking? 41: 67-82 Available at https://prostitutionresearch.com/does-legal-prostitution-increase-trafficking-2/; and Farley, M. (2007) *Prostitution and Trafficking in Nevada: Making the Connections.* San Francisco: Prostitution Research & Education. *Connections.* San Francisco: Prostitution Research & Education.

104 Cordelia Meyer, Conny Neumann, Fidelius Schmid, Petra Truckendanner, & Steffen Winter (2013) Unprotected: How Legalizing Prostitution Has Failed. *der Spiegel.* http://www.spiegel.de/international/germany/human-trafficking-persists-despite-legality-of-prostitution-in-germany-a-902533.html. The der Spiegel investigative journalists report that "The Netherlands chose the path of legal deregulation two years before Germany. Both the Dutch justice minister and the police concede that there have been no palpable improvements for prostitutes since then. They are generally in poorer health than before, and increasing numbers are addicted to drugs. The police estimate that 50 to 90 percent of prostitutes do not practice the profession voluntarily." Dutch Social Democrat Lodewijk Asscher considers the legalization of prostitution to have been "a national mistake."

105 Inge Schepers (2011) Public Prosecutor, National Public Prosecutors' Office Rotterdam, based in Zwolle Operation Sneep: "The frayed edges of licensed prostitution." Paper presented in Vienna 4 October 2011. Available at http://www.osce.org/secretariat/84652?download=true.

106 Helmut Sporer (2013) Kriminalpolizei Augsburg, Vortrag zum Seminar der European Women`s Lobby, Reality of Prostitution am 01.10.2013 in Brussels.

107 Ingeborg Kraus (2016) The German model is producing hell on earth! *Trauma and Prostitution* website. https://www.trauma-and-prostitution.eu/en/2016/11/02/the-german-model-is-producing-hell-on-earth/.

108 Euronews (2020, March 9) Coronavirus: one of Europe's largest brothels files for bankruptcy.

https://www.euronews.com/2020/09/03/coronavirus-one-of-europe-s-largest-brothels-files-for-bankruptcy.

109 Prostituting and trafficked women rent rooms in the brothel where they live. "Pascha's [German brothel] main income is the rent we get from the girls," explained Hermann Müller, the pimp/manager of Pascha. Women pay €175 for 24 hours' use of a room at Pascha. They must service least four men to break even (Dia, N.L.D (2015, January 29) Germany's Mega-Brothel Left Me Cold. Telegraph UK. https://www.telegraph.co.uk/women/sex/germanys-mega-brothel-left-me-cold/).

110 Battered women are in great danger from abusers when they are quarantined with no escape from the abuse or have no privacy for phoning for help.

111 Huschke Mau (2020) Coronavirus and prostitution – urgent! https://huschkemau.de/en/2020/03/14/coronavirus-and-prostitution-urgent/.

112 According to government evaluations of the Swedish sex buyers' law, men's rate of buying sex dropped from 13.6% in 1996, before the introduction of the law in 1999, to 7.9% in 2008. Selected extracts of the Swedish government report SOU 2010: 49 "The Ban against the Purchase of Sexual Services. An evaluation 1999-2008" S.32 Public attitudes about prostitution also changed. In 1996, 67% of the public did not consider sex buying to be a crime. Three years later, after the introduction of the law and public education and campaigns about prostitution, 76% of the public accepted the law. Since then, support for the Swedish law continues to be more than 70%. (Same evaluation, p. 30) http://www.government.se/contentassets/8f0c2ccaa84e455f8bd2b7e9c55 7ff3e/english-translation-of-chapter-4-and-5-in-sou-2010-49.pdf. See also Coalition for the Abolition of Prostitution (2016) *France's new prostitution law*. Available at http://www.cap-international. org/activity/understanding-frances-new-prostitution-law-briefing-infographics-and-more/. See also Max Waltman (2020). The politics of legal challenges to pornography: A comparative analysis. *Wisconsin Journal of Law, Gender, & Society*, 35.

113 Sweden (1999), Iceland (2008), Norway (2009), Canada (2014), Northern Ireland (2015), France (2016), Republic of Ireland (2017), and Israel (2018).

114 The adoption of neoliberal economic policy – the idea that anything that can be sold should be sold – by these organizations has caused untold damage to those in prostitution who seek escape it rather than receive a few dollars more in payment for their abuse.

115 Annegret Wittmann und Beate Hilgendorf, "Die Rechte der Prostituierten nach dem neuen Prostitutionsgesetz," Freie und Hansestadt Hamburg, Behörde für Umwelt und Gesundheit, Amt für Gesundheit und Verbraucherschutz, Fachabteilung.

116 Kassandra e.V. (2015) "Sonderregelung für Sexarbeiterinnen unter 21 Jahren" (07/2015). Pamphlet available from second author. Trafficking under the German law is defined as placing a person aged 18-21 in a legal brothel or helping her locate sex buyers.

CHAPTER 17

"But What About *Feminist* Porn?"
Examining the Work of Tristan Taormino

by Rebecca Whisnant

[This article was originally published in Sexualization, Media, & Society (SMS), part of SAGE Open, at https://journals.sagepub.com/ doi/full/10.1177/2374623816631727. Reprinted with permission.]

For over two decades now, I have taught, written, and spoken publicly about pornography from a critical feminist perspective. In the 1990's, the most common critical questions I received involved censorship and the law. In recent years, the focus has changed: when there are critical questions, they most often concern feminist pornography. What about it? Does it exist? Could it exist? Do I, or would I, object to it? What is it like, or what could it be like?

I do not find the "what-if" and "could-there-be" questions particularly illuminating, nor am I skilled at prognosticating what media forms might exist in possible post-patriarchal futures. Furthermore, as in discussions of pornography generally, sometimes people are motivated to defend "feminist pornography" in the abstract while knowing little to nothing about the actual material in question. Thus, it seems more fruitful to bring the discussion down to cases: that is, to investigate what some of those who claim to be making feminist pornography are actually making, and what they are saying about what they are making. People can then judge for themselves whether that material reflects a sexual ethic, and a conception of feminism, that they wish to endorse.

Case study: Tristan Taormino

This article focuses on one self-described feminist pornographer who looms large in the contemporary "sex-positive" and "sex radical" firmament. Tristan Taormino first came to prominence in the late 1990's and early 2000's as, among other things, editor of the lesbian porn magazine *On Our Backs* and a sex columnist for the *Village Voice*. In 1999, she collaborated with mainstream pornographer John Stagliano and fetish-porn producer Ernest Greene on *The Ultimate Guide to Anal Sex for Women*, a porn film based on her book of the same title. In more recent years, Taormino's porn productions have included the *Chemistry* series, the *Rough Sex* series, and *Tristan Taormino's Expert Guides* to various sexual acts.

Author, speaker, educator, editor, TV host, filmmaker, and more: when it comes to the various self-styled "sex-positive" movements, venues, and endeavors of roughly the last twenty years, Taormino has done it all, and she has been at the center of much of it. The variety and reach of Taormino's work illustrates that, as Lynn Comella observes, "Feminist pornography is not a series of stand-alone texts that exist outside of a much wider cultural context—and history—of sex-positive feminist cultural production and commerce" (2013, p. 91).

In addition to being prominent, Taormino is intelligent, reflective, and articulate about the choices she has made, and about the politics and assumptions underlying those choices. Furthermore, her body of work exemplifies themes and commitments that are largely consistent among those who produce, perform in, and/or support feminist pornography.

My discussion is based partly on Taormino's published writings and interviews, as well as on an admittedly small selection of her films—one full-length, and several extended clips. While I see no reason to believe that the selections I viewed are unrepresentative of her film work as a whole, readers should take into account that my critique is based on a limited sampling of that work.

As will quickly become evident, Taormino's feminist politics are different from my own, and my take on her work is a critical one. My aim is not to write a hit piece, however, but rather to articulate clearly the political and ethical worldview that underlies Taormino's body of work—thus, again, enabling more informed discussions of feminist pornography and related issues.

"An industry within an industry"

Feminist critics of pornography frequently emphasize that, whatever else it may be, contemporary pornography is above all an industry within a capitalist marketplace. As Robert Jensen points out, "the DVDs and internet sites to which men are masturbating are not being made by struggling artists who work in lonely garrets, tirelessly working to help us understand the mysteries of sexuality" (2007, p. 79). Even once we understand that mainstream pornography is driven by profit, however, we may tend to assume that *feminist* pornography emerges from utopian enclaves where people produce exactly what they want to produce, based on their own unique, creative, and egalitarian visions of sex.

Of course, no such enclaves exist; or, if they do, then few people will ever see whatever erotic materials are created therein. As Taormino and her co-editors write in their introduction to *The Feminist Porn Book*,

> *feminist porn is not only an emergent social movement and an alternative cultural production: it is a genre of media made for profit. Part of a multibillion dollar business in adult*

entertainment media, feminist porn is an industry within an industry. (2013, pp. 15-16).

In a 2014 interview, Taormino comments further that

> *In the United States there is not necessarily a clear, discrete division between "feminist/queer/indie porn" and "mainstream porn" . . . . I situate my own work in both worlds: I make feminist pornography that is funded and distributed by mainstream companies and features primarily mainstream performers.* (Voss 2014, p. 204).

In fact, perhaps more than any other figure, Taormino has occupied and helped to shape both mainstream and alternative spaces within the sex industry—as evidenced by, among other things, her having repeatedly won both Adult Video News awards *and* Feminist Porn awards.

Taormino is well aware of the trade-offs attendant on working with mainstream porn companies and reaching mainstream audiences. As she put it in the 2003 documentary *Hot and Bothered*, "Funding is always an issue . . . . people always ask why isn't there more feminist porn, why there isn't more lesbian porn, and the truth is, you need money" (Goldberg 2003). She continues,

> *I basically had two different ways to go. I could try the feminist way, which is that you beg, borrow, and steal, you do it on a shoestring, you ask all your friends to do stuff for free, and then you try to distribute it yourself. Or, I could go directly to the man and sell out, and go to a mainstream adult company, where I would have to compromise some of my, like, artistic integrity.* (Goldberg 2003).

Indeed, one can only be so critical of mainstream porn if that is the venue within which one works, and within which one hopes to maintain friendly ties and funding sources. Similarly, one can only diverge so far from the tropes of mainstream porn while still appealing to any reasonable subset of its consumer base.

Like all pornography, and indeed all media, feminist pornography can be analyzed in terms of its production, its content, and its consumption (Jensen 2007); and when media is produced and sold within a capitalist marketplace, such analysis must keep a clear eye on how each dimension is shaped by the imperatives of profit.

Production: From consent to authenticity

Taormino's most extensive discussion of what qualifies some pornography, including her own, as feminist involves the dimension of production—in particular, how she hires, treats, and works with performers. Her approach to making porn production "safe, professional, political, empowering, and fun" (Taormino 2013, p. 264) involves a number of practices that diverge from industry standards—from performers setting their own pay rates and choosing their own sexual partners, to providing a clean and safe work space with healthy snacks and performers' preferred drinks and hygiene products. In addition, her decision in 2013 (virtually alone among mainstream pornographers) to require condom use on her sets manifested a level of human decency and concern for performers' safety (Cohen, 2013).

Perhaps most central to Taormino's own definition of feminist porn production, however, is the role of collaboration between director and performers. In "Calling the Shots: Feminist Porn in Theory and Practice," she writes:

> Before we step foot on set, I have conversations with my performers, get to know them, ask them questions about their sexual likes and dislikes, favorite activities and toys, and what helps them have a really great work experience. I design their scenes around this information. (2013, p. 260).

Taormino's approach thus implicitly challenges one common refrain of feminists who oppose both pornography and prostitution: that these industries by their nature require people, primarily women, to have *unwanted* sex—sex that at best bores them, and at worst repels and traumatizes them—out of economic need (Tyler 2015, Moran 2013). Her ideal is that, on her film sets, people are having sex that they *do* want to have, in the very ways that they want to have it. Discussing her *Chemistry* series, she writes:

> *I'm interested in allowing the action to unfold organically (as organically as it can with lights, cameras, and people standing around you) and for people to move and fuck in ways they want to, for however long they want to . . . . So much of porn asks performers to act out someone else's fantasy or do what someone else thinks looks sexy: what if they were given the opportunity to do their own thing?* (2013, p. 259).

Thus, Taormino's performers choose their sexual activities and partners, she says, "all based on what feels good to them, all based on their actual sexuality, not a fabricated script" (p. 261). In this way, she moves beyond the view commonly articulated by defenders not only of feminist porn, but of porn generally: that everything is fine so long as everyone involved is freely consenting. To her credit, she sees that, for porn as for sex generally, mere consent is a low threshold.

For Taormino, then, the defining feature of ethical and feminist porn production is not consent but *authenticity*. She traces this emphasis back to her experiences directing explicit photo shoots for *On Our Backs*, noting that "what readers responded to most was the level of authentic desire and connection between the people. If I could capture that in a moving image, it could be even more palpable and powerful" (2013, p. 258). Her emphasis on authenticity is also evident in her practice of including extended performer interviews in her films. Unlike the brief and formulaic interviews found in most mainstream porn, she says, her interviews allow

342

performers to speak more genuinely and at greater length about their feelings, desires, and experiences, both within and outside the industry, thus both giving them an authentic voice and humanizing them for the viewer.

Authenticity: Constraints and complications

Since authenticity figures so prominently in Taormino's claim to be creating feminist pornography, it is worth examining this concept and the realities behind it in some depth.

There are many possible conceptions of authenticity when it comes to people's desires and choices (sexual or otherwise).[1] Taormino's is an exceptionally thin one: when she calls a performer's desire or choice "authentic," she means only that this is something the person sincerely wants to do, or from which s/he derives real (rather than faked) pleasure. As I will show, however, even given this minimal conception of authenticity, her claims about its role in her productions are open to question. While Taormino's pursuit of authenticity in her filmmaking is neither meaningless nor trivial, it is considerably more complicated than she makes it out to be.

At the very least, we should note the built-in limitations on authenticity in the context of pornography production. For example, Taormino describes as follows the production of her *Chemistry* series:

> *I take a group of porn stars to a house for thirty-six hours. There is no script and no schedule and everything is filmed. They decide who they have sex with, when, where, and what they do. I tell the performers before we begin shooting: forget everything you know about porn.* (2013, p. 258).

That is, she explains, the performers are to forget all the formulas and tropes that define mainstream porn: two minutes of this position, three minutes of that, ending with the "money shot" (of male ejaculation). Rather, the performers should do what *they* like to do sexually: all and only those sex acts that they authentically wish to perform, in the ways they wish to perform them.

Needless to say, not having sex at all during this rollicking weekend, or having sex only once or twice, is not among the options—at least if one wants to be paid much or hired again. And having sex in ways that are not camera-friendly, or that for any reason cannot reasonably be expected to appeal to viewers, is similarly not on the agenda. It is unsurprising, then, that in the scene I viewed from *Chemistry, Vol. 1*—in which two interracial male/female couples have sex in various positions, with the aid of various sex toys—there are no positions that are not highly visible to the camera. The scene ends in an entirely standard way, with a man ejaculating into a woman's face while she intones "oh yes, give me that cum" (Taormino 2006).

In short, it is impossible to participate in the production of a commercially viable porn film while "forgetting everything you know about porn." Perhaps a more realistic instruction to performers would be "forget as much as you can about porn, consistent with getting paid, maintaining your reputation and marketability in the industry, and ensuring enough viewers for this film to make it commercially viable."

In addition to the constraints on authenticity that are built into pornography production *per se*, recent developments in the industry impose further such constraints. As Taormino observed in a 2014 interview,

> *Ten years ago, I had more time and more money to make a movie than I do today. Budgets have decreased, yet the demand for new content remains high, so companies want filmmakers to create a unique product with fewer resources.* (Voss 2014, p. 203).

She does not explain how these market conditions affect her own work, including her often-mentioned practice of allowing performers to set their own pay rates. (Again, built-in limitations should be noted: surely a performer who demands pay significantly higher than standard market rates is less likely to be hired, or hired again.) Taormino notes further that, unlike in decades past,

> *today the majority of performers have agents . . . Agencies keep track of performers, make sure they arrive to set on time and prepared, and if someone is a no-show they have a pool of possible replacements. As in the mainstream entertainment industry, porn agents run the gamut from professional to unscrupulous.* (Voss 2014, p. 203).

The prevalence of agents in the porn industry is indeed important to consider, particularly the constraints it imposes on performers' choosing to do all and only those sex acts that they authentically desire to do.

Agents make money—again, as in the mainstream entertainment industry—by taking a percentage of performers' earnings. They thus have a financial interest in performers' accepting as many jobs as possible and having as few limits as possible on what sex acts they will perform and with whom. In particular, they benefit financially from performers' willingness to perform what are widely considered more unpleasant, dangerous, and/or degrading acts, since those acts typically pay more.[2] Even setting aside the financial interests of agents, these market dynamics clearly affect performers' choices. As porn performer Carter Cruise explains,

> *I know girls who only do vanilla boy-girl scenes. . . . If you're only doing those scenes though, you limit your audience and you don't make as much money. If you do things like anal, kinks, taboos, fetishes, girl-girl, boy-girl, you reach a much larger audience and you make a lot more money.* (Moneybags, 2014).

As Cruise further explains, not all agencies even allow their performers to limit the jobs they will take: "the agency that I'm with only represents 25 girls at a time, so they require all their girls to do everything. . . . we aren't allowed to have no-lists. I can't say I don't want to work with a guy because I don't like him."

Taormino says little about how she responds to this complex set of realities in her own work. How does she take account of the fact that her performers' putatively authentic choices are constrained not only by their own financial interests, but often by those of their agents as well? Would her ethical stance allow her to employ a performer who, in turn, works with an agency like the one Cruise describes? Does she pay performers more for engaging in more painful, risky, and/or degrading sex acts? If not, how would she explain this divergence from industry standards? If, on the other hand, she does pay more for these acts, then it's not clear why: after all, as she repeatedly assures us, her performers engage in those acts only if—and only because—they truly want to do them and are sexually gratified by doing them. So why would they expect, or deserve, to be paid more for them?[3]

The economic realities underlying performers' choices, then, are considerably murkier than Taormino's cheerful celebration of "authenticity" suggests.

The persistence of trauma

Porn performer Sinnamon Love has observed that, when it comes to porn production, "female directors have an advantage." She explains:

> *directors like Joanna Angel, Belladonna, Julie Simone, and Chanta Rose . . . manage to produce beautiful images of women but still get these women to push their limits in intense scenes. Perhaps some women feel more comfortable with a woman behind the camera asking them to do things*

that might be deemed degrading if asked by a male director.
(2013, 99-100).

The dynamic Love describes here may be exacerbated when the director is not only a woman, but a self-described feminist who emphasizes making her sets ethical, fun, and so on. How could anything upsetting or harmful happen here, where we're all safe and professional and here to get empowered?

As I'll detail later, at least one performer in Taormino's films appears, in an accompanying interview, to be describing a traumatic reaction. It is also instructive to look at Taormino's comments about her first and only experience performing in her own films. Her first film, 1999's *Ultimate Guide to Anal Sex for Women*, culminated in an anal gangbang performed on Taormino herself. While some of her later descriptions of this experience have been glowing, in a 2000 interview she gave a different impression. After explaining that, because the action was supposed to take place in one day, she had to wear the same outfit every day of filming, she goes on to say that the shirt she wore in the film "was a favorite of mine, which now I can't bear to wear." Asked what she would do to unwind after a day of shooting, she responded:

> *I don't drink or do drugs . . . . Usually we'd go to dinner and then we'd watch TV and go to sleep. I'd also take long walks with my dog . . . For me my dogs are very grounding and simple in their unconditional love for me. I'd come home to my dog with the bug eyes and feel comforted.* (Hernandez-Rosenblatt, 2000).

While it is reassuring that Taormino did not feel the need to drink or do drugs to cope with her experience, her immediate reference to these measures suggests that they are not uncommon among porn performers. Her reference to feeling "comforted" by the loving presence of her dog also suggests that her experience of being anally penetrated by ten people on film was not as fun or empowering as some of her later comments would suggest. Perhaps it is not surprising that she has since confined her own participation in pornography to directing and producing, rather than performing.

Content: Is anything off-limits?

Beyond issues of production, Taormino clearly intends for the content of her films to differ in important ways from mainstream (non-feminist) pornography. In fact, she cites disturbing developments in mainstream gonzo pornography as a key impetus for her decision to make porn production a central element of her work. Referring to the mid-2000's, she writes:

> *The trend in gonzo was the more extreme, the better . . . . It was as degrading and offensive as any antiporn feminist's worst nightmare. The scenes were not about exploring dominance and submission, being rough, or pushing the envelope. The spirit of some seemed downright hostile.* (2013, p. 257).

She does not explain the differences between porn's being "hostile"—or, as she puts it elsewhere, "joyless and mean" (2002, p. 134)—and its "exploring dominance and submission, being rough, or pushing the envelope."[4]

Taormino's films, however, include many of the same acts common in (other) mainstream pornography, such as gagging, choking, slapping, and misogynist name-calling.[5] When it comes to content, the similarities between her films and the rest of mainstream pornography are readily apparent; the question is, what are the differences?

Compared to mainstream gonzo, Taormino's films include marginally less robotic fucking, and more emphasis on activities such as cunnilingus and vibrator use. There is some kissing, and even some laughing here and there—neither of which is common in mainstream porn (unless the laughter is at women's expense). The core of Taormino's approach to pornography's content, however, is captured in the continuation of the quote above. Having decried the "hostile" nature of many mainstream gonzo films, she goes on to observe that such films:

> *lacked a fundamental component: female pleasure. I mean, if you're going to go to the trouble of calling a woman a slut and smacking her while you fuck her, there damn well better be an awesome orgasm in it for her. If she's not having a great time, what's the point?* (2013, p. 257).

Aside from the flippant attitude it displays toward misogynist epithets and violence, this quote exemplifies a tenet basic to the ideology of pro-porn feminism: that it is perfectly fine to portray dominance, submission, pain, and hierarchy as sexually exciting. As Taormino explained in *Cosmopolitan*,

> *Images of dominance and submission are not anti-feminist in and of themselves, but one of the reasons feminists critique them is because consent is not always explicit and because of the repetition of men dominating women . . . . Feminist pornographers don't want to do away with sexual power dynamics; many of us want to explore them in an explicitly consensual and more diverse, nuanced, non-stereotypical way.* (Breslaw 2013).

In fact, according to this view, it is rebellious and liberatory for women to claim traditionally male roles and prerogatives in sex. Taormino bemoans the fact that "women are still not seen as sexual aggressors, predators, or consumers" (2002, xiv); feminist porn aims, among other things, to fill this representational gap. As we will shortly see, however, depicting women in submissive and subordinated sexual roles is also seen as liberatory and feminist—provided, of course, that it is all consensual and authentic.

Taormino explains that she "place[s] so much emphasis on the process of making porn because it's difficult to designate what a feminist porn *image* looks like" (2013, p. 263). It is, indeed: if celebratory eroticized depictions of female pain, abject submission, and even violence against women need not disqualify something as "feminist pornography," what exactly is left?

Representation and personnel

One often-cited difference between "feminist pornography" and other pornography involves *who* is seen performing: as Taormino and her co-editors explain, feminist pornography emphasizes "the inclusion of underrepresented identities and practices" (2013, p. 15). More specifically, Taormino says, feminist pornography is "committed to depicting diversity in gender, race, ethnicity, nationality, sexuality, class, body size, ability, and age" (2013, p. 262). She always includes performers of color in her own films, and she seeks to increase the visibility in porn of trans and genderqueer performers. This emphasis on diverse personnel unites many advocates and creators of queer, indie, and otherwise alternative porn, as well as of self-described feminist porn.

Without dismissing the value of diverse representation, it is worth noting that marketplace constraints are once again germane. Take, for example, diversity in women's body size: having admittedly viewed only a small subset of Taormino's films, I would be surprised if any women appear in them who weigh over two hundred pounds. While there are niche and fetish markets for porn featuring such women, Taormino aims to appeal to mainstream audiences, and that means the women's appearances (and the men's too, for that matter) can be "diverse" only within fairly narrow parameters. It is thus not surprising that most of the women performers in Taormino's films also sport entirely hairless bodies (including pubic areas); like porn depicting fat women, porn displaying female pubic hair constitutes a niche/fetish genre.

Because both commercial and ideological considerations prohibit placing many (if any) constraints on content, it makes sense that diversity of personnel figures so prominently in explanations of what makes "feminist porn" feminist. It is not so much that different things are being done in feminist porn, but rather that more different kinds of people are shown doing them.

"What a feminist porn image looks like": Three illustrations

We can best discern Taormino's beliefs about what counts as feminist content in pornography by looking at what she includes in her own films. Consider, for instance, the following three examples.

Facials

In "Calling the Shots," Taormino describes the development of her perspective on the ever-popular "facial" (in which one or more men ejaculate on a woman's face). In her first film, although she succumbed to her male mentors' expectation that each scene end with the standard external cum shot, she insisted on no facials: "*It's a porn trope! It's degrading! Women don't enjoy it!*" (2013, p. 256, italics in original). She goes on to explain, however, that her perspective on facial cum shots has evolved in the intervening years: "I believe viewers appreciate consent, context, chemistry, and performer agency more than the presence or absence of a specific act" (2013, p. 263). Taormino's evolving principles may well have coincided with the increasingly apparent demands of her consumer base: again, when making mainstream porn, you make what sells in a mainstream market. Taormino's ambivalence about her choices in this regard is reflected when she goes on to say:

I'm conscious of the dangers of repetition of a specific act like a facial cum shot and what it could signify, specifically

351

that men's orgasms represent the apex of a scene . . . and women's bodies are things to be used, controlled, and marked like territory. Although I am trying to make a different kind of porn, once I put it out in the world, I can't control how it's received. (2013, p. 263).

While it is true that she cannot control how a facial cum shot is received or interpreted by viewers, she can and does predict quite accurately how it *will* be (mostly) received. The quote makes clear that she has decided to include these images in her films, knowing full well what they mean in a broader cultural context and why they are rewarding for the average porn consumer.

Racial language

Taormino criticizes the "inequality, stereotypes, and racist depictions" common in mainstream porn, where, she says, "race is exoticized, fetishized, and commodified in very particular ways" (2013, p. 261). Noting the industry's tendency to cast performers of color either not at all, or only in ethnically-specific and often overtly racist films, she touts her own divergence from this pattern:

I'm committed to combatting stereotypical portrayals on every level: I refuse to use race-specific, and often demeaning, language on box covers and in marketing materials. (2013, p. 262).

It is rare to see Taormino articulate such a firm limit on content. As it turns out, however, her specification "on box covers or in marketing materials" is significant, as even my limited viewing of her films yielded two instances of race-specific language.

In a scene from *Chemistry 1* portraying two interracial couples, an off-camera voice asks a female performer, "What do you see?" The performer responds, "I see a pink pussy . . . it looks so tight, like it's squeezing your black cock" (Taormino 2006). While this racialized reference to the black penis was presumably not scripted, Taormino could have edited it out. She chose to keep it in.

The second racial reference occurs in *Rough Sex 3*. In an interview prior to her scene, while discussing her feelings about being asked to dominate star Adrianna Nicole, African-American performer Jada Fire relates a prior experience of racist abuse on a porn set:

> *You can dominate a woman but you don't have to degrade her. Because I've been called a black piece of shit before.* [Off-camera female voice, presumably Taormino: In a scene?] *Yeah.* [By a woman?] *Yeah. She fucked me up like mentally, with the stuff that she said. . . . I know the boundaries, how far to go.* (Taormino 2010).

In the ensuing scene, Jada Fire wears a standard dominatrix outfit in order to boss around, push, shove, and humiliate Adrianna Nicole. At one point, she dons an impressively large black strap-on dildo and orders Nicole, "you suck this fucking black dick . . . let's see you fucking choke on this."

Thus, it is indeed just in marketing materials that Taormino eschews "race-specific and often demeaning language." Again, while the racial references are not Taormino's own words, it is her call whether to include them. She could, if she chose, instruct her performers never to employ such terms. She has made her decision, not only with respect to racialized language, but also with respect to the misogynist epithets—such as "bitch," "whore," and "slut"—that pervade both her films and her writings.

"Cash"

The second scene of *Rough Sex 3*, entitled "Cash," features Adrianna Nicole as a woman in prostitution, and Ramon Nomar as a man buying sexual access to her. In the interviews preceding the scene, each performer offers his or her perspective on the nature and/or appeal of prostitution. Nomar explains that it's:

> *about the power . . . this afternoon is gonna be like I say, and you cannot say anything. You get the money, and – shh – zip.* [mimes "zipping lip," laughs]. *It's simple . . . . it's about the person who wants to dominate the other.* (Taormino 2010).

Nicole then observes that:

> *when you walk into a scenario like that, you kind of don't know what you're gonna get, and you feel like you have to put up a front, and be on your game . . . . There is always a danger element to it. I mean you really don't know, walking in, what you're gonna get.* (Taormino 2010).

Thus, no comforting myths are rehearsed here about prostitution as empowering or liberating for women. Rather, between them, Nomar and Nicole make it abundantly clear that, in their minds, prostitution is about men's control and women's submission, men's speech and women's silence, men's sexual imperatives and women's fear of those imperatives.

These performers' comments strikingly parallel the insights of some women who have exited prostitution. For example, in her memoir *Paid For*, Rachel Moran observes of her experience in so-called "high-class" prostitution that "the attitude was clear: 'I have paid you two hundred pounds—therefore I will do whatever I feel like doing to you, and you will keep your mouth shut about it'" (Moran 2013, p. 91). Regarding uncertainty and fear, Moran sums it up as follows: "you don't know who or what you're dealing with until the door has closed behind you, and by the time the door has closed behind you, it's too late" (2013, p. 93).

The scene itself is mostly predictable, including plenty of aggression, both verbal and physical. "What do you think I pay you for?" Ramon demands of Adrianna at one point.

> *You think I can do this with my fucking wife, hmm? You think she will allow me to do this?. . . You are my whore now, you're my fucking whore, that's why you take it like this.* (Taormino 2010).

Later on, he instructs her: "Don't move from there, open your fucking mouth . . . there you go," as the scene ends with—what else?—a facial cum shot. Thus, beyond what the performers have already articulated, the scene conveys at least the following messages: that men demand sexual acts, and forms of sexual submission, from women in prostitution that they cannot get other women to perform to their satisfaction; and that the resulting sexual encounter is sexually exciting, not only for the male buyer but for the prostituted woman herself.

Before leaving this scene, let me draw one further connection, this time regarding the prominent role of strangulation therein.[6] Less than five minutes into the scene, Ramon strangles Adrianna, and in among all the slapping, bossing, pushing, arm-twisting, head-yanking, gagging, and more that ensues, strangling is unquestionably the main attraction.

Kathryn Laughon et. al., reviewing a range of studies, found that between 34 and 68 percent of women experiencing intimate partner violence reported strangulation (2008, p. 504). Joshi et. al., who conducted a series of focus groups and interviews at a domestic violence shelter, found that "*all* of the participants had been strangled and, among them, almost all were strangled multiple times. The loss of consciousness was common" (2012, p. 798). Furthermore, abusers who strangle their victims are especially dangerous, as Laughon et. al. observe:

In addition to the direct health consequences, a partner's use of nonlethal strangulation may indicate increased risk of later lethal violence . . . . women who experienced nonlethal strangulation were at increased risk for attempted and completed homicide when controlling for other demographic risk factors. (2008, p. 504).

To sum up, then: a great many abusive men strangle their female victims, causing both physical damage and psychological trauma; and murderous abusers are more likely than non-murderous abusers to have strangled their victims in the past.

What shall we make of "Cash," in light of this information? Nothing at all, some might say: of course it is terrible that some women get strangled when they don't want to be strangled, but this woman—Nicole, and/or the character she portrays—*does* want to be strangled, because she finds it sexually exciting. And some other women (and perhaps men) do too. Furthermore, Taormino even includes, in a DVD featurette, a tutorial on how to strangle your partner *safely* during sex. So what is the problem?

The question I mean to raise here is not whether viewers may be caused, or even encouraged, to strangle women by viewing this material. Rather, my concern is with the ethics of representing a key method of misogynist torture and terror as a sex game. Perspectives on this matter clearly vary, and reveal much about the politics and priorities of those whose perspectives they are.

Before leaving the "Cash" scene, one final note is in order. In a "behind the scenes" section following the main scene, some seemingly spontaneous sex acts occur (for instance, additional instances of Nomar ejaculating on Nicole). In a subsequent interview, Nicole says that after this performance, she did not leave the set for two or three hours, as she felt "really fucked up," as if she shouldn't be on the road: "I needed to get back to reality a little bit . . . all that was like a big extended scene, and that's why I didn't feel ready to get in my car" (Taormino 2010). We cannot know for sure to what extent the spontaneity here was merely apparent. But to this

356

observer, it seemed that this sequence of events—following, as it did, an already violent scene—took Nicole by surprise, and that as a result, she experienced traumatic dissociation from which it took her several hours to recover.[7]

This won't be pretty: Framing the content

The content of Taormino's films, then, might surprise anyone who expects feminist pornography to represent egalitarian sex, or even to eschew misogynist epithets and violent acts against women. It is thus important for Taormino and other creators and defenders of feminist porn to find ways of framing its apparently not-so-feminist content as progressive and liberatory. At least the following three ways of doing so are common in these discussions.

First, ridicule any ethical concerns or constraints as naïve and pollyanna-ish about the nature of sex. As Taormino and her co-editors put it,

> *sex-positive feminist porn does not mean that sex is always a ribbon-tied box of happiness and joy . . . . Feminist porn explores sexual ideas and acts that may be fraught, confounding, and deeply disturbing to some, and liberating and empowering to others.* (Taormino et. al. 2013, p. 15).

Feminist porn, they explain, represents "the power of sexuality in all its unruliness . . . that unruliness may involve producing images that seem oppressive, degrading, or violent" (p. 15). This framing is aided by the claim that power hierarchy is an inevitable component of all sexuality. As Betty Dodson puts it in the same volume, "Gradually I began to understand that all forms of sex were an exchange of power, whether it was conscious or unconscious" (2013, p. 26). On this view, aspiring to egalitarian sexuality—or expecting representations of such sexuality from self-described feminists—simply reveals one's failure to understand sex itself.

Second, emphasize the importance of accepting and celebrating all forms of sexuality, as a way of resisting puritanical and oppressively judgmental sexual attitudes. Taormino explains in the 2003 documentary *Hot and Bothered* that "feminism taught me all body parts, all erogenous zones, all sex acts, all fantasies were fair game" (Goldberg 2003). "We need to represent sex in positive ways," she urges, "to counteract all the shame, guilt, and judgment that our society heaps on sex" (Blue, 2011).

Third, suggest that portrayals of inegalitarian and/or violent sex can constitute a bold blow against sexist stereotyping. As Taormino puts it,

> *The dominant view within the industry is that couples and women want softer, gentler porn. This notion both reflects and reinforces stereotypes about female sexuality: we want romance and flowers and pretty lighting and nothing too hard. And that's true for some women,* but not all of us. (2013, p. 258).

On this view, one way to validate female sexuality and rebel against sexist constraints is by showing that women can (really, authentically) like it just as aggressive and nasty as men do, and to see to it that women—both performers and viewers—get what they authentically want. Taormino's emphasis on the stereotype that women only like gentle, romantic sex enables her to cast her own approach as rebellious and groundbreaking—as in the promotional copy for *Rough Sex*, according to which the series "dares to challenge conventional wisdom about the fantasy lives of women" ("Tristan's Films," n.d.). In fact her work reinforces a much older and more damaging stereotype: that deep down, women want to be sexually used, objectified, and dominated.

Consumption: "Guilt-free" porn use

Those who promote feminist and other "alternative" pornography frequently make connections between the ethics of production and those of consumption. For example, Tina Vasquez notes that in "ethical" pornography, "everything is safe and consent is part of the narrative, which enables viewers to watch whatever plays out guilt-free" (2012, p. 33). Men as well as women are encouraged to accept their own porn preferences, whatever those may be: as Taormino and her co-editors put it, feminist pornography "acknowledges multiple female (and other) viewers with many different preferences" (2013, p. 10). Indeed, part of the point of porn generally, including feminist porn, is to reassure consumers that their sexual desires, preferences, and fantasies, are perfectly fine and shared by others (Whisnant 2010): as Taormino observes, "[it] validates viewers when they see themselves or a part of their sexuality represented" (2005, p. 95).

Most feminists agree that it is important to challenge conservative sexual restrictions and judgments, and to affirm and enjoy sexuality in ways that do not harm oneself or others. However, many feminists also encourage critical reflection on sexual desire—including one's own—and the cultural forces that shape and direct it. In fact, it may be that, as D.A. Clarke suggests, "this question of the legitimacy of desires, and whether the fulfillment of desire is the same thing as 'freedom,' is at the heart of a feminist critique of pornography and prostitution" (2004, p. 188). Given the content of Taormino's films, evidently she finds unproblematic the desire of her male and female viewers to masturbate to films of women being strangled, slapped, gagged, called bitches and whores, and more.

It is worth reflecting, in this connection, on the message sent to viewers by Taormino's relentless focus on authenticity. For instance, a description of her *Rough Sex* series reads, in part, as follows:

> *the scenes are based entirely on the real fantasies of female performers, which run the gamut from dominance to submission . . . . Through dramatic roleplaying, each woman shares her most intimate desires, tests her own boundaries, and rides the seductive line between pleasure and pain.* ("Tristan's Films," n.d.).

While other films in the series may explore male submission, all scenes in *Rough Sex 3* involve the submission of Adrianna Nicole and her often-violent domination by female and male co-performers. The message, repeatedly reinforced in performer interviews, is that the scenes represent Nicole's *true* desires and fantasies, and that everything has been designed and choreographed to give her exactly what she wants. The film's subtitle, *Adrianna's Dangerous Mind*, reassures the consumer that—notwithstanding one's arousal to scenes of violence against a woman—it is *her* mind that is "dangerous," not one's own.

Thus, the tacit deal that most pornography strikes with the viewer—"she'll fake orgasm, we'll tell you the story that she loves it, wink-wink, and you believe what you want"—is off here. The viewer is told in no uncertain terms, including by the performer herself, that what the film depicts really *is* what she wants and craves. Whether this is true is not, for the moment, the point. The point is that the films take on a certain kind of ideological power that trades precisely on their claim to represent women's *authentic* desires—and that, depending on what those desires are, that ideological power is far from benign or feminist.

"Run out and do it": Feminist porn as sex education

Many defenders of porn, feminist and otherwise, urge attention to the distinction between fantasy and reality, pointing out that viewing some act onscreen does not necessarily mean one even wants to do it, let alone that one actually will. Taormino, by contrast, has stated repeatedly that she means for her films to inspire viewers to, as she puts it, "run out and do it" (2014, p. 256). Feminist porn, she observes, "gives [women and men] information and ideas about sex. It teaches. It inspires fantasy and adventure ..." (2005, p. 95). Because her writings, workshops, and films depict fully consensual and mutually rewarding sex acts, presumably, this will all be to the good.

360

As I will further elaborate in the next section, however, what viewers are inspired by Taormino's work to "run out and do" may be a considerably more mixed bag. A hint can be found in one of Taormino's first major media interviews, with misogynist "shock jock" Howard Stern on his radio show in 1997. Taormino chose to debut her book *The Ultimate Guide to Anal Sex for Women* on Stern's show, where it no doubt found a receptive audience. A telling moment occurs during a discussion of digital anal penetration:

Stern: *And what if she says, "Ow, that hurts, I don't want it, I don't like that. Get your fingers out of there." That means, go ahead anyway?* [Taormino laughs]

Robin Quivers: *No, that means you're going too fast.*

Taormino: *That means you're going too fast, or you're not using enough lube, or she's having anxiety and she's tensing up.* (Stern, 1997).

Coming from a feminist who claims to promote consent above all, this reply is shocking. The only defensible response would be that it means you should, in fact, immediately "get your fingers out of there." Taormino's reply, intimating that the woman does not know what she wants or will ultimately like, so the man should keep trying in a different way, replicates rape myths and promotes the sexual violation of women.

[Un]marked by a threat: Banishing social context

In their introduction to *The Feminist Porn Book*, Taormino and her co-editors observe that the writings therein "[defy] other feminist conceptions of sexuality on screen as forever marked by a threat. That threat is the specter of violence against women, which is the primary way that pornography has come to be seen" (2014, p.

13). Presumably, then, they believe it is both possible and desirable to produce sexual representations that are wholly *unmarked* by the threat (and pervasive reality) of sexual violence and exploitation. On the contrary, however, Taormino's own body of work is deeply marked by that threat, in ways that—though she determinedly ignores them—are likely both to harm many individual women and to deepen some aspects of women's group-based subordination to men. In what follows, I explain this claim with reference to one central example: that of anal sex.

The most cursory glance at Taormino's career trajectory reveals her messianic enthusiasm for anal sex. Her first book, *The Ultimate Guide to Anal Sex for Women*, launched her as a highly visible spokeswoman for "sex-positive" feminism; and her identically titled porn video (1999) marked the beginning of her career as a porn director. Another book (*The Anal Sex Position Guide*, 2009) and several additional porn films on the topic have ensued, and since 1999 Taormino has written the "Anal Advisor" column for the BDSM/fetish porn magazine *Taboo*, part of Larry Flynt's *Hustler* empire.

In this sense, Taormino's focus overlaps with that of the pornography industry generally, which during roughly the same period has increasingly fixated on anal penetration. Robert Jensen explains that:

> As legal constraints on pornography relaxed in the mid-1970's and the normalizing of pornography began, pornographers started to look for ways to make their products edgy, and the first place they went was anal sex. (2007, p. 58).

Over time, as the market became glutted with titles such as *Backdoor Baddies* and *Ass Factor*, even plain anal penetration became boring and humdrum. Pornographers thus looked for new ways to push the envelope, and practices such as double penetration (two men penetrating a woman simultaneously, one vaginally and one anally) and double anal (two men penetrating a woman's anus at once) become prevalent. As one female porn vendor observes, referring to the industry's relentless preoccupation with anal sex, "I think they forgot the other hole existed" (Goldberg 2003).

It should thus not surprise us that rates of heterosexual anal sex have risen dramatically in the past two decades (Fahs and Gonzalez 2014, 502). Nor is it surprising, given the primary consumer base of mainstream pornography, that many heterosexual men are urging their female partners to accept anal penetration. Often, they do not expect that the women will find the experience pleasurable. One man comments that "for most of my friends, it's sort of a domination thing . . . basically getting someone in a position where they're most vulnerable" (Rubin, 2007). Another observes that "Once a guy has anal sex, he's put on a pedestal by his peers." According to a third, "The physicality of it, being painful or whatever, shows how comfortable the girl is with you" (Rubin, 2007).

In this context, researchers Fahs and Gonzalez found, "submission to anal sex became a form of emotional labor women engaged in for their partner's pleasure" (2014, p. 509). As their research showed,

> *women simultaneously respond to external pressures to accommodate male fantasies (e.g. a boyfriend "begging" or directly requesting anal sex) and they create internal pressures to be sexually "normal" (e.g. believing they should compete with porn stars, hearing their friends describe anal sex as "cool," etc.).* (2014, p. 513-14).

Similarly, a study of 130 teenagers in Britain found a "climate of coercion" surrounding anal sex, with "consent and mutuality not always a priority for the boys who are trying to persuade girls into having it" (Culzac, 2014). In Fahs and Gonzalez's sample of 20 adult women, fully one-quarter reported "overtly violent encounters with anal sex" (2014, p. 510).

What, then, should we make of the striking convergence between Taormino's agenda and that of the pornographic mainstream, when it comes to anal sex? While undoubtedly some women genuinely enjoy being anally penetrated, at least the following is undeniable: Taormino's goal is to get *more* women to like and accept the same act that their male partners are also urging them to accept. Her work puts a happy, shiny, "feminist" gloss on the very set of expectations that many women and girls are already having difficulty fending off in their sexual lives.

In this connection, it is instructive to look to the beginning of Taormino's porn career, to see what loyalties she demonstrated and what messages she chose to send. The opening scene of her *Ultimate Guide to Anal Sex* shows Taormino entering the offices of prominent pornographer John Stagliano, widely known as "Buttman," to try to convince him to fund and produce her film. She pleads with him:

> *I know that people are probably here all the time, asking you to make their movie, but I really, really, really want you to make my movie. . . I want it to be hot, really hot . . . I want to inspire women everywhere to get into anal sex.* (Taormino, 1999).

Stagliano displays reluctance, noting that Taormino is inexperienced and that his is "a high-class company." He then continues,

> *if you can get somebody like* [performer] *Ruby in the movie having anal sex, then I might be interested. Because Ruby, I can't get nothing in her fuckin' ass. She won't take nothing in her ass . . . If you can get her to take that* [gestures] *in her ass, then I'll help you produce the movie.*

Taormino immediately agrees, and we cut to a man bringing Ruby into the room. Stagliano explains the "proposition" to her: "We want to find out if you'd be interested in, maybe, uh, doing that thing that you always said that you didn't wanna do. . . . Tristan claims that anybody can do anal sex, and it doesn't have to hurt at all." Ruby expresses doubt and giggles nervously, but within seconds

364

we see Taormino penetrating Ruby both vaginally and anally with different objects, while Ruby uses a vibrator. Ruby moans, "Oh, I *like* this toy!" The scene ends.

Of course, we cannot know whether Ruby was truly reluctant to be anally penetrated, or to what extent this scene was choreographed versus authentic. The point is that Taormino made a decision to tell a particular story, and that the story she tells sanitizes sexual pressure and manipulation while reinforcing rape myths—not least the idea that women who express disinclination to engage in particular sex acts, once pressed to do so anyway, find out that they love them. Despite the scene's inclusion in a celebratory 2003 documentary on feminist pornography, it is unclear what overlap exists between the messages of this scene and those of feminism.

Conclusion: Sex, ethics, and authenticity

Let me draw together some of the themes discussed herein by considering a three-column series that Taormino wrote for the *Village Voice* in 2006, entitled "Tomatoes Can Be Torture." In this series, Taormino recounts attending, as part of a BDSM event, a class on "erotic humiliation" taught by a couple who go by the names Femcar (the woman) and Phantom (the man). Their demonstration ventures into extreme territory: Phantom ties up Femcar, gives her an enema, throws tomatoes and other food on her, and urinates on her, inviting audience members to join in on both of the latter activities, which a number of them do. Taormino reports feeling distress at what she is witnessing:

> *All I could think was, who are these guys? Their behavior just disturbed me. None of them seemed ambivalent, they just stepped right up, whipped out their dicks, and started calling her names. It's like someone gave them permission to be brutes and they went for it.* (2006a).

Much of the remainder of the series can be read as Taormino's attempt to talk herself out of her own discomfort. Above all, she reminds herself, it is all Femcar's own idea:

> *While their scenes might appear to . . . go beyond what is considered "edge play," they were absolutely consensual. In fact, the architect of their most extreme scenes, down to every last degrading detail, was always Femcar.* (2006b).

Here, again, we see Taormino's apparent conviction that any kind of sexual activity is impervious to criticism, provided that it is not only consensual but authentically desired. Ultimately, Taormino decides that she wants to "play" with Femcar herself, although she wonders if she can manage to be as "rough, cruel, and unrelenting" as Femcar wants. (She can, as it turns out.)

My point here is not merely to be damning, but rather to expose a tension in Taormino's views about authenticity. In part three of the series, reflecting on her own reactions to Femcar and Phantom, she says:

> *Whenever I see any scene that disturbs me, I am usually projecting my own shit onto it. It's tapping into something in me, so I look inward, whereas most people are quick to say, "Those people are fucked up."* (2006c).

Taormino does not explain what kind of "shit" she harbors that leads her to have initial, misguided concerns about a crowd of men brutalizing and humiliating a woman sexually. Her view seems to be that one's *sexual* desires and responses are fully authentic, emanate apparently from nowhere, reflect one's deepest inner being, and are thus wholly self-justifying. Ethical concerns about virtually anything sexual, on the other hand, are just one's "own shit," which can and should be interrogated, reinterpreted, and/or suppressed. Such concerns are inauthentic and *not* self-justifying. Indulging them might lead to "policing or judging [someone's] desires, fantasies, and porn preferences," which, as Taormino assured *Cosmopolitan* (Breslaw 2013), she has no interest in doing.

In conclusion, I do not know whether feminist pornography is possible. But even assuming it is possible, I have explained herein why I believe Taormino's work falls radically short of the mark.

Either it is feminist to celebrate and advertise women's "authentic" desire to be sexually dominated, or it is not.

Either it is ethical and honorable to "play with" and promote dynamics of humiliation and violence that terrorize, maim, and kill women daily, or it is not.

As Andrea Dworkin once put it (1983, p. 237), "decide one more time."

Works Cited

Blue, Skye. (2011). Tristan Taormino: Interview. Retrieved from http://www.metanotherfrog.com/2011/06/19/tristan-taormino/

Breslaw, Anna. (2013, November 6). "So, What *Is* Feminist Porn? Find Out From a Woman Who Makes It." Interview with Tristan Taormino. *Cosmopolitan.com*. Retrieved from http://www.cosmopolitan.com/sex-love/news/a16343/tristan-taormino-feminist-porn-interview/

Bridges, A., Wosnitzer, R., Scharrer, E., Sun, C., & Liberman, R. (2010). "Aggression and Sexual Behavior in Best-selling Pornography Videos: A Content Analysis Update." *Violence Against Women.* 16(10), 1065-1085.

Clarke, D.A. (2004). "Prostitution for Everyone: Feminism, Globalisation and the 'Sex' Industry." In Whisnant, R. and Stark, C. (Eds.), *Not For Sale: Feminists Resisting Prostitution and Pornography* (pp. 149-205).

Cohen, Elizabeth. (2013). "Porn Producer Vows to Mandate Condoms After HIV Scare." Retrieved from http://www.cnn.com/2013/09/20/health/porn-industry-condoms-hiv/

Comella, Lynn. (2014). "From text to context: Feminist porn and the making of a market. In Taormino, T., Parrenas-Shimuzu, C., Penley, C., & Miller-Young, M (Eds.), *The Feminist Porn Book: The Politics of Producing Pleasure* (pp. 79-93).

Cummings, Christian. (2003, May) "Buttgirl: Tristan Taormino takes anal liberation to the streets." *Exotic*. Retrieved from http://www.xmag.com/archives/10-11-may03/buttgirl.html

Culzac, Natasha. (2014, August 15). "Anal sex study reveals climate of coercion." *The Independent*. Retrieved from http://www.independent.co.uk/life-style/health-and-families/health-news/women-being-coerced-into-having-anal-sex-researchers-say-with-persuasion-normalised-9671395.html

Dines, Gail. (2011). *Pornland: How Porn has Hijacked our Sexuality*. Boston: MA: Beacon Press.

Dodson, Betty. (2013). "Porn Wars." In Taormino, T., Parrenas-Shimuzu, C., Penley, C., & Miller-Young, M (Eds.), *The Feminist Porn Book: The Politics of Producing Pleasure* (pp. 23-31).

Dworkin, Andrea. (1983). *Right Wing Women*. New York: Perigee Books.

Fahs, Breanne, & Gonzalez, Jax. (2014, November). "The front lines of the 'back door': Navigating (dis)engagement, coercion, and pleasure in women's anal sex experiences." *Feminism & Psychology*, 24(4), 500-520.

Goldberg, Becky (Director). (2003). *Hot and Bothered: Feminist Pornography* [Film]. U.S.: National Film Network.

Herman, Judith. (1992). *Trauma and Recovery*. New York: Basic Books.

Jensen, Robert. (2007). *Getting Off: Pornography and the End of Masculinity*. Cambridge, MA: South End Press.

Joshi, M., Thomas, K.A. & Sorenson, S.B. (2012). "I Didn't Know I Could Turn Colors: Health Problems and Health Care Experiences of Women Strangled by Intimate Partners." *Social Work in Health Care*. 51(9), 798-814.

Khader, Serene. (2011). *Adaptive Preferences and Women's Empowerment*. New York, NY: Oxford University Press.

Laughon, K., Renker, P., Class, & Parker, B. (2008, July 28). *Journal of Obstetric, Gynecologic & Neonatal Nursing*, 37(4), 502-507. Retrieved from http://onlinelibrary.wiley.com/doi/10.1111/ j.1552-6909.2008.00268.x/abstract]

Love, Sinnamon. (2013). "A Question of Feminism." In Taormino, T., Parrenas-Shimuzu, C., Penley, C., & Miller-Young, M (Eds.), *The Feminist Porn Book: The Politics of Producing Pleasure* (pp. 97-104).

Mackenzie, C. and N. Stoljar (Eds.). (2000). *Relational Autonomy: Feminist Perspectives on Autonomy, Agency and the Social Self*. New York: Oxford University Press.

Moneybags, Rich Uncle. (2014). "An oral history with Carter Cruise, Sorority Girl Turned Porn Star." *Total Frat Move*. Retrieved from http://totalfratmove.com/an-interview-with-carter-cruise-sorority-girl-turned-porn-star/

Moran, Rachel. (2013). *Paid For: My Journey Through Prostitution.* New York: W.W. Norton & Company.

Rubin, Peter. (2007, July). "Is anal sex the new deal breaker?" *Details.* Retrieved from http://www.details.com/sex-relationships/ sex-and-other-releases/200707/anal-sex-new-deal-breaker

Simonton, A. & Smith, C. (2004). "Who Are Women in Pornography?: A Conversation." In Stark, C. & Whisnant, R. (Eds.), *Not For Sale: Feminists Resisting Prostitution and Pornography* (pp. 352-361).

Stagliano, John; Taormino, Tristan; and Greene, Ernest (Producers), & Taormino, Tristan; Stagliano, John; and Greene, Ernest (Directors). (1999). *The Ultimate Guide to Anal Sex for Women* [Motion Picture]. U.S.: Evil Angel Video.

Stern, Howard. (1997). Interview with Tristan Taormino. Retrieved in 2013 from http://www.youtube.com/watch?v=lziirxmWZ4g.

Taormino, Tristan. (2002). *Tristan Taormino's True Lust: Adventures in Sex, Porn, and Perversion.* San Francisco, CA; Cleis; London: Turnaround.

Taormino, Tristan. (2005). "On Crossing the Line to Create Feminist Porn." In Milne, C. (Ed.), *Naked Ambition: Women Who Are Changing Pornography* (pp. 87-98).

Taormino, Tristan (Producer), & Taormino, Tristan (Director). (2006). *Chemistry, Vol. 1* [Motion Picture]. U.S.: Vivid/Smart Ass Productions.

Taormino, T. (2006a, January 31). "Tomatoes Can Be Torture, Part 1." *The Village Voice.* Retrieved from http://www.villagevoice. com/news/tomatoes-can-be-torture-part-1-6400327

Taormino, T. (2006b, February 14). "Tomatoes Can Be Torture, Part 2." *The Village Voice*. Retrieved from http://www.villagevoice.com/news/tomatoes-can-be-torture-part-2-6400032

Taormino, T. (2006c, February 28). "Tomatoes Can Be Torture, Part 3." *The Village Voice*. Retrieved from http://www.villagevoice.com/news/tomatoes-can-be-torture-part-3-6399899

Taormino, Tristan (Producer), & Taormino, Tristan (Director). (2010). *Rough Sex 3: Adrianna's Dangerous Mind* [Motion Picture]. U.S.: Vivid/Smart Ass Productions.

Taormino, T., Parrenas-Shimuzu, C., Penley, C., & Miller-Young, M. (2013). *The Feminist Porn Book: The Politics of Producing Pleasure*. New York, NY: Feminist Press at the City University of New York.

Taormino, Tristan, et al. (2013). "Introduction: The Politics of Producing Pleasure." *The Feminist Porn Book: The Politics of Producing Pleasure* (pp. 9-20).

Tristan's Films. (n.d.) Promotional text, retrieved from http://puckerup.com/feminist-porn/tristans-films/

Tyler, Meagan. (2015). "Harms of Production: Theorizing Pornography as a Form of Prostitution." *Women's Studies International Forum* 48, pp. 114-123.

Vasquez, Tina. (2012, Spring). "Ethical Pornography." *Herizons*, 25:4 (pp. 32-36).

Voss, Georgina. (2014). Interview of Tristan Taormino. *Porn Studies* 1:1-2 (pp. 203-205).

Walker, Stephen (Director), (2001). *Hardcore*. [Film]. Retrieved from http://hcdocu.blogspot.com/

Whisnant, Rebecca. (2010). "From Jekyll to Hyde: The Grooming of Male Pornography Consumers." In Boyle, Karen, [Ed.], *Everyday Pornographies*. New York, NY: Routledge (pp. 114-133).

Endnotes

1   A number of philosophers have developed accounts of what it means for choices to be authentic, often as part of discussing concepts such as autonomy and/or adaptive preferences. See, for example, Mackenzie and Stoljar (Eds.,) 2000 and Khader 2011. Beyond broad philosophical definitions, it is also important to consider the specific social, cultural, and economic forces and personal histories that shape porn performers' preferences. While a consideration of these factors lies beyond the scope of this essay, many feminists—including women who have performed in pornography—have written insightfully about this set of issues (Dines 2010; Jensen 2007, Simonton & Smith 2004).

2   For a disturbing look at these dynamics in the case of one young British woman who traveled to California to perform in pornography, see the documentary *Hardcore* (Walker, 2001).

3   Taormino might respond that the question is otiose since, again, her performers set their own pay rates. Most likely, her performers do typically require more for performing acts such as anal, gangbangs, etc., regardless of their own desires and preferences: since standard industry practice is to pay more for these acts, arguably they would be foolish not to.

4   Regarding the use of similar euphemisms by male pornography consumers and reviewers, see Whisnant (2010).

5   See Bridges et. al. (2010) regarding the prevalence of these forms of aggression in mainstream, best-selling pornography.

6   Although the term "choking" is more commonly used colloquially, it refers to having foreign objects (such as food) blocking the windpipe. "Strangulation" is the correct term for having one's airflow cut off by something external, such as hands or a ligature.

7   Regarding dissociation and other typical reactions to trauma, see Herman (1992).

CHAPTER 18

Andrea Dworkin: Teller of Hard Truths

by Janice G. Raymond and H. Patricia Hynes

[Originally published in Truthdig, at https://www.truthdig.com/articles/andrea-dworkin-teller-of-hard-truths/. Reprinted by permission].

When Andrea Dworkin was alive, she despaired that her work would never be given its due. Writing was Dworkin's life, and she once said, "To communicate and to survive, as a writer and as a woman: the two are one for me." The publication of a new collection of many of Dworkin's well-known works of both theory and fiction, "Last Days at Hot Slit," has, simply by virtue of its publication, stimulated a reassessment of Dworkin's work by taking her writings seriously—a far cry from the way her books were treated when they were originally published.

Along with a timely introduction to Dworkin's writing, the book contains excerpts from "Woman Hating" (her first book, published in 1974), her epic analysis, "Pornography: Men Possessing Women," and her soul-wrenching novel, "Mercy." Other selections are letters Dworkin wrote to her parents and an unpublished essay called "Goodbye to All This," a biting retort to the "proud, pro-sex, liberated" women who, in her words, fought "for the right to be humiliated … for the right to be tied up and proud, for the right to

375

be hurt." "Last Days at Hot Slit" ends with "My Suicide," a previously unpublished essay written before Dworkin's death in 2005 from myocarditis, an inflammation of the heart.

When we interviewed women about the impact Dworkin's writing had on their lives and work, Australian novelist, poet and feminist book publisher Sue Hawthorne singled out Dworkin's fiction:

> *I recall the visceral response I had to her short story "Slit" and to her book, "Ice and Fire." But the greatest effect on me was reading "Mercy" … which has the most extraordinary detail about how it feels as a girl and a woman to be sexually violated for a significant part of her life. It is intense and difficult to read. But many significant works of literature are difficult to read. If she were a man, I'm pretty sure "Mercy" would be accorded the same status as James Joyce's "Ulysses."*

Reading "Mercy" inspired Hawthorne to write her own novel, "Dark Matters," about the erasure of lesbians and violence against lesbians, "a book I had to write as an action and in the hope that through fiction I might be able to change the world. At the very least, I should attempt to do so."

In reading the various reviews and media features that have accompanied this Andrea Dworkin revival, we are struck by how even writers who pen favorable words about her work seem compelled to mention her appearance. The initial sentences of the editor's preface to "Last Days" highlight Dworkin's "uniform of denim overalls and sneakers." Whereas Dworkin's opponents used her "uniform" to discredit her work and her words, the editors view her legacy more positively. However, an allusion to her attire in an otherwise approving introduction comes across as unwarranted.

Co-editor Johanna Fateman lists in the preface some of the caricatures of Dworkin's works, yet she doesn't refute or dispel them. Dworkin, for example, is said to have introduced "a vision of sex that would repel many … a sharply constrained and prescriptive menu of behavior." Yet many others understand that Dworkin's "vision of sex," so powerfully wrought, exposes the granite of women's suffering. It invites readers to question what sex is in a culture where gonzo pornography and the transformation of prostitution into ordinary work have ruined women's lives.

Gena Corea, author of the "The Mother Machine: Reproductive Technologies from Artificial Insemination to Artificial Wombs," told us that the clarity of "Pornography" prompted "one of Andrea's insights that will not quit me: When men experience the extreme pleasure of orgasm at the sight of women degraded and less-than-human, the inequality of women is something learned in the very cells of their bodies ... Pornographic propaganda against women infiltrates the body, waves of pleasure teaching that women are sub-human," thereby building "the emotional structure" for the inequality of women. In recent years, Corea has worked with a group of male prisoners who have committed violence against women and underscores the significance of "Pornography" in exploring their crimes.

Commenting on Dworkin's testimony before the 1986 Meese Commission on Pornography,[1] Fateman states in the preface to "Last Days" that Dworkin's "image would never recover from this strategic alignment with anti-obscenity conservatism." This is a curious statement. Has Malcolm X's alignment with the Nation of Islam damaged his image in perpetuity? When the American Civil Liberties Union joined with evangelicals to pass the Prison Rape Elimination Act,[2] did the organization's collaboration do permanent damage to its image? Rather than "never recover[ing] from this strategic alignment with anti-obscenity conservatism," Dworkin's "image," for many women, was enhanced by her courageous testimony in a government forum that otherwise would never have heard a radical feminist analysis of pornography. Dworkin understood the boundaries of engagement—that a commission appearance is not an alliance and that individuals and groups that strive to advance political change search for ways to act across differences in ideology and tactics.

In a preface to her essay, "Pornography Is a Civil Rights Issue," included in "Letters from the War Zone," Dworkin responded to these criticisms of collusion with conservatives:

> *I testified ... [because] pro-pornography "feminists" had already testified in other cities. I spoke to the Commission because my friends, feminists who work against pornography, asked me to ... A campaign costing nearly one million dollars would effectively discredit the findings of the Commission by smearing those who oppose pornography, creating a hysteria over censorship, and planting news stories to say that there is no proven relationship between pornography and harm to women and children ... Representatives of Penthouse sat with the ACLU lawyers and so-called feminists organized to defend pornography; and they heckled me during this testimony.*

What is missing in "Last Days," an otherwise laudable testimony to Dworkin's greatness as a feminist thinker, writer and activist, is a perspective on her political theory and its import. The editors—mainly Fateman—acknowledge Dworkin's influence. The preface recognizes that Dworkin "helped shape the historic grassroots feminist organizing of the late 70s and 80s; she rallied the forces of the antipornography, antirape and battered women's movements." However, there is uneasiness with her uncompromising writing even as it is portrayed as "empty of caveats, equivocation, or the endless positing of one's subjective limits." Dworkin understood, as British abolitionist Elizabeth Heyrick wrote, that "truth and justice make their best way in the world when they appear in bold and simple majesty."

Two generations after Dworkin's first book was published, New Zealand writer Renee Gerlich comments insightfully on Dworkin's "uncompromising writing":

> *Uncompromising refusal is a definitive feature of her work, refusal that stands in direct opposition to the*

accommodation expected of women. For this, Andrea was monsterized. The smearing of Andrea's work also acts as a lesson to women including myself. Whatever bravery it took Andrea to confront and reject men's abuse of women, and however patient, considered and gracious her writing and speaking reveal her to have been, Andrea's name is associated with an ugly volatility. Her detractors made an example of her, so that other women would not want to do what she did—namely reclaim our own creative energy and love for one another, our clarity of perception and moral instinct, and our ability to speak truthfully and powerfully from the gut. Of course, women can't be stopped from wanting these freedoms—and Andrea's work stirs us to claim them and sustains us in this effort.

In the 1980s, Dworkin and Catharine MacKinnon, along with a dedicated band of radical feminist activists, launched a courageous and groundbreaking civil rights ordinance against pornography. Dworkin, in one of our favorite passages, wrote:

> *The creative mind is intelligence in action in the world ... The world is anywhere that thought has consequences ... Creative intelligence is searching intelligence: it demands to know the world, demands its right to consequence ... Women are not supposed to have creative intelligence, but when they do they are supposed to renounce it. If they want the love of men, without which they are not really women, they had better not hold on to an intelligence that searches and that is action in the world; thought that has consequences is inimical to fettered femininity.*

This insistence on consequence, this attempt to make things real for women, is what Dworkin was most reviled for. She dared to think that she could transform her insights and intelligence into legislation that could help provide some legal means of redress to women who had suffered from pornographic violence. When FACT, the so-called Feminist Anti-Censorship Task Force, attacked the anti-pornography legislation that was supported by many women's groups, neighborhood organizations, women in prostitution, survivors of sexual exploitation, lesbians, ethnic and civil rights organizations, and by the hundreds of women who risked public exposure and harassment testifying on behalf of this legislation, the personal and political attacks on Dworkin escalated.

When violence against women can be rationalized or, more to the point, marketed and valorized as "sex," common agreement falters. Prostitution and pornography are the not-so-popular issues of violence against women, continually depoliticized and reduced to private choices. The endorsing of pornography and prostitution, especially from progressives and champions of women's human rights—those who should be radical feminist allies, those who should have been Dworkin's allies—is inexcusable.

When a woman works against pornography and prostitution, her reputation is destroyed, like the women who are exploited in prostitution and pornography. The latter are branded as sluts, whores, hookers, hoes and tarts, while the former are cast as up-tight, anti-sex, extremist, fundamentalist, right-wing, conservative, moralistic, anti-feminist, and against a woman's right to use her body in a self-determined way. If she is a writer, she gets censored from many publications that would be a natural outlet for her work. Rather than they, it is she who is portrayed as censorious and an opponent of free and progressive speech. In contrast, the pornographers and pimps are garlanded as human rights heroes and defenders of free speech.

Over the last several decades, it is Dworkin's work that has been most influential in bringing pornography and prostitution "out of the closet" of the private sexual realm and into the public forum of male violence against women. From our own work against the global sex industry, we know that there are many who argue that prostitution and pornography can be "made better" for women. These advocates promote a "sustainable prostitution and pornography," in which women are rendered "safer" for men's use—in reality, no safety for women at all.

Dworkin knew that there is an urgent need for courage and for the political will to act against the global sexual exploitation of women and children. She possessed that courage and political will. She was among the first to name all practices of sexual exploitation for what they are. Not sex work, but sexual violence. Not human rights, but a human rights violation. Not the product of women's consent, but the result of women's compliance with the only options available.

In both the written and spoken word, Dworkin coupled sexual and economic degradation of women with a country's national and foreign policy. In her 1983 speech to a conference of 500 men that is included in "Last Days," she underscored the gendered war waged against women and our perpetual wars conducted abroad.

> *Rape and war are not so different ... [Y]ou're turned into little soldier boys from the day you are born and everything you learn about how to avoid the humanity of women becomes part of the militarism of the country in which you live and the world in which you live ... Equality is a practice ... an action ... a way of life. It is a social practice. It is an economic practice ... It is a sexual practice ... It is a political necessity to create equality in institutions ... It cannot coexist with rape ... or with pornography ... or with prostitution or with economic degradation of women on any level.*

Decades since her speech, a team of researchers created the largest global database on the status of women, WomanStats,[3] and compared the security and level of conflict within 175 countries to the overall security of women in those countries. Their findings are profoundly instructive for global security and world peace. Democracies with higher levels of violence against women—including pornography, rape and prostitution—are less stable and are more likely to choose force rather than diplomacy to resolve conflict. Their empirical findings simply corroborate the luminous political insights that course through Dworkin's work.

Dworkin was a teller of truth, a thinker, a writer, an activist and a generous human being. She gave many women the confidence of their convictions that sexual violence is not natural and normal and that in the chronicle of human atrocities, pornography is not trivial or incidental but a gigantic industry— a rotten enterprise—built on male power in which "the degradation of the female is the means of achieving this power."

May this new collection of Dworkin's writings, "Last Days at Hot Slit"—a panoply of Dworkin's hard truths—lead many to reading her complete works.

Endnotes

1   Attorney General's Commission on Pornography, Final Report (July 1986) ("Meese Report"), https://babel.hathitrust.org/cgi/pt?id=m dp.39015058809065&view=1up&seq=1. *See also* https://catalog. hathitrust.org/Record/000824987.

2   Prison Rape Elimination Act of 2003, https://www.congress.gov/108/ plaws/publ79/PLAW-108publ79.pdf. *See also* https://www.ojp.gov/ program/programs/prisonrapeelimination.

3   WomanStats, http://www.womanstats.org/mobile/index.html.

CHAPTER 19

Genderberg Prostitution FAQ

by Samantha Berg

I wrote the Genderberg Prostitution FAQ in 2005 to emphasize reason over statistics and it remains the most popular page on my archived website Genderberg.com. Few emotions are more satisfying to me than occasionally seeing someone repeat my point, "There is no 'job' where a 13-year-old with zero experience can be sold for 100 times the price of a 23-year-old with ten years of experience."

--Samantha Berg

Q**uestion**: Isn't prostitution mostly a choice?

Answer: When prostituted women are asked if they want to leave prostitution, consistently around 90% say they want out immediately but the decision is out of their hands and in the hands of their pimps, their husbands, their landlords, their addictions, their children's bellies. A study of street prostitutes in Toronto found that 90% wanted to leave but could not, and a five-country study found 92% wanted out of prostitution. If they are there because they cannot leave, they are not choosing to be there.

If prostitution were really a choice, it would not be those populations with the least amount of choices available to them who are far disproportionately pushed into it. If prostitution were a choice, there would be no billion-dollar black market trade in coerced, tricked, kidnapped and enslaved people known as human trafficking.

Question: Sex is a powerful commodity.

Answer: Tulips were once considered a powerful commodity, which is to say that what men place value on is up to men's subjectivity and not a human universal. The same was said about trading black flesh once and it was proven incorrect. We're not talking about "commodities to be traded," but human beings. In prostitution it is not sex that is sold, it is power over women.

Question: Men will treat prostitutes better if it is legalized.

Answer: This has not borne itself out in legalization trials in Australia, the Netherlands, and Germany. All attempts to lessen the harms of prostitution have failed because men have not lessened their debasement of female sexuality and propensity to commit gendered violence in any significant way. There are plenty of medical records, police records and personal testimonies to substantiate men's violence towards females in places where prostitution has been legalized. Where prostitution thrives the value of women's lives is low, and the gendered violence they suffer has not decreased. In fact, the legalized province of Victoria, Australia has both the country's highest domestic violence rates and child prostitution rates.

In theory it sounds good to say sane, reasonable people should have the right to sell a kidney for $500 or more if they choose to. But opening the door to body organ selling would not lead to nearly as many middle-class American white men selling organs as other populations whose social circumstances can't seriously be said to allow an uncoerced choice. I'm glad we are willing to sacrifice the theoretical capitalistic rights of a very few possible body organ sellers for the greater benefit of preventing widespread exploitation of less privileged people.

Question: Hasn't prohibition been shown to fail?

Answer: Depends on what you're prohibiting. We as a culture prohibit child porn, and it's true that their prohibition doesn't work, but that doesn't mean the only other option is legalization.

When we stop focusing all attention on whether or not poverty-stricken teenage girls with abusive histories really want to be prostitutes and begin asking why so many men are unbelievably, horrifically violent towards prostituted people then we'll get to where Sweden is, a place that stops blaming females for their own rape, torture, and captivity. Without men's demand for bodies to abuse there would be no supply.

Question: Prostitution is the world's oldest profession and will always exist.

Answer: Prostitution is not the oldest profession; slave trading is: men selling or trading bodies amongst each other for profit. Saying prostitution is the oldest profession makes it sound like prostituted women have always been cunning initiators wielding their mighty sexual power over men like powerful vampiresses of the night. That's the misogynistic lie men have always wanted promoted because it absolves them of responsibility for what they do to children and women and makes them look like the victims of women's seductive wiles.

Question: Shouldn't prostitution be legalized and thought of as a normal job?

Answer: There's no reason to believe there will be a day when being naked won't make people feel vulnerable and exposed. It's a universal human experience of being naked to feel more vulnerable than having clothes on and there is no human society that doesn't have clothing of a sort. Moreover, it is inherent in having a part of someone's body penetrate another person's body to feel what thousands of prostitutes interviewed say they feel: like a human toilet, like they are being raped over and over again.

Contrary to what pro-prostitution advocates claim, the worst thing prostitutes face is not social stigma, it is rape, strangulation, beatings, burnings, and other violence from johns and pimps. Pimps are the people johns pay to outsource the violence necessary to keep sexual abuse victims obedient.

The Swedish model decriminalizing victims and putting the emphasis for change on prostitute-using men is the way to go because men should not have a right to sex on demand. The belief that men are entitled to sex on demand fuels prostitution, rape, street harassment, workplace sex harassment, anti-choice dogma, and every other gendered ill that makes up what we call "sexism."

Question: Why pretend prostitution isn't a part of everyday life?

Answer: I don't see anyone pretending our culture isn't saturated with the selling of female bodies, especially not the social workers and researchers trying to find solutions to the misery. When I hear people talk of legalizing it, I see a whole lot of pretending the misogyny and abuse intrinsic to the act of prostitution can somehow be wished away if only more laws making rape and assault more illegal than they already are get passed. It can't, as Sweden's own decades-long experiment with decriminalized prostitution demonstrated.

Question: Don't a lot of women enjoy it?

Answer: There is no research or collected evidence supporting this claim. When proponents of legalization talk about legitimizing prostitution, they talk a lot about theory and rights and ethics, but they don't let prostitutes themselves speak what they want. A five-country study of prostitutes found 92% wanted help getting out of prostitution immediately. 100% said they didn't want anyone they loved to ever have to prostitute their bodies for survival.

There is no sensible reason to ignore the 92% of prostitutes who do not consider it work but slavery in favor of the 8% minority, especially when doing so only affirms the rape culture that affirms men's entitlement to use women's bodies any way they desire, any time they want it.

In Germany the service union *ver.di* offered union membership to Germany's estimated 400,000 sex workers. They would be entitled to health care, legal aid, thirty paid holiday days a year, a five-day workweek, and Christmas and holiday bonuses.

Out of 400,000 sex workers, only 100 joined the union. That's .00025% of sex workers in Germany. Women don't want to be prostitutes.

Question: Do you think prostitutes should be arrested?

Answer: Absolutely not. Being desperately poor and/or abused is not a crime. But johns, pimps, and other sexual predators need to stop their criminally abusive behaviors and other options, like legalization, have been tried and failed. Sweden has had great success criminalizing sexual predation while attempting to assist people in getting out of "the life."

Question: But people need sex, and some have no other way to get it than from prostitutes.

Answer: No one needs sex like they need food, water, and air, and no one has the right to purchase access to another person's reproductive organs in order to masturbate themselves. 85% of American johns have regular female sexual partners and 60% are married men.

Sex is fun and feels good, and it is widely available to anyone who treats others respectfully with kindness and asks. An exchange of equal partners means there's always the risk of disagreement and the need for compromise. Buying prostitutes is less about sexual gratification than power gratification.

Question: But you agree porn and stripping aren't prostitution, right?

Answer: Of course they are. If getting paid to perform sex acts is prostitution, using a camera to record people paid to perform sex acts is recording prostitution. It is comforting for people to call porn performers "actresses" to distance themselves emotionally from the truth that they pay a third party to view recordings of prostitutes being prostituted, but porn actresses have a lot more in common with other prostitutes than with other actresses, such as poverty, a history of child sex abuse, and drug addictions.

Strip clubs, porn, Hooters, mail order brides, and other "sex work" are the prostitution of female sexuality for male consumption. In one study, 100% of strippers interviewed said they had been propositioned as prostitutes by patrons, so if you don't think strippers are prostitutes please recognize that your opinion differs greatly from that of men who spend money to make women submit sexually in strip clubs.

Question: Can't prostitution be made medically safer with regulations?

Answer: Sometimes more safe is still not safe enough. Unless prostituted women are sterilized, they can expect to get pregnant and must have repeated abortions. Neither the option of sterilization nor submission to repeated abortions is acceptable, and humans have not yet figured out a 100% effective method of containing the spread of deadly STDs.

I'm much more concerned about preventing rape and battery than I am in wondering how to patch women up after men torture them. When doctors, police, priests, NATO soldiers and refugee working men use their position of power to prey upon vulnerable and traumatized populations, as many prostituted people have reported, regulating prostitution is really about men organizing to provide other men easy access to disease-free bodies, and not about the welfare of women.

Question: If you try to stop prostitution, won't it just go underground?

Answer: This is extortion. It assumes men currently abuse prostitutes in horribly high numbers and if feminists don't agree to provide clean bodies for men's sexual self-gratification, their entertainment, then johns are gonna really beat the living shit out of prostitutes and it will be feminism's fault.

Basing public policy measures on the extortionist threat of increased violence in an already very violent environment is no way for a civil society to operate. Also, legalization has not only not stopped the violence prostituted people face, it actually makes it harder for victims to prove they were forced, and legalization increases the number of people involved with the sex industry overall without stopping male violence.

I am not persuaded that letting men masturbate themselves with a woman's body should be normalized as a "profession" and good-enough work for poor women based on threats of worse violence. Prostitutes are already at the bottom of the social totem pole, more raped, killed, exploited, and reviled than any group of women. Brothels are rape rooms and the daily systematized atrocities happening in them right now are compelling enough to take action stopping them.

Question: What about women like Annie Sprinkle, Nina Hartley, etc. who say they enjoy being prostitutes?

Answer: As with antiwar leaders, many former prostitutes (Andrea Dworkin, Norma Hotaling, Kelly Holsopple, Carol Smith, Anne Bissell) are themselves survivors of the commercial sex industry.

That a few paid prostitutes have learned to profit from advocating the legalization of prostitution does not hold water next to the overwhelming number of prostitutes without columns in porn magazines, book deals, their own websites, nationwide tours, and scheduled appearances on the talk show circuit booked by an agent. Some leading advocates of legalized prostitution such as Robyn Few, Norma Jean Almodovar, and Margo St. James have been convicted on pimping charges though they continue to present themselves as common prostitutes and not bigger players in organizing crimes against prostituted women. Sex worker rights leader Carol Leigh, aka Scarlot Harlot, has said herself in a 2004 debate, "95% of my friends want out of prostitution."

Don't you think tons of studies on legalization have been done by all sorts of parties? If the wealthy pimps, pornographers, and governments who want legalization and taxation had solid information proving legalization has met its stated goals, why wouldn't they spread that information across the Earth? Hugh Hefner would probably make a centerfold out of such "women like it and it's healthy" research.

If you know of a piece of quality research where a majority of prostitutes responded that they enjoyed being sexually used by several men a day, day after day, please present it to me. I have read a lot about this and I have never seen any evidence to support that prostitutes enjoy their job, paid celebrity spokeswomen for the billion-dollar multinational sex industry aside.

Question: Aren't you making personal moral judgements about prostitution and pushing them on others?

Answer: While the inherent intimacy of sexual acts is often a part of some people's belief that sexuality is unique to personal identity and possibly even sacred, most of what I've seen is research focused on the harms done to prostituted people. In other words, I'm not against legalizing prostitution because I'm uncomfortable morally with selling sex or have questions about my own sexuality, I am against legalizing prostitution because I have seen how it destroys health, hope, communities, and many lives.

Question: Isn't it better to make lots of money as a prostitute than working a minimum wage McJob?

Answer: Pimps ask themselves the same question, "Isn't it better to make lots of money controlling prostitutes than working a minimum wage McJob?"

Prostitution is not work like any other forms of employment, which is why I have come to see it as the Swedish do, as institutionalized sexual oppression instead of work. There is no other job where a person is expected to have their bodies penetrated repeatedly and exposed to contagion-carrying human fluids. There is no "job" where a 13-year-old with zero experience can be sold for 100 times the price of a 23-year-old with ten years of experience. There is no other job an emaciated homeless person strung out on heroin can do (or, more accurately, have done to them) as they're lying limp on the floor.

What has happened in the Netherlands is that johns seek out the most dejected and desperate women and children to sexually prey on because their powerlessness and addictions make them more willing to do violent, unsafe acts of prostitution for less money. The relatively small number of Dutch-born sex workers have complained of being undercut by drug addicted and severely abused women and "prosti-tots" (pimp joke) offering sex for their next fix.

Question: Men prostitute too, so it's not just about women.

Answer: Prisons develop systems of prostitution, not surprising since prostitution is big $$$ among gang members not in jail, and there is a specific loss of power, prestige, self-determination and spirit among men who are pimped. Men who are prostituted in prisons are treated much differently than the men who pay to rape them, and no one is treated better than the pimps.

Question: Legalizing prostitution is part of a wider campaign of sexual liberation.

Answer: Liberation for who is the underlying question. What is it about sex and women that lowers a woman's perceived cultural value if she has sex even without money or forcibly, as in cases of rape? Changing the cultural connection that makes women engaging in sex (paid for, raped, or consensual) worthless, low class sluts needs to be changed before legalization can be honestly considered.

There is the unfortunate neoliberal misconception that free markets are the best kind, that the economic marketplace can regulate itself through the cause and effects of competition, supply and demand. Ask yourself if Wal-Mart is really the world's largest private employer because they are truly better than other companies. In light of the evident failures of free marketism to produce diverse, consumer-driven, and fair business practices, how well should the free marketplace of ideas fare under the same laissez faire system? Why wouldn't we expect the same opportunistic consolidations, money equals the right to speech, more powerful exploiting the less powerful?

Question: Why can't you see johns/tricks who pay for prostitutes as just customers of sexual service?

Answer: The man with the money has all the power, not the moneyless prostitute. It's impossible to say men spend their money to create the exact sexee scenario they desire and this somehow means prostitutes have the power to dictate what happens, how far it goes, and other aspects of the fantasy the customer pays for. Johns are the demand that keeps the prostituted bodies moving, and the economic model is "demand creates supply."

Johns do not go out of their way to forcibly abduct women, get them hooked on drugs, take total control of their lives, or in any other way trap them in the sex trade because they don't have to. The pimps do it for them. They don't trap their prey; they are vultures who prey on the down and out, who pay specifically for their victims to be down and out. Johns have sex with women being held captive because of the expectation (an expectation rooted in reality) that johns will pay good money for it, then they say it's not their fault because they weren't the ones holding prostituted women captive.

Prostitution Is Not Work: The Crib Sheet

by Samantha Berg

A research paper promoting the legalization of prostitution was released titled *Associations between sex work laws and sex workers' health: A systematic review and meta-analysis of quantitative and qualitative studies.* The report was funded by the staunchly pro-legalization Open Society Foundation in service of "tackling the structural drivers of HIV."

Investigating the structural drivers of HIV transmission is a noble public health goal; however, it is not a specifically feminist goal. Feminism centers its advocacy and education on bettering the lives of women and girls, and feminists read prostitution research through a lens that centers the question, "How does this serve women and girls?"

Expecting people to pore through the daunting statistics and methodologies that sometimes spin my academically-inclined head is unrealistic and also unnecessary. Statistics are useful to quantify the severe harms of prostitution, but I have found more success convincing people that legalization exacerbates prostitution's harms when I lay off numbers and lay into common sense rationale connecting my audience to recognizable elements in their own lives.

Here are ten statistic-free explanations for how prostitution is harmful exploitation and not any kind of work.

1. No job title is threateningly flung in the faces of women and girls all over the world the way "whore" and its many synonyms in many languages are used to commit verbal abuse.

2. Prostitution is often compared to coal mining. Harms to coal miners are accidents that safety equipment aims to reduce; harms to prostituted women are intentionally inflicted on

them. Advertisements for pornography commonly portray harming women as an attractive goal for consumers.

3. Prostitution is often compared to low-paid McJob work. Fast food employees don't need specialized social services to help them quit the way prostitution survivors need protecting from pimps. When prostituted women escape, they are more often in the same situation as domestic violence victims, fleeing from imminent harm with only the clothes on their back and the fear of being recaptured in their minds.

4. Prostitution is often compared to cleaning toilets. Being forced by economic necessity to clean toilets every day would be deeply unpleasant, but it isn't rape and it doesn't leave people with PTSD, sexually transmitted diseases, or unwanted pregnancies. Anyone who has both cleaned a toilet and engaged in sex could explain the vast differences in these two activities.

5. Prostitution is not service work; it is bodily exploitation. The sex, race, and age of who provides a legitimate service doesn't matter for cashiers, plumbers, accountants, cab drivers, etc. the way it matters to prostitute-using men who won't accept sexual services from a man's body when they want a woman's body or from an elderly woman's body when they want a young girl's body.

6. There is no occupation that can be done while the worker is unconscious. Prostitutes are often drugged, passed out from unendurable pain, or have head trauma inflicted on them before and during being sexually assaulted.

7. Prostitution is not an entertainment media profession like modeling or acting. Actresses pretend to have sex, but prostituted women are not pretending having sex and the harm

to their bodies and minds is evidence of exploitation, not an occupation. There is no trafficking ring forcing teenage girls to perform Shakespeare for men's leisure.

8. Basic work safety conditions are impossible to reconcile with prostitution. Laws about occupational exposure ("reasonably anticipated skin, eye, mucous membrane, or parenteral contact with blood or other potentially infectious materials") mandate latex gloves, eye goggles, face masks, and aprons to protect employees. Prostitution can never be OSHA compliant.

9. Unionization is not possible. Pimps and pornographers call themselves sex workers because they are employed in the sex industry as they lobby for deregulation and exceptions to worker safety laws. You can't negotiate your way out of being raped when enduring unwanted sex is the job.

10. "I'll give you a dollar if you let me punch you in the face," is not a freelance job offer and neither are prostitution so-licitations. Men soliciting for prostitution in public are not magnanimously offering women jobs, no one approaches strangers in the street with offers of gainful employment.

CHAPTER 20

"The Handmaid's Tale" Offers a Terrifying Warning, But the Hijacking of Feminism is Just as Dangerous

by Gail Dines

[This article was originally published in Feminist Current on May 1, 2017, at https://www.feministcurrent.com/2017/05/01/the-hand-maids-tale-offers-a-terrifying-warning-but-hijacking-feminism-just-as-dangerous/. Reprinted with permission.]

In April 2017, two new series were released which, at first sight, seem to tell very different stories about women.

Netflix's Hot Girls Wanted: Turned On (HGWTO), produced by the same team as the 2015 documentary Hot Girls Wanted,[1] was described by many media critics as taking a more nuanced approach to the porn industry[2] than the earlier documentary, by showing how women can be empowered by both making and performing in porn.

Hulu's The Handmaid's Tale, on the other hand, is a terrifying "fictional" account of a patriarchal dystopia, where women cannot hold jobs or own property, and serve as either breeders, cleaners and cooks, or trophy wives. Those who resist are exiled to toxic waste dumps or worse. Atwood has asserted many times that her book, on which the series is based, is not really fiction — she drew inspiration from accounts of how women are actually treated around the world.

So while HGWTO purports to show how we can beat men at their own game, The Handmaid's Tale portrays how men beat women into submission. The contrast seems stark.

But in reality, both shows have a common underlying theme: that women's true role is to be fucked. In HGWTO women are fucked to make money; in The Handmaid's Tale women are fucked to make babies. Both narratives convey a form of biological determinism; that women are subordinate sexual vessels whose primary purpose is to serve the needs of men. And in both shows, it is women who, in the name of sisterhood, do the dirty work of men by playing the role of taskmasters to control the lives of other women.

The first episode of HGWTO featured "feminist pornographer" Erika Lust waxing lyrical about how women need to own their own sexuality by becoming pornographers. The tale told here by Lust is that when women get behind the camera, they can make artistic "erotic" movies that speak to women's sexual fantasies, instead of mainstream porn's focus on men pounding away at women's orifices. This episode was carefully crafted to tell a story of women's liberation from patriarchal oppression via empowered porn sex. But this narrative unraveled very quickly when we saw what Lust actually meant by "feminist porn."

Lust's rather bizarre idea of a compelling "erotic" movie for women was to portray a woman pianist living out her fantasy of playing the piano naked while being "pleasured." So Lust finds Monica, a woman who is both a pianist and willing to play out this fantasy, concocted by Lust. The problem is that Monica is new to porn and lacks any experience, while Lust hires a mainstream male porn performer, resulting in the usual degrading porn sex — pounding penetration and hair pulling included. Monica finishes the scene in obvious pain and traumatized, looking like a deer caught in the headlights of an oncoming truck. But remember, this is a "feminist" porn film, so Lust, acting all sisterly, gives Monica a big hug and a glass of water to make her feel better. And then asks her to fake an orgasm for the final scene. So much for authentic female sexuality!

400

It was stomach churning to watch Lust manipulate and cajole Monica into making this film, and lying through her teeth as she explained that she is doing something different from the boys. Despite all the talk about aesthetic value and women's sexuality, HGWTO is just a clever piece of ideological propaganda. Lust, just like the boys, is making money from sexually exploiting women; unlike the boys, she wraps herself in a feminist flag as a way to differentiate her brand in a glutted market. In Lust's world, sisterhood is powerful because it provides cover to pimp out women in the name of feminism.

Lust's duplicity would fit perfectly into the Republic of Gilead, the fictional country in The Handmaid's Tale. The Handmaids are sent to a kind of patriarchal boot camp run by "Aunts," who do the dirty work for the men. The Aunts manipulate and cajole the Handmaids into believing that they are on their side, by training them to fulfill their God-given roles of producing babies. Of course, should a Handmaid step out of line, there is always a handy cattle-prod nearby that the Aunts use to shock the Handmaids into submission. And when the Handmaid fulfills the duty of reproducing, then there is a sisterly hug from the Aunt.

Watching both shows brought to mind what Mary Daly called "the sado-ritual syndrome of patriarchy,"[3] where atrocities against women are ritualized as a way to render women's humanity — and suffering — invisible. One key element of the ritual is an "obsession with purity." In porn and the Handmaid's Tale, the women are "ceremoniously bathed" albeit in different ways. Monica's "bathing" takes the form of being plucked, shaved, and worked on by makeup artists and hairdressers who collectively turn her into a generic looking hypersexualized porn performer, thus erasing her identity and individuality. The Handmaids, on the other hand, have to cleanse themselves in a bath and then put on a ritualized garment for the "ceremony," an Orwellian term for being raped by her master.

Another key element in this ritualization is the use of women as "token torturers," which, Daly argues, both exonerates the men and turns women against each other. Lust and other "feminist pornographers" talk as if they are producing erotica for women when, in actuality, the porn movies they produce serve the male gaze and male sexual pleasure. Similarly, the Aunts with their cattle-prods are the front line enforcers, but in the background are a bevy of machine-gun toting men chomping at the bit to kill a woman should she step out of line.

In one telling scene in The Handmaid's Tale, the narrator tells us that she can't trust anyone, including other Handmaids, because they could be agents of the state. As feminism becomes increasingly watered-down by a neoliberal ideology that rebrands the sex industry as female sexual empowerment, we have to ask: Has our movement been colonized and hijacked to the point that it is now the Handmaiden of patriarchy?

Endnotes

1   Hot Girls Wanted, https://www.imdb.com/title/tt4382552/

2   Porn Again: Rashida Jones talks Hot Girls Wanted, April 27, 2017, https://www.bigissue.com/interviews/porn-rashida-jones-talks-hot-girls-wanted/.

3   Mary Daly theorizing the "sado-ritual syndrome," part I – the elements, April 4, 2015, https://scholarsandrogues.com/2015/04/04/mary-daly-theorizing-the-sado-ritual-syndrome-part-i-the-elements/.

PART IV:

LESBIAN RADICAL FEMINISM

CHAPTER 21

From Bars to Parades to Michfest and Beyond: Lesbian Feminist Organizing and Women-Only Space

by Tamarack Verrall

[This essay was originally a talk given by the author for Women's Studies Online, on April 2, 2020. Printed with permission of the author.]

When I wake each day I'm glad to be alive, glad for my life, glad for what I'm able to do. And then this wave comes over me of profound pain. I feel the pain of women in this world, knowing that with every breath I take, a woman or girl is being raped, banished, tortured in the cruelest way possible, held captive, murdered. I feel this every day. I live to see this change. I live to see women in leadership of this world, to heal all of the people, and our mother earth herself. I wake each day the lesbian feminist that I am.

I am going to take you on a journey. My particular journey over the past half century. I am 71 years old now, 50 years of living my life to the fullest, and consciously as a lesbian feminist. The how and why, and as always, the hope that our meeting together today will give us a chance to talk about what this topic means to you, and where we are headed.

My feminism came early, and it came naturally. I am told I was born yelling. And I was the only girl with five brothers, a rich field of study. I also had a forward-thinking mother who declared in the 1950's that as a family we were a collective, and that all members were expected to do housework. None of my girlfriends had the same. My childhood was loving and protected. Nevertheless, I met my first stranger in the park at the age of seven. I never told my parents as I instinctively knew that my freedom to roam would be reined in. I was frustrated that I had to wear shirts in the summer after the age of nine. I did not understand why I couldn't go off biking with my girlfriends to picnic in the fields at the age of 10. And at 11 my mother was forced to carry a dead foetus for two months, I presume the doctors suspected her of wanting an abortion. I remember her pain at this loss, and I realized much later that she must have been terrified that she could have died. The hospital operated on her finally on Valentine's Day. The cruelty of misogynist enjoyment of mental torture of women.

In high school I asked why there were no books on the curriculum written by women. I was told that no woman has ever written anything worth printing. Such was my introduction into the censorship of what unknown to me, so many women had accomplished. At that point I knew nothing about the fight for women to be doctors, the stolen discoveries of Science, the history of the fight for the vote, the civil rights movement happening in the US and in my own country, the African-American women heroes working the underground railway, the racism faced by Viola Desmond in Nova Scotia, the fight for women's suffrage in Canada which began in 1916 and did not end until 1960 when finally indigenous women and men were able to vote. I had no history of the truth of what was done as Canada formed, to Indigenous peoples here, and I had no idea of how much was being hidden from us of our own history of matters of importance to us as women.

In my teens I worked as a lifeguard being mocked as a small woman, that I would never pass the tests. I passed them. When they were planning to hire a younger man I had taught swimming to, as the next assistant manager, I fought it. It was my turn, and I became the first woman assistant manager in my area. In University I got

408

onto the Student Council to challenge that birth control was not allowed on campus. That was the late 1960s. On campus I met some women who were writing the Birth-Control Handbook which was published as an illegal book at that time.

Six of us opened the first English Women's Centre in Vancouver in 1969. Within three months we were hundreds, holding consciousness-raising groups, affectionately known as CR Groups, on all sorts of topics from what to do about violence by men, to shared unpaid home labour, to what orgasms were all about. This was the first women space I had ever experienced, apart from my always cherished conversations with my closest girlfriends. In that Centre we discussed things that we would not have allowed ourselves to even think about if we had not been women only. We could speak about things we were unsure of without being labelled ignorant or insignificant. We spoke openly about our lives, including sexual assaults, which in public would have carried stigma.

When the Centre was up and running, we decided to advertise a party, a celebration of what we were building together. The topic of men came up. Women wanted to invite their boyfriends to see this special place and to understand its importance. After a long discussion we agreed to open the doors to men, hoping that through that one night they would have a better understanding of the importance of Women's Centres. One of the main reasons we needed these Centres was that in the 1960s through the 1970s we had one Doctor in Montreal who was committed to providing abortions, to prevent women from dying as they were, from back street abortions. Women came here to Montreal from many parts of Canada the US and other countries looking for his help. So we had one room with pillows and blankets as a safe and a comfortable place for women to come before and after having abortions.

Well, that evening one man went upstairs and threw black paint everywhere with ugly slogans slapped onto the walls. I know it was only one man, but it caused a mess and it took a lot of energy to clean it up and to settle feelings of invasion. We realized how important it was in many ways to be able to trust who was in that Women's

Centre for our own discussions, and for women coming in. It was the only way for women coming in to even dare to let our thoughts, needs, and stories flow.

There was no such thing as a computer. We communicated and learned from each other through telephones, letters and visiting each others' Women's Centres when we could. Very occasionally we made a big enough noise to get on the news. We continued to grow.

In the 1970s and increasingly the '80s, the women's and lesbian movements grew powerful through books. Women wrote about past women activists hidden from history and we began to understand on a deeper level how long we had been silenced.

Books and newsletters began to flow. A book all about women is another form of women only space. A time finally focused on what was happening now and throughout time - to women.

Cables of Rage, Audrey Lord
Sexual Politics, Kate Millet
Sisterhood is Powerful, Robin Morgan
Against Our Will, Susan Brownmiller
Gyn/Ecology, Mary Daly
On Secrets and Lies, Adrienne Rich
When God was a Woman, Merlin Stone
Lesbian Woman, Del Martin and Phyllis Lyons

And a special shout out to The Suppressed Histories Archives, Max Dashu, celebration of this being the 50th year of researching and providing us with these archives, ongoing.

And through music. Nina Simone; Alix Dobkin; Sweet Honey in the Rock. It is impossible to do justice to them all here, but now that we have computers we are still able to find them, read them, and listen to the ways that they built lesbian and feminist culture.

During this time I travelled through Europe alone. Why not me, as a woman, I thought. A feminist action! My right to see the world! It was a defiance that taught me how many men feel they have the right to grab at any woman travelling by herself. I wanted to travel to North Africa and went with an ex-boyfriend, a good friend, knowing it was the only really safe way for me to go. This too was an eye-opener for me, reading La Femme Algerienne as I travelled, meeting 4 women in four months. Had stones thrown at me by boys, and barely escaped an attempt to kidnap me into trafficking. I was 22. My commitment to women everywhere profoundly deepened.

In my early 20s I felt an expectation, not so much from family but from society, that as a young woman I would marry. I had a recurring dream that I would agree to marry and that my mother and aunts were thrilled. But I was full of dread that this was not what I wanted to do with my life. I would agree to marry, the day would arrive, and I would be heading into the ceremony and thinking "If you don't leave now it's going to be even harder to get out of this later." Every time, I would run, jump into my car (a convertible in those dreams) and I would drive off to go camping with the wind blowing in my hair. So I listened to this.

And one day I met a woman, and in becoming friends she asked me if I had ever met a lesbian. I said "no" but that I imagined I might meet one, one day. She asked me how, and I said, "I don't know, maybe meeting one walking in the street by chance." I barely knew the word. She said, "Well, I am a lesbian." She became my first woman lover and I will never forget that first kiss. In my mind I thought, "This is what I've been waiting for." I stopped dating men. Not from a hatred of men. For the love of a woman.

A new and magical women-only space. My first love had come out in the bars, at the age of 16. "You show me the women's movement and I'll show you the bars," she said. I found out about the protocol at that time for butches and femmes, that certain butches had their own tables, that you didn't mess with tradition. My generation brought a free-flowing bunch of loving women dancing alone, in pairs, and in circles, dancing our feet off till dawn. A new women's space. New places to grow to celebrate our love for each other, our lesbian culture, in all of its variety, celebrating our cultures

411

within lesbian culture, falling in love, dancing, dancing, dancing. At that time, a half dozen of us met to discuss forming a lesbian movement in addition to our work in the women's movement. The 1970's brought a lot of movements - antiwar, for the earth, the lesbian movement, and a gay movement. Alliances were formed, as the then GLBT which became the LGBT to rebalance an early dismissiveness of lesbians, was born. Parades in June in memory of the Stonewall riots were now enormous spectacular celebrations across North America. It became somewhat easier to be "out."

Being both a lesbian and a feminist I never understood the antagonism of some heterosexual women toward lesbian feminists. I knew that there was a fear that we would make the feminist cause seem too radical. This was one of the early divisions within the women's movement. Was it a movement for every woman or was it to open doors for some women who fit in culturally, racially, class wise to society as it was? Here is a description of feminism by Barbara Smith, quoted back to her by Cherrie Moraga in a discussion they were having about a third world feminist perspective, both lesbian feminists teaching women's studies:

> *Feminism that is not about freeing all women which means working class women, women of colour, physically challenged women etc. is not feminism, but merely female self-aggrandizement. Lesbian Studies (1982).*

In 1973 and 1974 I travelled back to Europe this time to a camp for women on an island called Femø in Denmark. That was my first experience on women's land. There were about 250 of us, mostly Scandinavian and from other parts of Europe. There were a few from the US, one who was thinking of organizing a women's camp back home. This was bigger than the Women Centres, and it brought women together from a few countries, and it was in nature. It was the first time I could dress as I wanted to as an adult. No shirt. I met the Danish Red Stockings, witnessed 20 feminists from Italy find each other there, none knowing another feminist existed in her country. They spent the entire week planning together. We cooked, and took care of the land and each other, and felt a freedom and a level of discussion with each other that we had not experienced before. The seed was planted. Our commitment to reach beyond our own countries to create change for women. And a commitment to creating these opportunities for women to meet, to heal, to plan, and to learn from each other. Men circled in their boats, but we were in a safe space.

Well, back in North America many lesbians were planning to find land, live freely, and offer this freedom and connection to land to others. Stories were beginning to circulate about the freedom and power of living together on land. I moved with friends from Montreal to Vancouver with the plan one day to be on land together. Eight of us formed a lesbian collective called Lavender Hill. A women-only space. We had a special time. We learned a lot. We listened to all the new women's music. We wrote and spoke and gathered with women and other lesbians. We organized women's dances. We wrote newsletters. We were exploring and expanding what happens when lesbians have time with each other. We began to learn how to speak with each other with respect and love. We were fledglings, but we grew. We were learning.

In the 1970's, Women's Studies began to pop up in Universities, and in the 1980's Lesbian studies were added. This was the outcome of those early Women Centre discussions which made it apparent that there was much to discuss that did not always involve all of the other subjects under the heading of women studies.

From Margaret Cruikshank's introduction to her book *Lesbian Studies* (1982):

> *By creating a climate in which some academic women could come out as lesbians, Women's Studies has allowed us to find each other, explore common concerns, and support each other's work.*

This was the outcome of a Women's Studies Conference supporting, not denying, the necessity for lesbians to meet as lesbians within the conference. Lesbian professors were able to find each other, be "out" in numbers, in their universities, and collaborate, bringing Lesbian Culture into Women Studies, and in carving out space for Lesbian Studies too. In this case, the hard-won space for Women Studies supported the harder won space for Lesbians to teach Lesbian Culture.

But here is also what happened, and I quote:

One of the chief characteristics of the lesbian feminist educational movement is simply the euphoria, of the women involved in it. This is due partly to emergence from the closet and recognition of our sheer numbers. The emotional high women experience when we feel for the first time a passionate connection between our lives and our work is hard to describe to someone who has not directly felt it. Our teaching takes on a whole new dimension when we can be ourselves.

From Margaret Cruikshank, *Lesbian Studies*, (1982).

I want to say again that there was such an outpouring of books written by feminists and lesbian feminists that continued through the1980s that I can't possibly do justice to them all. But to name a few of them tells the story.

Remember, no computers. These were our lifeline.

--*This Bridge Called My Back: Writings by Radical Women of Color*, a feminist anthology by Cherrie Moraga and Gloria E. Anzaldúa.
--*Woman Hating*, Andrea Dworkin
--*Lesbian Nation*, Jill Johnson
--*Of Woman Born*, Adrienne Rich
--*Surfacing*, Margaret Atwood,
--*The Paradise Papers*, Merlin Stone

--*The Color Purple*, Alice Walker

--*The Coming Out Stories*, Julia Penelope and Susan Wolfe

--*Only Words*, Catharine A. MacKinnon

--*Don't -- A Women's Word*, Elly Danika

--*Ripening, Dreaming, Awakening, 3 Almanacs of Lesbian Lore and Vision*, Lee Lanning and Nett Hart

--*Molly Mollasses and Me*, Ssipsis and Georgia Mitchell

--*Cultural Etiquette, A Guide for the Well Intentioned*, Amoja Three Rivers

--*We'Moon*, Mother Tongue Ink

Reading a book by a feminist about her feminism for me, gives me time in women-only space. Reading a book by a lesbian feminist is time for me, in lesbian feminist space. As a lesbian feminist I enter the space of learning from a sister, as if I have the chance to be sitting with her, listening to her.

Consciousness-Raising Groups grew and matured. Some were for planning, some were for healing, some were for spiritual ceremonies. Some were women circles; some were lesbian circles. We learned how to raise healing energy for ourselves and for each other because almost all of us have experienced some if not multiple violence from men in the past. By this time, I had lived 10 years in Vancouver working in social services and had pushed to be able to create the first groups for girls who had been sexually violated by men and boys. In the community I led groups for women and for lesbians. For me lesbianism and feminism have a tight bond. I have always cared deeply for women and by my early 30's had met hundreds who needed to sit with someone who cared, individually and in circles, with others who had been through the same experiences.

The 1980s was a time in which we fought and won government funding for many women shelters. Shelters that were in secret locations so that women would feel safe, would be safe, having escaped violence from men. In the 1970s we had exposed the amount of violence towards women by men, and the number of women needing to escape from violent husbands. Many of us had learned self-defence to protect ourselves. Now we were pulling incest out from under the carpet. I went across country in my van, meeting women working at rape crisis centres and women shelters. At those meetings we spoke freely with each other. We spoke in that protected Women Space that we had come to depend on. We knew the importance of this safe women space for the women escaping and needing to heal from violence. We knew the importance of speaking in that women-only space where we were not accused of being biased, exaggerating or being too radical.

My next home was in Ottawa. I began to hold healing circles there for women and got entry to the Prison for Women, hearing stories from women inside, over a period of 10 years. I also set up a non-profit organization, a Healing Centre for Women, meeting with women individually and in groups to make sure that they could get support for free. This too, was women-only space. Without that space many women would not have had the time or feeling of safety to even allow themselves to remember and explore what had happened to them. I also contacted the Children's Aid Society in Ottawa to offer groups for girls, as a volunteer. The CAS was glad to support the idea. It was as new to them as it had been to the Social Services in Vancouver. But when I was asked to speak to a group in the community about the plan, a newspaper article got printed, titled Children Almost Sent to Lesbian. Right Wing women appealed to the Federal Government to fire me because my salary was Government based. Luckily, my boss at work backed me. So did Children's Aid. The groups happened. It is times like this that I personally need to recuperate in women only space.

I'm telling you that story because it infuriates me, not just for myself, but because most of the lesbian feminists I know are passionate about doing something to help in particular children and women who have been harmed, usually by men. It infuriates me that we are cast as the biased enemy, when we are focused on a global crisis in which women and girls, not only but most often, are being violated, kept in servitude, beaten, brutally attacked and killed. It infuriates me that while we donate our time because our hearts are breaking at the treatment of our sisters and daughters, that men in power have not stepped forward in large numbers to stop other men from this behaviour, and work with us to undo this patriarchal system, teaching boys that it is not only okay but essential to be gentle and respectful toward women and girls, and toward each other. That schools have not been given the means to turn this around in one generation. That men who are violent continue to be free to repeat their violence at will. And that these men continue to complain about our selfish focus on those who are losing their lives, most often women and girls. It is because of this that I personally need to recuperate in women only space. It is in women's space that have learned to transform that fury into positive action.

So, by this time in history, there was news of a giant festival for one precious week every summer, held in Michigan USA, for women. A festival that was built by women, for women to experience one week of peace in the year, a place to gather to share stories, and make plans, a place full of primarily lesbian feminists who knew that we needed the chance to be in the woods together and to experience what we could build together as a community, to strengthen ourselves for the work we did and do in the other weeks of the year. It was a place for women musicians, dancers, comedians, and poets, who like all women were having a hard time getting access to stages could come, and perform, and get known. And where we could all learn the power of changing this around, booking these extraordinary artists in our home communities. It was a time to be alone together in the woods to gather ourselves for the work we were all doing in our own communities toward a peaceful world.

I got myself there by the 1980's and felt free in a way I had never before. Inspired on a level I had never imagined. Healed to a depth I had not even dreamed was possible. Learned what women are capable of accomplishing. We were in the woods together learning how to build a community to build our own strength, for our own inspiration for what we were all doing to heal society, outside that one week, in our own communities. It was a time to watch our daughters run safely in the woods. It was a time to encourage the boys that gentleness is more fun. It was precious time together, and we took what we learned home with us for the benefit of everyone. This was time uninterrupted, to experience what we as women, and famously in the majority as lesbians and as feminists, inspired in each other to continue our work.

This was Women-Only space. This was that little camp of 250 in Denmark magnified to 8 to 10,000 at its highest numbers. One small week in the year to gather our strength, deepen our connections with each other, learn how to do what we were doing at an even higher frequency. Michigan became famous because it was that special.

I had to miss going for 20 years, because I wanted to do organic farming, on women's land. By the 1980s to1990s many women's lands had sprung up. Women alone, in couples, in collectives, in communes. Some had men visit at times, some were women only. All of them were havens where women could live close to the earth, not for one week, as Michigan was able to offer, but as a way of living. These women's lands dotted across North America, countries in Europe, Australia, New Zealand, and other parts of the world, stayed in touch with each other and shared ideas of how to plant, build things, fix equipment, hold events, and offer safe haven for women escaping violence, needing time in nature. Many of us had been to Michigan and because of that we were able to understand the power and the healing that comes from creating a space in the country for women and girls to be in nature, and free of all we experience in the larger world.

We knew it from Michigan, and other festivals that have also been happening for years now. And we knew it from living in the woods ourselves. After 20 years I did move back to the city where I live today in Montreal. By stopping farming I was once again free to return to Michigan and to go to a local drum camp for women as well. As always, being on land with women feeds my soul. I always leave stronger, filled with new ways to take care of myself, stay strong in body and spirit for the work I believe I am here to do on earth.

To do everything I can to end this violence and suppression of women and girls. I had had many chances to meet with women over the years. But I had missed Michigan fiercely, because of being able to experience what 6 to 10,000 women are capable of creating together. So I was beyond thrilled to be able to go back and especially as Michigan as we knew it was about to close. I had the unforgettable chance to experience how this festival had grown in the 20 years I had missed it, by attending the final two years of Michigan as it had become.

Here is what I want everyone to know and understand. In the 1980s to mid-90's when I went, there was a deep learning curve in how to do this. How to be together on the land in women-only space. How to build together the ability to grow and change, the ability to talk through differences, the ability to create healing energy for all the wounds that women arrived with from our lives, from our treatment as women in our home communities, from the psychological and physical harm we had endured recently, as well as past wounds surfacing there on that land because, often for the first time in our lives, we felt safe. And cared for. Where we could drum together and learn from women who have been beaten for drumming, knowing that in the distant past women drummed. Where we could learn dance that strengthens and heals us for the work we do in our home communities. Because most of the women dedicated to Michigan and other women's festivals know that these are the oases of healing for the work we do in our home communities. And that that feeling of safety is something that women rarely feel anywhere.

But I want to express what I found after missing 20 festivals, returning for the last two. As the festival opened, the level of energy, the depth of the healing powers, the music, and messages from the stages, had moved to a higher level than I had, in my absence, ever imagined possible. The performers and teachers were primarily women of colour. The community who have been meeting all these years had developed ways to solve problems peacefully. The girls who had experienced years of Michigan knew that freedom of walking through the woods in complete safety. The ceremony was powerful and magnificent, capable of transformation. And we were in deep pain that the festival as we knew it was about to close. But we carry it in our bones. As I looked over the crowd toward the end of that 40th year, I could see the wisdom of, and the strength of the women who have been to this festival over the years. What we learned and experienced stays with us, and we are all still here in our communities, finding new ways to stay in touch with each other, knowing that being in contact with each other with what we know, with what we have learned together through women only festivals or woman to woman discussions, is part of who we are, part of what we needed, to be the activists and healers that we are today. We know the value of women meeting with each other, unfettered, and not holding back on the conversations we need to have, to create the changes we know need to happen in this world. This is the power of women only space. This is why we need to be with each other sometimes. This does not mean that we are not busy, attentive to, working with everyone else to create a better world, when we are not in meetings with each other. It does mean that when as lesbian feminists and as feminist women we have the chance to meet, share news, plan and heal with each other, we emerge stronger for our work with this world still so full of violence, still so full of silencing women, still so full of women and girls imprisoned, horrendously treated, maliciously tortured and murdered.

For me it has been 53 years as a feminist 49 as a lesbian and only now am I realizing the determination behind this stranglehold that the majority of men continue to impose on women and girls. I hear "Change takes time." I hear "It has always been this way." I hear "Some things will never change." I hear "Men expect to be in control in that culture." And in 50 years in a country that prides itself on being an egalitarian free society, men and boys are still getting away with violence towards women and girls. My hope these days lies in holding onto what we know is possible from our experiences together.

Before I close, I want to talk about World Pulse. Because World Pulse has become my home base. Because I want you all to know about it. It is what so many of us have hoped for all our lives. A global movement of loving, dedicated women, and others who understand and are committed as well, to ending every form of violence and suppression of women and girls globally, and for a better life for everyone, and for the Earth herself. At this point we are 70,000 from 190 countries. Membership in World Pulse is free.

The love that I felt in Michigan, and at other women's events, is the same as the love flowing in World Pulse as we draw close to each other, getting to know each other, reading each other stories, knowing each other's work, finding ways to support each other, toward freedom for women and girls everywhere. The message is global. Listen to the women. The world is starving for women's leadership. It is in women's voices that I see change happening. It is in women's leadership that I see what is possible. It is from global networks like World Pulse, and from sister organizations whose focus is also global.

Women who were scheduled to take place at the UN have written a blueprint for dealing with this new virus. A feminist plan. A plan that begins with those who have the least. Let's lift up each other's work. We have computers now. Log on, read some stories jump in! World Pulse has become my home base. World Pulse gives me, every day, the chance to be part of building this global network, with powerful, dedicated women, all over the world.

I have said it before, and I will say it again. Finding and becoming part of World Pulse is a dream come true for me.

Just to finish. About women-only space. Why would anyone want to object to women meeting sometimes as women? We are stronger when we emerge from these times to meet everyone and every problem in our communities. We have healing to do of ourselves and each other because of the violence we have experienced in the past and in everyday life. We are in deep pain with every story we read. We are in deep pain knowing what so many women and girls are facing still daily. But now we have each other. We need to continue to find ways to meet with each other, to talk freely, and to heal. To continue our work for the benefit of everyone. It is the patriarchy that is threatened by our meeting with each other. We are demonized for wanting this time with each other despite the pain we carry, and despite or perhaps because of the ideas we spark when we speak freely together. We are breaking the rules. Despite the pain, we are continually working to heal, and continue to come forward as leaders toward a new world society.

It is Indigenous women in Canada who continue to hang red dresses out, to remember the missing and murdered Indigenous women in this country. It is women in Mexico who went on strike against the violence against women in their country. A day without women. Another way to create women only space for a day. It is the Indigenous women of the Amazon who are protecting their land. It is the women in Brazil, Argentina and Colombia who are in the streets to end violence against women now. It is the women in Cameroon and Sudan and Yemen and the DRC who are calling for peace and an end to rape, destruction, and ruin. It is the women in Pakistan who are calling for an end to the imprisonment and killing of women. It is the women in 190 countries in World Pulse who are calling for change and documenting the changes needed. It is the women of World Pulse who are forming a global sisterhood, who are continuing with our messages of love to each other. This is feminism. Working to end violence against anyone, working against poverty, working to protect the Earth.

And for many of us this is lesbian feminism. Women who dare to step out of the patriarchal norm know the full brunt of this patriarchy. Know its lies, and its tricks, and its violent means to stay in place. We love women. And we are here to create change.

I'm going to finish with a quote from Audre Lorde, and look forward to discussion. And after this is over, now we have computers and cell phones, and so we have each other.

You do not have to be me in order for us to fight alongside each other. I do not have to be you to recognize that our wars are the same. What we must do is commit ourselves to some future that can include each other and to work toward that future with the particular strengths of our individual identities. And in order for us to do this, we must allow each other our differences at the same time as we recognize our sameness.

--Audre Lorde

CHAPTER 22

Lesbians Are Under Attack

by BigBooButch, a.k.a. Parker Wolf

L esbians are under attack. Some of the attacks are coming from the usual places: heterosexual women throwing us under the bus, ignoring our contributions to feminism, and ignoring their own privilege;[1] bisexual women appropriating our lives and culture by claiming to be lesbians or worse, "bisexual lesbians" (context: there is no such thing – it's a lesbophobic concept);[2] and of course, men beating, raping, and killing us in the most grotesque ways possible. Oh, we experience violence from heterosexual and bisexual women as well,[3] but not to the degree, the depth, the depravity of men.[4] We lesbians have been dealing with the aforementioned for centuries. We're used to it. We expect it. It's part of what makes us such strong women, sisters, and friends. But there is another group of people attacking, both verbally and physically, lesbians and lesbianism today: transgender activists and their allies.

I saw a joke on Twitter the other day. It said that "the homophobia is coming from inside the community," humorously referencing the tag line of an old horror movie, *A Stranger Calls*, where the police trace phone calls coming into the house to terrorize a woman and the police tell her, "the calls are coming from inside the house!" It's terrifying because we are supposed to feel safe in our own homes.

Surrounded by our things, our family, our pets, and behind locked doors, we all feel safe inside our own homes. Lesbians have never had that safety inside of the LGBT community. We were on the front lines of the AIDS crisis in the 1980s, taking care of our gay brothers, marching with them to bring attention to the crisis, etc.[5] But those deeds were never reciprocated. Most gay men don't really care about lesbians or women in general and some are downright misogynistic. For decades, they took most of the LGBT resources and used those resources on themselves, not bothering to address anything to do with their lesbian sisters.

But, as bad as all of that seems, nothing prepared us for what came next: transgenderism. The vast majority of trans women are heterosexual: straight men claiming to be lesbians;[6] and a good number of trans men are straight women claiming to be gay men. Almost all of them are homophobic to one degree or another, hence "the homophobia is coming from inside the community." For the past few decades, heterosexuals have been encroaching on LGB spaces, lives, and culture. They go to our bars, they take over our Gay Pride events, and pretty much the only people calling themselves "queer" these days are heterosexuals, in an attempt to be cool and edgy.[7]

There's another reason for that phrase about homophobia coming from inside the community: young lesbians (and gay men, but I am focusing on lesbians for this essay) are transitioning due to homophobia – their own internalized homophobia and/or the homophobia they face from family, friends, their church, and/or their government. That homophobia pushes young lesbians into transitioning so they don't have to be homosexuals, they can be "men" loving women, aka, "straight."[8] This makes transgenderism the new gay conversion therapy for young lesbians (and young gay men).[9] The young lesbians of today feel lost and without community. That is, until they start searching online and find the transgender community, made up of mostly men claiming to be women, most of whom call themselves lesbians. They drill the transgender ideology into young lesbians' heads, convincing them that they are attracted to other women because they are, in fact, not women at all, but

426

are really men, trans guys. Transgender activists convince young lesbians that they are not homosexual, but they are actually straight men interested in women. Because so many people are in their ears about transitioning, these young lesbians take testosterone, bind their breasts, causing permanent damage – or worse: have radical mastectomies – and start living "as men."[10] As I stated earlier, these young lesbians are then preyed upon by men calling themselves lesbians. You can see this happening everywhere; even the media supports this by publishing essays about how lesbians have sex and focusing almost entirely on PIV (penis in vagina) sex and how to have sex with trans lesbians who still have their penises, because almost all of them keep and use their penises.[11]

Young lesbians are also being coerced into having sex with trans women (men), lest they be labeled "transphobic" and shunned from the community they so need, especially at a young age.[12] Of course, this isn't just happening to young lesbians. Lesbians the world over are being called bigots for not wanting to date and sleep with males calling themselves lesbians.[13] Transgender activists call this the "cotton ceiling" (its counterpart for gay men being the "boxer ceiling") and it describes what trans women feel they are entitled to and how they should go about getting: what is on the other side of our cotton underwear.[14] I mean, that's exactly what it is: male privilege and entitlement to women's bodies. Men the world over tend to get violent when women say "no" to them and they can lash out in myriad ways: beating, raping, throwing acid, killing, etc., the women who say "no" to them;[15] and since studies prove that trans women commit violent crimes (rape, murder, etc.) at the same rate as other men,[16] lesbians have to endure not just being shunned and name called, but also the possibility of violence and rape from men claiming to be women who feel entitled to our bodies when we say "no."

The transgender lobby is very, very powerful.[17] They have lots of money and backing by the left who have taken "politically correctness" to a whole new level. Laws and languages are changed in the name of "inclusivity" – including everyone but women. Women become things – objectified and dehumanized by being called misogynistic terms such as "menstruators," "uterus havers," and "bleeders" instead of women.[18] Lesbians of color are attacked for the same reasons, but also when talking about the Female Genital Mutilation (FGM) that they have endured because transgender activists and their allies object to the use of "female" in FGM. Lesbians of color are even accused of lying about their FGM.[19] Women who dare to stand up and be heard when it comes to our bodies, our lives, our language, and basic biology are not just called "transphobic," we are harassed both on and offline, we get rape and death threats, we are doxxed, our employers are contacted in an attempt to get us fired (which happens all too often to women), and we are no-platformed from speaking and performing in venues from public libraries to universities – the very places where ideas are supposed to be exchanged, challenged, and debated.[20] We have to hide behind pseudonyms online and keep our online groups private, vetting each person requesting to join so that we are not infiltrated by transgender activists and/or their allies wishing to attack or out us; and we have to keep our offline meeting places secret, sending out emails at the last minute with their locations so that transgender activists and their allies don't show up to harass and attack the women attending the secret event. This all isn't just happening to lesbians, but lesbians are taking the brunt of it.

For us older lesbians, this is both heartbreaking and infuriating at the same time because we remember what it was like to be young lesbians (in my case, a "baby dyke") trying to navigate in a world that hates us because we have no need or use for men or sometimes, femininity itself. We remember the lesbian bookstores, the stores where we got our Gay Pride gear, going to Gay Pride to get even more gear, riding with the Dykes on Bikes in Gay Pride parades, visiting with and meeting each other at Gay Pride festivals and even festivals like the Michigan Women's Music Festival (MichFest) held each August for 40 years, until its closing in 2015. We remember lesbian bars where we would hang out on the weekends or after softball games in lesbian leagues, where we could meet, dance with, and pick each other up in relative safety. We remember all of this and are deeply saddened that these things are not available for today's young lesbians. We all want so badly to be there for young lesbians as friends and mentors, to help them navigate a world that hates them, to help them to love themselves and their bodies, to convince them that hormones and radical surgeries are not needed, that they don't have to transition, and that they can be out and proud women and lesbians. So we write blogs, make videos, take to Twitter, Facebook, Instagram, Reddit, and Tumblr in an effort to be visible and to try to find young lesbians. We create groups on Facebook specifically for lesbians and hope that they can find us. We are doing everything we can to find our young sisters and to help them find a community of lesbians, not a community of homophobes and lesbophobes who only want to use them for their bodies and as fodder for the transgender ideology movement.

But it's hard. So many young women are being brainwashed into believing the transgender narrative and rejecting us older lesbians as transphobic, bigots, and TERFs, which is an acronym created by a straight woman[21] and it stands for trans-exclusionary radical feminist, but has now been characterized by courts and other organizations as a slur to silence women who understand biology and know that one's sex is immutable.[22] This slur is sometimes used on men and even transsexual males who understand that they are men and not women, but overwhelmingly, TERF is directed at women, most especially lesbians. See, transgender activists and their allies don't want us talking to young lesbians. They know that their smoke and mirrors of misogyny and lesbophobia gets blown away when young lesbians actually talk to the older generations and realize that they have been sold a bridge to nowhere. That's why they no-platform, doxx, and threaten women and lesbians: to keep us silent. Because they know if they let us speak, more women and lesbians will follow and our movement against their hate will grow as their movement crumbles.

Now, thanks to women like author J.K. Rowling, who came out in support of women a short time ago and has been battling a sustained attack on Twitter and in the media by transgender activists and their allies who have been threatening and harassing her,[23] everyday people who never knew this battle was going on are starting to see with their own eyes the madness that women, especially lesbians have been dealing with for decades. People are seeing how transgender activists operate: threatening women, "canceling" women, calling women names, heaping all manner of misogyny and hate onto women who know that the transgender movement is based on misogyny and homophobia. More women are becoming gender critical, gender abolitionists, and even radical feminists than ever before because they can see that what transgender activists are doing to Rowling and other women is wrong on so many levels. I've seen women and even lesbians subjugating themselves to men who call themselves women and lesbians. It is maddening because I can see that they want to be good people and that they think they are doing the right things, but they are merely throwing other women and lesbians under the bus in order to gain male approval. My hope, though, is that now that this issue is becoming more mainstream and more and more women & lesbians are waking up to the misogyny it takes to call women "menstruators," etc., we will start to see a change for the better.

My hope is to be able to give these women whose eyes are opened to the misogyny of the transgender movement a soft place to land so that they can start to undo their conditioning and start centering women instead of men. So, I will keep writing, keep running lesbian and radical feminist groups on Facebook, still tweet about lesbians and the hatred, lesbophobia, and misogyny we face on a daily basis. All of this so that other women, but especially lesbians can see that it is possible to be okay in your own body, it is okay to love other women, it is okay to exclude men from our spaces and our beds. Because the only way we are going to be able to defeat the misogynistic homophobes in the transgender movement is if we all stick together and center women. Women are powerful. Lesbians are powerful. Together, we can defeat transgender activists, come out of hiding, meet whenever and however we want, and show the world that we not only don't need men, but we can exist happily without them because we have our sisterhood.

Endnotes

1   Giang, Vivian "Stop Throwing Hairy Lesbian Feminists Under The Bus." FEM News Magazine 2015, https://femmagazine.com/stop-throwing-hairy-lesbian-feminists-under-the-bus/; Czyzselska, Jane. "Lesbophobia Is Homophobia With A Side-Order Of Sexism." The Guardian 2013, https://www.theguardian.com/commentisfree/2013/jul/09/lesbophobia-homophobia-side-order-sexism.

2   Valens, Ana. "The Phrase 'Bisexual Lesbian' Is Perfectly Valid." @ acvalens 2019, https://twitter.com/acvalens/status/115260129271 7641728?s=20; Lana_003. "Top Definition of 'Bisexual Lesbian.'" Urban Dictionary 2020, https://www.urbandictionary.com/define. php?term=Bisexual%20Lesbian.

3   Newberry, Laura. "Two Women Face Civil Rights Violations After Allegedly Attacking Lesbian Couple at Six Flags New England." Advance Local Media 2015/2019, https://www. masslive.com/news/2015/07/women_facing_civil_rights_viol.html.

4   Listening2Lesbians, https://listening2lesbians.com/.

5   Taylor, Jeff. "Watch Lesbian Activists Talk About Their Work During the AIDS Epidemic." Logo-NewNowNext 2018, http://www.newnownext.com/lesbians-hiv-aids-epidemic-round-table/08/2018/.

6   "Transgender Sexuality." Wikipedia 2020, https://en.wikipedia.org/wiki/Transgender_sexuality.

7   Levin, Sam T. "Too Straight, White, And Corporate; Why Some Queer People Are Skipping SF Pride." The Guardian 2016, https://www.theguardian.com/us-news/2016/jun/25/san-francisco-gay-pride-corporate-orlando-shooting.

8   "Lesbian Erasure." Wikipedia 2020, https://en.wikipedia.org/wiki/Lesbian_erasure.

9   Gender Heretic. "BBC Newsnight: Gay, Lesbian Kids Pushed To Transition." BBC Newsnight via GenderHeretics.substack. com 2020, https://genderheretics.substack.com/p/bbc-newsnight-gay-lesbian-kids-pushed.

10 Doward, Jamie. "Politicized Trans Groups Put Children At Risk, Expert Says." The Guardian 2019, https://www.theguardian.com/society/2019/jul/27/trans-lobby-pressure-pushing-young-people-to-transition.

11 Ferguson, Sian. "How Do Lesbians Have Sex? 28 Things to Know Before Your First Time." Healthline 2020, https://www.healthline.com/health/healthy-sex/how-do-lesbians-have-sex.

12 Robertson, Julia Diana. "Anonymous Letter By A Terrified Lesbian." The Velvet Chronicle 2019, https://thevelvetchronicle.com/anonymous-letter-from-a-terrified-lesbian-thoughtcrime/; Anonymous. "Get The L Out: Shame Receipts." Lesbian Rights Alliance, Aotearoa 2020, https://lesbian-rights-nz.org/shame-receipts/.

13 Anonymous. "Lesbophobia - Violence Against Lesbians Online." Google Drive 2020, https://drive.google.com/drive/u/0/folders/13vfYxPdJ-HeeLfk_ED g9fR9lUx2NFWpd?fbclid=IwAR2tYUzwEU6C7_GPY5PbpgefGJ0zsDbPzBvSlN8q6oDb7gnkMUaMyVyTlkE.

14 Girl Dick. "The Cotton Ceiling And The Cultural War On Lesbians And Women." https://medium.com/@mirandayardley/girl-dick-the-cotton-ceiling-and-the-cultural-war-on-lesbians-and-women-c323b4789368; Anonymous. "Get The L Out." Lesbian Rights Alliance Aotearoa 2020, https://lesbian-rights-nz.org/shame-receipts/; Wild, Angela C. "Lesbians At Ground Zero: How Transgenderism Is Conquering The Lesbian Body." Get The L Out UK Report 2019, http://www.gettheloutuk.com/attachments/lesbiansatgroundzero.pdf.

15 When Women Refuse, https://whenwomenrefuse.tumblr.com/.

16 Dhejne, Cecilia; Lichtenstein, Paul; Bowman, Markus; Johansson, Anna L.V.; Langstrom, Niklas; and Landen, Mikael. "Long Term Follow-up of Transsexual Persons Undergoing Sex Reassignment Surgery: Cohort Study in Sweden." Edited by James Scott. The National Center for Biotechnology 2011, https://www.ncbi.nlm.nih.gov/pmc/articles/PMC3043071/.

17 Williams, Joanna. "How Trans Ideology Took Over." Spiked 2020, https://www.spiked-online.com/2020/06/19/how-trans-ideology-took-over/; Bindel, Julie. "International Women's Day Has Been Hijacked By Trans Activists." The Telegraph 2020, https://www.peaktrans.org/international-womens-day-has-been-hijacked-by-trans-activists-julie-bindel-in-the-telegraph-06-03-20/.

18 Berger, Miriam. "A Guide To How Gender Neutral Language Is Developing Around The World." The Washington Post 2019, https://www.washingtonpost.com/world/2019/12/15/guide-

how-gender-neutral-language-is-developing-around-world/; Sole, Elise. "People Are Angry Over This Safe Sex Guide Which Calls A Vagina A 'Front Hole.'" Yahoo Lifestyle 2018, https://finance. yahoo.com/news/people-angry-safe-sex-guide-calls-vagina-front-hole-012527170.html; Murphy, Meghan. "Are We Women Or Are We Menstruators?" Feminist Current 2016, https://www.feministcurrent. com/2016/09/07/are-we-women-or-are-we-menstruators/.

19 Cornel, Jana. "Thread On FGM Harassment." @RadFemJana 2019, https://twitter.com/RadfemJana/status/1206052001399873536?s=20.

20 Anonymous. "Object's Doxxing Dossier." ObjectNow.org 2019, https://objectnow.org/objects-doxxing-dossier/; Forester, Maya. "I Lost My Job For Speaking Up About Women's Rights." Medium 2019, https://medium.com/@MForstater/i-lost-my-job-for-speaking-up-about-womens-rights-2af2186ae84; Pettersen, Thistle. "Thistle Pettersen: How I Became The Most Hated Folk Singer in Madison." UncommonGroundMedia.com 2019, https:// uncommongroundmedia.com/thistle-pettersen-how-i-became-the-most-hated-folk-singer-in-madison/.

21 Smythe, Viv. "I'm Credited With Having Coined The Acronym TERF, Here's How It Happened." The Guardian 2018, https://www. theguardian.com/commentisfree/2018/nov/29/im-credited-with-having-coined-the-acronym-terf-heres-how-it-happened.

22 Jaspert, Bea. "Twitter Thread On TERF Being A Slur." @ HogoTheForsaken 2019, https://twitter.com/hogotheforsaken/status/ 1158355043667664896?s=09.

23 Rowling, J.K. "Tweet About Menstruation." @jk_rowling 2020, https://twitter.com/jk_rowling/status/126938251836250931 3?s=19; Rowling, J.K. "Tweets About Biological Sex." @jk_rowling 2020, https://twitter.com/jk_rowling/status/1269389298664701952; Rowling, J.K. "J.K. Rowling Writes About Her Reasons For Speaking Out On Sex And Gender Issues." JKRowling. com 2020, https://www.jkrowling.com/opinions/j-k-rowling-writes-about-her-reasons-for-speaking-out-on-sex-and-gender-issues/; Tausz, Ramona. "J.K. Rowling Stands Up For Feminism Against Trans Extremism." New York Post 2020, https://nypost. com/2020/06/17/j-k-rowling-stands-up-for-feminism-against-trans-extremism/; Boodleoops. "J.K. Rowling And The Trans Activists: A Story In Screenshots." Medium 2020, http:// archive.is/DGKqt.

CHAPTER 23

My Year on Planet Lesbian

by Giovanna Capone

An earlier version of this piece was previously published on the website Lesbians Over Everything and also in Rain and Thunder: A Radical Feminist Journal of Discussion and Activism. Reprinted with permission.

Coming of age and coming out as a lesbian in the freezing tundra of upstate New York was a confusing yet exciting time in my life. Winter weather in Ithaca was often a blizzard of snowflakes burying every bush and parked car in a snowdrift. The wind was a blinding force of crystals whipping my face like tiny blades and leaving my cheeks rosy as I trod across campus day after day. Needless to say, my young blood was on fire. So I wasn't too focused on the weather. I was 21 in the early eighties and enrolled at Cornell University, a lucky working class kid with a high GPA and a scholarship. That was the only way I could be enrolled there and live so far from my family in the dorms. I was studying English Lit with a minor in Women's Studies - there was no major at that time in Women's Studies. In fact, there were only a handful of women focused courses, mostly taught by TA's. I gravitated to them gratefully. In the 400 years of English Lit contained in my comprehensive text the width of a telephone book, we had managed to cover only two women writers over four centuries. The rest were all men. I was aghast. I was angry.

To augment my studies, and to my delight, I managed to find a yearlong literary program at The Women's Writers' Center in Cazenovia, NY, just an hour away. Little did I know, this off-campus program was a cadre of feminist writers, all of them lesbian. One glance at the syllabus might have tipped me off: Judy Grahn, Adrienne Rich, Audre Lorde, Rita Mae Brown, Alice Walker, Olga Broumas, Maxine Kumin, and several others. But I was too naïve to make the connection. This Women's Writers' Center was probably the only such program in existence anywhere in the world: women only space, for female students to focus specifically on women's literature. I was thrilled and glad I discovered it from a modest flyer pinned on a bulletin board in the English Department.

After arriving in town, myself and four other female students would be housed together in an old Victorian on Lincklaen Street for the entire year. We would attend classes in a building a few blocks away with twenty other women. When I think of it now, this center was not unlike the academy of young women run by Sappho, the prolific Greek poet from the 7th century BC. As Sappho herself once proclaimed in a famous love poem whose fragment is now etched into history: *"Someone, I tell you, in another time, will remember us."* And it's true, we have! At that time, I was a big fan of Sappho and had another one of her famous fragments committed to my memory: *"Although they are only breath, words which I command, are immortal."* At 21, I had a serious interest in pursuing the life of a writer, but no exact idea how to do so.

Also at that time, everything in my life was pointing toward coming out as a lesbian, but the veil had yet to be lifted. That is, my feminist politics, my lesbian identity, and my writer's sensibility were rapidly coalescing. My life was progressing like some graffiti I'd seen scrawled on a bathroom wall in black ink, killing me softly with its words: **Feminism the theory, lesbianism the practice**. I knew I was in the midst of a powerful life change, yet unable to talk about it. The year before, I had taken subconscious note of my lesbian tendencies after a distracting crush on a female friend, which I kept a secret to all but myself. So I knew it was only a matter of time before this would become my reality, and not just something I pondered in the chaos of my dorm room, surrounded by the loud and obvious couplings and uncouplings of the heterosexual students around me.

One afternoon, I was on the wall phone in the dorm at Cornell, curling the long plastic cord between my fingers and pacing the hall. I was talking to my mother, telling her my decision to attend this women's writing program for a year. There wasn't much privacy in that hallway. As soon as I said the words, with a force akin to a winter gale blasting my face with icicles, she flew into a rage and screamed. "You're gonna get mixed up with a bunch of dykes!"

"What the hell are you talking about?" I screamed back at her in shock. "No, I'm not." A few minutes later, I got off the phone, shaking. To my surprise, I had hung up on her. It was the first time I ever did that. It took me a full hour to calm down, sitting on the edge of my bed. How dare she talk to me like that?

In the room next door, I could hear my dorm mate Brandon, an effeminate 6' 2" Black theater major, loudly playing Gloria Gaynor, "I Will Survive," a tune he played over and over on his stereo several times a week, driving everyone crazy. For once, this time it felt like the perfect ambiance for the moment.

About four days after that earth shattering call with my mother, I got a letter from my father in the mail. This was unusual because he never wrote me letters. Well, it was more of a note, dashed off quickly on company letterhead, obviously written in the office on a workday. When I opened the white envelope, inside were just two sentences, written in large cursive handwriting: "Re-consider! You are going down the wrong path!!!" The three exclamation points placed at the end imbued his words with an urgent tone. I pinned his letter to the cork board above my desk.

Despite my parents' best efforts at expressing their caution, I proceeded full speed ahead with my plan. Like the old Sinatra song, the record shows, I took the blows, and did it my way.

Upon arriving to town, I soon learned that my mother's observation was spot-on. I had fallen into a den of lesbians. How did she know? My circuitous path to self-actualization instantly got easier. It was like a tree trunk had been removed from my road.

Interestingly, the majority of women attending our program that year also ended up coming out. By the end of our final semester, nearly all of them were dating other women, either the other students in our program, or the diehard graduates who were hanging around town from previous years. Women were wont to stay in that town after finishing that writing program. Maybe they put something in the water.

In this altered universe is where I met my first girlfriend, Nell, a young woman who had driven nearly two thousand miles with her mother to attend this women's writing program. Her mother, an older replica of Nell, deposited her daughter and flew back to Texas, complaining first about the comments they'd received travelling cross-country with noticeable southern accents. Nell was so different from me, with her smooth southwestern twang and her endless proverbs from an east Texas past. I was raised in an Italian American neighborhood near The Bronx. I'd never come across such colloquialisms, the meanings of which were sometimes vague, sometimes clear.

"The things you see when you ain't got a gun." She spouted regularly. She was full of such pithy sayings and was quite the talker too. Her proverbs along with her southern accent and beautiful green eyes were for me part of her charm. As luck would have it, Nell ended up rooming in our large female household on Lincklaen Street.

Actually, every one of us in that program was a lucky duck. The feminist movement was in full swing, vibrant and exciting. Women writers were being published every day. Radical women's presses were debuting their work, and independent women's bookstores were setting up shop in town after town to promote them. There was a growing network of women's bookstores across the United States in the 60's, 70's, and 80's, part of the dynamic second-wave of the feminist movement. There was even a newsletter connecting them all: The Feminist Bookstore News, edited by Carol Seajay. It was a way to connect booksellers, printers, and publishers. Over two hundred feminist bookstores had opened throughout the country, hawking their tomes of revolutionary fervor penned by well-known sheroes or newly emerging women writers of the day, all passionate and smart. Bookstores popped up across the country with unique names like A Woman's Place, Bluestockings, Antigone Books, Old Wives' Tales, Mama Bears Books, Bloodroot Bookshop & Restaurant, New Words, A Room of One's Own, Women and Children First, Smedley's, and BookWoman. They soon became popular community centers run by strong-minded women in nearly every major city in America. Some had cafes selling food, in addition to books, periodicals, t-shirts, and music. Some hosted women performers every weekend and held open mics for local women authors. They became our gathering spaces and our community hubs, with bulletin boards in the back for finding a roommate or posting a flyer about an event. They employed and trained women as booksellers and café workers. They had stages to showcase women musicians and vocalists who often landed paid gigs on the weekend, filling the store with more foot traffic. These literary community centers incited our feminist fervor and our activism. They became excellent places to organize for social change nationwide. At last, we were reading material relevant to our lives. As a popular bookmark of the day proclaimed, "Freedom of the Press Belongs to She who Owns the Presses." We were creating a strong and vibrant women's culture, and we knew we were changing the world.

In my college town of Ithaca, New York, there was one such feminist store: Smedley's Bookshop, named after Agnes Smedley, the American journalist and writer. One afternoon, feeling bold, I took a bus downtown on a beeline to check out that store. The minute I walked in the door, I locked eyes on a lesbian album, the first I'd ever seen: *Alix Dobkin: Living with Lesbians*. I stared at the bright red cover with a photo of a short haired, intense looking woman wearing Vans exactly like mine. I was curious, but too terrified to actually pick up that album of women's music for closer inspection. What if the bookstore clerk thought I was a dyke?

On their shelf I found another book called **Women Who Kill**. At the time, we were learning about Bernadette Powell and Inez Garcia. Bernadette was a local black woman, a battered wife convicted of killing her abusive husband. Inez Garcia was a Latin woman charged with the murder of a man who raped her. Women who fight back against their abusers was a regular topic in our class. I remember listening deeply when we discussed Bernadette's case – a travesty of justice. The gross injustice toward women of color, and toward many women who fight back against their abusers and then have to serve jail time was a regular source of our collective rage. I was learning to view life from a female-centered point of view. I was given a clear analysis of race, class, and sex in a patriarchal society – so empowering. I was also acutely aware of my awakening attraction to women, and my emerging feelings for one woman in particular, that new one from Texas.

Within the first month of being thrown together in that communal household, Nell and I were both sorting out our mutual attraction. It was brewing like a strong pot of coffee, amidst the piles of lesbian novels, essays on radical feminism, and heavy doses of women-centered lit we were consuming every day.

I soon found out Nell, who was 19, was more experienced than I was regarding love between women. At the time, she was bisexual. This newsflash emerged late one night in the living room. It must have been a night when Sherry, our other housemate, wasn't home. Sherry routinely paced in wide circles on the living room rug while chain smoking Camel lights for hours. She said it calmed her down and was her form of meditation. However, if she was home "meditating," it was impossible for anyone else to use the living room.

On that night, Nell told me about an earlier relationship with a female friend of hers while in school in Norfolk, Virginia. Clearly, she had had relationships with women, while I had not. So I was the newbie in this equation. On top of it, I was painfully shy and had little idea how to proceed in these matters. To make things more stressful, we had a fourth roommate who was homophobic. She was from a religious family, and would occasionally drop comments to that effect. Even so, Mary Jean, for some strange reason, was extremely curious about developments between Nell and me.

Little did we know, Mary Jean had started tracking our movements. As we grew closer and began acknowledging our mutual attraction, Mary Jean was never too far off. She observed our blossoming relationship, from the first kiss in the living room, to the first time we spent the night together, in Nell's room, to the first time we made pancakes for breakfast in the morning. Nothing like having a persistent shadow when you're painfully self-conscious to begin with.

By the time our relationship had gotten off the ground, and we not only acknowledged our mutual interest, but acted on it enthusiastically, Mary Jean was never too far behind, expecting us to get home from class around 3pm and being pretty damn obvious about it too. During several romantic moments we enjoyed, whether it was listening to Joan Armatrading, Holly Near, or Teresa Trull, or dancing together in the living room, Mary Jean was sometimes hovering in the vicinity like a bad smell, watching us with an eagle eye. Eventually, we figured it wasn't just a coincidence. One day, after an evening of tentative love making in Nell's room, Mary Jean got bolder than ever. In the hallway outside, she loudly dropped a stack of books right near Nell's door. The door was slightly cracked - we knew it was her. Who else could it be?

The very next morning, as we put on our coats and hats and grabbed our backpacks to venture into the tundra for an early class, Mary Jean accosted us in the hallway. She blurted out "Are you two....uh uh...?"

She couldn't finish her sentence. It might have been: getting involved, having sex, or dating, but she couldn't actually say it out loud. All she could do was stutter and repeat herself. "Are you two.... uh..?" She toggled her hand back and forth, a gesture that usually means so-so, more or less, or maybe yes, maybe no. The French say: comme ci, comme ca. She wasn't French. It was all she could manage

441

to say, while peering at us. We well understood her meaning. Nell and I looked at her, then looked at each other. Then we burst out laughing. Mary Jean fled into her room and never referred to our relationship again. Finally, some peace.

By the end of the school year, as we were preparing our term papers and studying for finals, Nell and I were reminiscing about this amazing program we were about to finish – everything we'd learned and every female student we'd met. Some we liked. Some we didn't. The teachers we adored. There were certain ones we were more curious about. I knew my life would be forever changed after leaving here. My sense of self was clearer and stronger. So was my writer's voice. I felt empowered. My life path had been revealed: lesbian writer and feminist activist.

Around this time, we heard a shocking piece of gossip from another student in the program. It raised a few eyebrows, to say the least. We wondered: could it be true? Mary Jean had found herself a new beau. To our surprise, we discovered it was Sapphire, another woman in our class. Sapphire was a longtime lesbian, a cultured woman with a theater background and a flair for giving dramatic readings of Gertrude Stein's "Patriarchal Poetry," and Sylvia Plath's "Daddy." We were treated to her many talents on various Saturday nights at the program director's home.

On the final day of the program, we all gathered together for one last night before the podium, to celebrate the school year's end and to share our admiration of all things literary and female. This time, the podium was draped ceremonially with a dark purple banner embroidered with a quote by Audre Lorde: "Women are powerful and dangerous!" Wow, we kept thinking, Mary Jean and Sapphire? That's cool.

As unreal as it seemed, we were happy to learn of this new coupling, happy for Mary Jean and Sapphire. As I mentioned, by the end of that school year, just about every woman in our class had found herself a girlfriend. We were wrapping up finals and saying our good-byes, and lesbian love was humming in the air. Maybe this place was something like the Isle of Lesbos thirteen centuries ago, where Sappho instructed an academy of young women in the literary arts, and where she introduced the powerful art of writing about your life in the first person. I can attest to this: when a designated and protected female-only space is created, powerful things will occur.

When I got back to Cornell that fall, my long hair had been shaved to a short, sporty cut, which I loved. I met with the dean of the English department, who commented on my short hair immediately. I soon learned he had decided not to give me full credit for my year of study off campus. He referred to the teachers at The Women's Writers' Center as "lightweights," and droned on, saying my major was English Lit, and we had been studying women's lit, so he would only give me half credit for my full year of study. He said furthermore, I had exploited a loophole in the major, which he was working on closing. I was aghast. I argued my case. But he was firm. His decision delayed my graduation from Cornell by a full semester. It cost me extra money in tuition, and I had to take out another loan to finish my undergraduate degree. I did not graduate with my class. I was furious!

I tried to get my advisor involved. She could give me no effective support. But she was concerned about my level of frustration. She asked me what my plans were, post-graduation. I said I wanted to write, that's all. "Well, she said, "that's admirable but what about work?"

Annoyed, I answered "I want to write. Those are my plans."

She said: "You'll be back in graduate school in a year."

"No I won't," I promised, disillusioned with university BS. "I just want to write." That was the last time we ever spoke.

From this pivotal experience, I came to understand the deep, longstanding misogyny of the Cornell tradition, where women writers are considered only half as important as the male literary canon, and worth only half as much, if we are recognized at all. At this time on campus, there was huge social change and upheaval in the air. Masses of students, myself among them, were protesting and doing sit-ins to get Cornell and other Ivy League schools to divest from apartheid South Africa. Divest all university assets from companies doing business with that racist regime. The movement was having an impact. Despite a vibrant atmosphere of change, this stodgy university with its high-paid male minions such as that dean, remained unbudgeable when it came to acknowledging any progress for women. Antiquated attitudes forced me to graduate a semester late. Two months after graduating, I moved to Texas to live with Nell.

In the long run, that final act of blatant sexism on the part of the English Department dean did not stand in my way. I had obtained my degree in English Lit with a minor in Women's Studies from a good university. I had honed my writer's voice and my feminist point of view. I had also grown enormously in those four and a half years. More importantly, I had reckoned with my destiny and claimed it. My life experiences had given me wisdom, grit, and stamina. Well worth it. And the best part of all: another radical feminist lesbian had emerged, fully formed and sprung into the universe – a hellion bent on rebellion.

CHAPTER 24

Shaming the Butches

by Tristan Fox

If I hadn't been shamed and judged by the following people, I wouldn't have wasted any time hating myself for being butch: parents, peers, friends, teachers, therapists, siblings, aunts, grand- mothers, cousins, neighbours, co-workers, radical feminists, an- drogynous lesbians, coaches, physicians.

I think the war with my parents began at 2 years of age. I crawled into my father's closet and came out in one of his po'boy hats then tried to grab his size 11 shoes and shove my feet into them. I wanted his briefcase, too. I'd crawl around and drag it with me until my exasperated mother would retrieve it and place it out of my reach. I was defining my butch style even then. But they'd have none of it. Years later, my father on his deathbed said to me, "you weren't like the other little girls. You had crushes on all the neighbours' girls. We were worried for you. We were embarrassed."

At 5, my mother kept pushing dresses on me. The most notable was a chartreuse number with some kind of ruffled neckline. I really looked like a character from a theatrical production when I wore it. Which was twice. It also made me feel restricted and it hampered my tadpole and frog collection expeditions and tree fort construction projects, of which there were always several on the go. A latchkey kid, I waited until my mother left for school one morning and I ripped the darn chartreuse dress off and buried it in the back vegetable garden under a squash plant.

By 8, I had a favourite orange plaid shirt and a pair of bell bottom jeans with a cool button fly. I always wanted boots. My dad finally relented and bought me a pair of desert boots. My nickname was Boots around the neighbourhood for a while, but it was misheard by all and some of the little girls sounded like they were calling me "Butch." It kinda stuck but when my father overheard it one day after work, he looked horrified and put a stop to it.

When my aunts arrived, they were equally ashamed of me. They scolded my dad for getting me the desert boots which I adored. They would descend upon the guest room and stay for a week. Soon, my plaid shirt would go missing and some frilly, scratchy, white blouse would appear in its place. I'd hide the starched monstrosity and do search and rescue missions for my favourite plaid shirt with the pockets. Then when my dad came home from work, I'd get a talking to and a spanking for just wanting to wear what felt most comfortable and most natural.

Later, teachers would send notes home that I had to wear a skirt or a dress---no pants. Mom bought me horrible, scratchy leotards and some kind of chocolate coloured corduroy dress from hell. That dress was so rigid it could stand up on its own in a corner! I would take pants and put them on underneath the awful thing. Then I'd go out on the monkey bars or have to defend one of the girls and fight the boys at recess. Which I did many times for my sister, too. Sometimes I'd even take off the leotards and put them in my lunch kit. I was definitely a rogue even back then.

Years later, in my 20s and a bit into my 30s, I was drinking a lot and very depressed. My life was already like a tapestry of shame and pushback. I was in and out of the butch closet. I tried to be androgynous, but it was a performance. I tried to wear less "shameful" clothing, but it was a performance. I visited a therapist wearing my black leather motorcycle jacket and my Levi's buttonfly 501s. She told me I was too defiant and had a chip on my shoulder. She said I needed to wear less "angry" clothing and be more pleasant and neutral. She would have transed me if it were today.

When I stopped drinking, it strikes me that my process was to keep telling my story and killing the shame. As I reflect back on it all, I realized it had been other people who were ashamed of me that started my fight. It was their war projected onto me. They could just never let me be a tomboy or a butch lesbian. It just made them too uncomfortable, threatened, ashamed.

I know the war. I finally won the fucking thing only to wake up and have to watch my younger butch and tomboy cohorts getting sucked into trans ideology. No wonder they want to be boys instead of girls like me who are a categorical embarrassment to their families. I shake my head because I know why. I know the war. It's the war to be yourself and then it's the war to kill the shame that all those people put on me.

It's the shame they put on me because they could not accept or tolerate a tomboy butch lesbian as a daughter, a sister, a friend, a neighbour, a co-worker, a pupil, a niece. I didn't fit the stereotype of "girl," so I was shamed out of accepting myself just as I was.

You win the war by telling your story. That's what eventually kills the shame.

It's painful to watch the young lesbians go through the same struggle; to watch the shaming of a new generation of women. To the point that they are told they are male. Imagine not being accepted for who you are. Imagine that kind of shame that actually pushes you to pretend you are not a woman and to subject your body to hormone blockers and surgery.

CHAPTER 25

The Last Tomboy

by Tristan Fox

My wish for 2021 is that several of you heterosexual radfems and lesbian radfems stop the attack on butches and femmes in our community. By stating that butch/femme is a mimicry of heterosexual you are placing our young tomboy lesbians (and our gay boys) in jeopardy. You are also viewing my culture through your specific lens. Something you would never do with other oppressed minorities. Don't you dare tell me that I am male-identified.

There is a repulsion in the world of academic radfems against the butch/femme culture of lesbians. One prominent theorist believes that until we "give" up who we are and become androgynous homosexuals dressed in some Chairman Mao neutrals, we will never have acceptance in our community. There is a public shaming of all that is butch/femme alongside the attempt to categorize our lives as some kind of performance along a spectrum of "heterosexual" as the default orientation—as if our lives are not valid in and of themselves and cannot be analysed without constantly referencing heterosexuality.

We are labelled as "mimickers of heterosexual stereotypes" and subjected to endless conjecture about "performance." We are never validated in our own right. This is killing our youth. This invalidation of butch/femme culture is contributing to a mass contagion of transing of butch and tomboy lesbians (and their gay counterparts). Even in our own community, sisters are trying to erase us by condemning the butch/femme dynamic. How does that type of ostracizing look to a young, confused tomboy? Not only does the dominant culture shame the fuck out of her, she looks to community and has to witness this age-old refutation of her existence as a proud young butch who loves who she loves by even the radfem community. No fucking surprise she believes she must be a boy! Let's just eat ourselves from within and let the transcult finish the job, shall we?!

I often hear radical feminists stating emphatically that we need to just let little fey boys dress how they want to and the same with little tomboy girls. But the theory seems to stop there. Or, at least, I dare not say my name out loud if I choose to wear what I want and love the way I want to. Butch. Radical. Feminist.

Got news for you. That's homophobia. You are actually endorsing the transing of GNC children by speaking out against butch/femme lesbian culture. Gay and lesbian youth are being "selected" for cleansing. In a recent article regarding a school in the U.S., teachers were being "taught" (read: groomed by the transcult) on how to "sort out" the GNC boys and girls from the pack. We all know that means tomboys (and gayboys). They certainly are not routing out the gender conformers from this pack.

Unless our homosexual youth conform to gender or sex role stereotypes, tomboy girls and fey boys are streamlined into the transing machine and readied for a life of "fake" heterosexuality. They are being shamed and pushed to get double mastectomies, puberty blockers and artificial cross-sex hormones and we already know that the research into the long-term effects of these drugs is scant. We already know that their sex drive can be neutered FOREVER. They will never experience sexual arousal or orgasm. They are effectively "neutered" in order to enforce heterosexuality and gender compliance. WE already know who benefits. We already know that Iran has had a program whereby they have paid for "sex change surgery" on the gays for years—to make them "straight" behaving and appearing. And this is NOT about the androgynes.

This is a time when radfems, in particular, need to muster every resource to save our children, rather than to support trans lines of gender box thinking. They need to take a step back and re-examine an erroneous framework that conflates butch with masculine and femme with feminine heterosexual stereotypes and/or performance. That stereotype is harmful and plays into the hands of the transcult by pathologizing normal GNC youth who, we know from recent studies, would overwhelmingly—as high at 80%—grow up to be well-adjusted butch lesbian (or gay) adults. These young lesbians want to be anything but women. And we all know it's overwhelmingly the GNC girls who are terrified to be lesbians hated by the left, the right and the radical feminists for being butch. Read the detransitioner stories that are on the rise. More butches coming out stating they were afraid of being shamed and judged. A justifiable fear given the attitude of radfems who police lesbians and use the language of identity politics to shame young butches as a "gender" or as an "identity." Well, 30 years ago they were still shaming my subculture and they had a completely different language. It appears that the very thought of a "masculine" woman is still problematic. It just couldn't be possible unless it's a performance.

By all means, keep scapegoating the butches and femmes right down to the last tomboy. Keep claiming that clothing has a gender. Keep claiming that a lesbian in a suit is doing "masculine." Butches and femmes can be found throughout the history books smashing the gender box. Tomboys (and gayboys) are doing the same kind of gender smashing today. But that's all over now as they are transformed into make-believe heterosexuals.

These are the death knells of a rich culture going down. Are you expediting the erasure of difference? Or are you shouting from the rooftops against this atrocity?

Because call it butch, call it masculine, call it whatever you want. We have always existed and our existence isn't contingent upon your acceptance of the moniker or not. And if you want to continue to partake in our erasure, of course every young tomboy lesbian is going to think she's a boy.

CHAPTER 26

We Were Once Amazons: Mourning and Rebuilding Our Lost Lesbian-Feminist Communities

by Ann E. Menasche

How they went out of the world
The women-loving-women
Went out one by one
Having withstood greater and lesser
Trials, and much hatred
From other people, they went out
One by one, each having tried
In her own way to overthrow
The rule of men over women,
They tried it one by one,
And hundred by hundred
Until each came in her own way
To the end of her life
And died.
The subject of lesbianism
Is very ordinary; it's the question
Of male domination that makes
Everybody
Angry.

    -"A History of Lesbianism," Judy Grahn (1971)

I feel very blessed to have come of age at a time when women were rising, fighting arm-in-arm for our liberation, and when many of us were discovering our ability to passionately love women, and taking each other home. Though in those days we lesbians had few laws to protect us from losing jobs or custody of our children because of who we loved, and many faced rejection from family and friends and hostile jeers when walking down the street, we were creating a vibrant culture and community of our own. More importantly, we were breaking new ground for our sex, changing the world for women.

Those who lived during that time will recall that lesbians of the 1970's through the 1980's did not see ourselves as biologically distinct from other women, with an inborn sexual orientation. We were a spirited and rebellious lot nurtured by the tenor of the times, questioning the normative and compulsory nature of the hetero-sexual institution and rejecting the guilt and shame placed on us who had the courage to follow our hearts and forge a different path. So whenever and however we came to our lesbianism, we proudly proclaimed our emotional and erotic lives centered on our sisters as a positive choice that any woman could make. And, in the context of a rising feminist movement, more women of all races and back-grounds actually made that choice during those two decades than at any time either before or since.

I was one of those women who discovered my passion for my women friends with the support of and in the context of my feminism. It was a long process to break that taboo, but once I came out, I never looked back. I was hooked on the greater equality and intimacy I experienced with other women compared to what I had with men, and further held there by my excitement about what we could accomplish together. Though I continued to do political work in the mixed Left, my heart and soul was with the women.

Our army of lovers was beyond a doubt a force to be reckoned with. Lesbian-feminist energies were primarily responsible for creating women's record companies, concerts, coffee houses, battered women's shelters, rape crisis centers, women's centers, theatre groups, newspapers, publishing houses, women's studies departments, women's bookstores and music festivals. Many of us also worked, as I did, with our straight sisters for the Equal Rights Amendment and in defense of abortion rights, and with our gay brothers against the post-Stonewall reaction in the form of the Christian Right which was already attempting to roll back the few gains we had made.

Our culture was as intensely political as it was spiritual. There was an amazing record album put together by Olivia Records in 1977 in response to Anita Bryant's anti-gay "Save Our Children" campaign in Florida in which a group of lesbian singers and poets including African-American lesbians Pat Parker and Mary Watkins, celebrated our love for other women and our determination to fight back. As Mary Watkins proclaimed in "Don't Pray for Me:"

> *I know why you cry Sister Nita,*
> *Life is passin you by while rules enslave you*
> *And it's your blind innocence that traps you*
> *That makes you think it's the wrong I do.*

I remember I would sit with my girlfriend and glance through the local feminist press in the heart of San Francisco around that time and we would have multiple women-only, feminist events to choose from for our Saturday night outing.

Indeed, there were lesbian community networks propping up all over, from women's hiking clubs to book groups to lesbian potlucks in many neighborhoods in San Francisco. In West Philadelphia, where I lived in 1976, we had women's parties and dances where 100 lesbians from the neighborhood would cram into a house.

A few dozen lesbians in a coffee house listening to Chris Williamson or other lesbian-feminist musicians mushroomed into women-only concerts including one featuring Chris and Meg Christian at Carnegie Hall in 1982, and festivals involving many thousands of women, the most famous being the Michigan Women's Music Festival. Though I never made it to Michigan, I attended the West Coast Women's Music Festival on at least three occasions.

It was like disappearing into another world, where women ran everything from installing stages and equipment, to running the sound system to the food, to performing the music, and running the workshops. It was a magical place where we women felt completely safe, and discovered a sense of strength and self-confidence that we never knew we had.

We also had access to a network of lesbian bars dating back to the underground lesbian culture of a generation or two before, spurred on by World War II - women exemplified by the story of "Rosie the Riveter" taking on "men's work" while men were away at war - and increasing the possibilities of female independence. The first lesbian bar was Mona's 440 Club that opened in San Francisco in 1936. By the 1950's, there was a network of lesbian bars in most major cities that were ready and waiting for baby boomer lesbians when we came on the scene. Though these bars were marred by mafia control, police raids, and high rates of alcoholism (not to speak of heavy cigarette smoke that clung to your clothes when you left at the end of the evening), they were places for women to be together and find each other. By the 1970's, bars became community centers with softball teams and special events.

Even as recently as the late 1980's and 90's, lesbian groups were still able to form. I was involved in a lesbian-feminist organization called Lesbian Uprising in San Francisco, with members' ages ranging from the 20's to the 70's. We held meetings to discuss feminist books, marched behind our banner in Take Back the Night, Lesbian and Gay Pride, and in defense of abortion rights, participated in clinic defense, put out a printed newsletter to about 1,000 readers, and held cultural events of 100 or more lesbians. By 1994 the group folded, in part because lesbians could no longer afford to live in San Francisco.

The aging and dying off of lesbian community

In 2020, virtually all of this vibrant culture has disappeared. This occurred despite greater social tolerance for same sex relationships, and significant gains on the legal front, through U.S. Supreme Court decisions legalizing same sex marriage in 2015, and then this year, the surprising decision by a conservative Court holding that sexual orientation discrimination is covered under Title VII as a form of sex discrimination. These days, I rarely meet lesbians under sixty. "Lesbian Connection," one of the few lesbian publications remaining, fills half its pages with obituaries. The Michigan Womyn's Music Festival closed down in 2015. Even the lesbian bars are gone.

What happened? What happened to the powerful Amazons we were in the process of becoming, the lesbian-feminist revolution that we envisioned and fought for?

There were multiple forces arrayed against us. By the 1980's we were entering a more conservative era, and the Second Wave of Feminism – the roots that gave the lesbian community sustenance and allowed us to flourish – hit a wall and turned into barely a ripple. The Equal Rights Amendment failed to be ratified by the Congressional deadline in 1982, constituting a demoralizing blow to our movement. Affirmative action came to a stand-still through court decisions and that passage of Proposition 209 in California in 1996 and many women including a large number of lesbians who had entered the trades were forced out through male bosses and coworkers subjecting them to severe sexual harassment and physical violence. One woman mechanic who worked for the City of San Francisco was shot at by a co-worker. Women's resistance to the Christian Right that continued into the late 80's with hundreds of thousands marching for women's lives delayed but did not stop the steady erosion of women's reproductive rights. The ability of many women to seek and obtain an abortion, and thereby avoid the economic and emotional burden of unwanted children, resulted in freeing up women from dependence on a man, allowing them to pursue their educational and career goals unimpeded. Thus, as ironic as it sounds, abortion rights opened up the possibility for many women of embracing a lesbian life that would have otherwise been unattainable.

Then there have been the huge economic changes that have occurred under the regime of neo-liberalism, which have increased poverty and made economic survival, especially for women (who have always constituted most of the world's poor) far more difficult. "Welfare as we know it," the safety net for single mothers, was ended with the Clinton administration and government disability and retirement benefits as well as wages have remained virtually frozen. Meanwhile, the cost of housing and the rental of commercial space have both risen astronomically. Women could no longer afford to work part-time and be activists or cultural workers, or be able to run coffee houses, bookstores and other collective cultural or political spaces or even afford to pay rent on them. More and more women, disproportionately women of color, began living paycheck to paycheck, many still stuck in lower paying "women's jobs" or more than one, just to survive. The persistent wage gap between men and women full time workers – now at 20%, and worse again for African-American women and Latinas – has a real impact on women's lives. And a growing number of women, especially survivors of male partner violence, were pushed over the edge into homelessness, living in vehicles with their children or forced onto the streets. These economic conditions increased the economic dependence of women on men – even though men too have been harmed by neoliberalism – reinforcing the compulsory nature of heterosexual marriage and therefore made a lesbian life farther out of reach. Such conditions also have fueled the rise of prostitution, pornography and commercial surrogacy world-wide as women sell their bodies to wealthy men in order to pay the rent or put food on the table.

Finally, there was the rise of a set of ideas I will refer to as transgender ideology that first became dominant in the lesbian and gay community, already tamed and corporatized away from its radical roots and transformed into a sea of corporate funded non-profits. These ideas then moved onto the larger society, resulting in the rewriting of law and public policy. Transgender ideology, at its essence, represents one face of the backlash again feminism, turning the feminist conception on the oppressive nature of gender on its head. Instead of liberating ourselves from the roles that feminists have always opposed, thereby freeing women from stultifying stereotypes of "femininity," the passivity and subordination that reinforces structures of male supremacy and that deny us our full humanity, and at the same time allowing men to escape the expectations of "masculinity" that can also be confining, transgender ideology declares that being a man or a woman is to be redefined as a role, not a sex. If you don't fit in, are unhappy with the limitations placed upon you, it is not society, but your body which is "wrong." And most women, dubbed "cis," are expected to happily "fit in" just fine, undercutting the need for feminist struggle.

Meanwhile, while lesbians have always experienced male domination in the lesbian and gay movement, conditions for lesbians dramatically worsened as a result of widespread acceptance of this ideology by the transgender-dominated community institutions that nevertheless continue to speak in our name.

The Lesbian and Gay movement, turned into the "LGBTQIA++," now focuses almost exclusively on supporting males who declare themselves women (more and more of whom are actually heterosexual) and who have claimed a right of access to women-only spaces, programs, organizations and political and cultural events, as well as the "right" to be seen and treated as "lesbians." Refusing access to women's spaces and even the bodies of lesbians is now deemed "transphobic hate."

Transactivists first targeted the Michigan Women's Music Festival through several years of protests and blacklisting of musicians who performed there, demanding that transgender- identified males be admitted. All this contributed to the pressures that finally forced the Festival to close. Soon, threats to the livelihoods and physical safety of any feminist, lesbian or not, who asserted the separate rights and needs of women as a sex or who resisted transactivists' demands to be able to enter and colonize our spaces and organizations (including battered women's shelters and rape crisis centers that were built by Second Wave Feminists as a refuge from male violence) soon became commonplace, creating a hostile environment that systematically intimidated and silenced us. This forced any genuine feminism, including lesbian-feminism, to operate in semi-underground conditions.

Transgender identified males also proclaimed themselves the most "oppressed" of the growing collection of identities grouped around the LGBT and began receiving the lion's share of the donations and resources. This is perhaps because transgenderism itself encourages extreme body modifications, creating a large market for hormones and surgeries, big money-makers for Big Pharma and other corporate interests, causing this phenomenon to be quite popular with the donor class.

Women who "transitioned" were virtually unheard of before the turn of the new century. "Transsexuals" as they were called, though existing in far fewer numbers in the 1970's and 80's than today, were so overwhelmingly male that sexologists writing at the time hypothesized that the phenomenon was a biological condition caused by male fetuses not fully "masculinizing" in the womb.

There were conservatizing and anti-feminist tendencies in the lesbian community as well, that facilitated the end of lesbian-feminism as a political force. Even as early as the 1980's, lesbians had become more integrated into the mores of the larger society, sacrificing community ties for isolated coupledom, bringing back butch-femme role playing, and producing pornography that included sado-masochistic practices that looked strikingly similar to pornography appealing to straight males. One such publication in the San Francisco Bay Area which produced such pornography was *On Our Backs*. JoAnn Loulan, author of a number of lesbian books, described such practices favorably and began to adopt an extremely "feminine" persona herself, proclaiming that equal relationship promoted by feminists were decidedly unsexual and sexual passion was simply not possible in the absence of butch-femme roles. Of course, what made a lesbian life so attractive to many women was precisely the ways in which two women could enjoy relationships of equality and mutuality. In light of this negative PR that lesbian relationships were also inevitably hierarchical, and in the absence of the support previously provided by feminism and strong community institutions to hold them there, the pressure to conform to heterosexist norms became overwhelming. This caused a good number of lesbians to "jump ship" and date and marry men. Loulan soon became one of them.

The other way to "jump ship," of course, is to "transition" – to claim yourself male and attempt to "pass" as a man and gain for yourself the power and privilege that men have. Since real power and freedom for women now seemed an impossible dream, if you can't beat them, why not join them? Soon women, young lesbians in particular, began "becoming men" and the numbers of females "transitioning" started catching up to that of men. Others, declaring that they weren't "feminine" enough to be real women, began to identify as "non-binary," i.e., "neither male nor female." Transgender ideology thus has been able to redefine being a "woman" or a "man" as not biological sex, but a set of sex stereotypes along with role-appropriate pronouns, that anyone can adopt.

In recent years, the "transitioning" of children and teenagers who exhibit gender non-conforming behaviors, have same sex feelings and and/or have come to hate their bodies has grown exponentially, disproportionately impacting young girls. Girls who hate their bodies are common enough given the patriarchal society they grow up in, which is often exacerbated by the male violence that girls may experience at a young age. Moreover, homophobic families may well prefer their daughters "becoming sons" so that their children may live a life which on the surface appears "normal." Some women are subsequently regretting what they did to their bodies and "de-transitioning" to only find that their erstwhile transgender community has shunned them.

Virtually all young lesbians nowadays have gone through some period of time identifying as transgender. They are often quite isolated from each other and may know little of recent lesbian-feminist history. Meanwhile, older lesbians, many already in their senior years, meet quietly in each other's homes and share memories of

461

a different era. The generations have minimal contact with each other, making cross-fertilization virtually impossible.

Lesbians have thus been pressured on all sides – pressured to declare themselves "men," and to have sex with males who declare themselves "lesbians." All this, and the rising influence of the religious Right that still deems lesbians "sinners," to be ostracized if they choose their "lifestyle" over obedience to church doctrine, has made a lesbian life, despite the civil rights victories we have won, on balance more challenging than it has been in decades.

Unquestionably, the total number living open lesbian lives have shrunk significantly from the heyday of the 1970s. As the lesbian possibility sinks beneath the tide, women who love women are doing what we have always done historically, submerge into straight marriages or pass as men.

Rebuilding a movement; reclaiming a community

The past cannot be recreated, but any future for lesbians depends on whether we can rebuild a mass radical feminist movement for women as a sex – one that defends past rights while challenging the myriad contemporary faces of patriarchy, capitalism, and backlash. It also requires that lesbians declare our independence from the "LGBTQIA++," which not only no longer speaks for us but that is actively challenging the very idea of a lesbian life.

The fight to preserve and extend women-only spaces and programs and our right to self-organization is key. We must create intergenerational networks of feminists where we can share this history so younger women do not have to reinvent the wheel. And we must break out of the underground nature of the resistance to transgender ideology by speaking out collectively and in solidarity with each other, i.e., having each other's back. They cannot silence all of us.

Already this is happening, with radical feminist groups forming in various countries around the globe, including groups collaborating in connection with the Women's Human Rights Campaign/ Declaration on Women's Sex-Based Rights. We must also separate the "L" or the "LGB" from the "T," as the activists both in the UK and Brazil have already done with the founding of LGB Alliances.

It is not enough to recognize the dangers of transgender ideology. We also have to keep our eye on all of our enemies, especially the powerful religious Right, which has been taking advantage of the absurdities of transgenderism and the betrayal of so much of the Left to woo some feminists into thinking the Right can be allies. However, their primary purpose is to pursue a misogynist agenda of rolling back the LGB, reproductive rights, and women's rights generally. And when the Right turns the tables on us, we can be sure that lesbians will feel the brunt of their attacks.

We must go beyond purely defensive battles to regain the radical edge of radical feminism and begin to envision once again what it will take to make women truly free. Because lesbians are women after all, and lesbian liberation and female liberation are deeply intertwined. Until women are free to love other women without penalty – without suffering stigma, violence, or economic privation – we cannot be free as a sex.

It's time to organize and fight back, sisters. For thousands of years men have had unimpeded access to and control over the bodies and lives, reproductive and productive work of women. Our bodies have been seen as a resource to use and abuse as they saw fit. Men defined who we are and who we could be. And lesbians were demonized and the lesbian possibility rendered invisible or impossible.

But we amazons are still here. Many of us are old Dykes, but we are not dead yet and are crucial voices in the new struggles now unfolding. We are determined to pass the torch to our younger sisters, just like we built our movement on the shoulders of the women who came before us. We were among the leaders and co-creators of the Second Wave of feminism. We are here as mid-wives to the Third (real this time). We women-loving-women did it before and we can do it again.

PART V:

WOMEN'S SEXUALITY AS A RADICAL FEMINIST ISSUE

CHAPTER 27

Understanding Heterosexuality: "Eroticising Subordination" and Colonisation, A Lesbian Feminist Perspective

by Angela C. Wild

I. Introduction:

I have run workshops on this topic for two consecutive years as part of the Womyn's Gathering -- A women-only international radical feminist gathering, in France, in the summers of 2016 and 2017.[1] The first day of the gathering was traditionally focused on questioning and challenging the institution of heterosexuality. It was a perfect place and time to run it because as part of a full women-only week dedicated to ourselves and the difficult questions we had to investigate, the Womyn's Gathering gave us the space and time to go deeper into topics like this one. We knew we had a full week to integrate the findings we had made without having to rush back into the patriarchy on the same night.

The first year's workshop was entitled "Intercourse and Colonisation." It was a presentation and a series of small-group exercises around the theme. Women who gave me feedback told me they got loads out of it and carried some of the questions and insights with them for a long time, sometimes leading to remarkable changes in their lives. The workshop itself and the feedback helped me develop my thoughts further and lead me to write the second workshop. It was a theoretical presentation followed by an open consciousness-raising dialogue between women. I am publishing below an updated version of the theoretical part of the workshop. The consciousness-raising part, by its nature, has to remain confidential. I have run the workshop and repeated the process a few days later as there was a demand for more on this topic. The second time I ran it that year, about 20 of us sat under a tree in the grass in a circle. The whole workshop lasted about 5 hours. It was an incredible experience. I am grateful to all the women who bravely shared their experience and feelings, or who just sat there listening or crying. The silences and looks exchanged between women about our shared experience and shared secrets, painful as they were, finally opening for all of us for the very first time, was as powerful sometimes as the words that were pronounced. The experience was heart-breaking as well as warm and healing because it is soul-destroying to know so many women share this issue. Still, together that day, we pushed against the shame and the deathly silence imposed on us, and we opened up each other's consciousness.

I am not a specialist. I am not and will never be one of these re-searchers who distance themselves from their topic, studying women's lives as a distant object of investigation. I am a woman, as such, I am oppressed in patriarchy, this topic is a very intimate and difficult one for me, which is why I do what I do. I presented myself as such to the group of women who chose to come to it: I am like them, part of them, not a remote expert standing on a podium and lecturing them about their experience. I do believe that as women, we are experts in our lives. I was assisted by A.F. who at the end gathered the finding of our discussion, questioning, and search for solutions into a construc-tive conclusion. The workshop and discussion were fully translated in French simultaneously. I am thankful to the women who translated this challenging and emotional topic. This is no small task. I am forever grateful to Anne Billows, the initiator of the gatherings who asked me to run these workshops and for her essential and patient input improving and sharpening this text.

The text you are about to read is best understood with some understanding of compulsory heterosexuality. Adrienne Rich: "Compulsory Heterosexuality and Lesbian Existence," Sheila Jeffreys: Anticlimax: A Feminist Perspective on the Sexual Revolution, Catharine A. MacKinnon: Chapter 7: "Sexuality," in Toward a Feminist Theory of the State, Andrea Dworkin, Intercourse, and Dee Graham, Loving To Survive were my companions when I wrote it. This text is a follow-up on their work.

II. The text of the workshop:

Understanding heterosexuality: "eroticising subordination" and colonisation, a lesbian feminist perspective

This workshop will look at the meaning of "eroticising subordination," discussing for example phenomenon such as "rape fantasies" for women. The question is, how do we, as women learn heterosexuality? How do we learn to enjoy sex with men? How do we as women learn how to eroticise subordination? How is it possible for women to internalise and eroticise the experience of lack of consent, powerlessness, lack of control, submission, pain, and humiliation? By investigating the ways in which intercourse, rape, pornography or BDSM practises are used against women, I will expose the process which makes it possible for women to sexually enjoy our status as subordinate, submit to men willingly even enthusiastically and explore in which way men use both the culture they have created and heterosexuality as an institution to gain a stronger social control of women and ensure our submission.

To start this workshop, I would like to briefly share my journey through the topic, my interest in running such a workshop, how this particular issue has affected my life.

Like many women, I have been exposed to pornography as a child. Pornography has been used against me routinely in my adult life. Like many women, I have been a victim of sexual violence from a very early age. I have memories of having masochistic fantasies from the age of 12 years old. These fantasies became a shameful and painful secret. I only gained awareness about pornography as an oppressive tool of abuse from the age of 25. After more reading, I came to the understanding that the fantasies I was experiencing were the result of something that had been done to me deliberately and systematically. I started to understand the depth of MacKinnon's point: "Sexuality is to feminism what work is to Marxism: that which is most one's own, yet most taken away."[2] I also realised rape fantasies are used against women to justify the sexual violence against us, which is why it is so difficult for us to talk about them. This growing awareness has led to much anger and depression over the level and depth of the colonisation I have been subjected to. This is a taboo topic very few feminists have dared to mention, yet we know many women have rape fantasies. Ultimately, I feel that until we are fully able to explain this, it is impossible for us to fight it. Indeed, there is no chance we can win against a system of oppression if women sexually enjoy being oppressed.

A few definitions:

To understand phenomena such as rape or masochistic fantasies, it is useful to recognise them as one aspect of a much broader issue, which is central to female sexuality: the eroticising of subordination.

It is Sheila Jeffreys who coined the term "Eroticising Subordination" in *Anticlimax*:

> *Women may be born free but they are born into a system of subordination. We are not born into equality and do not have equality to eroticise. We are not born into power and do not have power to eroticise. We are born into subordination*

470

and it is in subordination that we learn our sexual and emotional responses.[3]

Eroticising subordination can be defined as the process women go through by which we learn to enjoy and want to submit to men in the act of heterosexual intercourse and beyond. It is a learnt behaviour, and it affects a wide proportion of women to some degree or other.[4]

Intercourse is the act of heterosexual sex involving the insertion of a penis into a woman's vagina for sexual pleasure, reproduction, or both. However, in a system shaped by power imbalance between men and women, intercourse is not a neutral act, far from it. It is a political one. Dworkin's defines intercourse ("the fuck") as the means "to create and maintain a social system of power over women, a social and political system in which the fuck, regulated and restrained, kept women compliant, a sexually subjugated class."[5] In the context of male supremacy, intercourse is defined as the act of heterosexual sex through which men seek to dominate, tame, colonise and destroy women.[6] MacKinnon tells us that sexuality is "constitutive of the meaning of gender."[7] It is through the act of intercourse that "gender" -- femininity as internalised inferiority for female and masculinity as internalised superiority for males -- is created and enforced. Intercourse is a tool used by men in patriarchy to dominate women, and as such, it is formative of women's oppression.

I define rape as any form of unwanted sexual contact a woman or girl experiences from a man that involves penetration by a penis (vagina, mouth or anus), whether physically violent or not, whether the woman is aware of its coercive aspect at the time or not, whether she can name it as rape or not. This definition includes any genital contact with a minor, marital rape, date rape, rape and violence in an otherwise consensual context (it starts as a consensual act and ends as a rape) because the woman withdraws consent for any reason or because the man used violence during the act), any form of sexual contact between a man and a woman where domestic violence is present, coerced consent in regular sexual intercourse or in paid intercourse (prostitution, the production of pornography, sex for rent...), sex when the woman is asleep, drunk or drugged, un-conscious for any reasons, whether the woman or girl feels scared, pressured, unable to say no, or freezes, whether the woman is in a situation of inferiority, vulnerability (significantly younger, dis-abled, ill, etc.) vis-a-vis the man, and that vulnerability is exploited by the perpetrator.

I define sexual violence as unwanted sexual contact that does not necessarily involve penetration. This includes flashing, un-wanted touching, sexual comments, sexual harassment at work, in the street, at school, catcalling, exposure to pornography, etc.

Eroticising subordination: some examples:

Women's eroticisation of subordination can take several shapes and manifests itself with different levels of intensity. The examples presented below are all interlinked, gradually developing from mild and mainstream to more extreme types of manifestations. They quite logically build up from one another and form a continuum. The list contains some examples; it is not exhaustive, and many more examples could be given.

Wanting a "real man" to treat us "like a real woman":

This is an idiom I have heard very often as a young woman. Heterosexual friends would often describe the kind of men they would be interested in: "manly-men" whose supposed power and physical force would protect them from other men. The male author-ity and physical strength is compared to the woman's (supposed) weakness, and I have always understood it to mean that the man was a potential threat to the woman herself if he decided to use his physical force against her. Implicitly, this was the sexually-exciting part. The terms "real woman" and "real man" are patriarchal terms: a "real man" is defined by his strength, dominant behaviour, and aggressive conduct; he is active and in a position of leadership. A "real woman" is beautiful, sexy, slim, on display for men's sexual pleasure, submissive, passive, accommodating, and showing deference toward men. We are in the presence of an obvious dichotomy: dominant /submissive, strong/weak, powerful/powerless, master/slave relationship. The keywords are: power and hierarchy. For a woman to say she wants a "real man" to treat her "like a real woman" sexually is to say she likes to be mastered during sex, owned and controlled, roughed up, dominated. She defines herself as passive, an object of his desire, at his mercy, a plaything for men's use, physically restrained, forced into, giving in, submitted, submissive, put in her rightful place, which is below him. There is a strong level of male identification as she derives her pleasure from his desire for her. It is a passive eroticism from the women she focuses on pleasing him. His pleasure through accessing her body is her pleasure.

Rape dream/rape fantasies:

Not many women willingly admit having rape fantasies, and yet studies suggest they are widespread.[8] These are more or less conscious and more or less acknowledged desires to be the object of male sexual violence, and that this sexual violence would be sexually pleasurable for the woman.

These desires are not necessarily conscious; they can take the shape of dreams/nightmares about sexual assault or rape, where the woman can wake up feeling sexually aroused. They can also happen through invasive images, flashbacks or thoughts of sexual violence or rape, happening more or less willingly to a woman who is awake. They can be triggered by images in the media, comments of a sexual nature made by men, harassment, etc. They can also be actively summoned by the woman. These fantasies are not necessarily acted upon.

Fifty Shades of Grey and erotic fiction for women:

The phenomenal commercial success of erotic fiction for women such as Mills and Boons novels, and of course, the book series *Fifty Shades of Grey* and its following film franchise, speak for themselves.

The tradition of erotic novels written by women and enjoying huge financial success starts in 1919 with the novel called *The Sheik* which depicts the kidnapping and rape of the heroine and her falling in love with the perpetrator.[9] The typical erotic fiction plot is incredibly predictable: it recounts the more or less explicit "forced seduction" of a young and inexperienced heroine by an older, stronger, more experienced and wealthier male character. He is hostile and sexually aggressive towards her, behaviour that will turn out to reveal his love and sexual interest for her. Her resisting his sexual advances will change him into a better man and lead to the protagonists getting married and living happily ever after.[10] *Fifty Shades of Grey* is the most recent and most sexually explicit example of this tradition. It also overtly displays the sadomasochistic ritual elements, which were only latent in previous erotic novels. Erotic fictions reinforce an ideology that is already prevalent in our culture. Here the fantasies start to be acted upon because they are normalised and romanticised by mainstream culture. It also acts as a call for action. Women actively buy the book or see the movie, looking for sexual arousal from the eroticising of women's subordination displayed in the text.[11] The fantasies are acted upon in real life; they work like a marketing strategy: "See it! Want it! Do it!" For example, DIY stores were reporting selling out of rope during the first month of release of the film, providing opportune publicity for the film as well as a suggestion that many people were becoming interested in BDSM as a result of watching it.[12] In this example, women in their real lives are encouraged to seek domination and pain in ritualised sadomasochistic practises, which are fantasised as being pleasurable for the woman.

Being aroused by porn:

Pornhub reports that its proportion of female viewers is increasing; female pornography watchers are reported to reach 32% of its overall audience.[13] Other studies confirm that a proportion of women watch pornography.[14] Women who have internalised some of the ideas above are likely to find pornography sexually arousing when exposed to it. The woman watcher identifies with the woman in the film: she feels pleasure at seeing her being used sexually/raped. She fantasises being her, and desires to become, as Dworkin says, "that thing that provokes erection."[15] Male identification is very advanced here as it is the narrative of pornography which is internalised by the woman. The focus and aim of the exercise is, as with all pornography, male's ejaculation.

Submissive women within BDSM:

On the extreme end of this continuum, are women who are submissives in BDSM. Submissive women often see themselves as innately sexually submissive: they think of themselves as born sexually submissive.[16] The pain/humiliation/submission and sexual pleasure are intimately associated sometimes from an early age with no possibility of experiencing any sort of sexual pleasure without the pain/humiliation/submission. The power dynamic is essential to any sexual encounter.

But this goes far beyond sexual practises as dominants (males) have total control over "their" submissives' lives, both body and mind: controlling every aspect of it, what and when they eat, what they wear, even when they can use the toilet.

Crucially, dominant men claim total control over the submissive woman's sexual pleasure: they control when the woman is allowed to experience orgasm. Sexual pleasure becomes a reward the man grants the woman if she has been a good submissive (positive reinforcement). Dee Graham explaining societal Stockholm Syndrome describes that in the condition of captivity if a member of the oppressor's class gives a small gesture of kindness (pleasure/relief) to a member of the oppressed class, he will be seen as a benefactor, creating a bond between them. [17] Giving pleasure or withdrawing pleasure are used against women. It is a powerful way to dissociate the colonised woman from her own body, as her pleasure is not hers anymore. At this stage, male identification is complete; the woman has fully accepted that he is in command of her and of her pleasure.

Eroticising subordination: a map

The examples presented above demonstrate that eroticising subordination is a reality in women's lives. The eroticising of subordination is not a topic that is usually discussed among feminists.[18] Anti-porn activists readily discuss the impact of pornography on men's sexuality but ignore women, like if pornography had no impact on women's sexuality. Discussions around *Fifty Shades of Grey* revolve around embarrassed laughter, sarcastic comments about the false consciousness attributed to the female audience or anger at the female writer. This silence suggests that we as feminists have internalised some shame and guilt. It suggests a taboo. Eroticising subordination is an inconvenient topic we would rather not think about, let alone discuss. This silence makes eroticising subordination a reality that is hidden from us.

How can we explain that women are not generally aware that we are sexually subordinate? What are the patriarchal structures, lies, cultural beliefs, behaviours, social norms preventing us from seeing our subordination and our own experience? How are we made to internalise it? How are we conditioned to find subordination pleasurable? How does eroticising subordination work? How does patriarchy ensure women's internalisation of subordination in a sexual way? This chapter is aiming to map out the elements necessary in a society for men to enforce eroticising submission to women as a class.

1. Patriarchy:

Patriarchy is an environment in which the systematic oppression of women by men for the benefit of men happens on a mass scale. In patriarchy, there are no safe spaces, no places to hide. That oppression is unavoidable; every single woman is born and will die in it. This is our culture. Through the myth that we live in a post-patriarchy, female oppression is often hidden from us, making us live through the denial of our own oppression as we are experiencing it.

2. A culture of grooming:

Patriarchy is a culture simultaneously teaching femininity to women and girls (where we internalise our status as inferior) and masculinity to men and boys (where they internalise their status as superior). As patriarchy teaches men to be aggressive, assertive, predatory, and violent, girls are taught the total opposite:

o   to be nice, pretty, sexy
o   to please others, to put other people before ourselves, and other people's needs before our own,
o   to accept that our body is not our own and that there are no safe spaces,
o   to have no boundaries,
o   to unlearn the word "NO" from the day we are born.

Males and females do not enter heterosexual partnership on an equal step, they do not share the same starting point, and both sexes do not want the same thing out of heterosexuality. Women's starting point is below men: our self-esteem shattered, we are often unable to defend ourselves. This conditioning and porn culture constitute a mass grooming of females. Women and girls are rendered vulnerable by the way patriarchal culture sexualises us and breaks our boundaries. Women as a class are groomed in patriarchy to be vulnerable to all men. After that mass scale patriarchal grooming, most women and girls enter heterosexuality broken, unable to set, let alone maintain boundaries. The grooming is in place precisely to ensure that in any heterosexual relationship every man, even the weakest one, has a clear advantage over the woman he shares his life with (or he takes on a date, or works with), even if legally they are supposed to be equal. There is no avoiding the power relationship that is clearly at play when a woman or girl comes into heterosexuality having been groomed and broken by patriarchy in that way.

3. The inevitability of heterosexuality, the inevitability of sexual violence:

The majority of women are in heterosexuality and consider themselves straight.[19] In patriarchy, heterosexuality is not only the norm; it is the destiny of the vast majority of women. In *Compulsory Heterosexuality And Lesbian Existence*, Adrienne Rich explains that women are compelled by force, fear, threat of violence or actual violence, social shaming and cultural conditioning to direct their affection to men and boys.[20] Most women end up married with children,[21] not because of some biological imperative and innate sexual orientation but because heterosexuality and motherhood are institutions enforced by men onto women on a mass scale. These institutions benefit individual men and men as a class and are cornerstones of patriarchy.

Heterosexuality and marriage are often portrayed as being freely chosen because women in the west can choose our husband. Supposedly this cannot be oppressive because there is a "choice." However, the choice is not between having a male partner or not. The choice is between which male partners to get. It is still seen as an abnormality for a woman to be single,[22] childless,[23] or lesbian. Women have no doubt fought for their right not to marry or not to have children (and women in the U.K. have fewer and fewer children) but are still shamed for not complying with those two imperatives. As we are living in a culture that grooms women into compliance, for many women not complying still means a total rejection from their family and communities. It is not impossible to resist, but there are severe consequences that women are not always in a position to face such as loss of support, loss of income, rejection, isolation, violence, threat of violence.

Sexual violence is also inevitable. The recent survey on consent by the French collective NousToutes surveying 100,000 women published in March 2020 exposes alarming statistics on sexual violence. The survey reveals that 90% of the respondents have experienced pressure to have sex at least once. 81.2% of respondents report having experienced psychological, physical, or sexual violence during sex. One woman out of six has started her sexual life with a non-consenting sex act. 50% of respondent have reported non-consensual penetrative sex (rape). One of 3 women report that a male partner has imposed intercourse without a condom against the woman's will. One woman in four has been in a situation where a male sexual partner has pursued intercourse despite her asking him to stop.[24] While it is true that not every woman will experience the same level of violence and that the level of colonisation and internalisation will be different depending on their experience, sexual violence is a foundational experience of sexuality for every woman in patriarchy. As part of our grooming, women and girls learn that as much as sex with men is unavoidable, sexual violence by men is also unavoidable.

MacKinnon explains the process by which women and girls embrace what they know they cannot avoid:

> Women who are compromised, cajoled, pressured, tricked, blackmailed, or outright forced into sex (or pornography) often respond to the unspeakable humiliation, coupled with the sense of having lost some irreplaceable integrity, by claiming that sexuality as their own. Faced with no alternative, the strategy to acquire self-respect and pride is: I chose it.[25]

Patriarchal culture presents heterosexuality as the default-setting for females. Additionally, sexual violence is quasi-universal, unavoidable. This sends the message to girls to "get on with it and brace ourselves," because it is going to happen either way, whether we like it, choose it, or not.

4. Gaslighting: sex is rape is sex is rape:

Gaslighting is a form of psychological manipulation aiming to encourage a person to doubt their sanity. Lying, denying something has happened or dishonestly interpreting something to create confusion and doubt are particularly effective when done repeatedly and consistently.

Patriarchal culture through the use of media, literature, and pornography use the words "sex" and "rape" interchangeably. They do this blatantly and repetitively. For example, journalists continuously use the word "sex" instead of "rape": "child sex," "child sex-worker," "forced sex," and "sex-work" are all words which describe rape, not sex. Activists who work against sexual violence, rape and pornography are routinely called "anti-sex." This is not accidental and indicates that men do not differentiate between sex and rape. Andrea Dworkin in *Intercourse* finds that men are saying the unsayable: "Sex is Rape."[26] Her study exposing "Male Truths" reveals that they have said so consistently and for a considerable amount of time. The idea that sex is rape is, in fact, mainstream male's definition of intercourse. Men as a class construct and impose gender, masculinity and femininity: what is the "normal" approved way for women and men to behave. Men as a class construct male sexuality as predatory and violent. When pornography presents female objectification, misogyny, brutality, cruelty and sadism as expressions of a normal healthy, disinhibited and creative sexuality and portrays women as enjoying this violence, we are experiencing the shifting of the definition of sex.

Who benefits from this shifting definition? Who would use one word instead of the other, and for what end? The consequence of this shifting definition for women is our inability to recognise and name sexual violence and rape when they happen to us.[27] When women cannot identify rape, this puts into question the meaning and relevance of the word "consent." Men also coerce women to give "consent" as we see daily in prostitution. Women "consent" to sex with men because they are coerced economically but also out of fear of physical aggression, because we cannot say NO, or simply because women think we owe sex to men.[28] As women are groomed to be unable to set boundaries and defend ourselves, rapists do not need to be physically violent to rape. This lack of physical violence adds to women's confusion, leaving women in indistinct limbo about the nature of the act that was done to them: If he was not physically violent, but she did not want it, was it sex or was it rape? Patriarchal culture operates a massive gaslighting of women.

5. Conditioning: pleasure and pain:

Women do sometimes experience a sexual response to rape,[29] a sexual response we call "orgasm" or "sexual pleasure," for lack of an adequate word. This is a phenomenon very few feminists have spoken about, a phenomenon not widely reported and often disbelieved or denied. One of the ways to understand it is that in a dangerous situation where a woman experiences intense stress or fear of rape, the vagina will lubricate itself to avoid injuries. The body can also be mechanically stimulated to orgasm whether the person wants it or not.[30] This involuntary bodily response is sometimes used by perpetrators in the justice system to prove the woman had consented and to justify sexual assault; this suggests that men know this. After all, the classic porn scenario is as Dworkin says: "the woman who resists only to discover that she loves it and wants more."[31] Sheila Jeffreys explains that as we do not have other words to describe a negative sexual reaction, women who experience this are often confused about the involuntary reaction of their body.[32] They consequently cannot appropriately define the nature of the act that was done to them.

Importantly, sexologists and psychologists also know that if a woman experiences "orgasm," it ensures our submission to men. Supporting Dworkin's theory on intercourse as a way to force women to submit, Margaret Jackson notes that it was "Freud's view that overcoming a woman's resistance creates a state of bondage in her which guarantees the man's possession of her."[33]

The heterosexual BDSM paradigm

I take BDSM as an example for two reasons. First, I believe that far from being an alternative subculture, lifestyle, sexual expression, or an extreme perversion from the norm of heterosexuality, BDSM represents the norm or rather heterosexuality in its purest, most condensed form. "As its defining qualities are hierarchy and power difference eroticised, sadomasochism is not a 'kinky' deviation from normal heterosexual behaviour. Rather, it is the defining quality of the power relationship between men and women."[34] BDSM practises are situated at the extreme end of the heterosexual spectrum; they do not constitute a break from heterosexuality. Heterosexuality is the eroticisation of power differences between men and women, sexual activities such as BDSM which are based on and construct power dynamic and hierarchy between extreme masculinity and extreme femininity are reinforcing male supremacy.[35]

The second reason for this choice is the pervasiveness of BDSM practises and ideology in mainstream culture and the previously mentioned shifting definition of sex. What can appear to be the most extreme sex acts have in reality introduced themselves in everyday life and can become the experience of any women whether they are part of the BDSM "community" or not. A recent survey uncovered that 7 out of 10 men have had "rough sex," a significant number of whom did not mention their intention to their partners.[36] The use of the term "rough sex" (a pornographic term taken from the BDSM vocabulary and practise) has now become a way for men to get away from a murder conviction.[37] The pornography industry is a global phenomenon affecting mainstream male sexuality; it dictates how men view sex, women and sexual behaviour. If pornography is a teaching guide for men, we need to look at what men are teaching each other and what they are learning from it.

BDSM training

One of the latest trends for pornographers is "BDSM train-ing." It comes under different names such as "BDSM training," "kink training," "sexual slave training," or "submissive training." A quick Google search of the term "sex slave training" reveals about 72,500,000 results in a few seconds. These trainings are delivered in various formats such as blog posts, books, videos, online games, online courses, real-life workshops, and pornography. The men writing those training guides are "dominant" BDSM practitioners. Some are expert in psychology, knowledgeable in brain study; understands how the brain reacts to pain and pleasure. These trainers are experts and skilled in different techniques of behavioural conditioning; they understand how to shape behaviour using positive and negative reinforcement, Pavlovian responses, etc.

Talking about his training program, one of the "dominant trainers" boasts: *"using these tools effectively, you can fully change the way that a person acts, not just when they are with you, but 24 hours a day."*

One of the tools men use to confuse women into accepting pain and humiliation as part of their sexual practice is to inflict pain and pleasure at the same time to confuse the brain: *"stimulating her clitoris while applying strong pain sensation."*[38]

> *The concept is that sexual arousal and pain are two of the most potent sensations the brain processes. One, the arousal, wants the brain to stick around and have an orgasm. The other, pain, triggers the fight or flight brain chemicals. Actually, both sexual arousal and pain share some brain hormones, so things get quite confusing for the bottom (the woman who is at the bottom NTA). I like to watch someone try to process these conflicting sensations. Their expressions are priceless. After the scene, let the bottom have some time to rest and process all that has happened.*[39]

To fully understand this quote we need to keep in mind the setting: the man calling himself "dominant" is in power (in patriarchy and in that room), the woman called "submissive" or "sex slave" or simply "meat," is not in power. She is born in a system of oppression; she has been groomed since birth to give up her boundaries. In that room, she is humiliated, vulnerable, naked and most probably tied with ropes, chains or handcuffs. When he hits her and gives her pleasure at the same time, knowing he reinforces his power over her every time, what we are witnessing here is not only about the sex, pleasure or pain. It is about the extreme power dynamic within the sex act itself, the will to confuse the woman's mind to submit her. We are witnessing an act of conditioning.

As a conclusion of his post about BDSM conditioning, another "dominant" man comments on the impact of the process:

> *This is not a game. This is serious shit. Psychological conditioning will have a long-term impact on people. (...) when you engage in a program of targeted and intentional manipulation of this magnitude, you are taking on the full responsibility of their psychological well-being until the moment that one of you dies or until you put them back the way you found them. If you train them to cum only at the sound of your voice, then you are responsible for fixing that shit when you break up, or at least helping someone else do so. Because if you send them off on their own to try and have their next relationship and you have taken away their ability to experience pleasure, then you are the highest degree of asshole there is.*[40]

Strikingly, these quotes are unmistakably showing the men who wrote them as some sorts of experts. They know that what they are doing is working. They have done it before, many times, with many women; they have perfected their techniques, they exchange tips on online forums, they train each other. They get the result they want; they get women to behave in the way they want; they shape women's behaviour and build in Pavlovian sexual responses. They know from experience that for woman, sexual submission is a learnt behaviour.

If the only thing what differentiates BDSM and heterosexuality is a matter of degree, we can argue that similarly women are trained by pornography, sexual violence and patriarchal grooming to respond sexually to male violence. Heterosexual pleasure is, as MacKinnon puts it, a "conditioned response."[41]

Construction of rape fantasies and eroticising subordination: conclusion

Women construct ourselves based on our experience of the world.

Women are born in subordination, and we internalise this status for ourselves. We also build our sexuality on that model.

We are raised in a culture that grooms us to give up our boundaries and make us unable to say NO.

Women construct our sexuality on our experiences of sex in this context. Women cannot always recognise a rape when this is done to us.

Men use sex and rape to force our submission.

Women ignore this.

Women also do not know that men do not differentiate between sex and rape. Women generally do not see it as the mass gaslighting this is.

Women "choose" intercourse by lack of other choice and because of the impossibility to escape from it.

If a woman has been raped and has not understood what has been done to her as a rape; if she has had some sexual response from it (response she would have called "pleasure" or "orgasm" for lack of a better word), then from now on, she will have learnt to eroticise that experience -- including the negative experience: lack of consent, powerlessness, lack of control, pain, humiliation, submission, etc. All this will be stored in her experience as "sex": "pleasure" and "positive." From now on, she will seek to reproduce that experience as she has received some positive reinforcement from it (pleasure, orgasm). This is how rape can become a fantasy.

To take this into the broader context, women in heterosexuality are "trained to come" only at the sound of man's voice, at their violence. Women are conditioned to accept the act of penetration and enjoy it in a similar way that women in BDSM are trained to enjoy pain as part of their sexual practice. In time, it becomes impossible to imagine sex without it; it becomes impossible to have any kind of sexual pleasure without it either. This is how women learn to sexually enjoy our subordinate status.

Endnotes

1   Womyn's Gathering 2016. https://womynsgathering2016.wordpress.com/.

2   MacKinnon, Catharine A. *Toward a Feminist Theory of the State.* Harvard University Press, 1991, p. 3.

3   Jeffreys, Sheila. *Anticlimax: A Feminist Perspective on the Sexual Revolution.* 2nd ed., The Women's Press, 1993, p. 302.

4   Bivona, Jenny, and Joseph Critelli. "The Nature of Women's Rape Fantasies: An Analysis of Prevalence, Frequency, and Contents." *The Journal of Sex Research*, vol. 46, no. 1, 2009, pp. 33-45, https://www.tandfonline.com/doi/abs/10.1080/00224490802624406.

5   Dworkin, Andrea. *Intercourse.* Twentieth Anniversary Edition. Basic Books, 2017, p. 200, https://www.feministes-radicales.org/wp-content/uploads/2010/11/Andrea-DWORKIN-Intercourse-1987.pdf.

6   I understand if you have resistance towards this idea, I had strong resistance myself, and I wrote about it here: https://notwhotheysayiam.wordpress.com/2015/07/13/thoughts-on-intercourse/. I would also strongly recommend reading her book.

7   MacKinnon, Catharine A. *Toward a Feminist Theory of the State.* Harvard University Press, 1991, p. 128.

8   Bivona, Jenny, and Joseph Critelli. "The Nature of Women's Rape Fantasies: An Analysis of Prevalence, Frequency, and Contents." *The Journal of Sex Research*, vol. 46, no. 1, 2009, pp. 33, https://www.tandfonline.com/doi/abs/10.1080/00224490802624406.

9   Hull, E.M. *The Sheik.* Hard Press, 2000.

10 Wild, Angela. C. "Erotic Fiction, Sadomasochism and Women." 2018,

      https://notwhotheysayiam.wordpress.com/2018/02/01/erotic-fiction-masochism-and-women/

11 Radway, Janice A. *Reading the Romance, Women, Patriarchy and Popular Literature.* Verso, 1987.

      Deller, Ruth A. and Clarissa Smith. "Reading the BDSM romance: Reader responses to Fifty Shades." *Sexualities* 16(8) 932–950, 2013, https://journals.sagepub.com/doi/abs/10.1177/1363460713508882

12 Halliday, Josh. "B&Q say Fifty Shades of Grey 'run on duct tape' alert – was just P.R. ruse." *The Guardian Website*, 11 Feb 2015, https://www.theguardian.com/business/2015/feb/11/bq-say-fifty-shades-of-grey-run-on-duct-tape-alert-was-just-pr-ruse

13 Pornhub. "The 2019 Year in Review." PornHub Insights, *Pornhub*, 11/12/2019, https://www.pornhub.com/insights/2019-year-in-review#gender.

14 Sandhu, Serina. "One in three women watch porn at least once a week, survey finds." *The Independent*, 21/10/2015, https://www.independent.co.uk/life-style/love-sex/one-in-three-women-watch-porn-at-least-once-a-week-survey-finds-a6702476.html.

De Cadenet, Amanda. "More Women Watch (and Enjoy) Porn Than You Ever Realised: A Marie Claire Study." *Marie Claire*, 19/10/2015, https://www.marieclaire.com/sex-love/a16474/women-porn-habits-study/.

Fight the New Drug. "Popular Porn Site Reveals Women Search for Hardcore Genres More Than You Might Expect." *Fight the new drug website*, 08/05/2017, https://fightthenewdrug.org/data-reveals-women-are-searching-hardcore-genres/.

15 Dworkin, Andrea. *Pornography: Men Possessing Women*. 2d ed., The Women's Press, 1982, p. 128.

16 Sex with Emily. "Confessions from a 22 year old submissive (and feminist)." *Sex With Emily Website*, 20/11/2016, http://sexwithemily.com/confessions-from-a-22-year-old-submissive/.

Lister, Kate. "He abused me and called it BDSM: the problem with pop culture's embrace of kink." *Inews Website*, 04/09/ 2018, Updated 24/10/2018, https://inews.co.uk/opinion/columnists/he-abused-me-and-called-it-bdsm-the-problem-with-pop-cultures-embrace-of-kink-508069.

17 Graham, Dee L. R., Edna I. Rawlings and Roberta K. Rigsby. *Loving to Survive: Sexual Terror, Men's Violence and Women's Lives*. NYU Press, 1994.

18 Morgan, Robin. "Politics of Sado-Masochistic Fantasies" in *Against BDSM: A Radical Feminist Analysis,* edited by Linden, Robin Ruth, Darlene R. Pagano, Diana E. H. Russell, and Susan Leigh Star, Frog in the Well, 1982, p. 109.

19 "Demographics of sexual orientation." *Wikipedia*, https://
en.wikipedia.org/wiki/Demographics_of_sexual_
orientation#:~:text=For%20women%2097.7%25%20identified%20
as,experience%20with%20the%20same%20gender.

20 Rich, Adrienne. *Compulsory Heterosexuality and Lesbian Existence.*
The Women's Press, 1981, file:///C:/Users/ATHENA~1/AppData/
Local/Temp/AdrienneRichCompulsoryHeterosexuality-1.pdf.

21 "Marriages in England and Wales: 2016." Office for
National Statistics: 2016, https://www.ons.gov.uk/
peoplepopulationandcommunity/birthsdeathsandmarriages/
marriagecohabitationandcivilpartnerships/bulletins/
marriagesinenglandandwalesprovisional/2016.

Rudgard, Olivia. "Proportion of women who never have children
has doubled in a generation, ONS figures show." 24/11/2017, *The
Telegraph Website*, https://www.telegraph.co.uk/news/2017/11/24/
proportion-women-never-have-children-has-doubled-generation/.

22 Gilmour, Paisley. "What single shaming is and how to respond if
someone does it to you." *Cosmopolitan,* 14/10/2020, https://www.
cosmopolitan.com/uk/love-sex/relationships/a32142296/single-
shaming/.

23 Stallard, Jenny. "Women like me, who don't have children, are
not damaged goods. The shaming has to stop." 04/08/2018, *The
Metro*, https://metro.co.uk/2018/08/04/women-like-me-who-
dont-have-children-are-not-damaged-goods-the-shaming-has-to-
stop-7794896.

24 NousToutes. "Enquete sur le consentement." *NousToutes.org
Twitter account* (In French), 03/03/2020, https://twitter.com/
NousToutesOrg/status/1234716966931369984.

25 MacKinnon, Catharine A. *Toward a Feminist Theory of the State.*
Harvard University Press, 1991, p. 149-150.

26 Dworkin, Andrea. *Intercourse.* Twentieth Anniversary Edition.
Basic Books, 2017, p. 200, https://www.feministes-radicales.org/wp-
content/uploads/2010/11/Andrea-DWORKIN-Intercourse-1987.pdf.

27 Warshaw, Robin. *I Never Called it Rape.* Harper, 1994.

MacKinnon, Catharine A. *Toward a Feminist Theory of the State.*
Harvard University Press, 1991.

28 B F Nkrumah. "Consensual Rape: She said yes, but did she?" 20/09/2017, *YouTube,* https://www.youtube.com/watch?v=SBZd9Y7WscA

29 Van Berlo, W., and B. Ensink. "Problems with Sexuality After Sexual Assault." Annu. Rev. Sex Res. 2000. 11:235-57, https://pubmed.ncbi.nlm.nih.gov/11351833/.

Millet, Kate. *The Prostitution Papers: A Candid Dialogue.* Paladin Books, 1973 (reprint).

Jeffreys, Sheila. *Anticlimax: A Feminist Perspective on the Sexual Revolution.* 2nd ed., The Women's Press, 1993.

MacKinnon, Catharine A. *Toward a Feminist Theory of the State.* Harvard University Press, 1991.

30 Nagoski, Emily. "The truth about unwanted arousal." *Emily Nagoski YouTube Channel,* 04/06/2018, https://www.youtube.com/watch?time_continue=2&v=L-q-tSHo9Ho&feature=emb_logo.

31 Dworkin, Andrea. *Pornography: Men Possessing Women.* 2d ed., The Women's Press, 1982, p. 215.

32 Jeffreys, Sheila. *Anticlimax: A Feminist Perspective on the Sexual Revolution.* 2nd ed., The Women's Press, 1993.

33 Jackson, Margaret. "Sexology and the universalisation of male sexuality (from Ellis to Kinsley and Masters and Johnson)." *The Sexuality Papers. Male sexuality and the social control of women.* Coveney, Lal, Margaret Jackson, Sheila Jeffreys, Leslie Kay, and Pat Mahony, Hutchinson, 1984, p. 82.

34 Roesch Wagner, Sally. "Pornography and the Sexual revolution: the backlash of sadomasochism." *Against BDSM, A radical feminist analysis*, edited by Linden, Robin Ruth, Darlene R. Pagano, Diana E. H. Russell, and Susan Leigh Star, Frog in the Well, 1982, p. 28.

Morgan, Robin. "Politics of Sado-Masochistic Fantasies." *Against BDSM: A Radical Feminist Analysis*, edited by Linden, Robin Ruth, Darlene R. Pagano, Diana E. H. Russell, and Susan Leigh Star, Frog in the Well, 1982, p. 109.

35 Coveney, Lal, and Margaret Jackson, Sheila Jeffreys, Leslie Kay, and Pat Mahony. Introduction. *The Sexuality Papers. Male sexuality and the social control of women.* Hutchinson, 1984, p. 14.

Farley, Melissa. "Lies About Sadomasochism." *Sinister Wisdom* #50, Summer/Fall 1993, pp. 29-37.

36 Mair, George. "Seven in ten men have had 'rough sex.'" *The Times Website.*

23/03/2020, https://www.thetimes.co.uk/article/seven-in-ten-men-have-had-rough-sex-jh9hvc98j.

37 We Can't Consent to This. https://wecantconsenttothis.uk/.

(At the time of writing, the British justice minister announced that the 'Rough sex' defence will be banned https://www.bbc.co.uk/news/uk-politics-53064086).

38 Dominant Guide. "Duelling Sensations: Playing with Multiple Points of Stimulation." 15/02/2016, http://dominant247.rssing.com/chan-41446771/all_p4.html.

39 Dominant Guide. "Duelling Sensations: Playing with Multiple Points of Stimulation." 15/02/2016, http://dominant247.rssing.com/chan-41446771/all_p4.html.

40 Cross, Isaac. "Submissive Training, Conditioning, and Development." *XC BDSM Kinky Essays, Events, and Education,* https://xcbdsm.com/educational-offerings/handouts-and-resources/sub-training/.

41 MacKinnon, Catharine A. *Toward a Feminist Theory of the State.* Harvard University Press, 1991, p. 148.

CHAPTER 28

My Sex-Positive Memoirs: How I Learned to Stop Drinking Kool-Aid and Start Judging

by Nina Paley

Youth is wasted on the young, and women's heterosexuality is wasted on men.

I was a very horny young woman in San Francisco in the early 1990's. Back then, I wanted more sex more often than my male partners did. A couple myths confused and distressed me: first, that "men just want sex." Second, that men peak sexually at 18, but women's desire increases with age, peaking around 40.

These are both lies.

The men I was with didn't just want sex. As a former friend explained, men don't want sex, they want *power*. It's possible that having a horny, sensual, desirous female partner turned my partners off.

Another myth of my youth, propagated by media and men and even some women, is that not only do men want sex, but women want babies. Women use sex to trap men in relationships. Men just want to be footloose and fancy-free, and those darn women push them into commitment.

I never wanted babies, which I would make clear up front when dating. That served only to freak out the men I was hoping to sleep with. It's not that they wanted babies; it's that they didn't want their female partner to determine it. If she wanted babies, he didn't. If she didn't, he did. Since most women (and men!) want babies, this commonly *looked like* men didn't want babies. But it was in fact men not wanting what their partners wanted, so they could feel in control.

A horny, childfree, sex-loving, non-monogamous (that's another story) heterosexual young woman should have had no trouble finding sex partners, yet this was not the case. I did find a few men to have sex with—once. They would have sex once, then I'd never hear from them again. Even finding such men was difficult.

Why was I pursuing non-committal, "empty" sex anyway? Sure I loved sex, but I didn't understand it.

I had received plenty of sex education: my mother worked for Planned Parenthood, and my childhood was filled with earnest Liberal sex-education books like "How Babies Are Made" and "What's Happening to Me?" Throughout my teens and young adulthood, I was encouraged to talk about sex, to "communicate," so I would be spared the repressive hang-ups of my mother's generation. I was naturally drawn to the Sex-Positive circles of San Francisco, where we talked and talked and talked about sex. But this "sex education"—all the Liberal discourse around sex—unwittingly encouraged dissociation: we could only talk about the body as a *thing* that does *acts*. Much of our intellectualism was a defense against vulnerability and what we dreaded most: shame. We separated sex from love and relationships; we thought that was progressive and empowering.

Overall, I wish we had shut up about sex more, and mediated it less. Mechanics aside, sex is a mystery, to be experienced directly and personally. Talking about sex is as useful as talking about God. Mediating spiritual experience does nothing to enhance such experience, but it does allow manipulation of seekers, giving rise to cults.

◇◈◇

By my early 20's, I had fallen in love a few times, and my boy-friends had broken my heart. The usual pattern was implosion: they withdrew, stopped communicating, shut down and shut off to me. I was inevitably left with my loneliness and horniness eating away at me.

I loved men. I identified with men. I thought I should be like men. Men seemed perfectly happy to fuck a woman and then never call her again, or be in a relationship for a while and then implode. Men liked sex without attachment; apparently it was the relation-ship part that drove them away, not the sex. I should try that, I thought. So, I decided to seek sex, men-style. I stopped caring if someone would make a decent partner, and focused only on if they would say yes.

Most men said no. There was no power to be gained from a woman who wanted it.

Then, I heard of SFSI: San Francisco Sex Information, a hotline requiring around 52 hours of sex education training, and was there-fore a community. A casual boyfriend told me SFSI was for "horny intellectuals." They had parties. I went. Some asshole said "yes." He was a terrible sex partner, but there were more where he came from. Finally, I thought, I'd get all the sex I wanted!

Again, I accepted this idea that sex could be independent of love and relationships. There was some talk at SFSI panels about love; people did acknowledge it, but it was like a thing that could or could not coincide with this thing called sex, which is what we were there to talk about.

We had panels about sex work, sex therapy, and porn. They said, "a prostitute is like a chef who serves you a delicious meal; a sex therapist teaches you how to make a delicious meal." We had to watch porn, lots of porn, culminating in a multi-screen sensory overload they called "Porn-O-Rama." This was a wall of video moni-tors playing all kinds of porn simultaneously: straight, gay, kinky, mainstream, fringe, and of course anime (including "tentacle porn" in clips from the 1987 Japanese film Wicked City,[1] which intrigued me as an artist and was easier to look at than the live-action videos).

Porn-O-Rama was supposedly designed to desensitize us so we wouldn't judge.

Not judging was a big thing at SFSI.

There were panels on anal sex. The book "Anal Pleasure and Health" by Jack Morin had recently come out and was well regarded in the community. I learned about nerve endings in the anus, different sphincters, and the imperative for lube.

There were panels on fisting, "the closest your hand can get to another's heart."

Bondage: "when the chains go on the outside, they come off the inside."

Sado-Masochism: nipple clamps, cock rings, paddles, pain being sexually exciting for some people (apparently most people in SFSI). Marks, like bruises and cuts, and when to leave them, or not. Scars, including "ritual scarification," which was popular. Piercings of all kinds.

Corsets, high heels, and other "body conscious clothing."

Dildos and vibrators. (SFSI was affiliated with the store Good Vibrations.)

Bondage and Discipline. Slaves and masters. Fun B&D activities like Masters controlling what food slaves get to eat.

Transsexuality. Here we learned that any skin surgically altered to contact other skin or tissue develops a mucus membrane. Hence, "neo-vaginas" are naturally self-lubricating. (This isn't true, but I believed it until very recently. It sounded science-y enough, why would I question it?)

SFSI's role models included Susie Bright ("sexpert," On Our Backs editor, "sex positive feminist"), Annie Sprinkle (stripper, sexologist, "pornographic actress," "sex positive feminist"), Pat Califia (Queer Theorist and "erotica" writer who, at the time, still called herself a woman) and stripper, author, and "pleasure activist" Regina Celeste*. Regina was our main facilitator, along with her partner Avery Marks*.

I ate it all up, and didn't judge, because I was horny.

I tried the things. Anal sex: check. Handcuffs: check. Nipple clamps: ouch. I didn't like pain, no matter how much I tried, but I liked the "pain community." Honestly I was disappointed in myself for not enjoying pain, just as I disappoint myself for not enjoying alcohol, when so many others seem to derive so much pleasure from it.

I did like the clothes. The Haight had stores catering to sex workers, and I looked great in that shit. Even the thrift stores had used fetish clothing, and I accumulated quite the wardrobe of vinyl dresses, including a long-sleeved zip-up red one my friends fondly called the "sausage casing." I was very thin at this time, practically "model thin," so I wanted to model. In sex-positive San Francisco in the mid-'90's, that meant porn.

The back pages of the local weeklies (the SF Bay Guardian and the SF Weekly) had lots of classified ads for "models." I responded to one for "Lingerie Models - no nudity."

Before I proceed to detail how I objectified and commodified my own body, and lost my libido as a result, I ask: what else would I have done? There's no way now-me could have convinced then-me that this was harmful.

I still can't easily explain why it was harmful; every time I try, I get into "spiritual" language, which, like talking about sex, is largely a waste of time. The harms of objectification and sexual coercion are to the soul and spirit, and I can't even intellectually justify the existence of these.

But I will try:

The more something is owned, the less alive it is.

This is an axiom of my Free Culture work.[2] When we pretend to "own" music and art, we commodify and kill it. Culture needs to be free, to flow.

This is true of all living things. Humans aren't objects. We have a material aspect, but the more we treat ourselves like objects, the less "human" we become. Treating animals as property gives rise to the horrors of factory farming; treating land, water, and the rest of the biosphere as property places us on the brink of environmental collapse.

In Civilization, women are objectified and treated as property—that is, owned to some degree—more than men. That doesn't change with "sex-positive feminism." The sex-positive idea is that women can gain some degree of control by *objectifying themselves*. Women remain objects, but if we play it right, the reasoning goes, we can partake in more of the profits of our exploitation.

Women are also human beings, with minds, ideas, desires, feelings, points of view, and consciousness. These are what make us *alive*, and that life is diminished by objectification.

I am less fully human when seen as an object by others, but I am even more troubled by my own participation in objectifying myself. I actively reduced my own humanity. The loss of my libido was only one measurable result. I was not only a victim of my commodification, but also a perpetrator.

Was I supposed to save myself for Love? I'd already been in love, several times, and my lovers imploded and left me. Men found me "too intense." No one wanted my love, not even me. The idea of men loving me for who I actually was, was long gone. No one wanted my soul, but some wanted my body, which was thin at last, and with makeup, a wig, and high heels was literally a hot commodity.

I was well aware I was supposed to be cautious, and took precautions; I only responded to solicitations specifying "no nudity" and "no sex" (both of which turned out to be laughable, and are tactics still used to this day to recruit young, vulnerable women).[3] I was also aware that I was supposed to feel ashamed. I spent a lot of time considering shame, and rejecting it: I wasn't harming anyone (ha!), my choices were informed, my eyes were open. Sex was nothing to be ashamed of. Objectifying my own body was nothing to be ashamed of: all the strippers, prostitutes, and porn models/directors who spoke at SFSI made that clear. It was work, it was art, it was expression. No shame in objectification: we are all objects, we live in a material world. Nothing wrong with exchange for money, either; we exchange all kinds of goods and services for money, why are bodies and sex any different?

Now-me knows sex is different, and bodies are not commodities. Then-me simply wouldn't have believed it. The body is sacred? Nothing is sacred in this world. Was I supposed to just cloister myself, be abstinent until Mr. Right came along? There is no Mr. Right, there was no one who would understand and respect and love me the way I needed to be loved, and time was ticking away while my very temporal body was at its peak of beauty and my hormones were screaming "fuck! fuck! fuck!"

Radical feminism might have helped me, but at the time I didn't know it existed. Dworkin was a dirty word. Plus, my craving for sex with men made it impossible for me to see men as they are, to admit how widespread misogyny really is.

Heterosexuality: it's a hell of a drug.

A hot body is often the biggest asset many young women have. We are lucky if we have hot, conventionally attractive bodies. All my years developing my mind and talents meant nothing compared to my brief moment of hot-boddedness. Men who were never impressed by my art would fall over themselves to buy me drinks and otherwise attend to me when I went out in a wig and makeup. I actually felt sorry for these men, so helplessly conditioned they were to respond to stupid gender cues, their feeble minds taken over by mediated programming. Do I pity them still? As much as I pity anyone who surrenders personal responsibility and critical thinking in favor of unexamined social programming. Such people are pathetic—and authoritarian, dangerous enablers.

For about a year, I enabled them myself, by dressing up as the male idea of a sexy woman: drag.

The first classified ad said, "Lingerie Models: no nudity." This couple took us young women to bars and clubs in San Francisco where we would talk to men and dance around in lingerie. Then they would auction the bras and underwear. We'd go to the ladies' room and change back into our clothes. The winning bidders would get duplicates of the lingerie we wore. So it wasn't that gross - they weren't even able to sniff our worn underwear. I have no idea why men would pay high prices for cheap Chinese lingerie except that they're idiots. Or they all knew they were paying for the "entertainment," which was us.

I only did the lingerie modeling a few times; the couple that ran it was flakey. Or maybe their deal was to always have new "girls," so none of us would be called back more than once or twice. The short shelf life of hot young women in "sex work" was sometimes mentioned in the community, but hard for us naive participants to comprehend.

Next I responded to an ad in the back of the paper for "Adult Models - no sex." "No sex" is a hilarious qualification. "Dental technician - no sex." "3-D Animator - no sex." "Accountant - no sex." Porn modeling is sex! But in sex-positive San Francisco, we didn't call it that.

The photographer lived in Berkeley and I posed for him several times. (Yes, it was explicit. It was porn.) He shot for various fetish magazines for fans of BDSM, fans of fat women, and fans of older women (at 28 years old, I qualified for "Over 30"). I was drawing my first syndicated comic strip, Fluff, at the time, and hired him to shoot my official author/artist photos for the press kit. I believe I traded him some porn modeling for it. His photos were well-lit and professional, but he also shot "amateur-style" photos for magazines that specialized in those. He helped me learn makeup and correct bra sizing (I'm sure he got off on measuring models' boobs). We went to a few clubs and social events together, with me in drag; he was intelligent enough to converse with, and since I had poor boundaries I considered him a friend rather than a total creeper.

I didn't judge.

Now I judge not judging. Do all cults train their members not to judge? In sex-positive San Francisco, we judged "prudes" and radical feminists like Andrea Dworkin[4] (whom I didn't bother reading, because she'd already been judged for me), in the name of not judging. Of course I didn't think about this critically; you need judgement for that.

Since I had a wardrobe full of thrift-store fetish wear, I responded to ads for "Dominatrix Apprentice - no sex." (There was sex.) One totally batshit lady in Richmond, CA, left me alone with her "slave" (a regular "client," or "customer," or perhaps "patron," or maybe even "husband" — she didn't say) and then screamed at me.

I eventually found a "safe" dungeon in the Lower Mission. I think I first visited this place for a rope workshop affiliated with SFSI. I loved rope work — very crafty, like macrame around human bodies. The dungeon had several dommes (aka "girls") working there; appointments were made and payments handled by others, it all seemed very professional. The boss/owner had a pet chicken. The girls ranged from kind of crazy (like me) to batshit insane — at least one was genuinely sadistic, acting out like a junior high "mean girl" on the rest of us. I sort-of befriended one of the other girls, a gentle and somewhat lost soul pursuing some esoteric spiritual knowledge from a Far Eastern guru. I wonder what has become of her. She was kind, if confused, like me.

So much of being young, confused, and selling your body is about believing you're not confused, you know what you're doing, your eyes are open, you have *choice*, you have *agency, stop kink-shaming!!* Certainly we all epitomized the privileged educated middle-to-upper-middle-class usually-white woman who dabbles in "sex work" for fun and "empowerment." We all had other opportunities to make money. I wasn't in it for the money at all; I had an internationally syndicated comic strip, after all (it didn't make that much money, but more than domming in a dungeon). I justified it by telling myself that I was learning — about sex work, men who pay for it, women who do it. It was an *anthropological experiment*, said me and countless other delusional young women who think we're special.

The stereotype that beautiful, hot, sexy young women are stupid made us feel so smug. *"They're* stupid, but I, as an intelligent, educated woman, am doing this for *research*! How clever I am! I'm not like those *other* girls, who really are stupid."

We were so stupid.

Also stupid: believing dominatrixing was different from other "sex work," that we had power, and that it wasn't sex. It wasn't *intercourse*, that is true. But it was definitely sex. I remember being with a client in Mistress Dianna's* apartment, who was allowed to jack off at the end of our session (I don't recall what that was about; did I spank him? Tie him up? Say dirty words to him?). Because I was "working," getting paid by the hour to be there, I sat at the other end of the room while this guy jerked off. And believe me, I *felt* it. We did not touch, there was much physical space between us, but it was definitely, unquestionably, absolutely sex.

It was sex controlled by the man paying for it, and since consent can't be purchased, some would call it *paid rape.*

"No sex" always turned out to be sex, after all.

Unfortunately, I had to experience this for myself to understand it. Actually, no one fully understands sex — it's not so much understanding as acknowledging. I can't say *why* some dude jerking off across the room profoundly impacts me, but I know from experience it does. I can't say why a year of porn modeling, dominatrixing, and "sex parties" made my libido disappear, never to fully return, but it did.

At this point I was in my first live-in relationship, and for the first time in my life I didn't want sex with my partner. Brett* became increasingly manipulative and abusive, and finally I was experiencing the dynamic I'd always heard about: the man just wants sex, the woman doesn't. What a sad way to come to understand that pattern. Our couples counselor, Marsha*, actually advised me to *trade* sex with Brett for things I wanted, like him taking a shower more than once a week. Marsha was a founder of SFSI. The counsel of this supposedly progressive, cutting edge sex-educator was indistinguishable from the Patriarchal 1950's status quo that SFSI and all my Liberal sex education was supposed to liberate me from. Maybe I was really a woman now, instead of the free (but often desperately depressed) genderless being I had been before. "Sex work" changed me. I'd made myself into an object to gratify men.

I guess many women learn this earlier, in high school or even junior high, when they start wearing makeup and getting into fashion. Many parents objectify their daughters even younger, dressing them in inappropriately sexual clothing and even entering them in child beauty pageants. I'd avoided all that as a child: beginning age 8, I refused to wear anything a boy wouldn't wear. T-shirts, corduroys, and running shoes were my daily uniform until I was 25 and living in the Castro. There, boys wore dresses and makeup and wigs, giving me permission to do so, too.

Had I been a teenager today, I likely would have insisted I was "really a boy" and demanded Testosterone and surgery. My liberal parents would have caved, too. I'm glad transitioning children wasn't a fad back then; much as I dislike being female in this society, I would like it even less as a permanent medical patient.

After Brett came Dick*, who turned out to be a serious porn addict. Once we were living together, he regularly turned down sex with me in favor of masturbating to porn in the kitchen. But I'd learned in SFSI that porn was harmless, so I didn't judge. When I finally started connecting the dots, our new couples counselor merely said, "maybe use porn less," which is like advising a raging alcoholic to "maybe drink less." Such were the mental health experts in sex-positive San Francisco.

I want to convey the SFSI people were nice. The San Francisco "kink community" of the 1990's included lots of gentle, kind, thoughtful, considerate members. They knew they were a minority and they always emphasized consent (although consent as a concept still leaves much to be desired, and is often equivalent to compliance). They had at least some sense of humor back then, referring to themselves as "perverts," just as transsexuals and cross-dressers called themselves "trannies." (A friend recently told me the venerable SF club Trannyshack shut down after being told its name was "transphobic." Trannies built that club!)

I often wonder where my old SFSI/kink friends stand on today's "queer" politics, especially transactivism. Do any of them feel dismay at "punch a TERF," transing children, and heterosexuals colonizing "queer"? Are there any SFSI or kink community defectors? Are any noticing the lack of consent in demands for public participation in fetishes like autogynephilia? Are any of them gender critical, as I am, or have gender-critical old-school transsexual friends, as I do? Do any of them mourn the sense of humor that drained away from the movement?

I especially wonder about Regina Celeste and Avery Marks. I used to cat-sit for them. Once, when staying in their apartment, I accidentally (duh!) menstruated on their sheets, staining them. They were extremely gracious about it, suggesting I had "blessed" them. Yes, they were cult-y, but also diplomatic. Do they have gender-critical friends, or did they help purge the movement of radical feminism?

So last night I looked them up. I felt affection for them, seeing recent videos and photos. They've aged, but kept their charisma.

I read Regina's website. She's still championing sex-positive ideology, zillions of genders, "networking with my clothes off." In one article she chastised a celebrity for saying "sex addiction" — that term harms people, wrote Dr. Celeste (always Dr., because she has a Ph.D in Sexology! as she and everyone who quotes her must mention at least once!).

Dr. Celeste didn't consider *why* someone would use the "harmful" term Sex Addiction: because people are actually experiencing *harm* from what Dr. Celeste calls "sex," but is really pornography, mediation, and misogyny — the *commodification* of sex. "Sex Positivity" is in fact Sex Commodification. That's what's "positive" about it: profit, its full absorption into Capitalism. Women especially become commodities, and many of us discover, too late, that

504

it *harms* us. The harms of porn and prostitution are of course legion, documented by numerous radical feminists, including Dworkin, who was no prude — she experienced the "industry" firsthand.

I learned the "adult industry" now goes by the name the Free Speech Coalition.[5] Thank you, Orwell.

Dr. Celeste writes copiously about how "sex negative" our "society" apparently is. Are we living in the same society? Because the society I'm seeing has images of sexualized women (and children!) everywhere on billboards, the sides of buses, magazines, TV shows, movies, etc. This one has porn driving the Internet, and teenage girls seeking cosmetic surgery on their labia. This one considers genital waxing and shaving standard grooming. This one has "Drag Queen Story Hour" at countless public libraries, including mine, and "I Am Jazz" on TV, and public education about gender for young children, and "gender identity" replacing sex. I suppose that is sex-negative, as sex—biological sex—is being erased.[6]

I want to, and can, savagely criticize Dr. Celeste. But I also liked her and Avery a lot, and when I see pictures of their smiling faces, I feel affection.

Life is all about making mistakes. No one has figured out how to get it right. If you keep sex sacred and private, your kids grow up repressed and ashamed (or so my elders have told me; I wouldn't know). If you make sex casual and public, it becomes a commodity and we lose our souls. Radical feminists rightly criticize porn, but banning porn outright is repressive — and almost certain to backfire, given the willful misapplication of porn regulations thus far. (In the 1990's, alternative comic books were regularly seized at the Canadian border because they were "mistaken" as porn. This effectively turned me against any and all porn regulation, but only later did I consider the border guards' frequent "mistakes" may have been on purpose, to manipulate people like me into opposing regulation I would otherwise support).

My 20's were hard. So was my childhood. So is right now. I'm not entitled to a do-over of childhood, youth, or last week. Do I regret the choices I've made? Yes, in the sense I wouldn't make those same choices again. But no in the sense that all of those choices made me who I am, and I like myself. I did stupid things because I didn't know any better, and the only way for me to learn was to do the stupid things I did. It's not like "sex work will hurt you" was any secret. Warnings against it were plentiful but not persuasive, and besides, I'd found my way into a kind of cult. The herd I homed to was all about sex work, porn, objectification, and "non-judgement"; who was I gonna listen to, them or a bunch of repressed prudes?

Now I'm in menopause, and have hardly any libido anyway. Whether that's due to the permanent scars of my "sex-positive" 20's, or the natural exhaustion of my ovaries, I do not know. Many or most women slow down a lot sexually in their 50's, yet sex is still worshiped throughout our culture. Much of our population couldn't care less about sex, even while it permeates all media as the be-all and end-all of life. Sex in advertising, sex in novels, sex in movies, sex on television, sex, sex, sex — and most women over 50 don't give a damn. Many women under 50 do, but we have to see sex from the male perspective all the damn time, because men still make most media. We objectify ourselves.

It is a relief to not be horny all the time anymore. It's also un-nerving, because in this society we're *supposed* to be horny. Except when I was horny, men didn't like that either. Women are either out-of-control nymphomaniacs, or dried-up prudes.

Or maybe, just maybe, women's sexuality doesn't exist to please men.

I just wish it had pleased *me*.

*names changed

Endnotes

1   https://en.wikipedia.org/wiki/Wicked_City_(1987_film).

2   https://blog.ninapaley.com/2019/01/01/press-release-seder-masochism-to-go-public-domain-january-31-2019/.

3   https://4w.pub/the-girlsdoporn-verdict-is-a-win-for-women-but-its-not-enough/.

4   http://radfem.org/dworkin/.

5   https://www.freespeechcoalition.com/.

6   https://4w.pub/the-move-to-erase-women-from-periods-pregnancy-and-parenting/.

PART VI:

ONLINE EXPLOITATION AND OPPRESSION OF WOMEN

CHAPTER 29

Creative Control: Woman as Intellectual Property

by Genevieve Gluck

"Once we have surrendered our senses and nervous systems to the private manipulation of those who would try to benefit from taking a lease on our eyes and ears and nerves, we don't really have any rights left."

— Marshall McLuhan, *Understanding Media: The Extensions of Man* (1964)

In recent years there has been a rapid deterioration of individual privacy, aided in large part by emerging media technologies. The boundaries between the public self and the private self have blurred to near transparency as we are encouraged to share information about our day-to-day lives online. What this means for the rights of women and girls, whose bodies were already treated as public property prior to this ongoing erosion of privacy, is a myriad of new methods for turning female flesh, and even the very identity of women ourselves, into intellectual property.

Through spy cam pornography, deepfakes, revenge porn, "female" AI assistants, sex dolls, gender ideology, and the trafficking of women and girls via social media, the bodies and images of women are being copyrighted and sold by men for a profit. The real woman has been disassociated, split from her own humanity, and reduced to hyper-sexualized images, or even an experience that men can try on for themselves. Advances in technology facilitate abuse against women with remarkably little oversight, and the speed of its development ensures that women's rights advocates are consistently on the defensive.

There have been some major gains made recently by campaigners, in various countries, who are utilizing social media to draw attention to the breaches of women's human rights enabled by the internet; however, unless the fundamental issue is confronted—the treatment of women as commodities, by men—women and girls will remain vulnerable and forced to react in self-defense to each new violation, facilitated by emerging media technologies that promote our dehumanization and motivate physical abuse.

My life is not your porn: South Korea's digital sex abuse epidemic

"Any violation of a woman's body can become sex for men; this is the essential truth of pornography."

— Andrea Dworkin, *Intercourse* (1987)

On July 7, 2018, tens of thousands of Korean women gathered[1] in the streets of Seoul, wearing masks to hide their identities. It was the largest women-only protest in the nation in recent recorded history; demonstrators claimed about 55,000 women took part. Many wore red T-shirts which said, "Angry women will change the world," and held signs that read, "My life is not your porn."

The issue that drove thousands of women to gather in the streets and protest against a single issue is the current escalation of spy cam pornography in South Korea, called *molka* in Korean, a portmanteau of "spy camera." Though digital sex crimes are increasing globally,[2] South Korea has been described as the "global epicenter of spy cam,"[3] with more than 6,000 cases[4] of illegal filming reported in 2017. That figure jumped to 6,800[5] in 2018 and continues to increase; however, that year only one-third of the reported cases were taken to trial. In 2019, 5,500 people were arrested for spy camera offenses, 97% of whom were men.

The motivation for filming women without their knowledge is an increased demand for the recorded violation of women's privacy as a form of pornography; those who stream women in public places of undress can earn money from paid subscription sites. Indeed, a new industry capitalizing on secretly recording women has been abetted by the recent explosion in streaming pornography. In 2019, two South Korean men were arrested for an organized spy cam syndicate that filmed and streamed the private activities of an estimated 1,600 female hotel guests; over a period of three months, the men had earned[6] roughly $6,200 from subscribers.

So widespread is the practice in South Korea that in 2019 two K-pop stars,[7] Jung Joon-young and Choi Jong-hoon, publicly admitted[8] to production and dissemination of spy cam pornography. Both men were found guilty of gang rape, filming the assault, and uploading the video online. This case highlighted how spy cam pornography has become so normalized in South Korea that even young and wealthy celebrities were participating in its production. To add insult to injury, both men had their prison sentences significantly reduced: Jung Joon-young's sentence was lowered from six years to five; Choi Jong-hoon's sentence was halved, from five years to 30 months.

In response to increased public demand for government intervention, the South Korean government in 2016 created a task force dedicated to investigating high-risk areas for hidden cameras, including public restrooms, changing rooms, and subway stations. Yet these meager attempts have not been enough to prevent abuse. In 2019, Lee Yu-jung became the first known casualty[9] of the recent spy cam pornography epidemic when she took her own life after a co-worker filmed her in the changing room of the hospital where they worked. Though footage of Lee was part of a larger cache of illicitly filmed women, the perpetrator received only a ten-month sentence. According to a survey by the Korean Women's Development Institute, the mental toll of digital sex abuse is devastating: nearly one in four women who has been secretly filmed has considered suicide.

The Nth Room

The "Nth Room" refers to a South Korean digital scandal[10] involving the sexual slavery of at least 76 women and girls. The victims, 16 of whom were minors, were forced to perform degrading and sometimes violent acts for the sexual amusement of the roughly 260,000 people who paid for subscriptions to view the content in a secret Telegram chat group. The group first appeared around early 2019 and quickly expanded into various "rooms," or messaging groups, with names like "slave room," "female child room," or "violate your acquaintance" room. The chat rooms were ranked by tiers; the lowest-priced room contained the least explicit and violent content, and users who paid more would have full access to videos sexualizing torture. "Let's rape" was a greeting used as often as "hello."

According to the website "Nth Room Awareness," published anonymously at nthroom.carrd.co,[11] victims were blackmailed by the group's organizer, Cho Ju-bin, and his accomplices. The men involved, called "operators," scouted the victims online and stole compromising information from their social media accounts. Using the threat of releasing personal information, such as sexual photographs, bank information, and addresses, operators forced women and girls to film acts of self-mutilation, including: carving the word "slave," on their bodies; cutting off nipples; and inserting scissors into their privates. Underage girls were forced to bark like dogs, or forced to lie naked on the floor of a man's toilet. Subscribers would also pay to rape or gang-rape victims. In one case, a subscriber paid[12] to have a schoolgirl murdered as revenge against her father, a middle-school teacher. However, the plot was discovered by the police before the murder was carried out.

There are various theories as to why South Korea in particular has become the global epicenter for spy cam pornography and online digital abuse. The nation has become an economic power-house in recent decades, allowing a generation of educated young women to enter the workforce in unprecedented numbers; the virulent misogynist attacks may be a backlash. According to Lee Mi-jeong,[13] a research fellow at the Korea Women's Development Institute, "Young people are very frustrated, especially men, if they compare their lives to that of their parents' generation. That frustration is projected onto women." In addition, South Korea boasts the world's fastest internet connection, widely available for free in its largest cities, and is home to the technology giant Samsung, all of which have enabled an online culture to develop at a pace that has surpassed other developed countries. However, the scourge of spy cam pornography did not appear suddenly and without warning. Prior to the *molka* epidemic and the Nth room, there was the revenge porn website called Soranet.

Soranet

Soranet was South Korea's largest pornographic website, founded in 1999. During the peak of its 16-year history, Soranet had over a million active users and hosted thousands of illegal videos filmed without women's consent. Crimes committed by Soranet and its users include: 1) brokering prostitution through advertisements; 2) hosting revenge porn, and abetting the extortion of victims via blackmail; 3) sex trafficking of minors; 4) installing spy cameras in public restrooms, dressing rooms, and upskirting; 5) filmed rape of women and real-time invitations[14] to join in the assault of a *golbaengi-nyeo* (a "sea snail girl"), the slang term for a woman who is unconscious due to drugs or intoxication.

515

The site was notorious for evading the law and several initial attempts to shut it down failed. The owners would purchase foreign domains and IP addresses, thus evading prosecution from Korean authorities, who had no jurisdiction over foreign-based websites. In addition, the owners would often change servers to escape detection and punishment, and would then use Twitter to advertise their most recent URL. According to Oh Ha-ryong, assistant director of the Korea Communications Standards Commission (KCSC), an internet watchdog, "They changed from Soranet.com to Soranet1.com, and so on. Site owners dodged us while continuously uploading more content. Even if we cracked down on them, we couldn't eliminate them 100 percent."

A few events in particular drew public attention to the ongoing abuses conducted through Soranet. In 2015, a user posted a photo of a partially naked and unconscious woman with the text: "Whoever posts the best sexual insult against my girlfriend will be invited to participate in a rape session at a motel in Wangsimni (Seoul)." Minutes later, the same user posted again, saying, "A guest has just been here and fucked her. Who's up for another round?" Police were flooded with calls from women reporting the incident, though authorities claimed they couldn't take action without more information.

The site was finally shut down in 2016 following public outcry to this incident, but only after several women victimized over the years took their lives. One of four co-founders, a woman with the surname Song, was sentenced to four years in jail; however, the three others involved, including her husband, escaped[15] conviction. As owners of foreign passports, the three left the country and remain at large.

Trafficking Hub

Between February and September 2020, more than two million people[16] had signed a petition to shut down PornHub, the largest streaming pornography website in the world. This is an astonishing achievement in itself, considering how normalized pornography has become in many parts of the world, but even more extraordinary is the speed and momentum of the backlash. The campaign, founded by Laila Mickelwait, is called "Trafficking Hub," and the petition states:

> Pornhub, the world's largest and most popular porn site, has been repeatedly caught enabling, hosting, and profiting from videos of child rape, sex trafficking, and other forms of non-consensual content exploiting women and minors. We're calling for Pornhub to be shut down and its executives held accountable for these crimes.

The grassroots movement was inspired by an op-ed by Mickelwait, published in *The Washington Examiner* on February 9, 2020, titled "Time to Shut Pornhub Down." Mickelwait mentions several cases of child trafficking and child rape videos hosted on the platform, including the case[17] of a missing Florida teen who was found after 58 pornographic videos of her abuse were uploaded to Pornhub. There are many documented instances of Pornhub profiting from rape and sex trafficking content, including 22 women who were coerced and manipulated into performing sex acts by Michael Pratt, owner of GirlsDoPorn. The video content, which they had been assured would not be seen by anyone, was uploaded to Pornhub against their wishes. These women organized together to file a lawsuit and won $12.7 million[18] in damages.

One of the most widely publicized cases of Pornhub profiting from rape involves a young woman named Rose Kalemba, who, at 14 years old, was abducted and raped at knifepoint by two men while a third filmed the attack. Within a few months, video of her rape was circulating on Pornhub. Her pinned tweet, which has been shared over 100,000 times, reads, "My rapists put me in a mental prison, but you gave me a life sentence by allowing 6 videos of my rape at age 14 to stay up for over 6 months until I impersonated a lawyer. The videos had views in the millions, & who knows how many downloaded them. You immortalized my torture."

Owned by parent company MindGeek, Pornhub averages 42 billion visits per year, or 115 million visits each day. Its content is user-generated, meaning anyone can upload content. As pointed out by Mickelwait, all that is needed to receive verification is to send in a selfie holding a piece of paper with one's username written on it. PornHub does not verify the age of the user uploading content or the age of those involved in the video. The lack of oversight by PornHub executives and staff results in videos of filmed rape and child sexual abuse remaining on the site and generating profit for the company, while fueling and incentivizing sexual violence.

PornHub has repeatedly refused Mickelwait's requests to release information pertaining to how many moderators are employed by the company. Instead, the CEO of MindGeek, Feras Antoon, appears to have created several Twitter accounts to stalk and harass Mickelwait. Moreover, according to screenshots shared on Twitter by Mickelwait, porn actress and PornHub representative Asa Akira has tweeted several disturbing comments in support of pedophilia, incest and rape, including: "shoutout to my pedophiles," "adulthood is knowing the difference between good rape and bad rape," "it only hurts if you resist," "nothing like a good raping to make u feel like a woman again," and "incest should be legal."

All of this behavior, says Mickelwait, is "on-brand for Pornhub," a company that "profits from and enables the trafficking and rape of women and minors." In a Twitter thread from May 12, 2020, Mickelwait cites several instances of trafficking and videos of rape posted to PornHub, including:

1) a nine-year long partnership[19] with a Czech sex trafficking ring, whose videos of sexual abuse exceeded 1 billion views;
2) A *Sunday Times* investigation[20] found "dozens" of illegal child abuse videos on PornHub within minutes, even of children as young as three years old, many of which had remained public for several years, prompting PayPal to sever[21] their ties with the company;

3) The Internet Watch Foundation confirmed 118 cases of child rape on PornHub in a two-year period, half of which were Category A offenses, including sadism;

4) Sex trafficker Michael Terrell Williams, verified and monetized by PornHub, arrested[22] in September 2020 for selling videos of a 16 year-old girl being raped, for which the company earned 35% of ad revenue profits;

5) Nicole Addimando was sentenced[23] to life in prison for killing her abusive boyfriend, who had uploaded to PornHub videos of himself sexually assaulting her;

6) Justin Lee raped 20 women, filmed[24] the abuse, and uploaded the videos to PornHub;

7) Avri Sapir discovered[25] monetized videos of her child sexual abuse posted to PornHub - at the time of the assault, she was a toddler.

In addition to the documented abuse freely available on PornHub, there are thousands of other instances of revenge porn which are uploaded to sites not named in media reports, or otherwise posted across social media. In September 2020, the UK reported[26] a 22 percent increase to a government-funded revenge porn helpline, with cases surging during lockdown restrictions imposed due to coronavirus. A 60 percent increase is predicted for the end of the year, and employees of the helpline service fear the trend will become "the new normal." In the US, at least one in ten women have been threatened[27] with the posting of explicit photos, placing them at risk of losing their jobs or being stalked, according to a 2016 survey. Women in Malaysia who infiltrated[28] secret Telegram chat groups discovered illegal pornography ranging from upskirt photos, to child sexual abuse, to ex-boyfriends revealing contact information. One woman involved in the sting operation said, "There was so much child porn being traded openly. There was a father who secretly filmed his own daughter and sent it to the group. I've seen boyfriends participating in a competition by sending their own significant other's photos to the group. I've seen

Photoshopped photos of women made to look naked or contact information shared with men claiming they are sex workers."

One particularly shocking report[29] revealed that across Australia, New Zealand, and the UK, one in three people had been a victim of image-based sexual abuse, with women overrepresented as victims and men making up the majority of offenders. Revenge porn is on the rise among youth, as well, with over 500 cases occurring in England and Wales during 2019.[30] Though the average age of victims overall was 15, there were instances of children as young as 8 years old coming forward. In addition, reports indicate that digital sexual abuse crimes are not being taken seriously by law enforcement. Data from the state of Victoria, Australia, found a correlation between revenge porn crimes and domestic violence: three-quarters of all image-based sexual abuse charges were brought to court with at least one other offense. Despite this, those who perpetrated revenge porn crimes alone did not receive prison sentences.[31]

In the U.S., the Indiana State Attorney General's Office overturned[32] a criminal case and ruled that the law against revenge porn was unconstitutional and violated free speech rights. Earlier the same year, a Tennessee court overturned a conviction for a man who followed women in public, filming their breasts and buttocks and groping women. David Eric Lambert was charged with unlawful photography and attempted sexual battery. However, three judges - all men - ruled[33] in an appeals court that women do not have a right to privacy or any claim to images of themselves being taken by men and used for sexual gratification or profit, saying:

> *Exposure to the capture of our images by cameras has become, perhaps unfortunately, a reality of daily life in our digital age. When nearly every person goes about her day with a hand-held device capable of taking hundreds of photographs and videos and every public place is equipped with a wide variety of surveillance equipment, it is simply not reasonable to expect that our fully clothed images will remain totally private.*

This ruling and sentiment contradict a 2019 decision made by the Supreme Court in the state of Illinois. While debating[34] whether revenge porn could be protected as free speech, Assistant Attorney General Garson Fischer stated:

> *It is not the case that one's right to privacy dissipates as soon as they communicate to one other person. If that is the limit on the definition to the right to privacy, then it essentially eradicates the right to private conversation at all. The vast majority of the victims of this crime — the overwhelming majority — are women. If the state can't proscribe this kind of speech, then it sends a message to women that they're not entitled to the same privacy, the same sense of safety.*

Deepfakes: Projected Rape

> *Deepfake technology is being weaponized against women by inserting their faces into porn. It is terrifying, embarrassing, demeaning, and silencing. Deepfake sex videos say to individuals that their bodies are not their own and can make it difficult to stay online, get or keep a job, and feel safe.*

— Danielle Citron, Professor of Law, Boston University, author of *Hate Crimes in Cyberspace* (2014)

While revenge porn—the sharing of explicit content without the subject's consent—is a relatively new type of crime, newer and more terrifying still is deepfake porn. "Deepfake" is a mash-up of *deep learning* and *fake*; using AI, the likeness of another person can be superimposed over existing video content with increasing accuracy.

Deepfakes are proliferating with accelerating speed, driven by unbridled objectification and the eroticization of violating women's boundaries. Media outlets frequently focus on the threat of deepfakes to political elections; however, a 2019 report from research group Sensity (formerly Deeptrace) found that 96 percent of deepfake content online is pornographic, and *all* of the faked subjects in the pornographic material were women. About a quarter of this content exploited South Korean women; the remainder, American and British actresses. The number of videos at the time the research was conducted was 15,000, twice the amount that existed only seven months prior.

The term, and mode of manipulation, originated in 2017 from a Reddit user called "Deepfakes" who was posting altered pornography that featured faces of celebrities on the bodies of porn actresses. The topic of deepfakes first reached the mainstream public through a *Vice* article[35] published at the end of that year, noting that celebrities such as Scarlett Johansson, Gal Gadot, Maisie Williams, Aubrey Plaza, and Taylor Swift had their likeness stolen and placed into hardcore porn.

As of this writing, there are already several websites dedicated to deepfake porn, as it is rapidly becoming normalized as a new genre, and indeed, a new form of terrorism against women. If any woman's likeness can be placed into hardcore pornography convincingly, then any woman who uploads a single photo of herself online may become a victim of digital sexual abuse.

And increasingly so, a single photograph is all that is necessary to supplant one digital visage over another. In 2019, a Samsung lab in Russia announced[36] that they had created an AI system which could generate an entirely fake clip from one image, and demonstrated this using celebrity photos and famous paintings, including the *Mona Lisa*, where she appears to be talking, smiling, even moving her head. The title "Living Portraits" appears at the top of the video, as though the viewer is meant to believe this technology has been spurred by an interest in history and art, rather than being almost entirely driven by the sexual exploitation of women against their will.

So far, up to 1,000 deepfake videos have been uploaded to porn sites every month of 2020, according to research group Sensity. The videos, hosted on three of the biggest porn sites (XVideos, Xnxx, and xHamster) rack up millions of views which in turn generate ad revenue. According to *Wired.com*,[37] one 30-second video of Emma Watson appears on all three sites and has garnered at least 23 million views. Other celebrities being digitally raped in this manner include Billie Eilish, Natalie Portman, and Anushka Shetty.

In October 2020, research team Sensity AI published a follow-up report: over 100,000 women had unknowingly had their image stolen and turned into porn through a deepfake bot freely available[38] via Telegram. Users could upload a photo and receive a nude version within minutes. According to Giorgio Patrini, CEO of Sensity and co-author of the report, "Usually it's young girls. Unfortunately, sometimes it's also quite obvious that some of these people are underage."

Video content from TikTok accounts, including of underage girls, have been appearing on PornHub. Nearly a third of TikTok users are under the age of 14, according to internal company data. An investigation[39] by *Rolling Stone* revealed more than two dozen instances of TikTok influencers having their likeness stolen and converted into deepfake porn. The publication spoke with the mother of a 17 year-old girl who discovered one of her videos posted to PornHub. In another instance, a Discord server was found to be dedicated to creating deepfake porn via user requests: "Do [name redacted], by the way she turns 18 in 4 days." The admin made the video and posted it to PornHub two weeks after she turned 18.

In October 2020, Tokyo police arrested[40] two men, Takumi Hayashida and Takanobu Otsuki — a university student and a systems engineer, respectively — for producing deepfake pornography using the faces of female celebrities and publishing the videos on pornography websites. Collectively, the two men earned about 800,000 yen, or $7,600, by releasing the videos on a website run by Hayashida.

This was the first-ever arrest of its kind in the nation, and the charges levelled against the men were telling of how this new form of terrorism against women is viewed in the eyes of the majority male lawmakers. Rather than labelling projected rape as a form of sexual violence, the police charged the men with defamation and copyright infringement. The crime was considered an affront to the companies that *owned the likenesses of both women involved*: the pornography studio, and the entertainment companies for which the women worked.

This is why we desperately need language to describe deepfake pornography for the form of sex-based violence that it is, and why I suggest the term *projected rape*.

This is the shocking reality of deepfake porn: a woman may be raped without ever being touched and that violation may be viewed endlessly by millions of men who participate in her degradation. We do not have the language yet to describe this type of projected rape, but that is precisely what it is. The separation of woman from her body, the supplanting of her whole self with fractured images and paraphernalia, the flattening of her humanity into intellectual property, makes possible new forms of rape and colonization which are more metaphysical than physical, but incites and even monetizes actual violence against women and girls.

The sex industry has been a driving force in the development of several media technologies, including pop-up ads, VHS, streaming video, and even aspects of the internet itself. Danielle Citron, who spoke at a US House Intelligence Committee on the impact of artificial intelligence and media manipulation, puts it bluntly: "At each stage we've seen that people use what's ready and at hand to torment women. Deepfakes are an illustration of that."

Deepfakes not only demonstrate that men use sex to terrorize women; they also show that men have vested interests, both personal and financial, in forcing women to conform to their sexual fantasies and expectations. The tools which allow men to project their desires onto women have developed rapidly, unchecked, and the lines between our reality and their pornified delusions are growing ever more blurred.

Conclusion

As media technologies advance, the accessibility of predation increases: those who prey on women and children and exploit their bodies for gain find increasingly easy avenues to do so. This is happening because of the already existent idea of woman as a commodity and object, and each new utilization of media to further this idea in order enact violence against women facilitates the sexual slavery of women and girls. The word "objectification" is used almost to the point of meaninglessness, yet the female, even the idea of her, has become a product, denigrated beyond recognition, to such a point where her torture is more than just entertainment, it is in fact furthering political ideologies and technological advances which seek new ways to capitalize on the sexual exploitation of the female body and image.

The concept of technological neutrality is outdated and must be re-examined. The idea that technology can exist in a vacuum, free from the bias and intent of its creator, is becoming irrelevant as the boundaries between technology and society disappear. The more technology blends with our personal lives, the less the distinction matters; artificial intelligence and streaming pornography are not the equivalent of technology that is, say, a spoon, or a book. We continue to lump many human creations under this term while technology becomes more interactive and enables profound human rights abuses. Moreover, abusive behavior that takes place online is intertwined with notions of "free speech," meaning that the existence of the medium placed between the perpetrator and victim transforms abuse into the self-expression of the abuser. Digital sexual abuse and projected rape then become classified as "free speech" simply because they are published online, and the theft of women's images to profit from their dehumanization becomes a protected right in the eyes of the law.

It is important to consider how many of our modern technologies we take for granted were advanced by men seeking to sexually exploit women, including streaming video, deepfake technology, and certain aspects of the internet. Therefore, it should not be surprising that men eagerly use these tools to further their subjugation of women and children and profit from their rape, both physical and mental. As Andrea Dworkin explained:

> *When your rape is entertainment, your worthlessness is absolute. You have reached the nadir of social worthlessness. The civil impact of pornography on women is staggering. One lives inside a nightmare of sexual abuse that is both actual and potential, and you have the great joy of knowing that your nightmare is someone else's freedom and someone else's fun.*

It will not be enough to continue to challenge emerging technologies as each human rights violation against women emerges. If we assume that approach, we will always be on the defensive, and we can't possibly keep up. We must 1) challenge the long-held idea of the neutrality of technology and 2) continue to work within our circles to change minds about the nature of women's reality and resist the commodification of women wherever we see it. We have truth on our side, whereas the images in pornography and shared elsewhere online are based in lies.

The men who are spreading these lies, profiting from digital sexual abuse, encouraging and participating in rape as a form of entertainment, are not separate from the technology they wield to do so: men are wielding emerging media to terrorize women. That such technology is considered to have a fundamental right to exist, whereas women do not have a fundamental right to safety, dignity, or bodily integrity is a violation and a hypocrisy that must be confronted.

Works Cited

"K-Pop Stars' Gang Rape, Spycam Jail Terms Significantly Reduced." *South Korea News | Al Jazeera*, Al Jazeera, 12 May 2020, www.

aljazeera.com/news/2020/05/pop-stars-gang-rape-spycam-jail-terms-significantly-reduced-200512091349608.html.

"South Korea Porn: Co-Founder of the Soranet Site Jailed." *BBC News*, BBC, 9 Jan. 2019, www.bbc.com/news/world-asia-46810775.

"Trailing Women With a Camera Was Legal, Appeals Court Rules." *The New York Times*, 12 May 2020, https://www.nytimes.com/2020/05/12/us/privacy-laws-public-tennessee.html.

"Two Men Arrested Over Deepfake Pornography Videos." *The Japan Times*, 2 Oct. 2020, https://www.japan-times.co.jp/news/2020/10/02/national/crime-legal/two-men-arrested-deepfake-pornography-videos/.

"Two Million People Sign Petition to Shut Down Pornhub for Sex Trafficking Videos." *Exodus Cry*, PR Newswire, 1 Sept. 2020, www.prnewswire.com/news-releases/two-million-people-sign-petition-to-shut-down-pornhub-for-sex-trafficking-videos-301122030.html.

Baraka, Jewell. "BREAKING: Young Women Trafficked onto Pornhub Via Fake Modeling Ads." *Exodus Cry*, 24 July 2020, https://exoduscry.com/blog/shiftingculture/breaking-young-women-trafficked-onto-pornhub-via-fake-modeling-ads/.

Bicker, Laura. "South Korea's Spy Cam Porn Epidemic." *BBC News*, BBC, 3 Aug. 2018, www.bbc.com/news/world-asia-45040968.

Boseley, Matilda. "Revenge porn: most perpetrators in Victoria spared jail for the crime, report finds." *The Guardian*, 26 Oct. 2020, https://www.theguardian.com/society/2020/oct/27/revenge-porn-most-perpetrators-in-victoria-spared-jail-for-the-report-finds.

Burgess, Matt. "Porn Sites Still Won't Take Down Nonconsensual Deepfakes." *Wired*, Conde Nast, 30 Aug. 2020, www.wired.com/story/porn-sites-still-wont-take-down-non-consensual-deepfakes/.

Burke, Minyvonne. "Florida Man Arrested after Videos of Missing Teen Surface on Pornography Website." *NBCNews.com*, NBCUniversal News Group, 25 Oct. 2019, www.nbcnews.com/news/crime-courts/florida-man-arrested-after-videos-missing-teen-surface-pornography-website-n1072141.

Chung, Lawrence. "Taiwanese Playboy Justin Lee Handed 80-Year Prison Term for Rape." *South China Morning Post*, 3 Sept. 2014, www.scmp.com/news/china/article/1583748/taiwanese-socialite-justin-lee-handed-80-year-prison-term-date-rapes.

Citron, Danielle. *Hate Crimes in Cyberspace*. Harvard Univ Press, 2016.

Cohen, Arianne. "Shocking study finds 1 in 3 are victims of 'revenge porn' or image-based sexual abuse." *Fast Company*, 2 Feb. 2020, https://www.fastcompany.com/90467411/shocking-study-finds-1-in-3-are-victims-of-revenge-porn-or-image-based-sexual-abuse.

Cole, Samantha. "AI-Assisted Fake Porn Is Here and We're All Fucked." *Vice*, 12 Dec. 2017, www.vice.com/en_us/article/gydydm/gal-gadot-fake-ai-porn.

Criddle, Cristina. "'Revenge Porn New Normal' after Cases Surge in Lockdown." *BBC News*, BBC, 16 Sept. 2020, www.bbc.com/news/technology-54149682.

Das, Shanti. "PayPal Cuts off Porn Site That Ran Child Abuse Videos." *News | The Sunday Times*, 17 Nov. 2019, www.thetimes.

co.uk/article/paypal-cuts-off-porn-site-that-ran-child-abuse-videos-98j2bdnjt.

Das, Shanti. "Unilever and Heinz Pay for Ads on Pornhub, the World's Biggest Porn Site." *News | The Sunday Times*, 3 Nov. 2019, www.thetimes.co.uk/article/unilever-and-heinz-pay-for-ads-on-pornhub-the-worlds-biggest-porn-site-knjzlmwzv.

Davies, Sophie. "Upskirting to Cyber-Flashing: Lawmakers Face Calls to Punish Digital Sex Abuse." *Reuters*, Thomson Reuters, 16 Mar. 2020, uk.reuters.com/article/us-women-laws-internet-trfn/upskirting-to-cyber-flashing-lawmakers-face-calls-to-punish-digital-sex-abuse-idUSKBN2100JM.

Dickson, EJ. "TikTok Stars Are Being Turned Into Deepfake Porn Without Their Consent." *Rolling Stone*, 26 Oct. 2020, www.rollingstone.com/culture/culture-features/tiktok-creators-deepfake-pornography-discord-pornhub-1078859/.

Do, Youjin, et al. "These Aren't Random Objects. They're Hidden Cameras." *KOREA EXPOSÉ*, 4 Sept. 2018, www.koreaexpose.com/south-koreas-spycam-porn-epidemic/.

Dworkin, Andrea. *Intercourse*. Free Press, 1987.

Dworkin, Andrea. *Letters From a War Zone*. Lawrence Hill Books, 1993.

Gallien, Stephen. "Tuscaloosa Man Charged for Producing Porn with a Minor, Uploading It to PornHub." *WBMA*, WBMA, 17 Sept. 2020, https://abc3340.com/news/local/pornhub-account-tied-to-tuscaloosa-mans-arrest-for-producing-porn-with-a-minor.

Hao, Karen. "A Deepfake Bot Is Being Used to 'Undress' Underage Girls." *MIT Technology Review*, 28 Oct. 2020, www.technologyreview.com/2020/10/20/1010789/ ai-deepfake-bot-undresses-women-and-underage-girls/.

Kakizaki, Makoto, et al. "Japan Police Arrest 3 Men over Deepfake Porn Using Faces of Celebrities." *The Mainichi*, 2 Oct. 2020, mainichi.jp/english/articles/20201002/p2a/00m/0na/027000c.

Lee, Sophia. "Cho Joo Bin Revealed to Have Plotted the Murder of a Young Girl With a Paid Member of 'Nth Room.'" *Koreaboo*, 26 Mar. 2020, www.koreaboo.com/news/ cho-joo-bin-plot-murder-paid-member-nth-room/.

Lenhart, Amanda, Michelle Ybarra, and Myeshia Price-Feeney. "Nonconsensual Image Sharing: One in 25 Americans Has Been A Victim of "Revenge Porn," 13 Dec. 2016, www.datasociety.net, file:///C:/Users/ATHENA~1/AppData/Local/Temp/ Nonconsensual_Image_Sharing_2016.pdf.

Marturello, Mike. "Indiana's revenge porn law ruled unconstitutional in Steuben case." The Herald Republican, 6 Nov. 2020, https://www.kpcnews.com/heraldrepublican/article_d67bfc4b-6dec-5d62-bf53-5d8b57b63590.html.

May, Tiffany, and Su-hyun Lee. "1,600 Motel Guests Were Secretly Streamed Live in South Korea, Police Say." *The New York Times*, 21 Mar. 2019, www.nytimes.com/2019/03/21/world/asia/ korea-spycam-hotel-livestream.html.

May, Tiffany, and Su-hyun Lee. "K-Pop Singer Jung Joon-Young Admits to Illicitly Filming Women." *The New York Times*, 13 Mar. 2019, www.nytimes.com/2019/03/13/world/asia/jung-joon-young-sex-videos.html.

McLuhan, Marshall. *Understanding Media*. McGraw-Hill, 1964.

Mickelwait, Laila. "Time to Shut Pornhub Down." *Washington Examiner*, 17 Feb. 2020, www.washingtonexaminer.com/opinion/time-to-shut-pornhub-down.

Park, Jun-hee. "What Is 'Nth Room' Case and Why It Matters." *The Korea Herald*, 24 Apr. 2020, www.koreaherald.com/view.php?ud=20200424000512.

Pinto, Anoushka. "Pornhub 'Profited from Child Rape' but Never Paid Compensation, Allege Victims." *MEAWW*, 8 Apr. 2020, https://meaww.com/pornhub-child-rape-victims-actively-profited-no-compensations-accusation-reparations-pornography.

Repard, Pauline. "22 Women Win $13 Million in Suit against GirlsDoPorn Videos." *Los Angeles Times*, 3 Jan. 2020, www.latimes.com/california/story/2020-01-02/lawsuit-girlsdoporn-videos.

Solsman, Joan E. "Samsung Deepfake AI Could Fabricate a Video of You from a Single Profile Pic." *CNET*, CNET, 24 May 2019, www.cnet.com/news/samsung-ai-deepfake-can-fabricate-a-video-of-you-from-a-single-photo-mona-lisa-cheapfake-dumbfake/.

Steger, Isabella. "An Epic Battle between Feminism and Deep-Seated Misogyny Is under Way in South Korea." *Quartz*, Quartz, 3 Apr. 2017, https://qz.com/801067/an-epic-battle-between-feminism-and-deep-seated-misogyny-is-under-way-in-south-korea/.

Sukumaran, Tashny. "Malaysian Survivors of Telegram Porn Scandal Lead Calls for Change." *South China Morning Post*, 1 Nov. 2020, www.scmp.com/week-asia/people/article/3107952/

malaysian-survivors-telegram-porn-scandal-abuse-and-exploitation.

Tai, Crystal. "'My Life Is Not Your Porn': South Korean Women Fight Back against Hidden-Camera Sex Crimes." *South China Morning Post*, South China Morning Post, 13 Oct. 2018, www.scmp.com/week-asia/long-reads/article/2168028/my-life-not-your-porn-south-korean-women-fight-back-against.

Vollmer, Dana, "Is 'Revenge Porn' Free Speech?" *NPR Illinois*, 14 May 2019, https://www.nprillinois.org/post/revenge-porn-free-speech#stream/0.

Webb, Caitlin, and Sally Weale. "More than 500 Child Victims of 'Revenge Porn' in England and Wales Last Year." *The Guardian*, Guardian News and Media, 9 Oct. 2020, www.theguardian.com/society/2020/oct/09/more-than-500-child-victims-of-revenge-porn-in-england-and-wales-last-year.

Wilson, Geoffrey. "Addimando Sentenced to 19 Years to Life in Murder of Boyfriend Grover in Poughkeepsie." *Poughkeepsie Journal*, 11 Feb. 2020, www.poughkeepsiejournal.com/story/news/crime/2020/02/11/nicole-addimando-sentenced-murder-christopher-grover-poughkeepsie/4694452002/.

Yi, Beh Lih. "Untouched Yet Ruined: The Toll of South Korea's Spy-Cam Epidemic." *The Japan Times*, 13 Jan. 2020, www.japantimes.co.jp/news/2020/01/13/asia-pacific/crime-legal-asia-pacific/south-korea-spy-cam-epidemic/.

Endnotes

1   Tai, Crystal. "'My Life Is Not Your Porn': South Korean Women
     Fight Back against Hidden-Camera Sex Crimes." *South China
     Morning Post*, 13 Oct. 2018, www.scmp.com/week-asia/long-reads/
     article/2168028/my-life-not-your-porn-south-korean-women-fight-
     back-against.

2   Davies, Sophie. "Upskirting to Cyber-Flashing: Lawmakers Face
     Calls to Punish Digital Sex Abuse." *Reuters*, Thomson Reuters,
     16 Mar. 2020, https://www.reuters.com/article/us-women-laws-
     internet-trfn/upskirting-to-cyber-flashing-lawmakers-face-calls-to-
     punish-digital-sex-abuse-idUSKBN2100JM?edition-redirect=uk.

3   Yi, Beh Lih. "Untouched Yet Ruined: The Toll of South Korea's Spy-
     Cam Epidemic." *The Japan Times*, 13 Jan. 2020, www.japantimes.
     co.jp/news/2020/01/13/asia-pacific/crime-legal-asia-pacific/south-
     korea-spy-cam-epidemic/.

4   Bicker, Laura. "South Korea's Spy Cam Porn Epidemic." *BBC News*,
     BBC, 3 Aug. 2018, www.bbc.com/news/world-asia-45040968.

5   May, Tiffany, and Su-hyun Lee. "K-Pop Singer Jung Joon-Young
     Admits to Illicitly Filming Women." *The New York Times*, 13 Mar.
     2019, www.nytimes.com/2019/03/13/world/asia/jung-joon-young-
     sex-videos.html.

6   May, Tiffany, and Su-hyun Lee. "1,600 Motel Guests Were Secretly
     Streamed Live in South Korea, Police Say." *The New York Times*, 21
     Mar. 2019, www.nytimes.com/2019/03/21/world/asia/korea-spycam-
     hotel-livestream.html.

7   "K-Pop Stars' Gang Rape, Spycam Jail Terms Significantly Reduced."
     South Korea News | Al Jazeera, 12 May 2020, www.aljazeera.com/
     news/2020/05/pop-stars-gang-rape-spycam-jail-terms-significantly-
     reduced-200512091349608.html.

8   May, Tiffany, and Su-hyun Lee. "K-Pop Singer Jung Joon-Young
     Admits to Illicitly Filming Women." *The New York Times*, 13 Mar.
     2019, www.nytimes.com/2019/03/13/world/asia/jung-joon-young-
     sex-videos.html.

9   Yi, Beh Lih. "Untouched Yet Ruined: The Toll of South Korea's Spy-
     Cam Epidemic." *The Japan Times*, 13 Jan. 2020, www.japantimes.
     co.jp/news/2020/01/13/asia-pacific/crime-legal-asia-pacific/south-
     korea-spy-cam-epidemic/.

10 Park, Jun-hee. "What Is 'Nth Room' Case and Why It Matters." *The Korea Herald*, 24 Apr. 2020, www.koreaherald.com/view. php?ud=20200424000512.

11 Nth Room Awareness, https://nthroom.carrd.co/.

12 Lee, Sophia. "Cho Joo Bin Revealed to Have Plotted the Murder of a Young Girl With a Paid Member of 'Nth Room.'" *Koreaboo*, 26 Mar. 2020, www.koreaboo.com/news/cho-joo-bin-plot-murder-paid-member-nth-room/.

13 Steger, Isabella. "An Epic Battle between Feminism and Deep-Seated Misogyny Is under Way in South Korea." *Quartz*, 3 Apr. 2017, https://qz.com/801067/an-epic-battle-between-feminism-and-deep-seated-misogyny-is-under-way-in-south-korea/.

14 Do, Youjin, et al. "These Aren't Random Objects. They're Hidden Cameras." KOREA EXPOSÉ, 4 Sept. 2018, www.koreaexpose.com/south-koreas-spycam-porn-epidemic/.

15 "South Korea Porn: Co-Founder of the Soranet Site Jailed." *BBC News*, BBC, 9 Jan. 2019, www.bbc.com/news/world-asia-46810775.

16 "Two Million People Sign Petition to Shut Down Pornhub for Sex Trafficking Videos." *Exodus Cry*, PR Newswire, 1 Sept. 2020, www. prnewswire.com/news-releases/two-million-people-sign-petition-to-shut-down-pornhub-for-sex-trafficking-videos-301122030.html.

17 Burke, Minyvonne. "Florida Man Arrested after Videos of Missing Teen Surface on Pornography Website." *NBCNews.com*, NBCUniversal News Group, 25 Oct. 2019, www.nbcnews.com/news/crime-courts/florida-man-arrested-after-videos-missing-teen-surface-pornography-website-n1072141.

18 Repard, Pauline. "22 Women Win $13 Million in Suit against GirlsDoPorn Videos." *Los Angeles Times*, 3 Jan. 2020, www.latimes. com/california/story/2020-01-02/lawsuit-girlsdoporn-videos.

19 Baraka, Jewell. "BREAKING: Young Women Trafficked onto Pornhub Via Fake Modeling Ads." *Exodus Cry*, 24 July 2020, https:// exoduscry.com/blog/shiftingculture/breaking-young-women-trafficked-onto-pornhub-via-fake-modeling-ads/.

20 Das, Shanti. "Unilever and Heinz Pay for Ads on Pornhub, the World's Biggest Porn Site." *News | The Sunday Times*, 3 Nov. 2019, www.thetimes.co.uk/article/unilever-and-heinz-pay-for-ads-on-pornhub-the-worlds-biggest-porn-site-knjzlmwzv.

21 Das, Shanti. "PayPal Cuts off Porn Site That Ran Child Abuse Videos." *News | The Sunday Times*, 17 Nov. 2019, www.thetimes.co.uk/article/paypal-cuts-off-porn-site-that-ran-child-abuse-videos-98j2bdnjt.

22 Gallien, Stephen. "Tuscaloosa Man Charged for Producing Porn with a Minor, Uploading It to PornHub." *WBMA*, WBMA, 17 Sept. 2020, https://abc3340.com/news/local/pornhub-account-tied-to-tuscaloosa-mans-arrest-for-producing-porn-with-a-minor.

23 Wilson, Geoffrey. "Addimando Sentenced to 19 Years to Life in Murder of Boyfriend Grover in Poughkeepsie." *Poughkeepsie Journal*, 11 Feb. 2020, www.poughkeepsiejournal.com/story/news/crime/2020/02/11/nicole-addimando-sentenced-murder-christopher-grover-poughkeepsie/4694452002/.

24 Chung, Lawrence. "Taiwanese Playboy Justin Lee Handed 80-Year Prison Term for Rape." *South China Morning Post*, 3 Sept. 2014, www.scmp.com/news/china/article/1583748/taiwanese-socialite-justin-lee-handed-80-year-prison-term-date-rapes.

25 Pinto, Anoushka. "Pornhub 'Profited from Child Rape' but Never Paid Compensation, Allege Victims." *MEAWW*, 8 Apr. 2020, https://meaww.com/pornhub-child-rape-victims-actively-profited-no-compensations-accusation-reparations-pornography.

26 Criddle, Cristina. "'Revenge Porn New Normal' after Cases Surge in Lockdown." *BBC News*, BBC, 16 Sept. 2020, www.bbc.com/news/technology-54149682.

27 Lenhart, Amanda, Michelle Ybarra, and Myeshia Price-Feeney. "Nonconsensual Image Sharing: One in 25 Americans Has Been A Victim of "Revenge Porn," 13 Dec. 2016, www.datasociety.net, file:///C:/Users/ATHENA~1/AppData/Local/Temp/Nonconsensual_Image_Sharing_2016.pdf.

28 Sukumaran, Tashny. "Malaysian Survivors of Telegram Porn Scandal Lead Calls for Change." *South China Morning Post*, 1 Nov. 2020, www.scmp.com/week-asia/people/article/3107952/malaysian-survivors-telegram-porn-scandal-abuse-and-exploitation.

29 Cohen, Arianne. "Shocking study finds 1 in 3 are victims of 'revenge porn' or image-based sexual abuse." *Fast Company*, 2 Feb. 2020, https://www.fastcompany.com/90467411/shocking-study-finds-1-in-3-are-victims-of-revenge-porn-or-image-based-sexual-abuse.

30 Webb, Caitlin, and Sally Weale. "More than 500 Child Victims of 'Revenge Porn' in England and Wales Last Year." *The Guardian*, 9

Oct. 2020, www.theguardian.com/society/2020/oct/09/more-than-500-child-victims-of-revenge-porn-in-england-and-wales-last-year.

31   Boseley, Matilda. "Revenge porn: most perpetrators in Victoria spared jail for the crime, report finds." *The Guardian,* 26 Oct. 2020, https://www.theguardian.com/society/2020/oct/27/revenge-porn-most-perpetrators-in-victoria-spared-jail-for-the-report-finds.

32   Marturello, Mike. "Indiana's revenge porn law ruled unconstitutional in Steuben case." *The Herald Republican,* 6 Nov. 2020, https://www.kpcnews.com/heraldrepublican/article_d67bfc4b-6dec-5d62-bf53-5d8b57b63590.html.

33   "Trailing Women With a Camera Was Legal, Appeals Court Rules," *The New York Times,* 12 May 2020, https://www.nytimes.com/2020/05/12/us/privacy-laws-public-tennessee.html.

34   Vollmer, Dana, "Is 'Revenge Porn' Free Speech?" *NPR Illinois,* 14 May 2019, https://www.nprillinois.org/post/revenge-porn-free-speech#stream/0.

35   Cole, Samantha, "AI-Assisted Fake Porn Is Here and We're All Fucked." *Vice.com,* 11 Dec. 2017, https://www.vice.com/en/article/gydydm/gal-gadot-fake-ai-porn.

36   Solsman, Joan E. "Samsung Deepfake AI Could Fabricate a Video of You from a Single Profile Pic." *CNET*, 24 May 2019, www.cnet.com/news/samsung-ai-deepfake-can-fabricate-a-video-of-you-from-a-single-photo-mona-lisa-cheapfake-dumbfake.

37   Burgess, Matt. "Porn Sites Still Won't Take Down Nonconsensual Deepfakes." *Wired*, Conde Nast, 30 Aug. 2020, www.wired.com/story/porn-sites-still-wont-take-down-non-consensual-deepfakes/.

38   Hao, Karen. "A Deepfake Bot Is Being Used to 'Undress' Underage Girls." *MIT Technology Review*, 28 Oct. 2020, www.technologyreview.com/2020/10/20/1010789/ai-deepfake-bot-undresses-women-and-underage-girls/.

39   Dickson, EJ. "TikTok Stars Are Being Turned Into Deepfake Porn Without Their Consent." *Rolling Stone*, 26 Oct. 2020, www.rollingstone.com/culture/culture-features/tiktok-creators-deepfake-pornography-discord-pornhub-1078859/.

40   "Two Men Arrested Over Deepfake Pornography Videos." *The Japan Times,* 2 Oct. 2020, https://www.japantimes.co.jp/news/2020/10/02/national/crime-legal/two-men-arrested-deepfake-pornography-videos/.

CHAPTER 30

A Chatroom of Our Own: Building Online Spaces by and For Women in the Era of Big Tech Censorship

by M. K. Fain

As a young feminist, I have always looked to my feminist foremothers for wisdom, guidance, and understanding of the world around us. Feminists before me have correctly anticipated the rise of porn culture, the limits of liberal feminism, and the dangers of gender identity ideology. We learn from the gains and losses of the generations of brave women before us to put our own wins and failures in a broader context.

But in one major area, feminists have come up utterly unprepared. The ground on which the war for women's humanity, safety, and dignity is being fought has shifted beneath us—and feminists were caught unaware. The tools of our past, like consciousness-raising groups or radical leaflets and zines, cannot compete with the new largest global force for patriarchy: technology.

In what feels like a blink of an eye, our world has changed. In 1996, the first time it was counted, there were about 40 million internet users.[1] In 2020 they are over 4.5 billion—about 60% of the world's population. Since the year 2000, this represents a 1,187% increase.[2] The overwhelming majority of those users (3.8 billion) are on social media.[3] The power to reach the population directly has changed how politicians, advertisers, and activists share and spread information. Social media has been a vital tool for everything from passing new laws to regime change. The means of communication, access to money, and the ability to gain power are increasingly occurring in the digital realm. Much like the "real world," these spaces are run by and for men.

Men control the tools we use to spread information to the masses, like Twitter. Men control the platforms we use to connect with like-minded groups, like Facebook. Men control the places where we can publish our ideas online, like Medium and Wordpress.com. Men control the ways we search for information, like Google. Men control the app stores we use download tools to our phones, like Apple.

The unprecedented rise in misogyny the West is experiencing is fueled by this technology. A porn-saturated internet is hijacking the brains of young boys and men, training girls to view themselves as objects, and shifting the expectations of female sexuality. Porn-sick boys raised on the internet-fueled degradation of women grow up to be porn-sick men working at companies like Google, Apple, Facebook, and Twitter, where they control what women can and cannot say.

These men protect their power, privilege, and access to female sexual objectification at all costs. That cost is often the censorship and silencing of feminists.

More feminists than I can name have been banned from Twitter for resisting patriarchal ideas, like the colonization of womanhood—Meghan Murphy, Claire Graham, and Maria MacLachlan, to name a few. Feminist writers like Issy Dickenson, Barra Kerr, and myself have all had content censored on Medium, a free blogging platform. Feminist websites like a site run by the Women's Liberation Front (WoLF) have been taken down by companies like Wordpress.com. Multiple radical feminist communities, such as r/GenderCritical, which had nearly 65,000 members, were banned from Reddit in June of 2020. Feminist censorship and #cancelculture is no longer just women getting fired, de-platformed from conferences, or socially shunned (although, all of those things have happened to me, too).

Misogynists are attempting to make it impossible for feminists to access even the most basic communication tools, and it is crippling our movement.

This is not just a problem of needing more women in tech. The problem is deeper than that, and goes to the very core of how Big Tech has been able to operate with virtually no oversight or accountability. The only solution is to separate from our reliance on male-controlled tech and to build our own spaces, tools, and networks run by and for women.

The problem with Big Tech

Most internet traffic today goes through one of a few companies. Fifty percent of internet sales go through Amazon.[4] Twitter has 166 million "monetizable daily active users."[5] Facebook has over 220 million.[6] One company, Google, controls 72 percent of mobile phone operating systems,[7] 64 percent of web browsers,[8] 87 percent of desktop web searches,[9] and 96 percent of mobile searches.[10] YouTube, which is owned by Google, has two billion active monthly users, and is used by 73 percent of US adults.[11]

This problem is called *centralization*: when a single company has a near-monopoly on communication or information in a particular area. Centralization gives the companies the ultimate power, and the user essentially none. This is because the user has basically nowhere else to go.

The problem is compounded by the widespread use of *proprietary software*. Proprietary software is code that is kept secret from the user, or is not licensed for re-use. This is a problem for tech activists who wish to push back against Big Tech centralization. Because the code is secret, it is hard to build comparable spaces that can compete with the money behind a site like Facebook, for example.

Free software aims to help solve this problem. Free software is code that is public and available for re-use, modification, and distribution. It is also commonly referred to as "open-source software."

When a platform is both centralized and proprietary, users of that software have essentially no recourse when the admins of that platform act in a way that harms the users—such as engaging in censorship. This is the problem that feminists are currently facing. Platforms like Twitter, Google, Facebook, YouTube, and Medium are both centralized and proprietary. When you are banned, censored, or silenced on one of these platforms, it can do major damage to your ability to get the word out about your cause, build an audience, raise money, or promote events—all which are important to a grassroots movement.

If you think simply following the rules of these platforms will protect you, you're in for a rude awakening. All of the above have demonstrated that they are not interested in fairly enforcing rules across all users. Women and feminists are particularly targeted. Take, for example, Twitter. Thousands of accounts remain on the platform after hurling misogynistic abuse at women, especially feminists or victims of male violence who have come forward. Yet, feminist writer Meghan Murphy was banned from the platform for tweeting the phrase, "Yeeeah, it's him." In this case, the word "him" was found to be a violation of Twitter's rule against hateful conduct, because it "misgendered" a male person who identifies as a woman. The double standard would be shocking if it was not so common.

Change.org, a popular petition site, removed a petition with thousands of signatures on it titled "Don't Call Us Menstruators," protesting the new word commonly used to refer to women by their bodily function. Change.org claims that, "As an open platform, we're committed to free speech,"[12] yet they deleted the petition after it was up for only three days.

On the blogging platform Medium, hundreds, if not thousands, of articles exist promoting porn, BDSM, and violent or degrading sexuality. "All About Double Penetration," "Drink Come Like a Vanilla Milkshake," "How to Use Pornhub Ethically," and "Why I Let My Partner Choke Me" are all articles that Medium deems acceptable. Yet, my own account was suspended after publishing an interview with Lesbian Youtuber Arielle Scarcella in which she discusses why she decided to "leave the left." The CEO and Founder of Medium, Evan Williams, was also formerly a co-founder, CEO, and chairman of Twitter. He also previously worked for Google. All of these men are connected. They control the internet which, today, means they might as well control the world.

The problem of misogyny in tech goes beyond Big Tech, though. From the very beginning of the industry, a concerted effort was made to pry any potential power away from the hands of women. Women were the original programmers since the job stemmed from typist and administrative positions that women were likely to hold at the time. Many of the early pioneers of computer engineering were women, like Grace Hopper and Ada Lovelace. Hopper identified the first computer "bug"—a month who had gotten trapped in the computer's wires.

Women were over 50 percent of the programmers selected to work on the first US Military computer in 1946.[13] They were using "pair programming" over fifty years before the concept took off in modern tech culture. Women are not only absolutely capable of good programming: we invented it.[14] Women were pushed out of the industry as it became increasingly clear that there was money and power to be gained.

Although there are many women in tech today, the bias persists. The net result is that women are not founding the companies that will go on to rule the internet, are not decision-makers at these companies, are not equally represented on tech teams, and, as a whole, lack the skills and resources that are necessary to win a culture war in the 21st Century. If we want to stand a chance at improving the lives of women and girls in the future, we must prioritize the digital battlefront.

The importance of online resilience

In a perfect feminist utopia, women would control the entire means of digital communication. In the not-so-ideal reality in which we currently live, this is essentially impossible.

Consider the process of baking a cake from scratch. Perhaps you mix the flower, sugar, water, and vegan egg alternative in a bowl. You pour that batter into a pan, and put the pan in the oven. A bit later you pull it out and enjoy your cake. You proudly announce that you "made the cake from scratch."

What you mean is, rather than buying a cake, you went out and bought the ingredients which you then turned into a cake. You may feel like you control the means of cake-making. But what if there was no flower available to you the markets? Would you have the ability to grow your own grain and convert it into the ingredient you need?

What if the utility company shut off your tap? Would you have another way to get water?

What if your oven broke? Would you be able to fix it?

We take for granted the infrastructure that allows us to build something "from scratch." If one point in the system breaks, our ability to make the cake goes out the window. We never really had the power to make cakes in the first place; we are utterly dependent on modern society functioning as we expect.

This is the same problem facing feminists who are looking to create autonomous spaces by and for women online. Becoming completely autonomous from the male-controlled internet infrastructure is unrealistic as we currently stand. Even if you know how to build your own website with code, you have to host that code somewhere for it to be "served" to your users (aka, a *server*). Examples of hosting providers include GoDaddy, Amazon Web Services, Google Cloud, and Bluehost. Any one of these companies could choose to kick you off of their servers at any time.

Should feminists create their own hosting providers? Absolutely. But the problem does not stop there. Hosts rely on Internet Service Providers (*ISPs*). An example of an ISP is Comcast, or Time Warner Cable. These companies deliver the data from the server where it is stored to the computer where the data is being requested. Those ISPs could limit or censor information they do not want to deliver to you. Thanks to the end of Net Neutrality laws in the United States, this is increasingly likely.

So should feminists build their own ISPs? Absolutely. But then what if there are blocks on accessing certain information in the hardware of your computer or phone itself? This isn't hypothetical. In China, the Communist Party uses a variety of tools to censor outside information from getting to the public. This censorship is known as "The Great Firewall" and impacts nearly every website or service Western internet users have come to rely on. One tool the CCP uses for censorship is by controlling the actual hardware devices themselves.

So should feminists build their own hardware? Absolutely. But you can see where this is going.

Control over the internet is intricately tied up in the control over means of production. Women, as a class, do not generally control the means of production. Until that changes, we have to accept that pure female separatism and freedom from male control online is nearly impossible. This does not mean that resistance is futile, though. It means that rather than focus on separatist purity, building spaces for women online, creating systems of communication we can rely on, and becoming independent from male-controlled Big Tech is a matter of building resilience.

In November of 2019, the blog Gender Identity Watch was suspended by Wordpress.com (their hosting provider). Wordpress.com locked the admin of the site out of their server and would not allow them to recover their media files. Years' worth of archiving work would be lost. Other gender critical blogs such as GenderTrender were also removed based on a selective application of Wordpress.com's Terms of Service.[15] GenderTrender lost eight years of work. Since these websites did not maintain their own backups of their data independent of their host, when Wordpress.com removed their sites they did not have the resilience to go elsewhere. Gender Identity Watch did end up getting their files back from Wordpress.com eventually, but only after threatening them with a lawyer.

What happened to these two blogs is an example of the importance of resilience when building subversive online spaces. If one host bans you, you must be able to pick up and go somewhere else. Single points of failure are the biggest issue facing feminist spaces online at the moment. Unfortunately, this lesson is too often learned the hard way, and years of feminist work is lost in the process. The more attacks we face, though, the more resilience we build.

Building (and protecting) online feminist spaces

Despite the apparent insurmountability of the problem before us, building and maintaining feminist spaces online is actually possible. In August of 2019, my partner and I launched Spinster.xyz, a feminist-centered alternative to Twitter.

Spinster was built using open-source software on a network of inter-connected servers called the *Fediverse*. The Fediverse is different from centralized social media. Rather than having a single company control every single user account, the millions of users on the Fediverse are spread out across thousands of different servers—each running their own version of open-source software. The servers can all talk to each other because they use the same core pattern of sending and receiving data, called a *protocol*. This means that when users join Spinster, they are not just connecting with other feminists. They get plugged into a potentially massive network to spread their message. Many prominent women who were banned from Twitter have joined Spinster to reconnect with their audience, including Kellie-Jay Keen-Minshull (Posie Parker), Meghan Murphy, and Claire Graham (MRKHVoice).

This solves a few problems facing women on Twitter. Spinster, while not a "free speech zone," allows women to discuss radical feminist concepts (like "men can't become women") without fear of being silenced. Since Spinster is not centralized, users who take issue with the politics or moderation practices of the site can join any of a number of other sites that connect with Spinster and still see and engage with our content (Glindr.org and Neenster.org, to name a few). Users are not stuck, beholden to admins or moderators with whom they may disagree. In the early days of Spinster, a group of young women did exactly that—created their own space which now runs parallel to Spinster. Users from Spinster and the new site may still follow and interact with each other. Using decentralized, open-source software made that possible.

Spinster, of course, has faced its fair share of attacks. Other servers on the Fediverse instantly blocked Spinster simply because we were a site for feminists. Trolls from 4chan, a notoriously anti-feminist site, organized DDoS (Distributed Denial of Service) attacks against us. Trans activists mass-reported the Spinster app to the Google Play store and successfully had the Spinster app removed. Each of these attacks trained us on resiliency, though. We learned how to resist attacks and how to build our own solutions when mainstream ones were not available.

This space has been important to many women who have been finding community, empowerment, and courage by connecting with one another. One user posted:

> I didn't really have expectations when I joined Spinster. I was curious and I was longing for a place for women, where we can freely express our opinions. It's been only a few days now and I already feel a sense of sisterhood, a deeper connection with such wonderful women. I love seeing your posts, reading about your experiences, your thoughts, and I am finding myself in so many of them. Being women is what unifies us.

Other women say that their time on Spinster empowered them to become more vocal advocates for women, taking that bravery into their life outside of Spinster. Arianna (@Ari), a user who joined on opening day, wrote:

> After only a few days here, I've noticed changes in my behavior on other social media (and even offline). I'm less

afraid of speaking out and being assertive, I care less about what others might think of my opinions, I feel overall more confident. Knowing that there are so many women who feel and think similarly to me, all compassionate and actively supporting each other, is truly meaningful!

Multiple women found the courage to use their real names while publicly discussing their radical feminist politics for the first time, a frightening and brave thing to do in the face of harassment and attacks. When women get together and speak freely, it results in consciousness-raising, support, and empowerment. This is one of the reasons that women-centered spaces are so vital, and are seen as a threat by men. This is why they need to be protected.

Spinster is not the end of creating feminist spaces online. In response to censorship on blogging platform Medium, many feminist writers have started creating additional platforms where women are freer to share their feminist analysis. 4W, the publication I founded after being kicked off of Medium, is one such example.

After the Reddit feminist purge, feminist technologists from multiple projects, including Spinster, joined together to create Ovarit.com—a radical feminist alternative to Reddit. Once again, we chose to build on existing open source software, working with the developers of that software to help make it feature-complete and scalable. Within a few weeks of Ovarit's invite-only launch, the site already had thousands of users. Now the freedom for women to share links and resources is not controlled by a male-owned company, but rather by the feminist community itself.

Other areas remain less-charted by feminists, though. In some cases, these are areas where we are particularly vulnerable. For example, many feminist women, organizations, and publications rely on Patreon or PayPal for processing payments and monthly donations. Patreon has a history of censoring groups with which it politically disagrees. Although they haven't started deleting feminist accounts yet, many are worried that future is on its way.

Feminists have few alternatives since payment processing is relatively centralized.

Online groups and forums have also struggled to migrate away from centralized social media, such as Facebook. Many women and feminist groups still rely on these platforms despite their blatant hostility to women. But since they are the best way to reach new members, groups feel forced to stay or risk alienating their audience. The risk is clear to users of these sites, though. What holds women back from creating feminist and women-owned online spaces is rarely the desire to do so, but actually finding a team of women with the skills, time, and resources to complete the project.

Making technology accessible to women

As discussed earlier, there is nothing inherent to technology that makes it inaccessible to women as a whole. Women were the first programmers, the first computer engineers, the first coders. Yet, women today face a variety of barriers of entry into technology, making overcoming the problems we face with male-controlled tech even harder to resist. The three major barriers I see for women getting into tech are socialization, culture, and time/money.

When generations of women and girls have been socialized away from an interest in technology, finding enough women who are interested enough in tech to pursue it as a career, let alone as a volunteer or activist, can be hard. Although "Women in STEM" programs can be aggressively liberal and even hostile to feminism, they are right that active effort needs to be put into changing the way women and girls are socialized around technology. The more girls across the board we encourage to gain technological skills, the more future feminist internet resisters we have.

Even when women do become interested in tech, the sexist culture of the field will quickly drive many women away. I lasted less than a year in my first programming job because the leadership was openly hostile to women and feminism. This deeply impacted my willingness to engage in tech communities going forward. I know I'm not alone—women leave the field at a rate nearly 50 percent higher than their male counterparts.[16] Women working in technology need to be supported by feminists, and feminists must make an active effort to build a supportive female community within the tech world.

And even when women do manage to stay in tech as a career, the excess burden placed on women outside of their jobs in their homes, relationships, families, and communities can make contributing to feminist technical projects a barrier. Women, as a whole, lack the time to spend volunteering to design, code, or maintain feminist technology. More importantly, they often lack the money—since money can buy time.

If the feminist movement wants feminist online spaces created and run by women to succeed, there has to be greater recognition of the monetary value of this work. Funding is always a problem in the Movement, and I do not suggest diverting funds from other important work. Yet, finding ways to fund feminist technology will be absolutely essential to building a feminist future in a society increasingly happening online. When we fund feminist technologists, we give women the time and freedom to build the spaces that we will all come to rely on as feminists are censored, banned, and disappeared from mainstream internet spaces. We can't afford *not to* support these projects. A feminist future depends on it.

Endnotes

1   Castells, Manuel. "The Impact of the Internet on Society: A Global Perspective." OpenMind, 2014, www.bbvaopenmind.com/en/articles/the-impact-of-the-internet-on-society-a-global-perspective/.

2   "Internet World Stats." World Internet Users Statistics and 2020 World Population Stats, 12 June 2020, internetworldstats.com/stats.htm.

3   "Global Social Media Research Summary 2020." Smart Insights, 1 June 2020, www.smartinsights.com/social-media-marketing/social-media-strategy/new-global-social-media-research/.

4   Lunden, Ingrid. "Amazon's Share of the US e-Commerce Market Is Now 49%, or 5% of All Retail Spend." *TechCrunch*, TechCrunch, 13 July 2018, https://techcrunch.com/2018/07/13/amazons-share-of-the-us-e-commerce-market-is-now-49-or-5-of-all-retail-spend/ .

5   Clement, J. "Twitter Global MDAU 2020." Statista, 4 May 2020, www.statista.com/statistics/970920/monetizable-daily-active-twitter-users-worldwide/.

6   Clement, J. "Facebook Users in U.S." Statista, 2 Dec. 2019, www.statista.com/statistics/408971/number-of-us-facebook-users/.

7   "Mobile Operating System Market Share Worldwide." StatCounter Global Stats, 2020, https://gs.statcounter.com/os-market-share/mobile/worldwide.

8   "Browser Market Share Worldwide." StatCounter Global Stats, 2020, https://gs.statcounter.com/browser-market-share.

9   Clement, J. "Search Engine Market Share Worldwide." *Statista*, 18 June 2020, www.statista.com/statistics/216573/worldwide-market-share-of-search-engines/.

10 Clement, J. (2020, April 28). U.S. organic search visits by engine 2020. Retrieved August 07, 2020, from www.statista.com/statistics/625554/mobile-share-of-us-organic-search-engine-visits/

11 Iqbal, Mansoor. "YouTube Revenue and Usage Statistics (2020)." *Business of Apps*, 23 June 2020, www.businessofapps.com/data/youtube-statistics/.

12 "Community." Change.org, 15 June 2020, www.change.org/policies/community.

13 Goldberg, Emma. "Perspective | Women Built the Tech Industry. Then They Were Pushed out." The Washington Post, WP Company, 19 Feb. 2019, www.washingtonpost.com/outlook/2019/02/19/ women-built-tech-industry-then-they-were-pushed-out/.

14 Böckeler, Birgitta. "Born for It: How the Image of Software Developers Came About." ThoughtWorks, 19 May 2016, www. thoughtworks.com/insights/blog/born-it-how-image-software- developers-came-about.

15 WoLF Board. "WordPress's Suspension of Gender Identity Watch." Women's Liberation Front, 21 Nov. 2018, womensliberationfront. org/wordpresss-suspension-of-gender-identity-watch/.

16 Florentine, Sharon. "Why Women Leave Tech." CIO, CIO, 16 Nov. 2018, www.cio.com/article/3321897/why-women-leave-tech.html.

PART VII:

"TRANSGENDER" POLITICS AND THE MEN'S SEXUAL RIGHTS MOVEMENT

CHAPTER 31

Against a Hierarchy of Oppressions

By Linda Bellos

I cannot write about contemporary radical feminist theory without addressing the current argument about trans politics, because it is not possible to meet another feminist without our meetings being sabotaged rather like the KKK disrupted meetings of Black activists fighting oppression.

I first wrote about race and gender in 1982 and I have written about this topic off and on since then. Now when asked to contribute to this anthology of contemporary radical feminist theory I find myself responding to the current discourse, or should I say argument between feminists and those men and women who support the new trans politics, and I wish to address it without being shouted down or threatened with violence.

It is now nearly 15 years since I realised that "race" was a concept created by White men as a justification for slavery and imperialism. Men had previously fought with each other and taken each other's lands (and women). But the wholesale theft of human beings and their transportation to the New World was quite another thing. As I write this piece today, people in much of the English-speaking world, as well as significant parts of Europe, are confronting that history of colonisation and the legacy of those European men who were engaged in the enslavement of African men, women, and children.

It is a painful history to consider, but one that must be exposed if the legacy of enslavement and colonisation is ever to be properly addressed.

I am a daughter of a Nigerian man who came Britain at the beginning of 1942; he remained here until his death in 2000, and as his daughter I have experienced racism in Britain that has left its mark. But that is not really the point; my point is that the personal experience of racism remains a current experience and is coupled with my knowledge of being oppressed as a woman, an awareness of which I have been conscious since I was a girl in the 1950's and 60's.

Being a Black woman is a matter of fact, and for the last over more than 60 years, of pride. Being a feminist and a lesbian, I have addressed the notion of gender with the same seriousness as I have the notion of race and sexuality. My view about gender comes from the same analysis which I have applied to race and class. They are man-made notions created to justify and enforce White men's dominance over others. I include here the notion of social class within this hierarchy. This does not make me hate others because they are different from me, or because they have been born into the "dominant" category. I hope that I continue to judge every human being by the content of their character.

But the new trans politics requires women to cease to be a biological category of humanity but instead the category of choice. I, for one, have over the last 20 or so years had as friends a number of people who have reassigned their gender. I am not hostile to those humans whose chromosomes are not clearly XX or XY, but I remain critical of the new politics of trans which has the effect of negating "women" as a category of humanity. What particularly disturbs me about the new trans politics is that it makes free speech of women, especially feminists, almost impossible. And it is often violent or threatens violence towards women. This is ironic since these men act like men whilst claiming to be women.

In Britain there have been several cases in which men who have broken the law and been imprisoned as a consequence, several of whom have been imprisoned for rape, have subsequently claimed to be women and been transferred to women's prisons and raped female inmates. I am not suggesting that all trans people have been similarly motived for claiming to be trans but the fact that it has occurred more than once leads me to the view that the lives of biological women are seen as secondary to those of men who claim to be women.

One good effect of this new trans politics is that it has resulted in many more women identifying as feminists, and the regrouping of many feminists who had not met for many years. Meetings of feminists are occurring in all parts of Great Britain in a way I have not seen since the mid 1980's. But what is disappointing about this new wave of feminists is that they are not building upon work done up to the mid 1980's. I do not mean that there should be no progress from those times but that the ways things are being done now do not reflect the feminist practices of equality and inclusion we developed in the 1970's and 80's. I myself contacted a number of feminists who had attended the court case in which I and Venice Allan had been found **not** guilty after we had been accused of the offence of questioning trans rights.[1] The pub was full of women and a few men who had come to support us in asserting women's rights.

We expressed and shared solidarity as though the demand for women's rights was in need of revival. I went round the large room and asked women if they would like to see the revival of the Women's Liberation Movement ("WLM"), and 90% of the women supported the idea, and 10 women said yes, they wanted to play an active part in restarting the Movement. But this time it would be more inclusive of the diversity of a wider range of women. After four meetings I and my good friend Sheila Jeffreys dropped out of this group because one thing we had not done was explain that how we did things as feminists was as important as what we did. The younger women knew nothing about feminist process, and it seemed to me that many of the younger women did not recognise that if you do things as men do them, for example with women going off and doing their own thing and bringing it back to the group as a done thing, what you get is lots of individual initiatives but no inclusive cohesion. The planning group did not continue.

I call this stuff about how we do things "process." And this attempt to restart the WLM without considering the "how" will remain a problem because it means that we generally excluded women who are "not like us." And if the Women's Liberation Movement does not include all women it will not benefit all women.

I have taken my feminist "process" into most of my work since the 1980's. It is harder to do when you are often the only women in a group of men, or the few other women in the room are not feminists of any kind. But I am still convinced that by the ways we organise our work, seeking it to be inclusive of the widest range of relevant Black or disabled or old or young, poor or rich, people, we might create answers to the question of achieving equality.

My politics has not fundamentally changed over the last 45 years and by that I really mean that my "process" has not really changed. I want to see all of the people impacted by a decision considered and this happens when they are consulted and listened to. They may have better knowledge of the subject than I, and good ideas as to making the issue more effective or less dangerous, and otherwise produce a better policy.

But my overall politics are based upon the notion that all people are of equal value. What do we with those people who have administrative and political power over others and use that power to benefit themselves and their friends? This is a long-standing problem usually benefitting men. And it is usually women who suffer from the consequences of this abuse of power. I have seen racism in these terms, a system which seeks to justify power over others, and as a Black woman I see the operation of a hierarchy of oppression whose purpose has been to divide and rule. Admittedly I have seen a number of White women who go out of their way to benefit from the oppression of Black women, but most are being challenged by Black women. And I am making this point because I do not believe that all Black women are perfect, nor that all White women are racists. But I do recognise that the notion of race is a man-made notion as is gender.

Racism is as real as sexism; these are the manifestations of ideologies which value humans differently dependent upon their genitalia. And what is so problematic about the new gender politics is that it is dependent upon a belief that humans may change simply by changing their outward presentation, but they bring with them their relative power over women and girls. This led to an extremely ironic example in 2018 in which a man who several years ago decided that he was a woman took me and Venice Allan to court because we had questioned his and other trans "women's" right to call themselves a woman.[2] Or at least he perceived that by my speaking to a meeting at which he was not present he had been harmed. The speeches were broadcast via the internet. The man went out of his way to listen to what I had to say about the physical attack on Maria MacLachlan.[3] I referenced that incident and said that if I were attacked as she was I would use the skills my father had taught me to defend myself. It seems that he sought out a recording of that speech presumably so that he could be offended by it. Anyway he did not win his case, but it is one that illustrates some of the foolishness of the argument of this, the new trans politics.

What it did do for me was bring me back to feminist politics which I had stepped away from whilst caring for my partner who died of cervical cancer five years from her diagnosis. Caroline died in September 2015.

All these matters have played a part in my revaluation of equality and I return to feminism to fill the gaping need to revisit the notion and practice of oppression. Not as a competitive reality but as a set of historical events that have shaped current events. These have been about power, not power to win a tennis championship. But power *over* others. The police officer in Minnesota who killed George Floyd[4] used his power to deprive another human being of oxygen. And he did so because he could. Just as countless men murder and rape women and girls because they can.

My politics have been about wanting to change the world, but first I have had to answer the question change it "from what to what?" As I finish this short essay, I am saddened by where we are at as a world, in which we see some lives as more important than other lives. What I know is that feminism has a methodology which has the potential to be useful to all to humans if we get away from the notion that some of us are more equal than others.

I am not sure how we measure oppression and how we might gauge it. Indeed, I am pretty certain that we should not try to measure oppression. Those of us who have a notion that the oppression of women is wrong, are, in my view going to have to stop being competitive about who is the most oppressed. I am not sure that it is a competition worth winning.

If we wish to change the world to make it a safe environment for all human beings and all living beings, significant changes have to occur and I hope that the politics that I engage with henceforth, will allow me and others to work in small groups respecting all others within that group, acting and listening respectfully with each other. I will not hold my breath, but I know that when there was a Women's Liberation Movement we got fairly near this practice of operating by this very unmale method. We did not get it right and I know for certain that there was little understanding of racism or discrimination because of disability and social class and that we struggled to listen to each other. But the politics I have engaged with which were not feminist, came nowhere near Women's Liberation's good practice.

My politics I hope, reflect the notion of equality as central. I do not know how painful your headache is, relative to mine, but I would like to see the end of all headaches.

Endnotes

1   "Gudrun Young Successfully Defends Leading Feminist & Anti-Racist Campaigner Linda Bellos OBE in Private Prosecution." *2 Hare Court website*, 30th November 2018, https://www.2harecourt.com/2018/11/30/gudrun-young-successfully-defends-leading-feminist-anti-racist-campaigner-linda-bellos-obe/?fbclid=IwAR08eqz0GNC36QDO8Qkjnpy5e-bU950c08n8Ufluz001-j1Ydx9j1WUfKZaM.

2   "Veteran Labour activist facing private prosecution over anti-trans comments." *The Telegraph*, 26 September 2018, https://www.telegraph.co.uk/news/2018/09/26/veteran-labour-activist-facing-private-prosecution-anti-trans/.

3   "Trans-identified male, Tara Wolf, convicted of assault after Hyde Park attack." *Feminist Current*, 27 April 2018, https://www.feministcurrent.com/2018/04/27/trans-identified-male-tara-wolf-charged-assault-hyde-park-attack/.

4   "How George Floyd Was Killed in Police Custody." *The New York Times*, 31 May 2020, https://www.nytimes.com/2020/05/31/us/george-floyd-investigation.html.

CHAPTER 32

Birth of a Radical Feminist

by Jamae Hawkins

Ireached my "peak trans" moment at the same time I was done being a Liberal. It occurred several days after I marched in the Women's March on January 21, 2017, shortly after Donald Trump's inauguration. Being a dedicated Democratic Liberal, I wanted to bask in the glow of being inclusive to everyone's issue and to object to Donald J. Trump being president. Women wore pink pussy hats and vagina costumes, I thought it was clever and expressive. I was participating in the march because I was just damn pissed that we elected a wannabe dictator and wanted to physically be in front of The White House to express displeasure. The march was peaceful and well attended by all people representing all different issues. I no longer saw it as just a women's march, but a solidarity of citizens disturbed about what is to come.

Days after the march, social media was flooded with trans activists complaining that they were violently excluded. Huh? They said that by women wearing pussy hats and wearing vagina costumes they were excluded because not all women have vaginas and by that exclusion those women were committing violence against them. WTF? What the hell does that even mean? From what I saw of the march, no one was excluded because everyone is pissed. I discovered that women describing their own existence is offensive to transgender women and their activists. In making the very statement of "Trans women aren't women, Trans men aren't men," women were slammed and labeled "TERFs" in comment sections of social media articles regarding trans issues. A "TERF" is an acronym that stands for "Trans Exclusionary Radical Feminist."

I FIRMLY believed that left wing politics did not deny science. I only subscribed to casual feminism at best; I didn't even know what a Radical Feminist was until I was called that name because I described basic concepts such as: Male is Male and Female is Female. The definition of WOMAN is an ADULT HUMAN FEMALE and a MAN is an ADULT HUMAN MALE. I have been labeled a bigot just for making that statement. Then it hit me how much it bothered me to be called a bigot and in that instant, I didn't give a care in the world. Who cares? I can be called any and every name in the book, but I will not deny reality for the likes of anyone. That was the moment when I realized that I that my political ideology as a liberal was dead.

Males trying to transition to female or females trying to transition to males are not a race or cultural group. They are a small number of men or women who for a range of reasons, usually some kind of mental illness or sexual fetish, wish to be of the opposite biological sex. The delusion of "being in the wrong body" is a symptom of underlying and untreated mental illness. My former views on transgender ideology were basic; I figured that people who wanted to be of the opposite sex would want to take on the issues of their desired sex. That has not been the case.

I have seen enough on social media to see a pattern of behavior in a large number of those who identify as male transitioning to female. What I have seen involves threats of violence if you don't subscribe to their way of thinking that biological males can be made female or biological females can be made male. I have witnessed liberal feminists immediately shutting down any immoderate opinions. As soon as someone makes a slightly critical comment or question, they are called a TERF, bigot, told to fuck off, die, be raped, and then immediately blocked, inhibiting any conversation at all. Another dismissive tactic is to minimize the issue as "just toilets," particularly with the disingenuous refrain "let them pee." This ignores that the push to substitute sex with gender identity affects everything from changing rooms, to women's sports, midwifery, lesbian spaces, media reporting on male violence, parenting practices, government policy, reporting, data collection, and women's rights to protest.

"Trans women" seem very detached from the true reality of women's lives, which is shocking in the sense they want to be female so bad. A lot of trans women seem to have an obsession with being "validated" by getting catcalled on the street by other dudes (even if they themselves aren't sexually attracted to other males) or being called derogatory terms associated with women. If trans rights were about being treated equally, I would reconsider showing my support, but these days trans rights is simply about women pretending trans women and women are the same. In the past few years trans women have campaigned to close women's domestic violence shelters for not accepting them, for trans girls to be able to harass girls in their own changing rooms, to allow trans women with male anatomies to go into women's changing rooms and make us uncomfortable, to co-opt every single women's cause for their own. Trans women are attempting to steal women's identities and be "better women than women" and then tell us that we're bigots for saying ENOUGH. This is no different than a white "trans racial" person who believes they are black telling black people who are born black to stop talking about their experiences because it's racist. That is exactly the same thing. Trans women seek to move women out of the way, to dilute what it means to be a woman; they are the neo-wave misogyny.

Trans people make up an incredibly minute percentage of the population, so why must women erase their identities to satisfy trans women? Why can't trans women claim their own identity instead of appropriating the issues of women? Stop trying to erase the female experience. There is no way to change BIOLOGICAL sex; GENDER is a societal construct that assigns characteristics and behavior in response to BIOLOGICAL sex. Sex reassignment surgery (SRS) is real and it involves sterilization and mutilation. For males, the full reassignment is a horror story of a wound that constantly needs tending for the rest of their lives. Many men who have gone through this are now feeling devastated but many are also in denial which is why they are so angry.

Sorry the truth hurts and life ain't fair. I do actually feel for some of these men and women but at the end of the day gender is not biological sex. They feel they were "born" the wrong gender when in fact our society has such rigid performance roles for males and females (gender = the performance of sex roles) that they will go to extreme lengths to become what they believe is the opposite gender. What they don't realize is that these gender roles are not real; they are social constructs and you can change your gender any time you like without mutilating yourself. It will not make you biologically the opposite sex, however. No one perfectly performs masculinity or femininity. People who feel that they cannot act/dress the way they want to because of their sex are not shrugging off the standard gender roles – they are buying into it. They are accepting the argument that a man cannot be feminine. So they change their bodies in some cases in order to "be women" and therefore be allowed to be feminine. In other cases, they do not change their bodies but demand to be called women, deny their male biology, etc. In both situations the person has changed their identity or body in order to conform to the expectation that women are feminine and men are masculine. Becoming "a woman" in order to be feminine in a socially-acceptable way is doing nothing to challenge gender stereotypes for males or females. It is literally buying into them. Shrugging off the standard gender roles would be to say, I am a man. I am male. I will dress femininely, so suck it up, and vice-versa.

There's my armchair analysis of what I've observed in these men and women.

CHAPTER 33

Yes, Women Have Vaginas. But That Is Not the Sum Total of What We Are

by The Chicago Feminist Salon

Women are not women because we choose to be women. Women are not women because we identify as women. Women are women due to the reality of our material bodies, as easily observed by other people. We are a class. We are female human beings, just as ewes are female sheep and does are female deer. There is nothing mysterious about this.

Bodies have social meaning. The collection of assumptions made about our personalities, our inclinations -- our "brains" -- as a judgement on the material reality of our female bodies, along with the rules and restrictions that are then imposed on us as a result of those assumptions, are what is known as "gender."

Female people, as a sex class, have the ability to produce the next generation of human beings, and to provide heirs. Male people desire to control this ability, and impose various rules on women to achieve that control. This is patriarchy. The specific form it takes, the specific rules imposed, vary across the world in different cultures, but the root, and the aims, are the same—male control of female reproductive power. Gender is the tool which upholds the patriarchy.

Female people, as a sex class, share the experience of being forced into the gender imposed on us as observed female people. We share the formative experience of being raised as girls, and then maturing into women.

This is true regardless of our own personal relationship with gender, whether we find strategies to accommodate it and "conform," or whether we struggle against it and suffer for not conforming. This is true across the world regardless of how the specific rules differ in specific cultures.

We are united as a class in our experience of having to deal with the externally imposed gender of "woman."

Belief in the doctrine of innate gender is incompatible with feminism

Gender is not innate. There is no "woman's brain," no "woman's personality." Indeed there is no normative relationship of personality or thought processes to sex/genitalia/reproductive system. There are only assumptions and rules, forced upon us due to our observed sexed bodies. Belief in innate gender is profoundly sexist, full stop.

We cannot identify out of having these assumptions and rules placed upon us. We need to fight the system itself, fight the rules.

We need feminism, not identity

Feminism is rooted in class consciousness. Feminism is rooted in shared experience, not only of our shared physical features but also of growing up with the social meaning of those features. Feminism is about fighting for the liberation of female people with concrete action.

Identity meanwhile is individualist, a product of post-modernity which enforces and encourages extreme individualism, and boils down to a series of language games. It's a false trap to imagine that we can change the power dynamics in the world merely by conceiving of ourselves differently or changing the labels for the boxes we're forced into.

Everyone knows what "woman" really means

Lately it's fashionable in certain postmodern queer-theoretical circles to play coy, to deny the reality that humans (like cats and dogs and marmots) are a sexually dimorphic species, to waffle and quibble and pretend that it's impossible to define just what "woman" really means. "If your mother has a hysterectomy, is she still a woman? What about infertile women?"

But the truth is that everyone on all sides of the "gender debate" knows what a "woman" really is.

The proof is in the fact that when those communities appropriated the term "woman" for their own ends, to include "males who identify as women" in it, they had to come up with their own new term to refer to what we all know as "women" -- because even they have a need to talk about us as a unified class. That's how obvious and united a group we are.

The term they chose to use? "AFAB" for "Assigned Female at Birth."

Next time someone from those circles asks you the gotchas, is so and so a woman, is your mother with a hysterectomy still a woman, all you have to do is answer back in their own language: "Well, was she AFAB? Because that's your answer."

The magic is that the word has been adopted for this use by the postmodern queer theory community itself. Males who "identify as women" won't use this term for themselves, because the fact of not being AFAB is indeed what makes them trans.

Meanwhile of course we all know that it is not at all random which children are "assigned female at birth." It's the children who sport a vulva rather than a penis. No expert is needed to decide which kids get slotted into "girl" and have "girl" gender with all its restrictive rules applied to them.

Born with a penis? Not AFAB, hence, not a girl, and not a woman. End of story. Males calling themselves "woman" are appropriating an experience which they do not, and cannot, understand.

Don't let anyone tell you they don't know what a "woman" is. We must stand up for the original use of "woman."

Your body and mind are fine as they are

Gender is oppressive. It is not surprising that girls in particular struggle with the rules applied to them due to their observed female sex.

It is not uncommon for this struggle to ramp up with puberty, as girls confront the horror that is being sexually objectified, and meet the restrictions and limitations that come with being an adult woman, meet the reality that still in many ways they are not regarded as full human beings in their own right, but rather accessories to men.

Girls and women are told in many ways that their bodies are wrong -- the wrong height, the wrong weight, the wrong shape. Gender ideology demands that the female body is to be shaped and restricted to fulfill the purpose of sexual objectification, while at the same time the sexed features of the female body are derided and mocked, portrayed as inadequate, weak, fleshy excess, vulgar in comparison to the male standard. The same breasts and curves that are demanded become "evidence" that women are sex-obsessed mindless creatures who have no higher ambition, no inner strength. Our monthly bleeding, the evidence of our unique power to create life, is twisted into an ugly taboo.

Women must at the same time be voluptuous, and yet take up no space.

Many a girl will internalize these messages and come to feel that the fault is in the body -- if only she were not a girl at all, all would be right. Surely the body is wrong. She has a full personality, after all, but in this "wrong" body that isn't permitted to have one. She chafes at the rules that come with this body, they don't fit, surely the body is wrong, a massive birth defect. She has dysphoria.

The new false promise of postmodern queer-theoretical circles is to say that those who do not wish to conform to these demands of gender may escape it, but indeed only by "no longer being women." Crucially however this process of becoming "not-women" is generally taken to involve artificially modifying the body to remove and blunt the sexually dimorphic features that mark it as female, in favor of attempting to mimic a crude facsimile of the male form.

Girls who have come to hate their bodies, to resent their breasts for the gendered social meaning that they hold, are told that this revulsion is a "natural" outcome of "not being women," rather than the internalized misogyny which it actually is. It is presented as impossible for a woman to be both observably female and free of the rules and stereotypes forced upon female people under the patriarchal gender system. Far from challenging gender, this is the ultimate capitulation to the system.

To be happy, she must either not be "woman" -- meaning not observably female -- or else acquiesce to the gender rules and sexual objectification.

We are our brains, so the saying goes, we can't (and shouldn't have to) change who we are, inside. It's far easier to change the body.

But the truth is, there is no normative relationship of personalities, of inclinations, of SELF, to genitalia and reproductive systems and sexed bodies. The postmodern and post-humanist mantra "Change the body or change the mind, we can't change the mind so we change the body" is a false dichotomy. Our bodies and minds are a valid combination just as they are. We need to come to a radical acceptance of ourselves. We are valid. Whatever, however, we are, we define what "woman" is and can be.

The true answer lies in changing the meaning that society assigns to the sexed features of our bodies. We don't need a bigger variety of boxes, of labels, of chains. We need to smash the boxes, break the chains, and be free. Indeed, we must...

Abolish gender and fight for true women's liberation!

CHAPTER 34

Men's Sexual Rights versus Women's Sex-Based Rights

by Sheila Jeffreys

[This talk was presented by Sheila Jeffreys as a Women's Human Rights Campaign ("WHRC") Webinar, on 18 April 2020. The talk is printed here with the author's permission.

The WHRC promotes the Declaration on Women's Sex-Based Rights (https://womensdeclaration.com/en/). The Declaration reaffirms women and girls' sex-based rights, and challenges the discrimination we experience from the replacement of the category of sex with that of "gender identity."].

We are all here because we are concerned about the destructive impact of the transgender activist movement which campaigns for "gender identity" rights is having on women's sex-based rights. I am going to talk today about where this problem came from. I shall argue that the transgender rights movement is actually a men's sexual rights movement. It is one aspect of the phenomenon that has been taking place since the so-called sexual revolution of the 1960s and 1970s, of establishing men's sexual freedom, their freedom to exercise the male sex right.

The so-called sexual revolution of the 1960s and 70s unleashed a men's sexual liberation movement which required that women and girls service men's sexual needs. From it grew the sex industry in the form of pornography and the toleration of legalisation of all forms of prostitution. What were once called the "sexual perversions" were also released and seen as an important aspect of men's liberation. Their practitioners were relabeled "erotic" or sexual minorities and they set about campaigning for their rights. The practices that men's rights campaigners sought to normalise included, alongside their use of women in pornography and prostitution, sadomasochism, paedophilia (a euphemism for child sexual abuse) and cross-dressing, now more commonly called transgenderism. A men's sexual freedom agenda is in opposition to the rights of women to be free from violence and coercion, the rights to privacy and dignity, and to the integrity of their bodies. The transgender sexual rights movement threatens the very existence of the category of women in law and social policy.

The transgender activists deny that their interest in cross-dressing is a form of sexual fetishism because this understanding is harmful to their endeavour. The legislators, parents, judges, wives, and offspring whose support they need to achieve gender identity rights are unlikely to take the desire to ejaculate into frilly knickers seriously as a rights issue. But because they pretend to be a special kind of person, one who through the exercise of a sorry fate was given a female brain in a male body in the womb, they are now receiving support from governments, councils, charities, human rights organisations, the UN, and the medical profession in their campaign to destroy women's rights.

Sexual rights

Do sexual rights exist? There are no UN documents which talk about sexual rights. When sexual rights are a part of rights' speech, they are generally seen as a part of women's rights and specifically women's reproductive rights. The struggle to get recognition that women's rights are human rights has been long and hard. The original UN conventions omitted the rights of women. They were based on what was important to men, voting rights, rights not to be unjustly imprisoned, the right not to be murdered by the state. This was only remedied to some extent in the "Women's Convention" or CEDAW in 1979, The Convention on the Elimination of All forms of Discrimination against Women. CEDAW though, seeks to expand traditional human rights understanding to fit women in. It does not cover issues that are fundamental to women such as violence against women and reproductive rights, though much work has been done by feminists to make these issues part of human rights discourse. On violence there is a Declaration on Violence Against Women from 1993 which forms a foundation for working against men's violence at the international level. Many other documents that are outside the UN system do address men's violence such as the Istanbul Convention from 2011 which was created by the Council of Europe. Reproductive rights are now defined as human rights by organisations such as Office of the High Commissioner for Human Rights. There is too much opposition within the Human Rights system from misogynist religious organisations both Christian and Muslim for abortion to ever have a place in a UN convention.

Sexual rights are commonly understood to be part of reproductive rights by rights bodies and in rights documents. They are seen as an aspect of health and tend to refer to women's right to the integrity of their bodies and to be protected from rape and sexual violence, unwanted childbearing and child marriage. There is no recognition of a separate category of men's sexual rights, because men are not a constituency in need of rights protections as a separate group. I shall argue here that men's sexual rights, which are about sexual access to women and children, are fundamental to male domination, they are assumed and they are protected. Women's "sexual rights" on the other hand, consist of women's rights to escape and be protected from the exercise of men's rights, or to survive the consequences of them as in abortion rights.

The Male Sex Right

Though there is no official recognition of men's sexual rights, there is a recognition so axiomatic, so generally accepted that it requires no mention, that men do have the right to use women and children for sexual pleasure and to treat them just as objects for their satisfaction. This is clear from the way that governments and legal systems the world over have traditionally protected and promoted men's rights to use women and girls in the sex industry. This is beginning to change, with a few countries now accepting that prostitution is a violation of women's human rights and enacting laws that penalise the male buyers in order to undermine the industry. But in the vast majority of countries, strip clubs, brothels, escort agencies, street prostitution, online prostitution, webcam prostitution and pornography thrive and are protected by the state. The assumption underlying this is that men do have what the feminist political theorist Carole Pateman calls the "male sex right." To satisfy men sexually male states, or pimp states, tolerate or legalise prostitution in which women are abused in the streets or hotel rooms or trafficked to the homes of abusers, are warehoused in strip clubs and brothels in which they often also sleep and spend their whole time. In some parts of Asia there are prostitution towns in which women and their girl children spend their whole lives servicing customers.

The slavish servicing of the male sex right in wartime and in peace is so egregious that it does suggest that pimp states, which is all states that do not have comprehensive legislation to protect women against exploitation in porn and prostitution, consider that men do have a right to be sexually satisfied by having women and girls presented to them in all possible ways for their pleasure. Men presently exercise their male sex right in myriad ways which harm or destroy the lives of women and girls. The male sex right is expressed in the sexual harassment and rape that create a sexualised environment which women have to navigate with extreme care at work, at home, in the street, on transport, in places of entertainment. This constant sexual pressure which women are under is seen as "natural," simply how men are, and women must accept it if they are not to be seen as manhaters.

In the book I am writing at the moment I am looking at the ways in which the male sex right constructs the world and women's experience of it. This goes far beyond what may be understood as male violence. The ordinary exercise of the male sex right, commonly just called "sex," involves men simply using women's bodies as masturbation aids whether women like it or not. The best example I have come across of this was listening to a Bangladeshi feminist, Farida Akhtar, explaining how men would come back to the hut from work at lunchtime to be fed by their wives, and would then take them out of the hut to penetrate them up against the back wall. In the UK marital rape was not a crime in UK law until 1991. Men still regularly use their wives despite their reluctance and advice books like those of Bettina Arndt in Australia who last year won an Order of Australia Award, tell women that they must service men for as long as those men require it. They must not, she says, "turn off the supply." We, women, are the "supply."

There are numerous other ways in which the exercise of the male sex right constructs the world for women. It determines where they can go in a city, whether they can enjoy a night out, whether they have to technologise their bodies to prevent conception or seek abortion, how many children they have, the advertising that forms the backdrop of the city streets they walk down, and whether they have to live with the stress of unwanted sex or their male partner's anger. It constructs how they have to dress, the crippling shoes they have to wear and the masks of makeup they have to put on their faces. There are so many ways and I can't talk about them all today. What I do want to talk about is the new problems for women that have been unleashed since the 1960s sexual revolution and particularly since the development of the Internet and the pornography industry. This consists of the normalizing of what the sexologists, the scientists of sex, used to call the sexual perversions.

The sexual perversions

The "sexual perversions" represent more unusual forms of male sexual behaviour. Until the gay liberation movement of the 1970s, homosexuality was included amongst lists of the perversions but the gay rights movement was successful in getting homosexuality destigmatised and in 1973 it was removed as a psychiatric diagnosis from the Diagnostic and Statistical Manual (DSM), the bible of U.S. psychiatry. Homosexuality is about wanted sexual relationships between adults and does not have victims. The perversions are forms of male sexual behaviour which do have victims and have harmful effects on women's lives. Male sexuality is constructed to be the sexuality of the dominant class, and in relation to women's oppression. Transvestism, or as it is more generally called these days, "transgenderism," is the most significant in the threat it poses to women's rights in the present. In the late nineteenth century the new science of sexology began to map these forms and give them names. Many took the form of what the scientists called fetishism i.e. concentrating sexual interest on objects that represented women such as high heeled shoes rather than on actual women. Men might then either wear large size high heeded shoes or ejaculate into high heeled shoes. The objects might be related to women's bodies, such as hair. Men who stole women's hair to masturbate on, cutting off women's plaits for instance, were called capillary kleptomaniacs. Men's hair fetishism is why the vast majority of young women today have long hair which is extremely inconvenient but exciting to men.

Men who liked women to be dirty were named saliromaniacs, one version of this is paying women to mud wrestle. There was a very wide range of perversions recorded. The perversions included renifleurism in which men would gain satisfaction from smells, particularly the smell of urine. In urolagnia men get excitement from watching women urinate. There were gay forms of urolagnia too. In one case in the medical literature, a man would go into the men's toilets and get other men to urinate into his coat pockets. In coprophilia men were excited by shit and in coprophagia men seek to eat women's shit, by visiting prostituted women and eating their shit off t-spoons for instance. There are occasional media reports of men doing any or all of these things today. Usually women and girls are the objects of these practices and experience distress if not more serious forms of harm. Women do not have "perversions" according to the sexologists, although they do not explain why. When it came to explanation, the sexologists very often said that the men's behaviour was the result of the way that their mothers having behaved wrongly towards them. They never mentioned the power relations between men and women which caused the sexual behaviour of the ruling class to be so distorted.

The normalisation of the perversions

One important tactic in the normalisation of men's sexual perversions, is changing the language. The language used by sexologists has changed markedly over the last half century. The changes were designed to reduce stigma. The word perversion could suggest disapproval, so it was replaced with sexual deviation and now paraphilia. Paedophiles (child sex abusers) became minor-attracted persons.

Paedophiles were the first group of men who had previously been seen as "perverts" to emerge demanding their sexual rights. Though the vast majority of the children who are sexually abused are girls, it is not heterosexual paedophiles that came forward to lead a movement for their rights, but gay men. The paedophile movement in the 1970s was composed of gay men. The groups that demanded abolition or reduction of the age of consent so that they could have legal sexual access to children were gay male groups like the Paedophile Information Exchange in the UK or NAMBLA in the US. They did not demand their own rights, however. No, they said, they were simply campaigning for the rights of children to have their own sexuality which would include wanting to be penetrated by middle-aged men. The paedophiles campaigned, they said, for children's sexuality rights!!! They demanded the lowering or abolition of the legal age of consent so that their access to children would be legalised. They were defeated at that time, particularly by radical feminists. I was in a group in the late '70s in Leeds, U.K., for example, which fought to keep the age of consent. They have started campaigning again in recent years as minor-attracted persons. They use many of the old arguments but also claim to be an oppressed group who are made very unhappy by social stigma and the difficulty of coming out to their families and friends. They are still predominantly gay. Heterosexual paedophiles who want access to girl children do not campaign in this way.

It is feminists who have fought to place limits on men's demands for the male sex right to be extended. We have had to fight the Left. In the 1970s the paedophile groups were supported by mainstream gay organisations and publications in the UK. But also, the Paedophile Information Exchange (PIE) was affiliated to the National Council for Civil Liberties, which is now Liberty, the main rights organisation in the UK, for several years without any objections. In the early 1980s a number of members of PIE were prosecuted for sexual acts with children and the group PIE was disbanded in 1983. The paedophile movement was as acceptable in the late 1970s and early 1980s as the transgender rights movement is today. Then, as now, feminists opposed the men's demands and the Left supported them. There are fascinating similarities.

The new movement of minor-attracted persons is seeking to gain recognition of paedophilia as a sexual orientation. By saying that they have a sexual orientation like homosexuals, paedophiles imply that they cannot help themselves and demand sympathy as an oppressed sexual minority. In the 1990s another group of those who would once have been called perverts, began to campaign for their rights and they are the transvestites.

The transgender rights movement

The transgender rights movement was created in the 1990s by heterosexual men who are transvestites. These heterosexual men are the force behind this movement and constitute the vast majority of those involved. I will not consider today the women or the gay men who transgender but concentrate on the most significant players. In the early part of the twentieth century the scientists said that these men simply had the sexual fetish of transvestism or cross-dressing. They did not suggest that they could change sex. In the mid-century the technologies that enabled the scientists to change people's bodies were developed, plastic surgery in particular. They began to create what they called transsexuals, and to see these men as a different category from the ordinary transvestites because they wanted to impersonate women all the time instead of just occasionally. To justify this, they developed the concept of gender identity disorder.

The name change

The diagnosis of gender identity disorder entered the DSM in 1980. Some saw it as a substitute for homosexuality which was removed from the DSM in 1973. The transgender activists of the new transgender rights movement did not like the fact that their sexual interests were called a disorder and applied pressure to get the name of the condition changed, in 2013, to "gender dysphoria." Transvestic fetishism remains so that there are now two diagnoses, men who are sexually excited to wear women's clothes and 'gender dysphoria' which supposedly represents a more permanent condition which, many of the scientists acknowledge, develops from transvestic disorder. Men can graduate into thinking they must really be women after years of cross-dressing.

The history of the changes in the way in which transgenderism has been understood and described in the DSM and sexological literature is fascinating and shows the degree of pressure that the transgender rights movement has been bringing to bear. Because the literature is technical, and not read by many feminists, we have not been able to observe how the ground has moved under our feet until recently, when the new confidence of cross-dressers has allowed them to step out of medical textbooks and into our toilets. The new confidence came from the way that the pornography industry normalised their fantasies and the Internet enabled them to create like-minded support groups and communities. Pornography has supercharged many of men's perversions, plushophilia, nappy fetishism, paedophilia, sadomasochism, and transvestism There are separate and profitable porn niches for all the perversions.

Though most of the medical profession now seems to accept that there can be such a thing as an innate but misplaced gender identity, many have resisted this idea and continue to see all the heterosexual men who cross-dress as sexually motivated, a problem they call autogynephilia, or love of the woman in themselves. They do not entertain the idea that their patients can really change their gender or sex. This group, including Ray Blanchard, Michael Bailey, and Anne Lawrence, who is a cross-dressing man, maintain the understanding that transgenderism is not about an essence of femininity, but sexual, and they use the term autogynephilia to explain this. On the basis of having studied and treated these men and collecting their fantasies and testimonies, they say that they seek masochistic sexual excitement by engaging in imitations of women in a variety of ways.

One group of autogynephiles is interested only in wearing what they see as women's clothes. They might only want to wear women's underwear, probably frilly and uncomfortable, under their work suits, or they may want to walk out in public looking like a porn star. Some of this group will have a past as teenagers when they were snowdroppers, meaning that they stole women's underwear from washing lines to masturbate in or on. Another group likes to engage in what practitioners see as women's activities. Some like to knit, for instance. Others in this group will visit prostituted women and demand to be "forced" to do the housework while dressed in a pornographic French maid's costume. These men will not do any housework in their own homes though, because they see it as degraded women's work. Another group of autogynephiles seeks to emulate women's biology. These men like to pretend to menstruate by using pads and red ink, or by seeking used tampons in the women's toilets and stuffing them up their bottoms. Others wear rubber female body parts, either just a vulva or a whole-body suit in which they will stand in front of a mirror and fondle their rubber breasts, for instance. The most dedicated seek permanent physical alteration by using hormones or having amputations, and these are the ones who would once have been called transsexuals. Almost without exception these men seek to censor any suggestion that they are doing these things for sexual reasons because that might inhibit the sympathy of the public and restrict their freedom.

Men who transgender are likely to have other sexual perversions as well, called co-paraphilias. These may include a clearly related paraphilia called apotemnophilia, or Body Identity Integrity Disorder, in which men are excited by the idea of being amputees and may seek to have legs amputated. One man who calls himself Chloe Jennings-White, real name Clive, has a female gender identity but also a paraplegic identity. He is very fit and a mountain climber but wants to find a doctor to break his back so that he can be paralysed and experience the excitement of being "transabled," as he calls it. He presents as a woman in a wheelchair but is in fact an able-bodied man. The co-paraphilias may include nappy fetishism in which men engage in what they call age regression and may imitate babies in nappies and even demand that their women university lecturers or social workers change their soiled nappies.

The threat to women's sex-based rights

The transgender rights movement has campaigned since the 1990s for their right to the protection of the law for the expression of their gender identities. Their demands have gradually escalated.

International bodies, national legislatures and many local governments and organisations have been overwhelmed by the huge money and influence that the pharmaceutical companies that profit from putting people, often from childhood, on their drugs for life, and billionaire cross-dressing philanthropists, have wielded over two decades to kowtow to these men's demands. They demand that they should be able to be recognised as women in law and have access to all the spaces, sports, opportunities that have been allocated to women to alleviate the severe disadvantage and violence that women suffer under male domination.

Women's rights are based on biological sex, not gender. The Declaration on Women's Sex-Based Rights explains the ways in which including men with "gender identities" in the category of women undermines or overturns the rights that CEDAW and subsequent international documents have assigned to women based not upon gender, but biological sex. All of these are explained in some detail in the document, so I will give only a couple of examples here. Where once transvestites would have quietly masturbated into high heeled shoes or dressed up in frilly underwear at special weekends away or attended special clubs where they could "dress" in private, they now feel entitled to pretend to be women in women's spaces. They get particular sexual satisfaction from being "recognised" as women. They might seek to shake a woman's hand in the women's toilets, for instance, and imagine that she sees them as female. They get naked in women's changing rooms and compete on women's sports teams. They do all this with the backing of large swathes of the Left, of governments, local councils, rights organisations. They have been much more successful even than the paedophiles were back in the 1970s, but the fightback is well underway.

The fightback

It is feminists who have fought the way in which exercise of the male sex right harms women and children. We have fought against rape, prostitution, pornography, paedophilia, and sadomasochism. We have a new fight on our hands against the transgender rights movement. In this fight we find ourselves up against men's fury at the idea that we might try to limit their freedoms, particularly their sexual freedom. We are struggling to get the weight of male sexual oppression off our backs and can seem to always be on the backfoot. But we have had some considerable successes and, in this struggle too, we are gradually making ground. It would be good to be able to concentrate instead on building women's community and women's culture, creating real alternatives for women and girls as we did back at the time of the WLM. That time will come again, but first we have to extirpate the idea that men's sexual fantasies give them rights to inhabit and thereby abolish women's rights as human rights.

CHAPTER 35

Symptoms as Symbols

by Lisa Marchiano, LCSW

[An earlier version of this essay appeared in *Transgender Children and Young People: Born in Your Own Body,* published by Cambridge Scholars.]

From the 15th through the 17th centuries, one of the most common psychiatric afflictions was called "the glass delusion." Sufferers believed they were made of glass and must be treated with extreme care lest their limbs shatter. One of the first cases was King Charles VI of France, who forbade people to touch him and swathed himself in protective blankets (Inglis-Arkell 2014).

This mental health disorder may have gotten a celebrity start with the French king, but it spread. For approximately 200 years, people all over Europe developed symptoms of the glass delusion; many of its victims were from the wealthy and educated classes. By the 1600s the glass delusion was a cultural phenomenon and the most noteworthy mental illness of the times. Cervantes wrote a short novel about it (Inglis-Arkell 2014). Rene Descartes mentioned it (Inglis-Arkell 2014). And then it disappeared. By the 1800s there were few reported cases (Inglis-Arkell, 2014). The cultural unconscious had found other images and symbols through which to express psychic pain.

The dictionary defines "delusion" as "an idiosyncratic belief or impression maintained despite being contradicted by reality or rational argument" (Stevenson 2010). It comes from the Latin word *deludere,* which means to mock. *Ludere* is Latin for "to play," and the prefix *de* gives the word a pejorative meaning. To play is to inhabit the space between what is fixed and what is false. A delusion then, is play that has become stuck. Play has degraded into dangerous fixity. To avoid falling into delusion, we must find a way to inhabit the *in between* space of authentic play, the realm of imagination, creativity, ritual, dreams, shamanism—and psychoanalysis.

The great British psychoanalyst D. W. Winnicott attached enormous importance to play, and felt that psychological health involved being able to relate flexibly to the inner world of fantasy as well as the outer world of consensual reality (Winnicott 2005). We need access to both. Winnicott coined the term "transitional space" to describe the in between territory in which play unfolds. The transitional space between external and internal worlds can be a place of encounter with new aspects of self, unthought truths, and creative solutions. "It is in playing and only in playing that the individual child or adult is able to be creative and to use the whole personality, and it is only in being creative that the individual discovers the self" (Winnicott 2005, 72-73). When we lose contact with the realm of *in between*, we lose access to the transformative space where change and healing happen.

When a client expresses a desire to change something in his or her external world, I hold it in Winnicott's transitional space. I often find myself saying: "I don't know what your feelings mean, but I do know they are important." I attempt to acknowledge the person's emotional truth while holding open the myriad ways it might be lived in the external world. My words express my belief that the voice of the soul finds ways of speaking that are surprising, weird, inconvenient, improbable, and disruptive. But to live a life awakened to individual meaning, we must take psyche's voice seriously.

To take something seriously, however, does not mean taking it literally. There is a space *in between* where metaphor proliferates, and curiosity is cultivated. If we cannot access the *in between*, we either reject expressions of soul as mere delusion, or we take such expressions concretely. The symbolic content that the psyche would have us look at becomes concretized and flattened, or brushed aside as "nothing but." Either way, we forfeit the ability to see a larger psychic and symbolic meaning. The work of attending to soul means trying to carefully inhabit that middle, *in between* space of the symbolic realm.

In listening for the voice of the psyche, we must listen into the *in between*, and neither dismiss our soul's messages nor construe them too concretely. Tuning into the poetic voice of the psyche can help us understand the recent surge in young people taking on non-traditional gender identities as a demand of a generation to have their struggles taken seriously in a world that has largely forgotten how to find this in between space. "There is no illness," Jung wrote, "that is not at the same time an unsuccessful attempt at a cure" (Jung 1966, 46). I argue that adopting a transgender identity may be just such an attempt at a cure on the part of young people struggling to find a meaningful initiation into adulthood. Transition comes from the Latin word "trans" which means to go across, to go beyond. In our culture of out-of-control materialism, is it any wonder that young people are desperate to go beyond? Identifying as transgender is an attempt to transcend the limits of biology to live out an *inner* reality. Feelings associated with gender take on the importance of personal revelation, compensating for a culture in which the literal and logical is so overvalued and soul is often denied. Ironically, in the case of medical transition, the compelling inner experience becomes hypostatized, metaphor made flesh. The young person falls into the sin of concretization even as he or she tries to break free from it.

In this essay, I will explore transgender identities among adolescents as a symbolic communication of psychic conflicts that are a normal part of the painful and often frightening passage to adulthood. In doing so, I will draw upon my clinical work with parents of transgender teens and with detransitioners. Jung taught us that our unconscious has important things to tell us, and that it does so in the symbolic language of myth, dream, and ritual (1970). Only by staying open to the psyche's strange symbolic tongue can we hear what it wants to tell us. To respond to the sudden rise in transgender self-diagnoses among young people in a manner that will enable personal and collective growth and transformation, we must be willing to engage the symbolic dimension of the symptom.

Liminal & literal

Winnicott's transitional space overlaps a great deal with the anthropological concept of liminality, a term coined by the French ethnographer Arnold van Gennep (1960). In his 1906 book *The Rites of Passage*, van Gennep wrote about initiation rituals around the world. He noted that such rites always follow a common pattern: separation, transition or liminality, and reincorporation. In the first stage, the initiate takes part in symbolic acts that separate him from his former self and his former place in his tribe. He leaves behind the person he has been, preparing to enter the liminal phase (van Gennep 1960).

Liminal comes from the Latin word for threshold. It describes a passage from one state to another, a crossing over marked by ambiguity and disorientation. Van Gennep also referred to this part of the rite as transition; things are in a state of flux. According to van Gennep, in this stage, social hierarchies are collapsed or dissolved. Norms are reversed, as one thing becomes its opposite. The middle liminal stage is where the main transformations of initiation occur.

Van Gennep described tribal rites characterized by a middle period of liminality, when monsters become incarnate, people die and are reborn, and the initiate is disoriented and unsure. Liminal experiences—such as religious rites, dreams, creative expression, and psychoanalysis—require things to be *both and*. We relate to the fantastic images that come up from the unconscious with a double stance—one from each side of the threshold—and allow that they express a legitimate psychological truth, even while we do not expect them to conform to objective consensual reality. *Harry Potter* author J. K. Rowling captures the essence of what it means for something to be psychologically true in a dialogue between the young wizard and the elder Dumbledore. When the pair meet in liminal space after Dumbledore's death, Harry asks whether the experience is real, or just happening in his head. "Of course it is happening inside your head, Harry, but why on earth should that mean that it is not real?" replies Dumbledore (Rowling 2007, 723).

Examples of engaging psychological truths seriously but not literally are easy to find. An indigenous shaman turns into an eagle at night, picks up the sick person he is to heal, and flies with him on his back to the Milky Way. Sticks are inserted into their bodies. They fly back, the shaman sucks the sticks out of his patient, and cures him (Bosnak 1996). Such liminal experiences are now being rediscovered by young people, who share them through social media. Nineteen-year-old John from Knoxville identifies as a fox:

> I started getting odd dreams where I would change physically into a fox, and they were very realistic—honestly. And after a while, in real life, it felt quite real, like I actually had a tail, I actually had ears, I actually had paws. At first it was one of those things that I freaked out over, and then after a while it was like "ah... I'm just gonna play with my tail for a minute." Every so often, John says he gets mental shifts: "I could just be at home, and all of a sudden, click, the fox part of me just kind of comes out for a while, and then it just goes." (Roberts 2015).

When John's experience of fox-ness is held as a liminal experience, it has all the richness and healing potential of the shaman's eagle flight. If understood as inner experience, it can lead him to greater appreciation of the spaciousness of soul. If, however, we make the mistake of understanding this experience concretely, it loses its symbolic potential for healing and veers alarmingly into delusion. Instead of leading us to curiosity about our inner life and an integration of our own mysterious and archetypal fox-like qualities, the experience becomes inappropriately transplanted to the realm of the literal, where it can lead not to wholeness, but to increased isolation and suffering. John's experience would then be reduced to pathology.

Dennis Avner was an American of Lakota and Huron heritage (Hall 2012). At ten, he was given the name "Stalking Cat" by a medicine man. Later, a chief exhorted him to "follow the ways of the tiger." Avner identified with his totem animal and appears to have understood this instruction concretely, for in adulthood he began to modify his body. Sometimes without anesthesia, Avner subjected himself to 14 surgeries to make himself look more feline. His septum was altered to flatten his nose, his teeth were capped and filed into points, silicone pads were implanted in his cheeks, and his upper lip was split. In 2012, at the age of 54, Avner was found dead in his apartment of apparent suicide (Hall 2012).

Although causes can only be assumed, Avner's search for transformation through surgery represents a collapse of the liminal, imaginal engagement of tiger-ness that might have transformed his life from the inside. When liminal space collapses, as it apparently did for Avner, we lose access to the renewing source of psychic life. Avner's quest for concrete realization of his tiger-ness apparently failed to lead to psychological health. So too we must be circumspect about a young person's desire to concretize a threshold experience via medical transition. Concretizing feelings by medicalized body alteration is likely to mean that the subtle messages from the unconscious are not being engaged symbolically.

Symbolic understanding

The middle, liminal space is the realm of the symbolic. According to Jung, a symbol does not have a fixed meaning but points beyond itself to a larger content that can never be fully encompassed by image or word 1975. It is the best expression for something unknown and essentially unknowable (1975). Understanding something symbolically is never a reductive process but one that adds layers of meaning. The image becomes larger and more spacious, getting both more specific and precise and less so at the same time.

When I was a child, my family owned a set of encyclopedias, and I used to love to sit and flip through the volumes. One of my favorite entries was the one for the human body. The illustration included an inset of the different systems—circulatory, digestive, muscular, skeletal, etc.—each printed on a separate sheet of clear plastic, so that they could be layered over each other, giving a sense of how the systems interrelated. Holding a symptom, feeling, or image in a symbolic fashion is somewhat like these illustrative overlays. Each layer adds something, perhaps obscuring something else, but not replacing it. Each level of meaning expands the experience of the original so that it is always more than the sum of its parts.

A teen "comes out" as transgender. If we understand this revelation concretely, we will see a girl trapped in a male body or vice versa, a cognitive construction that wasn't even possible until recent advances in medical technology. We are then held fast to this one-dimensional, limited understanding, and as with Dennis Avner's facial surgery, a literal understanding may seek external world realization. A symbolic perspective allows us to find companionship and encouragement in the universal human experience of feeling estranged from ourselves and our bodies. We are no longer fixated on those aspects of our experience that separate us and mark us as different, but find instead reassurance and connection with all who live and who have gone before us.

Taking symptoms concretely means that we may miss the meaning behind how our suffering has expressed itself. We focus on the wrapping, not the contents. This is always a possibility in the case of psychological symptoms. With body dysmorphia, for example, cosmetic surgery is contraindicated, for follow-up data show that the patient's obsessive dissatisfaction with one body part doesn't disappear after the "flaw" is corrected with surgery. Rather, it migrates to some other part of the body, which then becomes the new focus of intense dislike. The real suffering has not been addressed through surgery.

Tyler, a young transman, had a phalloplasty, leaving him with a large scar on his arm. He posted a video entitled "I Hate My Arm."

> *I worked so hard for this body, and now I'm not ashamed of the parts I was before. I don't experience dysphoria, I don't hate my body. Now it's all about my arm. I can go out shirtless, I can go out naked if I want, but my arm would be covered, no matter what. I want to start forcing myself out of sweatshirts and long sleeved shirts and forcing myself to go out and show my arm, but any time I think about it I just get sick to my stomach 'cause I'm so afraid (Tylerjvine 2016).*

This is what Jung meant when he said the "neurosis is always a substitute for legitimate suffering" (Jung 1969, 75). When we focus on the outer manifestation of the trouble, we are avoiding a genuine encounter with suffering. If we cannot encounter our suffering, we cannot hope to discover the kernel of transformative potential within it.

In the case of a transgender teen, I argue that the cure is not to fix the symptoms in objective reality, where the treatment dictated is a medicalized, concretized changing of names, hairstyles, and bodily appearance. Altering appearance is often a futile effort to capture the elusive intricacies of the psyche in fixed, physical form. That the "cure" for transgenderism has been reduced to commodified medical procedures focused on external appearance indicates that we may be addressing a soul problem in the superficial realm of persona, as the pathos of Dennis Avner's history attests.

Does the psyche ever want the concrete thing? The body of a tiger or the opposite sex? Could it be that a symbolic experience of our inner reality might also need to be lived out concretely? Possibly—but let's be wary. Without a willingness to explore, to be curious, or even mistaken, a rigid definition of the problem usually indicates an ego-driven stance. When someone comes into treatment and is certain that the only solution to the presenting problem is something in the outer world—a new job, a new partner, a new body—in my experience, it is almost always the case that the person is avoiding the deeper message conveyed by the pain.

The current cultural prescription for how to work with transgender youth does not allow for doubt. Transgender advocates aver certainty about innate gender: that we definitively know our own "authentic self," and that physical transition is the right course toward this authenticity. They exhort parents that full affirmation of a child's self-diagnosed identity is crucial for that child's well-being (Brill 2016). Part of the appeal of these beliefs is that they offer such a certain way to understand the ordinary tragedy of passing over the threshold to adulthood, along with a clear prescription to fix it. Let's reclaim the psychic space *in between* and engage the mysteries of symbol to help us understand the recent surge in young people taking on non-traditional identities. Such an approach can open up multiple ways of relating to a child's identity exploration and help us to divine the underlying issues, as described in the following case example.

Mikayla/Mitch*

Vicky is a middle-aged woman in my practice. She had been in treatment with me for some time before her daughter Mikayla began to struggle with gender. The following is a summary of her experience dealing with her daughter's transgender identity in the context of the work she and I did together to understand Mikayla's experience within a developmental framework that considered the symbolic aspect of adolescent identity exploration. For clarity's sake, I will refer to Mikayla by masculine pronouns and name when recounting the part of the story during which she identified as trans.

Mikayla is the only child of Vicky and Tom, who divorced when Mikayla was six. After the divorce, Vicky went through a period of depression. Tom traveled much of the year, and was in Mikayla's life only sporadically. Most of the time, Mikayla lived with her mother. Vicky states that Mikayla's childhood was mostly unremarkable. She fell in love with horses as a little girl, and rode at a nearby stable for many years. Vicky also remembers that Mikayla and a neighborhood friend used to like to pretend that they were dancers in a music video, and would spend hours making up their own dances in the garage.

Mikayla was academically advanced, and loved to read. Science fiction was always a favorite genre. Throughout grade school, she tended to have one or two friends with whom she was very close. Her mother described her as intense, quiet and somewhat anxious. Mikayla was nine years old when her cat died. Mikayla stopped eating for several days and refused to go to school for over a week due to grief and a paralyzing fear that the same fate would befall her.

When Mikayla was thirteen, her father relocated overseas for work. Though he tried to reassure her by promising fun summers in Europe, Mikayla was devastated. She recognized, as her father did not, that their relationship would become more difficult to sustain than ever.

Around the same time, an older boy cornered her backstage during a school play rehearsal and made lewd and threatening remarks while friends of his laughed nearby. Mikayla had felt the boy was a friend and was deeply shaken by this incident. Her mother reports that Mikayla started wearing baggy, oversized sweatshirts after this. She stopped doing the play or singing in the choir, activities she had previously enjoyed.

Mikayla became withdrawn and unreachable, and spent long hours in her room on her computer. Vicky admits that she was aware that Mikayla was probably on her computer late into the night, but felt that separating her from her friends on social media would only make her more alone and unhappy.

A few months after the backstage incident Mikayla gave her mother a letter stating that she was transgender. To Vicky, the wording of the letter seemed formulaic and unlike Mikayla's own style. She is pretty sure that Mikayla copied a template letter from an online site. The letter stated Mikayla's desire to be addressed as Mitch and referred to as "he." The letter also included a plea for hormone blockers, along with a vaguely worded threat: "If I am not able to interrupt the wrong puberty my body is starting to go through I am afraid for my future."

At first, Vicky was shocked and saddened. Vicky had never seen any behavior in her child that would lead her to believe she was struggling with gender. In addition, the idea that her daughter might really be her "son" made her grieve for the child she had always known and loved. But she was worried about her child, and she wanted to be as supportive as possible. Worried about Mikayla's recent tendency toward isolation and depression, Vicky quickly conceded on the matter of pronouns, name, and haircut. She even bought the child she was now calling Mitch a breast binder. However, she stated that she needed more time to consider before she would agree to Mitch taking medication.

Now in the 9ᵗʰ grade, Mitch began presenting as male at school. He was readily accepted in a peer group that was predominantly other natal females who identified as "transmasc," gender fluid, nonbinary, or some other designation. At first, Vicky was pleased to see Mitch gaining confidence and having friends after being socially isolated. But she also felt uneasy. "When they came over to the house or I drove them somewhere, gender issues were all they ever spoke about," she said. "It seemed to me there was something unhealthy about their preoccupation with all of this. I could see Mitch was getting swept along by them. I just hoped it was for the best."

After a few months, Vicky's hope was waning. The more time Mitch spent presenting as a transman, the unhappier he seemed. He became obsessed with passing as male. His academic performance worsened. He became further isolated from anything not trans related. His preoccupation was ruminative, leading him to focus on perceived slights or threats. When a family friend accidentally "misgendered" him by using female pronouns at a dinner gathering, Mitch became sullen and quietly enraged. He left the table and retreated to his room. When Vicky eventually forced her way into his room, she found that he had cut the word "die" into his arm with superficial scratches; he confessed contemplating taking a bottle of pills.

Mitch was hospitalized briefly for suicidal ideation. Gender issues were not a focus in the hospital, and Mitch had a break from the Internet and obsessing about identity. Vicky reported that he seemed a little better once he was home. The hospitalization also gave Vicky a chance to take a brief break from her constant worry and think; she made some changes when Mitch came home. First, she made a point of not talking about gender issues.

Engaging Mitch on this topic seemed to make him more spun up and anxious, and led to conflict no matter how carefully supportive Vicky attempted to be. It seemed that when the two of them discussed anything having to do with Mitch's gender, Mitch began the conversation from a standpoint of being certain that his mother would not understand. Not surprisingly, he usually had this expectation met, and the talk ended with Mitch more withdrawn and anxious. So Vicky quietly avoided the subject. But she did not avoid Mitch.

She made a point of spending more time together, doing things he had always enjoyed. They took a weekly creek walk as they had often done when Mitch was younger. She started to ask Mitch to walk the dog with her in the evenings, and he often came. Vicky told me she had decided it didn't matter whether the two of them talked when they were together. She didn't try to fill the space. But they were together, and most of the time after one of these brief trips around the block with the dog, things felt a little easier, a little less strained, even if neither of them had spoken a word. Vicky started suggesting the two of them go to a movie every Friday. She was surprised when Mitch almost always said yes, often even turning down invitations to spend time with friends. Vicky and Mitch were developing a connected routine that was fun and pleasant for them both.

Vicky began to see that Mitch's trans identification was in part an effort to separate from her, while at the same time asking for more care, attention, and connection from her. When Vicky responded to the latter request by spending time with Mitch without bringing up gender, there was a de-escalation in household tension.

If Mitch did bring up gender, Vicky attempted to address the issue in a neutral manner. When it came time to go to a family wedding and Mitch stated that he wanted to wear a tuxedo, Vicky didn't make a big deal out of it. "It's just clothing," she said. Occasionally, Mitch would try to bait her with provocative statements. For example, when he was feeling particularly distressed, he would blame Vicky, saying that he was miserable because she didn't believe he was truly trans. At these times, Vicky attempted to validate Mitch's feelings of distress without getting sucked into an argument about transgenderism.

Mitch's discharge plan from the hospital had included a recommendation that he start attending a weekly support group for trans-identified teens at a local center. In the weeks after Mitch's return from the hospital, Vicky noticed a pattern. The support group met on Wednesday evenings. Mitch would return from the support group sullen, withdrawn, and self-righteously argumentative. Thursdays were often difficult days as well. However, within a day or two, Mitch started to settle down again and be more relaxed in his mother's company. By Saturday or Sunday, Mitch would appear less anxious and depressed, and more able to engage in helping around the house, or doing his schoolwork. This would be the case until Wednesday evening, when the cycle would begin again.

Of course, there were sometimes angry outbursts and times when Mitch withdrew even during the "good" part of the week. Vicky noticed these often occurred around something that made Mitch anxious, such as final exams. Though Mitch's rants would focus on Vicky's lack of support for his trans identity, Vicky began to suspect that these episodes were mostly about Mitch's fear of failure, which stemmed from his perfectionism.

Throughout, Mitch continued to find satisfaction in sketching, an activity that had always been a favorite. Even at his most depressed, he would draw for hours and always signed up for an art class in school. Mitch's art teachers nominated him for a summer art program in Italy for talented high school students. Mitch's first reaction was ambivalent. He was thrilled by his teachers' confidence in him, but felt anxious about traveling alone and navigating identity issues overseas. He would have to live in a dorm, for example, and the dorms were grouped by sex. Vicky saw this as an opportunity for Mitch to have a significantly broadening experience. She gently encouraged the idea. Mitch was accepted to the program and agreed to go.

With minimal discussion, Mitch agreed to be housed in the girls' dorm, though his presentation when traveling continued to be androgynous. The program rules stipulated that phone calls were allowed only once per week. The program's website, however, posted photographs from time to time, and Vicky had glimpses of Mitch engaged in art projects or attending museums with other participants. She was delighted and relieved to hear excitement in Mitch's voice during their weekly phone calls. Mitch was swept away by all of it: new friends, the ambience of Italy, and the professional art instruction.

Mitch's absence gave Vicky a chance to step back and look at the bigger picture—something that she and I were able to do in our work together. We had often discussed the possibility that the trauma Mitch had experienced backstage may have made him feel frightened to be perceived as female. We also discussed the probability that constant exposure through social media and his peers may have convinced him that identifying as transgender made sense for him. But Vicky had another interesting insight.

"I am realizing that I never gave Mitch his own space around the separation and divorce. I never intended to ask him to take on my stuff, or turn him against his dad. But when I got depressed, it really affected him. I thought I was just being open, but I can see now that telling him about my own struggles was too much for him."

Movingly, Vicky had come to see the ways in which she and her child had become psychologically fused. She speculated—and I agreed—that Mitch's transgenderism was perhaps in part an effort to separate from her and develop a unique identity, while simultaneously signaling distress and anger at Vicky for her post-divorce collapse.

Mitch's summer in Italy gave him some space that he badly needed. He was able to experience some autonomy away from Vicky's scrutiny. Upon his return, Vicky noticed some loosening around the trans identity. Mitch mostly gave up wearing the binder, though he still often wore a sports bra. When he got "misgendered" in stores, he no longer seemed to get as upset. It took Mitch several years to step away entirely from his trans identification. For Vicky, these years were a painful process of trying to support her child as he found his way through being ideologically committed to being trans to his eventual desistence. Only after graduating from high school did Mikayla reclaim her birth name and begin reidentifying as female.

Vicky and I came to understand that, for Mikayla, adopting a transgender identity seemed to be both a plunge into depths of dark emotions and an attempt to avoid growing up. Binding her breasts, cutting her hair and begging for hormone blockers were efforts to deny her maturing female body. Her focus on being trans was also a way to avoid developmental challenges by displacing them onto gender, and her mother and school personnel avoided stressing her due to perceived fragility around gender. Like a bird feigning a broken wing to draw a predator away from a nest, Mikayla used gender confusion to draw attention away from developmental demands she was unready to face.

Mikayla's trans period served both as a defense against unbearable present reality, and provided something transcendent to bridge the impasse. As with all psychic products, Mikayla's trans identity may also prefigure in symbolic language the direction in which her soul needs to grow. As Mikayla continues to mature she can claim her "masculine" traits, becoming fearless, boisterous, loud, opinionated, strong, and confident.

Initiation

Throughout human history, cultures have developed rites of passage to help young people cross the threshold into adulthood, and from this we can surmise that adolescents have an ancient need to undergo initiation. If there are no elders present who can lead them through a meaningful initiation, teens unconsciously seek other ways. As youth approach adulthood, their developmental need to discover meaning and purpose draws them into the fires of life. They look for intense and even dangerous situations in which to test themselves, and they seek a tribe to which they can belong. Identifying as transgender may in some cases be an attempt to self-initiate, to slip the bounds of banal ordinariness and seek meaning and transcendence.

All initiations have at their core a death and rebirth experience as has been documented by anthropologists (Eliade 1975, van Gennep 1960). Initiates are often considered dead during the liminal/transitional period of the rite so that they may be resurrected in adult form. Often, they receive a new name upon completing their initiation. Many trans-identified children and their parents view transition as the death of an old self and the rebirth of someone new. Nine-year-old Ash, for example, thinks of the male part of herself as an older brother "that died or fell off a cliff" (France 2016). Indeed, a trans person's birth name is universally referred to as a "dead name" (Talusan 2015).

In indigenous initiations, the initiate sometimes undergoes a painful scarification or mutilation of his body in a "procedure of collective differentiation" that connects him forever onward with other initiated adults and conveys his new status in visual form (van Gennep 1960, 74). The ritualized hair and clothing styles, body piercings, tattoos, and even surgeries involved in social and medical transition mark the nonbinary or trans teen as part of a tribe. The young person has achieved a new status indicated by physical difference. He or she is no longer a child. By claiming a trans identity, the young person may be attempting to separate herself from her childhood and mark an initiation into adulthood.

However, for initiations to do their work, they must engage the unconscious and be negotiated in the liminal realm, for the passage from childhood to adulthood is an existential crisis at the heart of which lies the question "who am I?" The initiate must die to childhood. This is an intensely painful and frightening process made more so today because many young people must undergo adolescent initiation unaccompanied by formal rites. The collective experience, elders, and the language of ritual that has historically made meaning of this momentous transition is mostly absent in our culture. Today, the developmental crisis of adolescence is no longer contained by collective structures designed to help the young person successfully negotiate this perilous psychological crossing.

Mythologist Michael Meade has noted, "literalism is the great spell that binds and blinds the modern world" (Meade 2006, 122). If elders can't help adolescents hold their quest symbolically, but collude in seeing their exploration as literal, there is a risk that teens will become stuck in this transition phase. Then the initiation will be incomplete. To help young people hold their transition into adulthood symbolically, we must be committed to the importance of their experience without shrinking it into its literal manifestation. I contend that we must see *beyond* the symptom to the meaning behind it and be prepared to look more deeply at what is getting expressed individually and culturally.

Initiations require ordeals, and these are always painful and frightening. As initiating elders, part of our role will be to witness our children's suffering and discern when it is senseless and ought to be stopped, and when it is the sort the broadens and deepens, awakening the young person to what is hidden in his soul. If it is the latter, we must avoid the temptation to "fix" the suffering by addressing it superficially. As elders, we understand that this painful trial has deep significance in the symbolic realm. We hold open the liminal, transitional space so that the young person can retain access to it, and so can experience her initiatory suffering as that which helps her to hear the story that came with her into the world.

The way of initiation for women has always entailed going down into dark earth. The earliest myths of feminine initiation—from Innana in Sumeria to Persephone in ancient Greece—depict it as a fearful journey into the depths. During such a journey, the world of childhood is left behind and innocence is sacrificed. With her mother's help, Mikayla experienced her descent as transformative, and returned from the depths a maturing woman.

Teens for whom gender exploration is a descent to the underworld of depression, anxiety, and rumination need us to meet their ordeal with the spaciousness of symbolic understanding rather than the rigidness of certainty. The word "metaphor" comes from a Greek word meaning "to carry over." As we try to make sense of a teen's descent, the poetic language of metaphor can help carry us over the gulf of understanding and break the spell of literalism, allowing the ordeal to become an experience that transforms.

The case of Mikayla/Mitch is a fictionalized composite of many stories I have heard from parents.

Works Cited

Bosnak, Robert. *Tracks in the wilderness of dreaming: exploring interior landscape through practical dreamwork.* New York: Delacorte Press, 1996.

Brill, Stephanie. *The transgender teen a handbook for parents and professionals supporting transgender and non-binary teens.* San Francisco, CA: Cleis Press, 2016.

Eliade, Mircea. *Rites and symbols of initiation.* New York: Harper & Row, 1975.

France, Louise. "Inside Britain's only transgender clinic for children." *The Times*, November 5, 2016. http://www.thetimes.co.uk/.

Hall, John. The Independent. November 14, 2012. Accessed January 08, 2017. http://www.independent.co.uk/news/people/news/stalking-cat-daniel-avner-found-dead-in-apparent-suicide-after-years-of-body-modification-to-look-8316569.html.

Tylerjvine. "I hate my arm." YouTube. September 26, 2016. Accessed January 08, 2017. https://www.youtube.com/watch?v=vseH5D8e3A8.

Inglis-Arkell, Esther. "The 'Glass Delusion' Was The Most Popular Madness Of The Middle Ages." Io9. September 18, 2014. Accessed February 24, 2017. http://io9.gizmodo.com/the-glass-delusion-was-the-most-popular-madness-of-th-1636228483.

Jung, C. G. *The collected works of C. G. Jung. The spirit in man, art, and literature.* Edited by Herbert Read, Michael Fordham, and Gerhard Adler. Translated by R. F. C. Hull. New York, NY: Bollingen Foundation, 1966.

Jung, C. G. *The collected works of C.G. Jung. Psychology and religion: West and East.* Translated by R. F. C. Hull. Edited by Herbert Read, Michael Fordham, and Gerhard Adler. 2nd ed. Princeton, NJ: Princeton University Press, 1969.

Jung, C. G. *The collected works of C. G. Jung. Symbols of transformation.* Translated by R. F. C. Hull. Edited by Herbert Read, Michael Fordham, and Gerhard Adler. 2nd ed. Princeton, NJ: Princeton University Press, 1970.

Jung, C. G. *The collected works of C.G. Jung. The structure and dynamics of the psyche.* Translated by R. F. C. Hull. Edited by

Herbert Read, Michael Fordham, and Gerhard Adler. Princeton, NJ: Princeton University Press, 1975.

Meade, Michael. *The water of life: initiation and the tempering of the soul*. Seattle: Greenfire Press, 2006.

Roberts, Amber. "Otherkin Are People Too; They Just Identify as Nonhuman." Vice. July 16, 2015. Accessed January 08, 2017. http://www.vice.com/en_ca/read/from-dragons-to-foxes-the-otherkin-community-believes-you-can-be-whatever-you-want-to-be.

Rowling, J. K., and Mary GrandPre. *Harry Potter and the deathly hallows. (Harry Potter series, year 7.)*. New York: Arthur A. Levine Books/Scholastic Inc., 2007.

Stevenson, Angus. *Oxford dictionary of English*. Oxford: Oxford University Press, 2010.

Talusan, Meredith Ramirez. "What 'deadnaming' means, and why you shouldn't do it to Caitlyn Jenner." Fusion. June 4, 2015. Accessed February 26, 2017. http://fusion.net/story/144324/what-deadnaming-means-and-why-you-shouldnt-do-it-to-caitlyn-jenner/.

Van Gennep, Arnold. *The rites of passage*. Chicago: University of Chicago Press, 1960.

Winnicott, Donald W. *Playing and reality*. New York, NY: Routledge, 2005.

CHAPTER 36

Queer Politics

by Sheila Jeffreys

[This talk was presented by Sheila Jeffreys as a Women's Human Rights Campaign ("WHRC") webinar, on 6 June 2020. The talk is printed here with the author's permission.

The WHRC promotes the Declaration on Women's Sex-Based Rights (https://womensdeclaration.com/en/). The Declaration re-affirms women and girls' sex-based rights, and challenges the discrimination we experience from the replacement of the category of sex with that of "gender identity."].

I will argue today that queer theory and politics is composed of the politics, culture and sexual interests of gay men. They were created in direct opposition to the lesbian feminism which had developed a powerful challenge to men's sexual rights in the 1970s and 1980s. Queer is the enemy of feminism and lesbian feminism, not just because it excludes, us but because the whole mindset and practice is based upon the degradation of women and the embrace of "gender" i.e. the sex roles and sex stereotypes that create and maintain women's oppression.

Introduction: where did queer politics come from?

Today the word queer means very different things from when it was invented in the very early 1990s. Queer politics and theory have become the orthodoxy in universities, where queer theory dominates the study of feminism and sexuality. Generations of students already have been brought up under the thrall of these ideas. Queer politics dominates entirely the communities in which young lesbians seek to come out. It is hugely influential in culture and entertainment. It is hard to imagine that once queer politics was seen as edgy and transgressive! Today it means homosexual, but also adventurous heterosexuals, transvestites, various forms of fetishistic and harmful sex, and a host of other identities. It has become a euphemism for gay so that many lesbians in particular are happy to call themselves queer but not lesbian. Lesbian is a bit too out there, too confrontational, too women centred, might even indicate not loving men, and loving men is compulsory. Bisexual or non-binary are acceptable terms because neither means rejecting men and queer is very safe. Queer culture and politics have always been diametrically opposed to feminism from its very beginnings and never included lesbians unless they imitated and assimilated themselves into gay male forms.

There was a time before queer. In the 1950s, the word for those attracted to the same sex was homosexual, a term from sexology textbooks. In the 1960s the term gay was adopted as a way to reject being defined by the medical profession and because it sounded joyful and revolutionary. Its usage to describe gay men originated in the demimonde or world of prostitution in the late nineteenth century. That was called the gay world. At that time homosexual men and prostituted women often socialised together as both were outcasts. In the late 1960s the word "gay" was promoted by the new Gay Liberation Movement as the correct term for homosexuals. Neither the term homosexual or the term gay originated with or described lesbians. The terms in their generic forms referred to men and if women were referred to, modifying adjectives were required, so lesbians were female homosexuals or gay women.

When the Women's Liberation Movement and lesbian feminism got going in the early 1970s, the term "gay" was rejected as specifically male and having no relationship to women's experience. As women who loved other women, we called ourselves lesbians. We were out and proud.

What was lesbian feminism?

Lesbian feminism was based on recognising the great political differences between lesbians and gay men. We considered that lesbians and gay men had little if anything in common. Lesbians are women and members of the oppressed sex class. Gay men are members of the oppressor class. In this way our interests are opposed. But gay men's relationship to women is different from that of heterosexual men. Gay men are taught to worship masculinity as everyone else in male supremacist culture is, and to despise women. But gay men are seen to lack masculinity themselves because they do not penetrate women. Gay male culture, therefore, embraces the default position, of subordinated and cringing effeminacy. I don't want to suggest that all gay men subscribe to this culture. Indeed, at the time of gay liberation for a few years after the Stonewall Rebellion of 1969, gay male activists were incisively critical of the adoption of sex roles and effeminacy by their brothers. Some still are. But for the most part, those cultural forms that are still and indeed increasingly seen to represent gay culture, such as camp and drag, are about derision towards and the despising of women. Queer culture and politics without the oppression of women is not imaginable.

In 1994 I wrote a journal article out of my fury and despair at the development of queer politics which seemed designed to destroy the theory and culture that lesbian feminists had created, it was called The Queer Disappearance of Lesbians (Jeffreys, 1994). Lesbian feminists, I said, refused to be assimilated into gay men's politics. We refused to be seen as related to gay men but just less interesting and adventurous. The gay male historian Jeffrey Weeks described lesbian culture at the end of the nineteenth century as being "a pale version of the male" (Weeks, 1977: 87). We did not see ourselves as pale versions of the male or indeed any kind of males at all. I explained that "Lesbian liberation requires .... the destruction of men's power over women" (Ibid: 459). We challenged everything that queer politics came to represent.

Lesbian feminists separated off from gay male politics in the early 70s. We had our own organisations, discos, theatre, all focused on loving women, creating spaces for women and campaigning for women's freedom. We developed a profound critique of the male view of the world, what the lesbian theorists Julia Penelope called the Lesbian Perspective. We had our own ethics and philosophy, all based on creating a world worthy of women and lesbians.

Lesbian feminists developed a profound critique of gay male politics and gay male ambitions, as is clear in Marilyn Frye's work in The Politics of Reality and my own Unpacking Queer Politics. Lesbian feminists criticised gay male politics on a number of very important grounds. We saw gay men as having a sexuality very similar to that of heterosexual men even though it was aimed at other men and not women. We saw male sexuality as constructed out of the power relations of male domination, as the sexuality of the ruling class. It was, we argued, formed from men's bonding through the sexual subordination of women, and out of men's "male sex right," the right of sexual access to women and children. It is centred on the penis and penetration, shaped by the eroticised power difference of sadomasochism, powered by the prostitution and pornification of women by the sex industry. This model is the basis of gay male sexuality too. Gay men saw their very identity as tied to the enactment of eroticised power difference and a profitable industry of sadomasochism developed in gay male culture in the 1970s and 1980s, with clubs and bathhouses, leatherwear and tor-ture implements, pornography and prostitution all based upon the eroticising of power difference. Gay men, like women, were likely to eroticise powerful masculinity. Most gay sadomasochists were "bottoms" rather than "tops."

A good example of the basis of queer politics in male sexuality is the lauding of sex in public toilets, which is called cottaging in the UK and is a part of cruising in the US. It is celebrated by queer theorists in academic writings, in poetry and novels. This is an exclusively male practice, providing enhanced excitement for the men by the chance that they would be caught, and, some said, by the degradation of choosing to do sex where there was the smell of shit and urine. It is a practice of objectification which lesbians do not take part in. Back in the 1980s some lesbians who were desperate to imitate gay men in everything did try to meet up for sex in public toilets, but it was a fad. Generally, lesbians are not interested in amassing numbers of partners for anonymous encounters. Though this practice was a big part of male homosexuality historically, it was certainly never so for lesbians. The celebration of anonymous sex continues in queer culture. Lesbians are not desperate to engage sexually with strangers in alleyways or parks. Public sex of any kind has never been an ambition.

Lesbians are so different from gay men politically, sexually, socially that a generic word could never suffice. Without the word lesbian for ourselves, lesbian feminism would not have been possible. You cannot create a liberation movement for a group that cannot define itself. Gay male politics was forced to respond to lesbian feminist demands that they recognise the existence of lesbians. The result was that the word lesbian was usually included with the word gay in the titles of events, journals, conferences or organisations. In the 1980s events would be advertised with the word lesbian first, as in lesbian and gay film festivals for instance. Even the phrase LGB has the word lesbian first. There may still have been very little lesbian content but at least the word was there to suggest that lesbians had been considered.

Use of the term "queer" to describe a politics developed in the very early 1990s out of AIDS activism. Male gay activists who came out onto the streets to protest the wave of anti-gay hatred that accompanied the AIDs epidemic used the term "queer" to differentiate themselves from what they saw as an older generation of men who used the term "gay." They saw the older generation as too accommodating and not sufficiently confrontational for the moment of emergency that the new activists saw themselves to be confronting.

We lesbian feminists were horrified; it clearly disappeared lesbians all over again. Lesbians were subsumed under gay men and this was clear in the fact that immediately lesbians needed special words to describe them. Queer meant men and lesbians were queer women or female queers, adjectives were needed to modify the generic male of queer politics.

An explanation of what queer meant was given in the editorial of a new academic journal, GLQ or Gay, Lesbian, Queer, founded in 1993. It says that the Q in the title has two meanings, quarterly and also "the fractious, the disruptive, the irritable, the impatient, the unapologetic, the bitchy, the camp, the queer" (quoted in Jeffreys, 1994: 460). All these adjectives describe the traditional culture of gay men. Camp and drag are forms of behaviour that imitate what are seen as women's mannerisms and dress. Camp behaviour was a sign of male homosexuality right up to the 1970s but is less common now. It consisted of men flapping their hands and being "limpwristed" and speaking in an affected way, "Oh Darling." High voices and wristflapping were associated with femininity. It became an aesthetic style which emphasised appreciation of bad taste in which gay men idolised extremely effeminised heterosexual women, particularly those with a tragic story, like Judy Garland. Camp is based on the sending up of womanhood. Drag, as everyone here will know, consists of gay men dressing up as extremely exaggerated versions of femininity for amusement and to excite other men. The culture and theory of queer depends upon the subordination of women and its exploitation by gay men.

Origin in the sex wars

Queer politics emerged from the so-called feminist sex wars of the 1980s. The "sex wars" consisted of a fightback by sexual libertarians, sadomasochists, and pornographers against the powerful campaign waged by radical feminists and lesbian feminists to change the way sexuality was constructed under male dominance, i.e. the eroticising of male power and women's subordination. Groups that I was in such as the London anti-pornography group which was set up in 1977, London Women Against Violence Against Women, set up in 1980, Lesbians against Pornography, set up in 1983 and Lesbians against Sadomasochism, set up in 1984, campaigned against male violence and sexual violence, against pornography and prostitution, and against the eroticising of power difference amongst lesbians in both sadomasochism and butch/femme roleplaying.

Lesbian feminists like me were horrified by the arrival of queer politics, but our adversaries, the sexual libertarian lesbians who were promoting the sex of dominance and submission, were delighted. They were happy to be absorbed into queer politics which was based on that kind of sex. They were delighted to swear loyalty to their libertarian gay male allies. They continued to excoriate lesbian feminists for their intransigence in resisting the male model of sex, but now they had new weapons. There was a whole new queer dawn which justified them in making the clearest possible separation from the boring, anti-sex, manhating lesbians who, in their opinion, gave lesbianism a bad name. These lesbians promoted the seamless disappearance of lesbian politics as a separate entity within the queer, and rapidly expanding, rainbow alliance.

Queer Theory

Queer politics constituted a defence of the male dominated sexual freedom agenda that feminism and lesbian feminism in the 1970s and 80s had sought to overturn. Queer theory was developed to accompany queer politics and activism and created a way of thinking about sex that supported that agenda. It emerged from postmodern theory, Foucauldianism and the work of Gayle Rubin. Queer theory and politics incorporated and promoted from the beginning those sexual practices by gay men that feminist critics had identified as most problematic such as sadomasochism, pedophilia and trans-genderism. They embraced the work of the American lesbian sado-masochist, Gayle Rubin, lesbian, anthropologist, sadomasochism proponent and theorist of sexuality. She argued in a very influential paper in 1984 that a historical moment had arrived in which the sexual perversions were being liberated from the sanctions of the law and the prejudices of religion and medicine. These practices included, she said, "fetishism, sadism, masochism, transsexuality, transvestism, exhibitionism, voyeurism, and paedophilia" (Rubin, 1984:151). Most of these practices were overwhelmingly if not entirely male and harmful to women and children.

Rubin's ideas emerged from the work of another great inspi-ration for queer theory, the French gay sadomasochist, Michel Foucault. Both Rubin and Foucault promoted the sexual use of children by adult men. In one of his published conversations he discusses with others the charging of Roman Polanski with the drugging and rape of a 13-year-old girl child. Foucault announces confidently, "She seems to have been a consenting party" (Foucault, 1990: 204). He supports this view with the statement that "There are children who throw themselves at an adult at the age of ten - so? There are children who consent, who would be delighted, aren't there?" (Ibid). He was one of a large group of French intellectu-als in the late 1970s who campaigned to protect men who sexually used children from prosecution. These are the progenitors of queer politics which was dedicated to the protection and promotion of all forms of problematic gay male behaviour such as prostitution, pornography, paedophilia and transgenderism, practices formed from women's oppression and immensely harmful to women and children.

Queer theory, as the name suggests, saw itself as daring, defend-ing male sexual outcasts against old-fashioned morality. Queer politics was based upon the notion that sexual transgression was revolutionary. This meant transgression of the old-fashioned sexual mores that had imprisoned gay men but it included all the rebels and revolutionaries that Rubin and Foucault championed. Queer politics was about outsiderhood. This was not helpful to lesbians who, as women, had a lot more to campaign for than outre sexual practices. Lesbians were struggling in the 80s and 90s, for instance, to assert their right to custody of their own children. Male partners were being automatically given custody because lesbianism was seen as perverted. Our campaigning for basic women's rights was not a good fit with queer theory or politics. A very early Queer Power manifesto from London in about 1991 shows the contradiction. It stated "Queer means to fuck with gender. There are straight queers, bi-queers, tranny queers, lez queers, fag queers, SM queers, fisting queers in every single street in this apathetic country of ours" (quoted in Jeffreys, 2003: 37). Fisting was a popular practice of male gay sadomasochism in which a man would insert his fist and forearm into the anus of an unfortunate partner with the risk of damaging tears that could lead to serious infection. Lesbian feminists like myself thought that such a manifesto, if introduced into a courtroom would certainly disadvantage a lesbian mother seeking custody. We did not see ourselves as permanent outsiders engaging in revolutionary sexual practices. We considered ourselves the very model of how all women could be, free of the rule of men. We wanted, and expected, that all women could become lesbians. We proclaimed and sang, that every woman can be a lesbian. Rather than outliers we were the forerunners. Queer is not a term which can encompass this.

The rehabilitation of gender

The most problematic part of queer politics from the point of view of feminists like ourselves, who are now resisting the politics of "gender identity," was the way in which queer politics and theory was based upon sex stereotypes, i.e. gender. Gender in feminist theory is the sorting system that is necessary to show who is a member of the ruling sex class and who is a member of the subordinate class. This system is sexualized to create what is understood to constitute sexual excitement i.e. the eroticization of dominance and submission through gendered roles, a form of everyday sadomasochism (Jeffreys, 1990; MacKinnon, 1989). It consists of the sex roles and sex stereotypes that created and maintain women's oppression. Feminists seeks to abolish gender.

Queer theory reduced "gender" to a form of personal expression or performance which disappeared the material power structure of male domination. In this queer interpretation, gender is "transgressive" when adopted by persons of one biological sex who would normally be expected to display different characteristics. There is, however, no way out of gender, it can be swapped but not abolished. In this respect queer theory suited the socially conservative times of the 1990s when the idea of social transformation was forgotten and various forms of cavorting in line with the system were relabeled as fun and rebellious. I shall argue here that queer theory on gender, rather than being progressive, is coquettish, flirting with male domination and reproducing its contortions. It locks lesbians and gay men into precisely the old heteropatriarchal forms that more progressive movements, gay liberation and lesbian feminism, sought to demolish.

Queer theory embraced the idea that gender was socially constructed, but took the liberal approach in which it could be tinkered with instead of being eliminated. This rehabilitation of gender as fun, even necessary, to lesbian existence, was justified using the ideas of such luminaries of queer theory as Judith Butler. Butler argued that not only was gender a social construction, which was an orthodoxy of feminist theory in general, but that those persons of one physiological sex who "performed" the practices of the "gender" most usually associated with the other sex were behaving in a way which was transgressive (Butler, 1990). Such "performance," she said, demonstrated that gender was indeed a social construction and could have a disruptive effect on the sex/gender system on which male dominance is based. That did not happen, of course.

Queer theory and politics created a gender rescue mission for the purposes of sexual excitement. For most women and men under male dominance sexual desire is constructed precisely from eroticising the power difference between the sexes. Equality is unsexy, and the very idea of dismantling gender is detumescent. Gender, they say, puts the pizazz into sex. Judith Butler argues this. She explains that she is someone whose sexual desire is constructed out of gender difference. In an interview she says that she "situated" herself "in relation to butchness" in her early twenties, and has had "an active and complicated relationship with both butch-femme discourse and S/M discourse probably for almost 20 years" (More 2000: 286). In *Undoing Gender* she explains that "There may be women who love women" who cannot do this "through the category women" and that "they/we" are "deeply…attracted to the feminine" (Butler 2004: 197). She asks, "why shy away from the fact that there may be ways that masculinity emerges in women" (Ibid). Lesbian feminists have been accused of being boring and sexless for their stance as conscientious objectors to the practice. Masculinity cannot, in a feminist understanding, "emerge" in women. It is the behaviour of male power. Women do not have this power. They can imitate the behaviour of the powerful, men, but they cannot access its reality. In the degraded and antifeminist queer culture of today, many lesbians call themselves "butches" with no understanding of the history of this term and the reasons it was rejected by feminists in the 1970s, many of whom had been "butches" themselves, like the wonderful lesbian feminist philosopher Julia Penelope.

Lesbian feminists argue that queer theory arose out of a conservative time in the 1990s when the radical politics of lesbian feminism and gay liberation were being disavowed as unrealistic. The heady days in which social transformation could be imagined were over, and instead, a theory and politics developed which argued that transposition, that is swapping roles, was a better strategy than changing the system itself. Queer politics coincided with the marketisation of many areas of life, including sex, and the queer consumer was born. More and more sex industry practices were incorporated into lesbian and gay social life, such as drag shows and strip shows.

Queer support for transgenderism

Queer politics was, and is, wholly supportive of transgenderism. This is not surprising considering the extent to which queer is based upon conservative ideas of gender. The lesbians and gay men who transgender use queer theory to justify their practice. Holly Devor, who is now Aaron, explains that queer politics enabled the emergence of "transsexual lesbians, of tranny fags and the men who love them, of lesbians and gay men who enjoy sex together, and of dyke daddies who live out their fantasies as SM gay men" (Devor, 2002: 16). The transvestite Susan Stryker explains that transgender became "articulated" with queer in the form of "an imagined political alliance of all possible forms of gender antinormativity" (Stryker, 2008: 146). These lesbians and gay men say that it is not possible to do without gender. Jamison Green, another lesbian who has adopted a male name, says that it is not possible to question the need for gender since it is the necessary basis of human interaction, "Everyone uses gender to communicate" (Green, 1999: 126). Clearly, within these understandings, there is no way out. Lesbians like me who are conscientious objectors to gender, who refuse gender, are seen as charlatans, failing to recognise the ways in which they too are inevitably and fundamentally gendered.

Judith Butler, the most famous and influential queer theorist whose ideas have been the orthodoxy of sexuality and gender studies for decades, is wholly supportive of transgenderism. She said in 2015, that transgender surgery is a necessity for those who want it, "we all have to defend those necessities that allow us to live and breathe in the way that feels right to us. Surgical intervention can be precisely what a trans person needs .... one should be free to determine the course of one's gendered life" (Butler, 2015). She does not like my feminist opposition to transgenderism and says of me, "She appoints herself to the position of judge, and she offers a kind of feminist policing of trans lives and trans choices. I oppose this kind of prescriptivism, which seems me to aspire to a kind of feminist tyranny" (Ibid). I am, it appears, a feminist tyrant. I am not very effective in my tyranny, however. It is Butler's work that generations of gender studies students have been taught as if it were the bible.

The impact of queer theory today

The point has been reached today where the word lesbian and the concept of being a lesbian have been almost eliminated in the queer culture into which young lesbians come out. They are likely to encounter a culture that has been entirely queered, and has not a trace, no historical memory of lesbianism, not even in a homeopathic sense. There is no model for lesbianism as a form of resistance to male domination.

References

Butler, Judith. *Gender Trouble: Feminism and the Subversion of Identity*. Routledge, 1990.

Butler, Judith. *Undoing Gender*. Taylor and Francis, 2004.

Devor, Holly. "Who Are "We"? Where Sexual Orientation Meets Sexual Identity." *Journal of Gay and Lesbian Psychotherapy*, 6:2, 2002, pp. 5-21.

Foucault, Michel. "Confinement, Psychiatry, Prison." In Michel Foucault. *Politics, Philosophy and Culture: Interviews and Other Writings 1977-1984*. Routledge, 1990 (1st published 1977).

Frye, Marilyn. *The Politics of Reality: Essays in Feminist Theory*. The Crossing Press, 1983.

Green, Jamison. "Look! No, Don't!" In Kate More and Stephen Whittle (eds). *Reclaiming Genders: Transsexual Grammars at the Fin de Siecle*. Cassell, 1999, pp. 118-131.

Jeffreys, Sheila. *Anticlimax: A Feminist Perspective on the Sexual Revolution*. The Women's Press, 1990.

Jeffreys, Sheila. "The Queer Disappearance of Lesbians: Sexuality in the Academy." *Women's Studies International Forum*, vol. 17, no. 5, 1994, pp. 459-472.

Jeffreys, Sheila. *Unpacking Queer Politics*. Polity, 2003.

MacKinnon, Catharine A. *Feminism Unmodified*. Harvard University Press, 1987.

More, Kate. "Never Mind the Bollocks: 2. Judith Butler on transsexuality." In Kate More and Stephen Whittle (eds). *Reclaiming Genders: Transsexual Grammars at the Fin de Siecle*. Cassell, 1999, pp. 285-302.

Rubin, Gayle. "Thinking Sex." In Vance, Carol (ed). *Pleasure and Danger: Exploring Female Sexuality*. Pandora, 1984.

Stryker, Susan. *Transgender History*. Seal Press, 2008.

Weeks, Jeffrey. *Coming Out: Homosexual Politics in Britain from the Nineteenth Century to the Present*. Quartet, 1977.

Williams, Cristan. "Gender Performance: An Interview with Judith Butler." *Transadvocate*, 2015, http://radfem.transadvocate.com/gender-performance-an-interview-with-judith-butler/

CHAPTER 37

Gender Colonialism

by Nina Paley

This essay was originally published on February 7, 2018 on Nina Paley's blog at https://blog.ninapaley.com/2018/02/07/gender_colonialism/. Nina says: "Copying is an act of love. Please copy and share."

Last week I posted on fecebook:[1] "If a person has a penis he's a man," which led to my widespread denunciation as a "transphobe." I've written about this before, and anyone paying attention should know better, but I nonetheless commented this:

> *No matter how many times I state that I have trans friends, was standing up for trans people before the current crop of MRA[2] "transactivists" was even born, and continue to defend the human rights of trans people, people accuse me of the opposite. I tire of defending myself, and it makes no difference anyway. I hated seeing the trans movement get taken over by misogynistic men's rights activists; I hate seeing the misogyny of the "left" growing. I am witnessing a new, deeper, "postmodern" colonization of women. I bear no ill will towards trans people and like and love several; my*

concern is for WOMEN, especially those who aren't white liberal middle-or-upper class, and especially lesbians. When an aggressive white male comes here and declares "I'm a dyke!", and other liberal men gather round to support him, I see this colonization in action.

Do stick around, it takes a while to see, but I promise you I didn't get to this place out of ill will. It's so easy to just say "trans women are women!" and not deal with anyone's hate. I'm resisting for a reason.

What do I mean by colonization?[3] I mean the literal occupation of women's spaces – rape shelters, prisons, locker rooms, bathrooms, swimming holes, and women-only events that women have fought very hard for. By men. Physically. But a huge component of this colonization is mental, existing in the realm of ideas and "identity." What is a woman?

A sex without a people for a people without a sex

In American Liberal thought, colonization is bad. But immigration is good. And taking in refugees is doubleplusgood. This is why Americans backed the Zionist colonization of Palestine. Israelis weren't regarded as colonizers; they were refugees! And Palestine wasn't even inhabited, not really. It was a land without a people for a people without a land. The only reason you could possibly object was if you were ANTISEMITIC. Even if you were Jewish yourself, you self-hating Jew!

Taking in trans "refugees from masculinity" is also doubleplusgood. This is why Liberals back the modern transactivist colonization of womanhood. "Transwomen," who I will henceforth refer to as trans-identified males, or TiMs, aren't regarded as colonizers; they're refugees! And womanhood isn't even inhabited, not really. Womanhood is a "land without a people," because women aren't viewed as people. We're an open space for men to define.

What is the difference between a refugee and a colonist?

A colonist has guns and the backing of another state.

Unlike yesterday's transsexuals – those "refugees from masculinity" – today's TiMs have penises and the backing of Liberal Patriarchy.

My trans pals of the 90's didn't have today's backing of Patriarchy. It was riskier to be trans then, even among Liberals. They more resembled refugees, and I welcomed them. They also either didn't insist they were women, or if they did insist they were women, they "disarmed," if you will, by actually going through genital surgery. Today's TiMs proudly keep their penises and testicles and demand to have them acknowledged as "female body parts."

Obviously, times have changed.

Men's Rights Activists eventually figured out they could eliminate the middleman – transsexuals – and colonize women themselves. This fits nicely with regular old run-of-the-mill male dominance. Heterosexual men "identify" as lesbians, and patriarchal Liberals enforce women's compliance. Women are not to resist or even question this program. To write, "if a person has a penis he's a man" is an act of resistance so powerful, it will get you widely denounced and blacklisted.

You know what else would get you denounced and blacklisted in recent decades? Questioning or criticizing the State of Israel. The thought-terminating memes, the refusal to discuss, the disproportionate outrage are all familiar to my anti-Zionist activist friends.

Under the spell of American Zionism, no right-thinking Liberal believed atrocities were happening in and on behalf of Israel. No matter how much evidence activists produced, Zionist Liberals always downplayed it, or ignored it, or justified it because whatever the Palestinians were doing was surely so much worse. Likewise, no matter how much evidence feminists produce, of death threats and rape threats, of actual physical violence, of blacklisting and purging and no-platforming, we are dismissed as "transphobic." Even when the people presenting the evidence are trans, such as Miranda Yardley[4] and Jenn Smith.[5]

Simultaneous marginalization and support

Of course no males would be "refugees" if they had a home in the male sex class. But it's in Patriarchy's interest to simultaneously marginalize and support trans people, just like it's in Europe's and America's interest to simultaneously marginalize and support Jews. The marginalization drives the pressure of expansion. When people are secure in their homelands, they don't emigrate. It's the tired, the poor, the huddled masses yearning to be free that up and move to a new land. Without antisemitism, the "west" would have no colony in the Middle East. Without patriarchal gender enforcement, TiMs wouldn't be spearheading the further colonization of women. So men simultaneously threaten TiMs, and demand the protection of TiMs as "the most oppressed." That male-imposed marginalization is what drives the whole project.

Trans people themselves are a tiny fraction of the population. So why are language, laws and institutions being changed just for them? Because it's not just for them, it's for all men. TiMs are the "settlers" of the latest patriarchal colonization project.

Religion

Both Zionism and transactivism have a religious component. In Zionism it's the Torah/Old Testament, which simply states that God gave the land to the Jews, His chosen people. In transactivism it's gender identity, as summarized by Miranda Yardley[6]:

* *We all have a "gender identity" which is innate. This "gender identity" can be at odds with the physical embodiment of our sex;*

* *This "gender identity" has more weighting to our sex than the physical embodiment of our sex; and so it follows that*

* *"Trans women are women and trans men are men."*

for transgender individuals, personality determines sex.

Philosophical analysis aside, the reality is that the concept of gender identity collapses into the statement "trans women are women," and this is the foundation of most of their other claims to rights, spaces and validity. It is also the single most defended claim in transgender ideology, so much so that no debate is allowed.

I support freedom of religion, and everyone is free to believe whatever they want. I oppose forcing everyone else to believe what you believe. Everyone is welcome to their "gender identity." If a male believes he is a female, that's fine with me. If I have to believe he's female, that crosses the line.

I oppose gaslighting. I oppose requiring others to deny the evidence of their own eyes and identify someone else as a sex they are not. Not because trans-identified males don't "deserve" to be called women. But because they aren't women. "Woman" is not a club or a prize or a reward. It's a sex.

But it's treated like a club and a prize and a reward. And like anything of value intrepid males "discover," it is being colonized.

Women are not a land without a people. Women have always been people, even if men don't acknowledge that. The trans colonization project is essentially misogynist, and is popular among male Liberals for this reason.

Why do I care?

Believe me, if I could *not* care about modern transactivism, I would. I think it's my Muse's doing, because my film Seder-Masochism is about the same story: the colonization of women.

God used to be female. All of Her attributes were taken over by the male God. Creation, fertility, vegetation, the bringing forth of food, life and death – all that was once the Goddess's is now God's.

623

It's like the male God put on Her clothes, and then "identified" as Her, and there's no Goddess anymore.

Our connection to ancient goddess worship is completely broken. There's some art, and some ruins, and some echoes in myths and fairy tales, but we have no idea how these religions were really practiced. Modern western goddess-worship is re-built, re-invented, and re-imagined; it is immature, instead of building on thousands of years of tradition.

The establishment of YHWH as the One, Male God effectively erased the Goddess, and most don't even know enough to grieve. We sense there's something missing, but most can't even name it.

Gods and Goddesses are fictional, of course. What's happening now is a continuation of the erasure of the Goddess: the erasure of womanhood itself. The erasure of biological reality isn't only of concern to biological women, but to everyone who values science and some relationship to reality beyond individual "identity."

Woman means adult human female.

Womanhood is a biological reality. That's it. It's not an identity, a prize, an "exclusive club," or a land to be conquered. The more men regard womanhood as any of those things, the more inclined they are to colonize. Patriarchy regards women as property already, with disastrous consequences.

I am a reluctant feminist. I don't particularly enjoy being a woman. I don't "identify as a woman." I AM a woman. It's not a choice, it's biology. It's not a special club I'm trying to keep men out of.

Biology is the beginning and end of "womanhood," the alpha and the omega. If I wear pants, I'm a woman. If I wear a dress, I'm a woman. If my hair is long or short, I'm a woman. If I take testosterone, I'm a woman. If I cut off my breasts (don't think I haven't thought about it, I have fibrocystic breast disease and they can be very painful), I'm a woman. If I identify as a man, I'm a woman.

And if a person has a penis he's a man.
If you think that's "hate speech," the colonist is you.

Further Reading:

The Colonization of Womanhood[7]

Liberals and the New McCarthyism[8]

Endnotes

1   https://www.facebook.com/nina.paley/posts/10156238975447642.

2   https://en.wikipedia.org/wiki/Men%27s_rights_movement.

3   https://melaninandestrogen.wordpress.com/2016/11/21/the-colonization-of-womanhood/.

4   https://mirandayardley.com/en/.

5   https://transanityca.wordpress.com/2017/08/13/synanon-the-brainwashing-game-and-modern-transgender-activism-the-orwellian-implications-of-transgender-politics-by-jenn-smith/.

6   https://mirandayardley.com/en/finding-the-middle-ground-between-womens-rights-and-transgender-rights/.

7   https://melaninandestrogen.wordpress.com/2016/11/21/the-colonization-of-womanhood/.

8   https://www.counterpunch.org/2015/08/10/liberals-and-the-new-mccarthyism/.

CHAPTER 38

A New Radical Feminist Approach to Challenging Gender Identity Ideology: The Feminist Amendments to the U.S. Equality Act

by Ann E. Menasche, Feminists in Struggle, https://feministstruggle.org/

Though written for this book, this essay was originally published in Redline (republished with permission).

The mess we are in

The impact of "gender identity" on women's rights has been a regressive and destructive one all over the world. As the category of "women" is redefined by powerful forces in our society from the material reality of biological sex to a gender role or set of sex stereotypes commonly known as "femininity" that any male can identify into and many women reject, women's hard-one gains have begun to be eroded. The catechism of "transwomen are women" has meant that women have begun losing any claim to privacy rights including the ability to set our own boundaries through the elimination of private female-only spaces including bathrooms, communal showers, and changing rooms. These were gains of the First Wave of Feminism that allowed women to enter the public sphere for the first time in relative safety and comfort. Such rights continue to be essential because the problem of male violence -- rather than disappearing -- continues in epidemic proportions, as the "Me Too" movement has attested.

Also put in immediate jeopardy by "gender identity" ideology have been the gains of the Second Wave of Feminism. These include female-only battered women's shelters, rape crisis centers, affirmative action programs, women's scholarships, women's sports programs, etc., which are all essential remedies for ongoing sexism, male violence, and sex-based inequality, remedies that are now being redefined by transactivists as "bigotry" and "hate." Anti-discrimination laws that provided protection against sex discrimination, and even the Equal Rights Amendment that is at the brink of final inclusion into the Constitution, are all in jeopardy as "gender identity" subsumes sex. Even documenting sex-based disparities such as the pay gap between the sexes or sex segregation in employment becomes near impossible. Merely talking about our female bodies, discussing abortion, pregnancy, birth, breastfeeding, menstruation and menopause as female issues, as well as the meeting in female-only groups to do consciousness-raising and political organizing have been redefined by transactivists as "exclusionary" and "hate," supposedly equivalent to the horrors of racial segregation and the Jim Crow south. At the same time, individual "solutions" to women's oppression have been sold by trans ideologists to women who supposedly need no longer engage in collective struggle with their sisters but can simply "opt-out" of a female "identity."

The canaries in the coal mine have been children, mostly young girls, who have been sold the narrative that their alienation from their bodies, their gender non-conformity, the male violence and abuse that they frequently have suffered, and/or their same-sex romantic feelings mean that they were born in the "wrong" body. They are thus encouraged to undergo dangerous medical interventions that prevent them from developing normally, cause permanent harm to their bodies, and will ultimately result in sterility. For many homophobic families, such a result seems more "normal" and more preferable to having a son or daughter who matures into an openly gay or lesbian adult.

To make matters worse, all these developments have come at the same time that neoliberalism and austerity have dramatically worsened the impoverishment of women, coercing more women to stay in abusive marriages or to engage in prostitution -- so-called "sex work" -- to survive, and forcing a growing number of women and their children into homelessness; and have also coincided with religious fundamentalism, especially that of the Christian Right in the United States, gaining in influence in society and in all levels of government. The Christian Right has already rolled back and is now poised to eliminate abortion rights and to limit access to birth control, and have in their target hairs lesbian/gay rights. With fetal heartbeat bills passing in many states and a right-wing Supreme Court in place, a nightmarish future seems within reach, one where women are jailed for every suspicious miscarriage and are in constant fear of unwanted pregnancy that could do serious harm to their education and careers prospects, and place their very economic survival in jeopardy; where "no fault" divorce is eliminated; and where lesbians and gay men are sent back to the time before Stonewall.

In essence, women are stuck between a rock and a hard place, between the institutionalization of gender identity ideology that would erase us, and right wing religious fundamentalism that would enslave us.

Some feminists who understand the seriousness of the attack on women by gender identity ideology and the transgender "movement" (which is more astro-turf than a real grassroots movement engaging in a genuine civil rights struggle) have adopted an extremely narrow focus in attempting to defeat it that has caused them to make serious strategic errors. Faced with the default and active betrayal of neo-liberal capitalist politicians in the Democratic Party as well as most of the far Left, which has shamefully turned a blind eye to the harassment, violent threats and silencing of women that has occurred in the name of "trans rights," these feminists, many of whom are members of an organization called Women's Liberation

Front ("WoLF"), have turned to powerful far Right Christian fundamentalist organizations as "allies." The problem with this goes beyond the "bad look" of holding a press conference where the one feminist is surrounded by people promoting an anti-abortion and anti-gay message, or putting out a joint statement with Concerned Women of America, a group renowned for its homophobia and opposition to the Equal Rights Amendment. And it is more than the disarming of this group of feminists who may now naively think that these "conservatives," the sworn enemies of women's liberation, are quite reasonable, "really care" and "are not so bad" after all.

More importantly, this narrow single issue focus doesn't work when it comes to defending sex-based rights under attack by gender identity ideology. That is because "gender identity" depends for its very existence on rigid gender roles which maintain patriarchal power relations (what we used to call "sexism") and homophobia, in other words, the very conditions that are fostered and promoted by the Christian Right. Thus, any campaign in defense of women's sex-based rights and opposing the ideology of "gender identity" that inevitably erodes those rights must by necessity address *in the same campaign* support for lesbian and gay rights and for the right of all people to dress and express themselves as they like outside of gender role norms or stereotypes for their sex, free of discrimination or stigma. But to do that means the end of such "alliances."

Enter the U.S. Equality Act

The U.S. Equality Act, ("EA") (H.R. 5) that was approved by the U.S. House of Representatives and is now pending in the Senate, is a double-edged sword. It includes at long last badly-needed federal protections against discrimination for lesbians, gay men, and bisexuals. The EA also affirms the modest current protections in case law (via the Supreme Court's *Price Waterhouse v. Hopkins* case) against sex stereotyping. Another positive provision of the EA is the prohibition against religious exemptions to civil rights laws, a potentially huge loophole and favorite of the Christian Right that is already being used to gut civil rights protections. Religious exemptions go far beyond whether a gay couple can purchase a cake to celebrate their wedding like everyone else. With religious exemptions, employers can deny employees birth control and fire gay employees, county clerks can refuse to marry same sex couples, and landlords can refuse to rent to same sex, unmarried and/or interracial couples on religious grounds. Such exemptions undermine the idea of civil rights law that covers everyone, and the very concept of separation of church and state.

However, the EA also contains provisions that range from problematic to extremely harmful to women's rights and which would have the effect of erasing women as a sex category subject to legal protections. The EA adds "gender identity" as a form of discrimination, a term that is vague and subjective, and has been used to reinforce sex stereotypes that oppress women and all gender non-conforming people (i.e., the idea that "feminine" males are not "real men," and that "masculine" females are not "real women"), eliminating distinctions based on biological sex. Just as "race blind" policies make it impossible to see and address racism, "sex blind" policies which arise from the embrace of "gender identity" likewise make it impossible to see and address sexism.

Additionally, the EA includes "gender identity," "sexual orientation," and "sex stereotyping" under the single category of "sex discrimination," potentially leading to lack of clarity and confusion that may have a negative impact on women's sex-based rights. Far more dangerously, the EA defines "sex" and "gender-identity" as synonymous terms. The current bill thereby explicitly allows "gender identity" to subsume sex-based rights by prohibiting female-only spaces, thereby guaranteeing male access to such spaces based on their proclaimed "gender identity" (which means any male who identifies as a woman).

The birth of Feminists in Struggle

Feminists in Struggle ("FIST") was launched on International Women's Day, March 8, 2019, as a female-only radical feminist organization based in the United States. FIST bases its unity on agreement with thirteen principles, including affirmation that women and girls are oppressed based on biological sex; opposition to the system of gender roles; support for reproductive rights and lesbian rights; support for the Equal Rights Amendment; support for the abolition of prostitution through the adoption of the "Nordic Model" (which criminalizes pimps and sex buyers while decriminalizing prostituted women and girls); opposition to male violence and racism; support for free childcare and paid parental leave; and support for female-only spaces, programs and organizations.

Though there are many points of agreement with the feminists in WoLF, FIST distinguishes itself by explicitly rejecting alliances with the Christian Right as one of its principles and adapting a grassroots democratic decision-making structure. FIST also emphasizes a multi-issue approach to the fight for women's liberation and a more integrated longer term strategy to fighting gender identity ideology and defending the sex-based rights of women and girls. FIST's strategy emphasizes winning the battle of ideas within the whole society, including within the broad Left, through creating a new wave of visible in-the-streets feminist organizing and activism. This is the same strategy that won women the vote and resulted in the *Roe v. Wade* Supreme Court decision legalizing abortion in the United States. These victories were not gifts bestowed from on high but were won by mass struggle of millions of women. FIST believes that such a strategy is ultimately more decisive in achieving the changes that we currently seek as compared to a focus on lobbying politicians in the two corporate parties or playing one wing of the patriarchy against the other.

The Feminist Amendments to the Equality Act

A committee of FIST lawyers collaborated in a major rewrite of the Equality Act which we have called "the Feminist Amendments to the Equality Act" or "FAEA." Our aim in proposing these Amendments is to support the claims of lesbian, gay, bisexual, and transgender-identifying people as well as all gender non-conforming people for freedom from discrimination without compromising the fight against oppression based on sex.

The Feminist Amendments include the following provisions:

1. The FAEA establish two new categories or protected classes in federal civil rights law based on sexual orientation (homosexuality, heterosexuality, and bisexuality) and sex stereotyping, separate from sex.

2. "Sex" is defined as "genes, gonads, and the gametes that an individual body is configured to produce" that cannot be changed. The FAEA recognize the existence of people with differences of sexual development (sometimes popularly referred to as "intersex" individuals), and also recognize that ordinarily such individuals can still be classified as male or female.

3. "Sex discrimination" is defined as discrimination against individuals based on sex and includes discrimination based on pregnancy, childbirth, lactation, and other related conditions.

4. The FAEA add robust findings on the systemic inequalities of power and resources between men and women in all areas of life, including employment and education, the denial of rights over our bodies and reproductive capacities, and the need for female-only space, programs, and services to combat discrimination and to provide privacy and refuge from male violence.

5. The FAEA delete references to "gender identity" from the Equality Act. In its place the FAEA provide a broad and com-

prehensive definition of "sex stereotyping" which includes the expectation that individuals will manifest behaviors, dress, appearance, grooming, etc. traditionally associated with their sex and refrain from exhibiting those associated with the other sex. The protection against discrimination based on sex stereotyping would cover not only transgender-identifying people such as by protecting them from being fired from their jobs as happened to Stephens in the *Harris Funeral Homes* case. The Feminist Amendments also provide stronger, more comprehensive protections to gender non-conforming people generally as compared to the current version of the Equality Act. Under the Feminist Amendments, for example, all sex-based dress and grooming codes by employers and schools would be clearly prohibited, not just those directed against transgender-identifying people. At the same time, the Feminist Amendments provide that sex stereotyping discrimination does not include merely recognizing or referring to the sex of an individual. This is essential to allow for meaningful protection against sex discrimination.

6. The FAEA provide that female-only facilities, programs and services are not prohibited under civil rights laws and neither is publication of statistics based on biological sex. The establishment of separate facilities for transgender-identifying individuals and the establishment of "gender neutral" facilities are also not prohibited "as long as such facilities do not reduce the availability of and access to single sex facilities for women and girls."

Why Feminist Amendments?

But why try to amend the Equality Act at all? Why not just oppose the bill outright as WoLF has done?

Clearly, if radical feminists were in Congress and we were faced with an up and down vote on the Equality Act *as is*, all of us would be forced to vote "no." The current version of the Equality Act has such a negative impact on our sex-based rights that even with its positive provisions we would have no choice but to oppose it. However, we would first try to amend the bill so that the positive provisions were maintained and the women-erasing provisions deleted.

This is even more imperative as feminists standing outside of Congress. We need to project a vision of what kind of world feminists are fighting for. The Equality Act's consideration in Congress allows us to educate the population on how to resolve in a radical feminist manner the conflict of rights that has emerged between women and transgender-identifying individuals. We plan to accomplish this through seeking individual and organizational endorsements for the Feminist Amendments and holding public events to discuss our proposals. When we approach Congress, we hope to have a movement behind us.

The presently existing transgender movement is thoroughly misogynistic and reactionary. But there is a thread of legitimacy that author J.K. Rowling put her finger on when she asserted on in a Twitter conversation the right of every person to "[d]ress as you please, call yourself whatever you like, sleep with any consenting adult who'll have you, live your best life in peace and security." That's the message that needs to be incorporated into the fight to preserve and expand the sex-based rights of women and girls. In its essence, this is the message of feminism itself.

For more information on the Feminist Amendments to the Equality Act, check out https://feministstruggle.org/faea/. And please consider signing on as an endorser and join the campaign!

Update: The U.S. Supreme Court's decision in *Bostock v. Clayton County, Georgia*:

The Feminist Amendments to the Equality Act were drafted by a committee of Feminists in Struggle lawyers prior to the U.S. Supreme Court issuing its surprise decision in *Bostock v. Clayton*

County, Georgia in June 2020. In a broad reading of the civil rights laws, the Supreme Court in *Bostock* ruled that the prohibition against discrimination based on sex under Title VII of the Civil Rights Act of 1964 includes both sexual orientation and something called "transgender status." In the wake of *Bostock*, is FIST's approach outlined above and incorporated into the Feminist Amendments still relevant? I believe that it still is.

The Supreme Court decision actually ruled on three cases, two regarding job discrimination against gay men. The Court's finding that employment discrimination based on sexual orientation constitutes sex discrimination and is therefore illegal, is a cause for feminists to celebrate. There is no conflict between women's rights and lesbian/gay rights with which to contend.

The third case, *EEOC v. Harris Funeral Homes, Inc.*, involved a transgender-identifying male, Aimee Stephens, who was fired from his job after announcing he was "transitioning" and would be returning to work in women's clothes. The result in itself -- that Stephens should not have been fired for not wanting to follow the employer's male dress code -- should not be at all problematic for feminists. In addition, the Court's reasoning makes sense. Justice Gorsuch does not actually adopt gender identity ideology, despite his use of "preferred pronouns" for Stephens. Instead, he embraces, at least for the purposes of this decision, a definition of sex based on the biological distinctions between males and females. Thus, the Court observed that "an employer who fires an individual for being homosexual or transgender fires that person for traits or actions it would not have questioned in members of a different sex." Discrimination based on transgender status (which per the above description sounds a lot like "sex stereotyping" as defined in the Feminist Amendments) was therefore held to be "in part" based on sex, rather than transgender identity being a synonym for sex itself or the new definition of sex. Moreover, the Supreme Court put off decisions about sex segregated bathrooms, etc. until another day.

However, given the tendency of courts and legislatures to erase sex as a distinct category in favor of "gender identity," will this decision provide more fuel to the fire? Will the Courts confuse discrimination on the basis (in part) on sex, with sex itself? There is undeniably quite a bit of ambiguity in the *Bostock* decision, including a failure to define "transgender" and to make it clear that sex cannot be changed. So the *Bostock* decision indeed created cause for feminists to worry.

As it turns out, it didn't take long -- only two months -- for a lower Court to run with it and cite *Bostock* as grounds for substituting "gender identity" for sex, and eliminating the right to separate bathroom facilities based on sex, even though such right is explicitly provided for in Title IX law and regulations. In *Adams v. School Board of St. Johns County, Florida*, the Eleventh Circuit Court of Appeal, relying on *Bostock*, ruled that denying a girl who identified as a "transgender boy" access to the boy's bathroom, despite the availability of a "gender neutral" facility, constituted discrimination based on sex in violation of Title IX. Then approximately two weeks later, the Fourth Circuit in *Grimm vs. Gloucester County School Board* came to the same conclusions based on virtually identical facts.

In light of this development, the general approach taken by the Feminist Amendments remains essential. In order to avoid confusion and end the conflation of sex and "gender identity" (or more accurately, the disappearing of sex completely in favor of gender identity), we need a bill with clear definitions of all the terms being used, and ideally, separate provisions protecting each class of persons, rather than merging distinct protections under the broad umbrella of "sex." Though "sex stereotyping" used in the Feminist Amendments is better than "transgender status," it is not immune from being misused in the absence of a clear definition of what "sex" is (and that it cannot be changed) and a definition of what "sex stereotyping" includes and does not include. Notably both the *Adams* and *Grimm* Courts also held that the School Board had discriminated against the transgender-identified females based on "sex stereotyping" by denying access to the bathroom "matching" their gender identity.

Most importantly, we need a federal bill (whether as amendments to the Equality Act or as a separate piece of legislation) to spell out the rights of women and girls to separate spaces for safety and privacy (including restrooms, changing rooms, dorm rooms, prison cells, battered women's shelters, etc.) and separate programs (affirmative action programs, scholarships, sports programs, etc.) that seek to advance our status in society, apart from males including those who identify as "transgender."

It is more imperative than ever that we organize to demand that our rights as females not be subordinated or eliminated based on the competing claims of any other social group, marginalized or not. Asserting the rights of women and girls to our own spaces and programs is not discrimination, but is one of the remedies needed to end discrimination based on sex.

PART VIII:

RADICAL FEMINIST FICTION, POETRY, PLAYS, MEMOIR, AND LITERARY ANALYSIS

CHAPTER 39

The Power of Sisterhood Voices

by Alyssa Ahrabare

[Alyssa Ahrabare is a 25-year-old French feminist from Moroccan and Algerian origins. With a Masters in International Law and a specialization in human rights and fundamental liberties, she is now an international consultant on women human rights. Alyssa is a spokeswoman for the French non-profit organization Osez le Féminisme! ("Dare to Be Feminist"). She is a Project Officer for the European Network of Migrant Women, which she represents in the Women in Politics group of the European Women's Lobby. In addition, she is a co-organizer of Radical Girlsss (young women's movement for a global radical feminist perspective). Alyssa also founded a theatre company which uses art and pedagogy to promote equality between women and men.

This extract from her play Walks and Talks addresses psychotraumatic disorders caused by pedocriminal violence. Mechanisms such as involuntary paralysis, dissociation, and traumatic amnesia are still widely ignored and not yet recognised by the justice systems, to the detriment of victims of sexual violence. Alyssa is in favor of the total suppression of statutory limitation of sexual crimes against minors, a provision reserved in France for crimes against humanity.]

◇◈◇

Winter dusk dropping down like snow. Shadows roaring outside. In the crisp air, hawthorns are dead seeds unable to blossom as the rain falls, and falls again.

He is often around. I am used to the cuddles of the prickly sweater. His big purple raincoat always drips on the entrance floor.

I am stranded in my room. Mom told me to go to bed, but I cannot sleep, mesmerised by the vanishing lights slithering from the window, transforming the floor into rippling water. Forgotten in my bed, the captain of a ship sailing in the midst of the storm, I steer to the rhythm of the howling wind, to the rhythm of lightning streaks, to the sounds of laughing coming from downstairs and crashing on my closed bedroom door, like the foam of the waves on the white sand of a beach.

Suddenly, the door opens, and I am drowning in light. In the bright frame, here he stands, a shadow with a purple raincoat. Usually, I like the hugs from the prickly sweater. But this one... This one I don't like. This one says no. A thundering no from inside of me. No, no. NO! My whole body screams in silence, but the hug keeps on itching, the hug keeps on burning.

He picks up his purple raincoat. Before leaving he smiles at me. Downstairs, the logs crackle in the fireplace. Outside, in the cold and gloom, the rain rushes on the leaves of old trees. In my bedroom, now wet with pain and shame, my boat is sinking. Once again forgotten in my bed, I fall, and fall again.

Hawthorns from the garden's May trees aren't blooming. The garden is filled with grey, empty bushes, like ghosts blocking the light. Flowers are nowhere to be seen. Colours are nowhere to be seen. I am cold, all the time. I stopped playing with friends at school. It's like I'm not even there. People say I'm nasty. My dad scolds me and I am cold. This winter has no end and I will always be cold. I fall, and fall again, surrounded by empty bushes that block the light, forgotten on my wrecked ship, a barrier of water between me and the world. Time passes, like I'm not even there. I see my body from the outside, like I'm not even there. As if ants had crept up inside and were slowly eating away my essence, without anyone noticing.

I have defected myself. Time passes and nothing's easy anymore. I am hurt by people's laughter. I am hurt by the sound of the rain. I don't sleep anymore, I sink. I fall. I fall, and fall again.

I am thirty. I woke up one morning, sweating in my bed.

At thirty I remembered… The hug from the prickly sweater, now I remember.

I'm a child still, a purple shadow is following me around, making me renounce everything. I tell my father; he does not believe me. He says I am lying; he says I am deranged. The purple shadow keeps pulling the strings, like I'm not even there. I tell the therapist, he says I am to blame, he says I asked for it, the hug from the prickly sweater. He says I wanted it. Blades, deep in my lungs. The sky remains iron, darkness dropping down like snow. The hawthorn bushes are grey and empty, they're closing in on me like ghosts blocking the light. I tell the policewoman; she says I should not expect miracles. She says it happened too long ago, the hug from the prickly sweater, she says I should get over it and stop wasting her time. The judge says the same thing as the therapist. I did want it, the hug from the prickly sweater, to satisfy my early sexual needs. I will not tell anyone anymore. Forgotten in my bed, wet with pain and shame, wide awake, I am haunted by the sound of the rain falling, and falling again.

I keep on sinking, petrified and barely existing, losing years and years of my life. I am forty now and I have a new job. I have a colleague from Czechia; her name is Neha. Neha in Czech means tenderness. It's raining tonight. Drops falling, and falling again like bombs. Their sound on the sheet metal of my car is filling up all the space in the world, driving me to terror. As I gasp for air, she's suddenly here. Neha. Her light curls tickle my skin as she takes me in. Within her embrace I feel warm… Floating. Neha, like a lifeline, takes me to the surface through the bright love of her sight. I don't realise I'm crying. I don't realise I'm speaking. Neha welcomes the clash of my words in the vivid clearness of her eyes, her hands strong around mine. Head above the water, I can breathe. My heart explodes when she tells me she believes me, when she tells me that, long ago, her body also screamed no in silence. When she assures me that these things are nothing like hugs. When she confides to me that we are not alone, that men have stolen many years from many of our sisters. That they have no right. That we can heal.

Today, night terrors torment me still, but less. My years of agony are softened by Neha's light and by the sweet presence of feminist women she has introduced me to. They call each other sisters. They help me recognise and separate who I truly am from what he left inside when he broke into my self, what remained walled in to control my very existence without me knowing. They have words, right words, proper words that can chase the night away, words that can help me survive it. They believe broken pieces can be restored with care and knowledge... Among them I feel I am worth something. Among them I feel! I want to relearn everything, be stronger, liberated, I want to stop giving up on joy. Above all, I want to be connected to women and girls. Now that I know what is done to us, I want for no one to ever lose herself at the bottom of a sinking ship again. That's what is giving me strength, actually. What I do for me, I do for them. Everything I do for them, I am doing for myself. In the hawthorn bushes, burgeons are finally blooming. The circle seems broken, like winter could end. I learnt a new word, sisterhood. It is this bond, between us women, this kind of deep, incomparable, unconditional and universal love that I never knew. I hear sisterhood can heal the world... It's so powerful it may even be true.

When asked to contribute to this feminist anthology, I chose to complement the extract above from my play *Walks and Talks* with an essay on the cultural aspect of the feminist fight. This subject, dear to my heart, is the reason why I find so much joy and relief writing plays denouncing male violence against women and girls. The essay follows.

"I've learned that people will forget what you said, people will forget what you did, but people will never forget how you made them feel."

When I read this quote from Maya Angelou, it resonated a lot with what I have experienced throughout my feminist journey.

I have always been a feminist, long before I actually knew what it meant, and even before I really learned about the patriarchy or about the continuum of systemic violence globally silencing, killing and erasing women and girls.

When I reached out to a feminist organisation for the first time, to meet other women, to understand, to fight, I fell headfirst into an infinite ocean that keeps on expanding. Even today, after so many years.

I discovered femicides, and I learned that these crimes are far from the random private events still widely described in the media. I discovered the reality of prostitution - and its filmed form, pornography - which is women and girls who are trafficked, held in unsafe and at-risk environments, raped and drugged. I learned about dissociation and involuntary paralysis, the lasting impacts of sexual violence and incest. I met women whose lives stopped when they were 10, 5, 17, 31, 97. I learned about forced marriage, genital mutilation and pedocriminality, sexual harassment and inequalities in the workplace, institutional and medical violences. I learned about society's obsession with controlling women's bodies in any and every way, the pervasive stereotypes that lead to disease or death. I learned about the absence of representation in politics, in culture, everywhere.

I learned about gynecide.

So, I went deeper and deeper, to the roots of things, every fiber of my body rejecting the usual outrageous explanations: "that's the way things are," "it's always been like that." Lies. Things don't just happen in society, they are constructed, they are the result of a series of causes and consequences that create History.

To be solved, a problem needs to be understood.

All our lives, as girls, and as young women, we have been told over and over that women never invented, women never created, women never existed.

When we first started to read, books told us that boys were able to do anything, explore and conquer, fight injustice, save others and themselves. And girls? Fairy tales warned us about predators lurking in the shadows, telling us to follow the rules, be careful and never venture outside. These stories omit the fact that most women's attackers are not actually random wolves wandering the forest but rather men they know and sometimes love. They taught us that a boy can kiss a girl in her sleep and that it will make her eternally grateful. That we should sell what we cherish most in order to achieve love, or not even love, the mere attention of a man. These stories taught us that a woman with power can be nothing but a heinous witch and that we should aspire to be longing princesses instead: nice and safe! Or else…we need to watch out.

Witches are burnt at the stake, we know. Witches are killed. Those witches, those women, violated, humiliated and executed through ages, for what? Being free, speaking loud, standing tall, having medical knowledge, writing or reading books, daring to gather outside of male control, or even less than that, for anything really. For being a woman, in fact. Burnt, in public, so that we could all see, learn, be terrorised into knowing that we should stick to our place. Far from sight, cloistered, far from the smells of burning flesh.

These stories also led us to believe that other women are the enemy. Every told tale built walls between my sisters and myself, leaving me empty, alone. Alone as prey. Alone at the mercy of predators that devour us with the very love that we are supposed to long for. They steal our voices, our lives, the end of our stories, our existence finished by their encounter and our abduction.

What these stories really tell us in the end, is that, as women, we only exist through the care and service of men, through our sacrifices to them. We are nothing but tools, ready to be erased for the real heroes to exist.

So where does the story end? Where does reality begin? I believe that these tales we are fed, the History we are taught, the language we speak, the media we watch, the toys we play with, I believe that every single aspect of what educates us, what creates our sense of right and wrong, our sense of normality - I believe that all of this is at the root of the problem.

The feminist fight is also cultural.

We need to take back the narrative. Tell our stories. Tell any story from a new perspective, a new vision, a point of view that is never seen or heard. That's why I love this quote by Maya Angelou: When you are finally exposed to one of these visions, one of OUR stories. When, as a woman, you finally hear your own voice through someone else's: that's an unforgettable emotion. It's inspiring and it's definitely something to cherish.

When we were young, in school, we were only told about what men created, what men experienced through History, the fights they fought, what they wrote, what they invented... We were never told about Alice Guy who transformed cinema, nor about Nellie Bly who revolutionized journalism against all odds, nor Emmy Noether, Daisy Bates, Mary Andersen, Maria Telkes, Harriet Tubman, Grace Hopper, Stephanie Kwolek, or Ann Tsukamoto.

We never knew that women invented life rafts, syringes, refrigerators, ice cream machines, data processing, telecommunication technology, wireless transfer, video surveillance, circular saws, central heating, distress rockets, clear glass, suspension bridges, submarines. We never knew that women discovered the structure of the DNA, the genetic code of bacteria, the chemical composition of stars, hundreds of planets, dark matter, nuclear fission, the treatment for leukemia, the treatment for human papillomavirus, X and Y chromosomes. We never heard about Enheduanna, the first known female writer; Fatima al Fihriya who founded the world's oldest university; Trotula de Salerne who was one of the first people to ever talk about women's health and gynecology. We never learned about the strong, courageous, resilient women who fought against colonialism on every single continent: Fatma N'Souer in Algeria

647

against the French, Manuela Saenz in South America against the Spanish, Tarenorerer in Australia against the British.

We never knew women fought wars and traveled, explored and discovered, we never knew women led people and armies, inspired and created, flew and sailed, as pilots and pirates. We never knew because no one ever told us. So many of us never thought it was even possible.

It's often said that girls start feeling like they are less than boys around the age of six. Why wouldn't we when everything is done to limit our universe? In a world where everything is masculine from the names of our streets to the heroes in the books we love, from gods to presidents, how can we dream of ourselves as strong, inspiring, and whole?

I want to tell stories about all the women who were and who are erased. All the women that we are prevented from admiring or aspiring to become. Their mere existence is obliterated to have us believe that we cannot accomplish anything, that we only exist to be beautiful and care for others.

I would have loved to know about all of them sooner, to learn their names. Our sisters. Artists, scientists, activists, heroines, survivors who disappeared from our collective memories because of patriarchy. To tell their stories is to tell our collective story. It is taking back our common consciousness, our voices, our places. And ultimately, our lives.

CHAPTER 40

Endangered = at risk

by Giovanna Capone

you're on the list
of those expected to vanish

I see the connection
a definite loss of direction
in the loss of our lesbian spaces

We're being crowded out and drowned
in the alphabet soup
a toxic goop
that's eating us alive

Are we the last spotted owl
in a ponderosa pine?

I do not accept
the demise
of my lesbian tribe
the L
of LGBT
is not a dying breed

We are the living seed
of future generations

a lesbian nation
that will swing back
robust and green
stronger than we've ever been
a modern day Amazon tribe
thriving and alive

a silver labrys
on every neck
connects us to the matriarchs of old
A golden age
of female power
even in our darkest hour

I see a day
when lesbians of every age are strong
exuberant in life and love
our bookstores, festivals, dances, films
in full swing

Extinction is a vanishing
a languishing
a death

But we are alive!

Walking in a redwood grove
is where you see it best
the tallest living beings on earth
encounter all extremes

the oldest ones stand strong
among the young
the dead remain intact

Wounded trees are living trees
still giving every molecule of power to the young
struck by lightning
bent by storms
scorched by fire
they live strong

Old wood is good wood
in two hundred years

In the undergrowth you'll see the evidence of green
a million needle leaves are sprouting
from the trunks of older trees.

CHAPTER 41

The Parents

by Nineveh Cehack

"Oh, my mother died a few years back," a co-worker said as I inquired about why she never seemed to talk about her mother as much as she did her father. We had spent the last few weeks getting closer and our conversations now constantly veered into deeper topics.

"Ah." I paused. "I'm sorry" was on the tip of my tongue, but I stopped myself. Instead, I asked, "Did you love your mother?"

This is a question that has been slowly working its way into my vocabulary. Do you want to be pregnant? Did you love or even like your uncle/sister/father/cousin? It was a brash question made out of genuine empathy. I did not want to assume anything about anyone. In the years since I had made this choice, amazingly enough, not a single person has reacted immediately to any variance of the last question. There's always a hesitation, a quick review of all the memories in their mind, and finally, the answer: "Yeah, I guess."

So, the obvious question: Do I love my mother?

The answer: One day, I joked about with my mother that she wouldn't have to worry about domineering men taking advantage of her daughters if she just had a gay daughter. She groaned, an exaggerated sound, and declared, "I'd die if I had a gay daughter." My little sister and I made eye contact across the kitchen table. I was thinking, at the time, "Well, I guess I shouldn't be gay" and also "That is the best goddamn incentive to being gay I've ever heard."

Years back, when I was a horribly awkward child in elementary school and my older sister was a rebellious teenager, I unwillingly found myself spending time with her first and only boyfriend and future husband—a Jewish boy. I was never sure which came first: the boyfriend or the interest in Judaism. Nonetheless, they began to represent the same thing in my parents' eyes. They were staunchly Christian, members of a Middle-Eastern ethnic group that continues to face genocide and cultural assimilation due to their Christian and non-Arab realities. The idea of escaping a war-torn country where their right to exist was being eroded and having their American-born daughter defect to another religion—even worse, the *Jews*—was too much for them to handle.

There wasn't anything I thought particularly special about our branch of Christianity. We didn't decorate our churches—a wise use of the donated money, I thought—we had no confessionals and, most scandalously to the Catholic Church, our priests could marry. I never felt any sort of holiness from my parents. I felt as if they thought themselves holy by virtue of existing. It could take them far enough, I supposed, but not far enough to strike their children until they sobbed.

Hitting your child wasn't an uncommon thing among Assyrian households. A smack across the face, hissed threats in Assyrian to stop that crying or else they'd get it later, so on and so forth. I never was comfortable with it, so I found a way to sink into my video games as my sister and mother shouted at each other until the hitting began and my sister's angry screams would switch to pleads to stop.

Even as I hated it, I found myself imitating their behavior, threatening to smack younger cousins if they didn't do what I wanted. The ugliness in me grew bigger and uglier and I prayed my cousins forgot with time, that they would never remember the cruel me.

They stopped hitting us a long time ago. Not because they had seen the error of their ways and not even because we grew too big and strong to quietly allow it to happen, but because it stopped working. Because it went beyond what most Assyrians find acceptable and the social stigma was too strong. The threat was still there, but now I had a challenging smile and the mutual knowledge that I could drag them down with me.

Another memory: Last week, I watched my parents as they passed through airport security, on their way to a European vacation. I lived in their home, so I had to help them get to the airport. I hugged them as they got in line and smiled as they waved. They would be gone for nearly two weeks. As I got back into the car, my father's car, I breathed a sigh of relief. When I woke up the next morning to an empty house, I grinned and giggled, even as I looked around in self-conscious embarrassment, and felt like a kid. Every morning that I woke up alone, I felt as if I were a little less ugly.

At one point in time, in the nebulous years of my older sister's high school experience, there was the social worker. My sister went to school with a black eye. She couldn't turn her head without it hurting her neck because my father's foot had landed against it one night when they tried to pull her out from the table she crawled under for protection. The social worker was a sweet woman with a sweeter smile. She sat across from me in the living room of my childhood home.

My parents sat next to me.

How is your home life? How are you doing in school? Do you like school?

Yes, okay, I guess, and yeah, I like it.

It would take until I was in high school to admit it to myself. This was abuse, wasn't it? None of my friends knew, but this was proof how well children could hide their pain. I'd spend one moment on the floor, reeling from a harsh smack to the face, my nose aching from where the bridge of my glasses were smashed roughly into it, and within 5 minutes I'd be smiling and courteous as we ate a wholesome family dinner. I could step into a room and sense the atmosphere immediately. Was she mad? Was he mad? Did I do anything to upset them? I was the animal sensing its predator, masterfully inching past as it slumbered. I tasted the air.

Let's think about this for a second: My mother was trying to revive her relationship with her father, a year before I had finished college. I had only seen the man twice in my lifetime. My grandmother, his wife, no longer acknowledged his existence. He was a physically and emotionally abusive man. My mother asked, in a terrifying moment of self-awareness, "Am I like my father?" I stared down at my dinner and screamed on the inside. She kept trying with her father and I stood behind her, hesitant but hopeful. "Remember," I'd tell her, "there's nothing wrong with wanting a relationship with your father, but it's not going to work out if he doesn't acknowledge that what he did was wrong." She would nod, taking the advice to heart, and I found myself happy for her chance at closure, at some semblance of healing. But in my mind, I begged that she would finally make the connection, that maybe she would see where she had gone wrong. That I was speaking about her relationship to her daughters as much as I was speaking about her relationship to her father.

Or maybe this one: My mother and I, sitting at the dinner table together. It's Wednesday night, it's Saturday night, it's right after work or maybe it's just before bed, but we're sitting, chatting, smiling and laughing as we gossip the hours away. When I'm done with my meal or ready to leave, I get up and push my chair in. I give her a hug and tell her goodnight. She hugs me back, sometimes with one arm, sometimes with both, and tells me she loves me. I would hum in acknowledgement, never saying it back to her—I am unable to recall when I last did.

My older sister ran away from home when she was freshly eighteen, a solid couple of years into her relationship with her boyfriend. Unbeknownst to anyone in the family, she had been slowly funneling out her essentials over the past few months. One day, her friends met her outside her bedroom window and helped her climb down. She officially converted to Judaism within the year. I was angry. I was upset. I thought, "Why didn't you take me with you?" I was twelve.

Months later, I popped open my CD player for the first time in a long time. The cover flew open easily, revealing the folded up pieces of paper between the cover and CD. It was a farewell letter from my sister. Even now, I couldn't remember anything about the letter except for the tears that fell, shaking my whole body. My parents walked in, likely hearing the sounds of my cries, and took the letter from my hands. They asked the cruelest question of all: "Why are you crying? Why are you crying?" I thought monsters could never understand how people feel and hurt.

Far into the future I could barely imagine as a child: I was moving out, fresh out of college and a year into my new job. I was moving in with two of my best friends. I stood in the garage beside a van that held the last of my possessions. My mother stood in the doorway, sobbing her eyes out. My apartment was a ten-minute drive from my parents'. She said, "If you leave, you'll never come back." I hugged and consoled her, my eyes burning. I thought, "God, I wish, I wish, I wish."

Later, I sat on the floor of my room in my apartment, crying. I ached at their disapproval and was angered some part of me still sought after anything resembling approval from them. They never cared about the person in front of them, only the doll that did and dressed as they deemed appropriate.

An example: My little sister was in high school. She brought home a 3.8 GPA every year. My mother inspected her report card, eyes skimming past all the As, and froze on her Math class. "This is a B. Do better." When she left, my little sister sat down at her desk and stared at her laptop. Her eyes glistened. I took her report card.

"This is great! You did an awesome job!" I said, smiling the biggest I could. "You're much better at this than I was."

She looked up at me and nodded, lips trembling only the smallest bit.

Another example: I was handed two copies of the massive poster that sported my image on it. I was an example for my university to show off to the world. I was a university student representative, often standing on stage during graduations to aid the administrators. "Here," the Student Life director told me, "one for you and one for your parents." I smiled and nodded. Both of the posters sit folded in one of my drawers. A lifetime of conditioning told me that my parents would never care about any achievement if it didn't mean good grades or money. I look at them every so often, alongside the other rewards and publications I've received, collecting dust.

The follow-up question: Do you love your father?

He had a heart attack one night. I was young, maybe ten, maybe eleven. He nearly died, or so the doctors say. He smoked often. I asked him, "Could you maybe please stop smoking?" I didn't want him to die. I was tired of the way the cigarette smoke made my lungs feel whenever he was near me. I was scared, in the irrational way of a child, that I was going to get asthma. He frowned at me, "The doctors also said it was stress that did it. And since your older sister can't stop stressing me out, why should I stop smoking?"

I began throwing out his cigarette packs if I found them. He got better at hiding them. Eventually, I gave up and he, too, gave up the pretense of quitting.

Every year, we have a feast for our church's saint. For the past few years, I've helped out with taking donations, if only because it kept me out of the actual boring festivities. My father sat on the committee that organized the feast. Without fail, he'd beam at me and thank me sincerely for my help. When his old friends would pass by, he would introduce me with pride, his warm hand on my back. I'd find myself smiling back, standing up straight, hating myself a little bit more as I preened under his attention.

Once he drove me back to my apartment, hell-bent on getting me to change from the dress pants I was wearing to something more respectable, a dress, before we left for a wedding. He likely didn't realize that my mind was made up and that I would walk into my apartment, take off my pants, crawl into bed, and not get up until tomorrow.

"Your mother just wants you to look good." He repeated to me, for the umpteenth time.

"Okay, but why isn't this good enough? What about this makes me look bad?"

He didn't say anything.

"She needs to get it through her head that I don't exist to do whatever she wants of me." I continued, undeterred, the bitterness seeping into my voice.

"Then what are children for?" He screamed and I jumped in my seat, pressing my back against the car door, even as he continued to calmly drive. "Of course, you're my kids, I decide what to do with you. If I want to hit you, I'll hit you!"

I swallowed the lump in my throat and told that small piece of my heart that hurt that this is what I deserved for trying to make him feel again.

"He just dances to the beat of her drum," I told my older sister one afternoon as I held my infant niece close to my chest, mindful of how my hands supported her. My older sister stood in the kitchen, preparing the dinner we would have later. "I feel like if she were gone, he'd be a perfectly decent human being. Not that this excuses him, but he hardly seems to start anything."

"No," she said. "You just didn't see it. He's got a nasty temper. One time, he smashed my head into the car window."

I didn't respond. My niece snuggled deeper into me, her head lodging itself under my chin. I held her close and timed my breathing with hers.

It wasn't until after college that I realized I was repeating myself far more often than normal. Nothing I said seemed to click in my father's head, as if he had just heard the beginnings and ends of sentences. I dreaded talking to him about anything more complicated than the weather. My mother complained that his brain was broken, that she could tell something was wrong with him after his heart attack many years ago.

Some part of me was relieved that there was something eating away at that horrid man that I knew. That, if I waited long enough, I'd have an absent-minded father who no longer had any of that anger. If I waited long enough, I'd have a completely new person: a benign old man. I wished for his mind to deteriorate faster.

I wondered if all he had left were his habits. As a child, I could remember him walking into my room when he thought I had finally fallen asleep and laying a kiss upon my forehead. I soaked up the simple affection. Even now, he remembers to do so and some strange, silly part of me smiles in my half-awake state.

The ultimate question: Do I love my parents?

I received my acceptance letter from the school I would later attend for my Masters. I spent weeks crunching the numbers. How much would I have to take out in loans? Is there any way I could make this work part-time, so I could keep my job? Could any of my savings survive this? Was there anyone else I could live with to save on costs? I decided to move back in with my parents.

A few months prior, I had called the police on my mother after she had waved a knife at my little sister and slapped her hard. My knowing smile had failed me and my only weapon were the finger-shaped bruises I left on my mother's arms as I held her back from hurting my little sister further. I sobbed to the police sergeant after his officers kicked me out—after all, I no longer lived there—sobbed in the shower at my older sister's home hours later and sobbed again the next morning as I walked back to my apartment, grateful that the myriad of strangers I passed paid no attention to the young woman crying into the folded comforter in her hands. I thought of a monologue I had come across during my theatre days of high school. The lines sat with me for days, even as I failed to understand why. The character pleaded for her sanity, trying to stop her parents from having her committed to a psychiatric facility. The lawyer asks her if she loves her mother. She pleads,

> *"Something happens to some people. They love you so much, they stop noticing you're there, because they're so busy loving you. They love you so much, their love is a gun, and they fire it straight into your head. ...Mama, I know you love me. And I know the one thing you learn when you grow up is that love is not enough. It's too much, and it's not enough."* *(Ritt, "Nuts").*

There is a girl, a young woman, in the minds of my parents. She looks like me, sometimes. She takes her glasses off more than I do and straightens her hair every day and grows it very long. She speaks Assyrian fluently and is surrounded by Assyrian friends. She wears heels and dresses and make-up and never swears. She shaves her legs and her armpits and puts her legs together when she sits. She honors her parents, but honors God above all. They love her to shreds. They want the best for her and want to help steer her on the right path to success and happiness, by whatever means necessary.

That girl doesn't exist. She never did.

References

Ritt, Martin, director. *Nuts*. Warner Bros, 1987.

CHAPTER 42

eternal until you are full

by Tristan Fox

3 times last night
i awakened to my beloved—my
heart ringed around by that
penumbra of black ache
i know
you know.
this will be our lot—
this year of distance;
of time moving away fast,
past our clutches on the
last day when I fly west;
when you fly east.

every ounce of my being is a rose garden for
you, and the ocean and the tides and the stars in
your belly touch
my tongue. this rosebud in my mouth blossoms as
your hands entwine beneath the feather pillow in that
tin ceiling art deco hotel where
we made love on friday night in the rain in
downtown chatham—-

my ancestor's imprints still lucid in the streets.
every fibre of me inside you now
my hands chart the tender map of you—map of joy
and heaven that I have taken into my core;
the way you yield, my love;
the way i place my dna strands like a delicate offering
against your womb.

always i will come to you.
always i linger with these love poems wrapped in opal bows—
one after the other loosed until you are full of the strands of me
unravelling, deepening, now unfurled
inside you. this ribbon of
eternal until you are full.

CHAPTER 43

Passionate Stone

by Tristan Fox

"Against you I fling myself, unvanquished and unyielding, O Death!

The waves broke on the shore." Virginia Woolf.

lilo berliner

was at the ocean today,

dancing in bull kelp which formed

an impromptu tutu

about her mid-section.

she might say

the tempest tossed her above the waves,

dripping granite from her pocket.

at first white light. the fact of surrender

and memory of her death dividing the urchins, velvet mussels

into two distinct groups. she is dead.

she is not dead. she is telling her story.

she cupped into the limestone bowl

(of course she is passionate.)

her stone white hand stirring up fragments

of stardust and fiddler crabs

trapped from the avenging tide.

it was a repeat performance

revealing darkness

and a paradox of suffocating starfish.

then split open her palm

fist full of red bright stone.

Did she see Virginia's pockets at the river?

What sirensong was this?
The weight of thought

of white

of love.

CHAPTER 44

Who Wins the War of Love in Shakespearian England?

by Julia Miller

William Shakespeare's *A Midsummer Night's Dream* tells three interconnected stories portraying love, marriage, and class among mythological Greek royalty, Athenian mortals, and fairies of the nearby woods. Shakespeare's use of language illustrates culture as he experienced it, particularly Elizabethan England around the time this play was written from 1595 to 1596 (Shakespeare xiii-xiv). *A Midsummer Night's Dream* depicts the dominantly patriarchal structure of society, as well as socio-economic disparities between noblemen and mechanical laborers. Shakespeare's stories are adapted from broader cultural narratives and experiences; however, his diction throughout the play provides insight into the world and culture as he knew it (Greenblatt 226-7). In relation to *A Midsummer Night's Dream*, the word "won" has two distinct connotations made of compiled definitions derived from the completed action of "winning." The first definition connotes conquest and defeat or seizure of a person as a spoil, particularly one of great value or desirability ("win, v.2."; "win, v.5b."; "win, v.6."). The more pleasing definition is gaining a woman's affection with her consent. which can include attracting and persuading if the individual is unwilling ("win, v.7."; "win", v.9a."). Shakespeare's stories of Duke Theseus' mar-

669

riage to Hippolyta and four competing Athenian lovers—Hermia, Lysander, Helena, and Demetrius—illustrate the male-centric makeup of Shakespearian society. In *A Midsummer Night's Dream,* Shakespeare uses the word "won" to depict marriage as men's conquest over women and to suggest women can desire men and pursue love, but ultimately exposes women's lack of autonomy over their romantic lives.

Shakespeare describes Theseus' engagement to Hippolyta in terms of his triumph and her subdual to illustrate men's possession of women in marriage. Theseus proclaims his love to Hippolyta by retelling how he "wooed thee with my sword" and attained their courtship through defeating her kingdom in battle (1.1.17). He proudly maintains he "won thy love doing thee injuries" (1.1.18). Hippolyta was a Queen of the Amazons, a fierce tribe of warrior women in Scythia who swore to never marry and only reproduced with men whom they took captive, banishing male descendants (Miles 40, 44). Shakespeare uses the word "won" to describe Theseus' defeat of Hippolyta to reflect men's complete social and political dominance over women having conquered the Hippolyta, a symbol of female power and women's independence from men. Additionally, Hippolyta's status as a queen is much higher than Duke Theseus's power, but her socioeconomic and political status is masked and degraded by her association with Theseus through marriage. Shakespeare's portrayal of Hippolyta's engagement to Theseus through violent means against her will represents the subdual of women in marriage at their personal impairment ("win", v.2.; "win", v.5b.). Theseus proudly celebrates his victory gaining Hippolyta's "love" similarly to a trophy to be won, despite the cost to her (1.1.18). The objectification of Hippolyta as spoils of war mirrors women's forced submission to husbands chosen by a dominant male figure and an impersonal quality to love depicted as a simple transaction. Shakespeare's use of the word "won" when discussing love between a proud duke and a vanquished queen highlights the gender inequality between men and women in Shakespearian England and the perception that love is easily transferable.

Helena's love for Demetrius is presented as his accomplishment, reflecting women's propensity for romantic desires despite their social inability to fulfil them in most cases. Lysander tries to prove to Hermia's father that he is a better choice of husband than Demetrius, Egeus' chosen suitor of Hermia's who claims to love her as well. Lysander points out how Demetrius has "won her [Helena's] soul" and therefore he is unreliable and undeserving of Hermia (1.1.110). The act of two men fighting over a woman echoes men's possession of women as material goods. However, Lysander's argument reflects his mutual love with Hermia, wooing her with song and gifts (1.1.30-37). Lysander's romancing rather than conquering gives the word "won" a different connotation whilst referring to Demetrius and Helena's dilemma. This reference portrays Demetrius as a victor whose prize is Helena's affection, but "won" is used ironically because while Theseus fought laboriously to accomplish his goal, Demetrius did nothing and attained a prize he does not desire ("win", v.7., 9a.). Shakespeare's ironic use of "won" here depicts how men are perceived to have benefited when women fail to get their desires; Demetrius is a victor while Helena pines after him and achieves nothing without magical intervention. As expressed by the reference to her soul and spiritual essence, Helena is fully committed to Demetrius, reflecting women's ability to desire their mate without a man choosing for her ("soul", n.2a.). Nevertheless, her ambitions appear futile, as she is only an afterthought to Demetrius rather than a victory. Shakespeare's ironic usage of "won" in the context of Demetrius and Helena exhibits the futility of women's efforts to pursue their romantic interests in a rigid patriarchal society.

Once the lovers escape to the forest, the fairy king Oberon orders his servant Robin to give Demetrius a love potion because "A sweet Athenian lady [Helena] is in love / With a disdainful youth" (2.2.289-9). Oberon's act of selflessness helps Helena win Demetrius and thus Helena win Lysander at the end of the play, suggesting that women can only get their true desires with the help of magical intervention at a benevolent hand due to the constraints of Renaissance society. However, it is important to note Oberon uses magical potions to deceive the fairy queen Titania to get his will, so it is questionable how much power women truly have and how generous the higher power is to women's desires (2.1). Once the love plot is fulfilled, Egeus admits his "defeat" and declares he lost "his consent" before Theseus and the lovers (1.1.110). The word "defeat" demonstrates Egeus's feelings of loss and inferiority due to Hermia's wishes being fulfilled without his permission ("consent," n1a.). Egeus's feelings of defeat parallel Hippolyta's defeat by Theseus, but exhibit a significant difference; Egeus feels like he lost a battle by his daughter getting what she wants, but Hippolyta was literally conquered—her people suffered and she is now to be married against the values of the Amazons. The contrast between these characters' defeats additionally begs the question of who is *winning* and who is *losing* when it comes to love and marriage in Renaissance society and how these perceptions of gains and losses are dictated by gender. Leading to the marriage plot, Theseus blesses the marriage, saying he "will overbear your [Egeus's] will," solidifying the daughter's desires over the father's. Theseus's declaration implies the marriage was in doubt due to Egeus's lack of consent, despite his daughter's wishes and Demetrius's new love for Helena instead of Hermia. Shakespeare's depictions of the relationship between Egeus and Hermia surrounding her marriage to Lysander reveal the almost complete control fathers possess over their daughters and over women's potential to attain their aspirations.

Shakespeare's use of "won" indicates women are passive actors in their own love stories, where men have the social power to acquire women's hand in marriage and therefore their love. *A Midsummer Night's Dream* complicates this outmoded notion by presenting Hermia and Helena as active agents who fight for their romantic desires and escape to the forest to pursue their love. Defeat and capture characterize Hippolyta's engagement to Theseus, as he obtained her courtship through battle at her and her people's expense. This portrayal of love as a war against women's wishes exemplifies women's lack of independence in their lives, particularly romantically, within Renaissance England. In contrast, Shakespeare's ironic manipulation of "won" when Lysander describes Helena's love for Demetrius reveals the universality of love which both men and women possess. However, Demetrius is portrayed as the winner, while Helena can only *win* him after he is enchanted with a love potion and approved by the Duke. Shakespeare toys with the idea that women can achieve their aspirations of love, but only with magical intervention and the blessing of a higher power. The connections between love, marriage, and desire stemming from the single word "won" in *A Midsummer Night's Dream* exemplify women's ultimate inability to decide their martial fate within a society promoting male dominance over women.

Works Cited

"consent, n." *OED Online*. Oxford University Press, 23 May 2020.

Greenblatt, Stephen. "Culture." *Critical Terms for Literary Study*. Ed. Frank Lentricchia and Thomas McLaughlin. 2nd ed. U. of Chicago P., 1995, pp. 225-32.

Miles, Geoffrey. *Classical Mythology in English Literature: A Critical Anthology*. Routledge, 1999.

Shakespeare, William. *A Midsummer Night's Dream*.

Barbara Mowat, Paul Werstine, Michael Poston, and Rebecca Niles, eds.*FolgerShakespeareLibrary*,20April2020,https://shakespeare. folger.edu/shakespeares-works/a-midsummer-nights-dream/

"soul, n." *OED Online*. Oxford University Press, 18 April 2020.

"win, v.2." *OED Online*. Oxford University Press, 18 April 2020.

"win, v.5b." *OED Online.* Oxford University Press, 18 April 2020.

"win, v.6." *OED Online.* Oxford University Press, 18 April 2020.

"win, v.7c." *OED Online.* Oxford University Press, 18 April 2020.

"win, v.9a." *OED Online.* Oxford University Press, 18 April 2020.

ABOUT THE CONTRIBUTING EDITOR

Elizabeth Miller, the Contributing Editor of *Spinning and Weaving: Radical Feminism for the 21st Century*, is a Chicago feminist activist who runs the Chicago Feminist Salon and co-organized the Women in Media Conference, a radical feminist conference held in Chicago in 2018. In recent years, she worked on the successful campaigns to get the U.S. Equal Rights Amendment ratified in Illinois and to enact Illinois House Bill 40, which ensured that abortion will remain legal in Illinois even if the U.S. Supreme Court overturns *Roe v. Wade*. Among other projects, she is currently working with the U.S. radical feminist organization Feminists in Struggle to lobby Congress to pass legislation protecting women's sex-based rights and the rights of lesbian, gay, bisexual, and gender non-conforming people, organizing two other radical feminist conferences in the U.S., and is the founder of the Radical Feminism Resources community on Facebook and an administrator of the Radical Feminist page on Facebook.

ABOUT THE AUTHORS

(in alphabetical order)

Alyssa Ahrabare is a 25-year-old French feminist from Moroccan and Algerian origins. With a Masters in International Law and a specialization in human rights and fundamental liberties, she is now an international consultant on women human rights. Alyssa is a spokeswoman for the French non-profit organization Osez le Féminisme! ("Dare to Be Feminist"). She is a Project Officer for the European Network of Migrant Women, which she represents in the Women in Politics group of the European Women's Lobby. In addition, she is a co-organizer of Radical Girlsss (Young Women's Movement for a global radical feminist perspective). Alyssa also founded a theatre company which uses art and pedagogy to promote equality between women and men.

Linda Bellos: I am a proud Black British lesbian feminist who does not think that feminism is only for White women. My mother was Jewish and I have been proud to share her knowledge and culture and my father, a man who came to England during WW2 knowing that if the Nazis won the war Africa would be even more damaged than under British rule. I hope that I reflect my parents. My personal belief remains "Be Bold."

Samantha Berg is a radical feminist journalist and event organizer focused on ending men's demand for prostitution and pornography. In 2005 Sam created the forum at Genderberg.com where abolitionists contributed to one of the earliest online radical activist communities, and her many published articles about the sex industry are collected at Johnstompers.com. Sam has organized more than a dozen feminist events since 2012 and is a co-founder of WoLF, the Women's Liberation Front.

BigBooButch, a.k.a. Parker Wolf is a butch lesbian blogger and vlogger. She speaks on issues concerning lesbians and women in today's climate of hatred for women who will not bend to the will of men and transgender activists. She is also a radical feminist who runs several lesbian and radical feminist groups and pages on Facebook. You can see her work at her website, BigBooButch.com, she has also contributed to the anthology, *Female Erasure*, edited by Ruth Barrett, and she was a presenter at the Women in Media Conference in Chicago in 2018.

Brid is a graduate student living in occupied Mohawk territory in so-called Upstate New York. She is studying the ideologies and structures of Western society with the hopes that by analyzing the particularly devastating destruction wreaked by the West, she might identify the fundamental principles of necrophilia.

Giovanna Capone is a poet, fiction writer, playwright, and editor. She was raised in an Italian American neighborhood in New York, whose strong immigrant influence still resonates in her life. In 2014, Bedazzled Ink published her first book *In My Neighborhood: Poetry & Prose from an Italian-American*. Giovanna's play *Her Kiss*, was produced and performed to sold-out audiences in San Francisco by Luna Sea Women's Performance Project, in their first Dyke Drama Festival. She also co-edited *Hey Paesan! Writing by Lesbians & Gay Men of Italian Descent*. Recently she has co-edited an anthology of lesbian authors, entitled: *Dispatches from Lesbian America: 42 Short Stories & Memoir by Lesbian Writers*. Giovanna lives in Oakland, CA where she has worked as a public librarian.

She has also taught poetry to children and teens, through California Poets in the Schools. More recently, Giovanna is working on a documentary film about Italian Americans in Oakland, California. It's an exciting new direction for her. For further information, please see: www.giovannacapone.com.

Nineveh Cehack (pseudonym) was born and raised in Chicago, Illinois. She firmly believes that same-sex attraction is real and that raisins do not belong in dolma.

Chicago Feminist Salon is a monthly radical feminist salon in Chicago. They have recently begun writing up some of their discussions as "pamphlets" to continue the tradition of radical feminist pamphleting to disseminate radical feminist theory to women worldwide. The article contained here is their first pamphlet.

Gail Dines is a professor of Sociology and Women's Studies at Wheelock College and author of *Pornland: How Porn Has Hijacked Our Sexuality*. She is founder and President of Culture Reframed.

Mary Kate (M. K.) Fain is a feminist writer, activist, and engineer. She is the co-founder of Spinster.xyz, Founder and Editor in Chief of 4W, and a volunteer and contributor to multiple other feminist initiatives. She has been published in Feminist Current, Reader's Digest, and Tenderly, and is a regular contributor on politics to Caracal Reports. You can find her (for now) on Twitter @mkay_fain, or on Spinster @mk.

Melissa Farley is a feminist psychologist who founded the nonprofit organization Prostitution Research & Education in 1995. With many colleagues, she has published 40 articles and book chapters on the sex trade including prostitution, trafficking and pornography.

Tristan Fox is a lesbian radical feminist. She studied radical feminist theory at the University of Toronto and has had her poetry published in some smaller Canadian poetry journals. She lives with her beloved MJ on Canada's beautiful west coast.

Renée Gerlich is a writer and artist based in the Wellington region, New Zealand. Essays from her blog, reneejg.net, have been translated into French, Spanish, German, Turkish, Norwegian and Serbo-Croatian. Her writing has appeared in Feminist Current and Rain and Thunder, and she was a panelist at Seeking Feminist Future, an event hosted by Sydney University in February 2020. Her 2019 talk delivered with the International Women's Day committee in Brisbane, Transgenderism, Neoliberalism and Rape Culture, can be viewed on YouTube. Renée wishes to thank Deidra Sullivan for her tremendously helpful feedback and suggestions on her chapter.

Genevieve Gluck is a writer and feminist advocate living in Japan. She previously lived in South Korea, where she taught English at a Woman's University. She is the founder of Women's Voices, an audio library featuring feminist speeches, lectures, and book excerpts.

Jamae Hawkins: I'm just an everyday American, Black Woman, law abiding taxpayer, living and working in the DC metropolitan area with 2 children, 3 cats, and a corgi. My professional background is public policy and victims' advocacy.

Sheila Jeffreys is a lesbian feminist author, academic and activist who has been involved in feminist politics, mainly around violence against women, prostitution, and lesbian feminism, for 47 years. She has written 10 books. She wrote the first two in the UK before moving to Australia in 1991 to teach feminist politics at the University of Melbourne. She retired back to the UK in 2015. Her autobiography, Trigger Warning, was published in September

2020. She is a member of the Women's Human Rights Campaign and Object UK.

Inge Kleine is a feminist activist in Munich Germany. She is a board member at Kofra (Kommunikationszentrum für Frauen), a women's advocacy center and meeting place in Munich, and has been active in campaigns against sexual violence and prostitution in Germany.

Lisa Marchiano, LCSW, is a clinical social worker, certified Jungian analyst, and a nationally certified psychoanalyst. She co-hosts This Jungian Life, a podcast devoted to exploring current topics through the lens of depth psychology. She lives in Philadelphia.

Ann E. Menasche is a life-long radical lesbian feminist, social-ist, writer, and political activist, who has a forty-year career as a civil rights lawyer. She is the author of *Leaving the Life: Lesbians, Ex-Lesbians and the Heterosexual Imperative*, published in 1999. She is a founding member of Feminists in Struggle (FIST), https://feministstruggle.org/.

Julia Miller is currently a second-year college student studying psychology and literature at Northwestern University. In her free time, she trains dogs and horses, does art and photography, and enjoys writing.

Natasha Noreen is a 26-year-old feminist and activist advo-cating for migrant and women's rights in Italy and Pakistan. She is a member of the European Network of Migrant Women and Radical Girlsss. Natasha volunteers in several local associations that promote the inclusion of economic migrants and asylum seeker migrants within Italian society. She is also the founder of Feminism Pakistan: a Facebook community that promotes feminist discussion in Pakistan.

Nina Paley (https://blog.ninapaley.com/) is the creator of the award-winning animated musical feature films "Sita Sings the Blues" and "Seder-Masochism." She has been deplatformed, banned, and blacklisted for saying penises are male. You can see her films at https://www.sitasingstheblues.com/ and https://sedermasochism.com/.

Thistle Pettersen: I grew up in a Scandinavian-American nuclear family with parents who continue to be kind-hearted and also firm in their resolve to heal, protect and enjoy nature. My song-writing reflects this upbringing along with my propensity for riding my bicycle long distances. From September 11th, 2003 - January 2007, I rode my bike across America in groups and in pairs to resist car culture and the oil and gas economy. I have always been a feminist but it wasn't until 2014 and my interview with Sheila Jeffreys on WORT 89.9 FM community radio station in Madison, that I understood firsthand that taking a feminist stance has dire social consequences for public women in patriarchy. I was smeared, harassed, scapegoated, and blacklisted in my hometown by dozens of people who formerly were colleagues and friends. I am resilient and playing the guitar and singing is in my blood, so I have managed to use my art to help me pull myself back up from the muck and continue on in the world of feminist activism. Currently, I serve as a reporter and organizer with Women's Liberation Radio News (WLRN).

Janice Raymond: A longtime feminist scholar-activist on violence against women and sexual exploitation, Janice Raymond is the former co-director of the Coalition Against Trafficking in Women (CATW). She is the author of many books and articles, most recently the book *Not a Choice, Not a Job: Exposing the Myths about Prostitution and the Global Sex Industry* (Potomac Press, US; Spinifex Press, Australia). Dr. Raymond is currently Professor Emerita of Women's Studies and Medical Ethics at the University of Massachusetts, Amherst (USA) where she taught for 28 years. Dr.

Raymond was awarded the International Woman Award from the Zero Tolerance Trust in Scotland.

Raquel Rosario Sánchez is a writer, campaigner and researcher from the Dominican Republic. Her campaigning specialises in ending male violence against girls and women. Raquel is a featured writer at Dominican newspaper El Caribe and Spanish platform Tribuna Feminista. As a researcher, she is currently pursuing a PhD with the Centre for Gender and Violence Research at the University of Bristol. Her MA and PhD work focuses on online communities for men who pay for sex.

Sekhmet She Owl is a radical lesbian feminist and female separatist. She lives in the deserts of the United States, where she was born. She has been a member of Women's Liberation Radio News since 2016. You can listen to her feminist thoughts on her YouTube channel and on the WLRN podcast.

Cherry Smiley is a feminist from the Nlaka'pamux and Diné Nations. She is proud to work with feminists as part of the women's liberation movement. She is the founder of Women's Studies Online. She's not so good at being on time or doing what she's told.

Dr Jessica Taylor is a feminist psychologist specialising in violence committed against women and girls, and the psychology of victim blaming and self blame of women and girls subjected to male violence. Jessica is the director of VictimFocus, an independent research, consultancy and training company dedicated to changing the way the world responds to abuse, violence, and trauma victims.

Adriana Thiago is a 27-year-old Portuguese-Brazilian feminist and graduated in International Relations. Born in Luxembourg to Portuguese and Brazilian parents, she currently lives in Belgium. She studied in Madrid and has lived in Rio de Janeiro to reconnect to her culture of origin. Adriana has worked both as an activist in civil society associations and governmental organizations within the migration sector in Europe and Latin America. She now works for the European Network of Migrant Women and is a co-convenor of its Young Women's Movement, RadicalGirlsss, where she strives for a global radical feminist perspective and the end of sexual exploitation.

Tamarack Verrall has been active in the women's movement since the 1960's. Her focus has been the empowerment of women through hearing their stories. Currently her home base is Montreal, Canada. Her political base is World Pulse, a global network of 70,000 women from 190 countries. Her life's work is to see women and girls free of violence, to end poverty and to protect our Earth.

Yagmur Uygarkizi is a 24-year-old feminist who was born in Turkey, grew up in Italy and France, and studied in the UK. She is interested in male violence or discriminatory practices against women that are not commonly perceived as such, specifically prostitution-pornography and veiling. She has translated, written, and spoken on those issues and she's always more than happy to sneak into random people's casual conversations about those practices if she senses nonsense. She is the co-creatress of Radical Girlsss, the young women's movement of the European Network of Migrant Women.

Dana Vitálošová: I am a 34-year-old Slovak radical feminist writer and activist living and working in Bratislava.

Agnes Wade: I found it nearly impossible to make the argument that women's liberation is intrinsically linked to the fight to defend the living planet succinctly. There is just so much to cover. As I wrote, it became clear that I would have to develop and support these ideas further into a book which is... forthcoming.

Rebecca Whisnant is professor and chair of the philosophy department at the University of Dayton. She is co-editor of *Not for Sale: Feminists Resisting Prostitution and Pornography* and *Global Feminist Ethics*, as well as numerous articles and book chapters. A longtime activist and public speaker on the harms of pornography, she serves on the board of Culture Reframed, a nonprofit organization addressing pornography as the public health crisis of the digital age.

Danielle Whitaker is a U.S. based writer and radical feminist. An unapologetic fighter for women's liberation, she has been fiercely supporting lesbian rights for the past two decades. She is also a passionate advocate for animal welfare and environmentalism. Dani lives with her two partners and travels as often as life permits.

Angéla C. Wild is a political artist, a Lesbian feminist activist, and a writer. Her work focuses on challenging compulsory heterosexuality in all its forms, understanding the nature of male sexual violence and its impact on women's lives, as well as promoting uncompromising Lesbian visibility and creating women-only spaces, women's art, and culture. She is a founding member of Get The L Out UK Lesbian activist group, and writer of the only research on the cotton ceiling: "Lesbians at Ground Zero," available at http://www.gettheloutuk.com/blog/category/research/lesbians-at-ground-zero.html. As an artist she has organised several feminist /lesbian art exhibitions and is the creator of Wild Womyn Workshop, a shop for radical feminist activists.

Bec Wonders is a Ph.D. scholar at the Glasgow School of Art, currently researching the history of feminist publishing during the Women's Liberation Movement. Bec co-founded the Vancouver Women's Library in 2017 while pursuing a Masters in Publishing. She also founded the Frauenkultur Archive: an online repository of second-wave feminist book titles. More information about ongoing projects can be found at www.becwonders.com.

CPSIA information can be obtained
at www.ICGtesting.com
Printed in the USA
BVHW041058250421
605816BV00017B/1456